Select World Constitutions

Other books by the same author

1. New Comparative Government
2. Indian Polity
3. Indian National Congress Since Independence

Published by :
Lotus Press Publishers & Distributors

Select World Constitutions

(U.K., U.S.A., Switzerland, Russian Federation, China, France, Germany, Canada, Australia, Japan, South Africa, Bhutan, India, Bangladesh and Nigeria)

J.C. Johari

Lotus Press

4735/22, Prakash Deep Building
Ansari Road, Darya Ganj,
New Delhi - 110002

Lotus Press : Publishers & Distributors
Unit No. 220, 2nd Floor, 4735/22, Prakash Deep Building,
Ansari Road, Darya Ganj, New Delhi- 110002
Ph.: 011-41325510, 98118-38000
• E-mail : lotuspress1984@gmail.com
www.lotuspress.co.in

Select World Constitutions

ISBN: 978-81-8382-275-6 (PB)

Printed & Published by : **Lotus Press Publishers & Distributors,** New Delhi-02

Preface

Society cannot exist without state and there can be no state without a constitution of its own. Society means peaceful and collective life of the people which requires an authority in some form for keeping it well organised and safe. State is an institution endowed with, what Max Weber says, the 'legitimate power of coercion' that is exercised by its government. Thus, the constitution comes to have a place of its own in the form of written rules and unwritten practices which determine the organisation and working of the political system and define relationship between the rulers and the ruled. What the rule of a 'superman' cannot achieve, is achieved by the 'super-science of law' having its place in the constitution regarded as the 'supreme law of the land'. The words of Aristotle ring true that 'to live under a constitution is not a matter of servitude, it is a matter of salvation'. Hence, society, state, government and constitution are tied to each other with an unbreakable chain.

A comparative study of the constitutions of leading countries of the world shows that they are either of the English model or of the American model or a paculiar hybrid of both. Britain is known for having parliamentary form of government whose replica may be seen in the constitutions of Canada, Germany, Australia, Japan and Bhutan. America has the presidential form of government whose replica may be seen in the constitution of South Africa. France has a peculiar blending of the two whose replica may be seen in the constitution of the Russian Federation. And yet it must be stressed that a constitution may have some distinctive features of its own not available in the constitutions of other countries as we may see in the cases of Switzerland and China. In a comparative study of the constitutions, significant points of variation must also be taken into account. However, this fact remains to be stated that, as Ian Gilmour says 'successful constitutions and institutions are not mere pieces of a machinery. If they work, it is because of the ideas and beliefs of those who try to work them. The constitution must be like a living instrument'.

The constitutions of some major countries have been included in the courses of many universities for graduate and post-graduate classes. I have covered all of them in this book. As the constitutions of some other countries have been included in the courses of some universities, I have also covered them for the benefit of the students offering this course. An attempt has been made to present the matter in a very interesting and easily intelligible form. All topics have been explained and evaluated with the help of latest information. The interpretations are lucid and every care has been taken to avoid confusing expressions. At many places, references to standard works have been made so that the readers may have a better and advanced knowledge of this subject.

I hope that this hand-book will serve the purpose of the readers offering this course at the degree and post-graduate levels or preparing for various competitive examinations. I shall feel obliged to the readers who convey their suggestions or critical comments to me so that I may make necessary changes or improvement in the next edition or print of this book.

—J.C. Johari

CONTENTS

Part VII: German Constitution

Part X: Japanese Constitution

Part XI: South African Constitution

Part XV : Nigerian Constitution

Part - I

British Constitution

British government and politics have long exercised a peculiar fascination over the minds of men everywhere. For three centuries Britain was the modern equivalent of Greece and Rome combined, embodying the political ideals of the one and the imperial grandeur of the other. The British empire was even more impressive than the Roman in the extent of its frontiers, the efficiency of its administration and the impartiality (so far as an imperial authority can be impartial) of its justice. At the heart of the Empire was the United Kingdom, a country which justly prided itself on the stability of its government and the adaptability of its political system to a rapidly changing world.

—***Doughlas V. Verney***

1

CONSTITUTION OF THE U.K.

A comprehensive study of the British political system, and that too with a first and foremost place for it in a comparative study of the major modern governments is necessitated by certain pertinent reasons. Britain is rightly regarded as the ancestral home of the parliamentary government; the British Parliament is happily described as the 'mother of modern parliaments; and her constitution, though unwritten, is appropriately lauded as a testament of democracy in a land without 'a declaration of independence.' Impressed with the facts of English constitutional history, Woodrow Wilson observed that it "has been its leading characteristic that her political institutions have been incessantly in a process of development, a singular continuity marking the whole of the transition from her most ancient to her present form of government." The secret of this glorious feature of the British political system should be traced in this fact: "Homogeneity, consensus and deference are often cited as outstanding features of British society. Britain is widely seen as being fundamentally homogenous in its ethnic, religious and socio-economic composition, while the British people are often said to exhibit a considerable degree of consensus on basic political issues and show a marked degree of defence towards political leaders."[1]

English Constitutionalism

The term 'constitution', when applied to a political society, embodies both a physical and a legal conception. In the former sense, it refers to the totality of constituent elements that form the physical make-up of the state as the factors of population and territory including the institutions of political machinery or administrative mechanism. But in the latter sense, it refers to a sum-total of statutes, charters, documents, and all

1. R.M. Punnett: *British Government and Politics*, p.3.

In an era of democratic upeavals and dangerous political transitions around the world, it is easy to think of Britain as an exception, because its political system has endured for so many centuries.

Historical Firsts

1. Britain was the first nation to industrialise and for much of the nineteenth century, the British Empire was the world's dominant economic, political and military power, with a vast network of colonies throughout the world.
2. Britain was also the first nation to develop an effective parliamentary democracy (a form of representative government in which the executive is drawn from and answerable to an elected national legislature).
3. As a result of its vast empire, Britain has tremendous influence on the form of government introduced in countries around the globe. For these reasons, British politics is often studied as a model of representative government.
4. Named after the building that houses the British legislature in London, the Westminster model of government emphasises that democracy rests on supreme authority of a legislature, in Britain's case the Parliament and the accountability of its elected representatives. Traditionally the Westminster model and the values of consensus building and stability on which it rests have served as one standard (the American political system has been another) for countries struggling to construct demoeratic political systems.
5. Britain has served as a model of gradual and peaceful evolution of democratic government in a world where transitions to a democracy are often turbulent, interrupted and uncertain. ***—Joel Krieger***

Mark Kesselman, Joel Krieger and William A. Joesph: *Comparative Politics at the Cross-roads* (Lexington: D.C. Heath and Company , 1996), pp. 31-32.

written as well as unwritten (conventional) rules that constitute the organic public law of the state. Obviously, while in the former sense, the constitution becomes analogous to the science dealing with some phenomenon of nature, in the latter sense, it constitutes a field of important study in the domains of law and politics. And thus inspite of the fact that the term 'constitution' has been variously defined by different writers according to varying conceptions which they hold, it is indisputable that the constitution is a legal instrument which "embodies the more essential parts of the organic public law of the state."[2] Such a definition of the term 'constitution' may create some difficulty for a student of constitutional law when he is concerned with a study of the English constitution. Hence, it should be added that the constitution, as Dicey observed, refers to all

2. J.W. Garner: *Political Science and Government*, p. 499.

rules and regulations which directly or indirectly affect the distribution or exercise of the sovereign power of the state."[3]

While constitution refers to a body of rules that are essential for every political community, constitutionalism desires appropriate limitations whereby power is proscribed and procedure is prescribed. In other words, constitutionalism has its libertarian as well as procedural aspects. While it is required that the state shall perform such and such functions, it is also made obligatory that it would not transgress its defined area of authority. Thus, the directions are set forth determining the manner in which the policy shall be formulated and implemented within the jurisdiction of the state. "Constitutionalism, then, governs two separate but related types of relationship. First, there is the relationship of government with citizens. Second, there is the relationship of one governmental authority to another, the dichotomy is not sharp, for the latter type of relationship is regulated largely as a means of increasing the effectiveness of the control imposed on the former type."[4]

If constitutionalism precisely means the existence of a constitutional state, Britain occupies the most significant place in this regard. Moreover, the growth of British constitution affords a brilliant case of the development of genuine constitutionalism. The age of Tudor despotism ended with the 'golden age' of Queen Elizabeth I. The Stuart monarchs had to face the opposition of the people. The Civil War of 1640-48 was conducted on the issue as to who was supreme-the law or the king. The defeat of the king and the victory of the people confirmed the principle of the sovereignty of the latter. What remained undone in the Civil War was accomplished in the Glorious Revolution of 1688 that laid the foundation of the sovereignty of Parliament. The movement for the democratisation of the system continued with the result that the great Reform Acts were passed in 1832, 1867 and 1884 which enfranchised more and more people. The Parliament Act of 1911 crippled the powers of House of Lords and its amendment in 1949 further reduced the area of authority of the House in matters of passing a non-money bill. The rise of the two political parties had its own contribution to the development of English constitutionalism. It made the functioning of the parliamentary government a possibility.

As a result of all these developments, the British sovereign stands away from the area of effective political authority; the power is exercised

3. A.V. Dicey: *An Introduction to the Study of the Law of the Constitution*, p. 23.

4. W.C. Andrews: *Constitutions and Constitutionalism*, p. 11.

by the ministers of the Crown accountable to the Parliament; and that all citizens of the country, irrespective of their social and political status, enjoy the boons of liberty and equality what Dicey calls the 'rule of law'. What is of special importance in this regard is that English constitutionalism has supplied "a continuity of life to liberal institutions through many centuries when elsewhere they were dead or had never lived, permitted the growth of its own institutions among those communities in all parts of the world of which England herself was the mother and supplied the pattern of a constitution when the moment came for any newly liberated community to found one."[5]

Controversy Regarding its Existence

As already pointed out, the constitution of a state consists of those fundamental rules which determine the form and functions of government and lay down the procedure by which the political authority is to be exercised. It is thus one of the celebrated axioms of the science of politics that there can be no state without a constitution. Curiously, a controversy has found its manifestation so far as the existence of the English constitution is concerned. The names of Thomas Paine of America and Alexis de Tocqueville of France are known in this direction who reacted against the classical defence of Edmund Burke regarding his argument of a prescriptive constitution. The central theme of the argument of Paine is that there exists no constitution at all unless it can be produced in a visible form, that is, in the form of a document. A generation later, Alexis de Tocqueville of France repeated the same argument. But while Paine examined the case on the basis of a written constitution, de Tocqueville studied the case on the basis of its flexible nature. Like Paine, he concluded that the English constitution did not exist owing to the fact that there was no difference between the ordinary law of the land and the constitutional law.

That the views of Paine and de Tocqueville are miserably misfounded and that a thing like constitution does exist in Britain becomes clear with a close look at its component elements. The English constitution not having been made at a particular period of history has grown like an organism and developed from age to age in which contributions have been made by six important factors:

5. *Ibid.* p, 54.

Some Important Statements

An understanding of British governance begins with the consideration of its constitution which is notable for two significant features: its form and its antiquity. Britain lacks a formal written constitution in the usual sense, that is a single unified and authoritative text that carries special status above ordinary law and can be amended only by special procedure. Rather, the British constitution is a combination of statutory law (mainly Acts of Parliament), common law, conventions and authoritative interpretations. — ***Joel Krieger***

A volume might seem wanted to say anything worth saying on the history of the English constitution, and a great and a new volume might still be written on it, if a competent writer took it in hand. The subject has never been treated by any one combining the lights of the newest research and the lights of the most matured philosophy. —***Walter Bagehot***

The British constitution is a democratic one, but poured into an antique medieval world. It is still full of official titles, terminologies and procedures that originated in the Middle Ages. The importance of this tradition is that it has preserved not only the medieval form, but the mediecval essence, which in sum said: the king governs but conditionally, not absolutely. —***Samuel E. Finer***

1. **Great Charters:** The great charters constitute the most important milestones on the way of struggle for personal liberty and responsible government. They are historic and have a very important bearing on some of the fundamental aspects of the practices and principles of the constitution. The Manga Carta of 1215 established that even the king is subject to the law of the land and that the people have certain liberties which must be respected by him. The Petition of Right of 1628 denied taxation without the consent of the Parliament, prohibited arbitrary imprisonment, and biletting of royal soldiers on private residences, and also outlawed certain abuses of the royal power. Then, the Bill of Rights of 1689 laid the foundations of constitutional monarchy. These charters are the product of political crises and they contain the terms of settlement between the monarch and the people which occurred at various stages of constitutional development.
2. **Great Statutes:** Numerous laws passed by the Parliament define the principles of organisation and working of British political institutions. They grant authority, establish administrative agencies, and lay down their tenure and jurisdiction. For instance, the Parliamentary Reform Acts of 1832 and 1867 ending with the People's Representation Act of 1970 determine franchise and

regulate elections in the country. The Parliament Acts of 1911 and 1949 establish the supremacy of the House of Commons over the House of Lords. The Habeas Corpus Act of 1679 secures personal liberty against arbitrary detention. The Judicature Acts of 1873 and 1876 provide for judicial organisations and procedure. Thus in Britain constitutional principles can be distilled from numerous important statues. The Statute of Westminster of 1931, the Abdication Act of 1936, the Ministers of the Crown Act of 1937 and the Peerage Disclaimer Act of 1963 may be mentioned as other leading instances in this regard. All these statutes are very important for the development of political democracy and any attempt to repeal them would be considered as unconstitutional.

3. **Judicial Decisions:** Another source is to be found in the decisions of the judges. While deciding cases, the judges interpret, define and develop the provisions of the great charters and statutes. They fix the meaning and the scope of the formal laws of the constitution. For instance, in the *Case of Impositions* (1606) the court defined the scope of arbitrary power of the Crown to impose duties for the regulation of trade. Likewise, it was reaffirmed in a modern case *(Attorney General vs. De. Kayser's Royal Hotel Ltd. Case of 1920)* how the discretionary powers of the Crown are limited by a statute conferring similar authority. The independence of jury was firmly established in the famous *Bushel's Case of 1670*. In *Eton's Case* of 1815, the court was called upon to interpret Art. II of the Bill of Rights (the dispensing power as it hath been assumed and exercised of late) and decided that the expression did not apply to a general dispensation for which there was a precedent in the times of Queen Elizabeth I. The great text-books and commentaries written on the country's constitutional law by men like Sir Edward Coke and Blackstone have also contributed to clarify and fix the meaning and limits of important constitutional principles. In a good number of cases the courts have upheld the sovereign position of the Parliament. It may, however, be pointed out that the task of interpretation for the courts is based on the principle that their duty is to ascertain the true meaning of the words used by the Parliament and that the policy of the Act and the intentions of the law-makers are irrelevant except in so far as they have been expressed in the words used therein.[6]

---

6. Wade and Phillips: *Constitutional Law,* VIII Ed., p.11.

Important Constitutional Landmarks

1. **Magna Carta of 1215:** It began the process by which the law acquired a status of its own, independent of the Crown. The liberties of the people must be respected by the monarch.
2. **Petition of Right of 1628:** It denied taxation without the consent of the Parliament, prohibited arbitrary imprisonment, and biletting of royal soldiers on private residences, and also outlawed certain abuses of the royal power.
3. **Bill of Rights of 1689:** It established constitutional monarchy implying sovereignty of Parliament.
4. **Reform Act of 1832:** First in a series of such legislations, it widened electoral franchise culminating in the Representation of the People Act of 1918 that introduced the system of universal adult franchise.
5. **Parliament Act of 1911:** It reduced the powers of the House of Lords and made the House of Commons the Parliament in the real sense of the term.

4. **Common Law:** Several matters of great constitutional importance are covered by the principles of common law. It is from these principles that the prerogatives of the Crown, the privileges of the members of Parliament and the liberties of the people flow. The origin of common law dates back to the fourteenth century when the courts began to lay down case law. They claimed authority to state the law at a time when the meetings of the Parliament were brief and infrequent and statute-making was in a stage of infancy.

   The courts exercised their independent role as time went on, often subject to coercion by the Crown. But the judges stated the law as in their authoritative books or according to custom or good sense and equity. Thus, they created new traditions and judicial precedents. They gathered and reconciled many local customs and composed their own resultant jurisprudence, the law common to the whole country: hence there grew a term common law. Side by side with the common law, there developed equity through the courts of Chancery division. Thus, from the principles of common law and equity many subtle adaptations in the governmental system were made. But it should be remembered that since there is legislative sovereignty in Britain, principles of both common law and equity hold good until the Parliament passes a statute on the same subject.

5. **Conventions:** However, the most important feature of the British constitution rests not upon formal law as upon the usages and customs technically called the 'conventions'. These usages are the unwritten

rules of political practice and they have been defined by John Stuart Mill as 'unwritten maxims of the constitution'. The most curious thing in regard to constitutional conventions is that although their validity cannot be a subject of controversy in a court of law, they cover some of the most important parts of the British governmental system and are most scrupulously observed. For instance, the entire apparatus of the Cabinet and its relationship with the Crown and the Parliament have no foundation in law, they are regulated by the usages and conventions of the constitution which have developed in the course of time.

6. **Standard Works:** Commentaries on the English constitution written by eminent figures are also important in as much as they have systematised the diverse written and unwritten rules, established an understandable relationship between one rule of the constitution and the other, and then linked them into some degrees of unity by reference to central principles of the fundamental law of the land. In certain cases, such writers have provided compendious and detailed accounts of the operation of particular categories of rule and their works have acquired the status of constitutional documents. Erskine May's *Treatise on the Law, Privileges, Proceedings and Usages of Parliament,* A.V. Dicey's *An Introduction to the Study of the Law of the Constitution,* Anson's *Law and Custom of the Constitution,* Walter Bagehot's *The English Constitution,* Jennings' *Cabinet Government,* Laski's *Parliamentary Government in England* and *Constitutional Law* by Wade and Phillips are some of the most celebrated works on the English constitution.

It is thus evident that the British constitution is a living organism which has been in a condition of perpetual growth and change. However, it should be remembered that since the English people are conservative by nature, their political institutions have seldom witnessed a radical change, though they have been under the process of incessant evolution. That is why, it is said that in the history of British constitutional development no revolution was thoroughly radical and that while the present has remained connected with the past, the future is bound to remain organically connected with the present. The fact remains that while the British people are conservative by nature, they are also realistic in their outlook. As a result, the British constitutional system has been remarkably dynamic and constantly growing in response to the changing conditions of the age. For example, what was once an absolute monarchy, has gradually been transformed into a political democracy. The great British empire of Disraeli and Chamberlain has now become a Commonwealth or an association of free and sovereign nations. It has given strength to the national pride that in less fortunate countries, such changes "take place to the accompaniment of protracted bloodshed and in the awful shadow of civil war. In Britain, they are announced in a Speech from the Throne."[7]

Constitutional Conventions

Conventions of the constitution, a term popularised by Dicey, mean practices and usages hardened into unwritten rules of political behaviour. That is why, John Stuart Mill has called them 'unwritten maxims of the constitution' and Anson designated them as 'customs of the constitution'. They constitute an extra-legal phenomenon in as much as they do not find their place in the written rules adopted by a legislative or a judicial body. In other words, conventions mean 'constitutional practices', as Prime Minister Asquith said in the House of Commons in 1910, and they rest upon the usages developed over a long period of history. Hence, conventions of the constitution "are rules, or unwritten principles, understandings or maxims, of political behaviour. They are not established in statutes or judicial decisions or parliamentary custom, but they are created outside of these to regulate political conduct that the statutes etc. have not embodied and may never embody."[8]

It follows that there is a technical point of difference between a law and a convention. While a law is made by legislative body, convention means a practice based on general acquiescence. Again, while law is precise because of being written into the shape of a document, convention is 'uncertain' as it is never formulated into words. Finally, while a law is enforced by the courts, judges cannot enforce a custom as it does not emanate from a legally constituted body. Apart from these technical points of difference between the two, the peculiar notion about the conventions in Britain is that no definite boundary line can be drawn between the two in as much as theirs is a fusion without any confusion. The law of the land pays recognition to the well-established conventions of the times and once their existence is recognised by legislations, conventions do not remain

7. See R.G. Neumann: *European and Comparative Government*, Ch.2.
8. Herman Finer: *The Major Governments of Modern Europe*, p.60.

really very different from laws. Jennings thus rightly asserts that the conventional system of the British constitution "is, in fact, much like the system of the common law."[9]

For the sake of convenience, we may put a long list of important conventions under these heads:

First, there are some well established *conventions relating to the monarch* which regulate the exercise of royal prerogatives. The monarch reigns but does not govern. As such, he is the titular head of the state acting upon the advice of his ministers. He can do no wrong which implies that the responsibility is of the ministers who carry on the administration of the country and who cannot take shelter behind the throne for their acts of commission or omission. The monarch does not attend the meetings of the Cabinet; he appoints the Prime Minister without using his discretion to reveal the fact of his political non-partisanship. The office of the Prime Minister goes to the leader of the majority party in the House of Commons and the monarch has hardly any chance to exercise his discretion in this regard–save in the exceptional times of national crisis. The monarch has got the power to veto a bill passed by the Parliament, but he gives assent to every bill as a result of which his veto power has been in disuse since 1707.

Second, there are important conventions *relating to the Cabinet system.* The Prime Minister must belong to the House of Commons and that he must be the leader of the party which commands absolute majority in the House. All ministers must belong to the party of the Prime Minister and they must have the membership of the Parliament. However, if a minister is not a member of the Parliament, he must find his seat within a period of six consecutive months. All ministers are appointed by the monarch (on the advice of the Prime Minister) and they take oaths of office and secrecy before him. The ministers are accountable to the Parliament which means that they must resign in case a vote of non-confidence is passed against them. The Prime Minister may submit his resignation to the monarch whenever he so chooses and then advise the monarch to dissolve the House of Commons in order to have the final verdict of the people in a general election.

9. Ivor Jennings: *Cabinet Government,* p.5.

Third, there are equally important conventions *relating to the Parliament.* The Parliament must meet once a year at least. The House of Lords is not only the upper chamber of the British Parliament, it is also the highest court of appeal in civil matters and when the House meets in a judicial capacity, only 9 Law Lords sit. The Speaker of the House of Commons is a non-partyman and his office is highly exalted. So goes the maxim that 'once a Speaker, always a Speaker'. The Prime Minister and his ministers can be removed by the House of Commons and not by the House of Lords. A bill must be passed by both the Houses after three readings. The session of the Parliament begins with the Speech from the Throne. The Army Act is passed every year. The ministers have full regard to the will of the House of Commons in the conduct of foreign affairs, and do not declare war or neutrality, or make peace or enter into important treaties without securing, as soon as possible, endorsement by the Commons.

Last, there are some important conventions *relating to the Commonwealth of Nations* which determine the relationship between the monarch and his Parliament on the one hand and the member-states on the other. In case there is a Dominion, the British monarch becomes the head of that State as well and he acts on the advice of the ministers of that Dominion and not on the advice of British ministers. The British Parliament cannot make law for a Dominion until so desired by the latter. The monarch has his agent in the Dominions called the Governor-General who acts as his nominee, but when present in a Dominion (as in Canada, Australia or New Zealand), the authority is exercised by the monarch himself. That is why, it is commented that today the Queen of Britain is at the same time the Queen of Canada or Australia acting through her Governor-General appointed by her on the recommendation of the Parliament of the Dominion concerned. This is called 'Dominion Status'. The membership of the Commonwealth of Nations is optional and, hence any member-state may abandon the membership at its will. Then, a member of the Commonwealth of Nations may be a Republic and thereby regard the British king as the 'symbol of friendship' instead of paying him final allegiance. It is also required by a convention that the members of the Commonwealth of Nations meet in the annual conference under the chairmanship of the British monarch and discuss matters of mutual concern and interest.

Important Conventions of the English Constitution

Relating to Monarch

1. Monarch above politics
2. Nominal authority of the monarch
3. Appointment of Prime Minister and other Ministers by the monarch without using discretion
4. Monarch acting on the advice of the ministers
5. Monarch's absence from Cabinet meetings
6. No use of veto power

Relating to Cabinet

1. Prime Minister from the House of Commons
2. Ministry of the party having absolute majority in the House of Commons.
3. Political homogeneity
4. Minister being members of Parliament
5. Ministerial responsibility- both individual and collective
6. Prime Minister's power to advise the monarch to make 'an appeal to the people'

Relating to Parliament

1. Session of Parliament at least once a year
2. Only Law Lords take part when the House meets as a Court
3. Speaker–a non-partyman
4. Ministers responsible to the House of Commons and not to the House of Lords
5. Three readings of a bill in both Houses
6. Speech from the Throne to inaugurate session
7. Parliamentary approval for Government's policies

Relating to Commonwealth of Nations

1. Optional membership of the association
2. British monarch as the final authority of the Dominions
3. British monarch acting through the Governor-General on the advice of Dominion ministers
4. British monarch as 'symbol of friendship' for the Republics
5. Annual conference under the chairmanship of the monarch to discuss matters of mutual interest

Now the question arises as to what is the sanction behind the conventions. When conventions are unwritten rules unenforceable by the courts, why are they observed? Different theories have been propounded in this regard which are correct in their own ways but which revolve round the fact that conventions form the wrap and woof of the British constitutional system and provide the lubricating oil which keeps the parts of mechanism well in operation. First, we take up the view of eminent English jurist A.V. Dicey who holds that there is an integral relationship between law and convention as a result of which conventions are observed, otherwise sooner or later a violator would find himself actually breaking a law. Dicey's explanation is that conventions are so intimately bound up. with laws that if the former are violated, it naturally leads to the violation of the latter as well.[10]

The American writer Lowell holds a different view. He relies on the factors of public morality and the force of tradition and public opinion. He does not dismiss the contention of Dicey but finds it inadequate. In his view, many conventions may be broken or disrespected and there would be no punishment as there is no violation of law. For instance, if a defeated Prime Minister does not resign, he cannot be arrested and put before a magistrate for trial and eventual conviction. What is more important is the force of public conscience which, in such a case, would result in the shape of mass upheaval and compel the defeated Prime Minister to resign and go. Any undemocratic behaviour of the House of Lords would open ways for further diminution of its powers.[11]

Another view is furnished by an eminent English writer, Jennings. He considers the government functioning on a cooperative basis where the rules of law alone cannot provide for common action. Both written and unwritten rules are followed because of the habit of the people to obey. Thus, conventions are rules of political behaviour first established to deal with specific problems and subsequently to be followed by the canons of expediency and reasonableness.

The fact is that now laws and conventions have become interwoven to constitute and keep into operation the English constitutional system. They consist of understandings, habits or practices which, through only rules of political morality, regulate a large portion of the actual day-to-day

10. See Dicey: *Law of the Constitution*, pp. 445-49.

11. A.L. Lowell: *Government of England*, Vol I, pp. 12-13.

relations and activities of even the most important of the public authorities. That is the reason which prompts Ogg and Zink to say that conventions "clothe the dry bones of law with flesh and make the legal constitution work and keep it abreast of changing social needs and political ideas."[12] In fine, men work the Constitution to make it attain certain ends they deem desirable, the theory is the expression of these ends. As Laski says: "But men regard constitutional principles as binding and sacred, because they accept the ends they are intended to secure."[13]

Basic Features

1. An Evolved Constitution: The fact that Britain does not possess a coherent, well-formulated and written constitution does not substantiate the charge that 'there is no constitution in England'. 'The true position is that the English constitution is a growth, not a make. It was never made in a way as the American constitution was made by the Philadelphia Convention in 1787. In simple terms, it means that it was never created by a stroke at any particular period of history. No constitution-making body ever met to formulate the fundamental law of the English people; no monarch proclaimed it as an instrument of government complete in all respects. And yet there is very much a thing like the English constitution despite the obvious political fact that the English "have left the different parts of their constitution where the waves of history have deposited them; they have not attempted to bring them together, to classify or complete them, or make of it a consistent and coherent whole."[14]

An exception to this can be found in the Instrument of Government framed in 1653. It was a written constitution prepared during the period of Oliver Cromwell. Virtually, it provided the model of a military government headed by the Lord Protector having several units under the charge of his lieutenants. It, however, could not work well and with the restoration of monarchy in 1660, England slid back into her traditional system of government.

The existence of the English constitution can be easily traced in its gradual change and remarkable continuity. It has been likened with an

---

12. Ogg and Zink: *Modern Foreign Governments*, p. 29.

13. Laski: *Parliamentary Government in England*, pp. 52-53.

14. Boutmy: *Studies in Constitutional Law*, Ed. II p.6.

ever-green tree bearing fruits and flowers in response to the climatic conditions, or it has been described as a living organism ever-growing and functioning without having sudden leaps or suffering from unexpected breaks. It may be called the lengthened shadow of the English people in as much as it well represents the gradually changed character of the English political system of a traditionally conservative nation. Leaving aside the only exception of the Protectorate Period (1649-60), the English people have never shown themselves as volatile as the people of France who switched over from monarchy to popular government and then swang back to an autocracy under Napoleon Bonaparte. The Glorious Revolution of 1688 can be cited as an example when the English people invited Mary and William to ascend the throne after King James II escaped–an event that laid down the foundations of constitutional monarchy. The stubborn attitude of the Lords as displayed by them in 1909 led to the passing of the Parliament Act of 1911 that virtually clipped the wings of upper chamber of the Parliament; the insistence of King Edward VIII on marrying Lady Simpson led to his peaceful abdication in 1936. As accidents have occurred, so the wisdom of the English people has shown itself in dealing with the problem of change. Thus, the English constitution is described as 'a product of accidents and designs', or 'a child of chance and wisdom.'

The result is that the English constitution has a different nature. It "is like a maze in which the wanderer is perplexed by unreality, by antiquarianism and by constitutionalism."[15] James Bryce calls it "a mass of precedents carried in men's minds or recorded in writing dicta of lawyers or statesmen, usages, understandings and beliefs, a number of statutes mixed up with customs, and all covered with a parasitic growth of legal decisions and political habits."[16] It is by all means a continuously changing blend of the ancient and the modern and herein lie the secrets of its strength. It is owing to this that the governments have been permitted to rule effectively without allowing them to govern for long in an arbitrary and irresponsible manner, disregarding the wishes at least of the more powerful and articulate sections of the government. Besides, no rigid constitutional or political orthodoxy has been able to ossify the institutions of government and it "has not been necessary totally and swiftly to reorganise them at the cost of destroying established habits of thought, behaviour and sentiment."[17]

15. Dicey, *op. cit.*. p. 7.
16. Cited in Garner: *Political Science and Government,* II Indian Ed., p. 516.
17. G C. Moodie: *The Government of Greal Britain,* p. 14.

2. An Unwritten Constitution: The British constitution is the model of an unwritten constitution. Its written part is limited to some important charters signed by the monarchs, statutes passed by the Parliament and decisions given by the courts. The larger part of the constitution is unwritten as it is available in the form of numerous usages and customs. A list of constitutional documents should be referred to in this connection having leading instances like those of the Magna Carta of 1215, Petition of Right of 1628, Habeas Corpus Act of 1679, Bill of Rights of 1689, Act of Settlement of 1701, Act of Union of 1707, First Reform Act of 1832, Second Reform Act of 1867, Third Reform Act of 1884, Parliament Act of 1911, Statute of Westminster of 1931, Abdication Act of 1936, Ministers of the Crown Act of 1937, Peerage Disclaimer Act of 1963, Representation of the People Acts of 1918, 1928 and 1970 etc.

The bulk of the English constitution is contained in the form of usages, precedents and customs what Mill has termed the 'unwritten maxims of the constitution' and Dicey denominated them as 'conventions of the constitution'. These customs relate to the office of the monarch, the Prime Minister and his Cabinet, the Parliament and the Commonwealth of Nations. We have already dealt with their meaning, leading instances and the reasons behind their observance. What is relevant for our purpose at this stage is to point out that these well-established practices having no written form of their own constitute an integral part of the English constitution and since they constitute the bulky part of the English constitution, they render to it the character of an unwritten constitution.

The unwritten character of the English constitution has created the anomaly of something in theory and something else in practice what is sometimes described as its 'penchant for disguises'. It is due to this that 'nothing is what it seems to be or seems to be what it is'. Several instances may be given to corroborate that it is characteristic of the English constitution that forms and symbols continue to exist, while the spirit behind them has been completely transformed.

The written and unwritten parts of the English constitution may also be described as its internal and external segments. While the written rules of the constitution contained in the great charters and statutes are very clear and they constitute the internal segment, the practices or customs hedging around them to supply flesh and blood to the dry bones of the written skeleton may be said to constitute the external segment. That is why, Dicey divides the English constitution into the body of written rules which constitute, what he terms the 'law of the constitution', the other part consists of well established practices what he designates as 'conventions of the constitution'. However, the growth of the English constitution signifies the development of its both segments and that makes the nature of the English constitution "essentially pragmatic."[18] Both the written and unwritten parts of the constitution are duly observed, rather the people attach due importance to the latter, as they "have a distinct dislike for declaring their political philosophy in terms of law."[19]

3. Unitary System: A unitary system is one in which there is no division of powers between the national or central government on the one hand and regional or provincial governments on the other. All powers are assigned to the central government and if some local units are created for the sake of administrative efficiency or convenience, they are the creation of the central government. The salient mark of a unitary system is that the units of the state enjoy no autonomy, as they are like the agents of the central government. As such, the centre may enlarge or reduce their area of authority, or make other incidental changes in the powers delegated to them.

The British constitution is unitary. The central government located at London is constitutionally supreme and the governments of the units like those of Wales, Scotland and Northern Ireland located at Cardiff, Edinburgh and Belfast respectively derive their authority from the central government. The British Parliament is sovereign that can make any law for the country as a whole or for its part, or it may delegate some of its powers to a local parliament like that of Northern Ireland. Besides, there are units of local government like counties, boroughs, parishes and the London Metropolitan Council etc. that work according to the laws made by the Parliament and the directions issued by the central government. The unitary system of Britain can be traced in the fact that though these areas "do enjoy a degree of regional independence, but nowhere does this extend to the creation of a federal relationship."[20]

---

18. J.P. Mackintosh, *The British Cabinet*, p. 13.

19. The Centre-Left Think Tank Institute for Public Policy Research (IPPR) drafted a constitution in 1991 which included most of the reform agenda. This programme closely resembled manifestoes of the two major political parties in the general election of 1997. It should not be taken as the written constitution of the United Kingdom. See Dennis Kavangh: *British Politics: Continuities and Change* (Oxford: Oxford University Press, 2000), p. 51.

20. R.M. Punnett: *British Government and Politics*, p. 162.

The units of British government enjoy a considerable degree of administrative devolution. For instance, the government of Scotland has control over education, agriculture, fisheries, home and health, while its M.P.s constitute the Scottish Grand Committee of the House of Commons that discusses all matters relating to this unit of the United Kingdom. Likewise, the government of Wales has its control over several matters and the M.P.s belonging to this part constitute a Grand Welsh Committee that discusses matters relating to this region of the United Kingdom. The administration of Northern Ireland is much different. There is a separate Parliament having two Houses (House of Commons and Senate), a Cabinet and a Governor-General and a minister for Welsh affairs in the British Cabinet. The Channel Islands and the Isle of Man have their own Parliament and, like Northern Ireland, they are largely self-governing in internal affairs. Despite all these administrative devolutions, Britain has a unitary system, because all units are ultimately subject to the legislative supremacy of the central government.

4. A Flexible Constitution: The British constitution is flexible in view of the fact that it can be changed very easily; moreover, there is no distinction between the higher (constitutional) and lower (ordinary) law as the Parliament may make any law by the same process of legislation. Any law passed by the Parliament by its simple majority may amount to a change in the constitution. That is, there is no special process laid down for passing a bill of constitutional amendment. The unwritten character of the constitution is responsible for making the English fundamental law as a highly flexible affair. That is why, we find that the slow and gradual way in which the power passed from the monarch to the Parliament and from Parliament to the Cabinet, thereon to the Prime Minister, speaks of the highly flexible character of the English constitution. Not being set out or declared in any sacrosanct document, nor hedged in by some special process of amendment, the British constitution "can be changed or modified in any or every particular way by the ordinary process of legislation. It can be reformed in any part by an ordinary act of Parliament assented to in the ordinary way."[21]

National character plays its own part in determining the nature of a constitution. A constitution may be flexible or rigid not only because of the process of its amendment, or the breadth of its written provisions, much also depends upon the character of the people. In other words, it

21. Chrimes: *British Constitutional History*, p. 9.

means that changes in the constitution depend upon the temperament of the people. Thus, the flexibility of the English constitution is qualified by the conservative character of the people. Since the people are the lovers of tradition, no sudden or radical change has so far occurred in the English constitution. Leaving aside the peculiar events of the mid-seventeenth century, nothing very astonishing has occurred in the direction of, for example, reforming the House of Lords. No Parliament and no Prime Minister can dare take a step that might create mass indignation. It is for this reason that no change in the constitutional sphere as occurred without a very thorough airing of the matter in public many years before it was actually attempted and above all without seeking a mandate in an election to the proposal."[22] As Munro says, the legislators "come from the people; they think and feel as the people do; they are saturated with the same hopes and fears; they are creatures of the same habits and when habits solidify into traditions or usages, they are stronger than laws, stronger than the provisions of the written constitution."[23]

5. Concentration and Diffusion of Powers: One of the peculiar features of the English constitution should be discovered in the unique manner in which powers have been concentrated in the executive and legislative organs of the government and, at the same time, these have been separated, rather, diffused, in the midst of what Bagehot calls 'supposed checks and balances' of the constitutional system of Britain. It should, however, be pointed out here that the meaning of the term 'separation of powers' does not have the same implications here that were given by Montesquieu and what we find in the American constitutional system. What should be taken note of is that the separation of powers does prevail in Britain to the extent and in a manner that is essential for the preservation of the essential liberties of the people. In the place of the rigid separation of powers into three compartments, the British have preferred to have many divisions each providing checks on the other.

The concentration of powers is traceable in the fact that the monarch is the head of the state whose prerogatives, though formal, cover all the three spheres of government. The Prime Minister and the Cabinet constitute the executive part, but they have usurped the powers of the Parliament. Moreover, all members of the Cabinet are the members of the Parliament and thereby they perform functions originally vested in the national

22. Herman Finer: *The Major Governments of Modern Europe*, p. 63.

23. W.B. Munro: *The Governments of Europe*, p. 23.

legislature. The Lord Chancellor is the peculiar authority whose range of functions defies the principle of separation of powers as he is in the legislature by virtue of being the presiding officer of the House of Lords; he is in the executive because of being a 'member of the Cabinet; finally, he is in the judiciary on account of serving as Lord Chief Justice while the House of Lords sits as the highest court of the country in civil and criminal matters for England and Northern Ireland and for Scotland in civil matters. In addition, he has executive duties connected with the courts, such as confirming the appointment of justices, clerks, sending out circulars on sentences and being responsible for prisons, the probation service, and the release of persons from Broadmoor and similar institutions. What engages our attention at this stage is that even judiciary is not a separate part of the English government in a manner we find in the United States–the land of the separation of powers.

The essential feature of the English constitution is, therefore, the concentration of powers and since most of the powers have been usurped by the Cabinet, it has become the single-most important piece of mechanism in the political structure of England. In terms of law, sovereignty lies with the Parliament; in terms of politics, the powers of the Parliament have been usurped by the Cabinet. The result is the omnipotent position of the Cabinet that is sometimes identified with its 'dictatorship'. The essential thing is that the liberties of the people be preserved: while the Americans have done it by following the principle of 'separation of powers,' the English people have accomplished the same by having the 'diffusion of powers.' As Bagehot appreciates: "But we happily find that a new country need not fall back into the fatal division of powers incidental to a presidential government; it may, if other conditions serve, obtain the ready, well-placed, identical sort of sovereignty which belong to the English constitution under the unroyal form of Parliamentary government."[24]

6. Sovereignty of Parliament: The Parliament of Britain affords the solitary case of a sovereign law-making body. While writing in 1885, Dicey said that "the sovereignty of Parliament is, from a legal point of view, the dominant characteristic of the English constitution." He further added that it "means neither more nor less than this, namely, that Parliament thus defined has, under the English Constitution, the right to make and unmake any law whatever, and further no person or body is recognised by law of England as having a right to over-ride and set aside the legislation of Parliament."[25] While highlighting the same position, another writer

24. Walter Bagehot: *The English Constitution*, p.224.

25. Dicey: *An Introduction to the Study of the Law of the Constitution*, pp. 39-40.

Some Important Statements

Parliamentary sovereignty refers to the absolute and unlimited authority of a parliament or legislature, reflected in its ability to make, amend or repeal any law it wishes. It is usually seen as the central principle of the British constitution, and results from the absence of a codified constitution, the supremacy of statute law over other forms of law, the absence of rival legislature, and the convention that no parliament can bind its successors. ***—Andrew Heywood***

The core constitutional principle of the British political system and cornerstone of the Westminster model is parliamentary sovereignty. Parliament can make or overturn any law without recourse by the executive, the judiciary or the throne. ***—Joel Krieger***

The power or jurisdiction of Parliament is so transcendent and absolute that it cannot be confined either for causes or persons within any bounds. It can, in short, do everything that is not naturally impossible. What Parliament can do, no power on earth can undo. ***—Sir Edward Coke***

mentions that in England Parliament is legally omnipotent and it "can do anything and achieve any result which can be achieved by man-made laws."[26]

This classical phrase has certain important implications:

1. It signifies that the legislative power of the Parliament is unlimited and absolute. As De Lolme said, it can do everything except changing the sex of a person; or as Bagehot commented, it can make any law to do anything except making a man a woman and *vice versa.* The reason is that there is no written constitution in the country to define the area of legislative power of the Parliament and there is no federal system forestalling the authority of the national government. As a result, the Parliament is all-powerful to make a law, then change it, or even repeal it.
2. There is no distinction between constitutional law and ordinary law of the land. In the absence of a written constitution with a special procedure of amendment, the British constitution is the model of a flexible constitution. As a result, the Parliament possesses full constituent powers. By passing a law with its simple majority it can lay down any constitutional provision or make any change in the existing arrangement.
3. It signifies that there is no judicial authority in the country which may question the validity of a law passed by the Parliament. The courts are bound to enforce every law made by the Parliament.

26. Quinton Hogg: *The Purpose of Parliament,* p. 52.

Latest Facet of Parliamentary Sovereignty

It can be argued, however, that the U.K. Parliament enjoys neither legal nor political sovereignty. Its legal sovereignty has been compromised by membership of ther European Union. As an EU member, the UK is obliged to the jurisdiction of the European Court of Justice in Luxembourg. This was underlined in the Factortame Case of 1991 when, for the first time, the European Court of Justice declared UK legislation to be unlawful, in this case the Merchant Shipping Act 1988, because it contravened European laws guaranteeing a free movement of goods and persons within the European Community (as it then was). If the Parliament can any longer be described as legally sovereign, it is only by virtue of the fact that it retains the legal right to withdraw from the EU. In political terms, it is unlikely that Parliament has ever enjoyed sovereignty, it cannot simply act as it pleases. In practice, a wide range of institutions constrain its behaviour, including the electorate, devolved bodies, organised interests, particularly those which possess financial or economic muscle, major trading partners, supra-national organisations, international treaties and so forth. Parliament's right to withdraw the UK from the EU is, for instance, only notional. As most UK trade is now with other EU states, revoking the UK's membership would involve such heavy economic costs as to be, for all practical purposes, unthinkable. Andrew Heywood: ***Political Theory: An Introduction***, p. 95.

4. The sovereignty of Parliament, in a more accurate language, means the supreme authority of the House of Commons. Legally speaking, the term King-in-Parliament means King and the House of Lords and the House of Commons. But now both the King and the House of Lords have lost their former position of power and become subservient to the will of the House of Commons.
5. The doctrine of Parliamentary sovereignty is a legal fiction. It is a patent truth to a man of law who finds that a law made by the Parliament is binding and enforceable by the courts of the country.

As Parliamentary sovereignty is a legal fiction, the doctrine has been criticised from other angles. A man of politics highlighting the fact of political sovereignty is not prepared to accept the view that Parliament is omnipotent to pass any law as it is always under the control of the electorate. Democracy means power with the people and thus no Parliament can do anything to disregard the weight of public opinion. In case the Parliament makes a law contrary to the premises of the rule of law, it imperils its own supremacy. As Barker says, the sovereignty of Parliament and the rule of law "are not only parallel; they are also inter-connected and mutually

Intrusion of Democracy in the Political Sphere

Extension of Franchise

(*i*) To the middle class in 1832
(*ii*) To the working class in 1867
(*iii*) To the agricultural labourers in 1884
(*iv*) To the married women and spinsters over 30 years of age in 1918
(*v*) To all women over 21 years of age in 1928
(*vi*) To all adults over 18 years of age in 1970

Tenure of the House of Commons

(*i*) Fixation at 3 years in 1694
(*ii*) Fixation at 7 years in 1715
(*iii*) Fixation at 5 years in 1911

Reforms of the House of Lords

(*i*) Composition relating to life peers (law lords) altered in 1876
(*ii*) Powers in regard to financial and non-financial legislation reduced in 1911
(*iii*) Powers in regard to non-financial legislation further reduced in 1949
(*iv*) Composition relating to life peers (including women) altered in 1958
(*v*) Peerage renouncability allowed in 1963

Ministerial Responsibility

(*i*) To the monarch until 1714
(*ii*) To the monarch and Parliament 1714-1841
(*iii*) To the Parliament and electorate until 1868-1911
(*iv*) To the House of Commons and the electorate since 1911
(*v*) Increasingly to the Prime Minister since 1940

interdependent."[27] So, while attacking the doctrine of Parliamentary sovereignty from moral and humanitarian standpoints, it is argued that no Parliament can pass a law going against the celebrated norms of decent human life. Jennings is of the view that no Parliament can make a law that all blue-eyed babies must be killed.[28] It shows that there are profound moral and psychological checks and voluntary self-restraints which come into operation when substantial changes in the constitution are under consideration.[29] The fact is that the supreme power of the Parliament is based on the confidence of the people in its being the temple of national glory and freedom. It stands on the political axiom that the consent of the Parliament "is taken to be everyman's consent."[30] In a word, the doctrine of Parliamentary sovereignty, so understood, "is one of the most treasured in British constitutional history. It signifies the glorious liberation of the people from royal tyranny."[31]

The case of the sovereignty of Parliament needs reinterpretation in the light of new developments. The fact (except for Europe and Scotland) that there are no formal checks on the sovereignty of the Parliament "does not mean that in practice there are no limits. There are political checks on the government in the form of self-restraint. Its need to bargain with powerful pressure groups and appease its own backbenchers, its duty to respect the rights of opposition parties in the commons, and, of course, fear that the voters may turn out at the next general election. There have also been cases of groups successfully defying Parliament, such as the trade unions, obstruction of the 1971 Industrial Relations Act, the government pay policy of 1974, or the strike in 1974 in Ulster that brought about the collapse of the power-sharing executive there. But these are not constitutional checks and balances."[32]

7. Rule of Law: The constitutional government of Britain represents democratic way of the people without a declaration of independence and

27. Barker: *Britain and the British People,* pp. 24-25.

28. Jennings: *Parliament,* p. 9.

29. Carter and others: *The Government of Great Britain,* p.42.

30. See Redlich: *Proceedings of the House of Commons,* p. 29.

31. D.V. Verney: *British Government and Politics,* p. 36.

32. Dennis Kavangh, *op. cit.*, p. 56. Since the Parliament passed the European Communities Act in 1972, Britain has accepted the superiority of European law. British Courts can review statutes in the light of this legislation. For example, the House of Lords judged the Merchant Shipping Act of 1988 to be unlawful, because it contravened European Union Law. *Ibid.*, p. 47.

a written fundamental law of the land. It is, indeed, astonishing to see that the British people feel themselves securely free in the midst of an unwritten and evolved constitution the existence of which has been doubted by the protagonists of a written and enacted constitution. The reason for this lies in a constitutional government what the English writers, particularly Dicey, call by the name of 'rule of law'. It is based on the common law of the land and is the product of centuries of struggle between the *rex* or king determined to rule by the virtue of 'divine rights' and the *lex* or law made by the representatives of the people to protect their inherent rights and privileges. Laski writes that it is through the rule of law that the Englishmen "have sought to avoid not merely the obvious dangers of unfettered executive discretion in administration; we have sought also to assure that the citizen shall have his rights decided by a body of men whose tenure is safeguarded against the shifting currents of political opinion."[33]

The rule of law does not mean rule by the supermen; it definitely means rule by the super-science of law. As such, it represents the antithesis of the rule of lawlessness. It stands on the premise that the welfare of the people is the supreme law. It implies a constitutional form of government which exercises power in accordance with law denying any change for the king or his ministers to identify themselves with the state in the fashion of King Louis XIV of France. Thus Lord Hewart of Bury defines the rule of law as to mean the 'supremacy or predominance of law as distinguished from mere arbitrariness."[34] In other words, as a fundamental principle of the British constitutional system, it signifies that the exercise of the powers of government "shall be conditioned by law and that the subjects shall not be exposed to the arbitrary will of their rulers.[35]

The essential principles of the rule of law may be pinpointed in the following manner:

1. The individual should be able, through his legal adviser, to ascertain the law fairly precisely so that he can plan his actions with some degree of certainty.
2. Encroachment on the freedom of the individual must be lawful. Hence:
   (*a*) any act of the Government or its officials must be backed by law;

33. Laski, *op. cit.*. p. 360.

34. Lord Hewart: *New Despotism*, p. 23.

35. Wade and Phillips: *Constitutional Law*, p. 48.

(*b*) no authority can interfere arbitrarily in the individual's way of life;

(*c*) a citizen can feel certain that he will not be arrested unless he is charged with some definite breach of law.

3. Before a citizen can be punished, a breach of the law must be established in a lawful manner before an impartial tribunal.
4. Justice must be regarded as an end in itself, interpreting the law as it stands and uninfluenced outside the law by the wishes of the Parliament or the Government.[36]

The concept of the rule of law was given a classical formulation by Dicey in the form of following propositions:

First, the rule of law guarantees liberty of person and property by implying that no person can be arbitrarily deprived of his life, liberty or property by arrest or detention except for a definite breach of law tried in and held so by a court of competent jurisdiction. Second, the rule of law ensures equality. That is, all persons are equal in the eye of law and subject to ordinary courts of the country regardless of their private or public positions. Every individual is under the control of the law made by the Parliament or common law emanating from judicial decisions and under the jurisdiction of ordinary courts. Last, the rule of law means that the general principles of the English constitution are a result of judicial decisions determining the rights of private citizens in particular cases brought before the courts. Simply stated, it implies that the legal rights of the people are not protected by the terms of a written constitution as in a country like the United States, they are safeguarded by the operation of ordinary laws and remedies available under these ordinary laws against those, whether public officials or private persons who interfere with these freedoms unlawfully.[37]

All the three implications of the rule of law, as explained by the eminent English jurist, signify the existence of a democratic government operating on the maxim that the welfare of the people is the supreme norm of the land. Not only various fundamental freedoms are guaranteed to the people, free access to the courts is also assured to prevent and punish the wrong-doers. The peculiar thing about this is that the rule of law makes an unwritten charter of the essential liberties of the English people. It

36. Harvey and Bather: *The British Constitution*, p. 10.

37. Dicey, *op. cit.*, p. 203.

demonstrates that in Britain, it "is not necessary that in order to exist, a given right or liberty be expressly guaranteed in a statute or other formal act; by common law, it exists and if in so far as, it is not expressly forbidden and does not conflict with the rights of other."[38] It is rightly commented that the rule of law "involves the absence of arbitrary power, effective control of and proper publicity for delegated legislation, particularly when it imposes penalties; that when discretionary power is granted and the manner in which it is to be exercised should, as far as practicable, be defined; that every man should be responsible to the ordinary law whether he be private citizen or public officer, that private rights should be determined by impartial and independent tribunals; and that private fundamental rights are safeguarded by the ordinary laws of the land."[39]

Devolution of Powers

In January, 1998, British Prime Minister Tony Blair and Irish Prime Minister Bertic Ahern published a significant document. It outlined a framework for negotiations. It envisaged balanced constitutional change by both Governments and proposed a devolved form of government within Northern Ireland. After intensive negotiations on 10 April, 1999 a settlement was announced. Known as the Good Friday Agreement or Belfast Agreement, it envisaged radical reforms of the political structure of Northern Ireland, its relations with Ireland, and its constitutional standing within the United Kingdom. Its main provisions are:

1. Establishment of 108-member elected Assembly of Northern Ireland with power to legislate on all domestic matters currently administered by the Northern Ireland Office.
2. Constitution of an elected Executive Committee headed by the First Minister and the Deputy First Minister, an obligation that the Assembly be established within one year, a North/South Ministerial Council at which the representatives of the Irish Government and the executive authority in Northern Ireland might consider issues of cross-border concern.
3. Holding of regular meetings of the representatives of the Irish Government with the members of the British Parliament, the Northern Ireland Assembly and other regional Assemblies of the

38. Ogg and Zink: *Modern Foreign Governments*, p. 44.
39. Wade and Phillips, *op. cit.*, p . 58.

United Kingdom under a new British-Irish Council, with the object of promoting cooperation, information exchange and agreement on issues of mutual interest.

4. Amendment of Art. 223 of the Irish Constitution, replacement of the 1985 Anglo-Irish Agreement with a new bilateral accord incorporating a British-Irish Governmental Council to oversee the Assembly and the North/South Council.
5. Making of commitment by all parties to achieve the decommissioning of paramilitary weapons within two years.

The Northern Ireland Assembly having 108 elected members was established in 1998 as a part of the multi-party agreement on the future governance of Northern Ireland. An Executive Committee headed by the First Minister was constituted from among the legislative members. Responsibility for all matters formerly implemented by the Northern Ireland Office was transferred to the devolved authority under new parliamentary legislation implemented in December, 1999. The Agreement of 1998 also provided for the establishment of a North-South Ministerial Council to facilitate cooperation between the Irish Government and the representatives of the Northern Ireland Executive on specific cross-border or all-island concerns, and a British/Irish Council comprising representatives of the British and Irish Governments, members of the devolved authorities in Northern Ireland, Scotland and Wales, and representatives of the Isles of Man and the Channel Islands. Full devolution under the terms of Agreement was completed in April 2010 with the transfer of powers over policing and justice.

In 1999 devolved legislative authorities were established in Scotland and Wales. In Scotland a new elected Parliament based in Edinburgh was established with powers to legislate on all domestic matters and to vary the taxes set by the British Government by 3 per cent. The Scottish Parliament has 129 members elected every four years by a combined system of direct voting and a form of proportional representation whereby additional members are elected at large from a party list. The National Assembly of Wales located in Cardiff now holds responsibility for issues covered by the Welsh Office of the British Government. The National Assembly of 60 members is elected under the same system as in Scotland.[40]

40. *The Europa World Year-Book* (London: Routledge, 2010), Vol. 2, pp. 4597, and 4605-06

2

MONARCHY

The office of the monarch constitutes, what Walter Bagehot says, the 'dignified executive'. However, the classical defence of the Victorian writer has undergone a great change. The fact that there is 'crowned republic' in Britain illustrates that the king "has been sold to democracy."[1] And yet the existence of the king or queen is a matter of some confusion to the students of comparative governments belonging to a non-English country. The formal duties of a President of any other country of the world are easy to understand as they are stated in the constitution. Different is the case of Britain where the prerogatives of the monarch are nowhere written in an explicit form and no act of Parliament has been formally made to give them a clear expression if circumstances so required. Owing to this, the prerogative "remains a vague twilight area of residual powers, some of which, like the treaty power, are considerable."[2]

King and Crown: The constitutional history of Britain represents a steady decline of the *body politic* in the sphere of Monarchy and the House of Lords. Before the Glorious Revolution of 1688 there was hardly any difference between the King and the Crown as the power of the state was vested in the wielder of the Crown. However, the growing process of democratization brought about a major change and the monarch was gradually compelled to transfer part of his powers to the other institutions like the Cabinet and the House of Commons. The result has been a twofold executive – a powerful head of the government called the Prime Minister and a relatively powerless head of the state called the King or Queen. This development has led to a situation calling for the English writers to make a legal distinction between the Monarch and the Crown of which he

---

1. H.J. Laski: *Parliamentary Government in England*, p. 392.
2. D.V. Verney: *British Government and Politics*, p.141.

is a part. The position becomes clear with this aphorism that while monarch "is a person; the Crown is a symbol – the symbol of supreme executive power. This power used to be wielded by the monarch personally, but in modern constitutional monarchies it is exercised by the ministers of the Crown who are still formally the Queen's ministers but who are very much masters in their own house.[3]

The English writers do not regard the Crown as a headgear of the king or queen; they consider it as an institution vested with all powers of the government. That is why, Sir Sidney Low calls it 'a convenient working hypothesis'[4] and Amos describes it as 'a bundle of sovereign powers, prerogatives and rights – a legal idea.'[5] The distinction between King and Crown may be made more clear with the help of a few noteworthy points. First, the former is a living person, while the latter is the institution. As a person, king is born and he is to die one day; while the Crown is the permanent institution of Britain. The phrase that 'king is dead, long live the king' really means that the king as a person is no more, but may the office of monarch live long. It makes it evident that while the Crown is the repository of all powers, Second, the king is just the head of the state with no authority in his hands. He is a titular head acting on the advice of the ministers who are accountable to the Parliament and ultimately to the electorate of the country. A long course of struggle between the kings and their people brought about a situation in which the real centre of power shifted from a concrete monarch to an abstract Crown. Today the Crown represents a synthesis of supreme authority vested in and exercised by the ministers and the Parliament acting in the name of the 'sovereign'. In a word, the Crown is the key-stone of the constitutional structure of Britain whose powers "are always used as the cabinet, supported by the Parliament, wants them to be used."[6]

Title and Succession: The title and succession of the monarch are governed by the laws made by the Parliament. The Glorious Revolution of 1688 established the fact of the supremacy of Parliament over the king and laws made by the Parliament after this bloodless revolution settled various issues relating to the title and succession of the monarch.

3. *Ibid*, p. 142.
4. Sidney Low: *Government of England*, p. 255.
5. Maurice Amos: *The English Constitution*, p. 88.
6. Carter and others: *The Government of Great Britain*, p. 43.

Some Important Statements

Sovereignty rest with the Queen-in-Parliament (the formal term for Parliament). Britain is a constitutional monarchy: the position of the head of state passes by hereditary succession, but nearly all powers of the crown must be exercised through officers selected and bound by convention and law. ***—Joel Krieger***

The Crown is a soaringly resplendent personification of men's government, of the abstraction and the fact known as sovereignty, supreme authority. It is the picturesque symbol of the unity known to the nation. It brings alive the dignity and authority known in social life majesty. It exemplifies the practice of civic virtue known as a moral society. It is the shining countenance of the glorious aspirations felt as empire. The monarch reigns, but does not personally govern at all. ***—Herman Finer***

The essential feature of the development of monarchy over the centuries has been its adaptability to changing patterns of political power and in particular, in the last three hundred years, its evolution into a Constitutional Monarchy. The Monarch is more a personalised and attractive symbol of national unity than a vague concept of the State, the flag, or even a president, and the hereditary system at least solves the problem of succession. ***—R.M. Punnett***

For instance, the Act of Settlement of 1701 provides that the Crown shall be hereditary in the line of the Princess of Sophia of Hanover so long as it remains Protestant. If a family has no heir within the prescribed degree, the Parliament may by its law bestow Crown on another family. However, the Statute of Westminster of 1931 has made it mandatory that such a decision of the Parliament shall be ratified by the Parliaments of the Commonwealth of Nations, if they pay final allegiance to the British monarch. The principle of heredity is determined by the rule of primogeniture at common law which means that an elder line is preferred to a younger one and that in the same line a male is preferred to a female.

There are other laws relating to the regency, incapacity of the king, and royal marriage. The Regency Act of 1953 lays down the first potential regent (below 18 years) shall be the Duke of Edinburgh and thereafter the Princess Margaret and then those in succession to the Throne who are of age. If the sovereign is abroad or unfit to work for some reason, there is a provision for the appointment of the Counsellors of State to act in the officiating capacity. The Royal Marriages Act of 1872 says that consent of the king is necessary to a marriage in case the person is below 25 years and the marriage might affect the question of succession; in case the person is above 25, no such consent is needed save a year's notice to the Privy

Council. In 1936 the Royal Abdication Act came into force whereby the king may give up his office and then he becomes free from the limitations enjoined upon the great office.

Formal Powers of the Crown: It is, indeed, a peculiar feature of the British constitutional system that while the powers of the king have declined, the powers of the Crown have increased.[7] The reason for this should be traced in the ever-growing process of democratisation. The powers of the Crown have emanated from two sources–the acts made by the Parliament and the prerogatives derived from the common law. While the laws made by the Parliament are explicit and are also amendable by it alone, "the prerogatives are the residue of discretionary or arbitrary authority which at any time is legally left in the hands of the Crown.[8] While keeping in view that the powers of the Crown are vast and they are exercised not by the king as a person but by H.M.'s Government, it shall be worthwhile to mention them in the following manner:

The Crown has very important executive powers. As supreme executive head, it sees that all national laws are duly enforced and observed. It directs, supervises, and controls the work of administrative agencies, collects and expends national revenue, appoints administrative and judicial officers, nominates ecclesiastical and defence authorities, regulates the conditions of service of the personnel, suspends and removes guilty officials, holds supreme command over the defence forces and in some respects supervises the work of local governments. It conducts foreign relations, sends and receives ambassadors and other diplomatic agents, makes war and peace, signs treaties and international agreements.

The powers of the Crown are vast not only in executive matters but also in the field of legislation. It summons the session of the Parliament, prorogues it, and can dissolve the House of Commons. It delivers inaugural address when the Parliament meets which is called Speech from the Throne. It can create peers. All laws passed by the Parliament receive its assent for the sake of constitutional validity. It can promulgate ordinances in relation to its colonies. However, in one direction where its powers have increased immensely is that of delegated legislation whereby the departments have the power of issuing statutory instruments in order to keep the parent legislation in operation. This device has contributed to an immense increase

7. Ogg and Zink: *Modern Foreign Governments*, p. 51.

8. Dicey: *Law of the Constitution*, p. 424.

in the powers of the civil servants. While it is required that such orders must be in conformity with the wishes of the Parliament and they, at a later date, must be approved by the parent institution, normally it happens that all such orders prevail as the Parliament suffers from shortage of time to discuss them in detail.

Then, the Crown has judicial powers. The judges of the local governments are appointed by the Crown. The Lord Chancellor is appointed by it. All issues which come before the judicial committee of the Privy Council are decided by it. It also exercises prerogative of mercy and may grant pardon to persons convicted of criminal offences. In this way, it is the fountain-head of justice. It is also head of the Church of England. As such, it appoints bishops, archbishops and deans. It also summons the ecclesiastical conventions of York and Canterbury and their acts require its assent. Besides, it also acts as the head of the Church of Scotland. By virtue of these ecclesiastical powers the monarch is called the 'defender of the faith'. It is required by the Act of Settlement that the wielder of the Crown must be a Protestant. Finally, it is said to be the fountain-head of honour and by virtue of this privilege, it bestows titles and honours and decorations on such subjects as have rendered meritorious services to the state.

Bagehot's Classic Interpretation: An eminent English writer Bagehot has given a graphic expression of the powers of the monarch. He says that the sovereign has still three rights – the right to be consulted, the right to encourage, and the right to warn. He continues that "a king of great sense and sagacity would want no others.[9] The three rights may be thus explained:

1. **Right to be Consulted:** The fact that the king acts on the advice of the Prime Minister does not imply that the sovereign has forfeited his prerogative of being consulted in the matters of public interest. It is possible that a Prime Minister like Palmerston may be admonished by a monarch like Queen Victoria for keeping her in the dark about certain important developments. He keeps himself in touch with important matters affecting his people and his country. If he so likes, he may call the Prime Minister for gathering necessary information. It is thus obligatory on the part of the Prime Minister to keep the monarch well-informed and obtain his consultation as

9. Bagehot: *The English Constitution*, p. 69.

well, since under the constitution, as Winston Churchill once said, the sovereign "has a right to be made acquainted with anything for which his ministers are responsible, and has an unlimited right of giving counsel to his government."[10]

2. **Right to Encourage:** Then, the king by virtue of his long life and experience may be better informed and more experienced than the Prime Minister and thereby act better as a friend and guide of the government. As Prime Minister Peel said that "a king after a reign of ten years ought to know much more of the working of the machine of government than any other man in the country." When Queen Victoria withdrew from public life due to the death of Prince Consort, even a great leader and Prime Minister like Disraeli had to say: "For more than 40 years Your Majesty has been acquainted with the secret springs of every important event that has happened in the world and during that time have been in constant communication with all the most eminent men of your kingdom. There must necessarily have accrued to a sovereign so placed such a knowledge of affairs and of human character that the most gifted must profit by an intercourse with Your Majesty and the realm suffer by Your Majesty's reserve." This statement makes it quite plain that even a leading political leader has to look to the sagacious king for some sound advice to clear his head. While the tenure of the Prime Minister is quite uncertain as he comes and goes with the political wind, the king enjoys a very long life and his association with many governments makes him a mentor by whom a wise minister is obliged. While recalling his personal experiences, former Prime Minister Clement Attlee once mentioned that the monarch by virtue of keeping himself continuously in touch with public affairs acquires great experience which the Prime Minister cannot have despite his long political career. Even a slight hint from the side of the king is a big counsel to the Prime Minister and he may easily depend upon it as the king is not at all involved in political intrigues of factions and groups.
3. **Right to Warn:** The advisory functions of the king have got an importance of their own and a wise and sagacious king should not press his counsels to the point of creating a crisis. The mystic aura of royalty and the traditional reverence for his highest office lend special weight to his counsels. A Prime Minister like Asquith in his

10. Churchill: *The Second World War: The Finest Hour,* p. 379.

memoirs notes that a monarch may not only advise his ministers, he can also point out objections and suggest alternative measures which the ministers accept with utmost respect. As he is the best informed member and the only one who cannot be forced, says Jennings, to remain quiet and his special status "gives him power to press his views upon the minister making a proposal and (what is sometimes even more important) to press them on the Minister who is not making proposals. He can do more, he can press those views on the Prime Minister, the weight of those authority may in the end produce the cabinet decision."[11]

Reinterpretation of Jennings: Bagehot's assessment of the functions and powers of the monarch reflects a situation considerably out of date, but Jennings presents a more plausible explanation in this regard. Much change in the sphere of monarch's functions and powers has taken place since the time of Bagehot and his 'favourite Queen'. Among modern writers, Jennings illustrates that the functions and constitutional position of the monarch are governed by four factors – his office as an integral part of the constitutional set up, his place in the Commonwealth of Nations, his status as a social figure and, lastly, his personal equation.

1. The monarch is the integral part of the British constitutional system. The framework of cabinet government is such that it cannot operate smoothy without the monarch. The monarch appoints the Prime Minister and other ministers and administers to them the oaths of office and secrecy; he summons and prorogues the Parliament and dissolves the House of Commons; he puts signatures on the bills passed by the Parliament and thereby accords them constitutional validity; he acts as the fountain-head of honour and justice as well as 'defender of the faith'.
2. The monarch provides the golden link of the empire, a lace that joins, like the different beads, the various parts of the Commonwealth of Nations. Though a titular head of the state, British king stands as the shield of imperialism and also as the symbol of peaceful relationship between the 'mother country' and its colonies whether dependent or self-governing dominions. The Commonwealth of Nations thus finds a cementing bond in the great office of the monarch as the dominions pay final allegiance to the king and the republics regard him as the 'symbol of friendship.'

11. Jennings: *Cabinet Government* , pp. 327-28.

Monarchy

Merits

1. It provides a solution to the need for a non-partisan head of state who is above party politics.
2. The monarch embodies traditional authority and so he serves as a symbol of patriotic loyalty and national unity.
3. The monarch constitutes a repository of experience and wisdom, especially in relation to constitutional matters, available to elected governments.

Demerits

1. It violates democratic principles in that political authority is not based on popular consent and is no way publicly accountable.
2. The monarch symbolises (and possibly supports), conservative values such as hierarchy, deference and respect for inherited wealth and social position.
3. The monarchy binds nation to outmoded ways and symbols of the past, thus impeding progress.

Andrew Heywood: *Politics*, p. 342.

3. Apart from being an integral part of the political system of the country, the monarch wields a great social influence. So exalted is the position of the monarch that the British people say that while the sovereign is in the Buckingham Palace, all is right with the realm. The monarch personifies the majesty of the state. Undoubtedly, the king holds the most dignified post of the nation. An appeal made by the king during the days of national crisis, vision granted by him to the people on ceremonial occasions, a word of counsel given by him to settle a major problem etc. all are the living proofs of the unique social position enjoyed by the monarch who by the long traditions of constitutional government has become representative of the people.
4. We come to the axiom of the personal equation of the monarch which is, indeed, the most important factor in determining his real and exalted position. His popularity and the role which he plays in the social and political life of his country is an undisputed affair evident from the fact that even now while the people think in terms of reforming the upper chamber of the Parliament on the lines of a democratic set up, no such thing is heard about the great office of the monarch.

Survival of Monarchy: Finally, we take up the issue of the survival of monarchy in this land of representative government. Much has already been discussed in this regard in the preceding pages and an account in this direction is rather like a recapitulation of what has been said earlier, though in a more systematic manner. It is a fact that the spirit of the time is going against the office of the king and over the last few decades the world has witnessed a steady decline of this ancient office at the sweeping hands of a democratic government. It is indeed, surprising to see that while the thrones are falling down with the lightning of the democratic thistle, the English people still sing the coronation chorus of 'Long Live the Queen' and thereby demonstrate the popular belief that five kings or queens can never go from this world–one of Britain and other four of the playing cards. We may now mention these important reasons of the survival of monarchy in Britain:

1. The English people are essentially conservative and they do not want to change their old institutions radically. The experience of the Commonwealth Period (1649-60) drove home the lesson of even a despotic king's being better than a military dictator.
2. Britain has a cabinet government in which the monarch finds a fitting place. He is the only non-political member of the political machine in the hands of a cabinet having a Prime Minister and other ministers of either Labour or Conservative party. The phrase that 'king can do no wrong', or 'that he reigns but does not govern', is a proof of the fact that real authority is exercised by the ministers responsible to the Parliament and the people, while the king is just a symbol of dignified executive.
3. It follows from the above point, that the existing system of British government cannot operate well without the monarch. No elected person can replace the king in an equally suitable manner. An elected person shall not be free from the shackles of party politics and his short tenure of four or five years shall forfeit stability. The people will never pay that much of reverence to their elected chief as they do for their monarch. It is also possible that an elected person being the representative of the people and thereby in tune with people's minds in all respects will fail to drive out extreme radicalism. Political disputes are also likely to crop up between two elected heads the President and the Prime Minister. Election of the head of the state shall also mean a lot of unnecessary expenditure and political convulsion.
4. The office of the monarch is not without many advantages on the

national plane. The king proves himself to be indispensable in the working of the government and the promotion of the interests of the English people. It is he who invites the leader of the majority party in the House of Commons to form the government as desired by the electorate and it is he who dissolves the House to seek a fresh verdict of the people. A money bill is presented to the Commons with his formal recommendation and every bill passed by the Parliament becomes an act after receiving his assent. In addition to this, he acts as the friend, philosopher and guide of the government–a lighthouse to show path in the midst of ruffled waters. He also acts as mediator to iron out party differences and smoothening many rough edges in the existing postures and diminishing the virulence of the opposition.

5. Apart from some advantages at the national plane, the British monarchy is of some more advantages in the international sphere. The king is the head of the Commonwealth of Nations and all members either pay him final allegiance (if these are Dominions) or regard him a symbol of friendship (if these are Republics). The king is a source of maintaining good relations with other countries of the world by means of matrimonial ties, grant of uniforms and personal goodwill visits.

In a word, the monarch "is essentially a personal trustee or guardian of the constitution."[12] The British monarch is not at all a mere figure-head as treated by the non-serious observers of British government and politics. True to say that he does not steer the ship, but he has to make certain that there is a man at the wheel. While admiring the system of constitutional monarchy in his country, Laski remarks: "Thus, far beyond doubt, the system of limited monarchy has been an unquestionable success in Great Britain. It has, so far, trodden its way with remarkable skill amid the changing habits of the time. Its success, no doubt, has been the outcome of the fact that it has exchanged power of influence; the blame for errors in policy has been laid at the door of ministers who have paid the penalty by loss of office."[13]

---

12. Quinton Hogg: *The Purpose of Parliament,* p. 20.

13. Laski, *op. cit.,* p. 395.

3

WESTMINSTER MODEL

A closer examination of the British political system leaves a strong impression that the fortunate tradition of institutions grown out of experience and fortuitous accident has produced a system known by different names in which 'cabinet government' has the greatest acceptability. It is due to this that cabinet constitutes the 'core' of the entire system.[1] It has entitled a land of monarchy to be called by the glorious name of 'crowned republic' for the reason that it 'vests real executive power, not in an untouchable king, but in a responsible cabinet–responsible, that is to the real sovereign, Parliament, and ultimately to the people. The cabinet system is one of Britain's outstanding gifts to the science and practice of government. Yet this institution, like so many others, was never 'created'. It grew imperceptibly with the result that when it was firmly established, it was already so generally accepted that no serious protests against it were forthcoming. This is generally the advantage of gradually developed institutions over the 'created' ones."[2]

Cabinet Government

The system of cabinet government has these important characteristics:

1. It denotes titular authority of the monarch, The king reign but does not govern. The well-known saying that 'King can do no wrong' means that real authority of the monarch is no longer the deciding and directing factor and his powers are exercised in his name by the ministers ultimately accountable to the people. As the king is the dignified executive, he takes no part in the politics of the country. He does not preside over the meetings of Cabinet which formulates

1. Jennings: *Cabinet Government*, p.1.

2. Neumann: *European and Comparative Government*, p.18.

Some Important Statements

On balance, cabinet government and the fusion of legislature and executive represent a durable and effective formula for governance. There is no Washington-style gridlock (the inability of legislature and executive to agree on policy) in London. On the contrary, if there is a problem at the pinnacle of national power, it is not the separation of powers, but the potential for excessive concentration of power by a Prime Minister who is prepared to manipulate cabinet and blunt the force of collective responsibility. ***—Joel Krieger***

The cabinet is the core of the British constitutional system. It is the supreme directing authority. It integrates what would otherwise be a heterogeneous collective of authorities exercising a vast variety of functions. It provides unity to the British system of government. If, therefore, a constituent assembly were to set out in a written document the present British constitution, as it is actually operated, the cabinet would be provided for a prominent place. ***—Ivor Jennings***

The loyalties which centre no. 1 (Prime Minister) are enormous. If he trips, he must be sustained. If he makes mistakes, they must be covered. If he sleeps, he must not be wantonly disturbed. If he is no good, he must be poleaxed. But this last extreme process cannot be carried out every day and certainly not in the days just after he has been chosen. ***—Winston Churchill***

national policy and takes decisions in matters of urgent public importance.

2. If the king is the nominal head, real authority is in the hands of the Ministers. The Cabinet is the central directing instrument of government. It meets and decides national policy, both domestic and foreign. The ministers are responsible for the administration of their respective departments. It is the Cabinet as a whole which accepts responsibility for the smooth execution of administrative policies by all departments for the prevention of what is called 'departmentalism' and also for the removal of friction and settlement of disputes which may come up between various departments. It is the Cabinet which makes policy regarding the preparation of budget and adoption of legislative measures by the Parliament.
3. If ministers constitute the real executive, they are under double authority–nominal headship of the King and real leadership of the Prime Minister. They are appointed by the king on the advice of the Prime Minister; they take oaths of office and secrecy before the king and submit their resignation to him. But the real leader of the Cabinet is the Prime Minister who presides over its meetings,

distributes portfolios, makes changes in the list of ministers and no longer lives like a *primus inter pares (first among equals).*

4. The cabinet system of government defies the principle of separation of powers save to the extent of keeping judiciary apart. The two organs of government, namely, executive and legislature, are joined together as the ministers are the members of Parliament. According to a well-established convention, the Prime Minister must hail from the House of Commons and his ministers must belong to his political party. By virtue of this inter-linking, ministers attend sessions of the Parliament, speak and put resolutions, pilot budget and bills, but they exercise their right to vote in the chamber where they have their membership. Convention requires that if a minister is not a member of the Parliament, he must have its membership within a period of six months from the date he takes the oath of office and secrecy.
5. The ministers are responsible to the Parliament. This is the most dominant feature of the British government. As a result, ministers can continue in office so long as they enjoy the confidence of the Parliament and through it of the electorate.
6. The point of ministerial responsibility needs some modification in the light of new developments. It is correct to say that now British Cabinet has become 'responsive' rather than responsible to the Parliament. When a question is asked, the Cabinet may take benefit of not answering it in the 'public interest'; when a matter is brought to the House for discussion, the Cabinet banks upon the support of its majority party.
7. The factor of secrecy contributes to the strong position of the Cabinet. Every minister is under an oath not to break the secrecy of the decisions and any violation in this regard amounts to a situation calling for the resignation of the minister with almost no prospects of his return to the high ministerial post.
8. The strong position of the Cabinet going to the extent of being dubbed as a 'dictatorship qualified by publicity under Parliamentary control' is a result of political homogeneity and party solidarity. All ministers come from the party having absolute majority in the House of Commons. It is rarely possible, and that too during times of grave national crisis, that a coalition government is set up that too happens with the consent and cooperation of the two major parties.

9. In a cabinet government, the existence of the popular chamber depends upon the will of the ministers, particularly the Prime Minister. The Prime Minister with or without the prior approval of his colleagues may advise the monarch to dissolve the House of Commons for seeking final verdict of the people on matters of great public concern.

The system of cabinet government as existing in Britain illustrates that the real authority is not in the hands of the king, it is with the Cabinet– a body of important ministers under the leadership of the Prime Minister belonging to the political party enjoying absolute majority in the House of Commons (either singly or in coalition with some other party) and having control over both the executive and legislative departments of the government.[3]

Prime Ministerial Government

The most astonishing development in the sphere of the Westminster model should be traced in the extremely powerful position of the Prime Minister calling for the rechristening of this form of political system as the Prime Ministerial Government. The classical doctrine of the Prime Minister's being 'first among equals' or *primus inter pares* now stands thoroughly discredited. Such an astounding development of the British constitutional system, however, found its best expression in the statement of R.H.S. Crossman who should be regarded as the author of a new doctrine. On the basis of his inside knowledge of the British government by virtue of having had close association with the Labour Prime Minister Wilson, Crossman could go to the final length of saying that the nomenclature of parliamentary or cabinet government was outdated in view of the very strong position of one man – the Prime Minister.[4]

The discovery of Crossman made him a well-known figure in the field of the study of modern political systems. His findings led to the emergence of ample literature on the subject that virtually created a sort of interesting controversy on the vast powers and real position of the 'first elected monarch' of England. He has listed following relevant powers that the Prime Minister now wields:[5]

3. See A.B. Keith: *The British Cabinet System*, p.304.

4. Crossman: 'Introduction' in Walter Bagehot's *English Constitution*, p.51.

5. Crossman: *Inside View: Three Lectures on Prime Ministerial Government*, pp.63-66

1. 'The Prime Minister is the master of his Cabinet. As such, any minister fighting in the Cabinet for his Department can be sacked by the Prime Minister any day. The ministers must be constantly aware that their tenure of office depends on his personal decisions.
2. The Prime Minister decides about the agenda of the Cabinet. Here the Prime Minister has the last word. He decides (though in consultation with the Secretary to the Cabinet) what issues shall be fought out and what not.
3. The Prime Minister decides about the organisation of the Cabinet committees. What committees exist, how they are manned, above all, who are the chairmen–all this is entirely a concern of the Prime Minister.
4. The Prime Minister has almost monopoly of patronage. He personally controls the Honours List. He has an unchallenged and free hand in selecting new members of the House of Lords. It gives him a useful device for retiring an ageing or incompetent minister without disgrace and purging his Government by promotions into the upper chamber.
5. Even more important than the control of the patronage is the control of the Civil Service which a Prime Minister has exercised–again since the period of Lloyd George.
6. The final power of the Prime Minister is his personal control of Government publicity. The Government's press relations are conducted by the Number 10 press department at its daily press conferences. That means, the people have a daily coherent, central explanation of what the Government is doing–an explanation naturally in terms the Prime Minister thinks right.

Thus on the basis of these 'relevant' powers of the Prime Minister, Crossman sums up: "It does not mean that he is a dictator; it does not mean that he can tell his Ministers what to do in their Departments. But it does mean that in the battle of Whitehall this man in the centre, this chairman, this man without a Department, without apparent power, can exert, when he is successful, a dominating personal control. This explains why a British Cabinet is always called a 'Wilson Cabinet' or a 'Macmillan Cabinet'. It is because every Cabinet takes its tone from the Prime Minister."[6]

---

6. *Ibid*, pp.67-68.

As already pointed out, the findings of Crossman invited comments from several eminent persons most of whom criticized him for going too much away from the plane of political reality. The sum and substance of the critics boils down to this essential point that though the powers of the Prime Minister have immensely grown, it is still incorrect to designate him as the singular ruler of the country. The position of the Cabinet is still quite strong and no Prime Minister can be in a position to arrogate to himself what really belongs to it. As such, the nomenclature of Cabinet Government is still in existence. While furnishing a plausible rejoinder to what Crossman has argued, G.W. Jones has put his own point to substantiate the existence of the 'Cabinet Government' in England. He has tried to assert: "Shared responsibility is still meaningful, for a Prime Minister has to gain the support of the bulk of his Cabinet to carry out his policies. He has to persuade it and convince it that he is right. Its meetings do not merely follow his direction. Debate and conflict are frequent. It cannot be bypassed and he cannot be an autocrat. To attempt to become one presages his political suicide."[7]

Patrick Gordon Walker, who had the privilege of serving as a minister in the Labour Cabinet of Wilson, endorses the same point. According to him, although by the 1950s and 1960s, the office of the Prime Minister has risen greatly in status and that he has acquired an authority different in kind from that of his colleagues, he is still not independent of the Cabinet. The Cabinet remains the sole source of political authority. On occasions and for a while, a partial Cabinet can act in its name, but the power of a partial Cabinet always depends upon the assurance that sufficient number of leading ministers share in its decisions to secure the full authority of the Cabinet in the end. As he says: "A strong Prime Minister can be very strong. He can sometimes commit the Cabinet by act or words. But he cannot habitually or often do so. A Prime Minister who habitually ignored the Cabinet, who behaved as if Prime Ministerial Government were a reality–such a Prime Minister could come to grief. He would be challenged by his colleagues in the Cabinet and on occasion overridden. Theoretically, a Prime Minister could dismiss all his Ministers; but then he would present his critics in the party with potent leadership: Mr. Macmillan's mass dismissal in 1962 were generally held to have weakened him. Macmillan was less dominant in the new Cabinet than in his old. Prime Ministers

7. G.W. Jones: "The Prime Minister's Power" in Anthony King (ed.): *The British Prime Minister*, p. 1 90.

may well, like Mr. Harold Wilson, regard Mr. Macmillan's slaughter as an example to be eschewed."[8]

In this direction, we may refer to a sharp rejoinder given by Labour Prime Minister Harold Wilson. He says: "Cabinet is a democracy, not an autocracy. Each member of it, including the Prime Minister, seeks to convince his colleagues as to the course to follow. The Cabinet bears his stamp, it is true, on each and every policy issue, but it is the Cabinet not the Prime Minister who decides. The growth of Cabinet committee system is one factor which would restrain the overwhelming desires of a would-be dictator."[9] In order to contradict the thesis of Crossman, he lays stress on the following propositions:[10]

1. In peace time in this century and earlier, the Prime Minister in each decade has exercised, or has been able to exercise, more powers than his predecessor. But this is because, over the whole period, governments have exercised more power and influence. The Prime Minister has shared in this increased power, and almost certainly has increased his share. Now every action of the Prime Minister is personalized in the daily dramatization of politics which makes him superior to, but by no means supreme over, his colleagues.
2. Arguments based on emergency situations such as world wars are inadmissible for peace time conditions. The Prime Minister is invariably accorded emergency powers, but these are limited in duration; still more, they are conditional on his maintaining parliamentary confidence, such as a coalition tends to ensure.
3. The arguments in support of the thesis of Prime Ministerial government entirely fail to allow for almost 180-degree differences in the style of individual, indeed successive, Prime Ministers. Constitutional rationalists fail to recognise that Cabinets, and Prime Ministers too, are essentially human and, being human, are essentially different. Harold Macmillan has been rightly praised as a successful Prime Minister, but this did not mean that he could impose his will.
4. Few Prime Ministers, except in war time and rarely then, could dictate to their Cabinets, except on the basis of consultation with their senior

8. Gordon Walker: *The Cabinet*, pp. 95-96.

9. Harold Wilson: *The Governance of Britain*, pp. 8 9.

10. *Ibid.*, pp. 9-11.

colleagues. Prime Ministers who have ignored or defied the maxim, particularly if they have refused to appoint anyone who has opposed their views or in any way given offence, and have instituted 'government by crony', have invariably paid the price. Chamberlain was an obvious, but not the only, example.

5. Another defect of the theorem of Prime Ministerial government is its unrealistic assumption that everything is static. There are things he might essay in a given situation, say after a successful government election, that he would hesitate to attempt if things were going badly for him in the Parliament.
6. If Richard Crossman is right in saying–and most historians support his thesis–that the situation Bagehot was describing was just about to end, so there is a case for saying that Richard Crossman's analysis failed to take account of the new checks and balances qualifying the power of the Prime Minister. These include certainly the greater power of Cabinet committees, not to mention the select committees, whose extended power is one of Richard Crossman's achievements.

Though one may agree wholly or in part with the argument of Crossman about redesignating the British form of government, one can not deny this fact that the Prime Minister has become the most powerful institution in the political system of England.[11]

Prime Minister

If the Cabinet is the most important institution of the English constitutional system, the Prime Minister by virtue of being its leader is the most powerful officer. He is the real head of the government, while the monarch above him is the titular head of the state. In the words of Ramsay Muir, while the Cabinet "is the steering wheel of the ship of the state, the Prime Minister is the steersman."[12] The peculiar thing about this great office is that it has irresistibly grown since the times of Robert Walpole. Curiously, it has no legal basis: it is based on usages and conventions. It is bound with the designation of the First Lord of Treasury since 1721. Historical information reveals that for the first time in 1878 the title of the Prime Minister made appearance in a public document when Lord Beaconsfield signed the Treaty of Berlin. The Chequers Estate

11. *Ibid.*, p.10.

12. Ramsay Muir: *How Britain is Governed*, p.63.

Act of 1917 made a passing reference, but the Ministers of the Crown Act of 1937 gave a legal recognition to this great office by assigning fifth position to the Prime Minister in order of precedence and also by specifying his salary and pension. It was reiterated in the Ministerial Salaries and Members' Pensions Act of 1965.

Appointment: The Prime Minister is appointed by the monarch. Invitation to form the government implies his appointment. Convention requires that the monarch must choose the leader of the majority party in the House of Commons who can run the government with a comfortable majority behind him. It makes the point clear that British government is plebiscitical. That is, the real choice is made by the people who register their electoral verdict by giving majority either to the Labour or to the Conservative party. The existence of two well-organised and disciplined political parties has made it virtually essential that this office alternate between the two according to the verdict of the electorate.

The question of the appointment of the Prime Minister is based upon some well-established conventions. First, he must be a member of the House of Commons. That is, a peer cannot hold this office until he renounces his peerage as Sir Alec Douglas-Home had to do in 1963. This convention started in 1902 (after the exit of Lord Salisbury) and was confirmed in the event of 1923 when after the resignation of Bonar Law, the King invited Stanley Baldwin in preference to the ambitious Conservative candidate Lord Curzon. Second, he must be the leader of the party having clear majority in the House of Commons. In case a Prime Minister dies or resigns and the issue of appointing his successor comes up, the monarch may either consult its top-ranking leader before making up his mind, or may ask the party concerned to apprise him of its decision in this regard. For instance, after the resignation of Sir Anthony Eden in 1956, the Queen invited Macmillan to form the government on the advice of Sir Winston Churchill; likewise she invited Douglas-Home in 1963 on the advice of the outgoing Prime Minister (Macmillan).

However, there is some scope for monarch to exercise his discretion in this regard either to start or confirm a healthy practice, or to solve a major crisis. For instance, the monarch chose Ramsay MacDonald in 1931 in preference to Asquith although the Labour Party had behind it only about 1/3 of the members of the Commons. So, in 1940 the King chose Winston Churchill (not Neville Chamberlain) on the conviction that during the times of national crisis only a man like him would be able to requisition the support of the Conservatives as well as of most of the Labour members of the House of Commons. In both these cases, the choice of the monarch was appreciated by the people. However, it all happened under 'exceptional' circumstances, otherwise a constitutional monarch is expected to exercise his prerogative in a way that his motives are taken as 'sincere' by the people of the country. Herbert Morrison's assessment is appealing that the sovereign's choice "has much constitutional significance'. The choice may be a very delicate one and involve embarrassing complications. The sovereign would, of course, take all relevant considerations into account, and be at great pains not only to be constitutionally correct, but make every effort to see that the correctness is likely to be generally recognised."[13]

Functions and Powers: The functions and powers of the Prime Minister not described in any law or any written part of the constitution but forming part of the world of unwritten maxims of the constitution are vast that make him capable of acting like an 'autocrat' in certain respects.

1. Soon after his appointment, the Prime Minister makes the list of his ministers specifying their portfolios. In this direction, he is caught up by some strong considerations which are of a political as well as personal nature. He has to include the names of his most loyal friends who constitute his 'inner cabinet'; then he takes those important men of his party who are the leaders of various groups and without their support it may not be possible for him to maintain unity and solidarity in the ranks of the party; then, the aspect of merit and competence has its own part and the Prime Minister pays due attention to the long experience and efficiency of his colleagues who would keep his government running well. In addition to these powerful considerations, the Prime Minister sees that various geographical areas of the country are, as far as possible, fairly represented; that some ministers are taken from the House of Lords and that some room is given to the men of younger generations in order to arrange for their political training. He cannot increase the total number of his ministers beyond 91.
2. If the Prime Minister is the maker of his government, he is also its unmaker. He may change the portfolios of his ministers and drop any offending colleague just by the hint of his displeasure. It has

13. Morrison: *Government and Parliament*, p.77.

almost become like a theoretical proposition that the ministers act during the pleasure of the Parliament and the sovereign: the actual position is that they continue in office during the pleasure of the Prime Minister. This reason prompts Laski to say that the Prime Minister is 'central to the life and death of his ministers.'[14]

3. The Prime Minister is not only the leader of the government, he is also the leader of the party. As such, he enjoys double leadership making his position unassailable on either front. When elections take place, the personality of the leader counts above all and a victory of the leadership is a reward given to him in the form of, what is called, the mandate of the people. Laski thus aptly suggests that a general election "is nothing so much as a plebiscite between two alternative Prime Ministers."[15]
4. The Prime Minister is the dispenser of great offices. Apart from ministerial assignments, many other high officials like ambassadors, Lord Chancellor, Justices, Chairmen and members of the statutory commissions etc. are appointed by the monarch on the recommendation of the Prime Minister. The monarch is also the dispenser of justice and for this he appoints the judges, including Lord Justice of Appeals, on the advice of the Prime Minister.
5. The Prime Minister is the chief policy-maker. He convenes and presides over the meetings of the Cabinet. He decides as to what the Cabinet shall deliberate and discuss.
6. The Prime Minister acts as the general supervisor of government and co-ordinator of various departments. He sees to it that there is no rift among his ministers and if a matter comes up, he sees that it is amicably settled. There are various committees of the Cabinet, permanent and ad hoc, which do the work of maintaining harmony and co-ordination. The Prime Minister may act as the chairman of any committee for this purpose.
7. The Prime Minister is the channel of communication between the Crown and the ministers. If the king wants to know anything about Cabinet's policy, the Prime Minister passes necessary information to him. So the ministers meet the monarch with Prime Minister's approval. There can be no communication between the monarch and the ministers without the consent of the Prime Minister.

14. Laski: *Parliamentary Government in England*, p. 228.

15. *Ibid.*, p. 241.

Prime Minister

Powers and Position

1. Working Head of the State
2. Head of the Cabinet
3. Leader of the party having majority in the House of Commons
4. Member of the House of Commons
5. Being choice of the electorate as nation's representative at international Summit Conferences.
6. The Minister whom the electorate regard as person responsible for the well-being of the country
7. The Minister with the power to request dissolution of Parliament, to appoint or dismiss Cabinet Ministers, to dispense an enormous amount of patronage

Immense Power limited by

1. Prerogatives of the Crown as a last resort to oppose him
2. The delaying power of the House of Lords
3. The nature of modern party system, a party being a coalition of pressure groups, making it necessary for him to propitiate all factions and thus to govern by means of continual compromise.
4. The risk that a docile majority in the House of Commons will in a crisis turn hostile and refuse to give him confidence any more.
5. The need to remember that the Leader of the Opposition is an alternative Prime Minister, and that the electorate is continually comparing the two men, showing their opinion ultimately at a general election

Powers dependent upon

1. His authority over the electorate
2. Party discipline
3. His control over the Cabinet
4. His widespread patronage

8. The initiator of all legislation of a fundamental nature which must be approved by him at a Cabinet meeting before it is submitted to Parliament.

9. The most influential and powerful man in the country who is for a period of time almost a benevolent dictator

10. The counterpart in some measure of the President of USA

6. The mass media by which builds up an image of himself as an infallible and omniscient statesman are equally capable of destroying the image and showing that it has feet of clay

7. The constant pressure of events over which he has little control, such as political events in other countries making it necessary and expedient for him to modify his policy according to what is feasible (as opposed to what is desirable)

Fundamentally it is the moral authority he has acquired which counts with the nation.

Source: F.W.G. Benemy: *The Elected Monarch : The Development of the Power of the Prime Minister*, pp. 262-63.

8. The Prime Minister is the link between the Parliament and the ministers. He is the leader of the House of Commons, though sometimes he may transmit some of his powers to his most trusted deputy. This privileged position makes his authority above that of his colleagues. In consultation with his Cabinet ministers, he decides the time of the session of the Parliament, prepares inaugural address of the monarch, decides about the time of adjournment and prorogation of the Parliament. He asks his ministers to move a bill in the Parliament, put some resolution for approval, and present budget or money bill after securing formal recommendation of the monarch. He also instructs his party whips to maintain discipline in the ranks of the party.
9. The Prime Minister performs many important functions in the international sphere. Either personally or through his nominees he attends conferences of the Commonwealth of Nations and the United Nations. The presence of the British Prime Minister or his nominee at international gatherings is seen with special significance. It is the Prime Minister who makes authoritative pronouncements of his government's policy in international matters. Prosecution of war, mobilization of troops, conclusion of peace, negotiation of treaties etc. all demand expression of approval from the statements of the Prime Minister.
10. The Prime Minister is the leader of the nation. During days of national crisis, if time does not allow him to take his ministers in confidence, he may personally act or give immediate authority to his ministers to do the needful for facing a serious problem.

Position: It is obvious that the Prime Minister occupies a position of unmistakable supremacy in the constitutional structure of England. Lord Morley has called him *primus inter pares* meaning' first among equals.' This observation is based on the view that the Prime Minister is like the captain of his team without any special power making him a master, if not the boss, of his colleagues. While all the members of the Cabinet stand on a footing of equality, speak with equal voice, and (excluding some rare occasions) are counted on the fraternal principle of one man one vote, the Prime Minister being head of the team enjoys no special position save that of being 'first among equals'. Another view is given by Sir William Vernon Harcourt that the Prime Minister is 'a moon among lesser stars'. This phrase seems to recognize a lower position of the ministers as compared with that of the head. A moon among the lesser stars certainly has a higher position, but Harcourt corrects his real interpretation by adding that even this 'may not really be strong enough'.

If the classical aphorisms given by Morley and Harcourt need revision in the light of latest developments, the observation of Ramsay Muir also goes beyond the limit of plausibility. The English Prime Minister is neither a mere first among equals, nor can he be identified with a dictator. The fact is that he is a democratic leader of a democratic government working with the support of his democratic party. In the event of his wise handling of the situation he may win the support of all parties as Churchill had during the Second World War[16]; on the other hand, by losing the confidence of his party or people, he may be 'dethroned' like Ramsay McDonald and Neville Chamberlain. He is, indeed, both a captain and a man at the helm. The dominant fact about the position of the Prime Minister "is that he must operate flexibly within the Parliamentary and Cabinet system in which power is distributed and which gives the Prime Minister as much command over the political situation as he can earn."[17]

What lends weight to the observation that the English Prime Minister has become like a President or even a dictator draws sustenance from these points:

1. The Prime Minister has become the deputy of the nation as a whole irrespective of the fact that he is chosen by a particular constituency. A general election is now an election of the Prime Minister.
2. A Prime Minister banking upon the force of electoral mandate feels amply free in the selection of his colleagues. He comes to have a strong position whereby he effectively controls his party without being restrained by it in a like manner. Important leaders of the party move around his table for the collection of ministerial awards.
3. The power of patronage has now enabled the Prime Minister to act as the master not only of his cabinet but of the administration as a whole. The monarch is the fountain-head of honour, but all honours can be awarded by him to one whose name is recommended by the Prime Minister.
4. The Prime Minister is not only the controller of his party as well as of government, he has also become the real controller of the army of civil servants.
5. The Prime Minister has become the controller of the Parliament. His will becomes a law when an official bill is carried through the

16. Amery: *Thoughts on the Constitution*, p.72.

17. Ronald Butt: *The Power of Parliament*, p. 421

House of Commons, it cannot be obstructed by the House of Lords for ever, and the royal assent is a matter of constitutional formality. Moreover, there is no judicial check on him as the courts have no power of judicial review the like of which we find in the United States.

Let us reiterate what we have said above. The Prime Minister is yet far away from being dubbed as the President, much less an autocrat. The fact of Cabinet's strong position wherefrom the strong position of the Prime Minister emerges cannot be lost sight of. Or as one leading English political figure endorses on the basis of his personal knowledge of the inside story of British government: "A strong Prime Minister can be very strong. He can sometimes commit the Cabinet by acts or words. But he cannot habitually or often do so."[18]

Cabinet

What really keeps the British government in operation is neither the King nor his Privy Council, it is the Cabinet–a body of very important ministers headed by the Prime Minister. By all means, the Cabinet is the central directing instrument of government occupying a pivotal position in the constitutional structure of the country. So strong a position has now been assumed by it that it has become almost improbable for the House of Commons to exercise its popular check of 'responsibility' in the traditional sense of the term. The fact is that the Cabinet has now become more of a responsive and less of a responsible body. Allied with this is another fact that the strong position of the Cabinet has remained despite an astonishing increase in the powers of the Prime Minister.

Composition: The Prime Minister is the architect of his government. So goes the classical saying of Lord Morley that Prime Minister is the key-stone of the Cabinet-arch. The monarch invites the leader of the majority party in the House of Commons to form government. This invitation means the appointment of the leader of the Cabinet. As there are two leading political parties and power alternates between the two, it is inevitable that the office of the Prime Minister goes either to the Labour Party or to the Conservative party whichever commands absolute majority in the House of Commons. There is almost no chance for the monarch to exercise his discretion in this regard, for before making up his mind the

18. Gordon Walker: *The Cabinet*, p. 95.

sovereign has to assure himself by consulting the prominent personalities of the party in power whether the name chosen by him would be able to win the confidence of the party as well as command a working majority in the House of Commons. It is this chosen leader (called the Prime Minister) who selects the team of his ministers.

While the theory of cabinet government implies that the monarch appoints his ministers, practice shows that he gives approval to the list of ministers submitted by the Prime Minister. As the king is above politics, he is not expected to make any interference. It, however, does not mean that the Prime Minister has an absolutely free hand in the making of his ministers.The Prime Minister has to keep in mind considerations of territorial representation, eminence and position of the leaders of various groups within his own party and, above all, the merit and competence of his colleagues in order to keep the machinery of government well in operation.

Besides these points of consideration, the hands of the Prime Minister are also tied by certain statutory measures passed by the Parliament to prevent the danger of increasing domination of the executive over the legislature. It has, therefore, been laid down that the Prime Minister cannot enlarge the size of his government as per his free will. For instance, he cannot enlarge the size of his government as per his free will. The Ministers of the Crown Act of 1937 provided that only 18 out of 21 senior ministers could serve in the House of Commons at one time. It also provided that not more than 20 junior ministers could sit in the House of Commons at a time. According to the recommendations of the Herbert Committee of 1941, it was suggested that not more than 60 ministers should serve in the House of Commons at one time. The House of Commons Disqualification Act of 1957 (based on the above report) provided that not more than 70 ministers of all categories could serve in the House of Commons at a time. The Ministers of the Crown Act of 1964 has increased the number of ministers of all categories from 70 to 91, but it has abolished the ceiling on the number of senior ministers drawn from the House of Commons. However, there is no law laying down qualifications of a minister and in that respect the Prime Minister is guided by personal and political considerations in making the list of his ministers.

The British government is like a wheel within wheels. As such, a line of difference is sometimes drawn between the Cabinet and the ministry. Simply stated, it may be pointed out that while ministry means a set of all ministers belonging to all categories, Cabinet is a body of selected ministers only. The ministers of the Cabinet hold important portfolios and constitute the decision-making body of the government. Other ministers may be invited by the Prime Minister to take part in the Cabinet meetings if so necessary.

The practice of working with the collaboration of all or of a few colleagues varies according to the predilections of the Prime Minister and also perhaps in response to the balance of opinion. The practice of acting, off and on, with the active assistance or cooperation of a few important ministers has led to the emergence of what is now called 'inner' or 'partial' Cabinet. Evidence shows that in the post-First War cabinet, Prime Minister Lloyd George had an inner cabinet of three ministers – Horne, Geddes and Greenwood; in 1938 Prime Minister Neville Chamberlain had a like informal body of three ministers – Simon, Hali and Hoare. The personnel of such a body of close confidants may also vary from time to time as Prime Minister Lloyd George replaced his body of three advisors by two – Churchill and Birkenhead.

It is also possible that the size of this small band of personal advisors may become quite large. Prime Minister Ramsay MacDonald was said to have a body of six ministers, called the 'Big Six' (Henderson, Clynes, Snowden, Thomas and Sidney Webb, including himself). The practice continued even after the Second World War. Prime Minister Attlee had such a body of two ministers like Bevin and Cripps, though sometimes he also banked heavily on the co-operation of Harrison. After the elections of 1964, Prime Minister Harold Wilson had such confidants in George Brown, James Callaghan and Patrick Gordon Walker. This point may be reiterated that the existence of such a small body of trusted colleagues of the Prime Minister functions under the leadership of the Prime Minister for discussing important matters like general conditions of the country, parliamentary situations, the state of the party and tactics to be pursued in the Parliament.

Though not so easily understandable, Patrick Gordon Walker, who had the privilege of serving as an important minister of the Labour Cabinet headed by Harold Wilson, endorses on the basis of his personal knowledge that inner cabinet cannot be likened with a partial cabinet. According to him, an inner cabinet is just an informal body of very few important ministers who are often consulted by the Prime Minister, while the partial cabinet is a large organization consisting of a fairly large number of the ministers who are consulted by the Prime Minister in a way as if he were speaking to them in a full-fledged cabinet meeting. Moreover, while the former has no formal recognition, the latter has it in the annals of the growth of cabinet system in England. What he attempts to lay down is that though the Prime Minister acts in close consultation with some of his very close confidants, it does not lead to the existence of, what is sometimes called, the 'inner Cabinet.'[19]

As a matter of fact, the idea of an inner cabinet refers to the central nucleus within the cabinet structure, a core of principal leaders with whom the Prime Minister confers more than with others. Thus, something like a hierarchy within the cabinet develops. However, this so-called inner cabinet is quite different from the War Cabinet. The latter is, as Churchill reminds us, like an official policy-making committee which consequently bears full and exclusive responsibility for the conduct of affairs. This informal inner cabinet is only a group of men who are closer to the Prime Minister and more important than other Cabinet ministers and who help him in the formulation of national policy. What is very important is that as a group of a few very important members of the Cabinet, they bear no former responsibility.

Grades and Portfolios: Under the leadership of the Prime Minister, there are different grades of the members of the ministry.

1. There is the inner Cabinet consisting of some four or five ministers. These are the most trusted men of the leader who are committed to do or die for the sake of a policy adopted by them. In war times smaller circle is also known by the name of 'war cabinet'.
2. There is the Cabinet consisting of some 20 senior ministers. These are very important ministers and they hold charge of important departments as foreign affairs, home, exchequer, Commonwealth relations, colonial affairs, defence, trade etc. Some of the Cabinet ministers may not have any department at all and may be made to have supervision over some other departments as we notice in the cases of Lord Privy Seal and Lord President of the Council. But the outstanding feature of the Cabinet system is that these ministers meet collectively at least once a week to discuss matters of public and national importance and take policy-decisions which must be respected and followed by all regardless of the personal views of anyone of them.

19. Gardon Walker, *op. cit.*, p. 88.

3. There are ministers of the Cabinet rank. They are junior to the Cabinet ministers. They have charge of their administrative departments. They draw the same salary as paid to a Cabinet minister, but they are not allowed to sit in the Cabinet meetings until so desired by the Prime Minister.
4. There are ministers of state or deputy ministers in administrative departments where the work is particularly heavy and complex. A minister of state may either hold independent charge of some less important department or be associated with some important minister of the higher grade. It looks that a minister of this category holds a position between a full minister and a parliamentary secretary.
5. There are parliamentary secretaries or junior ministers associated with the ministers, they have no 'independent' charge of a department and, as such, they have no ministerial powers. They are not counted as ministers of the Crown. They are appointed by the monarch on the advice of the Prime Minister who sometimes takes the advice of his ministers concerned in this regard. The main work of a parliamentary secretary is to assist his minister in his work relating to the Parliament as answering questions and taking part in parliamentary debates.

The principle of responsibility of the ministers to the Parliament demands by virtue of a very well-established convention that all ministers belonging to any category, right from the Prime Minister down to a parliamentary secretary, must belong to the party having absolute majority in the House of Commons. In case the Prime Minister takes one who is not a member of the Parliament, it is required that he must find his place in either House within a period of 6 months. It also depends upon the discretion of the Prime Minister to have a minister without portfolio entrusted with the work what he likes to be done by him. It also depends upon the personal choice of the Prime Minister to designate the senior-most minister of the Cabinet as his 'Deputy'.

Responsibility: The most essential feature of the cabinet government is that the ministry remains accountable to the Parliament for its acts of commission and omission. To say that a minister is responsible for some action may, however, mean several different things. It may mean that he is the actual agent, the person deserving blame or praise therefor, in other words, the author of the action. Alternatively, it may mean no more than that he is accountable for the action in the sense that he is the proper person to be visited with the constitutional consequences or that he is the person under whose authority it was taken. In either case, the responsibility may be taken either as legal or conventional. As a matter of fact, the responsibility is of two types–individual and collective. As the ministers share collective responsibility for the general policies and record of government and also bear an individual responsibility for the actions and record of that portion of the administrative machine placed directly in their charge. Let us study both in the following manner:

Each minister is understood to be responsible for his own decisions and for all the actions of the department or office under his control. It is based on the notion that the minister should be a public spokesman and a defender of that part of administrative structure within his competence. It is he, or his absence his deputy, who explains the policy of the department in Parliament and elsewhere and upon him falls the task of answering criticisms directed at his department. As the Cabinet is said to have the final word in all matters of general policy, so the minister may have the last word in his own so far his department is concerned. It is required that a minister must resign in case he ceases to satisfy the House of Commons as was done by War Minister Profumo in 1963. It may, however, happen that a Prime Minister does not allow his minister to resign for the reason of his great utility, or the minister concerned may take the benefit of a wrong committed not by him but by some of his subordinate officials against whom suitable action would be taken. In 1954 Agriculture Minister Sir Thomas Dugdale took the plea of his ignorance about the land-purchase deal of his department and sought to save himself from the charge of administrative mismanagement, though he made it clear that he would take immediate steps to end wrong procedure. Strachey's failure to resign from the Ministry of Food after the collapse of Labour's 'groundnuts scheme' in West Africa and Lennox-Boyd's continuance as Colonial Secretary after the disclosure of negligence in the Kenya prison administration which led to the death of 11 prisoners at the Hola Camp in 1959 may be cited as other examples in this regard.[20]

As a matter of fact, the case of individual responsibility has lost much of its weight, since the Prime Ministers have converted it into the doctrine of a minister's being individually accountable to their own side. In case the Prime Minister wants to defend his minister, he faces the angry House with all skill at his disposal; in the event of his feeling dissatisfied with

20. G. C. Moodie: *The Government of Great Britain*, p.96.

the behaviour of his minister, the Prime Minister asks him to resign before the matter is taken up in the House of Commons. It depends upon the stand of the Prime Minister alone to take action against an erring minister or defending him by involving his case with the issue of collective responsibility. No minister can be sure so far as the support of the Prime Minister is concerned. He may, however, take it for granted that instead of remaining accountable to the Parliament individually, he has now become responsible to his party and its leader holding the office of the Prime Minister.

Collective responsibility signifies that all ministers must come and go together. All members of the government are expected to support publicly the official policies and actions regardless of their private feelings about the matter. In case any minister is not in agreement with the official line, he must resign. In other words, as Lord Melbourne once said, 'all must tell the same story.' In practical terms, it is impossible for the House of Commons to vote for the removal of a particular member of the government without voting against the whole government, unless it is clear that government is prepared to sacrifice that individual either as a scapegoat or because no collective responsibility is involved. The performance of the government as a whole should be judged while lauding or denouncing its performance. "In short the administration must stand or fall together. All its members must submit its policy to Parliament, must defend that policy, and, without exception, must resign or submit themselves to a general election if the House of Commons refuses to support it."[21]

The doctrine of collective responsibility has certain important ingredients. First, it covers the Cabinet and not the ministry as a whole, since the members of the former take part in the decision-making process. It is a different matter that even non-Cabinet ministers must support the official line, or they should resign. Second, sometimes the Prime Minister may take a decision with the advice or consultation of his inner Cabinet, what Prime Minister Lloyd George called 'inner Council', and may hope to have its endorsement in time to come by the Cabinet as a whole. Even in such a case no Cabinet minister may take the plea of being no party to the official stand as he was not consulted. Third, the principle of joint responsibility restricts the authority of the Prime Minister in the sense

21. Gardon Walker, *op. cit.*, p.88.

that it informs him to work in consultation with his ministers, particularly the very important ones for no other reason than to keep his hands strengthened and to avoid the position of a formidable onslaught on his own authority by his own colleagues. In this way, the principle of joint responsibility not only strengthens the position of the Cabinet vis-a-vis the Prime Minister, it also enables the ruling party to face the opposition in a vigorous manner.

In fine, the responsibility of the ministers to the Parliament has brought the legislature and executive together in a state of fusion that defies the principle of the separation of powers the type of which we find in the United States. It is due to this that we never find in Britain, what the Americans call, the 'deadlock of democracy'. Situation has changed over the recent years and for this reason the Prime Minister may hardly take the course of advising his colleagues for having agreement to differ'. Such a course is most likely to visit retribution as the well united and disciplined party in the opposition would exploit it in its favour and a cautious Prime Minister must know that it would lead to a general election in which the electorate would 'heavily work against a disunited party.'[22]

Functions: The Cabinet meets under the chairmanship of the Prime Minister at least once a week and its meetings may be called by the leader at any time if the circumstances so require. The meetings usually take place at the residence of the Prime Minister. The agenda is circulated by the Cabinet Secretariat in advance. But the meeting takes place in a closed room and minutes are kept confidential. As the Cabinet performs very important functions, it takes the help of various committees like Legislation Committee, Defence Committee and Economic Policy Committee. Some committees of an ad hoc type may also be set up to provide means whereby certain important issues and problems may be studied and discussed before a decision is taken.

---

22. S.E. Finer, "Great Britain" in Ward and Macridis (eds.): *Modern Political Systems: Europe*, pp. 108-109. Sometimes, Prime Ministers may find it politically expedient to suspend the doctrine of collective responsibility. For instance, in 1975 Harold Wilson allowed the members of his Cabinet publicly to differ during the campaign for European Community referendum. He justified it as an exception to prove the rule, limited to the period of the referendum and the specific topic of continued EC membership. Dennis Kavangh: *British Politics: Continuities and Change*, p. 51.

23. Ramsay Muir: *How Britain is Governed*, pp. 68-69.

On the issue of the functions of the Cabinet, mention should be made of the Haldane Committee Report of 1918. It described three functions of the Cabinet in the following manner:

(*i*) **Final Determination of Policy to be Submitted to Parliament:** The first and foremost function of the Cabinet is to frame national policy after discussing various important national and international issues. As the real executive, it "has to define the lines of national policy and decide how every current problem which may arise at home or abroad is to be treated."[23] After a policy-decision is made, it becomes the duty of every minister to carry it out either by means of an administrative action or by seeing to it that a bill is passed by the Parliament to give to it the shape of a statutory arrangement. In case a minister disagrees with the official line, he should tender his resignation. The linking up of administrative function with the legislative has empowered the Cabinet to usurp the inherent power of the legislature in a masterly way.

(*ii*) **Supreme Control over National Policy Approved by Parliament:** National administration runs under the supreme direction, control and superintendence of the Cabinet. All ministers are responsible for the policies pursued by their departments as well as for their administrative efficiency. They also issue necessary instructions to their subordinates. As the ministers are accountable to the Parliament, they keep the work of their departments well so that there is no serious objection to their lapses. In case a question is asked in the Parliament, the minister concerned has to give a satisfactory reply. In order to issue and implement some order without undue delay, the Cabinet may put it in the shape of order-in-council and get its approval by the Parliament within the period of 28 days. The delegated legislation has empowered the department to issue necessary statutory orders for keeping a law made by the Parliament in operation.

(*iii*) **Continuous Co-ordination and Delimitation of Activities of Departments:** Finally, the Cabinet performs the work of maintaining co-ordination among various departments. It also delimits the activities of various departments in a way that governmental machinery runs smoothly and successfully. In case there is some point of disagreement between the ministers, the matter should be settled by mutual deliberations or be referred to the Prime Minister for arbitration. In 1951 Prime Minister Churchill introduced the system of keeping some peers – called 'overlords' for the purpose of maintaining inter-departmental co-ordination. But this novel arrangement could not continue as the peers performed a very important function without being the members of the House of Commons. In the event of dis-satisfaction posed by the lower (rather powerful) chamber of the Parliament, the arrangement had to be abandoned after a period of four years.

Cabinet Dictatorship: Much water has flowed down the Thames since the time of Haldane Committee Report and a serious examination of the real powers possessed by the Cabinet has enthused some modern commentators to call this situation by the nickname of 'Cabinet Dictatorship.' The argument of Cabinet dictatorship is based on the enumeration of important functions and powers which the Prime Minister, in cooperation with his senior ministers, possesses. Some of the functions have already been discussed. Here we shall refer to three 'great directions' where Cabinet has assumed an 'omnipotent' position.

First is administration. The Cabinet formulates policy–both domestic and foreign–and takes decisions on all matters of public importance. It might well demand all the time and all the thought of the group of men who have to undertake it. As the Cabinet ministers have to give their minds to the problems faced by the government, they are not expected to remain immersed in the work of their respective departments; rather they are assisted by their junior ministers in the management of their departments. The cabinet ministers mainly look to the running of the government according to the policy decided by them and as they are accountable to the Parliament and to the people, they try to keep the administrative machinery going well. Moreover, as the prosecution of administrative work needs many high officials, they are appointed by the monarch on the advice of the Prime Minister who, in turn, counts upon the views of his colleagues. It is the Cabinet which decides important matters relating to the prosecution of war and conclusion of peace.

The point of the 'omnipotent position' of the Cabinet in this regard is supported by the statement that the Prime Minister and his ministers do not live under effective parliamentary control. When asked to form the government, the party in power sometimes does not even care much for the promises it had made in its election manifestos. When the Cabinet enjoys the majority of its pledged supporters, a three-line whip is sufficient to keep the big following in order to defeat the move of the opposition in the House of Commons. Sometimes, the ministers succeed in evading answer to a question on the plea of 'public interest'; sometimes an adjournment motion may be appreciated by the Prime Minister to be taken to the point of discussion culminating in the giving of some assurances by the government which may, and may not, be properly fulfilled in time to come. Obviously, the biggest weapon of removing a government by a vote of no-confidence can seldom be exercised by the Parliament as the majority is always with the Cabinet.

No less penetrating is Cabinet's control over the legislation formally made by the Parliament. The session of the Parliament runs according to the schedule prepared by the Cabinet. The text of the speech to be delivered by the monarch is prepared by the Cabinet which highlights government's programmes in the year to follow. The Cabinet looks to it that so much time shall be allotted to the Parliament for such business. It also decides as to what opportunities shall be given for the discussion of the way in which its gigantic responsibilities are to be met. As the Cabinet decides, the bills are moved in the Parliament by the ministers called official bills. These bills get four days of the week (Monday to Thursday) for discussion, while a bill moved by a private member (called unofficial bill) gets only Friday for discussion. Here again the Cabinet makes use of its pledged supporters to see that every official bill is passed by the House of Commons in order to save the life of the government. A private member's bill has almost no chance of being adopted by the House until supported by the Cabinet. It thus becomes clear that the Cabinet has usurped the inherent power of the Parliament. However, in case of a stiff opposition staged by the public the Cabinet may agree to withdraw that bill or abandon its legislative programme which would amount to a change of decision by its own will.

It follows that the Cabinet has deprived the Parliament of its inherent powers and made the latter like a rubber-stamp to put the seal of constitutional validity on the bills moved by the ministers according to its official policy. However, one thing which has further increased its authority in the legislative sphere is the growth of delegated legislation. Faced with the acute shortage of time, the Parliament has delegated its power to the departments to make statutory orders for the implementation of its laws according to its wishes. It is required that departmental orders, circulars and notifications issued in this regard must be ratified by the Parliament at a later date. What actually happens is that a host of statutory orders are placed before the Parliament for approval and they are passed within seconds. It is very seldom that a member raises some points of objection and a debate takes place to strike down some portion of an impugned order. These administrative regulations have the force of law as something made by the Parliament itself.

The issue of Cabinet's responsibility to the Parliament is a political and not a legal matter. It requires majority in the House of Commons to pass a vote of censure. However, when the Cabinet commands majority in the House and keeps its pledged supporters in order by the use of whips, it is highly improbable that the opposition may succeed in outvoting a ministry. It is possible only when there is a serious rift in the ranks of the majority party which a wise Prime Minister must never allow to creep in. More astonishing is the fact that the Prime Minister has the House of Commons in his control and he may crush any revolt of the 'dissidents' by posing a threat of advising the monarch to dissolve the House for seeking verdict of the people.

Apart from these two significant spheres of administration and legislation, the strong position of the Cabinet covers the area of finance as well. It is just a theoretical statement to lay down that the House of Commons controls the purse of the nation. The actual position is that Cabinet makes the budget and drafts money bills and presents them to the House of Commons with the formal recommendation of the monarch. It is impossible for a non-minister to move a money bill in the House as the formal recommendation of the monarch may never be available to him. So no member can move that the amount demanded by a department be raised. A private member may put a cut motion which is bound to be defeated as the Cabinet sees to it that a money bill is passed by the House in the same manner as it desires.

An assessment in this direction confirms the view of many recent commentators and text-book writers that there is a thing like Cabinet omnipotence in Britain. Despite the fact that Cabinet is the most important single piece of mechanism in the constitutional structure of England, it is wrong to dub its strong position with the appellation of 'dictatorship'. Several reasons may be advanced in this regard. First, Cabinet's responsibility to the House of Commons is still a fact no matter it has assumed the form of 'responsiveness' in the present context of political developments. The inherent powers of the Parliament have been definitely usurped by the Cabinet, yet the very principle of cabinet government has survived to prove that a Prime Minister like Eden would go if he commits a mistake on the' Suez affair'. The resignation of Prime Minister Macmillan after the publicity of the Profumo scandal is a further proof in this direction. Laski is right in his judgement that the Cabinet is no doubt a master of the House of Commons, but there "are always limits to its mastery of which it must take account."[24]

The most important check on the dictatorship of the Cabinet is exercised by a strong public opinion. The Cabinet is responsible to the Parliament; it is ultimately accountable to the people. No Cabinet and no Parliament can afford to go against the impact of public mind in a democratic state. A popular resentment in the shape of demonstrations, processions, strikes etc. reveals public mind and the Cabinet is bound to respect it for the sake of its own survival as well as for the sake of returning to power after the ensuing elections.

The charge of 'cabinet dictatorship' is thus contradicted. The actual position of the Cabinet in the present constitutional structure of England is wrongly depicted by the use of these epithets like 'dictatorship' or 'omnipotence'. A more plausible argument is to say that Cabinet enjoys a very dominant position in the British constitutional system subject to the pleasure of the people though not so much to that of the House. of Commons.

Shadow Cabinet

Now the leaders of the opposition are organised in a highly formalised team of 'shadow ministers' as both major parties, while in opposition, form a committee of some 20 important leaders who meet on a regular basis to co-ordinate the activities (of the opposition) that may be described as the running of the 'shadow government'. Leading party leaders are chosen as spokesmen for particular subjects by virtue of being known as party's 'experts' in their assigned areas of leading the attack upon the government, playing a prominent part in the formulation of party policy in their subject, and generally acting as a link between the parliamentary leadership, the back-bench M.Ps and the party outside Parliament.

Though the term 'shadow cabinet' came into prominence in 1955 when Clement Attlee (former Prime Minister) undertook such a step, its history is quite old if we try to trace its genesis. There is evidence to show that in the seventeenth and eighteenth centuries, groups of leaders and 'out of office' factions met together in order to organise and co-ordinate opposition to the ministers of the day. The Rockinghamites' 'Concilibalum' of the 1760s may be cited as a concrete example of this kind. There

24. Laski: *Reflections on the Constitution*, p.96.

appeared such bodies in the eighteenth century at different intervals that were named 'directing councils' and 'anti-ministerialist cabinets'. Such arrangements were, however, like a make-shift affair. It was in 1955 when Attlee organised his Labour Shadow Cabinet and since then all opposition leaders "have followed his precedent and named their terms of spokesmen so that the concept of publicly announced shadow government is now a well-established feature of opposition party organisation in Britain."[25]

Though both major parties form their shadow cabinets, while in opposition, the nature of the composition is different. The Labour Party calls it officially as 'Parliamentary Committee'. Elections take place at the beginning of each session, but the Leader may appoint Parliamentary Committee members and other leading M.Ps of his party. Different from this, the Conservatives call it by the name of 'Leaders' Consultative Committee'. Here all members are appointed by the Leader of the Party. In this way, each of the two major parties, while in opposition, "creates large and complex shadow government which broadly reflects the ministerial structure that it faces across the floor of the House."[26]

The system of having a shadow cabinet has certain merits. The members of the shadow cabinet tend to concentrate on their assigned aspects in their contributions to Parliamentary debates. The Leader of the Party does get a certain amount of the power of patronage by making the nomination of his shadow ministers who may treat it as a stepping stone to their bright future when power alternates from the ruling party to their side. It elevates the status of ordinary M.Ps in the eyes of the back-benchers. It increases the overall efficiency of the opposition. The existence of recognised specialist spokesmen for various subjects provides a ready source and authoritative statements of party attitudes and helps the opposition to achieve the kind of news coverage that it desires. "It provides pressure groups and the parties outside Parliament with a distinct point of contact with the opposition in each subject area. Further, by appointing senior and assistant spokesmen to cover each subject, and by giving them direct responsibility for organising and leading the attack upon the government in the subject, the opposition can make best use of its own resources in the Parliamentary battle."[27]

25. R.M. Punnett: "Her Majesty's Shadow Government: Its Evolution and Modern Role" in Valentine Herman and J.R. Alt (eds.): *Cabinet Studies: A Reader*, p.141.

26. *Ibid*, p.145.

27. *Ibid*, p.147.

4

PERMANENT EXECUTIVE

Cabinet being the supreme directing and controlling authority of the state stands at a three-dimensional cross-section constituted by the Party, the Parliament and the Civil Service. The study of civil service or non-political/permanent executive has an importance of its own in the sense that the Cabinet is linked with the administration by the presence within it of the heads from 16 to 19 ministers or so.[1] The executive of Britain consists of two parts – the political or non-permanent executive represented by the ministers who are chosen by the Prime Minister and who live in office so long as they enjoy the pleasure of the Parliament, and the non-political or permanent executive represented by high civil servants who are recruited on the basis of ability and, from time to time, promoted on the grounds of their semiority and efficiency and who enjoy a permanent tenure. A study of the non-political executive has its 'last but not the least' significance in as much as the senior ranks of the civil servants, if not the very large army of public officials, "play a cardinal role in shaping government policies.[2]

---

1. H.R.G. Greaves; *The British Constitution,* p.144.
2. S.E. Finer: "Great Britain" in Ward and Macridis (eds.): *Modern Political Systems: Europe*, p. 125. It is well observed: "Like ministers, civil servants are servants of the Crown, but are not part of the government. A change of minister or government, whatever the cause, does not involve a change in departmental staff. Civil servants are highly respected for their traditional anonymity and political neutrality, and for the technical expertise and countinuity they contribute to policy-making. The structure and behaviour of the British civil service is often considered a model of politically insulated efficient administration, free of the partisanship, insider dealing, and corruption found in many bureaucracies, particularly in post-communist, post-authoritarian and post-colonial regimes." Joel Krieger:" 'Britain" in Mark Kesselman, Joel Krieger and W.A. Joseph (eds.): *Comparative Politics at the Cross-roads*, p. 66.

Civil Services: The non-political or permanent executive of Britain is organised in a number of departments and their dependent boards and agencies. What is, however, important to note here is that each department is the responsibility of a single civil servant who works under the control of some minister. The highest permanent official is called the Permanent Secretary. The Treasury Department (known as the Department of all Departments) has two Permanent Secretaries. This official concentrates on particular aspects of the Department; he is charged with overseeing all the operations of the Department and is assisted in this regard by one or more Deputy Secretaries. Under his central direction come the Under-Secretaries, each in charge of a section and below them the Assistant Secretaries who head up the lower echelon divisions of the Department. Within these divisions, smaller units are administered by the Principals and Assistant Principals. Attached to most of the departments are several boards and commissions etc. for which the departmental minister concerned takes parliamentary responsibility.

The ministers may come and go with the wind of politics, but the work of public administration continues without missing even a single heart-beat. This is ensured by the large army of civil servants who execute the policies of individual ministers and, at the same time, play their own part in the formulation of national policy in their own ways. In its present form, the British civil service is a product of the last 150 years or so. In the beginning, it was a gift of political patronage and, for this reason, dubbed as 'outdoor relief department of British aristocracy'.

The Fulton Report (1966) suggested important changes in the organisation and working of the British Civil Service. It examined the issue of the management of civil service and visualised the following functions as correctly falling within the purview of the body formally charged with the responsibility of the Central management of the civil service:

1. To stimulate and assist the Departments in reviewing the kinds of skill and forms of organisation needed for their tasks as they change and develop;
2. In the light of this view, to determine man-power requirements both in quality and quantity, agree with the Departments how these requirements should be met, provide the necessary common services for new recruitment and internal transfer, and satisfy itself that the Departments are efficiently and economically satisfied;

Some Important Statements

Viewed from 10, Downing Street, the policy-making functions of the state may appear to be increasingly concentrated in the Prime Minister's hands. At the same time, viewed from Whitehall (the London nerve centre of civil service), the executive may appear to be dominated by its vast administrative agencies. The expanded range and tremendous complexity of state policy-making mean in practice that cabinet's authority must be shared with a set of vast unelected officials.

—Joel Krieger

Indeed, it is my general experience that the Minister-in-charge knows what he wants and is intelligent in going about it, he can command the understanding and cooperation and support of his civil servants. The kind of Minister who is most tiring to the officers of a Department is the minister who does not know his own mind and cannot make it up. If the policy of a Department is hazy, vacillating and ineffective, it is, after all, the responsibility of the Minister; it is quite likely to be his fault as that of his civil servants. ***—Lord Herbert Morrison***

No longer can civil servants be dismissed as mere administrators or policy implementors; instead, they are the key figures in the policy process and even sometimes run their countries. A reality of 'rule of the officials' may lie behind the facade of representation and democratic accountability. The organisation and control of bureaucratic power is, therefore, one of the most pressing problems in modern politics, and one that no political system has found easy to solve.

—Andrew Heywood

3. To specify in consultation with the Departments the qualities, qualifications and experience required of new recruits to the services;
4. To determine (after such negotiations as are necessary in each case) pay, pensions and other conditions of the service;
5. To determine training policy in consultation with the Department, conduct central training courses, arrange external training, and stimulate and guide training within the Departments;
6. To promote career development throughout the service and in particular to co-operate with and guide Departments in fostering the promotion and planning the future development of the most promising members of all disciplines;
7. To promote mobility both between the Departments and between the services and outside employments;
8. To discuss with the Departments (which should be required to consult central management on the matter) all promotions to the Senior Policy and Management Group, and to take the initiative in proposing

individual moves between the Departments both within the Group and the lower levels:

9. To advise the Prime Minister on:
   (*i*) the appointment at the salary-level of Deputy Secretary and above, and
   (*ii*) the most efficient division of responsibility between the Departments.
10. To study new developments in methodology of organising works in management techniques and in office machinery, and promote their use throughout the services.

The recommendations of the Fulton Committee mainly hinging on the abolition of Separate Classes or Services and their substitution by, what may be called, 'Classless Services' recruited by means of open competition and tests conducted by a Civil Service Commission (working under a Civil Service Department) were accepted by the Labour Government headed by Wilson in 1968. Lauding the aspect of egalitarianism as contained in the Report, Prime Minister Wilson said in the House of Commons on June 26,1968; "Everyone in the Civil Service, whether from a college of technology, or from university, whether he or she comes in from an industry or from a profession – all in future, the school leaver, the graduate, the accountant, the engineer, the scientist, the lawyer – for all of them there will be an open road to the 'top' which upto now has been, in the main, through the administrative class."

Ministers and Civil Servants: A representative democracy assumes the form of bureaucratic government when the real authority slips into the hands of permanent officials who make the elected deputies of the people their tools. These government officials by virtue of their high education, training, experience, long tenure and permanent posts often rule with a sense of self-aggrandisement jeopardising the liberties of ordinary citizens. Being non-political officers of the government, they are not accountable to the Parliament and any lapse of the department is interpreted as a fault of the minister concerned. The people and their elected representatives criticize the minister and when the popular resentment mounts heavily, it is not the civil servant but the minister who has to go.

What Bagehot called the 'efficient' executive really consists of two parts – the political or the non-permanent executive and non-political or the permanent executive. The former includes ministers, with Prime Minister at the head, who belong to a political party having majority in

Ministers and Civil Servants

What Ministers require of Civil Servants

1. Loyal implementation of ministerial or party objectives and programmes in cases in which they have been publicly stated and reasonably clearly specified.
2. Advice on a range of alternative objectives, priorities and programmes in cases in which form commitments have not been made in advance of taking office.
3. Expert advice (i.e. advice based on uptodate specialised knowledge) on the probable and possible problems and consequences of implementing alternative policy programmes.

What Civil Servants require of Ministers

1. The taking of decisions resaonably rapidly, the department's business must be despatched.
2. The winning of cabinet battles.
3. The defence of the Department from Parliamentary criticism.

Bruce Heady: "Cabinet Ministers and Senior Civil Servants: Mutual Requirements and Expectations" in Valentine Herman and J.E. Alt (eds): *Cabinet Studies: A Reader*, p. 125.

the House of Commons, while the latter are public servants having a permanent tenure. The former live in office during the pleasure of the Parliament, the latter retire on the completion of the age limit.

However, the working of modern representative governmental system requires that there must be close relationship between the two for the simple reason that while the minister is the 'layman', the civil servant is the 'expert.' While the minister is the policy-maker, the civil servant is the policy-implementor. While the ministers take decisions on matters of public importance in accordance with the policy contained in the election manifesto or rules of the party, the civil servants are expected to implement them faithfully like loyal servants of the department. The ministers cannot run the department without the help and co-operation of their subordinate officials, though the latter may do without the former either totally by making the government bureaucratic or partially by working under the formal framework of ministers and making that system known by the name of bureaucratic democracy.

The issue of relationship between the ministers and the civil servants is of two types – theoretical and practical. Theoretically, the minister is the master of the department and his staff (right from the secretary of the department down to the clerks) works under his command. The policy-making job belongs to the ministers and not to the civil servants. Whether the policy is socialistic or capitalistic, the civil servants must implement it with equal zeal as they have nothing to do with the politics of the country. In case an administrative officer violates the rules of service even by disobeying the decision of the Cabinet, he is liable to be punished, at least transferred to some other perhaps less significant post. But the practical side of relationship is different. The fact of the skilled work of the civil servants over the amateurish conduct of the ministers has reversed the real state of affairs. The old example of Palmerston is often cited who, on being the in-charge of Colonial Office, summoned his secretary to come upstairs and show his minister the colonies of the British empire.

The minister is often called an amateur or a layman as he has practically no knowledge of the way his department functions, while his secretary is an expert due to his high education and long training in office. Sidney Low comments that a youth "must pass an examination before he can hold a second class clerkship in the Treasury, but a chancellor of exchequer may be a middle-aged man of the world who has forgotten what little he ever learnt about figures at Eton and Oxford."[3] A minister's life engaged in party work, making speeches, conducting tours, and, above all, sudden reshuffles of the departments etc.. is responsible for his short and insecure tenure as the minister which negatively adds to the powers of the bureaucrats. The net result is that the minister has no other better and more useful alternative than to count on the support of his expert.[4]

Nothing but a close and harmonious relationship between the minister and his administrative staff is required. Both constitute the department. While the minister constitutes the higher managerial and policy-making level of the administrative system, the civil servants are the experts to run the department.

Hold of Bureaucracy: No government can run without the civil servants. But the matter of anxiety arises when they assume dominance over the ministers. A civil service keeping the ministers (elected by the people) under its thumb converts democracy into bureaucracy – a form of government which, as Laski says, jeopardises the liberty of ordinary citizens. Highlighting the recent phase of the growth of bureaucracy,

3. Sidney Low: *The Government of Britain*, p. 208.

4. Ramsay Muir: *How Britain is Governed*, p. 43.

Ramsay Muir says: "In short, in our system of government, the power of bureaucracy is enormously strong, whether in administration, in legislation, or in finance. Under the cloak of ministerial responsibility and cabinet dictatorship it has thriven and grown until, like Frankenstein's monster, it sometimes seems likely to devour its creator."[5]

The role of bureaucracy having so important, even formidable, dimensions is evident in three significant directions, namely, administration, legislation and finance.

Administration: A minister takes his office by virtue of his political craftsmanship; he must be a strong leader of the party, a good speaker and a capable parliamentarian having a place in the mind of the Prime Minister. When he enters his office, he has practically no knowledge of the way his department functions. Naturally he takes his secretaries and under-secretaries into confidence who enlighten him with practical difficulties in the way of the implementation of the pledges made by him or his party to the people. They also suggest possible alternatives which would save his face without making too great a breach with the accepted policy of the office. When a minister has to give answer to a question raised in the Parliament or when he has to make some important statement, he is supplied with all relevant information by his department.

As a minister is responsible to the Parliament and ultimately to the people, he is expected to speak and act in a manner showing him a monument of knowledge and such a credit can be achieved by him only when he safely depends upon the experts of his department. Very seldom it happens that a minister has the talent of doing much with his own judgment and thereby putting a heavy hand on the heads of the administrative staff. Such a man may go to the extent of making a remarkable change in the running of the department by breaking the conservative line of action. It enables Ramsay Muir to observe that bureaucracy "thrives under the cloak of ministerial responsibility."[6]

Legislation: The role of bureaucracy is not less real, though less obvious, in the sphere of legislation if we look at the drafting of the bills and the promulgation of orders, notifications, circulars etc. to keep the acts made by the Parliament in operation. The Cabinet decides the policy and accordingly bills are drafted to be introduced in the Parliament. But

5. *Ibid.*, p. 69.

6. *Ibid.*, p. 44.

drafting is a very technical work and can be done only by the experts. The minister may give an idea or an outline, but the actual language is to be given by the departmental experts who, while interpreting a clause, may make a change in the body of the bill by adding or deleting a particular phrase. It is noticed that despite Cabinet's open commitments to the people either in the shape of a manifesto issued on the eve of the polls or after that, radical changes in the sphere of legislation are not brought about as the civil servants are there to interfere in a negative but effective manner.

The bills moved in the Parliament by the ministers are not drafted by the movers responsible to the people but by these public officials who become arrogant and self-aggrandised due to the windfall of power. But more sinister is the sphere of delegated legislation. A law made by the Parliament is 'blanket' in the sense that it just has outlines to lay down something. However, its details are to be supplied by the department in time to come in the form of clarifications, notifications and letters. The fact is that the minister virtually leaves it to his administrative staff to issue regulations and notifications and hardly any member of Parliament puts objections to see that an impugned order is struck down. It is just a formality that hundreds of such orders come before the Parliament and are passed within minutes in the absence of any objection from any side. Ramsay Muir thus holds that cabinet dictatorship "is the bulwark behind which the power of bureaucracy has grown."[7]

Finance: Finally, there is the sphere of finance. It is true to say that the House of Commons controls the strings of the purse of the nation. It passes the budget and money bill which must be passed by the House of Lords within a period of one month. But the role of bureaucracy in financial matters must be examined in the light of the great work done by the departments at the time of budget-making. It is the administrative staff which gives appropriate shape to the estimates of various ministries. It is quite possible that the experts may advise the departmental head to impose a new tax on a new item; it is equally possible that the same expert may force the minister to change his mind for want of funds. Thus, Muir concludes: "The power of bureaucracy is to be found not only in administration, but also in legislation and finance; it not only administers the laws, it largely shapes them, it not only spends the proceeds of taxation, it largely decides how much is to be raised."[8]

---

7. *Ibid.*, p. 49.

8. *Ibid.*, p. 58.

The bureaucracy takes the benefit of anonymity. Since the minister is responsible, the civil servants under him find a natural defence. If there is an achievement, the credit is enjoyed by the government; if there is a lapse, the minister is in the dock. Lord Hewart of Bury calls this situation by the name of 'new despotism'. His argument is that the growing power of the departments at once and at the same time "places government above the sovereignty of Parliament and beyond the jurisdiction of the courts."[9]

Despite their serious revelations, the views of commentators like Muir and Lord Hewart of Bury look like crossing the frontiers of plausibility in some respects. It is too much to say that ministers are like 'puppets' in the hands of their administrative staff. The fact of the personal equation of the ministers and the over-riding control of the Parliament and the vigilant public cannot be easily dismissed. What is required is that the ministers and the civil servants "*must* work in team spirit to run the government smoothly for the simple reason that if things go well, he (minister) gets the credit. If they go ill, he shoulders the blame. So far as responsibility is concerned, he is the department."[10]

9. Lord Hewart: *The New Despotism*, p. 14.

10. Ogg. and Zink, *Modern Foreign Governments*, p. 138.

5

PARLIAMENT

The British Parliament is a bicameral body having monarch and the two chambers – House of Lords and House of Commons – respectively as the upper and the lower ones. It is, however, important to note that the House of Lords, despite being the older chamber and one time being the Parliament of the land, has lost its former power and glory and become hardly anything more than a revising and delaying institution subservient to the will of the House of Commons. It is rightly commented that after Monarchy, the House of Lords represents another major institution of the British government in decline. Though abolished with the Monarchy in 1649 and restored with it in 1660, this House has been in a state of increasing control of the Commons so much so that the Parliament Act of 1911 (with its amendment in 1949) has clipped its wings and thereby left it in a helpless situation of being more or less like an ornamental chamber. More astounding is the fact, that unlike Monarchy, the Lords have not given a tough fight to protect their old rights in the face of their grim opposition by the people of their popular chamber. [1]

House of Lords

Composition: The House of Lords consists of the members of six categories. In the first place, there are the princes of the royal blood who usually take no part in its proceedings. Second, there are the hereditary peers and peeresses of England above the age of 21. This category of peers constitutes a large number of the members of the House of Lords and the eldest of a peer of this category gets peerage in succession after the death of his father unless he disclaims it within a year of the death of his father. Third, there are Scottish peers. Prior to 1963, there were only

1. D.V. Verney: *British Government and Politics*, p. 154

16 peers from Scotland elected for each Parliament by the body of peers, but the Peerage Act of 1963 has conferred membership of the House on all peers. Fourth, there are life peers and peeresses created under the provisions of the Life Peerage Act of 1958. Fifth, there are 9 Law Lords appointed by the monarch under Appellate Jurisdiction Act of 1876 for the performance of judicial functions during their life only. Last, there are 26 spiritual peers including two Archbishops of York and Canterbury and three bishops of London, Durham and Winchester respectively. The rest 21 are taken on the basis of seniority list of the bishops.

In November, 1999 the British Government made a law to reduce the number of hereditary peers (who had the right to sit and vote in the Lords) from 750 to 92. In May, 2000 the Government set up the House of Lords Appointment Commission to make recommendations for the appointment of non-political peers including people's peers. It has taken over the role previously played by the Political Honours Scrutiny Committee. The Commission is an independent body responsible for vetting all nominations to the Sovereign for membership of this House to ensure that they meet the highest standards of propriety. In order to make the House a more representative body, now anyone in the United Kingdom is entitled to nominate himself-herself or any other person. But this Commission would expect that such a person is known for his/her integrity and independence and has a significant record of achievements in the chosen field or way of life. In April, 2001 the Queen announced her intention to bestow non-political life peerages on 15 people preferred by this Commission.

Peerage is a great privilege to those who want to receive certain political advantages without oscillating through the channel of the House of Commons. The Lords enjoy freedom of speech and also freedom from arrest while the House is in session. They can individually approach the king to discuss public affairs or record their protest against decision of the majority in the House in its Journals, But the biggest disqualification of a peer is that he can not take part in the elections of the House of Commons. The Peerage Act of 1963 enables a peer to disclaim his peerage and thereby seek election to the House of Commons. Thus, a man of political ambitions may disclaim his peerage and thereby seek election to the House of Commons to become the Prime Minister of the country if circumstances so favour as we find in the case of Sir Alec Douglas-Home.

Functions and Powers: The House of Lords is summoned and prorogued simultaneously with the House of Commons but adjourned separately. It meets for four days a week – Monday to Thursday – and for about two hours a day unless the matter before it is of an exceptionally important nature. Its quorum is 3, but a minimum attendance of 30 is required to pass a bill. Its average attendance (particularly after the Reforms Act of 1957) is about 200. Its presiding officer is the Lord Chancellor who takes his chair called the 'woolsack', But his position is very weak as contrasted with the office of the Speaker of the House of Commons. Convention requires that the members must address the whole House as 'My Lords' instead of addressing the chairman only. The questions regarding procedure are decided by the House and not by the chairman, For instance, if two or more members stand up to take the floor of the House, not the chairman but the House decides the issue of recognition. The proceedings are normally conducted in a very orderly manner and if there is some lapse, the matter is to be dealt with by the House itself. The Lord Chancellor may take part in the deliberations of the House if he is a peer. But while doing so, he must step away from the 'woolsack' and even vote on party lines like any other member of the House. He has no casting vote. It is, therefore, obvious that the position of the Lord Chancellor is not strong as that of the Speaker of the House of Commons.

It has now become an established fact that the House of Lords is a weak chamber as it has become subservient to the will of House of Commons. Its functions are rather ceremonial which may be classified into five parts. First, as an upper chamber of the Parliament, it has legislative powers. It is required that a bill must be passed by both the Houses of the Parliament before going to the monarch for his assent. The Parliament Act of 1949 has given to it the delaying power over non-money bill for a period of one year only in as much as if a bill is passed by the House of Commons in two successive sessions with the interval of one year between its first introduction and third reading of its second attempt, the bill shall be presented to the monarch without the concurrence of the Lords. The House of Lords has the power of delaying the passage of a money bill for a period of not more than a month. That is, the House of Lords is a quite powerless chamber in money matters.

In addition to these legislative and financial powers, the House of Lords has executive powers – control over the ministers. Its members may ask questions from the ministers, put resolutions and motions for discussion, appreciate or criticize the policy of the government and may go to the extent of rejecting a statutory instrument. A serious constitutional crisis took place in June, 1968 when the Lords rejected an order-in-council issued by the Labour Government of Prime Minister Wilson desiring imposition of sanctions against the illegal white government of South Rhodesia. The Lords exercised the logic of the difference between a bill and an order-in-council. Thus, the Lords manifested an attitude of hostility towards Labour Government's Rhodesian policy and a Tory peer (Lord Salisbury) went to the length of calling the government 'a criminal in policeman's uniform.'

The House of Lords has some judicial powers. It is still the highest court of appeal in civil and criminal cases for England and Northern Ireland and in civil cases for Scotland. These cases are heard and decided by the Lords of Appeal only. It is still a court for people impeached by the House of Commons. Finally, it has constituent powers. For example, the duration of the House of Commons as determined by the Parliament Act of 1911 cannot be changed without the concurrence of this chamber. In this regard the provision of time-limit (as given in the Parliament Acts of 1911 and 1949) are not applicable. Hence, the Lords can block a bill desiring any change in this direction by an adverse vote.

Reform Movement: The weak position of the House of Lords has been a matter of much discussion, even merriment, and many attempts have been made to make some reforms in its composition and ways of functioning. The reform movement of the House of Lords dates back to the middle part of the 19th century when democratisation of the House of Commons started. The first Reform Act of 1832 and the Chartist agitation thereafter added to the growing importance of the lower house of the Parliament. This process had its definite impact upon the issue of democratization of the House of Lords in some measure. In 1869 Lord Russell proposed the creation of life-peers and in 1888 Lord Salisbury desired the gradual creation of 50 peers, but both these ideas were rejected. The Lansdowne Plan of 1909 proposed a House of Lords of 330 members – 100 chosen by the whole body of peers, 100 to be appointed by the Crown, 123 to be elected by the House of Commons sitting in regional groups bishops to be chosen by the body of clergymen and 2 from the princes of the royal blood. This scheme was also rejected.

The first important event took place in 1918 when a committee of 30 members chosen equally from both the Houses was set up under the chairmanship of Lord Bryce. It recommended that the total membership of the House be reduced to 327 out of whom 3/4 be elected by the members of the House of Commons by the method of proportional representation, the rest of the members be selected from amongst the peers by a joint Standing Committee of the two Houses. It was also provided that the members be elected for a period of 12 years out of whom 1/3 would retire after every fourth year. Then, it proposed that a joint committee of the two Houses would decide whether a bill was money bill or not, and if there was any disagreement between the two, the matter be settled by a joint committee of 60 members, 30 from each chamber.

This scheme had the same fate. In 1922 the House of Lords debated and adopted a resolution declaring that it would welcome a reasonable measure limiting and defining the membership and dealing with defects inherent in the Parliament Act of 1911. In 1925 there was discussion of a plan brought to the House of Lords by Birkenhead. In 1928 Lord Clarendon suggested that the House of Lords should consist of 150 members elected by the body of peers and 150 nominated by the Crown according to the strength of various parties in the House of Commons. In 1932 Lord Salisbury proposed a House of Lords consisting of 300 members – 150 to be elected by the peers for 12 years and 150 to be nominated by the Crown for the same period. It also desired that the power of deciding whether a bill was money bill or not should be transferred from the Speaker to a joint body of both the Houses.

The Labour Party has been highly critical of the anachronistic character of the House of Lords. When the Labour Government came into being in 1964, the way was opened. The Government presented a White Paper on November, 1, 1968 highlighting: (*i*) Right to vote in the upper chamber to be restricted to about 230 created peers, (*ii*) Selection of some members on the basis of special knowledge, experience and interest in the problems of Scotland, Wales, North Ireland and other regions of the United Kingdom, (*iii*) Right of participation in the debates of the House of Lords to all hereditary peers and retention of their membership till the end of their life; (*iv*) Permission to the peers for taking part in parliamentary elections. (*v*) Number of ecclesiastical peers to be reduced from 26 to 16; (*vi*) Delay of public bills by the House of Lords for a period of not more than 6 months from the date of disagreement between the two houses; (*vii*) Increase in the number of ministers from the House of Lords; (*viii*) Review of the procedure and functions of the House of Lords after the implementation of these proposals. A bill based on these points was moved in the House of Commons and, despite its crossing the stage of second reading, was withdrawn by the Prime Minister in April 1969 in the face of strong opposition in the committee by some Labour back-benchers.

Parliament Acts of 1911 and 1949: What has given a great blow to the powers and prestige of the upper and the older chamber of the British Parliament is not the movement for its reform in the direction of its democratisation as desired by so many leading politicians but the acts of the Parliament passed by the obstinate House of Commons over the head of 'reluctant' but helpless House of Lords. The first legislative measure of 1911, as well shall see, definitely reduced the Lords to a subordinate position and the amended act of 1949 put a further check on its rump authority in non-financial matters. However, the effect of both these acts has been to demonstrate that the upper house of the English Parliament is no longer a co-ordinate authority with the lower one and even its usefulness as a revising chamber is quite doubtful.

The Lords could not read the writing on the wall and they chose a wrong wicket by rejecting the budget of the Liberal ministry in 1909. Prime Minister Asquith sought the verdict of the people on this issue and when the same party returned to power, it became clear that the people were with the government of the Liberal party. In this triumphant situation the monarch agreed with the proposal of the Prime Minister to swamp the House of Lords with newly created peers. The threat of the Prime Minister worked and in the absence of a hostile opposition from the side of the Lords, the bill was rushed through both the Houses and became the Parliament Act of 1911 after receiving royal assent.

The Parliament Act of 1911 has important provisions. First, it makes the House of Lords powerless in matter of money bills by specifying that such a bill must be passed by this House within a period of one month. That is, a delaying power of one month is sanctioned so that the House of Lords must adopt it despite its reluctance, otherwise it would go to the monarch for his assent. Any change in the money bill, according to this Act, is possible if the Commons is agreed with certain points raised in the House of Lords and thereby takes the bill back from the Lords in order to incorporate that change.

Second, in non-money matters, it limited the power of the Lords to delay the passage of a bill for not more than two years if the House of Commons obdurately desired to adopt it. It provided that a bill passed by the House of Commons three times in successive sessions and each time rejected by the Lords might be presented to the monarch for his assent provided a period of two years had elapsed between the initial proceeding of the bill in the House of Commons and its final adoption in the House in the third session.

It has defined the term 'money bill' so as to include measures relating not only to taxation but also to audits and appropriations and authorised the Speaker of the House of Commons to decide the issue whether a bill, in question, is money bill or not. This Act specified the normal team of the House of Commons of five years.

The Parliament Act of 1911 was a triumph of the Liberal genius; the amended act of 1949 marked the same for the Labour party. As a result of the victory of the Labour party in the elections of 1945, the passage became clear and the amended act of 1949 came into being. This act makes an improvement upon the former in the sense that now the House of Lords can delay the passage of a non-money bill for a period of one year only. It provides that a non-money bill may become law despite its being rejected by the House of Lords if it has been passed by the House of Commons in two successive sessions and if one year has elapsed between the date of the second reading in the first session in the House of Commons and the final date on which the bill is passed by the House of Commons for the second time.

The effect of these acts has been to deprive the House of Lords of any real power in matters of passing a bill already adopted by the House of Commons. It has confirmed the conviction of Spencer Walpole that when a minister "consults the Parliament, he consults the House of Commons," and when the Queen dissolves the Parliament, she "dissolves the House of Commons". What Ramsay Muir wrote about the Parliament Act of 1911 is applicable to the amended Act of 1949 as well that it "has reduced the House of Lords to a definitely subordinate position. It is no longer, in any sense, a co-ordinate authority with the House of Commons, but only a revising and delaying body; and not very effective even for that purpose.".[2]

Conclusion: Some reasons are given to prove that the House of Lords should be ended as it is a political anachronism in the country serving no useful purpose like the fifth wheel of a coach.

1. It is said that its composition is thoroughly undemocratic. It consists of the peers, mostly hereditary and life peers, who represent nobody but themselves.
2. The House of Lords is a body of very rich persons and it protects their interests alone. It has been called a citadel of wealth. Most of

2. Ramsay Muir: *How Britain is Governed,* p. 188.

its members are managers and proprietors of big industries and many of them are related to the leading business magnates. It shows the class character of the House of Lords.

3. It is irrevocably wedded to the policies and programmes of the Conservative party. The result is that whenever there is a Conservative government, it finds its natural support in the House of Lords, but when there is a Labour Government, it finds its natural opposition, sometimes hostile, in this body.
4. The House is characterised by mass absenteeism. Its quorum is only three, while total membership exceeds seven hundred. It is essential that there be at least 30 members to pas a bill. General attendance is hardly one hundred.
5. It performs hardly any useful service to the country. It has become so powerless that it cannot exercise effective control over the government and can do nothing beyond the delay of one month in the passage of a money bill and of a year in the case of other bills.

In contrast to the argument of abolishing the House of Lords, some reasons are given to justify the existence of this body on account of some of its useful services. There are:

1. The British people are essentially conservative and they do not favour any radical proposal of finishing their old institutions.
2. An argument applicable to the utility of an upper chamber, that it acts as a check on the hasty, rash and ill-considered legislation, is applicable in this direction as well. A bill passed by the House of Commons (other than a money bill) can be revised by the Lords in a way possibly acceptable to the House of Commons causing no disagreement between the two chambers; it can also be rejected by it to cause the delay of at least one year in which a healthy public opinion may emerge to act as a potential check on the haste of the lower chamber.
3. The House of Lords still performs some useful services. It acts as the highest court of appeal in civil and criminal cases for England and Northern Ireland and in civil cases for Scotland and Wales. A look at the history of British politics shows that it has seen the services of many distinguished leaders of the country. The quality of the debates is of a very high order.

House of Lords

Among the many quaint and ancient institutions which exist in the United Kingdom, the House of Lords is one of the most archaic. It nature, role and composition are unique in comparison with the second chamber of other countries.

—***R.G. Neumann***

The general weight of opinion seems to be that a Second Chamber is necessary and a convenient part of the Constitution; convenient to assist in originating and revising legislation and as an auxiliary forum of debate necessary to ensure (by interposing a minimum of delay) that public opinion really has declared itself concerning measures of fundamental importance which might be rushed through by a single Chamber. —***Stathearn Gordon***

In modern times, the Lords has served mainly as a chamber of revision, providing expertise in redrafting legislation. Although the Lords does not serve as a serious impediment to the government, it can slow down legislation and encourage modifications. —***Joel Krieger***

By was of conclusion a political anachronism and its reformed character does not come into the way of the authority of the House of Commons. It should neither be a replica of the lower House rendering it superfluous; nor should it be entrusted with some potential power making it a mischievous organ of the Parliament. Indisputable is the fact that the House of Lords, a rendezvous of retired statesmen and a storehouse of knowledge and administrative experience, has proved to be a very good revising and delaying chamber.[3]

House of Commons

The House of Commons is not only the lower chamber of the British Parliament, it is the only powerful wing of the King-in-Parliament. Since the monarch never makes use of his veto power and since the wings of the House of Lords have been clipped by the Parliament Acts of 1911 and 1949, what is called sovereignty of Parliament has really come to mean the supremacy of the House of Commons – something that has been appreciated as the 'most characteristic institution of British democracy'.[4]

3. Laski, *Parliamentary Government in England, op. cit.*, p. 138.
4. Hill and others: *The Background of European Governments,* p. 91.

House of Lords (2010)

Political Parties	Life Peers	Hereditary Peers	Bishops and Archbishops	Total
1. Labour Party	207	4	—	211
2. Conservative Party	139	47	—	186
3. Liberal Democrats	67	5	—	72
4. Democratic Unionist Party	3	—	—	3
5. Ulster Unionist Party	3	—	—	3
6. Crossbench	153	22	—	186
7. Others	18	2	26	46
Total	590	91	26	707*

*Excluding 12 members on leave of absence, 18 disqualified as senior members of the Judiciary and one disqualified as a member of the European Parliament. Lord Speaker is Baroness Hayman.

House of Commons (2010)

Political Parties	Seats
1. Conservative Party	30
2. Labour Party	258
3. Liberal Democratic Party	57
4. Democratic Unionist Party	8
5. Scottish Nationalist Party	6
6. Sinn Fein	5
7. Plaid Cymru	3
8. Social Democratic and Labour Party	3
9. Others	4*
Total	649

*It includes the Speaker. At present John Bercow holds this office.

Source: *The Europa World Year Book* (London: Routledge, 2010), Vol. II. pp. 4616-17.

Note: Legislation providing for the abolition of all but 92 hereditary peers and the establishment of an interim second chamber pending a definitive reform of the House of Lords took effect in 1999. *Ibid.*, p. 4605.

House of Commons

The deliberations of the House of Commons are dramatic and exciting, because they do more than decide the contents of law; they decide the reputations and fate of men who are or want to be in ministerial office. —***Woodrow Wilson***

The Constitutional powers of Parliament are subject to the constraints of party government; the significance of Parliament, however, lies not in its powers, but in its existence, for we do not have a system of government by Parliament but of government through Parliament. —***Michael Rush***

The main task of the House of Commons is still what it was when it was first summoned; not to legislate but to secure full discussion and ventilation of all matters, legislative or administrative. —***L.S. Amery***

It has also been described as the "major political body in a bicameral legislature, omnicompetent and sovereign.'[5] What Woodrow Wilson wrote it may be pointed out that the House of Lords should not be ended but mended in a way that it no longer lives like in 1885 still holds good that the deliberations of the Commons "are dramatic and exciting, because they do more than decide the contents of a law; they decide the reputations and fate of men who are or want to be in ministerial office. For the cabinet is a small group of members of Parliament who sit in and lead the Commons in legislation and the conduct of the administration."[6]

Composition: The House of Commons consists of the elected representatives (649 in 2010) chosen from single-member constituencies on the basis of one adult, one-vote system. All British subjects of either sex of above 18 years of age living in whatever part of Her Majestry's Dominions are eligible to vote. However, the minimum age of 21 is required to be elected to the House or serve in the Jury. Disqualified are the lunatics, bankrupts, persons convicted of high crimes, clergymen of the established Churches of England and Scotland and the peers of the United Kingdom, the holders of certain offices under the Crown, holder of judicial offices, civil servants, members of the regular and banned police services, members of the legislature of any country outside the Commonwealth and holders of other public offices listed in the House of Commons' Disqualifications Act of 1957.

The normal tenure of the House of Commons (as provided by the Parliament Act of 1911) is of five years. If a member resigns or dies in

5. Herman Finer: *The Major Governments of Modern Europe*, p. 97.

6. *Ibid.*,

office, bye-election is held to fill that seat. However, the process of resigning a seat is fictitious. In view of the established convention, a member of the House is expected to discharge a public duty and he should, for this sake, not resign his office until he accepts some other office under the Crown. Thus, a member intending to resign applies to the Speaker for his appointment as the Steward of Chiltern Hundreds or the Steward of Manor or Northstead; he soon gets appointment and thereby relinquishes his membership as well. The House can prolong its life beyond five years in times of grave national crisis. For instance, elections due in 1940 remained postponed till 1945 on account of Britain's involvement in the Second World War. The normal duration of the House cannot be changed until the Parliament Act of 1911 is revised with the concurrence of both the Houses of Parliament.

According to a well-established convention, the Parliament must meet at least once a year to pass certain essential bills (like renewal of Army Act) and the budget. The session normally begins in October and continues till the autumn of next year with certain breaks on holidays. Then it is prorogued and the unfinished business lapses. The session begins with an inaugural speech delivered by the monarch in the House of Lords where the Commoners are also present. The House meets for five days a week (from Monday to Friday). Certain business is exempt from normal closing time and other business may be exempted if the House so chooses, so that it often sits later than 10 p.m. on the first four days of the week, and all-night sittings are not uncommon.

Functions and Powers: The House of Commons is essentially a law-making body. The Parliament Act of 1911 lays down that a money bill shall be initiated in the House of Commons and the Lords must pass it within a period of one month. As regards non-money bills, the powers of both the Houses are co-ordinate, though the real situation is different. A non-money bill passed by the Commons must be passed by the House of Lords to avoid a crisis leading to further dimunition of its rump authority. It is provided by the Parliament Act of 1949 that in case a non-money bill passed by the Commons is rejected by the Lords and if the Commons re-adopts it in its successive session causing an interval of one year, the concurrence of the Lords is not needed. That is the obduracy of the Lords cannot do anything beyond the delay of one year against the determination of the Commons. Facts show that all important non-money bills are normally introduced in the House of Commons.

Curiously, now the executive powers of the House of Commons are more important than its legislative powers. The fact that the king can do no wrong implying responsibility of the ministers has left in the hands of the Commons a major power to exercise control over the ministers. The members may ask questions from the ministers to show that they exercise check over the government. Motions of adjournment may be moved (generally by the members of the opposition) to hold discussion on a matter of urgent public importance. The opposition may go to the last extent of tabling a censure motion to highlight the 'crimes' of the government and, if such a motion is carried through, it amounts to the fall of the government. All statutory instruments issued by the departments to keep the laws of the Parliament in operation are placed before the House for approval. When the statutory instruments are put before the House, any member may raise a point that such and such instrument has violated the decision of the House and then the House may hold a debate to pass or reject the order in question. The House may outvote the government by disapproving its policy, rejecting a bill moved by a minister, cutting the budget, or passing a motion of no-confidence.

The House of Commons has financial powers as well. It is said that the purse of the nation is in the hands of the Commons. All money bills and budget must be passed by the Parliament. It is the government which prepares a money bill and budget and presents them to the House with monarch's formal recommendation. Until the budget is passed by the Parliament, no part of it can be implemented. The Cabinet sees to it that the budget is passed by the House according to its policy. The discussion over the demands of ministers gives to the members (particularly of the Opposition) an opportunity for accusing the government of its acts of commission and omission. No member of the House can propose a new tax, he can certainly propose a cut. In case a cut motion is carried through, fall of the government follows. True to say that the Cabinet depends upon the support of majority behind it and the budget is passed by the House as it decides and desires, but the weight of criticism does not go in vain and a sensible Prime Minister pays attention to the various 'crimes' of the government highlighted by the fiery critics.

Then, the House has certain judicial powers as well. If a person contempts the privileges of the House, he may be arrested under a warrant signed by the Speaker and brought before the bar of the House. It depends upon the House to release him after admonition or award punishment. No judicial body can sit in judgement over the verdict of the House given in this direction. The House has its privileges committee to study a matter referred to it and then submit its report to the House for necessary action.

It is sometimes said that the House of Commons has transferred much of its real power in favour of the government (Cabinet) and consequently become subservient to the ministers. Samuel H. Finer holds that its primary function "is to sustain a government; its secondary function is to criticise it."[7] That is, the House has hardly any real power beyond the ventilation of grievances. It has no legislative initiative as hardly any bill moved by a private member has the chance of being adopted until it is supported by the Cabinet. The House is thus a registering body for passing a bill or a budget or approving a policy measure presented by the Cabinet. It is, likewise, argued that such a body of more than six hundred members can neither legislate nor govern; its main task "is still what it was when it was first summoned; not to legislate, but to secure full discussion and ventilation of all matters, legislative or administrative, as the condition of its giving assent to Bills whether introduced by the government or by private members or its support to ministers."[8]

Speaker: The Speaker is the presiding officer of the House of Commons. His designation is derived from the fact that in the early days of the twelfth and thirteenth centuries, only the presiding officer of the House of Commons – which was then a petitioning and not a law-making body – had the right to speak on behalf of the House to the monarch. It was this officer who took the petitions and resolutions of the House to the king and had a talk as the only 'speaker' (representative) of the House. Situation has fundamentally changed now when the House of Commons has become the real Parliament of the country in which the Speaker speaks very little and whenever he opens his lips, he speaks not to the House but for the House. On the occasion of his re-election to this office in 1945, Douglas Clifton Brown said: "As Speaker, I am not the Government's man, nor the Opposition's man. I am the House of Commons' man' and, I believe, above all, the back-benchers' man.. ..as Speaker, I cherish the dignity of the office very much."

It follows that the Speaker is a member of the House of Commons and he is elected by it. There is a very healthy convention that 'once a Speaker, always a Speaker.' It implies that the Speakership is a very exalted office and its holder may continue to occupy it till he likes. When the House of Commons is dissolved, he still continues to hold his office until

7. S.H. Finer: "Great Britain" in Ward and Macridis: *Modern Political Systems: Europe,* p. 109.

8. L.S. Amery: *Thoughts on the Constitution,* p. 12.

the new Speaker is chosen. However, it is required by a well-established custom that the Speaker returns unopposed as he contests election from some constituency as a man of no party. His non-political character is his best qualification entitling him to seek reelection and return unopposed.

Whenever there is a vacancy due to death or voluntary retirement, the nomination is made by the leader of the majority party after consultation with the leader of the opposition. Hence, names of those members are withdrawn where there are objections and, in these conditions, the name of a backbencher is preferred as he is an unknown or a non-controversial figure. After this formal nomination, the ceremony of his election in the House of Commons takes takes place. His name is proposed by a member and seconded by another and soon the result is out as there is no other name in the field. After the elections when the new House meets, the name of the same Speaker is preferred and his election is just a formality. However, the House elects the Deputy Speaker. As another convention has come up to elevate the Deputy Speaker to the post of the Speaker, it may be said that the formality of the election has more importance in the case of Deputy Speaker than that of the Speaker. This is called the tradition of continuity.

The functions and powers of the Speaker may be discussed under three heads - as presiding officer of the House, as executive officer of the House and, finally, as the defender of the dignity of the House. In the first place, the Speaker is the chairman of the House and by virtue of this capacity he acts as its presiding officer. He acts as the chairman (unless the House meets as Committee of the Whole House) when the House meets, calls the meetings in order, recognizes the members who want to speak, asks a member to withdraw words or apologise in the event of making an unparliamentary expression, names a member if his behaviour is repeatedly offensive to the dignity of the House, maintains discipline in the House and even asks his Sergeant-at-arms to push out a member if he refuses to leave the chamber. He conducts the business of the House and gives his ruling on the points of order raised by some members. He has casting vote to break a tie. The Parliament Act of 1911 has given to him the exclusive power of deciding whether a bill, in question, is a money bill or not.

Then, the Speaker has some executive powers. He issues writs and warrants. He appoints the chairmen of various committees. His staff includes Clerk, Librarian and Sergeant-at-arms who are always at his call.

If a person is found to have contempted the dignity of the House, he is arrested and brought before the House as per orders signed by the Speaker. It is up to the House to free the detained person after verbal admonition, or give a sentence of imprisonment. Such a decision of the House is implemented by the Speaker. Occasionally, he presides over constitutional conferences. It is his business to maintain discipline in the galleries and the lobbies and any violation of the rules by a person is subject to the judicial authority of the Speaker.

Finally, the Speaker is the defender of the dignity of the House. He acts as the spokesman of the House before the House of Lords and the monarch. If there is any encroachment on the powers of the House, the Speaker defends the House. For instance, when a minister refuses to answer a question despite persistent demands of the opposition, the Speaker rules whether the minister must give an answer or not, or whether he should be allowed to protect himself behind the cover of public interest. He also protects the interests of the minority sections and other back-benchers. It is his discretion to rule whether a question or a resolution is admissible or not. The debates of the House are published under his authority and he may order any portion of the minutes to be expunged if there is anything violative of the parliamentary behaviour and decorum.

In fine, the office of the British Speaker is the most dignified for the simple reason that he is taken to be infallible like the Pope. His non-political character is the best asset to command respect and discipline from all sides. Even the rustle of his official robe, once Disraeli said, is enough to check an incipient riot. His office is the peculiar example in the world to be synonymous with political neutrality. The reason of his greatness lies in the fact that soon after his election to the august office, he rises above party strife and rigorously cuts off his party affiliations. He gives no chance of suspicion and even when he has to exercise his casting vote, he behaves in a way as to maintain the status quo. It is commented: "Outside, no less than inside, of the House of Commons, the Speaker abstains from every form and suggestion of partisanship. He never publicly discusses or voices an opinion on party issues; he never attends a party meeting; he has no connection with party newspapers; he never sets foot in a political club; he never mingles with his fellow members socially in the (Westminster Palace's) tea rooms: he does not even make a compaign for his own election."[9]

9. Herbert Morrison: *Government and Parliament,* p. 204.

Speaker's Powers

As Presiding Officer of the House

1. To act as the chairman of the House, maintain order and discipline and conduct the business of the day
2. To allocate time for different kinds of business
3. To interpret the laws and rules of procedure
4. To recognise a member
5. To name a member, warn him, or ask him to withdraw from the House, or order his Sergeant-at-arms to push him out for disorderly behaviour
6. To admit motions, resolutions and points of order
7. To allow a member to ask questions or their supplementaries
8. To put matters to vote and then announce the result
9. To exercise casting vote in the event of a tie
10. To allow a minister to make or not to make a statement, and
11. To adjourn the House in the absence of quorum

As Executive Officer of the House

1. To issue writs and warrants of arrest for a person involved in the contempt of the House
2. To appoint chairmen of various committees
3. To supervise his staff—Clerk, Librarian, Marshal etc.
4. To have the punishment awarded to a person as decided by the House
5. To preside over important constitutional and inter-Parliamentary conferences
6. To make arrangement for the publication of the proceedings of the House
7. To make arrangement for the meetings of the committees, and
8. To certify a bill after it is passed by the House

As Defender of the Dignity of the House

1. To act as the spokesman of the House of Commons in the House of Lords and in a meeting with the monarch
2. To order expunction of unparliamentary references from the proceedings of the House, and
3. To safeguard the interests of the minority sections and the back-benchers

Legislative Process

Laws are made by the King-in. Parliament. It means that the monarch and the House of Lords and the House of Commons share the power of making laws. It is true that the sovereignty of Parliament really signifies supremacy of the House of Commons, but even the formal jurisdiction of the Lords and the monarch cannot be dismissed. It is the monarch who summons the session of the Parliament, inaugurates it with his Speech from the Throne, gives formal sanction to move a money bill in the House of Commons, and, in the end, puts his signatures on the bill passed by the Parliament in order to have it placed on the statute book. Then, the authority of the House of Lords has its own place. A non-money bill may be initiated in the House of Lords. The Lords can delay the passage of a money bill for a month and of a non-money bill for a year. Besides, the Lords, in stead of rejecting a bill, may return it to the Commons for reconsideration and it is possible that some of the points raised therein may be accepted by the members of the lower house. Even the rejection of a bill forcing the Commons to readopt it in the successive session after the lapse of a year may generate a healthy public opinion preventing the Commons to readopt it. Finally, the Lords can reject a bill of major constitutional significance. It makes the point clear that legislative process includes the Commons, the Lords and the monarch.

The Parliament deals with several kinds of bills. If a bill is of a general character affecting the people as a whole or their major part, it is called a public bill; otherwise it is a private bill concerned with a particular section or part of the society. Then, a money bill is concerned with the authorisation of government to raise or spend money in the form of taxes, surcharges, loans etc.; otherwise, it is a non-money or ordinary bill. Lastly, a bill moved by a minister is called a government or official bill; otherwise, it is a private member's bill. There is difference between a private bill and a private member's bill. If a bill is moved by a member of Parliament who is not a member of the ministry, it is called private member's bill; such a bill is taken up for discussion only on Friday and it has hardly any chance of being adopted unless it requisitions the support of the Cabinet. In sharp contrast to it, a private bill is one which affects a particular place or section of the country. Such a bill may be moved either by a minister or by a private member.

A bill is a well-written resolution specifying title, objects, area of application, and punishment in the event of its violation. It is required that it must be written very clearly so that there is, as far as possible, no scope for litigation or diverse interpretations. It is also needed that the various clauses of a bill must not be in contradiction with one another or with any other law in force in the country. As the laws are enforced by the courts and they are interpreted by men of law, it is further required that the language of a bill must be very specific and unequivocal. All parts of a bill are written number-wise, with sub-numbers and clauses, which are called sections or articles. It is, therefore, understandable that the drafting of a bill is a very technical matter which can be performed by the experts. The Cabinet has the department of legal experts for this purpose and a bill moved by a minister is well-drafted, while a private member has either to write a bill himself, or he takes the help of some expert confidentially.

The passing of a bill by the Parliament has different stages from initiation to the royal assent. Some important points must be kept in mind. First, a money bill can be moved only by a minister (as it is initiated with monarch's formal recommendation which cannot be secured by a private member) in the House of Commons and, after its adoption by the Commons, it goes to the Lords to be passed by them at most within a month.[10] Second, a non-money bill may be initiated in either chamber. If a bill is first passed by the Lords, the Commons may reject it any number of times, but if it is first passed by the Commons, the Lords may either return it with some recommendations or reject it. If there is some possibility of return, the matter is to be settled by the exchange of written messages and it depends upon the Commons to accept or reject all or any of the recommendations. If it is rejected, it depends upon the will of the House of Commons to readopt it in the successive session after a lapse of one

10. The Parliament Act of 1911 defines the money bill thus; "Any public bill which, in the judgment of the Speaker, contains only provisions dealing with all or any of the following subjects: the imposition, repeal, remission, alteration or regulation of taxation, the imposition for the payment of debts or other financial purposes or charges on the consolidated fund, or on money provided by Parliament or the variation or repeal of any such charges, supply the appropriation, receipt, custody, issue or audit of accounts or public money, the raising or guarantee of any loan or the payment thereof, or subordinate matters incidental to those subjects or any of them."

Legislative Process

Kinds of Bills

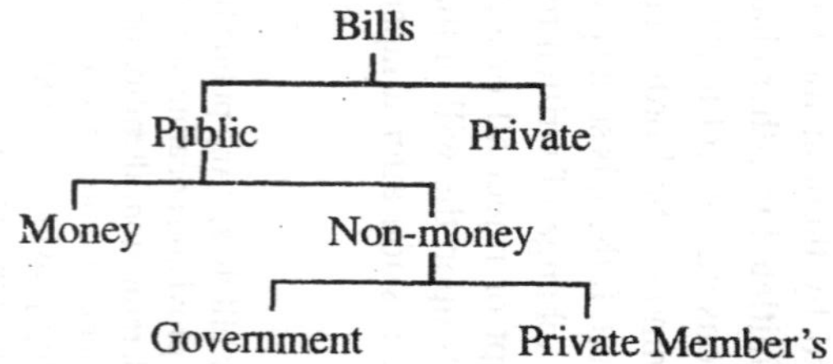

Important Points

1. Money bill can be initiated in the House of Commons.
2. Money bill is always an official bill moved with monarch's recommendation.
3. Money bill can not be rejected by the House of Lords.
4. Non-money bill may be rejected or returned by the Lords with some recommendations and it is for the Commons to accept them or not.
5. Non-money bill may be returned by the Lords once and if passed by the Commons after a lapse of one year in two successive sessions, it overrides the requirement of the concurrence of the Lords.
6. Royal assent is a formality, for the monarch does not use his veto power.

House of Commons

1. First Reading (a formality)
2. Second Reading (important general debate)
3. Committee Stage (consideration of bill in detail)
   (*i*) Committee of the Whole House (for money bills and very important bills)
   (*ii*) Standing or Select Committees (for others)
4. Report Stage (consideration of Committee Report)
5. Third Reading (limited debate)

House of Lords

1. First Reading (a formality)
2. Second Reading (important general debate)
3. Committee Stage (consideration by a Committee)
4. Report Stage (consideration of Committee's Report)
5. Third Reading (limited debate)

Final Stage

1. Consideration of amendments, if any proposed by the Lords (exchange of messages)
2. Royal Assent
   (*a*) No use of veto
   (*b*) No judicial review

year and thereby override the requirement of the concurrence of the Lords. Third, since the Cabinet has a comfortable majority behind it, it is certain that a bill moved by a minister must be adopted and a bill moved by the private member has no chance of passage, unless supported by the government. Official bills have four days for discussion (from Monday to Thursday), while private business takes place on Friday. Legislative process must, therefore, be studied in the light of Cabinet's usurpation of the inherent power of the Parliament.

Let us now consider the case of a public bill moved by a minister first in the House of Commons:

First Reading: The first stage is the introduction of a bill called 'first reading'. The mover gives his intention to the Speaker who, on the appointed time, calls him to introduce the bill in the House. Then, the mover, after taking leave of the House, stands up and reads the title and some important passages of the bill. There is usually no debate and a bill soon crosses this stage. If it is so required either by the House or by the mover for some important reasons, the mover may make a speech under the '10 minute rule' to highlight the objectives and motivating purposes. Then the bill is taken to be passed and printed at government expenses in order to be circulated among the members well in advance for making preparations for the forthcoming debate.

Second Reading: The most important and crucial stage in the life of a bill is second reading. On a day and at a time fixed by the Speaker, the bill is taken up for discussion and a general debate covering all parts of the bill begins. The 'friends' and 'foes' of the bill have their chance of either supporting or opposing the bill or putting some amendments. As bills are mostly moved by the ministers, the leaders of the opposition try to defeat the government for the sake of registering their vote of censure. Naturally the Cabinet tries to make use of the majority behind it and the bill after voting in favour is declared to be passed. Bills moved by private members fall through at this stage. The leaders of the opposition may take any course: they may oppose the bill and demand division to defeat the government; they may propose major amendments —virtually hitting at the form and nature of the bill; they may propose that the bill be taken up for discussion after an interval of six or seven months, that is, at a time when the House is already adjourned *sine die* and the bill automatically lapses with the prorogation of the House.

Committee Stage: Then follows the committee stage. A bill passed by the House after its second reading is 'committed' to a standing committee. If it is a money bill or a bill of extraordinary importance to be passed expeditiously, it is referred to the committee of the whole house; if it is referred to a select or sessional committee, it is subsequently examined by a standing committee. The committee holds its meeting in a separate room upstairs where the bill is discussed in detail. The mover of the bill is there to defend his bill, but the opposition takes another chance of defeating or destroying it. In discussion over the bill line by line and word by word, several amendments are moved. There is no use of closure motion as a result of which discussion becomes lengthy. After the bill is passed by the committee, it is reported to the House.

Report Stage: The bill is once again brought before the House as a whole and once again the members have the chance, though the last one, of ventilating their views on it. On the fixed date and time, the mover of the bill requests the House to allow him to present his bill with committee report for discussion. Now the discussion proceeds clause-wise. It is a different thing that various parts of the bill are grouped to save the time of the House and finish discussion within the allocated time. This is called 'closure by compartments'. However, in order to save the time of the House, other types of closure motions may also be invoked. It may be decided to take up only important portions of the bill and the rest to be taken as passed. This process of skip-over is called 'kangaroo' closure. 'Simple closure' may also be used to cut the debate short and put the matter for division. If the time is over and some parts of the bill remain to be discussed, it may be decided by the House to take vote on all parts of the bill (including the untouched ones) and it is called the 'guillotine' closure. The use of closure motion is the best safeguard to check the tendency of making irrelevant expressions called 'filibustering' in the United States.

Third Reading: A bill after crossing this stage comes for the third reading before the House which is just a formality. On a fixed date and time, the bill is taken up for last discussion. A general debate ensues but no substantial amendment can be moved; only verbal changes may be suggested or made. Naturally, the bill crosses this hurdle in no time.

Bill in the Second House: A bill passed by the House of Commons goes to the House of Lords for its concurrence. There the bill passes through similar stages. If the Lords concur, the bill is supposed to be passed by both the Houses of Parliament; if there is mounting opposition in the House, the matter is sought to be settled by the exchange of written messages. In case the bill is rejected by the Lords, it depends upon the will of the House of Commons to re-adopt it in the successive session creating a lapse of one year at least between the introduction stage of the first attempt and the third reading of the second one. It is obvious that the House of Lords cannot do anything more than the interposition of delay of one year to face the unbending will of the popular chamber.

Royal Assent: A bill passed by both the Houses of Parliament (or passed by the House of Commons alone a second time in its successive session after a lapse of one year of its rejection by the Lords) finally goes to the monarch for his assent. The veto power is in the hands of the sovereign. It is a well-established convention that the monarch does not exercise his veto power and thus a bill presented to him receives his assent. Then, the bill is placed on the statute book and becomes an act. As there is no judicial review in England, an act made by the Parliament cannot be struck down or repealed until the Parliament itself so pleases.

Private Member's Bill: A word may be said about private member's bill. Such a bill is moved by a member (who is not a minister) in the form of a petition. This petition is deposited with the minister concerned who holds an enquiry and hears interested persons. The matter in question is advertised and the possibly affected-persons and parties are requested to represent their cases personally or through attorneys. If the matter is approved, the minister concerned issues a 'provisional order' embodying the proposed bill. A number of similar provisional orders may be grouped into a Provisional Orders Confirmation Bill which is, at a later date, introduced by the minister. This type of bill passes through all stages (as discussed above) and faces less hostile opposition as it has already been scrutinised by the department concerned. This system is, indeed, expensive and time-taxing though better and more useful. Hence, the older method may also be made use of whereby a petition submitted by the private member is examined by two parliamentary officials (one from each House) called Examiners of Petitions for Private Members' Bills. After their certificate, the bill is moved and then it passes through various stages discussed above with the only difference that the matter is taken up for discussion on Fridays and that it is referred to a committee on private member's bills. However, as already pointed out, a private member's bill has almost no chance of being adopted until it requisitions the support of the Cabinet.

Financial Business: The passage of a money bill follows a procedure somewhat different from that of others. Even a budget is a money bill and its passage requires a special procedure. A money bill or a budget is first introduced in the House of Commons with formal recommendation of the monarch. It makes a money bill always a government bill and its defeat amounts to the vote of no-confidence in the government. The members of the opposition cannot propose a new tax or a new channel of earning the revenues, they can propose a 'cut motion' that is, the demand for appropriation made by a department be cut. A money bill based on the estimates of the departments and approved by the Treasury and the Chancellor of Exchequer are presented to the House in January or February. When a money bill crosses the second reading, it goes to the Committee of the Whole House which considers it in detail. This committee is called the Committee of Ways and Means when it discusses the revenue side of the budget; it becomes the Committee of Supply when it deals with the appropriation side of the budget. The estimates of revenue and appropriation approved by the Committee are then given the shape of two bills–revenues in the form of Finance Bill and expenditures in the form of Appropriation Bill–which pass through the same legislative process.

A study of legislative process makes it clear that it is the Cabinet and not the ordinary member of Parliament who makes laws. A bill moved by a private member has no chance of being passed by the Parliament as the Cabinet is there to oppose and see to it that it is defeated. The use of party whips and strict rules of party discipline enjoin upon the members to come to the House to support the government instead of putting their own bills. Hence, the better and more useful alternative before a private member is to influence the minister with the need for a particular type of legislation. Until the Cabinet is prepared to support the private member's bill (which is rather rare) or until a private member is very tactful and shrewd to get his point incorporated into the legislative policy of the Cabinet, there is no chance of enactment, as the majority in the House of Commons is in the tight grip of the Prime Minister and his Cabinet to decide the fate of every bill according to the policy of the government. It is thus commented that the legislative initiative has gone from the private members and come to the departments under the discretion of the Cabinet which together "have become in practice the first Chamber in our law-making mechanism."[11]

11. H.R.G. Greaves: *The British Constitution,* p. 31.

Committee System

A reference to the committee system must be made in the study of legislative process. Both Houses of Parliament have their committees for the detailed consideration of their business. This machinery of committee system saves the time of the House and enables the members (particularly the more competent ones in specific directions) to ventilate their views under the relaxed rules of procedure As Friedrich says: "Since the pressure is undeniably great in the English Parliament as in others, the critics of the system of closure have been looking for relief in other directions. As a consequence, they have advocated an expansion of the standing committee system in the House of Commons."[12] Sir Courtenay Ilbert, one time Clerk of the House, adds: "It proceeds on the view that when the general principle of a bill has been affirmed, a reasonable chance ought to be afforded for having its provisions discussed, that this chance is improved by sending a bill to a Standing Committee that, as a general rule, discussion in a Standing Committee is more business-like and effective than the discussion in a Committee of the Whole House, and that the time of the House is saved by dividing the bill into compartments for discussing ,the details of legislative measures."[13]

Purpose: The committee system is centuries-old. It is found in historical references that the king used to consult some committees of the House of Commons. However, its present form came into being in 1882 to discover a better and more workable alternative to the problems of the House of Commons. The main purpose behind it was to affect decongestion so that the House would be able to perform much of its business without the loss of time and skill of its members. The way out was the devolution of the business of the House to its committees working under the control and authority of the House itself. As such, the procedure provides a useful means of increasing expertness and conserving the time of the House of Commons.

Kinds: The committees of the House of Commons are of five kinds. In the first place, we take up the case of the Committee of the Whole House. As its name indicates, it consists of all the members of the House with the single exception of the Speaker. Hence, when the House sits as a committee of this type, the Speaker is absent and the meeting is presided over by some other member or Deputy Speaker who takes the chair of the

12. Carl J,. Friedrich: *Constitutional Government and Democracy*, p. 330.

13. *Ibid.*

Clerk. The Speaker's chair remains vacant and the mace is also removed. The rules of procedure are also relaxed whereby a motion proposed by a member need not be seconded, he may speak for a longer duration of time, he may speak more than once and closure motions are not put to restrict the scope of discussion. However, apart from these technical differences the political atmosphere of the committee remains the same for the obvious reason that it consists of all the members of the House. All money bills, urgent bills requiring to be passed expeditiously, one-clause bills not needing a detailed Committee examination and bills of major constitutional significance are taken up by this committee. While dealing with money bills, this committee acts with a double nomenclatures —Committee of Ways and Means when it deals with the revenue side of the budget and Committee of Supply when it considers the matter concerned with the appropriation side.

Then, there are 8 Standing Committees called by the names of A, B, C, D, etc. One of them is the Committee for Scotland. Normally all public bills, other than money bills are referred to these committees. The members of these committees (about 20 in each to whom additional 30 may be added) are nominated by a selection committee (consisting of members chosen by Party leaders) and their names are confirmed by the House. The Speaker designates their presiding officers, but if the designated chairman is absent for some reason, the members may choose someone else from amongst themselves to work in his place. Each standing committee consists of some 50 members in accordance with the proportional strength of various parties in the House. These committees consider bills referred to them after their second reading in the House and, as such, they have to keep their scope of discussion confined to the general decision taken by the House. The Committee for Scotland (in a larger form called the Grand Scottish Committee) deals with matters relating to Scotland. When a standing committee meets, its members may raise a point of discussion and put some amendments. Decisions are taken by majority vote.

Apart from these Standing Committees, there are select committees (each consisting of 15 members) set up for the purpose of examining special matters of great importance or to study bills of a radical nature. Normally such committees are appointed to discuss a very complex matter requiring special technical knowledge. Hence, these committees may hold a public hearing as well in which interested people of certain groups may seek participation either personally or through their solicitors. Hence, it is said

Committees of the House of Commons

Committees

Committee of the Whole House	Standing Committees	Select Committees on	Sessional Committees	Private Members' Bills Committees	Joint Parliamentary Committees
(Concerned with finance, legislation and matters of first-class constitutional importance) (a) Committee of Ways and Means (when dealing with revenues) (b) Committee of Supply (when dealing with appropriations)	(Concerned with legislation) 1. A Committee 2. B Committee 3. C Committee 4. D Committee 5. E Committee 6. Committee on Scotlaned* 7. Committee on Wales 8. Committee on Private members' Bills	1. Privileges 2. Estimates 3. Public Accounts 4. Statutory Instruments 5. Nationalised Industries 6. Agriculture 7. Science and Technology 8. Procedure 9. Publications and Debates 10. Kitchen and Refreshment	(Concerned with some matter not covered by other committees most of whom have now been replaced by: 1. Royal Commissions 2. Departmental Committees for Enquiries 3. Committee for Judicial Enquiries		

*There is also a Grand Scottish Committee consisting of all 71 MPs from Scotland plus 10 to 15 more to maintain the balance among different parties.

that they conduct the work of enquiries and eliciting public opinions rather than discussing the aspects of a legislative measure as happens in other committees. They have about 15 members who are supposed to have a special knowledge and awareness of that problem. These committees are set up for a definite purpose and, hence unlike standing committees, they do not live in existence till the prorogation of the House. They are dissolved after the business-in-hand is over.

In addition to these three types of committees, there are sessional committees set up at the beginning of the session. Instances may be cited of the committee on privileges, committee on estimates, committee on public accounts, and committee on Statutory Instruments. They are called sessional committees as they remain during the life of the session of the House. Like select committees, these committees may hold public hearings, call the minister or his departmental officers for some examination, and give report to the House.

Last, there are committees for private members' bills. Such a committee usually consists of 4 members chosen by the committee of selection of the House and the members of this committee are required to sign a declaration that they would not feel personally interested in the bill coming before it and that their constituents would not be locally affected by its passage. All private members' bill passed after the second reading are referred to these committees. It has already been visualised that as a bill moved by a private member has almost no chance of being passed until supported by the Cabinet, which is rather rare, committees dealing with such bills do not have much significance.

The House of Lords has its own committees. But if a bill is of an exceptionally important nature and its adoption is needed as early as possible, a joint committee consisting of equal number of members of both the Houses may be set up at the instance of either House, though the proposal must be initiated by the House where the bill has originated. In a word, the committees of the House of Commons play a very important and useful part in the working of the House and it is good that the English people have disallowed the tendency of having their mushroom growth as we find in America. The House of Commons has adhered to the advice of R.H.S. Crossman, Leader of the House, that they "must take care to see them up in the right way" and that they "cannot make the American-style committees. They must be in our tradition."[14]

14. See Bernard Crick: *The Reform of Parliament,* p. 303. (Appendix D)

Criticism: It is sometimes said that the committees have taken away the powers of the Parliament and a tendency, though scrupulously checked, to set up more and more committees for the consideration of more and more complex matters is not without dangers. In a mood of resentment Winston Churchill seems to have exclaimed: 'We are over-run by them like the Australians were by the rabbits.'[15] It has also been pointed out that the officials "fortified by the committees upon which experts and interested parties have set, are enabled to present to Parliament, through their ministers, proposals which are so formidably supported that the lay members of the House are unable to criticise them effectively."[16] It has further been maintained that these specialised committees would constitute a radical constitutional innovation amounting to a challenge to the accountability of the ministers. In view of this position, Birch comes to hold the view that it "may be appropriate to reconsider the nature of responsible government in Britain."[17]

But the fact remains that committee system is an inescapable necessity. No legislative body can do its work without the help of its committees if it has to avoid the wastage of its time and maintain efficiency. Two special features of the Committees of the House of Commons are noteworthy. First, some of the committees have come to hold quasijudicial function inasmuch as they hold public meetings, call ministers and their administrative staff for some interrogation and hear interested parties before making their report. Second, their way of doing involves a greater degree of bureaucratic mechanism and thereby more room is accorded to the reconciliation of representative government with bureaucratic administration.

The Opposition

While keeping in view the case of English representative democracy, Macaulay once remarked that the Government and the Opposition 'constitute the fore and the hind legs of a democratic stag'. Truly so, the cabinet government in England finds opposition as 'an integral part of the working constitution' what is called 'H.M.'s Loyal Opposition.'[18] What was regarded as 'immoral', 'unpatriotic' and 'factious' by the favourite politicians of King George III, has now become an essential part of the parliamentary government having five cardinal characteristics. First, it is

15. See K.C. Wheare: *Government by Committees*, p. 1.
16. *Ibid.*, p. 246.
17. Birch: *Representative and Responsible Government*, p. 164.
18. Quinton Hogg: *Purpose of Parliament*, p. 85.

'organised' as it presents a united challenge to the government on all issues it chooses to contest. Second, it is 'permanent' as it does not band and disband according to the waves of political ups and downs. Third, it is 'representative' as it consists of dedicated political leaders originally connected with the people of the country. Fourth, it is 'alternative' as it remains ready to form an alternative government if the Cabinet falls. Last, it is 'participant' as it takes part in the deliberations of the House and remains prepared to co-operate with the government chiefly during times of grave national crisis.[19]

The Opposition has a well-recognised and respected place in the British parliamentary system of government. Since Britain is a two-party state, one party wins absolute majority and forms the government, the other forms the Opposition. Political power alternates between the Conservative and the Labour parties according to the verdict of the electorate. The most notable characteristic of the Opposition is that it is well-organised. It has its leader and also a 'shadow cabinet'. The Leader of the Opposition draws salary from the exchequer and has his office inside the building of Parliament. He has his own whips and holds separate party meetings. He is rightly taken as the "obverse of the leader of the House."[20]

The Opposition performs certain important functions. In the first place, as its name indicates, it opposes the government. Lord Randolph Churchill observes that the business of the Opposition is to oppose. This is, however, an advance on the earlier formula of Tierney that the duty of the Opposition is to propose nothing, to oppose everything, and to turn out the government. It is due to this that the Opposition criticises the government with the intention of exposing its weaknesses ultimately amounting to its downfall. The Leader of the Opposition and his team (called shadow cabinet) ask searching questions from the ministers, demand debate on adjournment motions, and sometimes try to carry through their cut motions in order to effect the 'defeat' of the government.

However, the real business of the Opposition is not to place obstructions in the way of the government by making unnecessary exressions at every step. It is required that the opposition must be constructive. The Opposition must oppose objectionable policies and try to force the government to modify them. The views of men like Sir

---

19. Samuel H. Finer in Ward and Macridis, *op. cit.*, p. 111.

20. Jennings: *Parliament*, p. 74.

Randolph Churchill and Tierney are out-of-date and they fail to depict the constructive side of the argument. Irrelevant arguments do not pay, rather they recoil and the opposition has to suffer. What is really needed is that the opposition must support the government where it is indispensable, it must oppose where it can put forward a better and more useful course. Herman Finer says: "The tight organisation of the Opposition confronts the Government with a planned, continuous and inescapable set of critics, who have assumed the responsibility for Opposition. The Opposition has status."[21]

This constructive aspect of the opposition has to be scrupulously kept in mind by the leaders of the Opposition for the simple reason that while it "puts the Government on trial, it too is simultaneously on trial. The character and ability of the leaders of the Opposition and the Prime-minister are being rigorously assessed in public contest every minute."[22] Since the final authority is in the hands of the people, the Opposition has to see that its line of attack on the Government must be appreciated by the people in order to have a favourable wind for elections to come. It is aptly said: "The most it can hope for is to shame so many of the Government's supporters into abstention that the Government's stand is morally condemned in the eyes of the nation; and it may well have to wait till the next election to reap the fruits."[23]

Then, the function of the Opposition is not to oppose the Government, even in a constructive manner, at all times. It should co-operate with the Government in times of national crisis. There may be a national government consisting of the leaders of the Opposition to save the country from disaster. Hence, the leaders of the Opposition, in addition to keeping the Government under searching criticism, place an alternative programme before the people and express their willingness and capability to form the government if the chance is provided. Says Herman Finer: "Indeed, its responsibility is so 'governmental', as it were, that rebellions sometimes occur within the Opposition among individuals who want to be more pugnacious. On every question, the Government presents a clear policy for all the nation to see, and the Opposition presents a searching alternative so that the pre-occupied masses are invited to compare and choose."[24]

21. Herman Finer, *op. cit.*, p. 149.

22. *Ibid.*, p. 150.

23. Samuel H. Finer in Ward and Macridis, *op. cit.*, p. 111.

24. Herman Finer, *op. cit.*, pp. 149-50.

As a word of conclusion, it is safe to say that without a concerted opposition, the collectively responsible Cabinet would not be spurred on its highest merits. Around the Opposition, there "is a nucleus of a dozen or so men who sit on the front Opposition bench with the leader. They are virtually the alternative Government."[25] Samuel H. Finer argues that the attacks of the Opposition "can create a mood among the electorate. Its speeches bring many tears, but never turn a vote, though it can capture votes outside the House of Commons. It is to the electorate that its criticism is directed. For though the cabinet has power, the power is contingent; it faces a dedicated enemy which is banned with procedural privileges and commands an organised national following. And all the Government says and does is staked on the hazard of the few votes – three or four in every hundred – that can turn it out."[26]

Decline of Parliament

A critical study of the real position of the English Parliament, as it now obtains, presents a very interesting as well as a perplexing picture that ranges from its classical reverence of being 'grand inquest of the nation' as eulogised by John Stuart Mill to a modern version of its being in a state of 'decline', nay 'demise' as bemoaned by Lord James Bryce. Important works like G. W. Keeton's *The Passing Away of Parliament* (1952) and Christopher Hollis' monograph *Has Parliament a Future*? (1960) furnish a serious, if somewhat melancholy, evidence of the prevailing mood in certain quarters. The charge of the decline of the Parliament draws sustenance from the following points of criticism directed against its present position, particularly of the House of Commons. These strictures may be broadly grouped and summarised as follows:"[27]

1. Under modern conditions Parliament can no longer cope with the enormous volume and complexity of its tasks.
2. Instead of controlling the Executive, the House of Commons is little more than a rubber stamp for all powerful Governments

25. *Ibid.*, p. 149.

26. Samuel H. Finer in Ward and Macridis, *op. cit.*, p. 112.

27. See Gordon: *Our Parliament*, p. 155.

and parliamentary government has given way to Cabinet government.

3. Many of the decisions which ought to be taken in the House of Commons are taken instead outside the Parliament by bodies such as the Trade Union Congress and the Federation of British Industries, or by technical experts and 'Managers' who are able to dominate the politicians by means of their specialised knowledge.
4. Political power is so far monopolised by the great parties as virtually to prevent the entry into the House of Commons of independently minded candidates (even under party labels) of the type who in the past have contributed so much to the prestige of Parliament. Further, even if such men should reach Westminster, they would find the time of the House monopolised by every Government to such an extent that the drive and initiative would soon be stultified.
5. Parliament has largely delegated its legislative powers to the Civil Service.
6. The existing system of voting does not accurately reflect the opinion of the electorate, since it exaggerates majorities and depreciates or suppresses minority opinions.
7. All the above factors are tending to transform the House of Commons into a helpless puppet and have already gravely damaged its reputation in the eyes of the public.

Keeping such factors in his view, Hollis has minced no words in saying: "Parliamentary Government has already very largely perished. The Member is the obedient servant of the party machine. He tramps into the division lobby voting for or against he knows not what on subjects upon which as a general rule no opinion save that of the specialist is of the least value. The matters which were the subject of legislation in Victorian days were matters upon which any educated man could form an opinion....As things are now, it would really be simpler and more economical to keep a flock of tame sheep and from time to time to drive them through the division lobbies in the appropriate numbers. Absurd and excessive hours of meeting, constant all night sittings do not prove, as is sometimes superficially claimed, that Parliament is working hard; they prove that Parliament is not working at all."[28]

28. Christopher Hollis: *Can Parliament Survive?* pp. 64-65.

If this matter is studied in the light of what we have said on Cabinet Government, the contention of the critics, as given above, cannot be refuted. However, it would be a far-fetched view to say that the Parliament has almost declined, if not demised. There is ample evidence even today to illustrate the "undoubted popularity of parliamentary broadcasts, including television, the widespread excitement revealed at general elections; the ready sale of books about every aspect of Parliament, the respect accorded to leading parliamentarians and, above all, the never-failing queues for seats in the galleries of the House of Commons. Perhaps the answer is that although our constitutional machinery has been used through the ages and enjoys high repute in the world, no machinery will run for ever without periodic overhaul and re-design. This certainly seems to be the meaning underlying a recent debate on Parliamentary Reform, at the end of which the House of Commons resolved to maintain Parliament as the paramount forum of the nation and to bring its practices and procedures into harmony with this end and in accord with the needs of 1963."[29]

29. Gordon, ; *op cit.*, pp. 180-81.

6

POLITICAL PARTIES AND PRESSURE GROUPS

Political Parties

It is one of the celebrated axioms of modern politics that the organisation and working of political parties is indispensable for running a political system particularly one committed to the ideal of a liberal-democratic order. Undoubtedly, it is the political parties which make the system of representative government workable in as much as without them there "can be no unified statement of principle, no orderly evolution of policy, no regular resort to the constitutional device of parliamentary elections, nor of course any of the recognized institutions by means of which a party seeks to gain or maintain power."[1] As such, Britain being a model of representative government can be no exception. Rather, the peculiar thing about this country is that here the distribution of power "is primarily a function of the cabinet government and the British parliamentary system. So long as the parties accept the system of government, effective decision-making authority will reside with the leadership groups thrown up by the parliamentary parties (of whom one of the most important individuals is the party leader); and they will exercise this authority so long as they retain the confidence of their respective parliamentary parties."[2]

Origin: British party system, like the constitution itself, has an evolved character. As such, the history of its origin and growth dates back to the early phase of the modern period when two conditions contributed to the evolution of the party system, namely, the movement that the Parliament should become a legislative body in all its essentials with its rights fully established and that there should be political issues of a broad and deep

1. R.M. MacIver: *The Modern State*, p.396

2. R.T. Mckenzie: *British Political Parties*, p.335.

character on which the people may combine themselves in a group. The rise of the political parties became natural after the Restoration Movement (1660) when in 1679 a conflict developed over the passage of the Exclusion Bill. This bill was designed to forestall the succession of James II as the King of England after the death of Charles II. When the line of cleavage grew very sharp, the monarch (Charles II) dissolved the Parliament. Soon after, the supporters of the bill strongly petitioned for the calling of another Parliament and thus they came to be known as 'Petitioners', while their opponents became the 'Abhorers'. In due course, the former became the whigs and the latter the Tories.

Liberals started thereafter. A remarkable development took place at this stage that resulted in the establishment of the third party, called the Labour party in 1920. It consisted of the representatives of several labour unions. In due course, the Liberal party declined and its place was taken by the Labour making Britain once again the example of a bi-party system. The Labour Party had first chance to be in power in 1929 when Ramsay MacDonald was appointed as the Prime Minister.

Main Characteristics: The party system of Britain has its own characteristics that may be discussed briefly as under:

1. Britain affords the brilliant case of a two-party system. Once there were two factions called 'Petitioners' and 'Abhorers'; then they became 'Whigs' and 'Tories'; the Whigs were replaced by the 'Labour' with the result that the country came to have two parties known as 'Conservative' and 'Labour'. In a wider sense, the party system of Britain does not rule out the existence of other or 'third' parties. Even now there are some small organisations like Scottish Nationalists in Scotland and Plaid Cymru in Wales. However, what entitles Britain for being a model of bi-party system is that only two major political parties play a determining part in the mechanism of representative government. Power generally alternates between the two parties.
2. Quite misleading are the names of the major political parties of Britain. While the Conservatives have not invariably been opposed to change tooth and nail, the Liberals and now the Labourites have also not been propagating reforms vigorously. Within the ranks of both there have been many shades of opinion. The only point that may be added by way of generalisation is that the persons of a conservative temperament have by tradition gravitated to the Tory

(Conservative) party, while men of a liberal disposition have done the same first for the Whig and now for the Labour party.

3. The two parties of Britain have their sharp ideological distinctions despite the fact that both have no faith in the doctrine of scientific socialism. While the Conservative party stands for the protection and promotion of the interests of the affluent class having control over the means of production and distribution, the Labour Party does the same by and large for the class of the workers. Moreover, while the Conservative Party stands for the survival of British imperial dignity and for this reason strives for the retention of British hold over the poor and backward parts of the world, the Labour Party desires peace and liquidation of capitalism in the national and of colonialism in the international spheres.
4. A very important feature of British political parties should be traced in their being well-organised and disciplined and by virtue of that in their enjoying a hard core of electoral support. There is rigorous discipline due to which political maladies like cross-voting and floor-crossing are uncommon. The well-organised and highly disciplined character of the party system has made the working of cabinet system not only successful but an ideal for other countries to follow and to emulate.
5. British political parties have their full and unflinching faith in using democratic and constitutional means to realise their aims and objectives. It is due to this that events of violent manifestations do not occur in this country the like of which we may find in a country like France. Influencing the electorate by means of publications, speeches and sometimes by strikes done by the labour organisations are the principal ways by which political parties take part in the political process of the country. Any attempt to make use of violence or undemocratic action is carefully avoided. The result is that the two major parties remain like well-organised bodies and act in a way that gives stability as well as strength to the cabinet system of government.

Conservative Party: As stated above, the Conservative party has never been a body of thoroughly superstitious men. Its name hardly denotes its essential nature. As such, instead of calling it an organization of the opponents of reform, democracy and social justice, it would be more appropriate to describe it as a body of those who obdurately value their traditions and precedents and desire change at a very slow pace as far as possible. Under the leadership of men like Peel and Disraeli, for instance, it showed its 'militantly progressive' orientation. Hence, no one, as says a leading American writer, with a knowledge of English political history, "would contend that it has always been the party of reaction, or of obstruction to progress." Normally, the Conservatives oppose change or reform, but they accept it willy-nilly when they have to do it. One of their leaders once rightly said that they are 'cautious and circumspect reformers.'[3]

What deserves attention at this stage is that the Leader occupies a very important position. He is appointed for an indefinite period as there is no provision for annual election, though he lives under strict supervision of his party MPs and he may be forced to quit in case he commits a serious lapse. If the party gets clear majority, he becomes the Prime Minister, if the party is in the opposition, he forms his 'shadow cabinet'. Whips are appointed by him. His authority is by no means absolute in as much as the committee of the backbenchers (1922 Committee as it is called) may impeach him for his acts of commission or omission and thereby force him to take a different line of action.

Let us now look into the factor of ideology. As already pointed out, this party stands for broad principles that may be enumerated as under:

1. It believes that the nation is sustained by the existence of different social classes playing their part on the basis of merit. Ability and not accidents of wealth or birth should be the guiding consideration. No class should be favoured over or against another.
2. Freedom is the *sine qua non* of human life and its progress. Stress should be laid on the significance of free enterprise. The wider the choice, the greater scope for the development of self-reliance.
3. State activity in the economic sphere should be limited. There should be no attempt in the direction of nationalisation of private industries until it is warranted by the exigencies of the situation.
4. National institutions should be protected and honoured. As such, due respect should be given to the honour and greatness of the monarchy and the House of Lords.
5. British imperial interests should be safeguarded. Britain should play an effective role in the European Union for maintaining her political and economic power and prestige.

3. W.B. Munro: *The Governments of Europe.* p.242.

Labour Party: The Labour Party is a more socially representative organisation. It draws strength mainly from the middle class intelligentsia and manual workers. Its members are of four main categories: 'professions' (like university and college teachers), 'minor professions' (like journalists, organisers, public lecturers, insurance salesmen), small businessmen (like shopkeepers, accountants and executives) and 'working class occupations' (like labourers, artisans, clerks, etc.). In the main, the composition of the party is dominated by the 'professions' and 'workers'. The members of this party are of two types – individual (belonging to a constituency branch) and indirect (belonging to an affiliated trade union or Socialist Society). Individual members are required to pass an eligibility test of not being a member of any other party or ancillary organisation. No such test is required for affiliated members, and some of these can not even be classed as party sympathisers. Officers at local and national levels must be individual members of the party.

The Labour Party is committed to the doctrine of democratic socialism. Different from the socialist parties of the European countries, it has a socialism of its own based on the doctrine of Fabianism. The writings of such thinkers as Morris, Shaw, Cole and Tawney have helped furnish a native socialist tradition more influential than imported continental ideas. On the other hand, such writers reflect the mood and the spirit of British socialism; they rarely mould it. The party's policies and aspirations seem to be determined far more by prevalent political circumstances than by the pre-conceived philosophies. For this reason, the socialism of the Labour Party is fundamentally at variance with that of Marx. Its commitment to the principle of "common ownership of the means of production, distribution and exchange" did become a hot gospel for stalwarts, but party policy was never subsequently moulded in such a way that wholesale nationalisation could be a real possibility. "The Labour Party's brand of socialism has been tempered by the exercise of power. The chief aim has become the establishment of a Labour government rather than the bringing about of socialism."[4]

The broad principles on which the Labour Party stands may be described as follows:[5]

1. Man is inherently good and that institutions and societies are mostly to blame for making him behave badly and live miserably.

4. Stanley Henig and John Pinder: *European Political Parties*, pp.107-08.

5. See S.E. Finer, *op. cit.*, pp.85-86

Some Important Statements

So long as the parties accept the system of government, effective decision-making authority will reside with the leadership groups thrown up by the parliamentary parties (of whom one of the most important individuals is the party leader), and they will exercise their authority so long as they retain the confidence of their respective parliamentary parties. —***R.T. Mackenzie***

Like the term parliamentary sovereignty, which conceals the reduced role of Parliament in legislation and the unmaking of governments, the term two-party system, which is commonly used to describe the British party system, is somewhat deceiving. —***Joel Krieger***

Although the association of the Conservative Party with the economic and social elite is unmistakable, it is also true that Conservatives in Britain are associated historically with the birth of modern welfare state during the government of Prime Minister Benjamin Disraeli (1874-80) the creation of a long-lasting alliance between an upper-class leadership and a lower-class following. —***Samuel H. Beer***

Democracy, therefore, should be extended from the sphere of politics to that of economics and society.

2. It follows that scramble for private profit should be substituted by cooperative fellowship. Private firms and economic enterprises should be brought under social ownership and control. Key industries should be nationalised, the rest democratised.
3. It stands for the establishment of a welfare state so that private economy is placed under the regulation of social control. Social welfare services are performed by the State.
4. It desires that national institutions conform to the establishment of genuine democracy. As such, the privileges of the Lords should go.
5. There should be collective co-operation among the nations of the world. The United Nations should be strengthened so that there is peace in the world. Dependent peoples of the world should have freedom.

Other Parties: As a result of the split in the Labour Party in 1981, Roy Jenkins, Owen Roger and Shirley Williams formed Council of Social Democracy committed to the values, principles and policies of social democracy. They had protested against the increasing hold of the trade unions on the Labour Party, that in their view, could cause erosion of parliamentary government. It came to be known as the Social Democratic party with a programme of 12 Tasks—reformed Party system, fair elections, consistent economic strategy, employment policies, mixed economy, fair distribution of wealth, decentralisation, welfare of the community, better environment, equality for women, society for all, and international cooperation.

It failed to win the favour of the electorate in 1987. So it had its merger with the Liberal Party as a result of which it became Liberal Democratic Party. It was resolved that the new party must be open, democratic and participatory with full faith in (*i*) one person, one vote, (*ii*) national membership lists based on locally administered membership scheme, (*iii*) a leader elected by all members, (*iv*) a federal structure with UK federal level of institutions distinct from the institutions of the parties in the nations and regions of Britain, (*v*) representative assembles which would be the sovereign part of a democratic and accountable process of policy formulation, which would determine policy at the appropriate tier of a federal polity and which would have sole powers to amend the constitution, (*vi*) a constituency basis of association, and (*vii*) the right of members having a common interest to organise in autonomous groups with defined procedures for recongnition and representation within the party.

A section of the Social Democratic Party maintained its separate entity. The Liberal Democratic Party could secure 19 seats in the House of Commons in the elections of 1992. In the elections of 2010, it secured 57 seats and forced the Labour Party to form a colition government. Hence, it got a change to share power and thereby give a setback to the well established two-party system of the country.

Pressure Groups

Pressure group politics has been defined as the 'field of organised groups possessing both formal structure and real common interests in so far as they influence the decisions of public bodies,"[6] or alternatively, in so far as they seek to influence the process of government.[7] A pressure group plays the role of hide and seek in politics and, as such, it becomes fundamentally different from a political party that plays its part openly in the political process of the country. Moreover, the range of interest of a

6. W.J.M. Mackenzie: "Pressure Groups in British Government" in *British Journal of Sociology,* 1955, p.137.
7. J.D. Stewart: *British Pressure Groups,* p. 1.

Some Important Statements

Pressure groups are necessary to the government of our complex society. The coherent expression of opinion they render possible is vital. They have been a fifth estate, the means by which many individuals contribute to politics. —***J.D. Stewart***

The pressure groups are not themselves political parties as they do not seek political power over the whole process of government. They are concerned only with a limited aspect of the field of public policy, and their efforts are more concentrated and perhaps more effective as a result. —***R.M. Punnett***

Any organised group (and this includes firms and business) which tries to influence the policy of public authorities in its own chosen direction (though unlike the political parties, never themselves prepared to undertake the direct government of other country) is a pressure group. —***S.E. Finer***

pressure group is so limited that its role in the politics of the country varies from one point of time to another. Thus, a group maintains the peculiar life of being in as well as out of politics as per the involvement of its specific interest. It may be found that by no means all organised groups, or even a majority of them, normally have the slightest concern in what the government is up to, but at any point of time they might be so concerned and might wish to try to influence the official policy.

Though a subtle line of distinction between the pressure groups and political parties can be drawn, it should be borne in mind that the relationship between the two has become quite inextricable. While the former perform the job of interest articulation, the latter perform the function of interest aggregation. Thus, both act like twins in giving representation to the interests of the people with this line of difference that while the latter provide the main representation, the former do the auxiliary one. In other words, while the political parties provide territorial representation, the pressure groups do the same for the sake of functional representation. The relationship between the two has become so close that, in practice, "functional representation exists side by side with territorial representation."[8]

General Characteristics: In Britain there are literally hundreds of pressure groups of varying size, structure, functions and influence from the Confederation of British Industries and the TUC on the one hand to local, social and cultural groups on the other although, as a political study, our concern is primarily with those principal organisations that seek to

8. Punnett, *British Government and Politics*, p.133.

affect public policy as long as they do so. The groups are, moreover, by no means a new phenomenon although detailed academic interest in the politics of pressure groups is of a comparatively recent past. The Convention of Royal Burghs in Scotland which can be traced back to the fourteenth century is generally regarded as the oldest surviving organized group in Britain. In the eighteenth century there emerged a good number of political associations that agitated for the democratisation of the Parliament. The name of the Committee for the Abolition of the Slave Trade formed in 1807 was a much successful body. The Anti-Corn Law League was an outstandingly successful pressure group of this period. A new development took place after the middle of the nineteenth century when several organisations, big and small, allied themselves with the leading political parties - Whigs or Liberals and Tories or Conservatives. However, the emergence of the Labour Party has a significance of its own as it grew out like "a combination of various pressure groups from the trade union and socialist movements."[9]

One of the dominant facts of the British political system today is that pressure groups have become 'a growing force'. However, certain broad features can be discerned in this regard:

1. Since Britain has a full-fledged democratic set up, there is no limit on the size and working of the pressure groups. As a result, numerous are the pressure groups right from business organisations to labour and professional unions.
2. Britain is a unitary state with a stable bi-party system. As there is the concentration of central authority in the hands of the government situated at London, pressure groups are bound to direct their activities towards the machinery of a single central government. Here the nature of pressure group politics becomes basically different from that of its American counterpart where federalism has affected not only the governmental but also the non-governmental spheres of life. Moreover, as Britain is known for having a stable bi-party system, most of the groups live in clandestine relationship with one of the major political parties.
3. British pressure groups scrupulously observe the norms of democracy and constitutionalism. Hardly we hear about the role of anomic organizations that emerge like spontaneous outfits to vitiate the normal atmosphere of the country.

9. *Ibid.*, p. 135.

4. The growth of lobbying and especially the emergence of professional lobbyists, invites obvious comparisons with the position in the United States. Many of the practices employed in the United States are now found in the United Kingdom. The emergence of the forms of political consultants—some having links with lobbying firms or Capital Hill—and the techniques they employ (wining and dining MPs and peers and arranging private meetings with ministers and civil servants) has led to a number of commentators to believe, or rather 'fear', the 'Americanisation of British politics. The perception is pluasible one. However, it is difficult to sustain."[10]

What is really impressive about the nature of the politics of pressure groups in Britain is that their number and nature are not of an astonishingly complex variety and that their political behaviour does not smack of an irresponsible way of doing things for the sake of protecting and promoting their specific interests. Unlike their counterparts operating in other democratic political systems like those of America and France, British pressure groups "today are more concerned with details and administration and are perhaps more powerful and successful (if vocal) as a result."[11]

Structure and Organisation: A major illustration of the British pressure groups can be presented on the basis of their general structure and organisation, kind and nature of the interests they represent, the weight of authority they seek to exercise, the methods they want to employ and the like. Broadly speaking, they fall into two main types with a hybrid in between. While some like business groups, cooperative and trade unions defend economic interest, others promote special causes such as pacifism, nuclear disarmament, protection of animals and children. An initial distinction can also be made between sectional interest groups like the Automobile Association or the Institute of Directors and cause groups like the League Against Cruel Sports or National Viewers and Listeners Association that are bodies created specifically to lobby on behalf of some general cause.

Though a detailed catalogue of the British interest groups can be made, it cannot be lost sight of that all of them do not have equal significance in the political process of the country. Sectional interests always dominate because they are specific, not general, and for this reason they have a potential membership of active workers and leaders. These sectional groups

10. P. Norton: "The Changing Face of Parliament: Lobbying and Its Consequences" in his (ed.): *New Directions in British Politics* (Brookfield, Vermont: Edward Elgar Publishing Ltd., 1991), pp. 78-79.

11. Punnett, *op. cit.*, p.136

may be classified as business, labour and professional groups. While the business groups include the vast number of industrial, commercial and managerial bodies like the Institute of Directors, Confederation of British Industries, British Bankers Association of British Chambers of Commerce, National Federation of Building Trade Employers etc., labour groups are primarily the TUC and the individual unions. Then, there are the professional groups like British Medical Association, National Union of Teachers and Royal Institutes of Architects and Surveyors. The cause groups are formed for some purpose of general good like prevention of cruelty to animals and children, abolition of capital punishment, reform of prison conditions, preservation of rural England, maintenance of international peace and security etc.

What deserves particular mention at this stage is that a neat and water-tight division of British interest groups cannot be made on account of the nature of their organisation and working. While the categories of business and labour groups can be chalked out without much difficulty in view of their economic character, others may not be categorised in the like manner. For this reason, any categorization of interest groups looks like being arbitrary or incomplete. By all means, it may be regarded as illustrative though not a conclusive presentation of the matter under study.

Operational Dimension: What is of special significance in the study of pressure groups is their operation in the political process of the country that varies from country to country according to the nature of the political system. Two important points should, however, be given at this stage that have their peculiar place in the British political system. First, Britain has a stable two-party system with the result that while business groups invariably support the Conservatives, the labour groups do the same for the Labour party. And though the professional groups are by and large free from such ideological ties, they change their stands from time to time as per their specific interests. Second, the operational dimension of pressure group politics covers three distinct areas – executive, legislature and the public in general.

Of the three levels of pressure group activity mentioned above, the exercise of pressure on the Government and Civil Service "is the most direct and most important sphere of influence, as the concentration of constitutional authority in the hands of the central government, and in the executive machine particularly, means that pressure on Parliament and the public is used only as a means of indirectly influencing the Government. Also the most likely success for pressure groups is in the field of administrative and legislative action, and here it is influenced with executive that is most valuable."[12] Government departments and private associations generally co-operate with each other, since both sides stand to gain through such activities as the exchange of information and the sharing of each other's goodwill. Between government administrators and private associations, there is an extensive system of both formal and informal contracts.

The nature of public administration has now become such that the Government relies upon outside bodies for technical advice and information, for co-operation in the framing of legislation, and for help in the implementation of its policy. For instance, the Ministry of Agriculture relies heavily upon the NFU for membership of some 50 agricultural advisory committees, from the Beer' Diseases Advisory Committee. The Government cannot ignore some organisations like County Councils Association and the Association of Municipal Corporations over the reform of local government. Some bodies actually administer legislation on behalf of the Government; for example, the Law Society administering Legal Aid and the Royal Society for the Prevention of Accidents acting as a Government agent. In addition to the formal machinery for contact between the Government and the outside bodies, pressure groups are able to exert influence upon individual ministers and civil servants in less formal ways. After having a close look at this development of the British political system, Beer has laid down his doctrine of 'quasi-corporatism.'[13]

Pressure group activity at the Parliamentary level is easily visible. A group that has failed to have satisfaction from a minister or a civil servant, may try to exert pressure by taking the matter to the Parliament. Thus figures in lobbying or contacting MPs for raising a matter, putting a resolution, demanding discussion, and supporting or opposing a particular measure. It may be done through the representatives sitting in the House of Commons who could win elections with the active help and cooperation of some interest groups, or other ways can be adopted to influence the MPs. Some pressure groups may engage the services of professional lobbyists called Parliamentary Agents. Some groups like the NFU have local Parliamentary correspondents to maintain contact with their local MPs. The role of these MPs may, thus, be seen in their actions, by words or deeds, in tabling a motion or supporting a bill whether in the House or in its committees. Amendments to the official bills can be made at the instigation of pressure groups, with the Confederation of British Industries

12. *Ibid.*, pp. 139-40

13. S.H. Beer, "Pressure Groups and Parliament in Britain" in *American Political Science Review* (March, 1956), p.7

and other pressure groups being particularly active with regard to the passage of the Finance Bill through the House of Commons each year.

The role of pressure groups in the working of the Parliament is usually checked by the very firm discipline exerted on each party by the Whips, but sometimes a particular interest group may win enough sympathy in the House with both the majority party and the Opposition to force a minister to change his mind. Pressure groups have the greatest chance of influencing legislation in Parliament when the normal party alignment is broken. If there is a dissension among Government back-benchers with regard to a particular piece of official policy, this can be exploited by the opponents of the policy. Thus, in 1964-66, Parliament business groups opposed to the steel nationalization benefited from the dissent among Labour backbenchers over Government's proposals. Earlier in 1957, a combination of the Labour Opposition and some Conservative backbenchers had persuaded the Conservative Government to postpone the operating date of the Rent Act to the satisfaction of the tenants' interest groups.

It should, however, be added at this stage that the influence of the business and labour groups waxes and wanes according to the complexion of the government in which the weight of the public opinion has its own place. Moreover, while the labour groups do enjoy the privilege of exercising influence on the Labour government, the influence of the business even on the Conservative government is not absolute but conditional. It is qualified by the voting power of the working class, for Conservative party has to keep the support of some 7 million labour voters in order to stay in or get back into power. The essential fact, however, remains that "for better or for worse, such self-government, as the English people now enjoy today is one that operates by *and through the lobby.*"[14]

Critical Appreciation: There is no doubt that pressure groups can be seen performing a number of valuable service in the British political system in various ways. Their activity smacks of participation in the decision-making process between general elections and also acts as a healthy check over, as well as a prime mover of, the parliamentary government. The groups provide information, administrative co-operation and public and political supports. It can be argued that those who are most closely affected by Government activity should be most closely consulted and should be able to influence policy. Indeed, pressure groups are

14. S.E. Finer: *The Anonymous Empire*, p.120.

indispensable to the executive for the part they play in policy-making and also in administration. Thus, pressure groups draw people into the process of government and at the same time break down party domination of political process, bringing to the fore issues like capital punishment, which might otherwise lie outside the sphere of party politics.[15]

The weak side of the pressure group politics cannot be lost sight of. It is rightly contended that pressure group politics cannot be identified with mass politics in as much as not all sections of the people take part in it, nor are they capable of exerting influence in a more or less equal measure. The 'concurrent majority' as represented by the powerful pressure groups is seen as having too much power as compared with the 'numerical majority' as represented in the Parliament. Thus, the rise in the importance of pressure group politics has led to the emergence of a new hierarchy of political influence, based on the organization of group interests, producing what has been described as 'new Medievalism'[16] whereby a person "is politically important only in so far as he belongs to a group. The leadership of pressure groups is often unrepresentative and authoritarian, as it has to be powerful if it is to be in a position to negotiate. The secrecy in decision-making is to a large extent inevitable."[17]

There should be no doubt that pressure groups influence government policy and, in turn, the government influences pressure group activity with limited amount of coercion. Each needs the other. For this reason, it shall be highly imprudent to suggest measures that may outlaw the operation of organized groups. As factions are bound to play their part in the democratic process, so is the case with interest groups. As in many relationships, close ties may at times produce harmony and at times strain. The process of continuous contact and bargaining is dialectical exchange of influence, resulting in policies that are often the product of the dialectic, and not specifically of one or the other group.[18] As a matter of fact, so close has been the relationship between the political parties and pressure groups on the one side and government activity and political process of the country on the other that the two cannot be extricated. It is due to this that there is a two-way traffic between those who really rule and those whose interest are at stake because of their ruling. The merit of the whole phenomenon is that a sort of workable and useful balance is established.[19]

15. Punnett, *op. cit.,.* p.153.
16. Mackenzie, *op.cit,* p.146
17. Punnett, *op. cit.,* p. 153.
18. Richard Rose: *Politics in England,* p.138.
19. S.H. Beer: *Pressure Groups and Parties in Britain,* p. 8.

Part - II

American Constitution

We ought to consider which is the end of government, before we determine which is the best. Upon this point all speculative politicians will agree that the happiness of society is the end of government, as all divine and moral philosophers will agree, that the happiness of the individual is the end of man. From this principle it will follow that the form of government which communicates ease, comfort, security, or, in one word, happiness to the greatest number of persons, and in the greatest degree, is the best.

—***John Adams***

7

CONSTITUTION OF THE USA

A comprehensive study of the American political system and that too with a place after the British political system in an advanced study of the modern political systems is not without some valid reasons. It is not at all due to America's being the most advanced nation of the democratic world, nor should its reason be traced in her being the most powerful country of the globe. Rather, the source of all pertinent reasons should be discovered in several momentous developments like the beginning of documentary constitutionalism, political and national integration, irresistible growth towards democratisation, freedom of the press, existence of an independent judiciary and a host of several other phenomena that constitute the model of a liberal-democratic order. More than all, the American constitutional system, like its English counterpart, has adapted itself to changing conditions. It is as a result of this that a "heterogeneous restless people have developed a continent, built a nation, achieved a standard of living the highest the world has ever known, given the masses greater opportunities educationally and economically .than any other people, preserved the great freedoms, renounced imperialism, successfully fought two world wars and has today assumed international leadership and international obligations unparalleled in history."[1]

American Constitutionalism

Like Englishmen, the Americans have the credit of being the constitution-worshippers with this line of difference that while the former do so without having a constitution in the form of an enacted document, the latter do it otherwise. However, the common point between the two is their conviction in this celebrated maxim that there should be a 'limited

1. E.S. Griffith: *The American System of Government*, p. 8.

government', or the political organisation of the country should be circumscribed by a set of restrictions conducive to the protection of the essential liberties of the people. In other words, both the Englishmen and the Americans have their unflinching faith in the principle that certain prescribed procedure must be followed by the political decision-makers in making authoritative decisions and in the sense that there are certain decisions they may not make at all. Allied to this is their strong faith in this constitutional maxim that there is no single means of achieving a limited, or, correctly stated, constitutional government and that a strong and well-written constitution in and by itself is no guarantee of limited government. But neither is it meaningless.[2]

Making of the Constitution: As the occurrence of a war seemed inevitable after the proclamation of the historic Declaration of Independence on 4, July, 1776 it was also felt necessary by the great leaders of the Second Continental Congress to establish a strong Central government working according to some precise documentary rules. Thus, the Congress that set up a committee to draft a Declaration also appointed another committee of one representative from each colony to prepare and digest the form of confederation to be entered into between all of them. As a result of this, a sort of formal Constitution came into being called the 'Articles of the Confederation and Perpetual Union' that was adopted at the next Congress on November 17, 1777 and that was subsequently ratified by all the 13 colonies.

Though the loose union of the American States made spectacular achievements under the Articles like the winning of war of independence, several inherent weaknesses were also felt. Thus, the eminent leaders thought in terms of revising them if the existing union was to be made 'perfect' and 'indestructible'. In not much time, opinion in favour of having a strong and perfect union of the American States gathered weight. The Annapolis Convention of Sept., 1786 attended by the delegates of five States resolved to call a convention of all the 13 States to revise the Articles "so as to render them adequate to the exigencies of government and the preservation of the union. Thus came into being Philadelphia Convention of May, 1787 having delegations appointed by all States except Rhode Island. In all 74 delegates were appointed, though 55 attended and, finally, 39 placed their signatures to testify the adoption of the Constitution.

2. Stephen V. Monsma: *American Politics: A Systems Approach,* p.50.

The Philadelphia Convention met on 25th May, 1787 with a mind to suitably revise the Articles of the Confederation. Discussions, however, took a turn as some of the delegates submitted their own plans to provide a radical cure to the ills of the Confederation. The first constitutional scheme prepared under the leadership of Madison and submitted to Governor Randolph of Virginia (called the Virginia Plan) proposed a national executive, a national judiciary and a bicameral legislature with a lower house chosen directly by the people and the second one consisting of persons nominated by the State legislatures. The proposed national government was to have vast powers. Naturally it was opposed by the delegates coming from small States. William Paterson of New Jersey thus put his own design (called the New Jersey Plan) emphasising, in the main, uni-cameral legislature giving equal voice to all States, though Congress could have enlarged powers. Two other plans (one submitted by Pinckney of Connecticut and the other by Hamilton of New York) leaned more towards centralisation.

The way was thus cleared for the adoption of a new Constitution drafted by the Committee of Style under the chairmanship of Governor Morris of Pennsylvania on Sept. 15, 1787. One hurdle still remained and that was its ratification by the apprehended States. Three great campaigners (Hamilton, Madison and Jay) wrote a series of 85 articles under the fake name of 'Publicus' to persuade the leaders of the States that were later published as *The Federalist Papers*. The mission of the great leaders triumphed and the necessary work of ratification was completed with a unanimous vote in 3 and with a division in favour in 10 other States. Thus, the new constitution came into force on March 4, 1789.[3]

Growth of the Constitution: The American Constitution has a distinguished record of its own growth that may be described as its incessant as well as organic development towards a successful democratic political system. However, when we compare the growth of the American Constitution with that of the British, the difference lies in the fact that while the latter is not a make but a growth, the former is both a make and a growth. Beginning from its grand inauguration in 1789, it has remained in a continuous process of growth and expansion. In many ways, the Constitution has grown and developed even beyond the expectations and plans of the Founding Fathers. Thus, the American Constitution, like every

3. C.A. Beard: *The Supreme Court and the Constitution*, pp. 86-87.

other Constitution of the world, is "not a static but a dynamic, a Darwinian not a Newtonian affair."[4]

If the American Constitution is no more than the 'sap centre' of a system of government vastly larger than the stock from which it has branched, following important factors have played their part in this regard:

1. **Constitutional Amendments:** The Constitution provides a process of amending its provisions. This channel has been employed as a result of which twenty seven amendments have taken place so far. Any provision of the Constitution is amendable by the joint action of the Congress and the State legislatures. However, what makes it very rigid is the provision of special majority by which a proposal in the form of a bill must be passed by the Congress and State legislatures. It is true that the process of constitutional amendment is too rigid, difficult; even cumbersome, it has so far yielded result twenty seven times. These amendments have changed the shape of the original document to a considerable extent. For instance, the First Ten Amendments contain the fundamental rights of the citizens. The thirteenth amendment abolishes the system of slavery. The seventeenth amendment provides for direct election of the Senators. The twenty second amendment debars a person to seek Presidential election for a third term. Thus, various constitutional amendments have effected changes in the governmental system of the United States as originally established in 1789.
2. **Congressional Statutes:** The legislative authority of the federal government is vested in the Congress having Senate and House of Representatives as the upper and lower chambers respectively. The acts made by the Congress from time to time have done much to cover what could not be provided by the terms of the original Constitution and subsequent amendments. But one thing should be noted here: we are not concerned with every act passed by the Congress. Since the Constitution has set limits to the authority of the Congress, the American national legislature is not a sovereign law-making body and as there is a distinct difference between the constitutional law and the ordinary law of the land, our concern is here confined to those statutes passed by the Congress which have covered the gaps in the provisions of the Constitution. However,

4. W.B. Munro: *The Government of the United States*, p.69.

since the process of amendment is too rigid, it can not be denied that the legislative authority of the Congress has done much to keep the Constitution in operation. For instance, the Constitution says nothing about the organisation of the cabinet, machinery of elections, composition of the various executive departments, organisation of the subordinate federal courts, management of national currency and banking, recruitment and working of the armed forces etc. All these matters have been regulated by the laws made by the Congress from time to time. The organisation and working of the constitutional committees, the requirement that all bills must be passed through three readings, the various rules for the regulation and control of debates etc. are governed by the acts of the Congress.

3. **Executive Decrees:** Likewise, the orders and decrees of the President have greatly contributed to the growth and expansion of the Constitution. It is observed that Presidents like Washington, Jackson, Lincoln, Wilson, Roosevelt, Kennedy, Nixon and Bush had an impact on the Constitution at least equal to that of any of the original framers. By their vigorous use of the Presidential powers, they made the Presidency an office of executive as well as legislative leadership. The institution of the cabinet, the practice of senatorial courtesy, the declaration of war and peace, the making of executive agreements, the use of extra-ordinary powers during the days of national emergency, the use of veto over Congressional legislation in an unqualified manner etc. may be cited among the leading instances of the fact that in the exercise of these powers, strong Presidents have taken and maintained positions virtually settling constitutional questions with some meaning or application never attributed to it. Some Presidents have even claimed that the Constitution means what they say and quite often their views have prevailed. Even the heads of the executive departments and other administrative officers have to act swiftly as per orders coming from the White House. It is the Supreme Court alone that can place an effective check on the administrative powers of the President, but it should be taken for granted that unless the executive orders and decrees are challenged, they remain the part of an ever-expanding constitutional fabric.

4. **Judicial Interpretations:** Certainly the judicial interpretations have played a very important part in the growth and expansion of the

American Constitution. The judges interpret the Constitution and in the course of their interpretations, new meanings are given to its provisions. Justice Hughes once claimed that 'although the Americans are under a constitution, the Constitution is what the judges say it is.' It is indisputable that the Supreme Court has heavily contributed to the sphere of constitutional development. By the doctrine of implied powers, it has vastly increased the authority of the Congress in matters of legislation. By means of various decisions, it has enabled the federal government to control and regulate commerce, trade, industry, transport, communications, defence etc. Moreover, by the power of judicial review, the Supreme Court has made itself the guardian or protector of the liberties of the people and secured the credit of being a 'continuous constitutional convention at work.' It is owing to the very important part of the Supreme Court that the oldest written Constitution of the world has, for all its rigidity, shown remarkable elasticity. The truth seems to be that the Supreme Court "has read into the American Constitution many things which are not there visible to the naked eye. It has read out of the Constitution other things which are there as plain as print can make them."[5]

5. **Usages and Conventions:** Finally, like its British counterpart, the American Constitution has also grown by usages and customs. These usages and customs are the product of the ages and though they have their basis neither in the laws nor in the judicial decisions, they are now essential parts of the basic framework of the fundamental rules of the government. The cabinet, courtesy of the Senate in matters of approving foreign treaties and appointments made by the President, working of the party system, and Presidential primaries and party conventions may be counted among the leading instances. Although the usages and conventions have attracted less attention than other methods of constitutional development, they have always been at work enlarging, altering and influencing the substance of the Constitution. It cannot be denied, however, that they have played a very important role in determining the actual governmental process, steadily developing the 'unwritten Constitution' and in some respects, turning the written provisions of the Constitution into unintended channels or into uses altogether

5. Munro, *op. cit.*, p.69

contrary to what the Constitution makers had contemplated. One writer goes to the extent of saying that the "most complex revolution in our political system has not been brought about by amendments or by statutes, but by the customs of political parties in operating the machinery of government."[6]

Thus, the bare outline of the American Constitution once drafted at the Philadelphia Convention of 1787 has been steadily filled in and expanded through formal amendments, Congressional enactments, Presidential decrees, judicial interpretations and customs and usages. This unbroken process of growth and expansion has enabled the Constitution to keep pace with time and to become increasingly democratic and thoroughly modernised. Thus, Lord Bryce once asserted that the "American Constitution has necessarily changed, as the nation has changed." Right is the observation of Charles Beard that it "is a printed document explained by judicial decisions, precedents and practices, and illuminated by understanding and aspiration."[7]

Critical Appreciation: By all means, the making of the American Constitution constitutes the first bold instance of 'documentary constitutionalism' in the world. For a very long time there was a tendency in the United States "to regard the Constitution as a new invention of political science."[8] And yet certain points of criticism have been made to highlight the weaknesses of the Philadelphia Convention, the manner in which the great task was accomplished, and the provisions that ultimately had their incorporation into the fundamental law of the land. These may be put as under:

1. The Philadelphia Convention was not a truly representative body. The delegates were not elected by the people, they were nominated by the legislatures of the then colonies that had become States after the declaration of independence in 1776. A suggestion that the draft constitution should be submitted to the people for their approval in a referendum was defeated in the Philadelphia Convention. Hence, there was no popular approval of the Constitution that was inaugurated some two years after its ratification by the 3/4 of the then States.

---

6. C.A. Beard: *American Government and Politics*, p.26.

7. *Ibid*, p.15.

8. Ferguson and McHenry, *The American Federal Government*, p.65.

2. The Constitution prepared by the Philadelphia Convention was not at all an original creation. It lacked originality in several important respects. Much was taken from the Constitution of the Massachusetts and the Articles of the Confederation.
3. The American Constitution is a product of the struggle between the Federalists and Anti-Federalists in which the former could impose their will on the latter. The Federalists (who desired a strong government at the Centre with President and Congress in opposition to far much power than really favoured by the Anti-Federalists) could win after a course of intense and bitter discussion. By virtue of having a good command over the art of argumentation and also because of having a higher national image, men like Hamilton, Madison, Jefferson, John Adams, Jay and, above all, George Washington could prevail upon the 'old patriots' like Patrick Henry, Richard Henry Lee, Samuel Adams, George Mason and Elbridge.
4. However, the most poignant criticism of the American Constitution is contained in the 'economic interpretations' furnished by a critic like Beard. According to him, the framers were largely motivated by economic self-interest. While substantiating his thesis, he says that most of the delegates were engaged in money lending, slave trade, using land for speculative purposes, and running mercantile and manufacturing concerns. No representation was given to the class of small farmers and wage earners.

As a matter of fact, the Constitution emerged as a 'bundle of compromises.'[9] A distinguished student of the American Constitution makes a plausible observation when he adds: "Great men there were, it is true, but the convention as a whole was composed of men such as would be appointed to a similar gathering at the present time: professional men, business and gentlemen of leisure, patriotic statesmen and clever, scheming politicians; some trained by experience and study for the task before them, and others utterly unfit. It was essentially a representative body taking possibly a somewhat higher tone from the social conditions of the time, the seriousness of the crisis and the character of the leaders."[10]

9. Monsma, *op. cit.*, p.52.

10. Max Farrand: *The Framing of the Constitution of the United States*, pp. 40-51.

Basic Features

The American Constitution framed by the Philadelphia Convention of 1787 and inaugurated two years after has served as a vital unifying force for the diverse population. Representing itself as the opposite model of the British fundamental law, it has offered an alternative design to the lovers of a liberal-democratic order. It has its peculiar significance to the people of the United States who hold with ample pride and satisfaction that though many other elements have provided the cementing force to the structure of their political life, the most obvious and the most universally accepted element is their basic law formulated by their Founding Fathers. To them, it is this document that has sealed the significance of their War of Independence and served as a unifying force for their nation by putting together and establishing the centrifugal forces. Its salient features may be put as under:

1. An Enacted and a Written Constitution: The first and foremost feature of the American Constitution finds place in its being a formulated instrument made by the eminent leaders of a nascent nation to establish what they termed 'limited government.' The Philadelphia Convention of 1787 was a grand assembly of the leaders chosen by the legislatures of the then States and the Constitution made by this great assembly of great men was ratified by those who were elected by the people to do the august job while keeping their social, political and economic interests in their minds. It is evident from the language of the Preamble that reads: "We, the People of the United States, in order to form a more Perfect Union, establish Justice, insure domestic Tranquillity, provide for the common Defence, promote the general Welfare, and secure the Blessings of liberty to ourselves and our Posterity, do ordain and establish this Constitution for the United States of America."

The Philadelphia Convention gave a Constitution having seven Articles some of them being large enough to have sections within their detailed elaboration. The three main organs of the federal government–President as the executive, Congress as the legislature, and Supreme Court and subordinate federal courts as the judiciary have their sanction in these provisions. Moreover, the functions and powers of the three major organs have been left to the States. The process of amendment has also been laid down so that the words and phrases of the Constitution may be amended according to the exigencies of the situation. However, what has added to the richness of the provisions of the Constitution in an ever more but never less manner is the interpretative role of the judiciary. The final interpretations of the federal judiciary have given new meanings to the original provisions with the result that the American Constitution is said to have 5 pages along with 5,000 pages of judicial decisions made for the sake of their amplification.

2. Separation of Powers and Checks and Balances: It is true to say that no feature of American political system "is more characteristic than the separation of powers combined with precautionary checks and balances."[11] It signifies that the power of Government is diverse and diffused in the hands of three organs–executive, legislature and judiciary. The Founding Fathers adhered to the idea of separation of powers for the reason that, as Lord Acton aphorised, 'power corrupts and absolute power corrupts absolutely'. Whether sovereignty rests in an absolute monarch or the people, it is potentially dangerous and the only possible way out is to realise the political truth that power checks power. Madison had warned that any concentration and accumulation of powers in the hands of one, or few, or many, whether hereditary, elected, appointed or nominated, amounts justly to the very name of a tyrannical government.

As a result, the American constitutional system is based on the idea of separation of powers coming from the monumental contributions of Locke and Montesquieu and also from the language of the Constitution of Massachusetts. Art. I of the Constitution says: "All legislative powers herein granted shall be vested in the Congress." Art. III begins: "The judicial power...shall be vested in one Supreme Court and in such other inferior courts as Congress from time to time may ordain and establish." In its most dogmatic form, the American conception of the separation of powers may be summed up in the following propositions:

1. There are three intrinsically distinct functions of government, the legislative, the executive, and the judicial;
2. These distinct functions ought to be exercised respectively by three separately manned departments of government; which should be constitutionally and mutually independent; and
3. A corollary doctrine stated by Locke–the legislature may not delegate its powers.

---

11. Ogg and Ray; *Essentials of the American Government*, p.38.

However, the Founding Fathers were scientists as well. They well understood that separation did not mean complete disconnection. Apart from incorporating the law as laid down by Locke and Montesquieu, they invented a new system of checks and balances whereby they enabled each organ of government to exercise control over others so that the fear of partial despotism could be dispelled. The new arrangement was devised to set off the disasters of water-tight compartmentalisation as well as to ensure that no branch of government would become autocratic or irresponsible even in its own sphere of activity. This means that no branch of government has been given unrestricted area of authority even in its own sphere in as much as the other two organs of government have been given a limited power of acting as checks in order to prevent the abuse of power. In a word, the principle of checks and balances "requires that after the main exercise has been allocated to one person or body, care should be taken to set up a minor participation of other persons or bodies."[12]

This type of adjustment may be seen in this manner. The executive authority is with the President checked by the Congress and the Supreme Court. For instance, all appointments and foreign treaties made by the President are subject to Senatorial confirmation. Besides, the Congress can remove the President from office by the process of impeachment. Then, the President takes the oath of office before the Chief Justice to defend and protect the Constitution and the Supreme Court and federal courts, by virtue of their power of judicial review, may declare any order given by him *ultra vires* if it is found against the provisions of the Constitution or the due process of law. Likewise, the legislative power is vested in the Congress. It is provided that a bill passed by the Congress is under Presidential veto, but if the President rejects a bill and the Congress re-adopts it with a two-thirds majority, the Presidential veto is over-ridden. Then, the federal courts with Supreme Court at the top can exercise the power of judicial review and thereby determine the constitutional validity of any Congressional legislation either on the basis of authoritative interpretation of the constitutional provisions or due process of law. Finally, judicial branch is checked by the fact that the Congress can determine the number of judges and their salaries and emoluments, or limit their appellate jurisdiction, or even remove a judge by the process of impeachment. It all demonstrates the fact that this separation of powers combined with the precautionary checks and balances is, indeed, the 'primary feature of American government.[13]

12. Carl J. Friedrich: *Constitutional Government and Democracy*, p.185.

13. C.A. Beard: *American Government and Politics*, p.16.

CONSTITUTIONAL POWERS AND PROHIBITIONS

CONSTITUTION

Powers Delegated to the National Government

1. To tax
2. To regulate interstate and foreign commerce
3. To borrow and coin money
4. To establish inferior courts
5. To declare war
6. To raise and support an army
7. To maintain a navy
8. To provide for a militia
9. To govern territories and property
10. To define and punish piracies and other felonies on the high seas
11. To establish post offices and post roads
12. To grant patents and copyrights
13. To fix standards of weights and measures
14. To make all laws necessary and proper to carry out the above

Concurrent Powers

1. Both may tax
2. Both may borrow money
3. Both may establish and maintain courts
4. Both may make and enforce laws
5. Both may take property for public purposes
6. Both may spend for general welfare

Powers Reserved to the States

1. To regulate *intra* state commerce
2. To establish local governments
3. To protect the health, safety, welfare,and morals of its citizens
4. To ratify amendments
5. To conduct elections
6. To specify conditions for suffrage (except for specific prohibition in Constitution)
7. To change state constitutions and governments

Prohibitions on the National Government

1. Direct taxes must be proportionate: to population of states (changed by Sixteenth Amendment, 1913).
2. Bill of Rights may not be abridged.
3. Preference may not be given to one state over another in matters of commerce.
4. State boundaries cannot be changed without consent of the states involved.
5. Newly admitted states cannot be placed or plane of inequality with original states.

Prohibitions on both the National Government and the States

1. May not tax exports
2. May not grant titles of nobility

Prohibitions on the States

1. May not enter into treaties.
2. May not coin money, keep troops, or ships of war in time of peace.
3. May not pass laws impairing obligations of contract.
4. May not tax imports.
5. May not violate federal Constitution or obstruct Federal laws.

It is often said that the principle of separation of powers works well in the United States for the reason that there is the complementary system of checks and balances. But the real operation has made the entire system of checks and balances has been undermined on the one side by the growing leadership of the President and on the other by the dominant position of the judiciary headed by the Supreme Court. The rise of political parties and their ways of functioning have tended to redistribute the power separated by the Constitution. This has established the leadership of the federal executive in the hands of the chief administrator called the President. Above all, there is the phenomenon of 'judicial despotism'. The federal judiciary, with Supreme Court at the top has read into the Constitution many things which are not visible there to the naked eye; it has read out of it other things which are there as plain as print can make them. That is, the Supreme Court has established itself as the sole guardian of the Constitution and by virtue of this unique position come to hold the authority of being the 'final interpreter of the fundamental law of the land'.

3. A Rigid Constitution: A rigid constitution is distinctly different from its flexible counterpart in the sense that its process of amendment is difficult as a result of which the difference between constitutional law and ordinary law becomes sharply visible. The laws of the Constitution and the laws made by the legislature in the normal course of its working are different from each other. The two flow in different channels, the former possessing a specially higher and sacred status than the latter. Thus, a special process is laid down in a rigid constitution to carry out the work of amendment. The authority of the legislature is limited and it can not pass a bill of constitutional amendment exactly in the same manner as it does in the case of passing an ordinary legislative measure. It is clearly laid down that the bill of constitutional amendment should be adopted either by a special convention, or by a constituent assembly, or by the existing legislature with a special majority, or by the people through referendum, or by a majority of the governments of the units in a federal system, or by a combination of them.

The most notorious example of a rigid constitution is afforded by the fundamental law of the United States. The system has been condemned as cumbersome and undemocratic and it has also been proposed to substitute it with a more flexible and democratic procedure under which an amendment might be proposed by a simple majority of the two houses of the national legislature (Congress) and ratified by a majority of voters in the majority of the States, provided the latter were a majority of the total votes cast throughout the country. It is owing to the extremely rigid nature of the Constitution that only 27 amendments have taken place so far ever since its inauguration in 1789.

Amendment Procedure

*Methods of Proposal**	*Methods of Ratification***
1. By two-thirds votes of both the Houses of Congress.	By legislatures in three-fourths (38) of the States or
2. By Constitutional Convention called by the Congress when petitioned do so by two-thirds (34) of the States.	By Conventions in the three-fourths (38) of the States.
* Either of the two methods may be adopted.	** States may select either of the two courses unless the Congress specifically provides for one.

The Founding Fathers of the American Constitution visualised that future situations would need a change in the constitutional provisions. Thus, Act. V provides: "The Congress whenever two-thirds of both houses shall propose amendments to this Constitution, or on the application of the Legislatures of two-thirds of the several States, shall call a convention for proposing amendments, which in either case shall be valid to all intents and purposes, as part of this Constitution, when ratified by the Legislatures of the three-fourths of the several States, or by Conventions by three-fourths thereof as the one or the other mode of ratification may be proposed by the Congress; provided that no amendment which may be made prior to the year one thousand, eight hundred and eight, shall in any manner affect the first and fourth clauses in the ninth section of the first article; and that no State, without its consent, shall be deprived of its equal suffrage in the Senate."

It may be pointed out here that the difficult process of constitutional amendment was adopted in order to meet the then requirements of a confederal set up. The passionate attachment of the States (which joined the Confederation) to their individual independence made them afraid of granting any authority to the Centre that might have ultimately deprived them of their sovereign rights. Hence, an arrangement was made whereby the power of constitutional amendment was given to both. As a result, the American Constitution can be amended with the bilateral action of the federal government located at Washington, D.C. and 3/4 of the State governments.

The language of the Constitution is certainly difficult, but it implies two things: First if the work of amendment is initiated by the Central Government, then the bill must be passed by the Congress with a two-thirds majority in each house and then referred to the State legislatures to be adopted by the two-thirds majority for the sake of its ratification. In case the three-fourths of the States so ratify, the bill shall be taken as finally passed. However, the Congress has the power of getting the work of ratification done either by the legislatures of States, or it may provide for special conventions there. In the case of 22nd amendment of 1951 the work of ratification in the States was done not by the legislatures but by special conventions.

Second, if the proposal of constitutional amendment is initiated by the State governments, it should be supported by at least two-thirds of the State legislatures. In such a case, the Congress shall convene a special convention where the proposal will be discussed and for adoption it is required that it must have the support of at least two-thirds majority. If the proposal is adopted by the constitutional convention, it shall be referred to the States for ratification. In the States the work of ratification will be done either by the legislatures or by the constitutional conventions as the Congress decides. However, for the sake of adoption two-thirds majority is needed and the proposal will be taken as finally passed when, in all, three-fourth (38) States give their verdict in favour of ratification. This method has not come into use so far.

The process of amending the American Constitution may be criticised on several grounds. First, it is extra-ordinarily difficult, for it is not an easy affair to obtain a two-thirds majority first of both the houses of the Congress and then such majority in three-fourths of the State legislatures. Second, it is undemocratic; since a sizable minority may veto the decision of the majority. A little more than one-third majority in the Congress and one-fourth majority in the States is sufficient to negative all achieved after great deliberations and efforts. Third, there is no prescribed time limit for ratification unless specifically determined by a resolution of the Congress. For instance, on one occasion the State of Ohio ratified an amendment bill after 80 years. Absence of such a prescription makes an important issue like a plaything for the States and an indefinite delay takes away the very purpose for which the work of amendment is initiated. Fourth, there is no popular check in the form of referendum over Central and State legislatures as we find in Switzerland and France. The entire work of making amendment in the Constitution is entrusted to a relatively small number of persons assembled in the Central and State legislatures.

4. Federal System: The American Constitution affords the first best example of a federal system in the world for the patent reason that it exemplifies, in the most marked degree, the three essential characteristics, namely, the supremacy of a written and rigid Constitution, the division of powers, and the existence of an independent and impartial judiciary. Of course, even the American federal system, as we shall later see, has imbibed many traits of centralism, it is certain that the autonomy of the States is still existent. In spite of the increasing control of the Central government, the States have not been 'finished' and they are still important political entities in the American political system so much so that the Constitution "is meaningless unless taken in conjunction with the State Constitutions, which are not merely useful additions to it but its indispensable complement."[14]

The American federal system meets the requirements of a true federal model. In the first place, it is written and rigid. It contains about 4,000 words and covers about ten printed pages and thus appears to be the briefest written Constitution in the world. It affords the first example of a written Constitution. Its rigid character becomes evident from the fact that it requires a special procedure to be followed for making an amendment. It has also been made clear that the Constitution is the fundamental law of the land. To quote the Constitution itself, "This Constitution and the laws of the United States which shall be made in pursuance thereof; and all treaties made, or which shall be made under the authority of the United States, shall be the supreme law of the land; and the judges in every State shall be bound thereby by anything in the Constitution or laws of any State to the contrary notwithstanding."

In the second place, the American Constitution specifies the distribution of powers between the federal government and the governments of the units. The division of powers is made in one of the

14. C.F. Strong: *Modern Political Constitutions*, p. 110.

three ways. First, the powers of the federal government are enumerated and the rest are given to the units. Second, the powers of the units are specified and the rest are given to the Central government. Third, the powers of the Centre as well as of the units are enumerated so that there remains, as far as possible, no chance of conflict. The first method comes from the United States, the second one hails from Canada and the last one finds a glaring instance in the case of Indian federal system. However, it may be observed that the position of the units vis-a-vis the Centre remains strong when the first method is followed. And it is owing to this reason that the position of the American States is stronger than that of the provinces of Canada or the States of the Indian Union.

It follows that, in the United States, the Constitution has enumerated the powers of the federal government. The Congress has authority to make laws on the following subjects:

1. To levy and collect taxes, duties, imports and excises.
2. To borrow money on the credit of the United States,
3. To regulate commerce with foreign nations, and among the several States, and the Indian tribes,
4. To establish a uniform rule of naturalisation, and uniform laws on the subject of bankruptcies throughout the United States,
5. To coin money, regulate the value thereof, and of foreign coin and fix the standard of weights and measures,
6. To establish post offices and postal record,
7. To promote the progress of science and useful arts,
8. To constitute tribunals inferior to the Supreme Court,
9. To define and punish piracies and felonies committed on the high seas, and offences against the law of nations,
10. To declare war,
11. To provide and maintain a navy; to make rules for the government and regulation of the land and naval forces; to provide for calling forth the militia to execute the laws of the Union, suppress insurrections, and repel invasions, and
12. To make all laws which shall be necessary and proper for carrying into execution the foregoing powers.

Division of Powers

National Powers	Concurrent Powers	State Powers
(A) Delegated 1. To tax and borrow money 2. To regulate inter-State and foreign commerce 3. To conduct foreign relations 4. To maintain defence forces 5. To declare war 6. To coin money 7. To provide for post-offices and postal record 8. To grant copyrights and patents, and ⟶ 9. To establish uniform laws on subject of bankruptcy **(B) Prohibited** 1. To abridge freedom and rights 2. To pass bills of attainder or ex post facto laws 3. To grant titles of nobility, and 4. To impose levy on import tax.	1. To tax and borrow money 2. To pass laws affecting bank-ruptcy, and 3. To charter banks and other corporations **Implied Powers** (more numerous and detailed than delegated powers, e.g., social security legislation, regulation of inter-state business and labour, banking and credit etc.)	**(A) Reserved** By virtue of Amendment X, the powers not delegated to the United States by the Constitution and prohibited by it to the States are reserved to the States **(B) Prohibited** 1. To deprive persons of life, liberty and property without due process of law 2. To deny persons equal protec-tion of laws 3. To abridge the privileges and immunities of citizens 4. To make treaties or alliances; and 5. To coin money and remit bills or credit

The last requirement of a federal system in the United States is fulfilled by the federal judiciary. The Supreme Court is the final interpreter of the Constitution. As such, it is this court which decides any dispute between the Centre and the States. Art. III. Sec.2 of the Constitution provides that to all controversies to which the United States shall be a party, to controversies between two or more States, between a State and a citizen of another State, between citizens of different States, between citizens of the same State claiming lands under grants of different States, and between a State, or the citizens thereof and foreign States, citizens or subjects, the Supreme Court has original jurisdiction."

Undoubtedly, the United States furnishes a brilliant instance of a federal system, but its evaluation in the present form reveals that much has now changed what was originally designed. As the growth of centralism has been an inevitable feature of every federal system, the American federation has been no exception. With the advance of time and change of conditions and circumstances, the elements of centralism have developed so much so that even the States of the American federation have been deprived of much of their autonomy what was granted to them under the Constitution. Truly speaking, the field of federal jurisdiction has expanded so greatly and the growth of centralism has been so unmistakable that many people in the United States have formed the opinion that if the movement in this direction is not checked, in near future the States "may be left like hollow shells operating primarily as field districts of federal departments and dependent upon the federal treasury for their support."[15]. In this direction, several reasons may be accounted for:

(*i*) Political, economic and social changes have played their important part. The expansion of territory, growth of population, increasing fields of science and technology etc. all have advanced America from the position of a small and isolated nation with simple and agricultural economy to that of the most highly industrialised and probably the most powerful nation of the world.

(*ii*) The civil war over the question of slavery (1861-65) gave a strong verdict against the trends of separatism and the victory of the national government cemented the fact that the broad acts of the President and the Congress in carrying on the war and in the reconstruction that followed "left a heritage of expanded federal power never subsequently to be surrendered."[16]

15. Leonard D. White: *The State and the Nation*, p.3.

16. E.S. Griffith: *The American System of Government*, p.22.

(*iii*) The Supreme Court has enormously increased the authority of federal government by laying down the doctrine of implied powers. As the final interpreter and guardian of the Constitution, it has ruled that such are the implicit powers of the Centre, if not expressed, inasmuch as with the march of time and the emergence of new conditions and circumstance the terms and phrases have developed such implications.

(*iv*) By the system of grants-in-aid the national government has immensely increased its authority at the expense of the autonomy of the States. He who pays the piper calls the tune, so the weight of obligation falls upon the State governments. It has rightly been visualised that the grants-in aid given by the Centre to the States "offer a middle ground between direct federal assumption of certain State and local functions and their continuation under exclusive-state and local financing with haphazard coverage and diverse standards."

(*v*) There has been the fear of another great war in general and that of the spectre of communism and terrorism in particular. Since the State governments cannot defend themselves against an onslaught of any external power and since the fear of communism and terrorism pervades, naturally the upper hand of the national government has gained excessive weight.

(*vi*) There is the factor of people's confidence in the national government. The Centre has fulfilled its promises and rendered essential services to the people in a way that the bonds of local loyalty have become weak and, as a result, the national government "is almost a model of perfection when compared to some State capitals which are graft-ridden, inefficient, and unable to provide the services that the people expected."[17]

5. Presidential Form of Government: Britain is known for parliamentary form of government, America has the model of presidential government. The President is the head of the State as well as of the government. He is elected for a term of four years and may be re-elected. He appoints his ministers and may remove any minister or change his departments as per his pleasure. Since the executive and the legislature have been separated, the President and his ministers cannot be the members of the Congress. The President may send his message to the Congress and

17. See Burns and Peltason: *Government by the People,* p.142.

may go there to deliver it personally, but he cannot vote. The Congress cannot throw out the ministry by passing a vote of no-confidence. If the President is guilty of treason or of some grave misdemeanour, he may be removed by the process of impeachment.

6. Senate as the Powerful Upper Chamber: In most of the countries of the world, legislature is bi-cameral in which the lower house is more powerful than the upper house. In the British Parliament, the House of Lords is a weak chamber while the House of Commons, for all practical purposes, means the Parliament. So is the case with the Senate of France and the Council of States of India. But in America Senate, being the upper chamber of the national legislature, is more powerful than the House of Representatives. It confirms all the appointments made and foreign treaties signed by the President. It sits as a court of impeachment to try the President, Vice-President, judges of the Supreme Court and federal courts etc. It is true that a money bill cannot be introduced in the Senate, but when it comes, after it is passed by the House, the Senate may make any number of amendments in it. In a situation of deadlock, the matter is sorted out by the compromise or conciliation committee having equal number of members of both the houses. On account of being senior and seasoned politicians of the country, the members of the Senate are expected to have their final say in this committee. So to call Senate as the upper house is to make a case of terminological inexactitude.

7. Judicial Supremacy: Whereas the English Constitution is known for the 'sovereignty of Parliament' as its dominant characteristic, judicial supremacy is said to be the outstanding feature of its American counterpart. The powerful position of the judiciary becomes a source of astonishment when one studies it in the context of the basic features of the American Constitution contained in the principle of separation of powers and checks and balances. The founding fathers vested judicial authority in the Courts as they vested legislative authority in the Congress and the executive authority in the President without making one superior to or supreme over another. It is clear from the language of the Constitution that the makers regarded the federal judiciary as "the third member of government trinity, no less important than the other two members." And yet the courts have enhanced their authority in course of time with the result that they have come to establish their supreme hold by virtue of this fact that they "have the right to review the activities of all agencies of government in order to determine whether they are legally and constitutionally valid."[18]

18. Griffith: *The American System of Government*, p. 159.

The vesting of the power of interpreting the words and phrases of the Constitution in the Court has proved a blessing of the founding fathers to the inventors of the great power of the federal judiciary known by the name of 'judicial review'. Ever since the days of Chief Justice Marshall, the judges of the Supreme Court and subordinate federal courts have been making use of this unique power in determining the validity of an impugned legislative or executive measure. Not only this, the judiciary has outstretched its arms so as to cover State legislation and administration as well for this purpose. Thus, a situation has come where the federal judiciary has converted itself into a final arbiter of determining whether a law made by the Central or State legislatures or a decree promulgated by the executive is valid and, therefore, enforceable or not. Matters have reached a stage that the American Constitution is said to be, in the words of Justice Hughes, 'what the judge says it is'.

The power of judicial review has certainly made the Supreme Court something more than an equal member of the government trinity. Viewed from one angle, it may be said to have become the third and super-chamber of the American national legislature; viewed from another, it may also be described as to have become a quasi-political body functioning not in a judicial vacuum but whirling in a political climate. The expression of 'due process of law' has become a dexterous tool in the hands of the judges to define what is due or not, and that too in the light of the obtaining political circumstances. The way the federal judiciary has acted in invalidating certain progressive measures has made it liable for the charge of being conservative and deliberately hostile to the advent of a system favourable to the interest of the economically weaker sections of the community. Thus, a critic like Laski has commented that the 'due process' has meant 'not a road but a gate and the thing it barred was an attempt to transform political democracy in the United States into social democracy."[19]

19. H.J. Laski: *The American Democracy*, p.115.

8

FEDERAL EXECUTIVE

Since the United States has presidential form of government, there is nothing like nominal or formal executive, what Bagehot calls the 'dignified executive', the type of which we may notice in the monarch of Britain, the Governor-General of Canada, and the President of Germany. Here the President is the head of the state as well as of the government. He governs with the help of his ministers who are appointed by him and who remain in office during his pleasure. There is a Vice-President who acts as his mate and may succeed him if the office of the President falls vacant by any reason whatsoever. Then, there is a large army of civil servants who work under the President and his ministers; they enjoy a permanent tenure and are required to keep themselves aloof from the politics of the country.

President

The most powerful and spectacular office in the American constitutional system is occupied by the 'Chief Executive' called the President. A close look at the potentialities of his great office confirms the view that he exercises' largest amount of authority ever wielded by a man in a democracy'.[1] A substantial change has undergone this great, rather the greatest, office over the course of more than a hundred years highlighting which Hayman has observed that Presidential powers have so much increased that now he "is the focus of federal authority and the symbol of national unity."[2] The reason for this should be discovered in remarkable developments in domestic as well as foreign, particularly the latter, spheres. In 1966 Aaron Wildavsky conducted a survey of Presidential initiative and Congressional response in both internal and external matters

1. W.B. Munro: *The Government of the United States*, p. 164.
2. Sidney Hayman: *The American President*, p. 4.

from 1948 to 1964 and came to present his striking conclusion that the United States has one President, but two presidencies, one for domestic affairs and the other for foreign policy. He noted with amazement: "Since World War II, Presidents have had much greater success in controlling the nation's defence and foreign policies than in dominating its domestic policies."

Term, Succession and Removal: The President is elected by the American people for a term of four years. The original Constitution was silent on the issue of his re-election. It simply stipulated that the President would hold office for a term of four years which undoubtedly allowed him indefinite re-eligibility. However, a practice developed whereby no President till 1940 ever held this office for more than two terms. In this way, a good tradition started by the earlier Presidents like Washington, Adams and Jefferson could not be broken by the coming incumbents until Franklin D. Roosevelt won election on the Democratic ticket for the third term in 1940 and then for a fourth one in 1944. It all happened against a resolution passed by the American Senate on the question of a third term for President Coolidge that any departure from the established tradition would be unwise, unpatriotic and fraught with peril to our free institutions. The result was the 22nd constitutional amendment of 1951 which debars a person to seek a third term and makes it clear that the period of the officiating President shall be counted as one term in case his stay in office exceeds the duration of two years.

We now turn to the important issue of Presidential succession. The original Constitution provides that if the President vacates his office, the Vice-President shall succeed him and in case both vacate it, the Congress shall settle the matter by means of a law. Vice-President-elect shall act as the officiating President until the next President qualifies. However, if both the President-elect and Vice-President-elect fail to qualify, then the Congress may provide by law as to who shall act as the President until the new President or Vice-President shall have qualified.

The American Congress adopted a resolution in 1965 which took the form of 25th constitutional amendment two years after. It provides: (1) The Vice-President shall become the President on the death or resignation of the President. (2) On vacancy in the Vice-Presidency, the President shall nominate a Vice-President who takes office on confirmation by both the houses of Congress. (3) On a written declaration by the President that he is unable to discharge the duties of his office, the Vice-

President shall become President (Acting) until the President declares his inability ended. (4) On a written declaration by the Vice-President and a majority of the principal executive officers or any other body provided by law that the President is unable, the Vice-President becomes Acting President.

The Constitution provides that the President can be removed by the process of impeachment in case he is guilty of treason, bribery or other high crimes of misdemeanour. The House of Representatives shall initiate the charges with a majority vote and the Senate act as the tribunal presided over by the Chief Justice of the Supreme Court. The President shall have every right of defence either in person or through his nominee. Resolution must be passed by two-thirds majority for conviction which makes the President liable to removal from office and any other disqualification. He is also liable for trial under ordinary judicial procedure. The instance of Andrew Johnson is available to show that the process of impeachment against a President was made use of in 1868. But the President was saved by one vote. In 1974 Nixon resigned against whom impeachment proceedings were initiated. In 1999 Clinton was impeached, but the motion could not be passed by the required majority of votes.

Election: The Constitution lays down three qualifications for the President, namely, that he must be a natural-born citizen of the United States, that he must be at least 35 years of age, and that he must have been a resident of the country for at least 14 years. The procedure relating to the election of the American President (and also of the Vice-President) may be clarified with the help of three stages—nomination, formation of the electoral college, and his election by absolute majority. A major change in the mode of election of the President has occurred owing to the rise and growth of a political drama that has become a concern of the two major parties in which a 'third' man has no place at all. Since 1832 the two parties have been following the practice of choosing their candidates at the national conventions.

The National Committee of each party consisting of one man and one woman elected from each State and territory plus the District of Columbia (in conformity with the rules and regulations laid down by its legislature and by party organisation) sets up machinery for the conduct of the national convention well in advance. The names of many 'favourite sons' are discussed, but in the end two names are chosen—one for the Presidency and the other one for Vice-Presidency. However, convention requires that the name of the sitting President must be approved, if he wants to run for a second term. Usage also requires that the team of two candidates must belong to two different States, even regions, of the country and the running mate (candidate for Vice-Presidency) should not come from a 'doubtful State', that is, from a State in which his popularity may swell the votes of party's Presidential nominee. This work is over by the summer or monsoon of the election year and then the party sets up its national and State committees and headquarters for the nation-wide campaign.

The next stage is the formation of electoral college. Each State elects members for this body according to its own laws. It chooses as many electors as it has Senators and Representatives in the Congress, the present strength being 538 (100 Senators, 435 Representatives and 3 others from Washington, D.C.) in all. A simple majority of 270 is needed to win, otherwise the matter has to be decided by the House of Representatives in the case of the Presidency and by the Senate in the case of the Vice-Presidency, each State having one vote irrespective of its physical size or population, or number of deputies in the Congress. Instances show that such has happened in 1800, 1824 and 1876 in the case of President and in 1837 in the case of Vice-President.

Polling day for the election of the electors falls on Tuesday after the first Monday in November. The ballot is secret and direct. Individual votes are counted State-wise and by custom the Presidential candidate receiving highest number of votes in a State is declared the winner of all the electoral votes of that State. After this the electors meet in their State capitals as required by the national law of 1934 on Monday after the second Wednesday in December to cast their votes—one for the President and the other one for the Vice-President. Then the ballot boxes are sealed and sent to the President of the Senate. Counting of votes takes place on January 6 and the President-elect takes oath of office on 20 January before the Chief Justice of the Supreme Court.

Functions and Powers: The American Presidency represents a curious mixture of the powers and position enjoyed by an executive potent enough to maintain order and ensure faithful execution of the laws but not so strong as to assume the character of dictatorship. His strong executive authority is circumscribed by the arrangement of checks and balances. His determining voice in the sphere of administration is integrally tied with the checks of legislative and judicial organs of the federal government. That is why, Lincoln's Secretary of State (W.H. Seward) could confidently say about this office: "We elect a king for four years and give him absolute power within certain limits which, after all, he can interpret for himself." Munro aptly observes: "Strength with safety was what the framers of the Constitution endeavoured to combine in the Presidential office adequate authority but with firm checks imposed upon it."[3]

The functions and powers of the American President may be discussed under five heads–executive, legislative, financial, judicial and emergency. These are:

In the first place, we refer to the most important powers of the President relating to administration of the country. The Constitution vests in him executive authority. As head of the national administration, he assumes high technical responsibilities in the sphere of enforcement of the fundamental law of the land, laws made by the Congress and decisions given by the courts. He can employ military force to suppress a recalcitrant mob or a State of the American union. However, he has some discretion in determining the degree of vigour or leniency with which a particular law or judicial decision is to be enforced. The Constitution gives him the power to appoint (with the consent of the Senate) ministers, ambassadors, federal judges and many other officers of the United States. The convention of senatorial courtesy has given a lot of free hand to the President in this regard.

The Constitution empowers the President to appoint principal officers of the various departments (ministries) with the approval of the Senate and require their opinion in writing upon any subject relating to the duties of their respective offices. In this regard he may obtain their views either orally in a meeting or in writing, but he is not bound to accept them. Then, he is the chief foreign policy-maker and the accredited official spokesman of the country in international affairs. For this he not only appoints ambassadors and consuls, he also negotiates agreements and concludes treaties with foreign governments and implements them after their ratification by the Senate. He has complete discretion in matters of recognising or derecognising a government and in his hands the act of recognition of a foreign government is both a constitutive and a declaratory function. However, the President has secured a novel way of implementing his foreign policy by circumventing the over-riding control of the Senate. He may make 'gentlemen's agreements' or 'executive agreements' and thereby effect certain important commitments which need not be ratified

3. Munro, *op. cit.*, p. 186.

by the Senate as they do not amount to being a foreign treaty. He may also resort to secret diplomacy and thereby make 'secret treaties' with foreign powers and refuse to make them public in the national interest.

Now we turn to legislative powers of the President. Here he plays a quite important part which becomes clear with the view of Potter that the Constitution puts him 'at the beginning and end of the legislative process'.[4] The President is not merely the chief administrator and chief foreign policy-maker and its executor, he is also the chief legislator though in a different way. He has the positive power of initiating legislation through his messages containing information on the State of the Union. It is within his authority to read the message personally in the Congress and thereby add a good deal of weight to its contents by the chain of his physical presence, or get it read by his nominee. He can call extraordinary session of the Congress to consider some urgent matter. He may also issue executive orders (ordinances) and regulations having the force of law to be adopted by the Congress in time to come.

The most effective weapon in the hands of the President is his veto power. The Constitution requires that all bills passed by the Congress (except constitutional amendment proposals) must be sent to the President for his assent. If he appends his signatures, the bill becomes law and is placed on the statute book. The President is given 10 days' time for taking action (Sunday excluded) and he may either give his assent or return it to the Congress with some recommendations. The veto of the President is absolute in the sense that he may reject a bill without assigning any reason. But the veto is qualified in the sense that if the Congress passes the same bill again with 2/3 majority, it becomes law without being referred to him for his assent. He has pocket veto also which means that in case the session of the Congress is adjourned within the period of 10 days and he takes no action on it, then the bill is automatically killed. Historical evidence shows that American Presidents have made use of this power on many occasions, while his veto has been over-ridden by the action of the Congress in a few cases.

While referring to the judicial powers of the President, we 'find that he can grant reprieves and pardons for offences against the United States except in cases of impeachment. His authority in this regard does not apply in cases of violation of the State laws. A reprieve means postponement of the imposition of penalty, while a pardon is a release

4. Potter: *American Government and Politics*, p. 197.

from liability for punishment and may be absolute or conditional. While an absolute or full pardon absolves the alleged offender of all charges and makes him innocent as if he never committed the offence, a conditional or partial pardon is subject to certain terms and may be withdrawn later if these are unfulfilled. The President may also grant pardon in the form of commutation of the sentence resulting in the shortening of the period of imprisonment or substitution of a big punishment with a lighter one. However, pardon may also take the form of amnesty granted to a group of offenders as Jefferson did for all persons convicted under the Sedition Act of 1798.

The financial powers of the President cover the area of budget-making. The Budgeting and Accounting Act of 1921 abolished the executive office meant to assist the President in the discharge of his responsibilities of a Manager with regard to the expenditure of administrative agencies and replaced it with a Budget Bureau empowered to supervise the spending activities of various agencies and to advise the President about steps to be taken to introduce greater economy and efficiency in administrative services. The Bureau is headed by a Director who is appointed by the President and acts under his direction and control.

Lastly, we refer to the powers of the President during wars and national emergencies. The Constitution makes him the chief of the armed forces called into the service of the United States. He, thus, appoints officers of the armed services (with the ratification of the Senate) but can remove them at his will particularly during war times. The power to declare war lies with the Congress, but he can make a situation in which adoption of a resolution by the Congress becomes inevitable. Presidents like McKinley, Wilson and Roosevelt did so.

Allied with it is the case of national emergency. While the Constitution specifically provides nothing about the existence of a state of emergency and even the Supreme Court has the view that such a situation creates no new powers for the chief administrator, facts reveal that during times of emergency his authority is immensely increased which suggests his position as a prelude to his dictatorship.

Keeping all such points in view, Laski has correctly emphasised that the range of President's functions is enormous. He is the ceremonial head of the State. He is a vital source of legislative suggestion. He is the final source of all executive decisions. He is the authoritative exponent of nation's foreign policy.[5]

5. Laski: *The American Presidency*, p. 37.

American President *Versus* British Monarch and Prime Minister: While drawing a comparison between American President on the one side and British Monarch and Prime Minister on the other, Prof. Harold J. Laski well commented that the former is both more and less than the latter, and the more closely his office is studied, the more unique does its character appear.[6] It means that the American President is similar to as well as different from the British monarch in several respects. A study of the resemblance between the two shows that both are the heads of their respective States. As such, entire administration is carried on in their names; they perform ceremonial functions, make high appointments, receive foreign dignitaries, issue important proclamations, give assent to bills passed by the respective legislatures and possess prerogative of mercy. One may say that these are just formal powers which the two heads possess, though a great difference of kind exists in the way of their actual exercise. While the American President does it all as per his individual judgement, the British monarch does it on the advice of his ministers. While the British monarch is just the head of the State, the American President is the head of the State as well as of the ,government and, for this reason, the ceremony in his case "is merely the decorative penumbra of office."[7]

Apart from some formal features of resemblance between the American President and the British monarch, the features of difference are many that may be boiled down to this essential point that while the former is the real executive, the latter is the nominal head or the dignified executive. While the British king can do no wrong, the American President can. In other words, it means that while the British monarch is like a 'magnificent cipher' doing hardly anything more than placing signatures on the papers prepared by the ministers, the American President rules according to his best judgement. He nominates his ministers and may remove them. He sends messages to the Congress and veto a bill though passed according to the intent shown therein. He makes important declarations relating to war and peace and signs treaties with foreign countries that he may submit for Senatorial ratification, or not by designating them as 'executive agreements'. Thus, the powers of the American President are vast so much so that by his critics he is labelled as 'the elected dictator for four years'.

6. *Ibid.*. p.33.

7. *Ibid,* p. 28.

Powers of the President

Executive	Legislative	Judicial	Financial	Emergency
1. To protect and defend the Constitution 2. To enforce Congressional laws and judicial decisions 3. To make high appointments 4. To remove high executive officials 5. To formulate national policy and effect its implementation 6. To conduct foreign relations including representation of US abroad, and 7. To conduct foreign treaties and executive agreements	1. To send messages to the Congress 2. To convene extra-ordinary session of the Congress in a special situation 3. To adjourn the Congress when both Houses fail to agree on doing so 4. To pilot bills in the Congress through his 'friends' 5. To influence legislation through patronage, bureaucracy and public opinion 6. To exercise veto power-absolute, qualified and pocket	To grant reprieve, pardon, or amnesty	Making of annual statement of income and expenditure of the Federal Government or budget and its presentation to the Congress	1. War (making a situation in which Congress has no other option but to adopt a resolution in this regard) 2. Emergency (its declaration and deployment of forces, suppression of rebellion, conclusion of peace)

Note: The President gets a salary of 200,000 dollars plus 50,000 dollars per year for meeting other official expenses. He may also spend upto 100,000 dollars (non-taxable) for travel and 20,000 dollars for official entertainments.

True that the American President is far more powerful than the British monarch, the former is less powerful than the latter in certain other respects. The American President is elected for a term of four years and that one person cannot enjoy more than two terms. In contrast to this, the tenure of the British monarch is permanent and hereditary. Moreover, the monarch has a mystic aura of glory that a President may never possess. Being a man of politics, the President is treated as a partisan person. As such, his actions are criticised and he may be removed from office by the process of impeachment. Opposed to this, the British monarch is treated as 'above politics'; he remains immune from public criticism and the people offer him their sincere loyalty. Hence, the American President cannot enjoy the position of a 'dignified executive' that is enjoyed by the English sovereign.

The points of resemblance and difference between the two may be easily mentioned after having a study of the American President versus British Prime Minister. Both are elected officials with supreme actual authority in their respective States. Thus, both are mighty figures in their respective States, both exercise leadership, both face public criticism, and both may be removed from office for certain acts of commission or omission. In fine, both govern and remain accountable for that. However, the points of difference between the two are vital that show each being more as well as less powerful than the other in certain important respects. For this purpose we may examine their position in the following directions:

1. In the sphere of administration, the American President is more powerful than the British Prime Minister. We have seen that the British Prime Minister is bound by the principle of collective responsibility. He has to bank upon the advice and cooperation of his colleagues. Moreover, the fact of Cabinet's being responsible to the Parliament restricts the executive powers of the Prime Minister. The Prime Minister is always under the searching criticism of the Parliament. His policies must be approved by it. At any time the House may pass a vote of censure against the government, or the weight of public criticism may force him to quit or remove his controversial minister. In this way, executive authority of the Prime Minister is subject to the control of the Parliament. Different from this, the American President uses his executive powers independently Nominations as well as foreign treaties made by him are ratified by the Senate as a matter of courtesy. His ministers are like his 'personal servants'. He acts according to his best judgement. Being the

> **Some Important Statements**
>
> The making of the President is one of the world's most mysterious and complicated transactions in power. ***—Theodre H. White***
>
> At the most, the President can initiate a matter in the Congress either through his forced message or through his loyal friends, he cannot control it, as he (limited by the will of the national legislature) is always like a sailor on an uncharted sea; he cannot proceed with certainty upon his course. ***—H.J. Laski***
>
> A striking example of the difference between British Prime Minister and American President occurred in 1941 during the discussion between Churchill and Roosevelt in Newfoundland over the Atlantic Charter. As President, Roosevelt could sign on his authority, but Churchill felt obliged to refer the matter back to Cabinet in London. Unlike a President, a Prime Minister cannot be over-ruled by his Cabinet.
>
> ***—Patrick Gordon Walker***

Commander-in-Chief of the armed forces, he may mobilise troops and make declarations regarding the conclusion of war or peace. The process of impeachment is too tedious that has so far remained virtually an otiose affair, while several Prime Ministers or their leading ministers have been removed or forced to quit by an adverse vote or unforgiving mood of the Parliament.

2. The British Prime Minister is more powerful than the American President in the legislative sphere. We have seen that the Cabinet decides about the time and dates of the session of the Parliament; inaugural address of the monarch is prepared by the Cabinet; daily proceedings of the House are conducted according to the time table prepared by the Cabinet; bills and resolutions are passed by the Parliament owing to the existence of majority behind it; and, above all, there is no fear of royal veto as the monarch acts on the advice of his ministers. It shows that the Prime Minister (along with his Cabinet) has usurped the inherent powers of the Parliament. In clear contrast to it, the American President can not usurp the powers of Congress. Though he may send messages to the Congress, or he may get certain bills passed by it, or that he may veto a bill passed by it, or that he may influence its working by some shrewd tactics like those of lobbying or charm of the patronage, he cannot be a master of the national legislature. Instances are there when the Congress turned down what the President desired in his message, or that an appointment or a foreign treaty made by the President was rejected by the Senate, or that a veto exercised by the President

was overridden by the second attempt of the Congress in passing the same bill.

3. Likewise, in the financial sphere, the British Prime Minister is more powerful than the American President. The budget prepared by the Cabinet must be passed by the Parliament, otherwise it would amount to the defeat of the ministry. The Prime Minister sees to it that his financial proposals are passed and all cut motions tabled by the Opposition are defeated. Thus, the budget is passed by the Parliament in the same form as desired by the Prime Minister. Different from this, the budget submitted by the President to the Congress may and may not be passed in exactly the same form. It is subjected to serious criticism in the House as well as in the Senate and quite often we find that several amendments are passed that change the shape of the original budget to a considerable extent. Though the President may make use of some shrewd political tactics to have his budget passed, it is certain that he would not be able to do what the Prime Minister does to save his government.
4. The American President is more powerful than the British Prime Minister so far as his relationship with the party is concerned. In Britain there is a very strong party discipline and no leader, even the Prime Minister, can flout it. The rules of the party bind all. In this way, the Prime Minister acts as an authorised spokesman of the party. He scrupulously tries to follow the rules of the party as he knows that his very existence in office depends upon the support of his party. Different from this, party system in the United States is a very loose affair and the hands of the President are not tied by the constraints of his being a man of the party that had nominated him.
5. Finally, there are some directions in which the American President is more powerful than the British Prime Minister. The latter is not the head of the State, while the former is. Thus, while the latter has several important things done by the monarch as he cannot do them himself, the former does by virtue of being the head of the State. Thus, the American President may exercise his prerogative of mercy and thereby grant pardon, reprieve or amnesty. He may adjourn the Congress in the event of disagreement between both houses in this regard. He may also take extraordinary steps to meet national crises by virtue of being the head of his state.

What it all reveals is that both are more as well as less powerful than each other in certain respects. The reason for this should be traced in different kinds of political organisations as well as in varying forms of political cultures. The entire study under this head may be epitomised in this statement: While the British king reigns and his Prime Minister rules; the American President rules as well as reigns though without wearing the crown. As President Theodre Roosevelt once said that his position 'is almost like that of a King and Prime Minister reeled into one'.

Vice-President

The office of the Vice-President has often been held by the 'forgotten men of American history.' The reason for this lies in the fact that its real significance is overshadowed by the massive value of the Presidency. That is why, various metaphors have been used to downgrade the worth of this office. Benjamin Franklin called the Vice-President 'His Superfluous Highness'; John Adams characterised it as 'most insignificant office'; Thomas Jefferson regarded it 'a splendid misery'; Franklin Roosevelt preferred to live like a teacher of history rather than to assume this post; Woodrow Wilson dubbed this office as 'one of anomalous insignificance and curious uncertainty'; Thomas R. Marshall expressed his experience of being 'a man in a cataleptic fit', J.N. Garner went to the length of naming it 'not worth a pitcher of warm spit'. Keeping these phrases in view, Clinton Rossiter holds that most men of ability and ambition "would still rather be a leading Senator or Secretary of State than Vice-President, even after all the good and exciting times that Richard Nixon had."[8]

However, these critical observations fail to depict the true state of affairs if we examine the post of the Vice-President in the light of three directions. First, the Constitution specifically lays down that he would act as the President whenever there is vacancy caused by the death, resignation, removal or disability of the President. It implies that he is the heir-apparent to the greatest office of the country. It is a stepping stone to future promotion as well. Historical facts show that Vice-Presidents took advantage of this situation and thereby saved themselves from being the 'forgotten men of American history'. Second, the office of the Vice- President is not without any dignity as it "is a preparatory school for the chief executive post."[9] Lyndon Johnson's succession to the highest office after the assassination of President Kennedy cleared his way for being the nominee of the

8. Rossiter, *The American Presidency*, p. 102.

9. Munro, *op. cit.*, 192.

Democratic Party a little after and to win the election enabling him to be the duly elected President of his country. Theodre Roosevelt's succession to the greatest office after the assassination of President Mckinley was seen with great horror by a man like Senator Hannor. The officiating period gives a lucky chance to the future aspirant to establish his image as a very powerful prelude to the time of coming election. Finally, the Vice- President is the ex-officio president of the Senate. Apart from these three points, one more point should be kept in mind that some Presidents have taken their Vice-Presidents in the cabinet and depended upon their esteemed co-operation which has contributed to the significance of this office mistakenly debunked by many people in so critical phrases.

The office of the Vice-President requires same qualifications as we saw in the case of President; his election procedure is also the same with the only difference that in case no candidate secures absolute majority of the electoral college, the Senate would choose one out of the two getting highest number of votes in the cancelled election. It happened once in 1837 but now its recurrence is out of question when only two political parties have a straight fight for the offices of the President and Vice-President. It may be safely concluded that any opinion debunking the real value of this office is unjustified. Cases of Theodre Roosevelt, Coolidge, Truman and Lyndon Johnson negative all views which ruthlessly underrate the value of this office assuming 'second' position in the American executive.

Cabinet

A study of the President's cabinet in a work on the political system of the United States is governed by certain unimportant as well as important considerations. It has little significance in view of the fact that it does not form an elemental part of the Presidential structure and therefore remains close to the heart of the decision-making process. However, facts indicate otherwise that enable a student of American politics to discover its really useful as well as important place in the structure of the Presidency. No doubt, the cabinet is best understood as a lengthened shadow of the President and it is often viewed by the people as a board of directors of the nation to which the President is never a hostage. Viewed thus, the cabinet as a collegial body has hardly more than a symbolic value; in actual operation, each member of the cabinet fends for himself and is judged individually.

Some Important Statements

The Cabinet is a mere creation of the President's will. It is an extra-statutory and extra-constitutional body. It exists only by custom. If the President desired to dispense with it, he could do so. —***William Howard Taft***

I expect each Cabinet officer to be the outstanding expert in his field and expect them to give me the best advice on matters in their field. If I have got an eye doctor, a head doctor, a doctor for my throat, and a doctor for my stomatch, I am not going to ask my eye doctor for advice when something is wrong with my belly. —***Lyndon B. Johnson***

The Cabinet has remained an informal group without legal sanction, its personnel is determined by custom and by the President. —***Ferguson and McHenry***

Origin: With the inauguration of the Constitution in 1789, President Washington sought the aid and advice first of the Senate and then of the Supreme Court on Indian Affairs. But when the former 'snubbed' and the latter 'rebuffed' him, he started the practice of consulting his principal officers. For this he summoned regular meetings of the key officials to discuss issues of general executive policy. The name 'cabinet' came to be applied to these meetings so much so that the Supreme Court gave judicial recognition to it in its historic decision in the case of *Marbury v. Madison* in 1803. It confirms the view that the American Cabinet is an advisory body having its origin in custom grown to meet the pressure or necessity.

Apart from its popular appellation, the American cabinet is also known by some nicknames. It is called a 'kitchen cabinet' when a President (like Andrew Jackson) dispenses with the practice of calling regular meetings of all principal officers and acts with the aid and advice of only few of them in whom he reposes his best confidence. It is also called a 'brains trust' when a President (like Franklin Roosevelt) enlarges this body so as to include the Vice-President and other confidants heading some boards and commissions. That fact remains that the President is not only the head of his cabinet, he is the sole maker and unmaker of this body. The cabinet is 'President's Family, 'whether it consists of his 'Palace Guards' only, or his 'official Harvard group', That is, the American cabinet, unlike its British counterpart, "is not a body with collective responsibility; it is a collection of departmental heads who carry out the orders of the President."[10]

10. Laski: *The American Democracy*, p. 23.

What really aids the President is neither the cabinet as a whole nor the 'brains trust', as it may be called; it is a small group of his most trusted persons that may, in the absence of a better term, be designated as the 'inner ring'. One may say that 'inner ring' is just an analytical concept as none is officially designated as its member whether regular or ad hoc. It includes someone who gradually comes to be so depended upon and trusted by the President that he can be considered as an integral part of this core circle playing an important part in the decision-making process. It is also possible that a person enjoying a comfortable position in this circle may fall from the presidential grace and his place may be taken by someone else.

Composition: The composition of the cabinet is determined by the number of various departments created by the Congress and the attitude of the President who keeps his confidence in a few or all ministers or even in some more important persons who, in his view, know 'more than him about public affairs', From time to time, the Congress has created new executive departments and now these are: State, Treasury, Defence, Post Office, Interior, Agriculture, Commerce, Labour, Health, Education and Welfare, Housing and Urban Development and Transportation. While all the heads of executive departments (called secretaries) informally belong to the cabinet, it depends upon the discretion of the head to exclude some of them on occasions or regularly, or even include others holding the charge of various independent agencies. Laski is right in his assessment that, in general, the American cabinet minister "lives and moves and has his being in the context of Presidential thought. Howsoever able and distinguished, he is bound to be eclipsed by the major significance of his chief."[11]

The authority of the President in regard to the composition of his cabinet is related to Congressional sanction in two important respects. First, it is the Congress that may create a new department, or change the name of an old one, or merge a department with some other department, or confer the status of a full-membership on some department and the like. It is due to this that the number of executive departments has increased from time to time. Moreover, the Congress may authorise the President to reshuffle independent bureaus and agencies. Second, all appointments made by the President are subject to Senatorial confirmation and, as such, the Senate may reject any nomination made by him.

11. Laski: *The American Presidency*, pp. 89-90.

President and Cabinet: As already pointed out, cabinet does not have an independent and, for this reason, a powerful position in the American political system so far as its relation to its leader is concerned. Though it has been suggested at certain times that the President should make greater use of his cabinet, yet to many it has not been clear as to how it would help in view of the fact that members of this informal body "are appointed for varying reasons; they do not necessarily have great administrative skills; they may not always agree with the President on policy; indeed, one task of the President, and no easy one, is to make sure that department heads follow his policies. The cabinet is, in any case, a large and unwieldy collection."[12] It is for this reason that the relationship between the President and his cabinet varies from person to person.

The way of Johnson had a setback under Nixon who subscribed to the view that the presidency and not any other formal or informal body had 'a vital place of action in the American political system'. He depended upon the Harvard Professor (Kissinger) over and above his Secretary of State (Rusk). Without consulting his senior cabinet colleagues, he ordered H.R. Headman to have the Central Intelligence Agency to request the Federal Bureau of Investigation to halt its inquiries into the sources of the Watergate burglars' funding on the pretext that national security would be threatened by the release of CIA secrets if the investigation proceeded. One may, however, add that such a behaviour of Nixon was different from what he showed in the early phase of his first term.

It shows that while every cabinet officer is responsible for directing and co-ordinating the operations of his particular department 'to promote the effective exercise of President's authority and to help implement his ultimate responsibilities',[13] beyond this the impact of the Cabinet as an advisory group has varied from President to President. While Presidents like Truman and Eisenhower used it more often than did Roosevelt and Kennedy, Johnson's approach was to go to the cabinet more often than his predecessor, but this was less for the purpose of securing advice and more in an effort to build consensus for a decision he had already decided to make.[14]

12. R.A. Dahl: *Pluralist Democracy in the United States*, p. 102.

13. Feno: *President's Cabinet*, p. 5.

14. L.W. Koenig, *The Chief Executive*, p. 160

American and British Cabinets Compared: A comparative study of the American and British cabinets shows that there are points of resemblance and difference between the two. So far as similarity is concerned, both have a conventional origin and growth. There is no written provision for their existence and working. It may also be said that in both the number of the members is determined by a law passed by the national legislature. However, the points of difference are vital that may be enumerated as under:

1. The American cabinet distinctly differs from the British cabinet in the manner of selection of its members. The hands of British Prime Minister are tied with the considerations of territorial representation, party solidarity, political homogeneity and the ability of his colleagues, the American President is mostly guided by the factors of national economic interests and his election debts. Other considerations like those of party bosses, geographical representation and fitness of the persons play a very minor role.
2. Naturally, the American and British cabinets differ very much on the issue of relationship between the captain and his team. The British Prime Minister has been called *primus inter pares* meaning 'first among equals'. That is, a minister of the British cabinet has a position of his own which cannot be paled into insignificance by the great boss. In sharp contrast to it, the American chief is the master of his cabinet and his ministers are no better than 'errand boys' in the eyes of a President like Wilson. It is true to say that the cabinet office "is an interlude in a career; it is not itself a career." (Laski)
3. The American cabinet is, therefore, not a body charged with the important work of making policy or taking decision on important matters of national interest. Every major issue is decided by the President and the minister concerned has to carry it out if he has to avoid the ordeal of his dismissal. President Lincoln's assertion on the question of slavery that 'seven nayes one aye, the ayes have it' is rightly contrasted with British Prime Minister Lord Melbourne's docile statement on the issue of Corn Laws that it 'does not matter what we will say, as long as we all say the same thing.'
4. In contrast to politically homogeneous character of the British cabinet, the American cabinet may have the character of heterogeneity. The two-party system of Britain has made the cabinet a committee of like-partymen. The Prime Minister and his colleagues

invariably belong to the same party which commands absolute majority in the House of Commons. It is rare (as in time of war or grave national emergency) that national government consisting of the talents of different parties is formed. But in the case of American cabinet the requirement of political homogeneity stands on the basis of flexibility. The President may include some leaders of the other party as well. Roosevelt took Henry L. Stimson and Franklin Fox (Republicans) and Nixon of the Republican party included a Democrat (Connally) in his cabinet.

5. The last point of difference between the American and British cabinets finds place in the relationship between the executive and the legislature. Britain has parliamentary system of government in which executive is a part and parcel of the legislature and thus accountable to the mother-body. The Prime Minister and his colleagues must be the members of the Parliament and they can retain their office so long they enjoy the confidence of the House of Commons. Contrary to this, the American system of government is based on the doctrine of separation of powers whereby the President and his ministers cannot become the members of the Congress at one and the same time. There is no question of outvoting the cabinet and if there is any charge of treason, bribery or other high crime of misdemeanour, then not a minister but the President may be removed by the Congress by the process of impeachment.

Owing to these reasons the American cabinet remains over-shadowed by the strong Presidency. Its net result has been in making the cabinet 'one of the least successful of American federal institutions.'[15]

Critical Appreciation: What we have seen in the preceding sections of our study leaves a striking impression that the cabinet holds a very weak position in the decision-making process of the United States. Three principal reasons may be accounted for this:

1. Not all the cabinet members are chosen by the President on the basis of his long association or their known competence. In every cabinet there is a large number of appointees whose selection represents virtually a reward for their having supported the President in his campaign for office.
2. Cabinet members also remain subject to conflict of loyalties. Since party organisation is very weak and group interest consideration is

15. Laski, *op. cit.*, p. 23.

very strong, most of the ministers are torn between their loyalty to the President and their emotional attachment to the interest of their own group or organisation.

3. Above all, the pattern of American political system is quite different from a country like Britain. There is nothing like cabinet solidarity requiring all members of this informal body to live in cohesion. The result is that the President counts upon some and ignores others.

Owing to these factors, the cabinet is prevented from becoming 'a part of the inner circle of intimate presidential advisers.'[16] As a consequence, the effectiveness of this body as an advisory or co-ordinating machinery is somewhat reduced. There is no dearth of evidence to substantiate that several Presidents have, in fact, reduced the cabinet meeting "to a little more than a ceremony with social trimmings."[17]

Permanent Executive

The role of bureaucracy in the decision-making process of the country constitutes the most important part of our study. The secret of this matter lies in the fact that the bureaucrats are the real decision-makers. The job of the executive is the application of rules. Since the bureaucrats constitute the lower layer, they can well be found associated with the President and his secretaries forming the upper layer of the government and charged with the task of running the administration of the country. What astonishes a student of politics at this stage is that, like Britain, bureaucracy plays a quite significant part in the operation of the political system so much so that not only the executive but also the legislative sphere does not remain immune from its influence despite the fact that the American constitutional system is based on the celebrated principle of separation of powers. For this, let us examine the role of bureaucracy in the following important directions:

Bureaucracy and President: There is a two-way traffic so far as the relationship between the President and bureaucrats is concerned in respect of influencing each other that has its definite impact on the process of decision-making. There are several means whereby the President may enforce his demands on the bureaucrats. The Bureau of Budget, which is a part of the Presidency, plays a general supervising and co-ordinating

16. Sigler and Getz, *Contemporary American Government.*, p. 507.

17. E.S. Corwin: *The President: Office and Powers*, p. 19.

role over the bureaucracy. The power of making top appointments, skilful use of rewards and sanctions, and the power over the organisation of the executive branch are useful instruments in the hands of the President whereby he may influence the top bureaucrats. The possibility that his agency or sub-division may be split in two or three parts or combined with some other department is always like a lurking fear in the mind of the bureaucrats. Above all, finding their budgets cut or losing a desired programme "are two possibilities that help keep bureaucratic officials eager to please the President and certain persons and agencies in the Presidency.'[18]

If the President can influence bureaucracy in certain ways, he may also be influenced by it in some other respects. Many actions are taken in the name of the President without his knowledge and the enormous problem of control of the vast bureaucracy is not solved merely by the cabinet heads' being responsible to the President. Facts illustrate that today no President can exercise full check on the role of bureaucracy and, as such, he may take many things for granted. So many administrators must report to the President that he is deluged with information that must be predigested by staff members before he can absorb it. Hostile, secretive, or incompetent members of the bureaucracy can conceal their mistakes or misdeeds for long periods of time in the realization that such actions can be lost sight of in the vast mass of data that comes to the President's desk. Although vigilance by Presidential advisers, departmental heads and bureau chiefs is a safeguard against inadequate bureaucracy, incidents inevitably occur that embarrass the President or make him appear to be out of touch with his subordinates. Furthermore, department heads and bureau chiefs "may sometimes openly contradict the policy stands of President; or worse still, unsympathetic bureaucrats may undermine his plans.'[19]

Bureaucracy and Congress: Likewise, a study of the relationship between the bureaucracy and the Congress is like a two-way traffic each influencing and controlling the other in its own way. Before making a decision, the bureaucrats must frequently ask themselves what the reactions of the Congress are likely to be. It is due to three reasons, namely, Congress's power of the purse whereby it sanctions grants to various departments, general power of the Congress relating to programme authorisation and amendment, and the committee system in which the

18. See Sigler and Getz: *Contemporary American Government*, p. 538.

19. *Ibid.*

senior members of the federal legislature act as chairman and thereby force the bureaucrats to have good relationship with the legislature. An unwary bureaucrat may suddenly find his funds being cut if he has forgotten to cultivate a favourable relationship with certain Congressmen and that he has spurned too many Congressional demands. Moreover, if a politically astute career bureaucrat has to choose between going against the demands of a powerful Senator, or the President or one of his appointees, he may well choose to keep peace with the Senator and go against the President or his appointee as the former enjoys a fairly long tenure and acts as the chairman of the powerful committees.[20]

Despite the fact that bureaucracy is the creation of the Congress, the former has its own influence over the latter by indulging in the technique of lobbying, no matter lobbying of this type (called 'administrative lobbying') is an illegal affair. It is found that most of the departments and agencies of national government attempt to maximise their influence and go to the extent of lobbying the legislators. Skilful bureaucrats may have the Congress influenced through its 'liaison officers' who work in much the same manner as do private lobbyists. Another useful method of gaining Congressional favour is 'reverse lobbying' that uses the clients or an agency to work for the desired ends. A sort of liaison between the bureaucrats and the manufacturers of arms, for example, may take place whose impact may be visualised on the passing of the budget relating to the grants of the Department of Defence.

Bureaucracy and Interest Groups: So powerful is the nexus between the bureaucrats and the interest groups that the task of the former is often described as 'not to serve but to regulate the interest'. The National Labour Relations Board and labour and management interests and the Securities and Exchange Commission and investors and brokers are its examples. The bureaucratic system may be found providing an interest group with certain services or regulating some interest group. It may be illustrated with the statistics prepared by various departments as by the Department of Commerce for the use of the businessmen or by the Department of Agriculture for the use of the farmers. In such cases, the role of the interest groups "is usually one of encouraging the bureaucratic sub-system, giving any help it can, and forming a united front with the bureaucracy whenever the programme is threatened by budget cuts or other curtailment."[21] Here one may find the penetration of the influence of bureaucracy in the financial

20. Monsma, *op. cit.*, p. 184.

21. *Ibid.*, p. 185

sphere also. The various interest groups running huge establishments depend upon the policies and programmes of the executive departments.

Critical Appreciation: The Americans are faced with the problem of controlling the bureaucracy. Numerous critics of the functioning of various independent regulatory commissions and agencies have engaged public attention and it has been demanded that all such bodies should be abolished, or the powers of each be carefully examined and re-defined. Since neither the Congress nor the federal judiciary can have an effective control over the bureaucracy, all have pinned their hopes on the action of the Presidents who have taken gingerly steps in this direction. For example, Eisenhower established a permanent office of Administrative Procedure within the Department of Justice to provide assistance to every federal agency on daily basis; Kennedy sponsored major re-organisation plans for every independent regulatory agency; and Johnson appointed H.S. Williams as chairman of the Administrative Conference in 1967. And yet the Presidents have been unsuccessful in their efforts to control the bureaucracy and keep various executive agencies working in hrarmony in view of the fact that in the vast federal administrative apparatus, there are many points of resistance and many breakdowns in communications.

The problem is how to control the vast bureaucratic set-up and, in particular, how to deal with the dissident bureaucrats. The proposal of having ombudsman is not appreciated by many people as he could be another invincible bureaucrat subject to Parkinson's law and Peter's principle. An answer to this problem should be discovered in the will of the President to have really competent men as his secretaries and that the control of Congressional committees should be made more effective. It is, however, not easily possible as the Americans have a different political culture that has its different impact on the running of their political system. Not much authority can be placed in the hands of the President as it would violate the spirit of the American political system. The net result of all this is that bureaucracy has come to have the position of a 'fourth estate' in the American political system. Only a vigilant and vocal public can exercise a really effective check on the abuse of authority by the permanent public officials. "Swift to censure and slow to praise, the public exerts its pressures upon the federal executive in no uncertain terms. The public, in making its demands known, makes use of (and is used by) a whole arsenal of weapons."[22]

---

22. Warner and others: *The American Executive*, p. 241.

9

FEDERAL LEGISLATURE

Congress

The legislative organ of the American federal government is known by the name of the Congress. Originally a body of 26 Senators and 65 Representatives, it now consists of 100 and 435 members in the upper and lower chambers respectively. In addition to this enlargement of size, a great deal of difference has occurred in other directions as well. The way its two chambers are organised, and, more particularly the manner in which they are influenced by local and regional considerations through the instrumentality of interest groups, has made its proper study a very complex affair. As Woodrow Wilson suggestively adds: "Like a vast picture thronged with figures of equal prominence and crowded with elaborate and obtrusive details, Congress is hard to see satisfactorily and appreciatively at a single standpoint. Its complicated form and diversified structure confuse the vision and conceal the system which underlies its composition. It is too complex to be understood without an effort, without a careful and systematic process of analysis, consequently very few people do understand it, and its doors are practically shut against the comprehension of the public at large."[1]

Special Features: The organisation, working and functions and powers of the Congress reveal following salient features:

1. It is a bi-cameral body having Senate and House of Representatives as the upper and lower chambers respectively. The Senate is organised on the federal principle of equal representation to all units of the Union regardless of their geographical or demographic compositions. Each State sends two members whether it is big like New York or small like Nevada. But the lower house is organised on the principle of territorial representation-on demographic basis

1. Wilson: *Congressional Government*, p. 58.

with the provision of at least one member from each State. Thus the quota of every State is fixed and the work of allocation of electoral districts is with the States subject to the over-riding jurisdiction of the Congress and the Supreme Court.

2. Originally the method of the election of the Senators was indirect. But the 17th constitutional amendment of 1913 made a change in this regard to combat the menacing tendency of electoral corruption. As a result, the Senators are now directly elected by the same body of voters in each State as the people choose their Representatives.
3. Each house of the Congress is the judge of the eligibility of its members and may even go to the length of disregarding a constitutional point while allowing or refusing a person to take his seat in either chamber. For instance, in 1806 the Senate admitted Henry Clay of Connecticut when he was below 30 years of age. In 1926 it refused to let Frank L. Smith of Illinois and William S. Vare of Pennsylvania take their seats in the house on the plea that they had spent too much money in their elections. Likewise, the House of Representatives in 1900 excluded Bringham Robert of Utah to take his seat on the charge that he was a polygamist.
4. There is a big gap in the duration of the life of a Senator and of a Representative. While the former is elected for a term of six years, the latter for two years. It is true that there is no bar on the times a person may be elected, yet it is clear that the life of a Representative is far too short a period which discourages eminent politicians to have their place in the popular chamber of the national legislature.
5. While the Founding Fathers wanted the House to act as the barometer of national opinion and the Senate as a body to protect the interests of the component units of the union, the situation has changed to the extent that the Senate alone has taken upon itself the onus of protecting the interests of the States as well as of the nation as a whole. Obviously, the position of the lower house has been overshadowed to a very large extent.
6. One more direction where the Senate has belied the hopes of the framers of the Constitution lies in the development of a custom called 'Senatorial courtesy'. The Constitution-makers wanted a salutary check on the authority of the President, but over the period of last 200 years or so, the check has developed into a system of organised political blackmail. Everything is determined by the yardstick of political friendship.

7. The two houses of the Congress work without strong party discipline. There are floor leaders belonging to both the parties, but they are no match to the whips of the English Parliament. The members act freely and the passage of a measure requires the support of each other on the basis of temporary alliances or adjustments. This is called log-rolling.
8. The character of the bills moved in the Congress shows that the members (particularly of the lower house) are much guided by local and regional interests for the sake of obliging their constituents with rewards and thereby keeping their electoral prospects high. Due to the usage of locality rule, the members of the popular chamber fight for petty gains (like the opening of some federal office in their constituency) and a legislative benefit secured for their sake goes by the name of 'pork-barrel'.
9. Owing to the absence of strict party discipline, the American Congress works under the influence of pressure groups fighting for their respective interests. While the candidate for Presidentship fights elections on the basis of national and international issues, Senators and Representatives solicit votes on the basis of local and regional matters. Besides, the legislators exist and thrive on the support of organised catalytic groups and they can not frustrate the expectations of their 'masters' in the interest of their own electoral prospects.
10. The Congress is not a sovereign law-making body like the British Parliament. Its powers of law-making are limited by the terms of the Constitution. Moreover, a bill passed by the Congress is subject to the veto of the President which may be over-ridden when it readopts the same bill by 2/3 majority. However, what can not be over-ridden is the veto of federal judiciary with Supreme Court at the top. The judges by virtue of their power of judicial review may declare any law passed by the Congress as *ultra vires* if it is found to be violative of the constitutional provisions or due process of law.
11. The Congress works on the principle of separation of powers and checks and balances. The Constitution has vested legislative authority in it. It has also put it under the control of the President on one side and of the courts on the other. Because of the system of separation of powers, the Congress and the President cannot combine and if there is any such tendency, the Supreme Court is there to undo it.

Powers of the Congress

Legislative

Power of making laws on
- (*i*) Enumerated subjects in the Constitution
- (*ii*) Implied powers as interpreted by judicial decisions given by the federal courts with Supreme Court at the top
- (*iii*) Concurrent powers for the Federal as well as State legislatures (with an over-riding authority in favour of the Congress

Non-Legislative

Constituent
1. Passing a bill of constitutional amendment
2. Calling a convention for passing a bill of constitutional amendment
3. Fixing time-limit within which State legislatures must ratify or reject a bill of constitutional amendment,

Executive
1. Confirmation of appointments and foreign treaties by the Senate
2. Declaration of war and peace
3. Appointment of its own staff

Electoral
1. Choosing of President and Vice-President by the House and the Senate respectively when a candidate fails to secure absolute majority of the electoral college
2. Choosing of Speaker by the House and President pro-tempore by the Senate

Directing and Supervisory
1. Sanctioning a new department or board or bureau or agency
2. Re-organisation of departments
3. Grant of appropriation of funds
4. Authorisation of employment of personnel and periodic review

Inquisitorial
1. Setting up of investigating committees and consideration of their reports

Judicial
1. Sitting in judgment over the eligibility of a member even after his being duly elected
2. Holding trial of impeachment

Financial
1. Passing budget and money bill

12. Lobbying is a peculiar American institution. The members of the Congress succumb to the techniques of the professional lobbyists who influence them with threat, inducement and promise to do or not to do a particular thing inside the legislative chamber. It is found that even Congressmen resort to the practice of lobbying for the protection and promotion of some specific interests.

Functions and Powers: The Congress has the power to make laws on the following important subjects:

1. To lay and collect taxes, duties, imposts and excises, to pay the debts and provide for the common defence and general welfare of the United States.
2. To borrow money on the credit of the United States; and regulate commerce with foreign nations and among several states.
3. To establish an uniform rule of naturalisation, and uniform laws on the subject of bankruptcies.
4. To coin money, regulate the value thereof, and of foreign coin, fix the standards of weights and measures; and to provide for the punishment of counterfeiting the securities and currency coin of the United States.
5. To establish post office and post roads; and to promote the progress of science and useful arts.
6. To constitute tribunals inferior to Supreme Court; and to define and punish piracies and felonies committed on the high seas and offence against the law of nations.
7. To declare war, grant letters of marque and reprisal and make rules concerning captures on land and water; to raise and support armies but no appropriation of money to that use shall be for a longer term than two years; and to provide and maintain a navy.
8. To make rules for government and regulation of the land and naval forces.
9. To provide for calling forth the militia to expedite the laws of the union, suppress insurrections and repel invasions.
10. To provide for organising, arming and disciplining the militia.

However, this is not all what comes under the authority of the Congress. Over a period of more than 200 years, it has gained other powers called 'implied powers', or those powers which can be reasonably inferred or deduced from the powers specifically mentioned in the Constitution, or powers which are necessary and proper for the execution of the delegated powers. Thus, for example, the power to establish federal banks, to create naval and military academies and to construct highways and bridges etc. have come within the scope of Congressional authority by virtue of the doctrine of implied powers laid down by the Supreme Court. It may, however, be kept in mind that implied powers "do not give the federal government a blank cheque to do anything it wishes. If that were true, the system would be unitary rather than federal. Implications be made only from some specifically delegated powers."[2]

However, the Congress has some other powers as well—electoral, constituent, executive, directing and supervisory, inquisitorial, judicial and financial.

1. Among its constituent powers, we find that a bill of constitutional amendment must be passed by both the chambers by 2/3 majority of the members present and voting. On a petition submitted by 2/3 States, it shall summon a constitutional convention and lay down rules of its business. The Congress has also developed some powers in this regard whereby it may lay down time-limit within which the States are required to ratify or reject a bill of constitutional amendment.
2. The electoral powers of the Congress are also important. The Constitution lays down that a candidate for Presidency or Vice-Presidency must secure absolute majority of the electoral college, otherwise the mater shall be decided by the Congress. The House of Representatives shall choose one out of the three securing highest number of votes for the Presidency and the Senate shall choose one out of the two having largest number of votes for Vice-Presidency. But the voting pattern shall be on the basis of 'one State one vote'. Besides, the House elects its Speaker and the Senate elects its President *pro tempore.*
3. The executive powers of the Congress include confirmation of all appointments and foreign treaties (made by the President) by the Senate and approval of the proposal of making war and peace by a resolution of both the houses. Both the chambers appoint their own officers and committees. Then, the powers of direction and supervision are directly related. It is resolved by the Congress

2. Ferguson and McHenry, *American Federal Government,* p. 265.

whether a new department, bureau or commission is to be set up. It may expand agencies, consolidate them or abolish them altogether. In addition, it defines their powers, sanctions appropriation of funds, authorises the employment of personnel and reviews their work periodically. For example, the Legislative Re-organisation Act of 1946, requires Congressional standing committees to exercise continuous vigilance over the execution of laws falling within their respective spheres.

4. The inquisitorial powers of the Congress include appointment of committees to investigate some matters of alleged misappropriation of funds or scandal.
5. We may refer to the judicial powers of the Congress. Both chambers are master of the eligibility of their members. Even a duly elected member may be disallowed to take his seat in the house on some ground of corruption after a resolution is passed by simple majority. Each house can expel a member if its 2/3 majority so desires. Besides, each house can also make some relaxation in the qualifications of a candidate for its membership. However, the most important task is the process of impeachment whereby the House of Representatives has power of initiating the charge against the President, Vice-President and other high public officers and the Senate, after hearing both the parties, gives its verdict by its 2/3 majority.
6. In regard to financial matters, the Congress controls the purse of the nation. The Constitution ordains the financial supremacy of the Congress by specifying that no money shall be drawn from the treasury but in consequence of appropriation made by a law. The money bill originates in the House of Representatives and becomes law after it is passed by the Senate. The budget is prepared by the bureau, but the President submits it to the Congress and its provisions are implemented after it is passed by the Congress.

Critical Appreciation: The fact of decline of the Congress can not be rebutted even by the American writers in view of the salient fact that the leadership of the executive has usurped the inherent powers of the legislature in every political system whether parliamentary or presidential. So far as the American political system is concerned, the Congress has lost much of its power curiously by playing a cooperative as well as competitive role in relation to the authority of the President. The problem is that it loses itself when it acts in a co-operative spirit and thereby becomes the object of criticism on the ground of being a second fiddle to the operation of the Presidency; likewise, it loses when it takes scuffle with the President as he perforce makes use of some shrewd ways to immunise himself from the control of the federal legislature and that causes the enhancement of the authority of the former at the expense of the powers of the latter. It is too much to talk of the power of impeachment whereby the Congress may remove a President in as much as the process is too tedious and cumbersome.

The American Congress is certainly a weaker organ of the federal government. It is weaker than the President on the one side and the Supreme Court on the other. The Senate has developed the convention of 'courtesy' and thereby given a long rope to the Chief Executive; the Supreme Court has taken advantage of the power of judicial review and thereby circumscribed the inherent powers of the representatives of the people. Certain 'notorious' practices (like those of gerrymandering, log-rolling, pork barrel, lobbying etc.) have contributed to the decline of the position of the federal legislature. Emphasis on local and regional interests and discreet role of pressure agencies have robbed the Congress of its real authority and significance.

Senate

Originally a body of 26 members (when there were 13 States) and now of 100 (as there are 50 States), the Senate is not only the upper house of the American Congress, but in order of importance it comes next to the President.[3] The fact that the Founding Fathers made it co-ordinate with the House of Representatives (with a minor difference in financial matters) and vested in it some more important powers relating to the imposition of check on the executive authority of the President shows that they never desired to keep this body as a mere ornamental chamber. Moreover, the actual exercise of authority by the Senate over a period of last century or so has confirmed the view of Munro that it is a 'terminological inexactitude' to call it a second chamber. So important a position is now held by the members of this body that a leading political figure prefers to join it instead of acting as the mate of the President or a representative of the lower chamber. That is why, it is believed that the Senators "are somewhat of a different breed of political animal from the average representatives."[4]

3. D.W. Brogan: *The American Political System*, p. 170.

4. Burns and Peltason: *Government by the People*. p. 420.

Some Important Statements

Probably no second chamber in the world today has an influence so real and direct, not only in the most obviously national concerns such as foreign affairs, but down to the very minutest business of federal legislation, including finance. So powerful is the Senate, indeed, that it is regarded by some as the sole effective Federal Chamber in the United States. ***—C.F. Strong***

The House of Representatives is the most shackled deliberative body in the world, the Senate is the freest. ***—D.W. Brogan***

The Senate is unquestionably the outstanding second chamber among national parliamentary bodies. The Congress provides one of the few remaining examples of two-house plan operating on a substantially coordinate basis. ***—Ferguson and McHenry***

Composition: As the Senate acts like the backbone of the American federal system, its composition gives equal representation to each State of the American union. Two members from each State are elected to this body if they have three qualifications—citizenship of the United States with at least 9 years' standing, above 30 years of age, and residence in the State from which they are elected. Besides, the Senate is the judge of its elections and other qualifications of its members and, as such, it can negative the electoral victory of a candidate in case he has committed grave irregularities or any such lapse amounting to electoral corruption. For instance, it refused to allow FL. Smith of Illinois and W.S. Vare of Pennsylvania to take their seats in 1926 on the charge that they had spent huge amounts of money in their elections. A resolution passed by the majority of votes is needed for this purpose.

According to the terms of the Constitution, two members are elected from each State regardless of its size and population for a period of six years, 1/3 retiring every second year. The original plan had provided for their indirect election. But the 17th constitutional amendment of 1913 made a change in order to eradicate electoral corruption. As a result, now Senators are elected by the body of voters in each State in the like manner as they elect their Representatives. In some States, it has become a matter of usage to elect two Senators from two different regions. But as there is no limitation on the number of terms a Senator may enjoy, it is easy to understand that a reputed person may have chances more than one and thereby serve even for a period of more than two decades. As required by the 20th constitutional amendment of 1933, the session of the Senate opens on 3rd January and runs till the end of June or July unless otherwise provided by a resolution passed by the Congress.

Filibustering: One thing that makes discussions and deliberations in the Senate as the most striking phenomenon is the use of filibustering or a device of free speaking for any length of time and without any care for the relevance of expression. It is a device of obstruction exercised by some members of the Senate to prevent the adoption of a measure under consideration, or to obtain certain concessions as the price or reward for allowing its passage. The exercise of this technique has become a very profitable business in the hands of professional speakers who squander the time of the house by making irrelevant speeches for no other reason than to carry their opposition to the point of a veto. This happens due to the fact that voting cannot be done until speakers are silent. Hence, the group of professional filibusters relays on the basis of prior agreement and the time of the house is wasted by the reading of excerpts from some novel, drama or private correspondence just to create unnecessary humour.

Since filibustering is "a means of preventing the passage of a bill by using long speeches and other parliamentary manoeuvres to prevent it from coming to a vote,"[5] one may ask as to what devices are available to the members of the Senate to put a check on this insidious practice. The answer is that they have three options. First, they can simply give in and agree either to drop the bill completely or to strike a compromise by accepting certain changes in the bill in return for the end of a filibustering. Second, the supporters of a bill can fight the filibuster and hope to wear out and outlast other. It includes keeping a quorum of Senators in hand in order to force those filibustering into nearly round-the-clock sessions. This tactic, however, works when there are few filibusters, or they are not very serious.

However the most effective way to stop filibustering is to apply closure motion. In 1917, it was decided by the Senate to apply this check if a move initiated by at least 1/6 members was adopted by the house with 2/3 majority of the members present and voting. This agreement was, however, revised in 1949 to mean that 2/3 majority would mean 2/3 of the whole house. It is clear that the revised arrangement made the application of closure motion more difficult, even impossible. The return to the old position in 1959, *i.e.*, 2/3 majority of the members, present and voting, has softened the position. One thing is, however, clear that the Senators do not want to deprive themselves of the 'great privilege' which is the best safeguard for their political and economic interests.

5. Monsma: *American Politics: A Systems Approach*, p. 138.

Senatorial Courtesy: According to a well-established constitutional convention, Senate is known for showing its courtesy. Senatorial courtesy "is a practice under which an appointment by the President will be confirmed only if approved by the Senator or Senators of his own party from the State concerned."[6] The Constitution requires that an appointment made by the President must by ratified by the Senate. That is, the appointing power of the President is shared by the Senate that may, and also may not, approve the nomination of one whose name is referred to it by the chief executive. However, a convention has developed which requires that before filling a federal post in a particular State, the President should consult the Senator or Senators of the State and obtain his or their consent in this regard. If the President shows courtesy to the Senator, the appointment is perhaps sure to be approved, otherwise a major opposition launched by the Senator concerned may lead to the rejection of the nomination. The result is that the President "has only half appointing power, the Senate has the rest."[7]

The Vice-President is the presiding officer of the Senate. The Senate elects its President *pro tempore* to act as the presiding officer when the Vice-President is not available for some reason. The office of the President *pro tempore* goes to the man whose name is chosen by the caucus of the majority party in the house. He is a member of the Senate and therefore exercises his right to vote, whereas the Vice-President (not being a member of this body) can do so only to break the tie. However, the chairman of this house has no effective power to control the debate because of the use of filibustering; he cannot recognise a member as he has to give him first chance who stands up first. The Senate expects no leadership from its presiding officer and an attempt by a headstrong chairman (like Vice-President Dawes) is sure to be defeated by the resenting house.

Functions and Powers: However, what has made the Senate more than a co-ordinate branch of the American Congress and assigned to it the name of being the most powerful upper chamber in the world is its strong position. A look at its functions and powers shows that the scope of its effective authority pervades every branch of the American government. For the sake of convenience, it is better to classify the functions and powers of the Senate under five heads-executive, legislative, judicial, financial and investigative.

---

6. Ferguson and McHenry: *American Federal Government,* p. 619.

7. W.B. Munro, *The Government of the United States,* p. 192.

The Founding Fathers vested executive authority of the Union in the President, but they empowered the "Senate to act as a powerful check on his discretionary authority."[7] Hence, it has been laid down in the Constitution that all appointments and foreign treaties made by the President shall be ratified by the Senate. As a result, a foreign treaty signed by the President cannot be implemented unless it is approved by the Senate by its 2/3 majority. It is true that the Senate normally approves a treaty signed by the President, but a situation may arise in which a treaty negotiated by the chief executive may be rejected as happened, for example, in the cases of the Treaty of Versailles of 1919 and the Comprehensive Test Ban Treaty of 1996. Likewise, it is needed that all appointments made by the President must be approved by the Senate by the simple majority of votes. As a matter of usage, the Senate normally approves appointments made by the President behind which lies the fact of political friendship between the two. Secret adjustments are often in operation and the position of gentlemanly compromise makes the machinery run smoothly. The convention of Senatorial courtesy requires that the President before making a 'minor' appointment of federal officers in a State must have the prior consultation and consent of the Senators from that State and this process of mutual consultation works to the advantage of both. When the Constitution gives first half power to the President and second half to the Senate, naturally both are expected to work in a way that the other does not feel offended.

It is clear that the executive powers of the Senate are not shared by the House of Representatives and thereby these enhance the authority of the former alone. Then, in the legislative sphere as well, the authority of the Senate is no less obvious as compared to the powers of the lower house of the American Congress. No bill can be deemed to have been passed by the Congress unless it is passed by the Senate after it is adopted by the Representatives. The concurrence of both the Houses is required. In Britain the House of Lords may defeat the passage of a non-money bill once and in case the same bill is passed by the House of Commons after an interval of one year, it over-rides the authority of the House of Lords. That is, the Lords cannot defeat the will of the Commons and can do nothing more than a delay of one year if there is a sharp disagreement between the two chambers of the English Parliament. In the United States, the Senate is not a weak chamber like the House of Lords. An adamant Senate can kill any non-money bill any number of times it likes. In the event of disagreement between the two Houses, the matter has to be settled by a joint conference committee having equal number of members of the two houses. It is clear that even in this compromise committee the Senate has no chance of losing at all, rather it has every prospect of having better of the bargain as it is represented by men of greater political skill and superior bargaining capacity.

The House of Lords of Britain is a weak chamber as regards financial business, for it can not defeat a money bill or a budget passed by the lower house. The only power with it is to delay the passage for a period of one month in Britain and 14 days in India. It is surprising to see that the Senate is no less powerful than the House of Representatives even in this direction. The only point of difference lies in the fact that a money bill can not be introduced in the Senate. This restriction is not very effective as there is no limit of time within which the Senate is required to pass that money bill or budget. Moreover, the Senate has the power of making necessary amendments in that bill and the financial business can not be taken as passed by the Congress until it has the concurrence of both the houses.

Then, the Senate has some judicial powers. It can refuse a duly elected member to sit in the house if a resolution is passed by the simple majority to denounce his corrupt practices in the election. It is also a court of impeachment—a legislative trial of public officials. The Constitution lays down that the President, Vice-President and all civil officers of the United States may be removed from office by the process of impeachment on the charges of treason, bribery, or other high crime of misdemeanour. It is provided that the charge shall be initiated by the House of Representatives if a resolution is passed by its majority vote and the decision shall be taken by the Senate by its 2/3 majority. When the Senate acts as the court of impeachment, it is considered the highest court presided over by the Chief Justice of the Supreme Court, unless the charge is against him, and the matter is decided by vote after both parties have their hearings. The only punishment which the Senate can give is immediate removal and future disqualification from holding civil offices under the national government.

In addition to these important functions and powers, the Senate has enhanced its authority by one more significant channel which invests it with the power of making investigations. That is, the Senate is not only a deliberative body exercising executive and judicial powers, it is also an investigating body. However, the exercise of this function has created an instrument of terror in its hand. If a resolution is passed by the Senate calling for investigation into an alleged scandal, the members of the nominated committee are given power of visiting the offices concerned, meeting their staff, checking papers and documents, interviewing witnesses and doing many other things to establish guilt upon the wrong-doers.

Critical Appreciation: It demonstrates that the American Senate has got a very important place in the constitutional system which is next to the Chief Executive alone so far as the area of wielding effective authority is concerned. However, certain points of criticism may be noted as under:

1. The Senate apart from being the upper chamber of the Congress, is a "millionaires' club". It has members drawing support from wealthy magnates who work for the advantage of their masters by posing as the servants of their constituents. Even the arrangement of direct election of the Senators has not served the desired purpose and it is found that with the passage of time and inflationary conditions of the country, it has now become a club of the multi-millionaires.
2. The investigating powers of the Senate developed over a period of years after the First World War have not only created an instrument of terror in the hands of a few powerful leaders of this house, it has in a way undermined the system of separation of powers and checks and balances so masterly devised by the Founding Fathers and so jealously safeguarded by the Supreme Court.
3. The device of filibustering is the most undesirable feature of the process of deliberations in the Senate. As already suggested, it is a mischievous trick in the hands of professional demagogues to coerce the house to bend in response to their intents. It affords nothing but spectacular legislative exploits. It is true that the closure rule is there to check any possible misuse of this old privilege, it is equally true that the revised position of 1949 has made its applicability almost rare, if not wholly impossible.
4. The political role of the Senators smacks both of conservatism and political chicanery. If the Senate has done to disappoint the wishes of the Founding Fathers (as for instance in the sphere of making investigations), it has done something to fulfil their expectations by maintaining a strong defence of constitutional methods and powerful opposition to violent and high-handed opinions and actions.

5. Last, it may be remarked that the American Congress has the reverse tradition of keeping its upper house in a strong position overshadowing the authority of the lower one. When the position of the Senate is contrasted with that of the House, it looks like an upper chamber for technical reasons alone, otherwise it may well claim to be the first chamber of the Congress on the basis of its real prestige and authority.

Apart from these weaknesses, it remains to be said that the Senate stands not only as the most powerful upper chamber in the world, it is also the most successful political institution of the American constitutional system. It consists of the leading political personalities of the country and acts as a potent check on the executive authority of the President and, as is said in defence of a bi-cameral system, acts as a check on the rash, hasty and ill-considered legislation adopted by the lower chamber. Laski says that the Senate "gives a vivid reality to political democracy in the United States which no other institution as fully or so gladly supplies."[8]

House of Representatives

The lower chamber of the American Congress is known by the name of House of Representatives. It is a national chamber in the sense that it consists of 435 representatives elected directly by the people of 50 States in proportion to their population. Obviously, the organisation of the lower house is democratic where units of the American union have their representation on the basis of their population as a result of which big States have greater number of representatives than the smaller ones. The Founding Fathers wanted to organise the Senate on the federal principle and that is why they allotted two seats to every unit irrespective of its area or population. As the leading American writers put: "Intended as the popular branch of Congress, the House of Representatives was made larger and more responsive to the public will than the Senate. The latter, as a deliberative upper chamber, was made smaller and more removed from the popular pressure."[9]

Composition: The Constitution does not specify the strength of the house. It simply lays down three points in this regard–that the

8. Laski, *The American Democracy*, p. 92.

9. Ferguson and McHenry: *The American Federal Government*, Ed: X, p. 269.

Some Important Statements

The House sits not for serious discussion, but to sanction the conclusions of its committees as rapidly as possible. It legislates in committee rooms; not by determination of majorities, but by the resolutions of specially-commissioned minorities; so that it is not far from the truth to say that Congress in session is Congress on public exhibition, whilst Congress in committee-rooms is Congress at work. —***Woodrow Wilson***

Intended as the popular branch of Congress, the House of Representatives was made larger and more responsive to the public will than the Senate. The latter, as a deliberative upper chamber, was made smaller and more removed from the popular pressure. —***Ferguson and McHenry***

Members of the Congress specially those in the House of Representatives often find themselves virtually in the pocket of pressure groups compelled to do their biddings with far greater strength than the Congressmen feel themselves obliged to do at the biddings of the party. —***D.M. Berman***

representatives shall be appointed among several States according to their respective numbers, that there shall not be more than one member for every 30,000 people, and that every State shall be entitled to at least one representative regardless of its size or population. Due to this, the apportionment of seats became a matter of controversy and revision took place after every census until the Act of 1929 fixed the total number of representatives at 435 which was then increased to 437 in 1961 with the inclusion of two States in the American union–Alaska and Hawai for some time. In 1962 the strength of the House was reverted to 435.

The Constitution has vested the work of conducting elections in the States as a result of which times, places and manners of holding elections are prescribed by the laws of the States. But the Congress has the overriding power of making laws which may alter State laws and regulations. It has been clearly provided that no State can make any discrimination in the sphere of suffrage on the grounds of race, colour, sex, or previous condition of servitude. The Congress has passed a law providing that franchise cannot be restricted by a State on the basis of non-payment of poll taxes.

It follows from the above that it is within the authority of a State government to delimit constituencies which need not be equal, compact and contiguous. This loophole has given birth to a notorious practice called 'Gerrymandering' after the name of Elbridge Gerry of Massachusetts. It means electoral district making on a partisan basis for political reasons. The practice of Gerrymandering signifies an unnatural or arbitrary arrangement of electoral districts for considerations of personal or partisan

Allocation of Seats for States in the House of Representatives

S.No.	States	Seats	S.No.	States	Seats
1.	Alabama	7	27.	Nebraska	3
2.	Alaska	1	28.	Nevada	1
3.	Arizona	4	29.	New Hampshire	2
4.	Arkansas	4	30.	New Jersey	15
5.	California	43	31.	New Mexico	2
6.	Colarado	5	32.	New York	39
7.	Connecticut	6	33.	North Carolina	11
8.	Delaware	1	34.	North Dakota	1
9.	Florida	5	35.	Ohio	23
10.	Georgia	10	36.	Oklahoma	6
11.	Hawaii	2	37.	Oregon	4
12.	Idaho	2	38.	Pennsylvania	25
13.	Illinois	24	39.	Rhode Island	2
14.	Indiana	11	40.	South Carolina	6
15.	Iowa	6	41.	South Dakota	2
16.	Kansas	5	42.	Tennessee	8
17.	Kentucky	7	43.	Texas	24
18.	Louisiana	8	44.	Utah	2
19.	Maine	2	45.	Vermont	1
20.	Maryland	8	46.	Virginia	10
21.	Massachusetts	12	47.	Washington	7
22.	Michigan	19	48.	West Virginia	4
23.	Minnesota	8	49.	Wisconsin	9
24.	Mississipi	5	50.	Wyoming	1
25.	Missouri	10			
26.	Montana	2		Total 435	

advantages. It is all done to assure maximum possible chances of winning elections by shaping and reshaping electoral districts in a way that 'doubtful' parts of the constituency are mutilated. Due to the application of this pernicious device, the shape of electoral districts looks like a scorpion, serpentine, lizard, shoe-string, sadle-bell etc. The technique of Gerrymandering signifies that "in districting a State or city, spread the majority of your party all over, or over as many districts as possible. If you have enough votes to control every district, concentrate the strength of your opponents in as few districts as possible, so that it will do them the least good."[10]

10. Ogg and Ray: *Essential of American Government*, p. 192.

Qualifications and Term: The Constitution requires that a member of the House of Representatives must have three qualifications–that he must be the citizen of the United States of at least 7 years' standing, that he must be of at least 25 years of age, and that he must not be holding any office under the government of the United States. In addition, it is also needed that he must be the resident the State from which he is elected. A convention has developed to require that the representative must belong to the same Congressional district. This is called the locality rule to close the door for an outsider called 'carpet bagger'. The reason behind it is that only a local man knows the problems of his constituents and is expected to be their genuine representative. In order to fulfil this conventional qualification, leading political figures of the country have their residence or office in several towns of the States so that the constituents may carry conviction in the fact that even after election he "keeps his ear close to the ground–so close, as someone has said, that he gets it full of grass hoppers."[11]

It is provided that in the case of death or resignation of a member of the House of Representatives, the Governor of the State concerned shall call a special election for the unexpired portion of the term or in special circumstances may nominate someone to represent the constituents. Like Senate, the House of Representatives has the power of disqualifying its duly elected member on a substantive charge. For this a resolution must be passed by simple majority. For example, it refused to allow a duly elected representative (B.H. Roberts) of Utah to take his seat on the charge that he was a polygamist. The House also adopted, at the same time, a new rule that required the members or officers of the House, their principal assistants, and professional staff members of committees to file with the committee on standards of official conduct each year a report disclosing certain financial interests–which were to be available to the public–and a sealed report on the amount of income from their interests. As under the Senate rules, the sealed report could be opened by the committee only if it so decided that it was essential for an investigation, while the data that might be made public, were extremely limited.

The House of Representatives is elected for a term of two years. After every second year, elections take place in the month of November which the Americans call an "off year" in case the Presidential elections do not

---

11. Munro: *The Government of the United States*, p. 314.

coincide with the elections of this chamber. The House meets at least once a year. Its regular annual session begins on 3rd January and continues till the end of June or July. Both the houses of the Congress hold their meetings separately but simultaneously adjourn their sitting according to the resolution passed by them. But the President may adjourn the session if there is a disagreement between the two on the date and time of adjournment. If circumstances so require, the President may call an extra-ordinary session of the House. A majority of the members of the House is required to constitute its quorum. However, when the quorum is not available, 15 members may compel the attendance of absentees by instructing the Sergeant-at-arms to arrest and bring them to the House in order to keep the running business under transaction.

Speaker: The presiding officer of the House of Representatives is known as the Speaker. He is elected by the members of the House of Representatives. As the term of the House is two years, it is obvious that the election of the Speaker takes place at the beginning of the new house. Besides, as the election is held on party lines, it is further obvious that the nominee of the majority party wins. It is a matter of usage to re-elect the same man if the same party secures majority again in the house. Two factors are taken into account when a party caucus decides the name of its nominee–the seniority of the candidate and his popularity. As such, the American Speaker is a partyman and his office has a distinctly political character, something quite different from the English practice. It has put a big premium on the real significance of the office which the Americans, just for patriotic reasons, consider 'both ancient and honourable.'[12]

Neither the Constitution nor the rules of the house make the Speaker more than a modest man to preside over meetings in a modest way. However, much depends upon the personal equation and some occupants like Reed, Cannon and Longworth used their power in a way that they were dubbed as the 'Tsars' and' Dictators' by the members of the House. As the American Congress works with the help of its committees, the Speakers started the practice of inducting their own men into them and thereby determining the fate of every bill as per their personal wishes. The Speakers abused their power of making committees in a way that what they 'let through, it went through' and what they 'vetoed was decently buried in the committees." This state of affairs deteriorated so much so that in 1910 a war against Cannonism (Speakership of Cannon) broke out

12. *Ibid*, p. 323.

in which Speaker's autocracy was crushed when it was decided todeprive him of the power of making committees.[13]

The revolution of 1911 gave a serious blow to the autocratic authority of the Speaker and restored to the House its power of making committees. Yet it does not imply that the Speaker has become without any power of his own, or his office has grown similar to that occupied by the chairman of the House of Lords or the Senate. Still, he possesses some important powers. He presides over the meetings of the House and can call upon any member to hold his seat when he vacates it for a short duration. He exercises his power of recognition. The Speaker maintains order and decorum in the House. He can name a member and also adjourn the house for some time in the situation of grave disorder. He can have the lobbies and galleries cleared and instruct his Sergeant-at-arms to push a recalcitrant member out of the chamber. He applies and interprets rules of the House and decides the points of order. If there is any ambiguity in the rules of procedure or in the event of conflicting interpretations of a situation, he gives his ruling by exercising his power of discretion. After a bill gets first reading, he refers it to the committee and "sometimes exercises considerable discretion but is ultimately subject to the will of the House.'[14]

The significance of the office of the Speaker should be examined from this point as well that he is next to the Vice-President in the list of President's successors. And yet the American Speaker cannot have that dignity as is possessed by his English counterpart. For the reason of being a political man, he is considered a partisan officer by the other side. He takes part in the politics of the country by living on the side of his own party. It is reported that some of the Speakers like Longworth won encomiums from the minority for defending their interests. The result has been that despite the fall of the 'Tsars' in the revolution of 1911, the American Speaker has retained some iota of authority without having a total loss of his leadership.

Committee System: The committees have a very important place in the working of the American Congress, since they determine the fate of a bill which is referred to them after the formal first reading without any discussion in the House. Thus, Woodrow Wilson called his government as 'government by the committees'. Others have used the phrase that the committees are 'little ministers with enormous power.' Both chambers of

13. Brogan: *The American Political System*, p. 194.

14. Ferguson and McHenry, *op. cit.*, p. 282.

the American Congress work with the help of Standing Committees, though other kinds of committees are also set up for special purposes. No doubt, these committees "are the most important class of committees, for they are a screen which sifts the great mass of proposed legislation."[15]

Following points deserve attention as regards the composition of the standing committees:

1. The standing committees in the House are constituted after every second year when the new chamber meets, while Senatorial standing committees never die and some changes in their composition take place after every second year when 1/3 seats are filled up.
2. The committees are elected by the respective houses which is just a formality as the slates of names are already made by the parties concerned in rough proportion to their strength in the chamber and those names are ratified by the house in a formal manner.
3. As far as possible, it is kept in view that a Representative serves on one of the major standing committees, while a Senator on not more than two.
4. The assignment is made on the basis of seniority as well as special interest of the member in various matters.
5. The chairmanship of a committee is given on the basis of seniority and the chairman has a free-hand in appointing his staff or in selecting members for any sub-committee, if so required.
6. These committees hold their meetings *in camera* or in public as desired by them and the people at large may be invited to give evidence for some important consideration.
7. The chairman by virtue of his special ability or personal equation may enhance his area of authority and exercise a more or less free-hand in making agenda, giving time for debates, deciding places of sitting, calling public for evidence and doing so many other dexterous things in order to influence the working and decision-making process of the committee.

Apart from these standing committees, mention may be made of other committees as well. For instance, there are temporary special committees which are set up to deal with a special kind of matter not covered by various standing committees. These committees are appointed by the chairman of the House for a definite period and for a specific work on the basis of a resolution adopted by the House or the Senate. Special

15. *Ibid*, p. 281.

investigating committees are a case in this regard. Then, there may be a joint conference committee to hammer out some agreement between the two chambers of the Congress if there is a matter of controversy. Such a committee consists of equal number of members of both the houses and its report is final. Last, we come to the committee of the whole house - a prototype of its English counterpart. This committee as its name indicates, consists of all the members of the house without the Speaker and also without the rigidity of the rules of procedure.

If the American committee system is compared and contrasted with its British counterpart, certain points of resemblance and difference appear. Similarity lies in the fact that in both countries legislative business is conducted in the committees; the committees are virtually constituted by the selection committees of different political parties in rough proportion to their respective strength in the house; and the principles of seniority and special interest have their definite part. However, certain subtle differences are there. First, the American committees play a more important role than the English committees for the reason that in America a bill comes for discussion first before the committee and then before the house, while in Britain a bill is referred to the committee after second reading. That is, the decision over the life and death of a bill is taken in the house in Britain but in a committee in America. Second, Britain has cabinet government in which bills are moved by the ministers and hence there is a difference between official and private member's bill. A bill moved by the minister has almost every chance of being passed by the committee as the cabinet has 'usurped' the powers of the legislature. This is not so in America where every bill is a private member's bill and its adoption does not depend upon the use of whips but on the process of log-rolling. Above all, there is a big difference in the way of their functioning. In America committees hold public meetings and invite the people at large for some evidence. This is not the case with the committees of the British Parliament.

Legislative Process: The legislative process of the American Congress is similar to that of Britain in many respects. The main point of difference lies in the fact that there is nothing like government bill in the United States sponsored by a member of the treasury which must be passed by the House of Commons in order to avoid the defeat of the ministry. As a result, every bill moved in the Congress is, what is called in Britain, a non-official bill or a private member's bill. Moreover, as there is want of strict party discipline maintained by the whips, the members have to requisition the support of other groups on certain promises–a practice that goes by the name of 'log-rolling.' This is in sharp contrast to the British practice. Again, pork-barrel is the main feature of American legislation. That is, the legislators endeavour to have laws for the benefit of their constituents just for the political reason of brightening their electoral chances in the ensuing elections. Apart from these major points of difference, there is similarity in the process that the bill must be passed by both the houses with simple majority after three readings and finally assented to by the head of the State.

The legislative process involves three stages which are as under: The first stage called the introduction of the bill requires that the mover drop his bill into the box (hopper) of the Secretary of the House of Representatives or deposit it with the clerk of the Senate in case he belongs to the upper chamber of the Congress. The first reading is a pure formality and it is taken to be completed as soon as the title of the bill is printed in the Congressional Record and Journal.

Then comes the second reading which determines the life and death of a bill whether it is public bill of general application or a private bill having its concern with a particular place or people. Unlike the British practice, a bill moved by a member soon after its first reading is referred to a committee with a specific number allotted to it. This is called the committee stage. The members of the committee make serious deliberations and either favourably report to the house, or reject it, or adopt it with some amendments, or rewrite it completely in the name of making necessary changes, or even pigeonhole it by making no report to the house at all. In case some relevant information is required for a proper discussion, the committee may take the help of the Congress library. Interested officials and heads of the departments may, either on the request of the committee or on their own initiative subject to discretion of the chairman or members of the committee, may appear to speak in favour of or against the bill. It depends upon the will of the committee to hold public session for eliciting more information. The rigorous sifting of bills at the committee stage is very important in the life of a bill as here the question of a bill's adoption or rejection is almost settled. Woodrow Wilson was right in his assessment that "Congress in its committee rooms is Congress at work."

After a bill is passed by the committee, it is placed on the Union Calendar; a public bill other than a money bill is placed on the House Calendar; a private bill is placed on the Private Calendar; if a bill has to be passed without much delay due to urgent circumstances, it is placed on the Consent Calendar. On the first and third Monday of the month, the clerk reads out its title and in case no objection is raised to its immediate consideration, the bill is deemed to have been finally passed by the House. Last is the Discharge Calendar on which a bill is placed if is forced out of the committee by a special resolution passed by the absolute majority of the House. If such a motion is carried, the bill is 'snatched' from the committee and placed before the House for its consideration and subsequent adoption within 7 days of grace. Sub a motion may be taken up only on second and fourth Mondays and requires a simple majority for its adoption."[16]

Discussion over a bill in the house or in the committee of the whole house marks the presentation of the matter before all members when general debate starts in which motions for amendments are put in order to add or delete something. There is no filibustering in the House and closure motions are applied to check irrelevant and time-consuming discussion. The Speaker has the power to disallow dilatory motions and Rules of the House allow a member to speak for not more than one hour save without the unanimous consent of the whole house. After the discussion is over, voting takes place to decide the matter.

A bill passed in the second reading signifies its final adoption by the House as third reading is just a formality. It involves merely reading of the title of the bill and a vote unless a member for hardly any other reason than obstructing it demands that the bill be read in full. Some minor amendments may be proposed by a member or members, but after a little interval, the bill is passed by the house and is transmitted to the Senate with Speaker's signature. When the Senate takes up a bill, same procedure is adopted as a result of which the bill passes through similar stages with two differences. The first point of difference is that there is no use of the teller plan in voting, and the decision is taken by the voice vote, or standing vote, or roll-call vote. But the second point is quite startling: there is no closure motion and the members can speak freely for any length of time individually or with the help of their professional groups to see that their purpose of political bargaining is served. This is called filibustering.

A bill passed by both the houses goes to the President for his assent. Ten days' time is given to him (excluding Sunday) within which he must

16. Wilson, *op. cit.* p. 79.

take action. He may give his assent and then the bill becomes an act. The President may veto the bill, or return it to the Congress with his objections or recommendations. If the bill is re-passed by the Congress, the President must put his signatures in order to have the bill placed on the statute book. In case a bill is rejected by the President, the Congress may over-ride his veto by repassing the same bill by 2/3 majority. It shows that the veto power of the President is both absolute and qualified. There is one more variety of the veto power which is called 'pocket veto'. If the session of the Congress is over within the period of 10 days given to the President and he takes no action on the bill, then the bill shall be taken as 'killed' and not rejected by the veto power of the chief executive. Unlike British monarch, the American President makes use of all varieties of his veto power.

Apart from certain points of difference between the English and American legislative processes, some more points may be taken into account at this stage. It is quite noticeable that there is no such thing as judicial review in Britain and, that is why, a law passed by the Parliament cannot be declared *ultra vires* of the Constitution by the courts. It reveals the sovereign character of British Parliament. Another point deserving our attention is that the veto power of the monarch is a 'dead' weight as he never uses it. Convention requires that a bill passed by the Parliament must not be vetoed by the monarch. As a result, every bill is assented to by the monarch, while some bills are vetoed by the President and sometimes some of them are re-passed by the Congress to over-ride the veto. It is also noteworthy that committees do not play a very important role to the extent of killing or pigeonholing a bill in the British legislative process as they do in the United States. The British Parliament is the master and its committees behave like its subordinate agencies. The reason for this lies in the fact that while in Britain a bill is referred to the committee after its full discussion in the house, it is referred to a committee in the United States prior to the decision of the house.

10

SUPREME COURT

It is quite clear from the language of the American Constitution that the Founding Fathers, while endeavouring to implement the system of separation of powers associated with the arrangement of checks and balances considered the Supreme Court sitting at the apex of the federal judiciary as the "third member of governmental trinity, no less important than the other two members."[1] Apart from setting up three separate departments acting as a check upon one another, equally more compelling reason was the federal pattern which informed the framers to install an independent and impartial judiciary for the sake of interpreting the words and phrases of the fundamental law of the land and acting as a referee in matters of constitutional dispute between the national and state governments. However, many important changes took place in the American political system as a result of which the original design of checks and balances could not survive as the judiciary assumed most powerful position. Munro rightly holds that the development of the Supreme Court into a final arbiter of constitutional disputes "is one of America's most important contributions to the science of government."[2]

Organisation: The Constitution is silent on the issues of number, qualifications, salaries, emoluments and period of service of the judges of the Supreme Court. It empowers the Congress to cover these matters by legislation. As a result, the Supreme Court came into being in 1789 according to a law made by the Congress with a Chief Justice and six associate Judges. The number of judges was increased to 9. The judges are nominated by the President subject to their ratification by the Senate. As there is no constitutional or ordinary law specifying the qualifications

1. E.S. Griffith: *The American System of Government*, p. 159.
2. W.B. Munro: *The Government of the United States*, p. 547.

Some Important Statements

I do not think that the United States would come to an end if we (the Court) lost our power to declare an Act of Congress void. I think that the Union would be imperilled if we could make that declaration as to the laws of the several States.

—***Justice Holmes***

The Supreme Court is the keeper of American conscience; it is essentially the conscience of the American upper middle class sharpened by the imperative of individual social responsibility and political activism and conditioned by the Conservative impact of legal training and professional legal attitudes and associations.

—***John R. Schmidhauser***

The 'due process' has meant not a road but a gate and the thing it barred was any attempt to transform political democracy in the United States into social democracy.

—***H.J. Laski***

of a judge, it is clear that the matter depends upon the political action of the President. In the absence of clear cut constitutional or legal requirements, the President is free to appoint anyone for whom Senatorial confirmation can be obtained. Terms are for good behaviour. Temporary suspensions are probably constitutional, if surrounded by safeguards, but short of impeachment there is no way of compelling an aged, lazy, incompetent, or corrupt judge to vacate his office. Facts illustrate that though the Constitution of the United States says nothing about the qualifications of a judge, actual practice may be found to have imposed three requirements in this regard - that he must have a formal legal training, that he must hail from a family having a high social status, and that he must be having a political standing in the country.

The appointment of a judge is made on a permanent basis for life and it is a matter of his will to retire at the age of 65 (after 15 years of service) or resign at the age of 70 after serving for ten years. His service is secure during his 'good behaviour'. In case the House of Representatives initiates a charge against a judge based on the allegation of treason, bribery or other high crime of misdemeanour, the matter goes to the Senate where a resolution passed by 2/3 majority is required to remove the accused from office and punish him with future disqualifications. So far 9 judges of constitutional courts have been impeached of whom 4 were convicted. Samuel Chase was the only judge of the Supreme Court to stand trial on the charges of impeachment.

Jurisdiction and Judicial Review: The annual session of the Supreme Court opens on first Monday of October and runs till the end of June or so. Special sessions may be called by the Chief Justice during the period of adjournment in the event of some matter of unusual or urgent importance. The Chief Justice presides over sessions and conferences of the Court and announces its verdicts, but he does not command a special position as a matter is decided by vote. In case the Chief Justice is absent, the session is presided over by a judge having precedence over others, the matter being settled by the rule of seniority based on the point of length of service and date of birth in case the appointment of judges is of the same date. The Court hears a case for a period of two weeks meeting on days from Tuesday to Friday. On Saturday the judges meet *in camera* and register their views so that the judgement is delivered in public on Monday.

The Supreme Court has both original and appellate jurisdictions which may be thus clarified:

Original Jurisdiction	*Appellate Jurisdiction*
1. Action by the United States against a State.	1. From lower districts courts.
2. Action by a State against a State.	2. From State courts when a federal question is involved.
3. Cases involving ambassadors and other public ministers.	
4. Actions by a State against citizens of another State or aliens (here jurisdiction is not exclusive).	

The Supreme Court does not exercise advisory jurisdiction. It has consistently 'rebuffed' the President and the Congress to advise on 'abstract' points. However, the judgement of the Supreme Court is final and no appeal can lie against it.

Apart from this, what has made the Supreme Court the most powerful organ of the federal government is the power of judicial review in the hands of the judges. It implies that the Supreme Court and Federal courts have the power to declare an order passed by the executive or a law made by the legislature inoperative in case and to the extent there is the violation of the constitution. In America the judges apply the second criterion of 'due process of law' as well while using the power of judicial review for the reason that, in the eyes of the judges, it is an historic safeguard against arbitrary governmental actions affecting life, liberty and property of the people. Prof. H.J. Abraham defines the term to mean the power of any court "to hold unconstitutional and hence unenforceable by law, any official action based upon it, and any illegal action by a public official that it deems...to be in conflict with the Basic Law, in the United States its Constitution."[3]

By virtue of this distinctive attribute, any federal court can declare an impugned executive or legislative measure unconstitutional, but the Supreme Court has final authority in this regard. It is a fact that the Constitution does not specifically empower the courts in this regard, but the power has been wielded by virtue of 'reading into the fundamental law of the land' by the judges of the Supreme Court. It is true to say that the power of judicial review in the hands of the judges has come by prescription. The first instance took place in 1803 when Chief Justice Marshall gave his historic judgement in the case of *Marbury* v. *Madison.* For the sake of clarity, four implications of this decision may be put as under:

(*i*) That the Constitution is a written document that clearly defines and limits the powers of government;

(*ii*) That the Constitution is a fundamental law and thus superior to the ordinary law passed by the Congress.

(*iii*) That the act of Congress which is contrary to and in violation of the fundamental law is void and cannot bind the courts; and

(*iv*) That the judicial power conferred by the Constitution together with the oath to uphold Constitution which the justices take on the assumption of office, requires that the courts should declare when they believe that the acts of Congress are in violation of the Constitution.

From 1803 onwards, the Supreme Court has made use of this innovatory power and thereby established a strong and also unchallengeable position that, as Justice Frankfurter once confidently asserted, it has 'become the constitution'. However, it may be pointed out that the scope of judicial review is not unlimited. The exercise of this distinctive attribute is tied up and these considerations ought to be kept in view. First, the power is a clear proof of the judicial supremacy empowering the judges to determine whether an executive order or a legislative measure is in conformity with the constitutional provisions and thereby 'valid' or

3. Abraham. *The Judicial Process,* p. 251.

not. Second, it is not a prospective but a retrospective power which means that an executive order or a legislative enactment made in the past is *ultra vires* of the Constitution and so unenforceable. Third, the federal judiciary of the United States can make use of this power in regard to 'federal questions' and also exercise this prerogative even in cases of executive orders and legislative measures issued by the State governments. Fourth, there is nothing like an automatic exercise of this power. The courts can not take any initiative in this direction; they can decide the matter only when it is brought before them by the aggrieved party. Last, the Supreme Court is the 'masterless man' in this regard and it can change its own view as the circumstances demand.

Critical Appreciation: Undoubtedly, the distinctive attribute of judicial review has exalted the position of federal judiciary at the expense of the powers of the executive and the legislature and thereby given a rude setback to the system of checks and balances so well devised by the framers of the Constitution. Laski calls it 'undemocratic' in view of the fact that five judges of the Court may invalidate any order of the President or a law of the Congress and thereby sit in judgement over the actions of those elected by the millions of voters of the country. In most of the cases, the view of the judges in informed by the canons of conservatism. For instance, the American Supreme Court struck down New Deal legislation that was made to deal with the serious crisis of Great Depression in the early 1930s. Then, in a mood of irritation, President F.D. Roosevelt had to debunk the American constitution as 'a relic of horse and buggy days' and he had to think in terms of 'packing up the Court.' It is a different matter that it could not happen.

However, it may be commented that the power of judicial review in the hands of federal judges is not without its utility. Apart from being a source of occasional irritation to the President, to the Congress and to the State governments, it has protected the republican-federal system of the United States. The Supreme Court has been lauded as the continuous constitutional convention at work. Through this power, the Supreme Court has acted as the guardian of the national constitution, protecting its fundamental principles from encroachments by legislative and executive branches of the national government and also from the governments of the component units of the American union.

11

POLITICAL PARTIES AND PRESSURE GROUPS

Political Parties

Like Britain, the emergence of party system in the United States is a matter of extra-constitutional growth. As already pointed out, it has belied the sincere expectations of the founding fathers who had deliberately sought to envisage a framework of government which, as Madison said, would be free from the 'violence of the faction.' In spite of the solemn warning issued by the greatest leader of the nascent American nation (Washington) against the sinister role of political parties, the growth of party system occurred gradually but incessantly. His successors took note of the same 'pernicious' development and Jefferson in his farewell address had to observe that political parties "are likely, in the course of time and things, to become potent energies by which cunning, ambitious and unprincipled men will be enabled to subvert the power of the people and to usurp for themselves the reins of government." "The inevitability could not be undone" and, as Munro says, the calls for a partyless politics "fell on deaf ears."[1] So much so that by the middle of the nineteenth century, party system became a recognised fact of the American political life. It is well observed: "The American party system consists of two major elements, each of which performs in specified ways or follows customary behaviour pattern in the total system. To remove or alter the role of one element would destroy the system or create a new one."[2]

General Features: Since the party system of every country has some special features of its own, the salient characteristics of the American party system may be enumerated as under:

1. W.B. Munro, *The Government of the United States*, p. 115.

2. V.O. Key, Jr: *Politics, Parties and Pressure Groups*, V.Ed., p. 206.

Some Important Statements

No America without democracy, no democracy without politics, no politics without parties, no parties without compromise and moderation.

—***Clinton Rossiter***

The party is more human than the state, more approachable, more intimate in its relations than the government. The party is in a sense a political church which does not require very regular attendance or have a very strict creed.

—***Merriam and Gosnell***

There are two great and several minor parties in the United States. What are their principles, their distinctive tenets, their tendencies? This is what an European is always asking of intelligent Republicans and intelligent Democrats. He is always asking, because he never gets an answer. The replies leave him in deeper perplexity.

—***Lord James Bryce***

1. America is known for having a bi-party system. The Democrats and the Republicans are the two major parties and the power alternates between them. In a strict sense, America may be described as having a multi-party system as there have been several 'minor' parties. But their value is equal to nothing as they have never been able to make a tilt in the distribution of power.
2. The American parties lack the essential ingredient of what is meant by the 'party' in other democratic countries of the world. The element of ideology is missing. The two parties differ on issues as they are, not on the lines of ideological commitments.
3. The American parties may be described as federations of specific interests. The absence of the ideological factor has made them like coalitions of interests. Leading American 'writers admit that no political association can be more motley than their Democratic Party and the Republicans, for all their sterner commitments to principle and respectability are very much less of an army with a hundred different banners. Both parties are happily described as a vast enterprise in 'group diplomacy'.
4. The structure of the American political parties is marked by decentralisation of authority and consequent enfeebling of discipline to an exaggerated degree. Both parties may be regarded as loose confederacies of States' parties since the locus of power is not there at the Centre. Each party has its units at the Centre and below, *i.e.*, at the State and local levels where its unit looks like an independent, self-sustaining, sovereign force in the balance of political forces.

5. The American party system not only exhibits the total absence of what is ill-named as 'bossism', it also shows that both parties pick up candidates for the Presidency or important seats in the Senate from amongst those who have never held their membership. That is, each party may go for the rank 'outsiders' in matters of nominations for the top elective posts.

In fine, the American party system displays "more *pluribus* (plurality) than *unnum* (uniformity)."[3] It would not be wrong to say that the structure of each American party smacks of a peculiar brand of feudalism "with few enforceable pledges of faith, feudalism in which the bonds of mutual support are also loose that it often seems to border on anarchy, feudalism in which one party does not even have a king."[4]

Absence of Ideology: The absence of ideology and its presence in a different sense in the American party system is certainly a surprising feature having no comparison with its British counterpart. An analysis of voting behaviour in the Congress reveals that there is hardly a single issue that brings about a clear-cut division between the two parties and a sizable proportion of their members is invariably found on each side of the controversy. Herman Finer goes to the extent of saying that in America there is only one political party–Republican-cum-Democratic Party–divided into two nearly equal halves by habits and the contest for office. In the earlier days of the Constitution the division appeared more clear, but with the passage of time, it blurred so much so that Lord James Bryce in his scholarly study could maintain that the great parties of America were like two bottles of liquor each having a different label but no wine.[5]

Much change in this regard has also occurred owing to quick progress of the country in the economic sphere. Now the factors of economics and regionalism are so inextricably intermixed with each that the basic elements of 'agriculture' *v.* 'industry', or the menacing features of 'solid north' *v.* 'solid south' no longer figure prominently. Each party, as says Brogan, is basically traditional marked off from its rival, not by any doctrine or class but by ancestry and geographical distribution of strength.[6] Leading American writers endorse that no party "ever enlisted the undivided support

3. Stephen K. Bailey: *The Condition of Four National Parties,* p. 7.
4. Clinton Rossiter, *Parties and Politics in America.,* p. 13.
5. Bryce: *The American Commonwealth,* Vol. II, pp. 344-45.
6. D.W. Brogan: *An Introduction to American Political System,* p.x.

of any entire economic interest or group or geographical section."[7] Laski has put his impression in these words that the American party system "is more like a bloc of interests than a system of principles."[8] It may be easily found that both parties "are interested in the votes of men, not in the principles, and they care not at all whether the votes they gather are bestowed with passion or with indifference–so long as they are bestowed and counted. The task that they have uppermost in mind is the construction of a victorious majority, and in a country as large and diverse as ours this calls for programmes and candidates having as nearly universal an appeal as the imperatives of politics will permit."[9]

Party System at Work: We have seen that the American party system lacks the essential traits of a responsible party system finding their place in a party's adopting a reasonably clear programme and having some centralised authority to exercise effective control over all subordinate units. Though either of the two parties wins national elections relating to the offices of the President, the Senators and the Representatives, it is difficult to say as to what mandate is with it. One may draw some broad points from the survey of important utterances made by the candidates during the time of election campaigns, but a thing like voters' mandate is either missing altogether, or it is too general, even vague, not explicit. And yet the working of the American party system shows that they perform, though with uneven success, on account of this fact that they are only one of the several forces working towards co-ordination in the government.[10]

A study of the American party system in its operational dimension reveals that they are very active at the time of the elections of the President, the Senators and the Representatives. It does not mean that they are of out of work after the election business is over. Their prominent role can be understood when the session of the Congress starts. Matters relating to the election of the Speaker, formation of the committees and the election of their chairmen, introduction of bills and debates thereon *etc.* are all conducted on party lines. The appointments made by the President are governed by party consideration, so is with their ratification by the Senate.

7. Ogg and Ray, *Essentials of American Government*, p. 41-42.
8. Laski: *The American Presidency*. p. 79.
9. Clinton Rossiter, *op. cit.*, p. 11.
10. Monsma, *op. cit.*, p. 308.

The result is that the highest bureaucrats of the country are usually of the same party as the President aids in communication and co-ordination. The members of the President's party in the Congress form a natural starting point for his attempts to influence the Congress and, for this reason, are called "President's friends". In this way, the party 'helps to bind the disparate formal institutions of the political system together."[11]

Since the American constitutional system is based on the principle of separation of powers, decision-making agencies are different and also disparate. The parties play the role of a co-ordinator. At the same time, the supplementary structure of checks and balances enables them to establish a sort of interlinking bond between different organs of the department. Thus, we find that President not being a member of the Congress manages to influence the legislative behaviour. It also happens that while the Presidency is captured by one party, the Congress by another. In such a situation there occurs the 'deadlock of democracy.' And yet it is the loose party system of the United States that acts as the resolver of conflicts. One may ask as to how does it happen? The answer is that often persons "jump the party tracks and work at cross-purposes with their fellow party members. This occurs within the Congress, within the bureaucracy, between the Congress and the President, between the President and the bureaucracy, and on and on."[11]

Critical Appreciation: The party systems of the United States and the United Kingdom resemble in a few but differ in many respects. First, we take up the case of some points of resemblance. In the first place, both countries are well-known for having a bi-party system. The Conservative and the Labour parties in England and the Democrats and the Republicans in the United States are the examples of the two major parties. Moreover, while some other or minor parties exist in both the countries, they have no real significance as the alternation of power invariably takes place between the two leading parties. One may say that, it is rather a superficial point as the very nature of the American party system is basically different from that of the United Kingdom. Second, party system in both countries is a matter of extra-constitutional growth. Political parties have no place in the written parts of the constitutions of the two countries under reference. The evolution of party system in both countries is a matter of conventional development.

The points of difference between the American and British party systems are vital. In the first place, while British party system stands on

11. *Ibid.*

the basis of the principles or a definite ideology, there is nothing like it in the case of the American party system. American parties have never been bodies of men united on some general principles into concrete form by legislation and by administration. "It is considered wise to begin by accepting the fact that the emptiness of the names of the two great American parties may be significant, not of the emptiness of the role of parties, but of the fact that they cannot be understood, if they are judged in European, or more strictly British, terms."[12]

Pressure Groups

A novel feature of the American political system should be discovered not in the operation of a representative democracy through political parties taking part in the biennial elections of the Congress and the quadrennial elections of the President but in the role of several interest organisations operating at every level through which the people sharing common economic or social characteristics or policy objectives struggle for the protection and promotion of their specific interests. There is no dearth of such groups, though only some of them may be taken for the purpose of our study as they play their part in the determination of an official policy or in the implementation of some governmental law or order.

General Characteristics: In the United States, there are literally thousands of pressure groups of varying size, structure, functions and influence ranging from the National Association of Manufactures (NAM) and American Federation of Labour–Congress of Industrial Organisation (AFL-CIO), American Medical Association, American Bar Association, American Civil Liberties Union *etc.* to local and social or cultural groups like Southern Christian Leadership Conference and Urban League. Our concern, in the main, is with those principal organisations which seek to affect public policy. The salient features of their operation may be put as under:

1. Pressure groups in the United States are numerous; they are also autonomous to a very great extent. The reason for this lies in America's being a vast democratic country with a federal system and having a huge population dedicated to the ideals of mammon-worship and pragmatism. The party system is too weak to keep the numerous groups in order. The result is that organised

12. Brogan, *op. cit.*, p. 46.

groups feel nothing like committed to a particular political party. Not only this, the role of groups is so potential that it determines the behaviour of the political parties in most of the cases and not *vice versa.*

2. The constitutional system of the United States is such that the pressure groups find ample scope for making their influence felt. There is separation of powers coupled with the system of checks and balances with the result that the decision of one department may be checked by another. Interest groups thus fix their attention at all centres of decision-making, including its implementation. American political system stands on the principle of separation of powers whereby the will of the President cannot become a law in every case and that the federal judiciary may strike down any order of the President or any law of the Congress on the ground of its being *ultra vires* of the Constitution. Mostly the groups have their eyes fixed on the President as he is the virtual ruler of the country, but when they fear some frustration, they make their potential articulation through the legislative bodies with the result that there is pressure and cross-pressure on the government. Sometimes, lobbying assumes a very serious proportion to act as a counter blast to the authority of the President as a result of which there occurs, what is called, the deadlock of democracy.
3. What makes the subject of American pressure groups a matter of interesting study as well as an object of denunciation is their technique of lobbying. It means exercising pressure on public officials in order to have the purpose served, though in a strict sense its application is taken as confined to persuade and influence the members of the Congress who are concerned with the business of legislation. In actual practice, the scope of lobbying has now covered almost every nook and corner of the American administration whether at the national, or state, or local level. Not only this, sometimes the lobbyists go to the final extent of bearing their weight upon the public officials by all means, whether proper or improper, that becomes 'grass-roots lobbying'. Though one may find glimpses of the use of this technique even in other countries like Britain and France, it may be said that the magnitude of lobbying in the United States has no parallel in the world. Legitimate use of this technique is contained in the observation of a leading Congressman: "Lobbying is an essential part of the representative government, and it needs to be encouraged and appreciated."

Some Important Statements

American pressure groups know no institutional bounds. They attempt to influence any decision of the political system that affects their interests, whether these decisions are made by the Congress, the Presidency, bureaucracy, or the judiciary.

—***Stephen V. Monsma***

When a number of men are united for the defence, maintenance or enhancement of any more or less enduring position or advantage which they possess alike in common, the term 'interest' is applied both to the groups so united as to the cause which unites them. —***R.M. MacIver***

Politics rests ultimately upon the conflict and accommodation of interests brought into being by the manifold inequalities of a society; broadly speaking, political decision will follow the course along which it is led by the relative strength of interests. —***J.D.B. Miller***

Lobbying: The technique of lobbying implies putting influence on the men in authority roles, it covers every sphere of the government whether legislative, or executive, or judicial. It would be too simple a view to agree with the phraseology of the law of 1946 or the interpretation of the Supreme Court of 1954 that the scope of this tactic is limited to influencing the members of the Congress only. Today no branch of American government can be said to be immune from the onslaught of the technique of lobbying. The strictly legal implication is thus totally unrealistic in view of the fact that the executive agencies "have given considerable leeway in implementing legislation through interpretation and administrative rule-making. In addition, the groups wish to influence policy proposals that are often authored in the agencies and then sponsored by Congressmen. For their part, members of the Congress branch want the co-operation and political support of their clientele in their dealing with the Congress.[13]

No doubt, the technique of lobbying has its own set of evils, but the Americans have their own notions about its legitimacy. To them it may be regulated but not outlawed as its abolition would amount to the infringement of the essential liberties relating to speech, expression and assembly as provided in the Constitution by the First Ten Amendments. To them the principal method of regulating lobbying is disclosure rather than control. They agree that the statutory definition of this term has been unclear and the enforcement of the Federal Regulation of Lobbying Act of 1946 minimal. It is clear from the fact that so far disclosures have been

13. Sigler and Getz, *Contemporary American Government*, p. 252.

few giving limited information and thus their effects have been of a questionable nature. It is also feared by many people that severe restrictions on the tactic of lobbying would hamper legitimate methods of influencing the decision-makers without checking more serious abuses. To them, the consolidated and highly effective opposition of the lobbies cannot be lost sight of. Moreover, it is also emphasised that there should be no ban on the desire of some capable men who want "to keep open avenues to a possible lobby career they may wish to pursue later."

Critical Appreciation: The existence and articulation of interest groups has been denounced by the critics for being opposed to the doctrine of the genuine representation of, what Rousseau called, the general will. It is also said that in this type of politics, very shrewd and corrupt leadership enjoys a position of special advantage at the expense of the position of others who are more deserving than them. It is also alleged that the behaviour of the interest groups is hardly democratic either towards their own members or other groups operating at the same level. The manner of ' hide and seek in polities' as shown by the groups not only differentiates them with political parties, it also makes them immune from public accountability. All these evils of the politics of influence are very much existent in the United States, though other democratic countries of the world cannot be said to be exceptions in this regard.

If the politics of pressure groups has its weaknesses, it has its strong sides also. According to leading American people, such type of politics makes its own important contribution to the successful operation of their democratic system. The interest groups "play an indispensable function in identifying the interests in the society to which the political system must respond. They also serve to increase participation and to clarify issues in connection with the other great input function of the political system - leadership selection. Pressure groups thus offer an important supplement to the official system of representation. By permitting a more precise expression of special interests than can be expected through the broad political parties or through district's Representative, pressure groups may prevent a sense of alienation and enhance the stability of the system."[14]

14. M.D. Irish and J.W. Prothro: *The Politics of American Democracy*, p. 254.

Part - III

Swiss Constitution

Among the modern democracies which are true democracies, the Helvetic Republic has the highest claim to be studied. It contains a greater variety of institutions based on democratic principles than any other country. The most interesting lesson Switzerland teaches is how traditions and institutions, taken together, may develop in the average man to an extent never reached before the qualities which make a good citizen—shrewdness, modernity, commonsense and sense of duty to the community. It is because this has come to pass in Switzerland that democracy is more truly democratic than in any other country in the world.

—Lord James Bryce

12

CONSTITUTION OF SWITZERLAND

A comprehensive study of the Swiss political system in a work on modern political systems has certain pertinent reasons of its own. Though Switzerland is a small and land-locked country of Europe, her political institutions occupy a very significant place in the sphere of major constitutional systems of the world. Indeed, the Swiss system has successfully integrated a population characterised by social, linguistic, religious and cultural diversities into a united nation and demonstrated the possibility of close co-operation between peoples who at one time "were independent of each other politically and who today are widely divided by language and religion."[1] Not only from a religious or ethnic but also from the political standpoint, the Swiss constitutional system is peculiarly important. It is primarily due to the fact that throughout the ages Switzerland has been a republic; the monarchist ways of thinking have been alien to the people. The Swiss, unlike the British or the French, has no understanding for the powers and privileges of a ruler, and thus for him the state "is an affair of all citizens, and its guidance is not to be hereditary, nor is it to be entrusted to an elected individual."[2]

Swiss Constitutionalism

Two strong impressions may be gathered from what we have said. First, democracy with its offshoots in the spheres of liberalism and federalism is the basic touchstone of the Swiss political system. Second, the history of Swiss political institutions is deceptively long owing to the

1. Buell and others: *Democratic Governments in Europe*, p. 558.

2. See Hans Huber: *How Switzerland is Governed.*

fact that the people of this country did not live under a strong and unified government until late in the eighteenth century. Though the Swiss Confederation being the oldest of the existing federal states of the world and founded in the successful struggle of three districts–called the Forest cantons–against the over-lordship of Austria in the 13th century, it expanded to 13 States (cantons) when it was recognised as sovereign and independent by the Treaty of Westphalia of 1648. It was by all means a loose league of States with no strong central power at that time. And so it continued to have its chequered career through the storms and confusion of the French Revolution and Napoleonic Wars so much so that even in the general settlement of 1815 it did not find its final basis of stability. It was still too loose, as was shown in a short civil war begun in 1847 by 7 Roman Catholic Cantons (Sonderbund) which, like the Southern Confederacy in the United States in 1861, attempted to secede from the general body. Revision of the Constitution immediately followed the defeat of the seceding cantons, and the constitution of 1848 transformed the old confederation (Staatenbund) into a federal State (Bunderstaat)[3]. The Constitution of 1848 was radically revised in 1874, and the Constitution of that year, subsequently amended in certain features, was the one under which Switzerland was governed till the inauguaration of the new constitution is 2000."

The Constitution of 1848 was essentially the creation of a committee of 23 men elected by their colleagues in the Diet or, in the case of a few recalcitrant cantons, appointed by its Chairman. As members of the Diet, most of them were also chiefs of their cantonal governments. The ones who came from the liberal cantons had also participated in the liberal revision of their cantonal Constitutions. The large majority were members of the legal profession, supplanted by a few merchants, two doctors and a few high-ranking officers who had just returned from the Sonderbund War. Perhaps the most interesting characteristic of the participants was their relative youth. Four, including the Chairman of the committee, were in their thirties, the great majority were in their forties, and only six were over fifty. Only Neuchatel which was still nominally a principality under the monarch of Prussia and Apenzell-Inner Rhodes were not represented on the drafting committee.[4]

---

3. C.F. Strong: *Modern Political Constitutions*, p. 114.

4. G.A. Codding, Jr. *The Federal Government of Switzerland*, p. 32.

Some Important Statements

The framers of the Swiss Constitution of 1848 had before them the normal task of the most constitution–makers: to create a system of government that would provide security against external enemies and internal conflicts and furnish the conditions necessary for the attainment of good life for a maximum number of individuals.

—***J.A. Codding, Jr.***

And yet the entire constitutional system (under the revised constitution of 1874) has been devised in such a way that the essential liberties of the people are bulwarks which protect the linguistic, religious, political and social minorities against any bias towards dictatorship on the part of a majority and guarantee a sphere of privacy to the human personality. —***Hans Huber***

Switzerland mocks all attempts to define nationality, for though the Swiss form a nation with a solidarity which has resisted, through the space of more than six centuries, the multifarious attempts which have been made to undermine, it, they have always lacked and still lack a common religion and a common language, while even their mountains do not form a ring which would make a natural boundary.

—***C.F. Strong***

Prior to its eventual ratification by the people and the cantons, the Constitution could be adopted as a result of compromise. While the advocates of centralism desired a strong Central government, the federalists were no less adamant on ensuring the principle of autonomy of the units. A bicameral legislative system was thus accepted so that the units of the confederation may have their representatives in the upper chamber of the Federal Assembly. Then, a peculiar pattern of a collegial executive was adopted so that no member of the government could exercise his authority in an arbitrary manner. Likewise, the idea of a powerful judicial authority as one having its manifestation in the United States was abhorred with the result that the Federal Tribunal was deprived of the power of judicial review of legislation. In fine, while the 'centralists' could be successful in devising a strong and unified government at the Centre, the federalists could emerge triumphant in reconciling the issue of a strong Central government with the freedom of the people and the autonomy of the cantons.

It was specifically given that the cantons would remain 'sovereign so far as their sovereignty is not limited by the Federal Constitution'. The powers of the Federal Government extended to diplomatic and military affairs as well as to certain other spheres such as posts, customs, weights, and measures and such other matters in which concerted action was deemed necessary with a view to achieving national unity. The executive power was vested in a Federal Council consisting of 7 members elected by the Federal Assembly. The legislative power was vested in a bi-cameral body called the Federal Assembly. While the National Council was given to represent the people, the Council of States was to have the representatives of the cantonal governments. The judicial authority was vested in the Federal Tribunal without power of judicial review. An important change in the direction of a strong and unified government at the Centre could be visualised in the provision that while the Constitution guaranteed sovereignty to the cantons, it authorised the Federal Government to intervene in the cantonal affairs without awaiting a request from the cantonal authority in the event of internal disturbances or threatened conflict between the cantons.

The most important feature of the Constitution of 1848 could, however, be traced in its provision for a strong and unified government system based on a federal model. It terminated the system of a loose Union of States as coming from five and a half centuries and set up a new model which, though formally designated as a 'Confederation', was the model of a federation. Thus, the transformation of a loose league of cantons into a federation of the units of 'Confederation' could be described as the dominant feature of the Constitution of 1848. Certainly it afforded "an even more striking example than the United States of how conflicting state interests can be overcome, without annihilating State identity, by the political device called federalism."[5]

The Constitution of 1848 underwent a total revision in 1874 and again in 1999 and it is in accordance with this Constitution, that Switzerland is governed today. It gave to the Federal Government centralised control over military affairs and initiative in unifying certain matters of commercial law. This was done to overcome the weaknesses observed in the army during its mobilisation in 1870-71. It also reinforced the anti-clerical provisions of the previous Constitution and added new powers to combat some of the abuses that had been observed in managing national economy. It introduced federal legislative

---

5. C.F. Strong, *op. cit.*, pp. 114-15.

referendum. It abolished separate judicial systems of the cantons and provided for the establishment of a uniform system. The Federal Tribunal, which under the previous constitutional dispensation had been more than a committee of the Federal Assembly entrusted with certain very limited judicial duties, was strengthened so as to make it a real federal court approximating to the model of the United States Supreme Court.

The most important features of the revised Constitution of 1874 could however, be traced in strengthening the hold of the Federal Government. It not only increased the control of the Centre over armed forces, it also provided for the nationalisation of the railways under federal ownership and causing legislation to be referred to the entire Swiss people not as inhabitants of certain cantons but as a single, unified Court of Appeal. By all means, it marked the triumph of the Radicals who continued their movement for the centralisation of powers after the inauguration of the previous Constitution. The result was that the federalists who could have their lines incorporated into the constitution of 1848 in the form of important compromises had their defeat at the hands of their traditional opponents who would now not let them have the development of the Constitution in the direction of social and municipal privileges of the cantons.

Framed and adopted by the Federal Parliament on 18 December, 1998 and ratified by the people in a referendum on 18 April, 1999, the new constitution came into force on 1 January, 2000. It is a big document having 197 articles. The structure is more or less the same. The names of the principal organs of the government have been changed. Federal Assembly, Federal Council and Federal Tribunal have been renamed respectively as the Federal Parliament, Federal Government and the Federal Court. There is House of Representatives in place of National Assembly and Senate replaces the Council of State. New provisions have been included to cover items like citizenship, environment, zoning, security, education, research, culture, public works and transportation. It makes Switzerland a republican, democratic and social welfare state.

General Provisions of the Swiss Constitution of 1999

Ideals of the Preamble

(*i*) Mindfulness of our responsibilities towards creation,

(*ii*) Renewal of our alliance to strengthen liberty and democracy, independence and peace in solidarity and openness towards the world.

(*iii*) Determined, with mutual respect and recognition, to keep our diversity in unity.

(*iv*) Conscious of our common achievements and our responsibility towards future generations, and

(*v*) Certain that free is only a person who uses his freedom, and that the strength of a people is measured by the welfare of the weak.

Swiss Confederation includes 26 Cantons

Zurich, Berne, Luccerne, Uri, Schwyz, Obwalden, Nidwalden, Glarus, Zug, Fribourg, Soluthurn, Basel (Town), Basel (Country), Schaffhausen, Appenzel, Outer-Rhodes, Appenzel Inner-Rhodes, St. Gallen, Grisons, Aargau, Thurgau, Ticino, Vaud, Valais, Neuchatel, Geneva and Jura.

Purpose

(*i*) The Swiss Confederation protects the liberty and rights of the people and safeguards the independence and security of the country.

(*ii*) It promotes common welfare, sustainable development, inner cohesion and cultural diversity of the country.

(*iii*) It ensures the highest possible degree of equal opportunities for all citizens.

(*iv*) It strives to safeguard the long-term preservation of natural resources and to promote a just and peaceful international order.

Rule of Law

(*i*) The law is the basis for and limitation of state activity.

(*ii*) State activity must be in public interest and proportional.

(*iii*) State institutions and private entities must act in good faith.

(*iv*) Federation and Cantons respect international law.

Individual and Social Responsibility

Every person is responsible for himself or herself and advances, according to his or her abilities, the goals of state and society.

Salient Features

The salient features of the Swiss Constitution may be thus enumerated:

1. **A Written and an Enacted Document:** Like the Constitution of the United States, it is a written document having 197 Articles. While the Constitution of 1848 converted the loose league of cantons into a federation of the units of the 'confederation', its revised form in 1874 gave to the federal government centralised control over military affairs and initiative in unifying certain matters of commercial law. As a matter of fact, it opened the way for the gradual infiltraton of centripetal tendencies. The new Constitution specifies the powers of the Centre and also enumerates some concurrent powers given to both the Centre and the cantons. It is the supreme law of the land.
2. **A Rigid Constitution:** Like the American Constitution, it is rigid as its process of amendment is very difficult. A bill of constitutional amendment passed by the Federal Parliament must be ratified by the majority of the cantonal governments as well as by the majority of the voters in a referendum. At least, 1,00,000 voters or 8 cantons may initiate a proposal to be adopted by the Federal Assembly. If it is passed, then it is to be ratified by the majority of the cantons and a nation-wide referendum. If compared, it appears to be more rigid than that of the United States, for here the ratification is to be done by the majority of the cantonal governments as well as by the majority of the votes taken in a referendum. But in a different respect, it is less rigid than that in view of the 'democratic' character of the people. The institutions of direct democracy (initiative and referendum) have made the matters easy. Moreover, at every stage the bill or proposal of amendment is to be passed by the simple majority of votes, while in America a bill of constitutional amendment must be passed by 2/3 majority in each house of the Congress and then by the same majority in the Congresses of at least 3/4 States.
3. **Plural Executive:** In all countries of the world, the executive is singular as it is headed by one person whether he is a President or a Prime Minister and the like. But the Federal government of Switzerland is a unique model of collegial or plural presidency. It has seven members (ministers) and all of them are designated as the 'Presidents'. The salaries, allowances and powers of all the Presidents are equal. It is just for the sake of performing certain ceremonial functions that on the basis of seniority, one of them is

designated as the President of the Federation and another as the Vice-President for one year. Healthy conventions prevail whereby the Federal Assembly elects the same persons again and again for a term of four years. Not more than one President can belong to the same canton, while the cantons of Zurich, Berne and Vaud are invariably represented. Not only this, not more than two presidents should belong to the same political party. Hence, it is always like a coalition government. The whole arrangement is unique and, as Lord Bryce says, it "deserves best study".

4. **Federal System:** As in the United States, so here a federal system has been set up in spite of the fact that the Constitution declares this country a 'confederation'. The Constitution is the supreme law of the land. The powers have been divided between the Centre and the units (cantons). The subjects of national importance (as foreign affairs, military affairs, declaration of war and peace, post and telegraph, currency and coinage, railways, banking and commerce, higher education, settlement of cantonal disputes etc.) have been given to the Centre. There are some concurrent powers (as regulation of industries, control of the press, construction and upkeep of highways etc.) which have been given to both the Centre and the cantons. The residuary powers have been given to the cantons. Federal Court has been set up to interpret the words and provisions of the Constitution and to settle legal disputes between the Central and cantonal governments. Like the States of the USA, the cantons of Switzerland enjoy autonomy and so it, like its American counterpart, is appreciated for having a true federal system.

5. **Direct Democracy:** Modern democracy is known as 'representative government.' Power resides in the people, but it is exercised by the deputies chosen by the voters in periodic elections who are said to be accountable to their electors. This system prevails in Switzerland. But it has three peculiar institutions of direct democracy-initiative, referendum and landsgemeinde. Initiative signifies the right of at least one lakh voters to send a proposal to the Federal Parliament and to ask it to either adopt it in the form of a bill or refer it back to the final verdict of the people in a referendum. Referendum means that a bill of constitutional amendment or any 'urgent' bill, after it is passed by the national legislature, must be placed for the final verdict of the people, before it is put into operation. At least 50,000 voters or 8 cantonal governments may demand a referendum on any other

bill. Thus, referendum places final veto power in the hands of the majority of the voters of the country. In five small cantons of this country, the system of town parliament prevails which is called 'landsgemeinde'. Each adult voter is the member of his town assembly and so elections for the cantonal legislature are not held here. Thus, Bryce lauds Switzerland as 'the ancestral home of democracy.'

6. **A Social Welfare State:** Chapter 3 of Title 2 makes Switzerland a social welfare state. It is given that the Federation and the Cantons strive to ensure that, in addition to personal responsibility and private initiative, every person benefits from social security and necessary health care. Each able-bodied person works under fair and adequate condition. Each family is protected and gets suitable shelter. All children have initial, and continuing education according to their abilities for the sake of their development and social and cultural integration. It is the obligation of the Centre and of the Cantonal governments to ensure that everyone is protected against the economic consequences of old age, disability, illness, accidents, unemployment, maternity, orphanhood and widowhood. They shall strive to realise the social goals within the framework of the constitutional powers and with the means available to them.
7. **Fundamental Rights:** An important features of the Constitution may be seen in its Title 2 having basic rights. The enumeration of rights is so comprehensive that it covers social, economic and political spheres and ensures the existence of a full-fledged liberal-democratic order. The authors of the Constitution have gone much ahead than what is contained in the Universal Declaration of Human Rights adopted by the General Assembly of the United Nations in 1948 and then described by T.H. Marshall in his 'Citizenship and Social Class' in 1949. Marshall's categorisation of rights as civil, political and social aligns them with the case of a welfare state and civic republicanism. But the novelty of this part of the constitution of Switzerland lies in the fact that here the case of basic rights is bracketed with the themes of citizenship and social goals. Chapter 1 of this Title enumerates 'basic rights relating to respect and protection of human rights, equality before law, no discrimination on the grounds of religion, race, age, sex, language, social position, way

of life etc., protection of life and personal liberty, protection of children and adolescents, social security, marriage and family life, freedom of faith and conscience, primary education, freedom of assembly, development of science and art, cultivation of good faith preservation of language and culture, long or permanent settlement or residence in a part of the country.

Some rights of economic character ensure free choice of a vocation of profession, free access to and exercise of any private economic activity, formation of unions or associations for the protection of such rights, settlement of conflicts between employers and employees by means of conciliation, maintenance of peace in the industrial sphere and good labour relations. The people have the right to keep property and to get full compensation in the event of its nationalisation by the state in the public interest, to resort to strike or lockout in a manner sanctioned by the law of the state.

The category of political rights includes a number of rights as freedom to form and express opinion, to seek information and disseminate it. Editorial secrecy is guaranteed. The radio, television and the press have the freedom to express news and views. Independence of judiciary has also been ensured for the protection of these rights. So the aggrieved person may move the competent court to get justice within a reasonable time frame. The aggrieved person has the right to free legal assistance. Exceptional courts or tribunals cannot be created. The case is to be heard and tried in a free and fair manner. Aribtrary arrest or detention of a person is prohibited,. The judgment of a court may be challenged in a higher court. Nobody may be punished physically or financially until declared guilty by a competent court. Thus the basic rights have a legal protection. However, such rights may be limited by reasonable restrictions imposed by the state in the public interest. As this country has a federal set up, the Centre regulates the exercise of political rights in federal matters, the Cantonal governments regulate the exercise of such matters in regional and municipal matters.

A novel feature of this part of the Constitutions is that the political rights have been integrated with the issue of citizenship. That is, such rights are available only to the Swiss nationals. The Federal Government has the power to regulate acquisition or loss of citizenship through descent, marriage and adoption. It may also make a law to set minimum requirements for the naturalisation of foreigners by the Cantonal governments and grant naturalisation permits. It may facilitate the naturalisation of stateless children. It may also make a law to encourage links among Swiss citizens domiciled abroad and their links with the home country. What strikes a foreign student at this stage is that the federal government may legislate on the rights and obligations of Swiss citizens domiciled abroad in particular on the exercise of the political rights at the federal level, the duty to render military or alternative service, assistance to needy persons, and social security.

As all modern political systems have undergone significant changes, the Swiss system cannot be taken as an exception. The State has increased its domain of activity and centripetal tendencies have also grown here. But the notable point is that the rulers of this country have been able "to realise the goal of a welfare state while preserving the wider domain of essential freedoms which constitute the principal heritage of a liberal tradition."[6]

Process of Constitutional Amendment

Let us now study the process of amending the Swiss Constitution that is, indeed, a quite difficult affair owing to the fact that various methods of effecting a total or partial change admit of both the legislative and popular participation in this regard. We have already hinted that in this country the process of constitutional amendment is not at all an exclusive concern of the federal and cantonal legislatures, it requires the ratification of such measures by the people as well. What makes it really democratic, but also very rigid, is the fact that it "makes in every case the final sanction of the people an indispensable condition for the adoption of a proposed amendment and its incorporation in the constitution."[7]

The process of amending the Constitution has been described in Title 6 of the Constitution. The distinctively peculiar thing in this direction is that the Constitution may be subjected to two types of revisions – partial or total – and in each case a different procedure has to be adopted. Thus, the process of amending the Swiss Constitution may be discussed under these two heads–partial revision and total revision.

Partial Revision: It means amendment of any particular clause or clauses of the existing Constitution. Its procedure is as follows:

1. If the proposal has been passed by both the chambers of the Central legislature (Federal Parliament), it is referred to the people for ratification at the polls. If in such a case the majority gives its vertict in favour, it comes into force.

Revision of the Federal Constitution

Art. 192. General Principles

1. It may be subjected to a total or partial revision at any time.
2. Where it and the implementing legislation donot provide otherwise, the revision shall follow the legislative process.

Art. 193. Total Revision

1. Total revision of it may be proposed by the people or one of the Chambers, or may be decreed by the Federal Parliament.
2. If the initiative emanates from the people, or if the Chambers disagree, the people shall decide whether a total revision shall be undertaken.
3. Should the people accept a total revision, both chambers shall be newly elected.
4. The mandatory provisions of international law may not be violated.

Art. 194. Total Revision

1. A partial revision may be requested by the people or be decreed by the Federal Parliament.
2. A partial revision must respect the principle of the unity of subject matter; it may not violate the principles of international law.
3. A popular initiative for partial revision must, moreover, respect the principle of the unity of form.

Art. 195. Entry into Force

The Constitution revised in total or in part shall enter into force as soon as it is accepted by the people and the Cantons.

2. The people may take the initiative. If the proposal is put forth through a popular vote and if it is supported by a majority of the voters, then the Federal Government drafts the amendment embodying the principles and the same is submitted to a fresh referendum. But the people may also present their proposal in the form of a complete draft of the desired amendment. In such a case, the proposal will be

---

6. Arnold Zurcher: "Switzerland" in J.T. Shotwell (ed.): *Governments of Continental Europe*, p. 340.
7. Strong, *op. cit.*, p. 165.

discussed in the Federal Parliament and after it has given in vote in its favour, it will be put to referendum. However, if the Federal Parliament does not agree with the proposed amendment, it may recommend its rejection or put forward its own counter-proposals and then submit them to a popular vote. In this way, the acceptance of the proposal emerging from a popular initiative or of an alternative proposal submitted by the Federal Parliament or the rejection of both, is left to the decision of the majority of voters and of the cantons.

Total Revision: It means replacement of the existing Constitution by an entirely new Constitution. It procedure is as follows:

1. The proposal of amending the Constitution in full may come from the House of Representatives or the Senate, each House approving of it in a separate resolution. If the two Houses of the Federal Parliament approve of it, it is submitted to the people for their verdict at the polls. If it is approved by a majority of Swiss voters, it comes into force.
2. If the proposal is accepted by one House and rejected by other house of the Federal Parliament, or if the proposal is put through popular initiative (supported by at least 1,00,000 voters), the matter has to be submitted to referendum. If a majority of the Swiss voters gives its decision in favour of total revision, then fresh elections to both the Houses are held for the purpose of undertaking the revision and the new Federal Parliament after adopting it has to submit it to the people for ratification. If in this second referendum, the proposed matter is approved by a majority of the voters, as also of the cantons, the Constitution is accordingly revised.

The rigidity of the Swiss process of constitutional amendment has been softened by the practice of popular sovereignty. The Swiss people are so sensitive to their rights that they have not pondered over the need for a strong and independent judiciary as we find in the case of other federal States particularly the United States. In 1939, they rejected a proposal that their Federal Court be invested with the power of judical review, because as a learned Swiss judge puts, they "saw in the judicial examination of constitutional law an infringement of the democratic principles."[8] When the proposals for constitutional amendment have too frequently been made by the people themselves, they have never felt

8. Hans Huber: *How Switzerland is Governed,* p.10

apprehensive of the legislative or executive despotism. Rappard lays emphasis on the fact that it "is easier for the Swiss people to amend their fundamental law than their ordinary statutes against the will of a hostile parliament."[9]

Direct Democracy

In the Swiss constitutional system nothing is more instructive to a student of comparative governments than the institutions of direct democracy–initiative and referendum. They are perhaps the most remarkable agencies that democracy has produced, for they afford the channel of direct legislation by the people. No doubt, the instruments of direct democracy have been introduced in other countries also in varying degrees, but Switzerland is known for their most distinctively extensive use. That is, while in other parts of the world the agencies of direct democracy are like frills to adorn the constitutional costumes, in Switzerland they form the warp and woof of the political system. Thus, Switzerland has been regarded as the ancestral home of the devices of pure democracy. In the words of Prof. W.B. Munro, "In one form or another these institutions of direct democracy have been used, but they have spread along the major routes of democratic infection to various other countries including the United States."[10]

Initiative: As pointed out above, initiative is one of the devices of direct democracy operating in Switzerland. It is a positive device in the hands of the voters whereby they may propose matters of legislation. Legislation is not an exclusive affair of the elected bodies as we find in other countries. In Switzerland the people may override the jurisdiction of the elected bodies; they may propose legislation and thereby justify their supremacy over their elected representatives. Moreover, in Switzerland, the scope of initiative covers not only the ordinary field of law-making, it also covers the sphere of constitutional amendment in part or full. Thus Hans Huber defines it as the right of a definite number of voters "to propose an amendment to the Constitution, the drafting of a law or a single constitutional or legal ordinance, or to demand a popular vote upon it."[11]

---

9. W.E. Rappard: *The Government of Switzerland,* p. 60.

10. Munro, *Governments of Europe,* p. 746

11. Hans Huber, *op. cit.,* p.27.

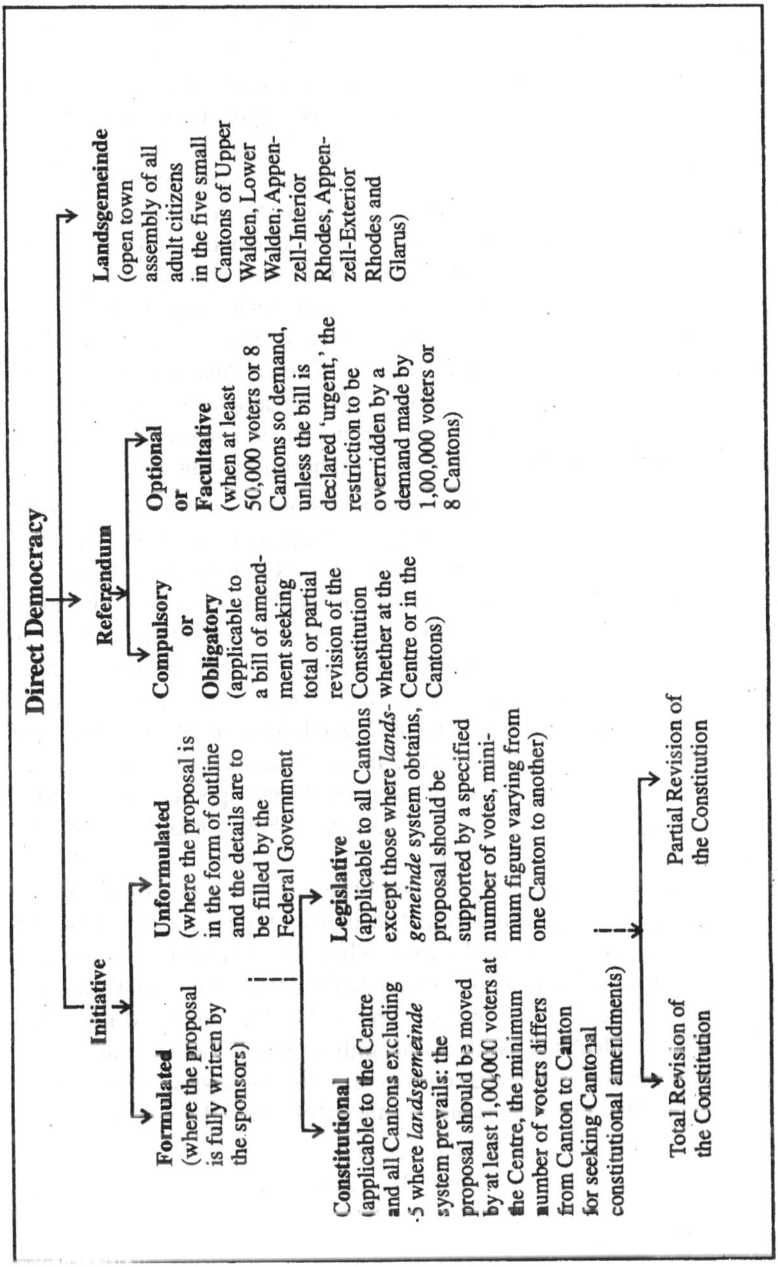
Direct Democracy
Initiative
Referendum
Landsgemeinde (open town assembly of all adult citizens in the five small Cantons of Upper Walden, Lower Walden, Appenzell-Interior Rhodes, Appenzell-Exterior Rhodes and Glarus)
Formulated (where the proposal is fully written by the sponsors)
Unformulated (where the proposal is in the form of outline and the details are to be filled by the Federal Government
Compulsory or Obligatory (applicable to a bill of amendment seeking total or partial revision of the Constitution whether at the Centre or in the Cantons)
Optional or Facultative (when at least 50,000 voters or 8 Cantons so demand, unless the bill is declared 'urgent,' the restriction to be overridden by a demand made by 1,00,000 voters or 8 Cantons)
Constitutional (applicable to the Centre and all Cantons excluding 5 where landsgemeinde system prevails: the proposal should be moved by at least 1,00,000 voters at the Centre, the minimum number of voters differs from Canton to Canton for seeking Cantonal constitutional amendments)
Legislative (applicable to all Cantons except those where landsgemeinde system obtains, proposal should be supported by a specified number of votes, minimum figure varying from one Canton to another)
Total Revision of the Constitution
Partial Revision of the Constitution

In this way, initiative exhibits the inherent right of the voters to make their influence felt even in those cases where legislature may like otherwise. Obviously, it is different from the right of submitting a petition. A petition is a mere submission by the people to a body praying for the commission or omission of a particular thing and it depends upon that body to do as it thinks fit. But initiative is the vindication of the sovereign power of the people as it takes effect without regard to the wishes of the elected bodies. It stands on the assertion that the voters have an inherent right to propose matters of legislation and when ratified by a majority of their votes, it becomes a piece of law or Constitution, no matter it goes against the wishes of the elected representatives. Thus, initiative has been considered an arrangement whereby a specified number of voters "may prepare the draft of a law and may then demand that it either be adopted by the legislature or referred to the people for acceptance at a general or special election. If approved by the required majority, it then becomes a law."[12]

As prevalent in Switzerland, initiative is of two kinds – constitutional and legislative. The right of constitutional initiative covers the whole or partial amendment of the Constitution of the Confederation. Under it a minimum of 1,00,000 voters may ask for a full or partial amendment of the Constitution. However, in the cantons there is legislative initiative as well. In all the cantons except where there is the system of town assembly (Landsgemeinde), a prescribed number of voters may either propose a new law or submit to the Cantonal Council the principle on which they desire a new law to be formulated. In the latter case, the Council may refer to the people the specific matter and if it gets support of the majority, the Cantonal Council prepares the law and submits it to the people for their final acceptance or rejection.

The device of initiative is important in cases of constitutional amendments. In this direction, it is of two types – formulated and non-formulated or in general terms. When the demand of the voters is contained in the shape of a draft or in specific terms, the Federal Parliament accepts it for the approval of the people and of the cantons. If the voters send a general demand giving outline only, then it is the obligation of the Federal Government to draft, consider and pass the laws as desired by the required number of voters subject to the ratification of the people.

Referendum: It is another device of direct democracy in Switzerland. It implies a process by which the verdict of the people is sought

12. Munro, *op. cit.*, p. 746.

on a proposed law and on which the legislature has already expressed its opinion. In simple words, it means reference to the people for final approval. It is a device through which the people may demand that a particular resolution passed by the legislature should not come into force unless it is ratified by the electorate at the polls by a majority vote. In the words of Munro, it "is a device whereby any law which has been enacted by the legislature may be withheld from going into force until it has been submitted to the people and has been accepted by them at the poll."[13]

The device of referendum was introduced in Switzerland in 1778 much earlier than the agency of initiative that was adopted in 1892. Like initiative, referendum is of two types – compulsory or obligatory and optional or facultative. All constitutional amendments, partial or full, whether of the national or of cantonal Constitutions, are subject to referendum and, as such, no constitutional amendment can be finally effective until the resolution is ratified by a majority of the voters and of the cantons in the case of federal constitution. But the application of optional referendum is limited to the cases of ordinary legislation. A federal law which is of general importance and which is not declared as 'urgent' by the Federal Parliament must be submitted to the referendum if the demand to that effect is made by at least 50,000 qualified voters or by 8 cantonal governments.

Criticism: The working of the agencies of direct democracy has its own merits and demerits. Its merits are:

1. It is the surest means of discovering the wishes of the people and an excellent barometer of the political atmosphere.
2. It lays down that in Switzerland elected bodies are subject to the sovereign control of the people and thus it is this country alone where the doctrine of popular sovereignty has been realised in actual practice.
3. These devices have established a living and unbreakable connection between the government and the people and thus the deputies chosen by the people may never gain the arrogant status of representative bodies.
4. The working of the institutions of direct democracy disseminates political education among the people and inculcates in them a keen awareness of public issues and a deep sense of responsibility in discharging their civic duties.

13. *Ibid*, p. 746.

5. The application of the devices of direct democracy imparts a moral character to the provisions of the Constitution and the laws and thus intensifies the forces of habitual obligation.

In a word, these devices justify the fact that the people in whom the sovereignty resides, "must themselves exercise the right of dissolution and the right of veto."[14]

The working of direct democracy in Switzerland has these demerits:

1. It adversely affects the prestige and responsibility of the legislature. The legislature remains like nothing more than a drafting committee of the people. It reduces the element of responsibility in the normal functioning of legislative bodies.
2. The agencies of direct democracy give to the people what they hardly deserve. The people, in general, vote for the measures about which they do not know much and hence the fate of the very technical and specialized measures is decided by the votes of the largely ignorant masses.
3. The working of referendum, in particular, has introduced a greater degree of conservatism. It is found that the people have often rejected a bill if it was found effecting a radical change. Finer has expressed the view that uninformed, unintelligent and vindictive people have very frequently wrecked progressive legislation.
4. The actual operation of referendum is so rigid that it leaves no room for a prudent voter to propose any amendment. He has to vote either 'yes' or 'no' and, thus, the result of the popular vote fails to produce a correct reflection of the public opinion.
5. It is also found that the people do not take active interest in the affairs of everyday elections. There is a lot of lethargy and indifference owing to election-fatigues and thus the results of voting are based on the actions of a minority of the Swiss population. Hence, it is difficult to see how a law ratified by a narrow majority vote may command the willing obedience of the people.

Christopher Hughes remarks that the Swiss themselves "are unanimous in deploring it."[15]

---

14. Simon Deploige: *The Referendum in Switzerland,* p. 284
15. Hughes: *The Federal Constitution of Switzerland,* p. 102

Federal System

The Swiss federal system presents a classic example of this type. It constitutes the basic feature of the Swiss governmental system and it is the chief instrument through which Switzerland has attained national unity without destroying the autonomy of the cantons. However, Switzerland is now by no means a confederation (as mentioned in the constitution) owing to the fact that the union is complete and secesion is not permitted. Art. 1 provides that the Swiss people and all the Cantons form this Federation.

The Swiss system meets every requirement of federalism. In the first place, it has a written and rigid Constitution. As a comparatively longer document, it goes into a good many details dealing with matters as fishing and hunting, qualifications of members of the liberal professions, sickness and burial of the indigent, cattle diseases, gambling houses, lotteries etc. Thus, the Constitution specifies much what otherwise should have been covered by ordinary legislation and its reason seems to lie in the fact that behind this plethora of details "is the desire for sharp delimitation of the respective competence of federal and cantonal powers."[16] It is also due to the fact that the Constitution represents a compromise between the advocates of cantonal rights and those in favour of a strong federal government and therefore "tries to anticipate and prevent causes of internal friction and possibility to the civil strife."[17]

The Constitution distributes the powers of government between the Central and cantonal governments.[18] It specifies the powers of the Centre which include foreign relations, military affairs, declaration of war and peace, railways and federal roads, bridges, aerial navigation, posts and telegraph, wireless communication, banking and commerce, conservation of natural resources, coinage, paper money, higher education, settlement of cantonal disputes, laws relating to marriage, naturalisation and extradition etc. It also enumerates certain concurrent powers under the jurisdiction of both the central and cantonal governments such as regulation of industry and insurance, construction and upkeep of highways, control of the press and encouragement of education. The rest are the residuary powers given to the cantons. Two special points may be noted here. First, if there is a conflict on a concurrent subject, the law of the Centre shall prevail over the cantonal law. Second, the cantons have also been given

16. J.B. Mason: "Switzerland" in Marx (ed.) *Foreign, Government*, p. 372.

17. R.C. Brooks: *Government and Politics of Switzerland*, p. 49.

18. In Switzerland there are 26 cantons (units) in all – 20 full and 6 half. It may sound strange to a student of comparative governments. While the full cantons have two votes, half cantons only one in matters of constitutional amendments. While full cantons have two representatives in the upper chamber of Federal Parliament, half cantons have one.

the power to make non-political agreements with foreign states subject to the approval of the federal government.

Finally, there is the Federal Court which takes cognizance of the conflict of competence between central and cantonal authorities. It also decides cases of public law between one canton and another. It hears appeals against violation of constitutional rights of citizens and appeals of private persons against violations of international treaties or agreements.

A word may be said about the constitutional status of the Swiss cantons. As we have already seen that the word 'confederation' is a misnomer, the cantons of Switzerland do not enjoy sovereignty. They have their share of autonomy. They are the original component parts of the federal system and they still retain their essential prerogatives. It is from them that the federal system draws its authority and derives its constitutional status. The Senate represents the cantons on the basis of equality and in this respect corresponds to the American Senate. The cantonal governments maintain law and order and manage for education, elections, public works etc. They also execute laws made by the Central legislature. The legal personality of the units is thus preserved and they have not been 'finished' owing to the paramount fact that the "reserve of power is left with the cantons."[19]

However, the Swiss federation is not immune from the elements of centralization of powers. With the march of time and change in the socio-economic pattern of life, the Central government has enhanced its authority. Since 1874 the federal authority has increased so as to cover civil and criminal law, alcoholic beverage, traffic, transportation, banking, social welfare projects, industrial legislation, public hygiene, etc. The financial position of the federal government has been strengthened by the creation of new sources of revenue. The factors of economic depression and demand for ever-increasing social services have played their part, but the factor of war has been very potent in this regard. During the Second World War, the Federal government was empowered to levy even direct taxes and excise duty, though the cantons received a share of revenue from these sources. Thus the augmentation of these federal powers "has necessarily exalted the prestige and influence of the government of the Confederation at the expense of the separate cantons."[20]

---

19. Strong, *op. cit.*, p. 116

20. Zurcher: "Switzerland" in Shotwell (ed.): *Governments of Continental Europe*, p. 338.

Division of Powers

Important Delegated Powers of the Federation	Important Residual Powers of the Cantons
1. Foreign-affairs including declaration of war and peace and conclusion of treaties with foreign states	1. Maintenance of law and order
2. Defence including maintenance and regulation of armed forces, military training and acquisition of private property for defence purposes	2. Establishment of courts and determination of judicial procedures
3. Customs and duties including imports and exports	3. Health and sanitation
4. Currency and coinage including banking and monetary system	4. Maintenance of public work
5. Communications including post, telegraph and telephone	5. Maintenance of schools, colleges and universities and professional and technical institutes
6. Weights and measures	6. Conclusion of treaties with foreign states concerning matters of public economy and neighbourly relations without violating the constitution of the Confederation or rights of the cantons
7. Manufacture and sale of gun powder, arms and ammunition, including atomic energy	7. Maintenance of the armed forces of not more than 300 men with the consent of the Centre
8. Extradition and movement of foreigners	8. Regulation of liberal professions
9. Broadcasting and television	9. Maintenance of recreational games
10. Ships, aerial navigation and railways	10. Maintenance of protection with the help of other cantons or of the Confederation.
11. Food and drugs including prevention of infectious diseases	**Restrictions**
12. Supervision of roads, bridges and national highways	1. No canton can make a constitution inconsistent with the Federal Constitution
13. Hunting and fishing	2. No canton can exercise political rights in a way going against the republican or representative system
14. Water, water power, river embankments and electrical engineering	3. No canton can make separate alliances or a treaty of political nature
15. Civil and criminal law including marriage and collection of debts	

Important Delegated Powers of the Federation	Important Residual Powers of the Cantons
16. Social security including elimination of unemployment and protection of family	4. No canton can restrict free passage of armed forces
17. Forest, wild life and ecology	5. No canton can face external aggression on its own.
18. Manufacture, refining and sale of liquors and distilled spirits	**Powers of Federation and Cantons**
19. Regulation of the employment of children in factories and working hours of the staff	1. Agriculture
20. Insurance against illness, accidents including family compensation funds	2. Regional planning
21. Labour management and employer-employee relationships	3. Protection of nature and landscapes
22. Establishment of bishoprics and religious orders	4. Encouraging housing construction
23. Lotteries	5. Trade and industry
24. Automobiles and bicycles	6. Harnessing hydraulic power
25. Granting subsidies to the cantons	7. Taxes
26. Civil protection of personal property	8. Insurance against illness and accident
27. Promotion of general welfare and economic security	9. Spirits
28. Regulation of trade and industry	10. Footpaths, roads and bridges, hunting and fishing
29. Establishment of federal university and polytechnical centres	11. Immigration, residence and naturalisation of aliens
30. Migration, immigration, residence and establishment of aliens.	12. State schools

Note: While the Confederation exercises general supervision over harnessing of hydraulic power and taxes, implementation of federal laws relating to national defence is shared by the cantons.

If the Swiss federal system is compared with the federal system of the United States, three leading points of difference arise. First, in Switzerland the spheres of central and cantonal governments have not been divided into water-tight compartment. For instance, the cantons execute the laws of the Federal Parliament and cantonal authorities assist the federal government in various matters of national administration. The cantonal governments organise courts, appoint judges and lay down the procedure to be followed in cases of settlement of disputes and through these agencies the laws made by the Centre are enforced. The federal government guarantees to the cantons their territories, constitutions and sovereignty within specified limits. Third, since the Swiss Federal Court, unlike the American Supreme Court, has no power of judicial review over federal legislation, the position of cantons in Switzerland has grown weaker than that of the United States. Obviously, the Swiss cantons cannot defend themselves from the onslaughts of central legislation.

The federal system of Switzerland needs proper appreciation in as much as the tendency of centralism does not vitiate its true character. Andre Siegfried fears that the danger of the tendency of centralism "is that to the extent to which they suffer encroachments of the federal power, the cantons will gradually cease to be sovereign states at all and become simple district administrations as carrying out the behests of the federal authority." The correct position is that, inspite of the extension of the federal powers, the cantons "remain important elements of the Swiss constitutional system and it is being a citizen of a canton that national citizenship is ordinarily required; and the laws and regulations of the respective cantons still determine many of the citizen's ordinary civil rights in Switzerland."[21]

21. Zurcher, *op. cit.*, p. 338.

13

STATE STRUCTURE

A study of the Swiss State structure should be made with this impression that while speaking of the legislative branch of the Federation as the supreme organ of government we must, of course, include not only parliament but the voters at large, who, exercise legislative power through the institutions of direct democracy.[1] Thus, one may find that though Swiss Federal Government is the national executive, it is very much a creature of the Federal Parliament in a correct sense, both the national executive and the national legislature are the creatures of the electorate. It is certainly because of these peculiar institutions that the Swiss political system is said to have "illuminated both the science and the art of government."[2]

Federal Government

Composition: The national executive of Switzerland known as the Federal Government (Bundesrat) stands as a class by itself in as much as it is not only unique to the students of modern political systems living in other countries of the world, even of all the political institutions of Switzerland it is characteristically Swiss. Apparently it resembles the marks of a parliamentary executive of the British model as well as of a presidential executive of the American model, essentially it is different from both. It frankly dismisses the case of a singular executive headed by a leader like a Prime Minister or a President and thus responds to the deep-seated and austere republicanism of the people who "might see therein an evidence

1. Arnold Zurcher: "*Switzerland*" in Shotwell (ed.): *Governments of Continental Europe*, p. 337.
2. W.B. Munro: *The Governments of Europe*, p.736.

of a monarchical or dictatorial tendency."[3] Prof. C.F. Strong is of the view that "no executive system in the world is so deserving of attention as that of Switzerland, for the founders of the Swiss Constitution of 1848 and 1874 would appear to have succeeded in a project which has baffled the ingenuity of all previous statesmanship, and especially that of France, namely to combine the merits and exclude the defects of both the parliamentary and the non-parliament systems."[4]

The Federal Government consists of seven members chosen every four years by the national legislature (Federal Parliament) in its joint session. In addition, one of the seven members is annually designated by the Parliament as its President, while the next one as its Vice-President. Although the Constitution does not so require, the members of the Federal Government are almost invariably chosen from among the members of the Federal Parliament and who, after being so chosen, resign their seats in the legislature. It is prescribed that not more than one person from one canton shall be chosen, but the usage demands that one member must invariably come each from the leading cantons of Zurich, Berne and Vaud. From the normal arrangement it appears that the Federal Government is composed of four from German-speaking cantons, two from French-speaking cantons, and one from Ticino or the Italian-speaking canton. In this way, a satisfactory regional and linguistic distribution is assured, because all the three major language groups are more or less fairly represented.

The term of the Federal Government coincides with that of the House of Representatives, since it is elected at the beginning of each House and is completely renewed after every general election. If there is a vacancy within the normal period of four years, it is filled at the next meeting of the Federal Parliament for the unexpired term of office. However, in practice, the Federal Presidents enjoy a very lengthy tenure because of the peculiar Swiss democratic traditions. Though chosen afresh after every fourth year, the old members are normally reelected so long as they desire to serve. In case the House of Representatives is dissolved earlier, the first business of the Federal Parliament is to reelect the members of the Federal Government and in such a case sitting members are generally reelected without any consideration of the change in the political complexion of the national legislature. The reason for this lies in the Swiss traditions whereby

3. Rappard: *The Government of Switzerland,* p.76.

4. Strong: *Modern Political Constitutions,* p.266,

it looks irrational for the state to lose a valuable administrator on account of mere difference of opinion. Thus, the Federal Government is virtually a permanent body where the average period of service is more than ten years.

Swiss State Structure

Federal Government

7 Presidents elected by the Federal Parliament for four years in a joint session holding these portfolios:
1. Political
2. Interior
3. Justice and Police
4. Military
5. Finance and Customs
6. Public Economy
7. Post and Railways.

One of them is designated as the President and the other as Vice-President for a year.

Federal Parliament

Senate

46 members elected by the cantons–2 each by a full and 1 each by a half Canton.

House of Representatives

200 members elected directly by the voters by proportional representation with list system for 4 years.

Federal Court

26 Judges and 12 alternates elected by the Federal Parliament in a joint session for 6 years–one of them is designated as the President and one as Vice-President for a year.

The work of the federal administration is divided into seven departments equal to the number of Federal Presidents. These are Political, Interior, Justice and Police, Military, Finance and Customs, Public Economy, Post and Railways. Each member of the Federal Government is the head of one department and the substitute head of another. The Federal Government decides itself how the functions are to be distributed. The allocation of departments is made among themselves by mutual arrangement. The assignment is made nominally afresh every year, but, for the reason of convenience, economy and efficiency, the same department is held continuously by the Federal President so long as he enjoys its membership. The deliberations of the Council are private, but the decisions are normally taken by the count of hands.

President: One of the ministers is designated as the President and the other as the Vice-President by the Federal Parliament for one year. According to an established practice, this is done on the basis of seniority and the office rotates among the seven ministers. A new member of the Government serves beneath all his seniors and the retiring President goes to the bottom of the Govt list. Hence, it is quite obvious that in case a Federal Minister serves for more than a period of seven years, he may get two terms (though not consecutively) of the Presidency. For instance, S.G. Motta enjoyed five terms, Herr Muller three, and Dr. Philippine Eter four.

The President of the Federal Government is also known as the President of the Swiss Federation. But the designation of the presidency is a matter of courtesy. The Swiss executive is plural or collegial which automatically implies that it has no single head. The Swiss President is neither the *primus inter pares*, nor the party boss, nor the chief administrator. After the expiry of his one year term, he becomes one like others and during the term as well, he acts like a chairman having formal precedence over others. He receives salary equal to his other colleagues except a small remuneration for meeting the cost of official entertainments; he gets no palatial residence or special transport, nor is there any grandeur of his high office. The decisions are taken by the majority of votes and the President has the right of casting vote to break the tie. It is thus clear that the Swiss President "is, strictly speaking, no .such person because there is no such office."[5]

Of course, the Swiss President neither reigns nor governs, he is given the position of formal precedence over his colleagues for the simple reason that there are certain ceremonial functions which cannot be performed simultaneously by persons more than one. He appoints ambassadors, receives and sees off foreign guests, represents the Federation at home and abroad, and to a limited extent, possesses emergency powers. The Swiss Presidency is thus a matter of ceremonial necessity. Unlike the American President, he does not select his colleagues, or appoint officials, or veto bills, or negotiate treaties, or send messages, or act as the real executive; nor like the British Prime Minister he plays instrumental in the choice of his colleagues and their ways of working. On the whole, it brings to its holder only a nominal honour, and thus the Swiss people "are apt to forget who their President is just now, although they are likely to know by name the majority of the members of the Federal Government."[6]

Functions and Powers: The Swiss Constitution contains a long list of the functions and powers of the Federal Government which for the sake of convenience may be grouped under these heads:

5. Strong, *op. cit.*, p.226.

6. John Brown Mason: "Switzerland" in Marx (ed): *Foreign Governments*, p.374.

1. The Federal Government is the executive of the federal state structure. It conducts the affairs of the Federation in accordance with federal laws and decrees. It must ensure due observance of the Constitution, the laws and decrees of the Federation and federal treaties. It supervises the guarantee of cantonal constitutions given by the Federal Parliament and, as such, it examines whether the cantonal constitution has anything contrary to the Federal Constitution. It looks into matters relating to the execution of judgements of the Federal Court and of agreements and arbitration awards concerning disputes between the cantons. All federal appointments, except those entrusted to the Federal Parliament or Federal Court, are made by the Federal Government. It examines the treaties made by the cantons either with each other or with a foreign state and may recommend their annulment to the Federal Parliament if they are detrimental to the interests of the Federation. It conducts foreign relations, safeguards external interests of the nation, ensures external safety of the country and looks for the maintenance of Swiss independence and neutrality. It also looks for the maintenance of law and order and if the cantonal governments fail in their task, it may intervene according to the directions of the Federal Parliament. It also supervises official conduct of all officers and employees of the federal administration. It has the charge of Federal Army and all branches of administration thereof vested in the Federation. In the situation of emergency, when the Federal Parliament is not in session, it is empowered to call out troops and deploy them as it thinks fit,
2. In the legislative sphere, the Federal Government submits projects of laws and arretes to the Federal Parliament and gives its preliminary advice upon projects which the cantons or Presidents may send up to it. The usual procedure is that the Federal Government submits a message or report accompanied by a draft embodying the action which Federal Government wishes the Federal Parliament to take. The draft forms the basis of the discussion in the commission of each chamber of the Parliament. Thus, the Government may initiate legislation and the Parliament adopt it with certain amendments. The Federal Government also examines laws and ordinances of the cantons that have to be submitted for its approval and supervises the branches of cantonal administration where such supervision is incumbent upon it. It gives an account of its work to the Federal

Parliament in each ordinary session, presents to it a report on the internal conditions in the country and foreign relations of the Federation, and recommends for its consideration such measures which it thinks necessary or useful for promoting general welfare. Although the members of the Government cannot be the members of the Parliament, they may sit in either House, participate in the debates and answer questions. They also attend the meetings of parliamentary committees which examine the bills and by virtue of their expert knowledge and their influence, they may succeed in having an effective say in the matter under discussion.

3. The Government administers federal finances and prepares the budget and submits accounts of federal receipts and expenditure. As such, it collects revenues and supervises expenditure authorised by the legislature.
4. It has some powers of a judicial nature. It hears appeals of private individuals against decisions of various departments and also against decisions of the Federal Railway Administration. It also has appellate jurisdiction over decisions of the cantonal governments in cases relating to discrimination in elementary schools, differences arising out of treaties relating to trade, patents, military taxation, questions about occupation and settlement, consumption taxes, customs, cantonal elections, and gratuitious equipment of the militia. However, the Federal Government does not enjoy full authority in this field, because the appeals against its decisions may be taken to the Federal Administration Court.

Special Features: From the preceding account of the organisation and functions of the Federal Government it becomes clear that it is a unique institution. However, its special features may by summed up as under:

1. The Swiss executive is plural or collegial. It means that it has no single head. The President enjoys nothing but a formal precedence over his colleagues and after a period of one year retires according to the principle of rotation by seniority.
2. Though elected by the national legislature after every four years, or even earlier, the Swiss executive enjoys a very long tenure of stability. This stability means more than the mere fact that once elected, the Federal Government unusually cannot be dismissed before the end of the normal term of four years.

3. Although the Federal Government is virtually a permanent body enjoying enormous powers, it is subordinate to the national legislature essentially owing to the theory of Swiss Constitution that the executive is not an independent or co-ordinate branch of government. The Government really acts according to the policy which originally emanates from the Parliament.
4. The Swiss executive does not correspond to the type of British cabinet. It is true that, like the British cabinet, it is the child of the legislature, and its members take part in the deliberations of the Federal Parliament, the Swiss executive is quite different. Its members are not picked up by a single leader; they cannot enjoy the membership of the legislature after being so chosen, their total number is fixed; they belong to different political parties and thus reveal unity in diversity; above all, they are not individually or collectively responsible to the legislature.
5. The Swiss executive is different from the American cabinet. Although, its tenure is characterised by stability and its members do not enjoy the membership of the national legislature, none of the seven Presidents is like the American President or his secretaries. Unlike the case of American cabinet, the seven members of the Government are elected by the national legislature in a joint sitting and the President possesses nothing similar to the American head of the state except the official designation. Besides, while the American executive works independently of the legislative control owing to the system of the separation of powers, the Swiss system is different where the Ministers take a very prominent part in the deliberations of the Parliament and pocket their pride if their wishes are turned down.
6. The Swiss executive is virtually a non-partisan body. The members of the Government are not chosen from the party having majority in the lower house of the national legislature. Rather they are a heterogeneous group of politicians belonging to different major parties who are chosen in view of their capability of administration. The party lines are not so rigid and it is administrative skill, mental grasp, good sense, tact and temperament by which the case of a particular person is adjudged.

On the whole, the Swiss executive is neither parliamentary nor presidential; it is unique by itself. Plurality instead of singularity, diffusion of executive authority instead of concentration, non-partisanhood in the midst of party politics, stability instead of periodic elections by the national legislature, and its working under the control of the national legislature and ultimately of the people may be cited as its special characteristics. Obviously, the Swiss executive is without its parallel. Naturally, it is a matter of pride to the Swiss people who have regard it as "the mainspring and certainly the balance-wheel of the national government."[7]

Federal Parliament

The national legislature of Switzerland is known by the name of Federal Parliament. It is a bi-cameral body having Senate and House of Representatives as the upper and lower chambers respectively. In the words of the Constitution, it is the repository of supreme authority of the Federation, subject to the rights of the people and the cantons. In this respect, Swiss Federal Parliament resembles the English Parliament and the American Congress. However, the striking point of difference is that the powers of both the chambers even under the present Constitution are equal. Hence, Strong says that the Swiss legislature, like its executive, "is unique; it is the only legislature in the world the powers of whose upper house are in no way different from those of the lower House."[8]

Composition: The Senate corresponds to the American Senate in respect of its composition. Every full canton has two seats in this house, while every half canton has one regardless of its size or population. As a result, its total strength is 46. Each canton has its own laws to determine the mode of election of the deputies, the length of their term of office and the allowances paid to them. This arrangement is certainly different from the patterns of American and Indian federal systems. This system of election does not prevail in the cantons having landsgemeinde.[9] The cantons also reserve the right to recall or replace their representatives. There is no uniformity in regard to their terms of office; in some Cantons it is four years, in others it is three years and, in some others it is for a year only.

---

7. A.L. Lowell: *Government and Parties in Continental Europe,* Vol.II, p. 205
8. Strong, *op. cit.,* p.206.
9. There are five landsgemeinde cantons, namely, Glarus, Appenzell-Outer Rhodes, Appenzell-Inner Rhodes, Obwalden and Nidwalden. These cantons, as Hans Húber says, "stand for the purest and most direct democracy." *How Switzerland is Governed*, p.2.

The House of Representatives is the popular chamber of Swiss Parliament. It has 200 members elected directly by the people by means of proportional representation with list system and secret ballot. The minimum age of a voter is 20 years and now discrimination on the ground of sex has been abolished. Each canton, whether half or full, forms an electoral constituency and seats are allotted to it according to the ratio of one for every 24,000 of the total population. It is required that each canton must send at least one representative to the lower house. As the cantons are represented in this chamber in proportion to their population, there are naturally wide differences in the allocation of seats. Thus, Zurich (because of being the biggest canton) has the highest number of seats (35). It is specified that a clergyman or a member of the Federal Government or of the Federal Court or of any department of the Federal Government can not be elected as its deputy.

Allocation of Seats in the House of Representatives

Cantons	Seats	Cantons	Seats
1. Url	1	14. Appenzell-Inner Rhodes	2
2. Upper Walden	1	15. Appenzell-Outer Rhodes	1
3. Lower Walden	1	16. St. Gallen	12
4. Luzern	9	17. Aargau	14
5. Zurich	35	18. Thurgau	6
6. Glarus	1	19. Grisons	5
7. Zug	2	20. Vaud	16
8. Berne	29	21. Ticino	8
9. Solothurn	7	22. Valais	7
10. Fribourg	6	23. Geneva	11
11. Basel Town	7	24. Neuchatel	5
12. Basel Country	7	24. Schwyz	3
13. Schffhausen	2	26. Jura	2
		Total	200

The term of this House is of four years. But mid-term polls may take place in case the two chambers fail to agree on a proposal for constitutional revision. It elects its President and Vice-President for one year. Neither of them is eligible for re-election in the consecutive year. Custom requires that the Vice-president should be elevated to the post of the President. When the House meets in its normal session in the months of March,

June, September and December or in any extra-ordinary session, the President acts as the Chairman. He regulates the business, protects privileges and dignities of the house, and uses his casting vote to break a tie. But his office is honorary, neither as exalted as of his English counterpart, nor as influential as we find in the case of the parliamentary leaders and those persons who have been so fortunate to attain it to enjoy a special prestige among their party associates.[10]

The sessions of both the chambers are held concurrently but in separate houses. However, joint sessions take place for definite purposes, as to elect the members of the Federal Parliament, Federal Court, Federal Insurance Tribunal, Chancellor of the Federation, Commander-in-Chief of the armed forces, grant of pardon or amnesty and resolution of disagreement between them. When such a sitting takes place, decisions are taken by the majority of votes and the President of the House of Representatives presides over the joint session.

Functions and Powers: The functions and powers of the Swiss Federal Parliament may be discussed under four heads—legislative, executive, judicial and constituent.

1. As regards legislative powers, it is competent to enact laws and decrees dealing with matters falling under the jurisdiction of federal authorities. It determines and enacts necessary measures to ensure due observance of national Constitution. It also votes on treaties and constitutional amendments. It passes federal laws and legislative ordinances, considers and passes the annual budget, approves state accounts and authorises public loans floated by the federal government. It can demand all kinds of information on the administration of the Federation and direct questions to the national executive.
2. It exercises important executive functions also. In its joint session,it elects seven members of the Federal Government and designates one of them as its President, elects 26 judges of the Federal Court and designates one of them as its President, elects twelve substitute judges for the national judiciary, also elects one Commander-in-Chief during war times, elects one Chancellor to work as the General Secretary of the Federal Government, and elects the members of the Federal Insurance Tribunal. It declares war and

10. Brooks: *Government and Politics of Switzerland*, p.80.

Some Important Statements

There is no bench for a Ministers nor for any Opposition, Since neither exists. The executive officials have seats on a dais right and left of the President, but not being members, they are not party leaders. *—Lord James Bryce*

There are few Parliaments which exercise more miscellaneous duties. *—Arnold Zurcher*

The Swiss Federal Councillor (President) is like a lawyer or an architect, in that his advice is sought and usually heeded, but he is not supposed to throw up his job when his employer insists on having something done differently. *—W.B. Munro*

This is the most important function of the Federal Tribunal (now Federal Court), because in the absence of inferior federal courts, the unity of civil jurisprudence could not otherwise be assured in Switzerland. *—W.E. Rappard*

peace and ratifies alliances and treaties. All treaties concluded by the cantons among themselves or with foreign states must be confirmed by the Federal Parliament provided they are referred to it either by the cantons or by the Federal Government. In case a cantonal government fails to execute federal laws and regulation, the Federal Parliament decides on the nature of intervention against the recalcitrant party.

3. As regards its judicial powers, it exercises the prerogative of granting pardon and amnesty. It deals with conflicts of jurisdiction between different federal authorities. It also hears appeals against the decisions of the Federal Government relating to administrative disputes.
4. It has powers of constitutional amendment. However, these powers are subject to popular verdict. When both Houses agree to revise the Constitution, either wholly or partially, the proposed revision is submitted to the people for their acceptance. In case one of the chambers does not agree to the proposed revision, the matter is referred to the people for their decision. If the majority of the electorate votes for revision, new elections to the Federal Parliament take place and when the new legislature adopts that bill (which is a foregone conclusion), the matter is referred to the people as well as to the Cantons for their final ratification.

Criticism: Despite the fact that the Swiss Parliament has been called by its Constitution as the repository of supreme authority, it remains to be pointed out that its real authority has much declined due to various reasons associated with the institutions of direct democracy and other practices of this ancestral home of democracy. The process of direct legislation has contributed to its decline in a very great measure. Its major decisions are subject to the veto of the people. Many important bills are piloted by the members of the Federal Government who submit them with a well-reasoned report highlighting the urgency of the matter. A well-known Swiss writer admits that the federal legislature "cannot be designated a parliament in particular, because it cannot be put out of office by a vote of lack of confidence."[11]

Federal Court

Composition: The youngest of the three organs of the Swiss national government is the Federal Court (Bundesgreriecht) consisting of 26 judges and 12 alternates or substitutes elected by the Federal Parliament in its joint session for a period of six years. It is taken into account that the judges represent all official languages. One of the judges is elected as its President and the other as its Vice-President for a term of two years, neither of whom can be re-elected for the next consecutive term. The Constitution does not lay down qualifications except that a judge may be eligible for the election of House of Representatives and that he should not be a member of the Federal Parliament, Federal Government or some other department of the government. The Constitution requires that all the three linguistic areas of Switzerland should find adequate representation. However, a convention has developed whereby only men of forensic abiiity and experience are elected and then re-elected as long as they 'live or care to serve'. It has its seat at Lausanne, the capital of Vaud canton, as a token of satisfaction to the French-speaking people of the country who have had some lingering feeling of.dis-satisfaction with the importance of Berne – German-speaking capital city in the canton of Berne.

Jurisdiction: The jurisdiction of the Federal Court covers civil and criminal cases and other issues of public law. Its civil jurisdiction covers all suits between the Federation and the cantons and between the Cantons themselves. Suits filed by an individual or a corporation on one side and the Federation on the other, provided that the former are the plaintiffs and the amount involved in the dispute is 8,000 francs or more, also lie with this Court. It also decides cases between the individuals where the amount exceeds 10,000 francs and when the two parties request to take the matter

11. Hans Huber, *op. cit*, p. 41.

under its jurisdiction. It further decides cases relating to loss of nationality or disputes concerning citizenship between the communes of different cantons. The Constitution further confers on it powers to ensure uniform application of laws relating to commerce and transactions affecting movable property, suits for debt and bankruptcy, protection of copyright and industrial inventions. Finally, it has appellate jurisdiction over cantonal courts in all cases arising under federal laws where the amount in dispute exceeds 8,000 francs.

On the criminal side, the Federal Court has jurisdiction, original and exclusive, in cases of high treason against the state and revolt and violence against federal authorities, crimes and offences against the law of nations, political crimes and misdemeanours which are either the cause or consequence of disorders and disturbances necessitating armed federal intervention and, finally, offences committed by the officials appointed by a federal authority before the Tribunal by that authority. In criminal cases the Tribunal holds assizes from time to time at fixed centres in which the country is classified for the purpose. In these assizes a section of the Tribunal sits with a jury chosen by a lot from the neighbouring villages.

Then, the Federal Court has a restricted constitutional jurisdiction. It takes cognizance of conflict of competence between federal authorities on the one side and cantonal authorities on the other, disputes in public law between cantons, and appeals against violation of constitutional rights of citizens and appeals of private persons against violation of international agreements or treaties. In all cases of conflict of competence, it is the power of this Court to uphold the federal Constitution against ordinary laws and decrees of the cantons and the cantonal Constitution against ordinary laws and decrees of the cantons. Its power of judicial review is limited to cantonal governments alone and, as such, it can invalidate cantonal laws and look into the constitutional validity of cantonal executive actions. It is not only that the Court has no power to question the constitutionality of federal laws or federal decreas, it is specifically required by the Constitution to treat all federal laws as constitutional and to enforce them.

However, the Swiss judicial system is quite different from the American model. There are no subordinate federal courts and the Federal Court stands alone. Nor has it separate officials to execute judgment. Its power of judicial review does not cover federal laws and decrees. It may further be added that although conflicts of jurisdiction between cantonal and Federal authorities are decided by the Federal Court, the conflicts of jurisdiction between the Federal Government and the Federal Court are decided by the Federal Parliament. As a result, the Swiss Federal Court cannot have the position enjoyed by its American counterpart where, as Justice Frankfurter once confidently asserted, 'the Supreme Court is the Constitution. It is pointed out that "to endow it with the right of disavowing federal statutes would therefore be to impose on a much weaker court a much heavier burden than that under the American judiciary sometimes seems to be staggering."[12]

12. Rappard, *op. cit.*, p. 91.

14

POLITICAL PARTIES AND PRESSURE GROUPS

Though, by all means, Switzerland is a free and 'open' country, its political panorama is unlike other democratic countries of the world. It has a multi-party system in the literal sense of term, which cannot be easily placed in the categories of the 'right' and the 'left', or the 'liberal' and the 'conservative' or the 'progressive' and the 'reactionary'. Sobriety, moderation and a 'communal' conscience of the people make the national highly pliable with the result that political cleavages created by the party system do not prevail in the country that have their manifestation in other parts of the world. Moreover, the Swiss people guard their individual liberty jealously. It is evident from the fact in a referendum after referendum they "have turned down even moderate encroachments which would hardly stir a ripple in other countries. The lesson of this impressive display of national sentiment has not been lost on the political parties, none of which can afford to deviate greatly from the clearly demonstrated popular will. Authoritarian parties have, therefore, led a very listless existence in Switzerland, and their prospects are dim."[1]

Political Parties

Inspite of the dominant fact of direct democracy in Switzerland, political parties have grown up as a natural concomitant of the present-day needs of the representative government. But while this country has a multi-party system, different from the bi-party system of Britain and the United States, it resembles both in respect of its conventional development. The Swiss political parties have an extra-constitutional growth; they are not recognized in the Constitution of the Confederation, though an indirect

1. R.G. Neumann: *European and Comparative Government*, p. 748.

mention has been made in the laws governing the legislative organisation and procedure and machinery of elections. Art. 73 of the Constitution, as amended in 1918, introduced the principle of proportional representation in the elections of the National Council. It is obvious that the principle of proportionality would be meaningless unless it is referred to the parties having their elected representatives in proportion similar to that prevailing between their electors, is to be established.

General Features: The Swiss party system has certain essential characteristics which may be put as under:

1. There are political parties without sharp cleavages. In spite of the fact that the Swiss people are characterised by diversities of race, language, religion and nationality, the party lines do not coincide with them. The party life is vigorous, strong and influential, and party rivalry is free from bitterness and violence.
2. The Swiss parties, are distinguished by their moderation (excluding the communists) and they show no tendency to swing to conservatism. The Social Democrats are far from being the doctrinaire Marxists and are really like a reformist labour party. The socialism of the socialists is more practical instead of being revolutionary. It is owing to this fact that the Swiss Federal Executive has been in successful operation.
3. All parties agree on three fundamental points, viz., independence, neutrality and trade of the nation. They may disagree on details, but on the importance of the three goals, there "can be no difference of opinion."[2]

As pointed out above, Switzerland is a country having many political parties, it will be worthwhile to discuss the organisation and principles of the major ones.

Liberal Party: It is one of the oldest parties of Switzerland, and although its influence has now declined, it is indisputable that it has played a very important part in shaping the political system of the country. To it goes much of the credit for the creation of modern Switzerland and the installation of the Constitution of 1848. It dominated the political scene throughout the second half of the last century, but gradually its control declined so much so that in the elections of National Council it secured only five seats in 1959. It hardly had any place in the Federal Council. Its

2. Munro: *The Governments of Europe*, p. 750.

offices are located in the principal areas of Geneva, Basel, Lausanne and Nauchatel. This party has stood for liberalism and as such it has advocated laissez-faire in economic policy and opposed the idea of increase in state activity.

Catholic Conservative Party: Also known as the Christian Socialist Party, it occupies a very important place. Its primary purpose has been to protect and preserve the doctrines and institutions of the Catholic Church specially in the rural cantons where its strength has been the greatest. Although many decades of participation in government have softened the early Catholic repugnance towards a federal state *per se*, its platforms usually contain exhortations against over-centralisation and any increase in the federal bureaucracy. It still makes a point of being the defender of individual liberty which includes property rights and protection of the family, preferring to rely on the church, private philanthropy and co-operative institutions rather than on the state to safeguard the welfare of individual. But the love for Catholicism is so great that Rappard calls it neither individualistic, nor liberal, but frankly theocratic.[3]

Radical Democratic Party: It has played a very prominent part in establishing a secular, liberalistic, centralistic and democratic government in Switzerland. It has stood for the widest possible extension of political democracy through the institutions of initiative and referendum. Whereas it still considers itself as the party of a strong Central government, in recent years it has not been averse to warning the nation about the dangers inherent in any further encroachment upon the powers of the cantonal governments. Secularism is one of its most outstanding planks and, as such, it can always be found in opposition to any issue that would tend to increase the power of the Catholic Church or, in any way, reduce the freedom of religious preference. Basically it favours non-intervention by the government, its attitude has been much less rigid than that of the Liberals. In this way, this party runs half-way between the extremes of Catholicism and Socialism.

Social Democratic Party: In recent years, this party has come to assume an important position in the Swiss political life and its influence is steadily increasing. It is supported mainly by the industrial workers, civil servants and professional classes. It advocates shorter working hours, guarantees full employment, expansion of social insurance, collective bargaining, direct federal taxing power, suffrage for women and the positive

3. Rappard: *The Government of Switzerland*, p. 100.

role of the state in the United Nations. One very important thing to be noted here is that this party has gradually softened its policies in order to shake off the influence of Marxism and come to stand for the principle of mixed economy. In the programme of 1959, it declared that every man, irrespective of his origins and possessions, shall be free to develop his faculties and capacities.

Labour Party: In a strict sense, it is the only party of the left wing and since its 'leftism' is not in conformity with the national culture and traditions, its strength is confined to a very small section of workers engaged in the industry or intellectuals. This party could never gain remarkable success owing to the strict control of the federal and cantonal governments and the prosperous life of the community.

Minor Parties: In addition to these parties, there are some minor parties in Switzerland. There is a party of Farmers, Artisans and the Middle Class now known as the Farmers' Party. It is the defender of the interests of the agrarian population. It is strongly anti-Marxist in outlook in regard to economic problems. It opposes intervention on the part of the State in the economic life of the community if it does not directly benefit the farmers. In the elections of 1959, it secured 23 seats in the National Council and 4 in the Council of State. There is the Independent Party founded by Gottlieb Duttweiler that stands for the defence of the interests of the consumers and opposes State intervention in the economic sphere.

Criticism: The Swiss political parties play a role that is less notable compared to the role of their counterparts in other democratic countries of the world. It is due to these reasons[4]:

1. The institutions of direct democracy have shifted the centre of contest from the legislative chambers to the polls. The last word in the law-making system rests with the people and not with the parties and this makes the prospects of strong party organisations in the legislatures unnecessary.
2. The sessions of the Swiss legislature are comparatively short. After sitting for about a month, the members return to their respective places and thus there is hardly any encouragement to professional politicians.
3. As in the case of legislature so in the executive, the prospects of strong party organisation have no ground to flourish. Since the Federal Government is a stable body and consists of various party representatives, its character becomes non-partisan. As it represents

4. Codding, *The Federal Government of Switzerland*, p. 113.

no single party and is not used as an instrument for the execution of a party programme, there remains no need for a strong party organisation to control the national executive.

4. The party organisation has also remained weak owing to the fact that in Switzerland there are no nation-wide elections like that of the American President. The parties are supported by local subscriptions and thus they are mainly concerned will local elections and local affairs.
5. Switzerland does not exhibit a complex variety of national issues. The people adhere to their neutrality in international sphere, independence and economic well-being in the national sphere, and thus they do not inculcate seriously divergent interests as is found in other countries of the world.
6. Above all, there is the most brilliant fact of unity in diversity. In spite of their religious, linguistic and racial differences, they are united.

Pressure Groups

Despite the fact that Swiss political life is 'strongly localised' and there is so much diversity in the socio-political life of different cantons making of any generalisation 'insecure'[5] political parties have their existence and operation in this 'tiny democracy' of Europe with this important line of difference that here party system has been immune from the tides of agitational upheavals or sharp ideological cleavages. One more significant characteristic of Swiss political pluralism that strikes us at this stage is not that various interest groups have their existence and operation at the stasiological map of this country, rather the Swiss political system "tends to provide more opportunities for the open and direct participation of interest groups in political process than does the system in the United States, for example."[6]

General Features: Let us look into the characteristics of the politics of organised groups in the political system of Switzerland.

1. The role of interest groups is, to a great extent, integrated into the normal political process in which multi-party system has its thorough

5. C.J. Hughes: "Switzerland" in Henig and Pinder (ed.s); *European Political Parties*, p.366.

6. Codding, *op. cit.*, p.114.

prevalence. True that there are no sharp ideological cleavages between the parties, they do have their different approaches towards the matters of social, political and economic importance. It provides ample scope for organized groups to have their relationship with this or that political party as per their specific interests. Interest groups can usually find a party whose attitude reflects their chosen position and common cause. Second, the system of proportional representation for elections to the House of Representatives encourages the existence and operation of the multi-party system. It has its own impact on the role of interest groups. As it makes it relatively easy to start a new party with favourable orientations at the national or cantonal levels, a new interest group may easily come into existence, or an existing one may easily shift its political affiliation in a way subserving its interest to its own satisfaction.

2. The lack of salaries and emoluments for the parliamentarians and the growing length of parliamentary sessions make it difficult for a professional politician to work in this field. Even a self-employed person like a private medical practitioner or a lawyer finds it difficult to perform parliamentary services. The result is that the places of professional politicians are being occupied by trade and industrial union officials and even by industrial executives all of whose salaries are continued during tenure and for whom replacements are hired to carry out their normal duties. Allied with this is the fact of national temperament. The people abhor professional politicians.
3. What, however, leads to brisk activity of interest groups in the Swiss political system is the prevalence of the institutions of direct democracy. The groups may indulge in getting signatures for sponsoring a bill of constitutional amendment at the Centre or in a canton, or an ordinary bill in the latter, or they may be doing the same for asking the Federal Parliament to put a particular bill for the verdict of the people after it is passed by it. Initiative and referendum are thus the two important weapons not as much with the people as these are in the hands of the politically wise interest groups whereby they can play their part in the political process of the country in consonance with their respective specific interests.

Varieties and Role: As in other plural societies so in Switzerland, there are organised groups of different kinds whose ranges of interests differ from purely business to labour, agrarian and professional. Some of the important interest groups may be enumerated as under:

1. Swiss Union of Commerce and Industry (VORORT). It includes:
   (*a*) Swiss Society of Machinery Manufacturers
   (*b*) Swiss Watch Chambers
2. Swiss Peasants (Farmers) Union. It includes:
   (*a*) Winegrowers Association of Western Switzerland
   (*b*) Swiss Brown Cattle Race Association
   (c) Swiss Association of Producers of Cattle for Slaughter
   (*d*) Association of Swiss Master Butchers
3. Swiss Federation of Trade Unions. It includes:
   (*a*) Swiss Railway Employees Union
   (*b*) Swiss Federation of Construction and Wood Workers
   (c) Swiss Federation of Metal and Watch Workers
   (*d*) Swiss Federation of Workers in Commerce, Transportation and Food Industries.
4. Swiss Association of Arts and Crafts.

These major groups either have their operation in the political process through some political party, or they take the advantage of constitutional provisions relating to the institutions of direct democracy. Available data shows that, on occasions, different interest groups have had the chance to induct their 'faithful agents' into the Federal Government. In every election, some leaders manage to have the membership of the Federal Parliament on the support of leading interest or pressure groups.

Criticism: It should, however, be added that the role of interest groups in the Swiss political system is not as potential or effective as we find in a country like the United States or France. The reason for this should be found both in the political make-up of the country and the traditional attitude of the people. In general, as we have already seen, the people are allergic to choosing professional politicians or leaders of an agitational disposition, nor do they approbate militant or highly shrewd methods of lobbying the like of which we find in other 'open' countries of the world. Though the issue of pressure group politics has sometimes cropped up to engage the attention of the people, it has failed to earn importance of the first rank. Codding rightly sums up: "If worst comes to worst, the Swiss voter has confidence in his own ability to choose right from wrong. After all, the majority still has its ultimate weapon, the referendum, backed by the constitutional initiative."[7]

7. Codding, *op. cit.*, p. 132.

Part - IV

Russian Constitution

In accordance with our theory, revolution means construction, but it also always implies demolition. Revolution requires the demolition of all that is obsolete, stagnant and hinders fast progress. Without demolition you cannot clear the site for new construction. Perestroika always means a resolute and radical elimination of obstacles hindering social and economic development of outmoded methods of managing the economy and of dogmatic stereotype mentality.

—***Mikhael Gorbachev***

15

CONSTITUTION OF THE RUSSIAN FEDERATION

A study of the Russian political system in an advanced study of the political systems of the world has its own significance. Russia is the biggest country of Europe that had the credit of being a super-power of the world until a few years ago. A liberal democratic system has now come into being after the disintegration of the Union of Soviet Socialist Republics (USSR) in 1991. The 'socialist system' established by Lenin in 1917 and consolidated by Stalin withered away to the astonishment of all. A new order came into being under the leadership of Boris Yeltsin. What was the Russian Soviet Federated Socialist Republic (RSFSR) as a unit of the Soviet Union became a fully sovereign State with the name of Russian Federation committed to the norms of a liberal-democratic order[1]. As President Yeltsin, in his message to the Federation Council on 21 December, 1996, reiterated: "I have no doubt that all of you are committed to the creation of a law-governed State. Many tasks are yet to be carried out for the idea of a law-governed State to triumph in our country. Among these goals is the criterion of a truly independent and authoritative judiciary."

Creation of the Russian Federation

The political and socio-economic order established by Lenin in 1917 and consolidated by Stalin started crumbling after 1970. The emerging wave of criticism hit at the era of Brezhnev (1969-82) as the period of slowing down (zamedleniye) and stagnation (zastoi). It paved the way for the inauguration of the new era of openness (glasnost) and restructuring (perestroika) under the leadership of Mikhail Gorbachov. 'He first used

1. John Sallnow: *Reform in the Soviet Union: Glosnost and the Future* (London; Pinter Pub., 1989), p.11

the word *glasnost* at a party conference on the point of ideology in December 1984 when he was Second Secretary to ailing Chernenkov. After taking charge in March, 1985 he put his 'new thinking' before the people in clear and strong terms.[2] On 21 May, 1988 he said in a party meeting: "Certainly it is impossible today to describe in detail the concrete image of the future for which we are reaching through *perestroika,* but the basic parameters and main features of which we call a qualitatively new state of society can and must be outlined. They can be outlined, because the chief orientations and tendencies of social change have already emerged."

The RSFSR was the biggest constituent unit of the USSR. In April 1978 it adopted a new Constitution. In June 1990 it passed a declaration of republican sovereignty by 544 votes to 271 in its legislature and adopted the name of the Russian Federation. In 1991 the post of the President of the Federation was created which was assumed by Boris Yeltsin as a result of his victory in the elections. He was the first executive head in the Soviet history to be elected by the popular vote.[3] He set up a Constitutional Court having 19 judges elected for 12 years on a non-renewable term. In October, 1991 he announced an economic programme to establish a healthy mixed economy with a powerful private sector. In the following month, a law was made that extended citizenship of the Russian Federation to all who lived in this country at that time and to those living in other Soviet republics if they so requested. In December, 1991 Yeltsin created the Commonwealth of Independent States that included the Russian Federation and other sovereign States which were previously the constituent units of the Soviet Union leaving the three Baltic republics of Estonia, Latvia and Lithuania.

On 12 June, 1991 Presidential election was held in which Yeltsin gained 57.3% of the votes by virtue of which he became the President of the Federation for next five years. In November, 1992 a bankruptcy law was made that permitted the winding up of the indebted enterprises. The system of central distribution of resources was established in 1993 and the work of overseeing privatisation was entrusted to the State Committee on the Management of State Property. It began with small and

2. Gorbachev says; "Perestroika is a word with many meanings. Its key or essence is revolution. A decisive acceleration of the socio-economic and cultural development of Soviet society which involves radical changes on the way to a qualitatively new state is undoubtedly a revoluntionary task." *Perestroika* (London: Collins, 1987), pp. 49-50.

3. *The New Encyclopaedia Britannica,* 1993, Vol. 10, p.255.

> **Some Important Statements**
>
> He who does not regret the passing of socialism has no heart, but he who wants to bring it back has no head. *—Vladimir Putin*
>
> Civil rights are a final area of concern. Under communism constitutions typically established an elaborate set of civil liberties, though in reality these were largely ignored by those in power. With the collapse of communism, the leaders were faced with deciding how civil liberties should be constitutionally protected. This meant not only strengthening the rule of law so that those once-hollow rights could be enforced, but also deciding what kinds of rights should be enshrined in the constitution. *—Patrick O'Neil*
>
> The new Russian constitution guarantees protection of those individual civil liberties traditionally emphasised in liberal democracies (speech, thought, association), as well as the right to housing, medical care, a decent environment, social security and free education–are also guaranteed, suggesting a continuing commitment to communal responsibility for the welfare of the individual. But the relative importance of individual and communal rights is left undermined, even though they may often collide with each other. *—Joan DeBardeleben*

medium-sized enterprises. The Constitution of the Russian Federation was passed by the legislature in 1992 and then ratified by the people in a referendum held on 12 December, 1993. The making and promulgation of the Constitution of the Russian Federation should be hailed as the first democratic experiment of the people who had so far been under the yoke of a totalitarian system. Yeltsin would be regarded as the Pericles of Russia in time to come. Russia is now a sovereign State as well as the most powerful member of a Confederation (Commonwealth of Independent States) created in 1991.

Salient Features

The Constitution of this country, known as the Fundamental Law of the Russian Federation, has these important features:

1. **A Liberal Document:** It establishes a popular system on the lines of other democratic countries of the world. It sanctions ideological or political diversity that automatically recognises a multi-party system. That is, now this country has no official ideology as was the case under the earlier Constitutions. All public associations have been made equal in the eye of law. No party or group can change

this system by forcible means. Freedom of thought and expression has been guaranteed and judiciary has been assured an independent position. The provisions of the Constitution ensure free and fair periodic elections. It protects right to private property with right of inheritance. Nationalisation of private property by the state for a public purpose by the authority of law has been recognised. As a result of this, the system of private economy has been introduced in the country that was not allowed under the erstwhile socialist system. The Government has been made accountable to the legislature for its acts of commission and omission. A long list of the human rights and civil freedoms of the citizens has been included in the fundamental principles of the constitutional system.

2. **Supremacy of the Constitution:** The Constitution of Russia is written. It has 137 Articles. Chapter 1 specifies fundamental principles of the constitutional order wherein the norms of liberal constitutionalism may well be noted. Chapter 2 has a long list of human and civil rights and freedoms. Provisions relating to the Federal Structure, the President of the Federation, the Federal Assembly, the Government of the Federation, and the Judiciary are contained respectively in Chapters, 3, 4, 5, 6 and 7. While some provisions relating to local government are contained in Chapter 8, the following chapter has provisions relating to amendment and revision of the Constitution. Art. 15 makes it clear that the Constitution of the Federation has the supreme legal force applicable to the country as a whole. All laws and decrees of the Centre and of the governments of the constituent units must conform to it. In this direction, a notable point is that all laws must be officially published for the sake of general information. Since the provisions of the Constitution may be amended or revised by special majority of the two chambers of the Federal Assembly and a bill of this kind is subject to the final verdict of the people in the form of referendum, it is rigid like the Constitutions of Switzerland and France.

3. **Fundamental Principles:** Chapter 1 has a set of 16 principles that constitute the basis of the Russian constitutional system. It is given that 'Russia is a democratic federative law-governed State with a republican form of government'. Man and his rights and freedoms shall be the supreme value. The recognition, observance and protection of human and civil rights and freedoms shall be an obligation of the State. Power is vested in the multi-national people

of the country who shall exercise it directly or through their elected deputies. Usurpation of power is prohibited. The Constitution shall be the supreme law of the land. The Russian Federation shall consist of the constituent units as republics (states), krays (areas), oblasts. (regions) and cities of federal significance. The Russian Federation shall be a social state whose policy is aimed at creating conditions ensuring a worthy life and the free development of human personality. Private as well as public property shall be recognised. The organisation of the government shall be based on the principle of separation of functions. The system of local government shall be guaranteed. Ideological and political diversity shall be recognized and, for this reason, multi-party system shall prevail. The Russian Federation shall be a secular state. Finally, universally recognised principles and norms of international law as well as international agreements made by the state shall be an integral part of its legal system. It shows that under this Constitution, Russia is a democratic, federal, secular and social welfare state.

4. **Internationalism:** The Russian Constitution goes much ahead in the direction of including provisions pertaining to an international order than what is given in Japanese and German Constitutions. While the Japanese constitution of 1946 declares renunciation of war as an instrument of national policy, and the German Constitution of 1949 says about the commitment of the State to observe the principles of international law, the Russian Constitution says about the commitment of the state to the principles and norms of international law as well as international agreements made by it. Human rights and freedoms shall be recognised and guaranteed according to the universally recognized principles and norms of international law. The enumeration of the basic rights and freedoms in this Constitution should not be interpreted as a denial or dimunition of other universally recognised human and civil rights and freedoms. The Russian Federation shall grant political asylum to foreign citizens and stateless persons in accordance with the universally recognised norms of international law. A bill passed by the State Duma must be compulsorily examined by the Federation Council if it is related to war and peace. The Constitutional Court of the Russian Federation may strike down a law or an order of the government of the Centre or of any constituent unit if it is inconsistent with an international treaty made by the Federation.

Some Important Statements

The spirit of liberty is the spirit which is not too sure that it is right:

—Vladimir Putin

Whoever would overthrow the liberty of a nation must begin by subduing the freeness of speech. ***—Benjamin Franklin***

Give me liberty or give me death. ***—Thomas Jefferson***

In the late 1980s, when *glasnost* permitted the formation of new and relatively autonomous social groups, the public life destroyed in the Stalinist and post-Stalinist periods had to be reconstructed. The process produced an outburst of public activity and many grassroots groups formed to express diverse interests and concerns.

—Joan DeBardeleben

5. **Environmentalism:** A novel feature of this Constitution should be traced in its recognition of the norms of sustainable development. It has provisions for the protection of a healthy environment. Everyone shall have the right to a favourable environment, reliable information on the state of environment and compensation for damages caused to one's health and property by the violation of environmental laws. Everyone shall have the duty to preserve nature and the environment and to treat the natural resources with care. Law-making on matters relating to land, water, forest, subsurface resources and environmental protection falls within the jurisdiction of the governments of the Centre as well as of the constituent units. The Government of the Russian Federation shall ensure the implementation of a uniform State policy in the spheres of culture, science, health, social security and ecology. It shows that this Constitution has paid heed to the new norms of internationalism in the direction of safeguarding the environment for the health and life of the people and thus contributed to the development of international environmental law.
6. **Federal System:** The Constitution establishes a federal system by dividing powers between the federal government and the constituent units which number 89 in all. The exclusive powers of the Centre have been spelt out which include adoption and amendment of the Constitution and of federal laws, securing compliance of the Constitutions (charters and laws) of the constituent units with the Russian Constitution and federal laws, making foreign policy and

conducting foreign relations, defence and security of the country, currency and money emission system, federal public services etc. It spells out concurrent powers of the Centre as well as of the constituent units as protection of human rights and civil freedoms, demarcation of State property, use of natural resources, safeguarding the environment, coordination of international and foreign economic relations etc. All other powers have been left to the constituent units. The Constitutional Court of the Federation has been given the power to interpret the terms of the Constitution and to settle legal disputes between the Centre and the constituent units or between the units themselves. The Russian Constitution has been declared the supreme law of the land.

7. **Quasi-Presidential Government:** The Russian Constitution has followed the pattern of the French Constitution by placing the head of the State (President) in a stronger position than that of the Government headed by the Prime Minister. The President proposes the name of the Chairman of the Government of the Federation (Prime Minister) that must be approved by the State Duma. In case the proposals of the President in this regard are rejected thrice, he shall dissolve the State Duma and then appoint a Prime Minister of his choice. He appoints Deputy Chairmen and other ministers of the Government on the advice of the Prime Minister. The ministry is responsible to the State Duma. This arrangement of ministerial responsibility resembles the parliamentary system of Britain, but the position of the President is not like that of a constitutional head who, like the British monarch, can do no wrong. The President has the power to accept, or not, the resignation of the Prime Minister and his ministers even after a motion of no-confidence is passed by the State Duma. Moreover, he can dissolve the State Duma in case it passes another motion of no-confidence against the Government within next three months. It shows that the responsibility of the Government to the State Duma is just a formality. The President presides over the sessions of the Government and, as such, his voice has its weight in the taking of decisions. He may dismiss the Prime Minister. He may remove the Deputy Prime Minister or any minister on the advice of the Prime Minister. It is clear that the Prime Minister has to act according to the wishes of the President, if he desires to live in office.

8. **Bi-Cameralism:** The Constitution has adopted the system of bi-cameralism by creating the Federation Council and the State Duma as the two chambers of the federal legislature. The old practice has been followed by not designating the two as the upper and the lower chambers as we find in other countries. However, the old tradition of declaring the national legislature as 'the highest body of the state' has been broken down. The State Duma looks like a lower chamber, as its 450 members are directly elected by the voters of the country. It approves the proposal of the President of the Federation relating to the appointment of the Chairman of the Government (Prime Minister) and may remove the Government by passing the motion of no-confidence. The Federation Council has 178 members as two representatives come from each constituent unit. In all other respects its powers are equal to those of the State Duma.
9. **Independence of Judiciary:** The Constitution has elaborate arrangements for the independence of judiciary. The work of administration of justice has been entrusted to the courts. It is required that the judges have higher education in law and must have been in the legal profession for not less than 5 years. Their appointments are made for a fixed duration. They are inviolable and, as such, a judge cannot face criminal liability save in accordance with the procedure established by law. The trial of the accused should be open and fair. The Constitutional Court has the final power of judicial review whereby it may strike down any law or decree of the federal government or of the government of any constituent unit in case it is repugnant to the provisions of the Constitution. This power is also given to the subordinate courts. Art. 120 says that the judges shall be independent and be subordinate only to the Constitution and the federal laws. If the court finds that the act of any government body conflicts with law, it shall take a decision in accordance with the Constitution and federal law conforming to it.
10. **Fundamental Rights and Duties:** Chapter 2 has a very long list of human rights and civil freedoms. Here we may find all the celebrated rights of the people as prevailing in a democratic country like equality before law and its equal protection, freedom of thought and expression, prohibition of discrimination on any artificial ground as that of faith or nationality, inviolability of person and family life,

free movement and residence in any part of the country, freedom to profess and practise any religion, right to form associations or unions, right to hold peaceful meetings, rigid to participate in the management of public affairs, right to elect and be elected and to take any public service, right to keep or dispose of private property, freedom for doing any literary or artistic activity, prohibition of making ex-post facto laws or putting a person in double jeopardy, right to social insurance in the event of old age or physical disablement, right to secure the nationality of a foreign state, right to have damages from the government in the event of its unlawful action, right to secure legal protection of these freedoms etc. At the same time, the citizens are duty-bound to abide by the Constitution and the laws of the land, to serve the motherland by rendering military service or service in any other form when called upon to do it, payment of legal taxes and levies, preserving the environment etc. The notable point is that here the Constitution has incorporated rights relating to the protection of environment and human rights as universally accepted.

A cursory look at the salient features of the Russian constitutional system leaves some strong impressions. First, Russia "is a semi-democracy by virtue of being a regime in which democratic and authoritarian forces operate along one another in a stable combination."[4] Second, this important fact should be taken into account that "in many post-communist states, the presidential system operates within what are parliamentary systems"[5]. Multi-party system is there of course, but independence of judiciary has not been ensured as it prevails in a liberal-democratic order inspite of fact that the present situation is far better than that prevailed in the Soviet Union.[6]

---

4. Andrew Heywood: *Politics*, p.35.
5. *Ibid.*, p.339.
6. As a critic says: "Concepts such as judicial independence had no tradition either in pre-revolutionary Russia or in the Soviet era. Under Soviet power, the Courts were answerable to the communist party and judges were selected through the *nomenklatura* system of party appointment. Likewise, the principle of 'rule of Law' was poorly understood, Joan DeBardeleben, "Russie" in Mark Kesselman, Joel Krieger and W.A. Joseph (eds.) *Comparative Politics at the Crossroads* (Lexington: D.C. Heath and Company, 1996), p. 336.

Fundamental Principles of the Constitutional Order

Section I of the Constitution has a number of principles which lay down the basis of the Russian constitutional system. These are:

1. Russia or the Russian Federation is a democratic federative law-governed State with a republican form of government.
2. Supreme value shall be attached to man and his rights and freedoms. It shall be the obligation of the State to recognise, observe and protect human and civil rights and freedoms.
3. Russia is a democratic and multi-national State.
4. The sovereignty of the Russian federation shall extend to its entire territory.
5. The Russian Federation shall have its constituent units, each shall have its own Constitution and laws, and all units shall be treated as equal.
7. The Russian Federation shall be a social state whose policy is aimed at creating conditions ensuring a worthy life and the free development of human personality.
8. The integrity of economic space, free flow of goods, services and financial resources, support of competition and the freedom of economic activity shall be guaranteed.
9. The principle of separation of functions shall be applied. As such, legislature, executive and judiciary shall be independent.
10. Local governments shall have a recognized independent status within the limits of their competence.
11. Ideological diversity shall be recognised.
12. Secularism shall be established.
13. The Constitution of Russia shall have supreme legal force and direct effect over the entire country.
14. Finally, no provision of the Constitution should be in conflict with these fundamental principles of the constitutional order and no principle may be changed except in accordance with the procedure established by the Constitution.

Human and Civil Rights and Freedoms and Obligations

Chapter II of the Russian Constitution specifies a long list of fundamental rights of the people which incorporate the points of 'human rights' as now accepted by all democratic countries of world. These are:

1. Equality before law and courts.
2. No discrimination on the grounds of sex, race, nationality, language, origin, descent, material and official status, place of residence, religion, beliefs, membership of public associations, or other circumstances.
3. Right to life, capital punishment to be given in rare cases.
4. Protection of human dignity, prohibition of torture, violence or severe humiliation.
5. Right to personal freedom or inviolability of person, freedom from arbitrary arrest and detention.
6. Inviolability of private and family life, protection of honour and good name, privacy of correspondence and communication.
7. Right to information, right of access to documents and materials affecting anybody's freedoms.
8. Inviolability of home.
9. Right to choose nationality and use native language and education.
10. Free movement, residence and settlement in any part of the country, right to go abroad and return.
11. Freedom of conscience and religion.
12. Freedom of thought and expression, prohibition of censorship of news.
13. Right to form associations or unions, including trade unions and to join or leave any association.
14. Right to peaceful assembly, marches and picketing.
15. Right to participate in the management of public affairs.
16. Right to elect and be elected or to secure a public service and take part in referendums.
17. Right to appeal to government bodies.
18. Right to private property.
19. Right to choose vocation and do labour.
20. Right to social security.
21. Right to protection of health.
22. Right to maintain favourable environment.

23. Right to education.
24. Freedom of literary, artistic, scientific, technical and other forms of creative activity and teaching.
25. Right to secure legal protection of freedoms.
26. Right to open and fair trial in a court.
27. Right to have qualified legal assistance.
28. Prohibition of ex-post facto laws.
29. Prohibition of double jeopardy.
30. Protection of the rights of under-trials and convicts.
31. Right to have damages from the State for its unlawful actions.
32. Recognition and honour of universal human rights.
33. State protection of Russian citizens living abroad, freedom from deportation and forced extradition.
34. Right to choose citizenship of a foreign State and enjoy double citizenship.
35. Right to political asylum.

The duties and obligations of the citizens are:

1. Caring for elders and parents by children above 18 years of age.
2. Payment of legal taxes and levies.
3. Preservation of nature, care of the natural resources and environment.
4. Defending the country and performing military service or services in any form for this sake.
5. Respecting the Constitution and laws of the Federation as well as norms of international treaties and universal human rights.

In fine, the Russian Constitution embodies all those rights which are honoured in a liberal–democratic system. If the words of Laski ring true that a state is known by the rights it maintains, then the Russian Federation is by all means a democratic State.

Federal System

The Russian Constitution establishes a federal system which is quite different from the system established by the Stalin Constitution of 1936 and by the Brezhnev Constitution of 1977 that was designated by the critics as 'quasi-federal', in spite of the fact that the complex mechanism of the constituent units remains by and large the same. It meets all the requirements of a federal system in the following manner:

First, the Constitution is written, rigid and supreme law of the land. It has 137 Articles and the method of amending it is quite difficult. It is the supreme law of the land. As such, all laws of the Centre as well as of the constituent units must conform to it.

Second, Art. 71 spells out following powers of the Federation:

1. Adoption and amendment of the Constitution and federal laws; control over, and compliance therewith,
2. Federation structure and the territory of the Russian Federation,
3. Regulation and protection of human and civil rights and freedoms; citizenship of the Federation, regulation and protection of the rights of national minorities,
4. Establishment of the system of federal legislative, executive and judicial bodies, the procedure for their organization and activities, formation of federal and State government bodies,
5. Federal and State property and administration thereof.
6. Establishment of the basic principles of federal policies and federal programmes in the sphere of State, economic, ecological, social, cultural and national development of the Russian Federation,
7. Establishment of the basic legal principles for the unified market; financial, currency, credit and customs regulation; money emission; the basic principles of pricing policy, federal economic services, including federal banks,
8. Federal budget, federal taxes and levies, federal funds for regional development,
9. Federal power-engineering systems, nuclear power, fissile materials, federal transport, railways, information and communication, activities in space.
10. Foreign policy and international relations of Russia, international treaties of the Federation, issues of war and peace.
11. Foreign economic relations of the Federation,
12. Defence and security, military production, determination of the procedure for selling and purchasing weapons, ammunition, military equipment and other military hardware, production of poisonous substances and the procedure for their use.

13. Determination of the status and the protection of the State borders, territorial sea, air space, exclusive economic zone and the continental shelf of the Federation.
14. Judicial system, public prosecution, criminal-procedural and criminal-executive legislation, amnesty and remission, civil, civil-procedural legislation, legal regulation of intellectual property,
15. Federal collision law,
16. Meteorological service, standards, metric and time systems, goods and cartography, official statistics and book-keeping.
17. State awards and honorary titles of the Federation,
18. Federal State services.

A novel feature of this Constitution is that it has included a list of concurrent powers on the pattern of the Australian and Indian Constitutions. Art. 72 says about the 'joint jurisdiction' of the Russian Federation and the constituent units in these matters:

1. Measures to ensure the correspondence of Constitution and laws of the republics and the charters, laws and other normative legal acts of other units,
2. Protection of human and civil rights and freedoms, protection of the rights of national minorities, ensuring lawfulness, law and order, public security, border zone regimes,
3. Issues of possession, utilisation and management of land and of subsurface water and other natural resources,
4. Demarcation of State property,
5. Use of natural resources, protection of the environment and provisions for ecological safety, specially protected natural territories, protection of historical and cultural monuments,
6. General issues of upbringing, education, science, culture, physical education and sport.
7. Coordination of health care issues, protection of the family, maternity, fatherhood and childhood, social protection, including social security.
8. Carrying out measures against catastrophes, natural disasters, epidemics, and the rectification of their consequences,
9. Establishment of common principles of taxation and levies in the Russian Federation,

10. Administrative, administrative-procedural, labour, family, housing, land, water and forest legislation, legislation on sub-surface resources and on environmental protection,
11. Personnel of judicial and law enforcement bodies, lawyers, notaries,
12. Protection of the traditional habitat and the traditional way of life of small ethnic communities,
13. Establishment of general principles of the organisation of the system of State government and local government bodies,
14. Coordination of international and foreign economic relations of constituent entities of the Russian Federation, and observance of international agreements of the Russian Federation.

Finally, the Constitution provides for the creation of a Constitutional Court to settle legal disputes between the Federation and the constituent units, to interpret the provisions of the Constitution, and to determine the constitutional validity of the laws and decrees of the Federation and of the constituent units.

Though the Constitution of the Russian Federation meets all the requirements of the federal system, it has its peculiar features which may be enumerated as under:

1. Admission into the Russian Federation and creation of a new constituent entity shall take place in accordance with the procedure established by federal constitutional law.
2. The status of a republic shall be determined by the Constitution of the Russian Federation as well as by the Constitution of the republic. But the status of all other units shall be determined by the Constitution of the Russian Federation and the charter of the unit concerned as adopted by its legislature.
3. Relations among the units of a republic may be regulated by a federal law or by a treaty between the government of the republic and the unit within it concerned.
4. The status of a constituent entity of the Russian Federation may be changed by mutual agreement between the Russian Federation and the constituent entity of the Russian Federation in accordance with federal constitutional law.
5. Russian language shall be the official language of the entire country. But the republics shall have the right to have their own official language.

6. The constituent units of the Federation have autonomy in respect of areas or matters which are not covered under the exclusive and joint control of the Centre and the units as given above.
7. No federal law or act should conflict with the provisions of the Federal Constitution and so no law or act of any constituent unit should conflict with the Russian Constitution and the law or act of the Centre.
8. With a view to encourage cooperation and coordination between the Federal and the constituent units, it has been provided that they shall set up a kind of 'unified system of executive authority'.
9. The Centre is all-powerful in matters of circulation and stabilisation of currency.
10. The Russian Federation may participate in inter-state associations and transfer some of its powers to those associations in accordance with international agreements, provided it does not entail restrictions on human rights and freedoms and does not conflict with the basic principles of the constitutional order of the Russian Federation.

The Russian federal system is in operation and sometimes we hear of the secessionist movements in the units of Chechnya and Daghestan. Keeping it in view, a critic says that many of the disputed issues between the regions and the Centre are not clearly resolved by the Constitution despite general statements about jurisdiction and shared responsibilities. Since 1994, individual treaties have been negotiated with some of the more recalcitrant republics within the Russian Federation such as Tatarstan and Bashkortostan. The process involves a continued reliance on an individualised ad hoc approach to constructing federalism, a process likely to endanger continuing perceptions of favouritism and discrimination towards particular republics and regions.

The fact that the Russian federal system has a fragile character cannot be overlooked. The Soviet Union was a multinational state. Leaders like Lenin, Stalin, Khrushchev and Brezhnev managed to maintain the superficial federal system with the iron hold of Communist Party. The principle of national self-determination was incorporated into the constitutions framed from time to time, but its realisation was an impossibility under the dictatorial rule of the Communist Party. This is the reason that as the hold of the party became weak, many republics took to the path of secession. All republics became independent states. Things have not taken a fundamental change under the constitution of the Russian

Federation as well. Secessionist movements may be seen in the provinces of Chechnya and Daghestan. The dissident elements are not prepared to honour the constitutional provision assigning seats to 89 units in the upper chamber of the Parliament (Federation Council). "The likely results are an escalation of demands for regional privileges and a drop in the perceived fairness of central policy."[7]

Amendment and Revision of the Constitution

Chapter 9 of the Constitution has provisions relating to its amendment and revision. These are:

1. Art. 134 says that such a proposal may be submitted by the President of the Federation, or by the Federation Council, or by the State Duma, or by the Federal Government, or by the legislative body *of* any constituent unit, or by groups consisting of not less than 1/5 of the members of the Federation Council or of the deputies of the State Duma.
2. Art. 135 says that the provisions of Chapter 1 (Fundamental Principles of the Constitutional Order) and of Chapter 2 (Human and Civil Rights and Freedoms) and of Chapter 9 may not be revised by the Federal Assembly of Russia. In case such a proposal is supported by 3/5 of the total number of the members of the Federation Council and of the State Duma, a Constitutional Assembly shall be convened. It may either reject the proposal or adopt a new draft by 2/3 majority of its total strength. After adoption., the draft shall be submitted for a referendum in which more than half of the electorate must take part and the decision in its favour must be supported by more than half of the voters taking part in it.
3. With regard to provisions contained in Chapters 3 to 8 of this Constitution, it is provided in Art. 136 that a proposal to this effect shall be adopted in accordance with the procedure established for the adoption of such a law and shall come into force after it has been approved by the legislative authorities of not less than 2/3 of the constituent units of the Russian Federation.
4. Finally, Art. 137 says that any amendment in Art. 65 of the Constitution (relating to the composition of the Russian Federation) shall be introduced on the basis of a federal constitutional law on

7. Joan DeBardeleben, *op. cit.* p. 331.

the admission to the Russian Federation and the creation within it of new constituent entities of the Federation or on changes in the constitutional and legal status of the constituent units of the Federation.

It shows that by nature this Constitution is rigid like the Swiss, French and German constitutions.

The procedure of amending the Russian constitution appears to be complicated in view of the fact that different provisions may be amended in different ways. Generally, one procedure is laid down in the constitution for amending any of its part or parts. Perhaps the makers of the Russian constitution have followed the Indian style where different methods have been prescribed for different categories of the provisions of the constitution. However, much depends not on the written provisions of the constitution as on the temperament of the people. English people have a flexible constitution which exists like a rigid constitution because of their conservative nature. Indian Constitution is a peculiar mixture of flexibility and rigidity and yet amendments after amendement have been made to alter the provisions where the procedure of amendment is difficult. The rulers of the Russian Federation may make amendments after amendments to meet the requirements of time and thereby dispel the fears arising out of its rigid nature.

16

STATE STRUCTURE

The structure of the federal government has the President at the apex, the Government (Prime Minister, the Deputy Prime Ministers and the Ministers) under his control, the Federal Assembly having Federation Council and State Duma, and the Judicial Authority including all federal courts with Supreme Court, Supreme Arbitration Court, Constitutional Court and prosecutorate. The pattern of the federal government is neither parliamentary nor presidential, it is a queer hybrid of the two as prevailing in France in view of the fact that the President overshadows the authority of the Prime Minister and his Council of Ministers as well as of the Federal Assembly in several important respects. However, it cannot be identified with the trend of, what the French call, Bonapartism in view of two salient facts. First, the President is responsible for his acts of commission and omission and, for this reason, he can be removed by the process of impeachment. Second, a person cannot have this office for more than two consecutive terms. The goal of eliminating all vestiges of a totalitarian system, as prevailing under the constitutional system of the former USSR, has been achieved to a considerable extent.

President

Art. 80 says that the President shall be the head of the State. He shall be elected for a term of four years by the citizens of the Russian Federation on the basis of universal, equal and adult suffrage. Any citizen of Russia who has completed the age of 35 years and has resided in the country on a permanent basis for at least ten years may be elected. The manner of the election shall be determined by a federal law. Like the German Constitution, the Russian Constitution says that one person cannot hold more than two consecutive terms. It is different from the American system where a person cannot have more than two terms either consecutively or otherwise. He shall take the oath of loyalty to the people in the presence of the members of the Federation Council, the State Duma and the Constitutional Court before assuming his office.[1]

Art. 92 makes it clear that the President shall exercise his powers after taking the oath until his term expires and a newly elected President has been sworn in. The office may fall vacant in the event of his death, resignation, persistent physical inability, or impeachment. In the event of his persistent inability for reasons of illness, his duties shall be delegated to the Prime Minister (Chairman of the Government of the Russian Federation), but he shall have no right to dissolve the State Duma, or call a referendum, or submit proposals for amendments in or revision of the Constitution. It is also provided that the next Presidential election shall be held before the expiration of three months from the date of the early termination of the Presidential office.

Art.93 has the provision of removal of the President by impeachment. He may be charged by the State Duma for high treason or some grave crime. A resolution to this effect must be passed in the State Duma by 2/ 3 majority of the whole House and then approved by the Federation Council in the like manner. It is required that such a move be initiated by at least 1/3 members of the State Duma that must be endorsed by a resolution of a special commission set up by it. Before the matter is finally decided in the Federation Council, it is also necessary that a decision be taken by the Supreme Court of the Federation in support of the allegation made by the State Duma and then a similar decision be taken by the Constitutional Court confirming that the established procedure for bringing charges against the President has been duly followed. Finally, it is required that the decision to impeach the President be taken by the Federation Council within three months after the charge is framed by the State Duma. In other words, the procedure of impeachment has these steps:

1. At least 1/3 members of the State Duma should initiate the move of impeachment. The charge or charges framed by them must be approved by a special commission set up by the House for this purpose.

---

1. Joan DeBardeleben: "Russia" in Mark Kesselman, Joel Krieger and W.A. Joseph: (eds): *Comparative Politics at the Crossroads* (Lexington: D.C. Heath and Co., 1996) pp. 330-31

2. The view of the Supreme Court of the Federation must be taken for ascertaining the commission of the crime by the action of the President.
3. The matter must be referred to the Constitutional Court for having its view whether the established procedure has been followed.
4. A resolution to impeach and remove the President must be passed in each House of the Federal Assembly by 2/3 majority of the total membership.
5. The Federation Council must adopt a resolution to this effect within three months after the State Duma brings the charges against the President.

The Constitution enumerates the functions and powers of the President in detail. First, in the executive sphere, his functions are as under:

1. To appoint the Chairman of the Government of the Federation (Prime Minister) with the consent of the State Duma, and to appoint ministers on the advice of the Prime Minister,
2. To preside over the meetings of the Government (Ministry) of the Federation,
3. To take action on the decision relating to the resignation of the Government,
4. To nominate to the State Duma a candidate for appointment to the post of a Chairman of the Central Bank of the Russian Federation and to raise before it the issue of his removal,
5. To appoint and remove the Deputy Chairman of the Government (Vice-Prime Minister) according to the advice of the Chairman (Prime Minister).
6. To recommend names to the Federation Council for the posts of the judges of the Constitutional Court, Supreme Court, Supreme Arbitration Court and the Prosecutor-General of the Russian Federation and judges of other federal courts.
7. To form and head the Security Council of the Federation whose status shall be determined by a federal law,
8. To approve the military doctrine of the Federation,
9. To form or organise the Administration (Secretariat) of his office,
10. To appoint and dismiss ambassadors and plenipotentiary representatives of the Federation,

11. To appoint and dismiss Supreme Commanders of the defence forces of the Federation,
12. After consultation with the appropriate committees and commissions of the chambers of the Federal Assembly, to appoint and recall diplomatic representatives of the Federation serving in foreign States and international organisations.
13. As Supreme Commander of the defence forces, to introduce martial law in the country or in some of its parts in the event of any aggression or its threat according to the terms of federal constitutional law and to inform the Federal Assembly in this regard immediately.
14. To introduce a state of emergency in the whole country or in its part according to the terms of federal constitutional law and then inform the Federal Assembly immediately in this regard,
15. To issue edicts and regulations with binding effect on the whole country in accordance with the terms of the Constitution of the Federation and other federal laws.

Art. 84 specifies his legislative powers as under:

1. To announce elections to the State Duma in accordance with the Constitution of the Federation and other federal laws,
2. To dissolve the State Duma in accordance with the terms of the Constitution,
3. To announce referendums according to the terms of the Constitution,
4. To submit draft laws to the State Duma,
5. To sign and promulgate federal laws.
6. To address the Federal Assembly with annual messages on the situation in the country and on the basic objectives of the internal and foreign policy of the State.

The diplomatic powers of the President, as given in Art. 86, are:

1. To frame or direct the foreign policy of the Federation,
2. To hold negotiations and sign international treaties of the Federation,
3. To sign instruments of ratification,
4. To receive letters of credence and letters of recall of the diplomatic representatives accredited to his office.

Besides, the President has some other powers which may be enumerated as under:

1. The Constitution spells out obligations of the President in general as (*i*) to protect and preserve the Constitution, (*ii*) to guarantee protection of the human rights and freedoms, (*iii*) to adopt measures to safeguard the sovereignty, independence and unity of the State, (*iv*) to ensure coordinated functioning and interaction of all bodies of the Government, (*v*) to determine the basic objectives of the home and foreign policy of Russia, and (*vi*) to represent the Federation in international relations. It must be done in accordance with the provisions of the Constitution.
2. To use conciliatory procedure so as to resolve disputes between the federal government and the governments of the constituent units and to refer that matter to an appropriate court in the event of non-agreement; to suspend any law or act of a constituent unit on the ground of being against the Russian Constitution, or against any federal law, or against international commitments of the Federation, or against human and civil rights and freedoms, until the issue is resolved by an appropriate court,
3. To settle matters relating to the citizenship of Russia and granting political asylum; to bestow State awards and confer honorary titles and supreme military and special titles and to grant pardon.

Government–Council of Ministers

By designating federal executive as the 'Government of the Russian Federation,' the Russian Constitution has followed the pattern of the French Constitution. It is the executive wing of the Federation. It consists of a Chairman (Prime Minister), Deputy Chairmen (Deputy Prime Ministers) and some ministers. The Chairman shall be appointed by the President of the Federation with the consent of the State Duma. Nomination for this post shall be submitted not later than two weeks after a newly elected President assumes his office, or after the resignation of the Government, or within one week after the State Duma rejects this nomination. The State Duma shall take decision on the nomination of the Chairman by the President within one week of its submission. The State Duma may reject two nominations. In case it does it thrice, then the President shall dissolve it and appoint a Chairman of his choice.

After his appointment, the Chairman of the Government shall submit to the President his proposal about the organisation of the ministry within a week. The list shall contain the names of the Deputy Chairmen and other federal ministers along with their portfolios. Then, in accordance with the provisions of the Constitution, federal laws, and decrees issued by the President, he shall determine the basic objectives of the activities of his government and shall organize the work of all ministers. The functions of the Government are:

1. To develop and submit to the State Duma a federal budget and a report relating to its implementation,
2. To ensure implementation of a uniform policy throughout the country in the spheres of culture, science, education, health, social security and ecology,
3. To carry out the administration of federal property,
4. To carry out measures for the defence of the country, national security, and implementation of its foreign policy,
5. To implement measures so as to ensure lawfulness and civil rights and freedoms, protect property and public order, and combat crime,
6. To exercise other functions entrusted to it by the Constitution, or federal laws, or Presidential decrees.

It is also given that the procedure of the working of the Government shall be determined by a federal law. Art. 115 makes it clear that the decrees or orders issued by the Government shall be binding. In case any decree of the government is inconsistent with the provisions of the Constitution, or federal laws, or Presidential decrees, the President shall have the power to strike it down.

The Government has been made responsible to the President as well as to the State Duma. It shall resign shortly before the new President assumes his office. It may submit its resignation to the President at any time who may, or may not, accept it. The State Duma may pass a motion of no-confidence by its absolute majority against it. In such a case, the President may either accept or reject it. In case the State Duma passes another no-confidence motion within three months, the President may either accept the resignation of the Government, or dissolve the State Duma. The Government may itself initiate the move by putting a confidence motion. In case the Government is defeated, the President may either accept its resignation, or dissolve the State Duma. After accepting the resignation of the Government, the President may instruct it to continue until the new Government is formed.

It shows that the Russian Constitution envisages a typical model of the principle of ministerial responsibility. Its responsibility to the popular chamber of the national legislature (State Duma) is nominal, to the Head of the State it is real in view of the fact that the President may either accept the decision of the House or reject it, and may even go to the final extent of punishing the House by ordering new elections. The making of the Government resembles the German model to the extent that the proposal of the President relating to the nomination of the Prime Minister (Chancellor in Germany) is to be accepted by the popular chamber of the Parliament. But other provisions have no parallel in any other Constitution of the world. By all means, it places the President in a very strong position. It may be said that the ministry lives and works under the thumb of the President, not of the popular chamber of the national legislature, the type of which may not be found in any democratic country of the world.

Federal Assembly

The Constitution establishes a bi-cameral legislature known as the Federal Assembly having Federation Council and State Duma as the upper and lower chambers respectively. Art. 94 defines it as 'the representative and legislative body of the Russian Federation'. The Federation Council shall have two representatives from each constituent unit of the Federation. As there are 89 units, so its present strength is 178.[2] It simply lays down that each constituent unit of the Federation shall send two deputies, one representing its legislative wing and the other its executive wing. The State Duma has 450 members directly elected by the voters of the country. Here the Russian Constitution has followed the German pattern. Half of its members are elected by means of proportional representation with list system. In order to be elected, it is necessary that the person must be a citizen of Russia, be over 21 years of age, and have the right to participate in elections. One person cannot be simultaneously a member of more than one house of the Federal Assembly or of any other legislature of the country.

The federal law relating to the elections has these important provisions :

2. *The Europa World Year-Book* (London; Routledge, 2010), Vol. II, p. 3772.

1. To qualify for candidacy, an individual must obtain signatures of at least one per cent of the voters of his constituency.
2. A party or an electoral alliance must obtain at least 100,000 supporting signatures from at least 7 regions, but not more than 15 per cent from one region.
3. In the election a party must get at least 5 per cent of the votes polled in respect of seats to be allocated according to proportional representation with list system.[3] In each house a party must get at least 35 seats to secure or maintain its registration as a 'faction' that would entitle it for chairing the commissions and committees of the house.

It should be noted here that the State Duma may be dissolved before the expiry of its term by the President in case it rejects the nomination of the Prime Minister thrice, or it passes second no-confidence motion against the Government within next 3 months. But under certain conditions it cannot be dissolved by the President. These are:

1. If it has not completed one year of its existence.
2. If it brings charges against the President of the Federation, until the Federation Council takes a decision on that issue.
3. If the state of emergency or martial law is in force in the country as a whole or in one of its parts.
4. If the term of the President of the Federation is to expire within next six months.

After making an announcement of the dissolution of the State Duma, the President of the Federation shall announce the dates of next elections so that the newly elected house may be convened not later than 4 months. The term of the State Duma is of four years. But the procedure relating to the composition of the Federation Council shall be determined by a federal law. The deputies of the State Duma shall work on a professional permanent basis; they may not be employed in State service or engaged in any other paid activity except for teaching or for some scientific or creative work. The members would enjoy immunity during the term of their office. They may not be arrested, detained, or searched except in the event of detention at the place of crime. They may not be subjected to personal searches

3. The election law of the Russian Federation permits a political party to 'delegate' some of its percentage in favour of another party so that it may cross the 'threshold' of 5 per cent of votes.

except in instances where so provided by a federal law in order to ensure safety of other people. The issue of the removal of immunity, or the matter of privileges as called in other democratic countries, shall be resolved in an appropriate chamber of the Federal Assembly on submission of the Prosecutor-General of the Federation.

The Federal Assembly shall be a permanently functioning body. The State Duma shall convene its first session on the thirteenth day after election, but the President may convene its session even earlier. The first session of this house shall be inaugurated by its oldest member. The business of the house shall lapse with its dissolution. The two houses shall meet separately. The sessions shall be open, but the State Duma may hold a secret session in a special situation envisaged by its procedural regulations. A joint session may be held to hear the message of the President or of the Constitutional Court of the Federation, or of some foreign dignitary. Each house shall elect its presiding officer and his deputy from amongst its own members. Both houses shall set up their committees and commissions and hold parliamentary hearings on issues under their jurisdiction. Each house shall set up its Accounts Chamber whose composition and working shall be determined by a federal law. Each house shall adopt decrees on issues relating to its authority by the Constitution. A decree shall be adopted by a majority of the total strength of the house, unless provided otherwise by a federal law.

The process of legislation has some unique features which may be noted as under:

1. The right of legislative initiative belongs to the President, Federation Council, State Duma, Government or Ministry, Constitutional Court, Supreme Court, Supreme Arbitration Court of the Russian Federation as well as to the legislative bodies of all constituent units.
2. Bills shall be submitted to the State Duma. However, bills on the introduction or cancellation of or exemption from taxes, issue of State loans, changes in the financial obligations of the State, and expenses to be covered by the federal budget shall be submitted upon a resolution of the Government of the Federation.
3. Bills shall be adopted by the State Duma and then submitted to the Federation Council within next five days for 'examination' who shall approve it by its absolute majority. In case the Federation Council takes no action within this period of 14 days, the bill shall be taken as passed. In case the Council rejects it, the two chambers may set

up a conciliatory commission to resolve the matter after which the bill shall be reconsidered by the State Duma. In case the Federation Council rejects the reconsidered bill of the State Duma, then the State Duma may pass it by 2/3 majority of its total strength.

4. A federal bill passed by the State Duma must be compulsorily 'examined' by the Federation Council if it is related to the federal budget, federal taxes and levies, financial currency, credit and customs regulation, money remission, ratification and denunciation of international treaties of the federation, status and protection of the State borders of the Federation, and war and peace.
5. The veto power of the President over a bill passed by the Federal Assembly is absolute as well as qualified. It is given that a bill passed by the Federal Assembly shall be placed before the President within five days of its adoption who shall sign and promulgate it within next 14 days. In case he rejects a bill, the two houses may reconsider it and in case the same bill in the same form is readopted by both the houses separately by 2/3 majority of their total strength, the President shall sign it within 7 days and then promulgate it.
6. Different is the case of the adoption of a constitutional bill. It is given that a federal constitutional bill must be passed by the Federation Council by 3/4 majority of its total membership and then by 2/3 majority of the total membership of the State Duma. The President shall give assent to such a bill and promulgate it within 14 days. It shows that the President has no veto power over a federal constitutional bill.

Judiciary and Prosecutorate

The Russian Constitution has made an achievement by making provisions for the independence of judiciary. Art. 118 says that the administration of justice shall be vested in the courts. Judicial authority shall cover civil, criminal, administrative and constitutional varieties. The creation of special or extraordinary courts shall not be permitted. The judicial system is established according to the terms of the Constitution and federal laws. With a view to maintain independence of judiciary these provisions have been made:

1. The judges shall be the citizens of the Russian Federation, be above 25 years of age, must have higher qualifications in law and have

served in the legal profession for not less than five years, the federal law may require additional requirements.

2. The judges shall be independent. They shall have the power to examine the validity of any act or of a law in the event of its conflict with the provisions of the Constitution and thereby hold supremacy of law.
3. More important is the provision that the judges shall be irremovable. The powers of a judge may be terminated or suspended only on the grounds of and in accordance with the procedure established by law.
4. The judges shall be inviolable. As such, a judge cannot face criminal liability otherwise than in accordance with the procedure established by federal law.
5. The hearing or examination of a case in all courts shall be open. Cases may be heard in close sessions in a situation permitted by a federal law. The examination of criminal cases by default in courts shall not be permitted except in a situation permitted by law. Judicial proceedings shall be conducted on the basis of controversy and the equality of the parties concerned. Where legally required, judicial proceedings shall be conducted with the participation of a jury.
6. Finally, it is given that the courts shall be financed from the federal budget and should ensure the possibility of the complete and independent administration of justice according to the requirements of a federal law.

The Constitution provides for three apex courts–Constitutional Court, Supreme Court and Supreme Arbitration Court. The President appoints the judges of these courts with the consent of the Federation Council. It implies that the nominations of the judges made by the President shall be approved by the upper house of the Federal Assembly. It resembles the American system where the appointments of the judges made by the President are ratified by the Senate. But appointments of the judges of other federal courts are made by the President according to the provisions of a federal law. The powers and procedure of all the courts shall be determined by a federal constitutional law.

The Supreme Court is the highest judicial body of the Federation for civil, criminal, administrative and other cases examined by courts of arbitration; it exercises judicial supervision over their activities in the procedural forms envisaged by federal law and shall provide interpretation on issues of judicial proceedings. The Supreme Arbitration Court of the Federation is the highest judicial body for settling economic disputes and other cases examined by courts of arbitration; it exercises judicial supervision over their activities in the procedural forms envisaged by federal law and provides interpretation on issues of judicial proceedings.

The Constitutional Court of the Federation consists of 19 judges. It is the custodian of the Constitution. At the request of the President, or of the Federation Council, or of the Government, or of the Supreme Court, or of the Supreme Arbitration Court, or of any legislative or executive department of any constituent unit of the Russian Federation, this Court hears and decides whether or not an impugned law or action of the Centre or of the government of any constituent unit is in conformity with the provisions of the Russian Constitution or of any treaty signed by the Centre. It also settles disputes between government bodies of the Centre and the constituent units of the Federation. It interprets the provisions of the Constitution at the request of the President, or of any chamber of the Federal Assembly of the Centre, or of some such body of a constituent unit. It also exercises the power of judicial review by looking into the validity of a law or action of the Central or regional and local governments as to whether it is in violation of the constitutional rights and freedoms of the citizens. It also decides whether a particular international treaty signed by the Centre is consistent with the provisions of the Constitution. In case the Constitutional Court strikes down any law or order or treaty on the ground of its unconstitutionality, it shall not be enforceable. At the request of the Federation Council, this Court may issue a resolution on the observance of the established procedure for bringing charges of treason or of other grave crimes against the President of the Federation.

The provisions of the Constitution demonstrate a marked change in the judicial process of this country by virtue of making arrangements for an independent judiciary. But in one respect the tradition of the earlier Soviet Constitutions has been maintained. The offices of the Prosecutor-General and of subordinate prosecutors have been included in the domain of judicial authority. More than this, the whole structure has been given a centralised form like the system of procuratorate as established under the Stalin and the Brezhnev constitutions. Art. 129 says that the office of the Prosecutor-General of the Russian Federation shall be a single centralised structure in which public prosecutors are subordinated to higher public prosecutors. The Prosecutor-General shall be appointed and dismissed by the Federation Council on the recommendation of the President. The prosecutors of the constituent units of the Federation shall be appointed by the Prosecutor-General with the consent of the government of the unit concerned. All other prosecutors shall be appointed by the Prosecutor-General of the Federation. The powers of the Prosecutor-General of the Federation shall be determined by a federal law.

The operation of the Russian political system should, however, be appreciated with a sense of caution. Democratic institutions are developing, of course, but things will take time to consolidate themselves. When the Constitutional Court established by Yeltsin in June 1991 over-ruled some of the actions of the President, he dubbed it as an activist role of the judiciary and dissolved it. He also dissolved the sitting Parliament in October, 1993. The result was that the Parliament and the Constitutional Court were recreated according to the wishes of the President. He also managed to restructure the powers of the Courts by urging the Federal Assembly to make laws in this regard. Hence, it is commented: "Executive centralism is prevalent at least in theory...Russia has traditionally lacked an independent judiciary., but since independence some steps have been taken towards the separation of the judicial system from the political authorities."[4] Those who see things from close quarters find that the dominant role of bureaucracy is still there. Prof. Garvil Popov, former Mayor of Moscow, testified it in these words: "The country's old command system, the core of which was the Communist Party viewed power exclusively as an instrument for achieving its own ends. It has gone now. But this does not mean that it has been replaced by democratic rule. Only a system capable of organising certain aspects of society's life outside the state system, that is on an independent basis, can act as a real alternative to bureaucracy. Today bureaucracy reigns everywhere."

An American critic thus says: "The new Russian Constitution adopted in December, 1993 shifts the balance of power decisively in the direction of the executive branch. The structure embodied in the new Constitution resembles the French presidential system in many ways, but some critics in Russia call it an authoritarian Constitution, because it places so many powers in the President's hands. As in France, the Russian Constitution creates ample room for conflict between the legislative and executive branches. However, a combination of factors (including constitutional provisions, political culture, political party fragmentation and regionalism)

4. *The Encyclopaedia Americana,* 1995, Vol. 24, p. 29.

work to give more powers to the Russian President than the French President. The constitution designates the President as the head of the state, but, unlike in Germany, he does not have a figurehead position. At the same time, the Constitution places executive power in the government of Russia, which is headed by the Prime Minister. The structure envisages conflict between the President and the legislative branch, because the President's party or supporters do not necessarily hold the balance of power in the Parliament."[5]

5. Joan DeBardeleben, *op. cit.*, pp. 331-32.

17

POLITICAL PARTIES AND PRESSURE GROUPS

One important point that makes the Russian Federation fundamentally different from the Soviet Union is the prevalence of multi-party system and the rise of a number of interest groups some of which are also known as social and protest movements. Gone are the days when the Communist Party was the state and only such groups could play their part in the political process of the country which had the patronage of the ruling party. Some of the parties are so small that they look like pressure groups and may be taken not as 'transmission belts' but as alternative political blocs. One of the most important of these new groups was the Democratic Russia Movement which formed the base of support for Yeltsin's leadership. It represented a broad coalition of forces, opposed to the dominance of the Communist party which wanted Russia to gain enough autonomy to move more quickly to the direction of market reform and democratization, concepts that were still only vaguely defined at that time.[1]

Political Parties

As already pointed out, now Russia has a multi-party system. About half a dozen parties take part in the Presidential and Parliamentary elections and manage to secure sizeable number of votes. Still, the party system is in a formative stage. These parties are known by the name of their supreme leaders which shows that they are formed not on the basis of some clear-cut programme but on the personality of a leader. They do not have a firm social base or their stable constituencies. The process of fragmentation and polarisation is also at work as a result of which the parties and electoral

1. DeBardeleben, "Russia" in Kesselman and others, *Comparative Politics at the Crossroads*, p. 343.

coalitions are fluid. Parties and blocs frequently splinter, join with others, and rename themselves making it difficult for the public to hold parties and politicians accountable for their actions (or inaction) and to know whom to vote for (or against). "Alternative policy approaches are not clearly articulated by a viable opposition party or coalition. As a result of all this fragmentation and flux, many voters have become apathetic or confused. The weakness of political parties has also hindered the government's ability to develop a firm base of political support for its policies."[2]

The multi-party system of the Russian Federation is dis-organised and indisciplined. There are more than two dozen parties and blocs, big and small as Agrarian Party, All-Russian Union for Reunion, Democratic Party of Russia, Majority Party, New Names, Our Home is Russia, Party of Economic Freedom, Russian All-People's Union, Russia's Democratic Choice, Free Labour Party, Peasants Party of Russia, Republican Party of Russia, Social Democratic Party of Russian Federation, Communist Party of Russia, Liberal Democratic Party, Congress of Russian Communities, Forward Russia, Party of Russian Unity and Accord, Democratic Russian Movement, Free Democratic Party of Russia etc. Some parties are like blocs as Women of Russia and Yabloko. Derzhava is an alliance of some parties as Russian Christian Democratic Movement, State Renaissance Party, Soyuz and Social Democratic People's Party.

None but the Communist Party of Russia has an ideology of its own. It stands on the principles of Marxism-Leninism. The policies and programmes of other parties are vague and when some party fights for the interest of a particular section of the people, it looks like an interest group. For instance, the Agrarian Party and Peasants Party of Russia fight for the interests of the farmers and demand agricultural reforms along with dissolution of collective farm system. Other parties as Party of Economic Freedom and Republican Party of Russia supports mixed economy and liberalisation in the economic sphere. The Social Democratic Party of the Russian Federation has a socialist programme as it desires a democratic

2. *Ibid.*

system ensuring social participation of the employers and the workers and protection of human rights. It may be taken as a mildly leftist organisation. The Russian Christian Democratic Movement and Majority Party have a rightist orientation.

Pressure Groups

In the Soviet Union several interest groups (as Komsomols, Octoberists, Pioneers, Writers' Union etc.) existed which were subordinate to the Communist Party and which served as a conduit for its ideological influence and political control. But now the conditions have basically changed. The workers, the employees and the professionals have formed their unions and the functioning of those associations has changed which existed under the rule of the Communist Party in the Stalinist and post-Stalinist periods. The Federation of Independent Trade Unions (FITU) is no longer an arm of the Communist Party. The workers have formed their trade unions at the regional and local levels. The Writers' Union and the Cinematographers' Union are the examples of professional groups. The Women Movement though registered under the election law, is not a party as such, it is an interest group of the women of Russia. The notable point is that now dissident and protest movements often occur here. Andrei Sakharov, who was thrown behind the bars, was freed in 1986 and then he freely participated in the reform process till his death three years after. Alexander Solzhenitsyn, who was exiled from the country, came back in 1994. It shows that in the Russian Federation led by Yeltsin, the people "increasingly refused to allow Communist Party organisations to define their interests for them, but instead expressed their interests for themselves."[3]

In the end, we may say that the political system of the Russian Federation is no longer totalitarian as it was in the Soviet Union. A liberal-democratic order replaced the communist order established by Lenin and strengthened by his successors like Stalin, Khrushchev and Brezhnev. Gorbachov read the pulse of the time and he started the process of change that saw its consolidation at the hands of Yeltsin. It had four integrated

3. *Ibid*, p. 351.

implications-liberalisation and then attempted democratisation of the political system, dismantling State dominance of the economy, a search for new forms of collective identity to replace those provided by the old communist ideology, and process of economic integration into the world of states and exposure to ideas and goods from the western world."[4]

4. *Ibid*, p. 357.

Part - V
Chinese Constitution

Because imperialism still exists, because domestic reactions still exist in our country, our present task is to strengthen the people's state apparatus--mainly the people's army, the people's police and the people's courts--in order to consolidate national defence and protect people's interests. Given these conditions, China can develop steadily under the leadership of the working class and the Communist Party, from an agricultural to an industrial country, and from a new democratic into a socialist and communist society, can abolish classes and realise the Great Harmony.

—***Mao Zedong***

18

CONSTITUTION OF CHINA

A study of the Chinese political system in an advanced study of the modern political systems is not without certain pertinent reasons. The Chinese civilisation is one of the oldest civilisations of the world. To a student of religion and philosophy, China represents a very old system of its own. Likewise, to a student of politics, she is important not as much for its centuries-old religious or cultural traditions but because of her inherent potentialities of a world power. When China was like a moribund entity in the 19th century, Napoleon Bonaparte could visualise: "There lies a sleeping giant. Let it sleep, for when he wakes, he will shake the world." The whole world is aware of the fact that the Chinese rulers have ever been obsessed with the idea of world domination. However, what has attracted the attention of the world at large towards the political system of this country is the fact of its becoming 'red' in 1949 under the leadership of Mao Tse-tung–the Red Father of China. The progress that this country made under this supreme leader and after him coupled with political developments that have taken place ever since the advent of communism unmistakably lead to this impression that "an ignorance of the nature and aims of this rising colossus, regardless of the attitudes taken towards it, is a serious chink in anyone's intellectual armoury."[1]

Making of the Republic of China

Japan's victory over Russia in 1905 gave a new impetus to the upsurge of Chinese nationalism. Now the 'maker of modern China' appeared. He was Dr. Sun Yat-sen. Inspired by the three ideals People's Nationalism, People's Democracy and People's Livelihood–he exhorted the people to follow him for making the revolution successful.[2] As a result, the revolution

1. Harold C. Hinton: "China" in Kahin (ed.): *Major Governments of Asia,* p. 41.
2. Bhatia and Tan Chung (eds): *Legal and Political System in China,* Vol. 1, p. 9.

of 1911 took place when the Manchu rule was overthrown and China became a republic. A new Constitution came into force and Dr. Sun Yat-sen made his nephew Yuan Shi-kai the President. However, the objective of the revolution was frustrated as the first President moved in the direction of establishing his personal rule. He abrogated the Constitution after a year of its inauguration and was prevented by death from crowning himself as the emperor. It shows that the revolution of 1911 failed the reason of which should be traced in the fact that the revolutionaries had little in common beyond overthrowing the Manchu dynasty, and because there "was little Chinese nationalism at the time to give support to the new republic."[3]

The message of the revolution of 1911 was now carried by the Nationalist People's Party or the Kuomintang (former Alliance Society) that posed a serious threat to the dictatorial ambitions of the first President. What, however, came into the way of Chinese progress was the imperialistic expansion of Japan that in 1915 made notorious 21 demands on China. Fortunately, due to the pressures of Britain and the United States, the Japanese rulers modified their demands and thereby secured a foothold in the mainland of China. The successor of the first President, Li Yung failed miserably and thus the Kuomintang (KMT) set up a separate government in the south with its capital at Canton. Moreover, the governors of certain provinces raised their own armies and they became 'war-lords'. Thus was ushered in the short era of war-lordism signifying that China "fragmented into a number of conflicting regional units, each based on locally recruited army, and often backed by one or the other of the great Powers seeking to defend their own interests."[4]

The deteriorating situation could be checked in 1921 when Dr. Sun Yat-sen became the President of Chinese government in the south. He reorganised his KMT and then moved towards the north to deal with the formidable forces of war-lordism. The expedition took place under the command of Chiang Kai-shek. A new Constitution was adopted in 1924 and the Organic Law of the National Government was enforced in 1928.

The momentous development that took place at this stage was Dr. Sun's getting close to the communists to deal with the forces of internal disruption. He appreciated the idea of including the communists in the

3. D.J. Waller: *The Government and Politics of Communist China*, p. 16.

4. *Ibid.*

KMT as 'individuals' and not as party members. The Russian emissary Michael Bordin could persuade Dr. Sun to reorganise his KMT on the pattern of the Communist Party of the USSR. He was also instrumental in the establishment of the Whampoa military academy which was headed by Chiang Kai-shek, though it had a large number of Russian military experts on its staff. The way for the infiltration of the communists was thus opened.

Differences between the communist and anti-communist elements grew after the death of Dr. Sun in 1925 when Chiang held the office of the President. In 1927 he took to the course of totally suppressing the communists. The result was the downfall of the leadership of Chen Tuhsiu. The communists could not improve their position until Mao Tse-tung assumed the undisputed leadership of the Chinese Communist Party in 1935 who had all along advocated guerilla tactics in place of positional warfare in meeting the KMT attacks and had looked upon the peasantry as the main revolutionary force in the country. However, as Chairman of the Chinese Soviet Republic set up in Kiangsi in 1927 (and abolished in 1937), he had earned popularity by advocating a policy of land reforms that tolerated small land-owners. What, however, forced Chiang Kai-shek to work in alliance with the communists was the imperialistic posture of Japan. It afforded a good occasion to the communists to fight against the Japanese forces during the Second World War and yet weaken the foundations of the KMT by perfecting their guerilla-based system and carefully building up their strength and popular support in the countryside.

When the second great war ended, China remained under the formal control of Chiang Kai-shek and his KMT, while the real power had well slipped into the hands of the communists. Facts indicate that by this time, the communists had established some 27 'liberated areas' with an aggregate population of 85 million and had enormously expanded the Red Army, now one million strong. A sort of civil war was now unleashed. To deal with this problem, the KMT government convened a national constituent assembly in November, 1946 that was boycotted by the communists and the Democratic League. The new Constitution was framed and enforced on the new year's day in 1947 that was declared invalid by the communists. Elections under the new Constitution took place in November, 1947 and Chiang was elected as the President. The KMT regime, however, lacked cohesion and corroded by snowballing corruption, rapidly alienated the sympathy of the people in the countryside as well as of the intellectuals and students in the towns. Despite the massive support of the United States, the KMT could not stem the tide of advancing communism and finally collapsed when Chiang Kai-shek escaped from the capital and sought refuge in the island of Formosa (Taiwan). Thus, on October 1, 1949 the People's Republic of China came into being. It heralded the significance of this remark that "under the communist dispensation, the monopoly of one would have to be asserted, something which even the strongest dynasties had never achieved."[5]

In short, the foundations of the political system of China are based on a particular ideology. It is the ideology of Marxism-Leninism that has been further tailored first by Mao and then by his successors to suit the conditions of Asia's biggest country. It is based on the Sinified Marxism of Mao who took upon himself the arduous task of modernising his country even at the expense of the traditional culture of his people. The way Mao could suppress his opponents in the 'great proletarian cultural revolution' could show that the system would not collapse under its own weight or through faulty construction. Even after the passing away of the Great Leader, the system has shown a remarkable ability to survive and thereby belie the almost incredible miscalculations on the part of a section of the leadership and heavy pressures from diverse outside sources. Even the critics admit that the People's Republic of China "promises to be an ambitious, dynamic, ruthless, and growing power. As such, it will require constant and increased understanding by all persons who are concerned not only with the future of the United States but with the future of Asia and, indeed, of the world."[6]

Chinese Constitutionalism

The story of constitutionalism in China begins from 1912 when she became a republic and gave to herself the 'most modern type of Constitution' whereby on January 1, 1912 Sun Yat-sen was formally instituted as the President of the provisional republican government. On the same day, the National Council at Nanking adopted a provisional Constitution and the first national flag with five stripes representing the five races of the Chinese, Manchus, Mongols, Tibetans and the Moslems. However, the period which followed the revolution of 1911 became ripe

5. H.McAkavy: *The Modern History of China,* p. 328.

6. A.S. Whiting: "China" in Ward and Macridis (eds): *Modern Political Systems: Asia.,* p. 213.

with vast problems, complexities and confusion as a result of which power fell into the hands of the military despots who had little sympathy either for the discarded system or for the adoption of political democracy. Moreover, Sun's action of making Yuan his successor resulted in the abrogation of the provisional Constitution in 1913 and the inauguration of a period of political instability that could not be controlled until the Kuomintang established its firm control in 1923 and then adopted a 'Permanent Constitution of the Republic of China.' As declared in the Preamble, the new Constitution was made "with the object of establishing the national dignity and maintaining the national boundaries and in order to promote the welfare of the people and uphold the principles of humanity."

After the seizure of power by the communists in 1949, the work of making a new Constitution was entrusted to a committee set up by the Central People's Government on Jan. 13, 1953. The committee met under the chairmanship of Mao that prepared the new Constitution of communist China. It was adopted by the National People's Congress on Sept. 20, 1954. As claimed by the founder of the new regime, the Constitution recorded five fundamental changes in his country since the inception of communism - China's emergence as a really independent state after shaking off all shades of colonial dominations, termination of the centuries-old hold of feudalism, achievement of internal peace and an unprecedented unification of the mainland after terminating the era of chaos, attainment of a higher degree of democracy after putting an end to the situation in which people had no power, and, finally, rehabilitation of the economy of the country with the cooperation of the Soviet Union. It was replaced by a new constitution in 1975.

The replacement of the Constitution of 1975 by a new one became a natural event after the death of Mao Tse-tung (Zedong) in Sept., 1976. The new regime under Hua Kuo-feng announced the revision of the Constitutions of the Communist Party and of the State as early as possible. It was officially declared that the new regime wanted to adopt a new constitution in order to make it more attuned to the economic and military modernisation which is the prime goal of leadership while possibly restoring a limited measure of liberalism in the treatment of diverse 'social groups and opinions'. It desired to pursue the policy of reverting to academic standards in education, introducing profit incentives for industrial workers and playing down the idea of 'class struggle' which had created so much disturbance over the last ten years.

Some Important Statements

The Soviet Union from 1917 to 1991 and China since 1949 are examples of countries where this communist ideology has been installed as the political regime through revolution, creating what these countries call (or called) 'people's democracies'.

—Patrick O'Neil

In China of today we can never dispense with leadership by the Party and extol the spontaneity of the masses. Party leadership is, of course, not infallible and the problem of how the Party can maintain close links with the masses and exercise correct and effective leadership is still one that we must seriously study and try to solve. But this can never be made a pretext for demanding the weakening or liquidation of the Party's leadership.

—Deng Xiaoping

The People's Republic of Chins is one of the few countries still governed by a Communist Party. Its political system reflects the general characteristics of a communist-party state, including a communist party monopoly on political power, party control of all government and social institutions, and the existence of an official ideology that the party claims the nation must follow if it is to reach its domestic and international goals.

—William A. Joseph

A brief survey of this Constitution shows that it presented a blend of the original provisions of the first formal constitution promulgated in 1954 and social and political development since then. It largely wrote off the 'radical' reforms of the era of the Cultural Revolution (1966-68).

The Constitution of 1978 was inaugurated as an important measure to do away with many steps taken by Mao during the horrible phase of the cultural revolution. Its makers, however, failed in accomplishing all that they had desired at this stage. Their movement of 'de-Maoisation' continued unabated. Success in this direction paved the way for the inauguration of a new Constitution in the light of what the new leaders had been able to achieve. Thus, at its III session the V National People's Congress (composed between November, 1977 and February, 1978) set up a revision committee in September, 1980. The draft Constitution framed by the revision committee was taken up for discussion by the National People's Congress when its session opened on 26 November, 1982. The NPC (presided over by President Zhongxuan) appreciated the Report of Peng Zhen and on 4 December, 1982 adopted the new Constitution by 3,037 votes (with 3 abstentions) after hailing it as 'distinctively' Chinese and suited to the needs of China's 'socialist modernisation.' Its preamble says: "This Constitution affirms the achievements of the struggle of the Chinese people of all nationalities and defines the basic system and basic tasks of the state in legal form; it is the fundamental law of the state and has supreme authority. The people of all nationalities, all state organs, the armed forces, all political parties and public organisations and all enterprises and undertakings in the country must take the Constitution as the basic form of conduct, and they have the duty to uphold the dignity of the Constitution and ensure its implementation. It is clear that the Chinese constitutionalism is based on the ideology of Marxism-Leninism as modified by Mao and his successors.

Salient Features

The new Constitution has four chapters. Chapter 1 contains a long list of 'General Principles'. Chapter II incorporates a comprehensive list of Fundamental Rights and Duties of the people. Chapter III specifies state structure. Its section (*i*) deals elaborately with the National People's Congress and its Standing Committee: section (*ii*) has some provisions for the President of the NPC; section (*iii*) covers the State Council in detail; section (*iv*) is about the Central Military Commission; section (*v*) has provisions for local People's Congresses and local people's governments at different levels; section (*vi*) deals with organs of self-government of national autonomous areas; and section (*vii*) provides for the system of People's Courts and People's Procuratorates. Chapter IV is about national flag, national anthem and national capital.

In first impression, the striking features of this Constitution are: restoration of the offices of the Head of the State with the designation of President assisted by a Vice-President (former chairman and vice-chairman), institution of a Central Military Commission to direct the armed forces, extension of the powers of the National People's Congress and its Standing Committee, introduction of the system of Premier's over-all responsibility for the State Council, change in the institution of combining rural people's communes, management with government administration and establishment of special administrative regions where necessary, constitutional recognition to the principle of family planning, softer orientation towards the political system of the USSR (now Russian Federation) and its foreign policy, invitation to foreign individuals and firms to invest their money in China and, above all, elimination of bold and frequent references to the ideology and leadership of Mao.

The salient features of the new Constitution may be enumerated as under:

1. **An Enacted and a Rigid Constitution:** Like its predecessors, it is an enacted Constitution having 138 Articles grouped into four

chapters. While the Preamble throws light on the achievements of the past and the goals of the future, Chapter I has general principles on which the new constitutional system is based. Chapter II deals with the fundamental rights and duties of the people. Chapter III deals with the structure of the State. It provides for the Central, provincial and local governments. It declares National People's Congress (NPC) as the highest organ of State power. Chapter IV mentions National Flag, National Emblem and the National Capital. The rigid nature of the constitution can be traced in the fact that the National People's Congress has been empowered to make any amendment in it by its 2/3 majority.

2. **Unitary System:** Though China is a very big country and the Constitution recognises the fact of multi-nationality, it, like its predecessor, provides for a unitary system of government. There is no division of powers. All powers, as a result, are with the Central government, while provincial, regional and local governments are under its full control. In other words, the entire administration of the country is done from the national capital–Beijing. The Central government has been empowered to make changes in the powers and status of the administrative units located at the lower levels. Under the Central Government, there are 22 Provinces and 5 Autonomous Regions including Tibet and 4 Municipalities. Hong Kong and Macao are China's Special Administrative Regions.
3. **Unicameral System:** Like its predecessor, the new Constitution provides a unicameral legislature. It is the National People's Congress having powers of legislation despite the fact that its deputies are to be chosen from the ranks of the people, units of provincial and regional administration, and armed forces. Though a quite unwieldy body, it has been given a Standing Committee that functions on its behalf during the inter-session period. One may marvel at the fact that not the Parliament as such as its small committee has been given the status of a continuously functioning national legislature.
4. **Vertical Rule and Dual Rule System:** State administration of China is based on two principles adopted by the Chinese founding fathers from the Soviet system. China is not a federal State and yet it has large units of regional and local governments which operate under the control of the Central government. Within 'vertical rule', central-level ministries and commissions under the State Council supervise the work of corresponding functional bodies at the lower levels of

government. Within 'dual rule', government agencies are subject to control by the Communist Party as well as being subordinate to higher government bodies. Under vertical and dual rule, a county government, for example, would be subordinate to both the provincial government and to the county-level Communist Party organisation. "Such a system leads to complex and sometimes conflicting lines of authority within the Chinese bureaucracy, but it also reinforces two key aspects of governance and policy-making in China–centralisation and Party domination."[7]

5. **Fundamental Rights and Duties:** Like its predecessor, the new Constitution provides fundamental rights and duties, now in a largely comprehensive form. The citizens have been given the right to education, to elect and be elected on completing the age of 18 years, to work, to have rest and leisure, to get material assistance in old age or in the event of physical inability, to prevent transgression of duty by a public servant, and the like. The state has been enjoined to grant equal rights to women, protect marriage and the family and the just interests of the Chinese living abroad. Besides, freedoms relating to speech, assembly, expression, and correspondence have been guaranteed. Inviolability of person and home has also been recognised. The citizens have been granted right to profess and propagate atheism. No person can be arrested except by a decision of a People's Court or with the sanction of a public security organ. The state grants right of residence to any foreign national persecuted for supporting a just cause, for taking part in revolutionary movements, or for engaging in scientific activities. Besides, fundamental duties have been mentioned like supporting the leadership of the Communist Party, strengthening the socialist system and abiding by the Constitution and the laws of the country, protecting public property, observing family planning, respecting social ethics, safeguarding State secrets, defending the motherland and resisting aggression.

6. **Democratic Centralism:** In accordance with the celebrated system of a communist State as adopted under the previous arrangement, the principle of democratic centralism has been sanctified under the

7. W.A. Joseph: "China" in W.A. Joseph, Mark Kesselman and Joel Krieger (eds.): *Third World Politics at the Crossroads* (Lexington: D.C Heath and Co., 1996), p. 61.

new dispensation as well. This system applies to the organisation of both the party and the government. Art. 5 of Constitution of the Communist Party of 1973 says: "The organisational principle of the Party is democratic centralism. The leading bodies of the Party at all levels shall be elected through democratic consultation in accordance with the requirements for successors to the cause of the proletarian revolution and the principle of combining the old, middle-aged and the young. The whole Party must observe unified discipline. The individual is subordinate to the organisation, the minority is subordinate to the majority, the lower level is subordinate to the higher level, and the entire Party is subordinate to the Central Committee." The idea of democratic centralism is contained in the official affirmation that the leading units of the Party and the Government at all levels shall regularly meet and report their working to the respective Congresses or general body meetings, constantly listen to the opinions of the masses and accept their supervision. Party members have the right to criticise organisations and leading members of the Party at all levels and make proposals to them. If a party member or an official holds different views with regard to the decisions or directions of the party or some governmental organisation, he is allowed to reserve his views and has the right to bypass the immediate leadership and report directly to highest levels, upto and including the Central Committee of the Party.

7. **Central Military Commission:** Another feature of the Constitution is the provision for the establishment of a Central Military Commission consisting of a Chairman, Vice-Chairmen and some members. Its term is linked with the term of the NPC. It function is to direct the armed forces of the country. (Art. 93) Its members shall be elected by the NPC (by the SC when the NPC is not in session) and they shall be accountable to the NPC or its SC (Art. 94). It has been done to reduce the hold of the military over the government.
8. **A 'Socialist' State:** Above all, the constitution declares China a committed State. It is peoples' democratic dictatorship led by the working class and based on the alliance of workers and peasants. There shall be only two kinds of ownership of the means of production–socialist ownership by the whole people and socialist collective ownership by the working people. The State may allow non-agricultural individual labourers to engage in individual labour involving no exploitation of others, within the limits permitted by

law and under unified arrangement by neighbourhood organisations in cities and towns or by production teams in rural people's communes. At the same time, these individual labourers should be guided on the road to socialist collectivisation step. The sector of the economy is the leading force in national economy. The state may requisition by purchase, take over for use, or nationalise urban and rural land as well as other means of production under conditions prescribed by law.

General Principles

One important feature of the Constitution is the incorporation of a very long list of 'general principles' in Chapter I that constitute the foundations of the new fundamental law as well as the goal of the Chinese state. These are:

1. China is a socialist state under people's democratic dictatorship led by the working class and based on alliance of workers and peasants; sabotage of socialist system is prohibited.
2. All power is vested in the people and it is to be exercised through people's congresses at local and national levels.
3. All state organs are based on the principle of democratic centralism.
4. Equality of all nationalities and protection of the rights of the minorities is guaranteed.
5. Upholding uniformity and dignity of the socialist legal system and observance of the Constitution by all people and their institutions is ensured.
6. The state recognises socialist economy with public ownership of the means of production in the hands of the people and collective ownership by the working class.
7. State protection of public property is ensured; damage to public property is prohibited.
8. The state recognizes right of the citizens to own lawfully earned income, savings, houses and other property with right to inheritance.
9. The state shall undertake economic planning on the basis of socialist public ownership.
10. The state shall give permission to foreign enterprises, whether individual or collective, to invest their money in China and enter into economic co-operation with Chinese enterprises according to the law of the land.

11. The state shall make primary education universal and compulsory and encourage higher education and learning in the fields of science, technology, medicine etc.
12. The state shall endeavour for building a socialist spiritual civilization and inculcate civic virtues for the love of motherland.
13. The state shall also look towards family planning and protect and improve living environment.
14. The state shall make efforts for strengthening revolutionisation, modernisation and regularisation of the armed forces.

Fundamental Rights and Duties

Like the previous Constitution, the new Constitution contains a long list of fundamental rights and duties of the citizens. The notable point in this direction is that the number of fundamental rights and duties has been further enhanced. The fundamental rights may be enumerated as under:

1. Citizenship to all Chinese nationals and equality before law,
2. Right to vote and seek election for every citizen above 18 years of age without any discrimination,
3. Freedom of speech, assembly, association and demonstration,
4. Religious freedom without foreign domination over religious bodies and affairs,
5. Personal freedom, no arrest without approval of People's Procuratorate.
6. Inviolability of personal dignity, prohibition of insult, libel, false incrimination,
7. Inviolability of home, prohibition of unlawful search,
8. Protection of private correspondence except in cases relating to public security or investigation of a criminal charge,
9. Right to criticise administration, lodge complaints against a public servant and make suggestions for streamlining administration.
10. Right to work, State to provide employment and improve working conditions.
11. Right to rest, State to give vacation and prescribe working hours,
12. Right to insurance allowance after retirement,
13. Right to material assistance in old age, illness, physical disablement, particularly for soldiers, destitutes and martyrs,

14. Right to education for all-round development of personality.
15. Right to pursue scientific research and literary and artistic activities,
16. Equality of sex, equal pay for men and women for equal work.
17. State protection to marriages and family life, and
18. State protection to the rights and interests of the Chinese living in the country or abroad.

The fundamental duties of the citizens are:

1. To work and cultivate labour emulation.
2. To observe family planning, parents' duty to look after their children and children's duty to take care of their parents in old age or in needy circumstances.
3. To use rights in a way conducive to the interests of the society.
4. To safeguard the unity of the country and of all its nationalities.
5. To abide by the Constitution, laws of the country, protect public property, keep State secrets, observe labour discipline and public order and respect social ethics.
6. To safeguard the security, honour and interest of the motherland.
7. To resist foreign aggression, perform military services and join militia, and
8. To pay taxes.

A critical study of this part of the Chinese Constitution shows that the nature of fundamental rights and duties is based on these principle: First, economic and social rights take precedence over civil liberties. Second, the civil liberties are to be enjoyed and exercised in conformity with the 'interests of the people' in order to strengthen the 'socialist system'. Third, the social and economic rights involve the direct intervention of the State and appear in the form of State services to the citizens. Fourth, there is not only a sort of formal declaration of a right by the State, but also a clear expression of the means by which it is to be achieved. Last, and most important of all, rights are not only formally coupled with duties, these are virtually subordinate to them. Thus, what a critic once said about the former Soviet Russia applies here too that everything is governed by " a duty to work in disciplined subordination to State's purposes."[8]

8. Merle Fainsod: *How Russia is Ruled,* p. 318.

19

STATE STRUCTURE

To a considerable extent, the new Constitution of 1982 is a refined and revised edition of its predecessor. As such, a study of the State structure of the People's Republic of China under the new constitutional dispensation of 1982 should be made with this impression that it is in one respect, as earlier claimed by Yeh Chien-Ying in his Report on the revision of the Constitution presented at the First Session of the Fifth National People's Congress on March 15, 1978, that it is a people's constitution' through the study of which the masses "should steadily raise their potential consciousness, heighten their awareness of being master of the country, enhance their sense of respect for law, correctly exercise the rights of citizens of the country, properly administer and build up our socialist state." Moreover, it has been prepared with a mission: "Let the whole nation work together with one mind, overcome all difficulties, defeat our enemies, transform China into a great modern, powerful socialist country and forge ahead towards the great goal of Communism."

National People's Congress and its Standing Committee

Like its predecessor, the new Constitution declares the NPC as the 'highest organ of State power'. During its absence its Standing Committee has the highest legislative authority. Its term is fixed at five years. As a unicameral Parliament, it consists of one house having Deputies elected by the provinces, autonomous regions, and municipalities under the Central government, and the armed forces. The number of Deputies and the manner of their election shall be determined by law. The Standing Committee will start work for holding elections two months before the expiry of the term of the NPC, but the holding of elections may be postponed in exceptional situations. A decision to this effect must be taken by 2/3 majority of the Standing Committee. The term of the NPC may be extended for any duration, but it is laid down that fresh elections shall take place within one year of the expiration of the abnormal situation. The NPC shall meet at least once in a year. The session shall be convened by the Standing Committee. The special or extra-ordinary session of the NPC may also be convened either by the Standing Committee or when 1/5 Deputies of the NPC so desire. Before the commencement of the session, the NPC shall elect a Presidium to conduct its proceedings.

The Constitution specifies functions and powers of the NPC in a very elaborate manner. These are:

1. To amend the Constitution,
2. To supervise enforcement of the Constitution,
3. To enact and amend basic statutes concerning criminal offences, civil affairs, State organs and other matters,
4. To elect President and Vice-President of the Republic,
5. To confirm the nominations of the Premier, Vice-Premiers, State Councillors, Ministers in-charge of departments and commissions, Auditor-General and Secretary-General of the State Council after their names are recommended by the President,
6. To elect the Chairman and members of the Central Military Commission,
7. To elect the President of the Supreme People's Court,
8. To elect the Procurator-General of the Supreme People's Procuratorate,
9. To examine and approve the plan for national economic and social development and report on its implementation,
10. To examine and approve the State Budget and report on its implementation,
11. To alter or annul inappropriate decisions of the Standing Committee of the NPC,
12. To approve the establishment of provinces, autonomous regions and municipalities directly under Central Government,
13. To decide on the establishment of special administrative regions and the system to be introduced there,
14. To decide matters relating to war and peace, and
15. To exercise such other functions and powers as the highest organ of State power should require.

Besides, the NPC has the power to recall or remove the President, Vice-President, Premier, Vice-Premiers, State Councillors, Ministers in-charge of ministries and commissions, Auditor-General and Secretary-General of the State Council, Chairman and members of the Central Military Commission, President of the Supreme People's Procuratorate and Procurator-General of the Supreme People's Procuratorate.

A technical difference is made between ordinary and constitutional legislation. It says that all bills and statutes must be passed by absolute majority of the House, but constitutional amendment bills proposed either by the State Council or by 1/5 members of the NPC must be passed by 2/3 majority of all deputies of the NPC. In this sense, the new Constitution has a rigid character at least for the sake of an argument.

With a view to retain the former system, the NPC has been provided with a Standing Committee consisting of a Chairman, Vice-Chairmen, a Secretary-General and some members, but none shall simultaneously hold any office in any of the administrative, judicial or procuratorial organs of the state. It is also provided that its term is linked with the term of the NPC, but it shall continue to work until the new SC is composed. A new arrangement is that its President and Vice-President cannot serve for more than two consecutive terms. Another important point to be taken note of at this stage is that now its functions and powers have been enlarged. These are:

1. To interpret the Constitution and supervise its enforcement,
2. To enact and amend statutes except those made by the NPC,
3. To enact partial supplements (when the NPC is not in session) and make amendments to statutes enacted by the NPC, provided they do not contravene the basic principles of these statutes,
4. To interpret statutes,
5. To examine and approve (when NPC is not in session) partial adjustments to the plan for national economic and social development and to the state budget that deem necessary in the course of their implementation,
6. To supervise the work of the State Council, Central Military Commission, Supreme People's Court and Supreme People's Procuratorate,
7. To annul those administrative rules and regulations, decisions and orders of the State Council that contravene the Constitution or the statutes,

8. To annul those local regulations or decisions of the organs of the State power of provinces, autonomous regions and municipalities directly under the Central government that contravene the Constitution, the statutes or the administrative rules and regulations,
9. To decide (when (NPC is not in session) on nominations by the Chairman of the Central Military Commission and other members of this body,
10. To appoint and remove the Vice-Presidents and judges of the Supreme People's Court, members of its judicial committees and the President of the Military Court at the suggestion of the President of the Supreme People's Court,
11. To appoint and remove the deputy Procurators-General and procurators of the Supreme People's Procuratorate, members of its procuratorial committee and Chief Procurator of the military procuratorate at the request of the Procurator-General of the Supreme People's Procuratorate,
12. To approve the appointment and removal of the chief procurators of the people's procuratorates of the provinces, autonomous regions and municipalities directly under the Central government,
13. To decide on the appointment and recall of plenipotentiary representatives abroad,
14. To decide on the ratification or abrogation of treaties and important agreements concluded with foreign States,
15. To institute systems of titles and ranks for military and diplomatic personnel and of other specific titles and ranks,
16. To institute state medals and titles of honour and decide on their conferment,
17. To decide on the granting of special pardons,
18. To decide (when NPC not in session) on the proclamation of state of war in the event of armed attack on the country and in fulfilment of international treaty obligations concerning common defence against aggression,
19. To decide on general or partial mobilisation,
20. To decide on the enforcement of martial law throughout the country or in some part, and
21. To exercise such other functions as the NPC may assign to it.

The Chairman of the NPC presides over the meetings of the Standing Committee. It has been made responsible to the NPC.

The present Constitution makes some important arrangements relating to the functioning of the NPC. For instance, Art. 70 provides that it shall appoint Nationalities Committee, Law Committee, Foreign Affairs Committee, Overseas Committee and other necessary committees to examine, discuss and draw up relevant bills and draft resolutions according to the directions of the NCP or its SC. These committees shall work under the control of the NPC or its SC, while the NPC or its SC may appoint, when necessary, inquiry committees to look into a specific question. The Deputies have been given the right to move bills and proposals, address questions that the ministers must answer in a responsible manner. No Deputy can be arrested without the consent of the President of the NPC, nor can be punished for speaking or voting in the NPC or its SC. The Deputies are enjoined to live in contact with their electors and play an exemplary role in abiding by the Constitution. The voters may exercise supervision over their elected Deputies and may recall them.

A critic may point out that the national legislature of China is neither a sovereign law-making body like the British Parliament, nor like a non-sovereign but by no means entirely powerless Congress of the United States. It is merely an ornamental organisation like the Supreme Soviet of the erstwhile USSR with this line of difference that it is a uni-cameral body. The Deputies of the NPC, one may easily understand, are the handpicked persons who assemble for a very negligible span of time just for putting a seal of constitutional validity on the actions of the elite of the ruling party. In view of the too unwieldy size (as consisting of 3,040 Deputies in 1993), the NPC may be said to bring representatives from the provinces and autonomous regions into a massive display of public unity.. Thus, what Linebarger said about the NPC under the previous constitution applies even now that it is the model of a 'sham parliament'.[1] Or, as a critic says, the NPC, like the earlier one, "may perform a communication and implementation role similar to that performed by the Central Committee of the Chinese Communist Party."[2]

In the states ruled by the Communist Parties alone, legislatures are condemned as 'rubber stamps'. It implies that their main function is to

1. Linebarger: *Far Eastern Governments and Politics*, p. 230.

2. A.S. Whiting: "China" in Ward and Macridis (ed.s): *Modern Political Systems: Asia*, p.179.

give to policies made by the party in power the appearance of being approved by the so-called representatives of the People. However, one may trace a point of difference in the case of National People's Congress of China. The label of 'rubber stamp' may be a bit extreme to describe it, but it does convey the fact that the Communist Party closely monitors every aspect of the national legislature's operations to ensure that it is in compliance with Four Cardinal Principles. Nevertheless, the NPC "is a very visible part of the Chinese political system, and it is important to understand its structure and function and to gauge whether the legislature could become an active force for democratisation in China."[3]

President

Since China is a republic, it is headed by the President with a Vice-President under him.[4] Both are elected by the National People's Congress for a term of five years. That is, the term of the President and the Vice-President is concurrent with that of the NPC and, as in the USA, it is limited to two consecutive terms. A citizen of China having right to vote and above 45 years of age may hold this post. He performs some important functions as:

1. To enforce laws and decrees made by the National People's Congress or its Standing Committee,
2. To appoint and remove the Prime Minister, Deputy Prime Ministers, Ministers, heads of the commissions, Secretary-General of the State Council and Auditor-General,
3. To confer awards and honours on the distinguished figures of his country,
4. To grant amnesty to the offenders or the sentence of a criminal,
5. To enforce martial law and to mobil is armed forces for the defence of the country,
6. To represent his country at international conferences,
7. To appoint and recall Chinese ambassadors to foreign countries and to receive foreign envoys for maintaining international relations, and

3. W.A. Joseph, "China" in Mark Kesselman, Joel Krieger and W.A. Joseph (eds): *Third World Politics at the Crossroads*, p. 412.
4. The Vice-President shall officiate when the President is absent. If none is available, then the NPC or its SC shall elect someone else for the purpose.

8. To confirm or repeal treaties made with foreign States.

It may, however, be pointed out that the Chinese President performs his functions with the formal nod of the NPC or its Standing Committee. He performs his executive functions through the State Council that is responsible to the NPC or its Standing Committee. He has no veto power over the bills passed by the NPC or the decrees promulgated by its Standing Committee. It shows that he is not a powerful figure like the Presidents of America and France. However, as this post is held by a powerful leader of the Communist Party, his actual position very much depends on his place in the Party hierarchy. It is well said: "The position is largely ceremonial, though it has always been held by a senior party leader and has sometimes been used as a base for advancing one's personal power."[5]

State Council

The State Council is the executive body of the highest organ of the state power as well as of the state administration. It is composed of the Premier, Vice-Premiers, State Councillors, Ministers in-charge of ministries and commissions, an Auditor-General and a Secretary-General. Its head is the Premier. He directs its working and presides over its meetings. Its term is linked with the term of the NPC, but it has been provided that no person shall hold an office for more than two consecutive terms. It conducts auditing of all state accounts by an auditing body. It is responsible to the NPC or (when not in session) to its Standing Committee. The functions and powers of the State Council are:

1. To analyse administrative measures, enact administrative rules and regulations and issue directions and orders in accordance with Constitution and statutes.
2. To submit proposals to the NPC or its SC.
3. To lay down the tasks and responsibilities of the ministers and commissions of the State Council.
4. To exercise uniform leadership over the work of ministries and commissions of the State Council.
5. To exercise unified leadership over the work of local organs of state administration at different levels throughout the country and to lay down the detailed division of functions and powers between Central

5. W.A. Joseph, *op. cit.* p. 61.

government and organs of State administration of provinces, autonomous regions and municipalities directly under the Central government.

6. To draw up and implement the plan for national economic and social development and the state Budget.
7. To direct and administer economic work and urban and rural development.
8. To direct and administer work concerning education, science, culture, public health, physical culture and family planning.
9. To direct and administer work concerning civil affairs, public security, judicial administration, supervision and other related matters.
10. To conduct foreign affairs and conclude treaties and agreements with foreign States.
11. To direct and administer the building of national defence.
12. To direct and administer affairs concerning nationalities and to safeguard the equal rights of minority nationalities and the right of autonomy of the national autonomous areas.
13. To protect legitimate rights and interests of Chinese nationals residing abroad and also protect lawful rights and interests of returned overseas Chinese and of the family members of Chinese nationals residing abroad.
14. To alter or annul inappropriate orders, directions and regulations issued by the ministries and commissions.
15. To alter or annul inappropriate decisions and orders issued by local organs of state administration at different levels.
16. To approve the geographical division of provinces, autonomous regions, and municipalities directly under the Central government and to approve the establishment and geographical division of autonomous prefectures, counties, autonomous regions and cities.
17. To decide on the enforcement of national law in parts of provinces, autonomous regions and municipalities directly under the Central government, to examine and decide on the size of administrative organs and in accordance with law appoint, remove or train administrative officers, appraise their work and reward or punish them, and
18. To exercise such other functions and powers as the NPC or its SC may assign to it.

Inspite of the fact that the State Council is headed by the Prime Minister and he as well as his ministers have been made accountable to the national legislature, it should not be inferred that the Central executive of China is analogous to that of the British cabinet, or the American cabinet, or the French cabinet as a curious mixture of the two, or the Federal Government of Switzerland. It cannot be identified with parliamentary executive in as much as the Chinese Premier is not taken from amongst the majority party, nor is there any room for the tradition of collective responsibility. Similarly, the State Council of China cannot be likened with the American cabinet that exists and works under the powerful leadership of the President and whose members are not accountable to the national legislature. The Chinese executive does not work on the principle of separation of powers as we find in the United States. Nor does it have its parallel in the French model where the President is the real executive and the cabinet headed by the Prime Minister works under the effective control of the President as well while remaining accountable to the Parliament. The Federal Government of Switzerland is a class by itself whose seven members belonging to different political parties and hailing from different cantons of the country act without living under the iron tutelage of any ruling party and also without being accountable to the national legislature. The hollowness of the provision of accountability of the State Council to the NPC is proved by the fact that no ministry has so far been put to a vote of censure and no minister outvoted or condemned by the Deputies of the people, while several ministers have been 'relieved' at the behest of the Chairman of the Communist Party. By all means, the State Council has been set up to act in co-ordination with the national legislature and work in a team spirit in the conduct of official business. In fine, the control of the Party over the organs of State "is formally asserted."[6]

Courts and Procuratorates

Like the erstwhile Soviet Union, the system of law and justice in China is characterised by the assumption that law is very much the product of national environment and material conditions in society. Much before being in power, the Communist leaders of China had made it clear that all laws, decrees and judicial system of the reactionary Kuomintang government "shall be abrogated and in their place all laws and decrees designed for the protection of the people shall be formulated and people's

6. J.P. Jain: *After Mao What'?* p. 210.

judicial system shall be established." The new line witnessed its adoption after the seizure of power by the communists. Thus, Art. 30 of the Organic Law of the People's Court of China said: "The task of the people's court is to try civil and criminal cases and by judicial process to punish criminals and settle civil disputes in order to safeguard the people's democratic system, maintain public order, protect public property, safeguard the rights and lawful interests of the citizens, and ensure successful carrying out of the socialist construction and socialist transformation in the country."

Section (vii) of Chapter III provides for the judicial system. People's Courts are the judicial organs of the political system of China. Art. 124 provides for a Supreme People's Court whose term is linked with the term of the NPC. All cases are heard by People's Courts except those involving special circumstances and the accused is granted right to defence. Supreme People's Court is the highest organ of judicial department. It supervises administration of justice by all local People's Courts. It is responsible to the NPC or its SC. The Constitution makes arrangement for the procuratorial system. It says that People's Procuratorates are State organs for legal supervision. The term of the Supreme People's Procurator is linked with the term of the NPC. The People's Procuratorates exercise their procuratorial powers independently and are not subject to interference by administrative organs, public organisations or individuals. The Supreme People's Procuratorate is the highest organ that exercises supervision over all subordinate procuratorates. It is responsible to the NPC. The citizens of all nationalities may use their own language in the courts. If so, the courts or the procuratorates shall provide translation for the party not familiar with court's language. All hearings shall be done in the principal language of that locality. Finally, the People's Courts and People's Procuratorates and all public security organs shall, in handling criminal cases, divide their functions, each taking responsibility for its own work and they shall co-ordinate their efforts and check each other to ensure correct and effective enforcement of law.

On account of being a communist country, the judicial system of China has its own nature. The "lawyers' regulations" stipulate that "our task is first to protect the rights of the state, the collective and the individual, and to safeguard implementation of laws." While a defendant is entitled to a defence counsel, there is no legal presumption of innocence and proven guilty. Trials almost never take place until the defendant has confessed his guilt under pre-trial interrogations. Huang Huing, the Supreme People's Procurator, told the NPC in December, 1982 that 99.97% of the criminals prosecuted during the first 9 months of 1981 were found guilty. A defence lawyer's task is not to suggest that his client is innocent but to protect his rights and look for extenuating circumstances that might merit a lighter sentence. Dilatory ways of defence (as prevailing in other democratic countries) are dubbed by the Chinese rulers as 'adversary tactics' and they are not allowed to visit his client, the lawyer needs prior permission of the government. A prominent jurist like Chen Yisong said that the defendants may appeal against their conviction to a higher court but only once, they cannot take the alternative of dragging litigation for years. A Chinese lawyer is not permitted to seek extension of the case of his client. A major trial might take about two months, but the wheels of justice can grind at dizzying speeds. Trials are sometimes made public to show that justice is being served and to warn against lawless behaviour. For instance, the televised trial of the Gang of Four (Madam Chiang Ching, Zhang Chung-qiao, Yao Wenhyuan and Wang Hongwen) gave millions of countrymen first look of the legal system of their country.[7]

One may easily take note of the fact that all norms of judicial sanctity stand sacrificed under the new constitutional dispensation. The new Constitution abrogates the cultural revolution practice of public trials that had spoken of the 'mass line' being applied in procuratorial work and in trying cases. It re-establishes the People's Procuratorates which are given considerable powers in matters of arrest and detention of the enemies of socialism. One may notice the terrible dimension of the provision whereby no citizen could be arrested without the permission of the local people's courts or of the People's Procuratorates, responsible to local people's congress at corresponding levels and exercise independent power in prosecuting officials or citizens free from the interference of local state organs. Thus, what Wint said about the old arrangement applies more rigorously to the present situation as well that the main duty of court in China "is not to distinguish right from wrong, it is to further the cause of revolution."[8]

7. Christopher S. Wren: "The Legal System of China" in *Amrit Bazar Patrika* (Calcutta), 17 December. 1982.

8. Guy Wint: *Commonsense About China*. p. 122.

20

POLITICAL PARTIES AND PRESSURE GROUPS

Typical is the case of China so far as party system is concerned. By all means, it a country ruled by the Communist Party on the model of the erstwhile Soviet Union, but the concluding words of the Preamble to the Constitution of 1982 proclaim that 'all political parties and public organisations and undertakings in the country must take it as the basic form of conduct, and they have the duty to uphold the dignity of the Constitution and ensure its implementation'. China is a Communist-Party State and yet it has 8 organisations known as 'non-Communist parties' which have some seats in the national legislature and are collectively referred to as 'democratic parties'. It is a strange designation that "is meant to signify the role they play in representing different interests in the political process and lend some credibility to China's claim that it is a democracy."[1] So, there are many interest organizations, social groups and protest movements which play the role of pressure groups in the political process of the country. But the fact cannot be lost sight of that they are like 'transmission belts' for communicating official policies to particular groups of citizens as well as for mobilizing public support for those policies.

Political Parties

To say that in China there are 'non-Communist parties' is to create a paradox to a student of comparative politics and government. A totalitarian regime adopts several shrewd methods to create a mask of democratic face and thereby hoodwink its critics. So is the case with China. The non-

1. W.A. Joseph. "China" in Joseph, Kesselman and Krieger (eds.): *Third World Politics at the Crossroads*, p.72

Communist parties of China draw their membership not from the people in general but from a particular segment of the people and thereby they become like interest groups pampered by the ruling party to establish the show of political pluralism in the country. For instance, China Democratic League consists mostly of the intellectuals, whereas the China Democratic National Constitution Association draws members mainly from the business world. In a sense they may be labelled as 'satellite parties'[2]

As a matter of fact, China has one-party system. The Communist Party is the state, the government, the country, and the nation. Its main tasks are:

1. To lead the members and non-party members in studying Marxism-Leninism Mao Tse-tung's Thoughts conscientiously and criticising revisionism.
2. To give constant education to the members and others concerning the ideological and political lines and lead them in fighting absolutely against the class enemy.
3. To propagate and carry out the policies of the party, implement its decisions and fulfil every task assigned by the party and the State.
4. To maintain close ties with the masses, constantly listen to their opinions and demands and wage an active ideological struggle so as to keep party life vigorous, and.
5. To take in new party members, enforce party discipline and constantly consolidate the party organisations, getting rid of the State and taking in the fresh so as to maintain the purity of the ranks.

The party is organised and functions on the principle of democratic centralism. It means that the branches of the party at all levels have members elected through democratic consultation. There is democracy in each unit of the party so that the members may discuss matters and arrive at a decision in a democratic manner. At the top is the National Party Congress that takes all decisions and, in its absence, it is done by its Central

2. J.D.Seymour: *China's Satellite Parties,* p.87.

Some Important Statements

Unlike the social democracy of some western European political parties, such as the British Labour Party and French socialist party, which is rooted in the commitment to competitive politics, and political pluralism, China's socialist democracy is based on the unchallengeable leadership of the Chinese Communist Party. —***William A. Joseph***

In China of today we can never dispense with leadership by the Party and extol the spontaneity of the masses, Party leadership, of course, is not infallible and the problem of how the Party can maintain close links with the masses and exercise correct and effective leadership is still one that we must seriously study and try to solve. But this can never be made a pretext for demanding the weakening or liquidation of the Party's leadership. —***Deng Xiaoping***

Committee. At the same time, it is required that a lower unit should work under the guidance and direction of the higher unit. Since National Party Congress (or its Central Committee) is at the top, its decision is final and binding on all the lower units of the party. It shows that while the element of democracy moves from bottom to the top, the element of centralism moves from top to bottom. It may be easily understood that while the element of democracy is a fiction, the element of centralism is a fact.[3]

The Communist Party is the guiding and directing force of the country. A leader like Mao, or Hua, or Deng or Jiang or Jintao is its Chairman who with the help of his trusted comrades rules in a dictatorial manner. Opposition is prohibited. Dissent is not tolerated. Even the peaceful protesters may be massacred as happened in the Tiananmen Square in June, 1989. A decade before this tragedy, Deng had flatly rejected any call for 'more democracy' and clearly spelled out his views on the role of his party in the political system of the country.

---

3. Political power is held by the Chinese Communist Party. Its highest authority is the Party Congress which is convened every five years. In October, 2007 its 17th National Congress elected a Central Committee of 204 full members and 167 alternate members. To direct policy, the central committee elected a politbureau of 25 members. Its standing committee and 9 members provincial people's congresses are the local organs of state power. Provincial People's Governments are responsible for local affairs. *The Europa World Year Book* (London: Routledge, 2010), Vol. I, p.1235.

Pressure Groups

Inspite of having a few 'satellite' parties in the country, China does not have a multi-party system. Similar is the case with many interest organisations which are formed around social or professional categories with a total membership in the hundreds of millions. Principal among them are such associations and unions which represent the workers, farmers, intellectuals, women, youth etc. In a non-democratic system such organisations are pampered by the party in power so as to legitimise its hold pretentiously in the name of a 'democratic order'. Such organisations cannot be numerous and they cannot play a competitive role. So, in China such organisations implement the 'mass line' of the ruling party by providing a means for them to express their views on policy within strict limits.

Reference may be made to some of these organisations. The urban industrial workers belong to the All-China Federation of Trade Unions. It is a umbrella organisation for occupation-specific unions as well as for workers unions in individual factories. The Communist Youth League is a body of the intellectuals. It is a vehicle for recruiting young people into the Communist Party and spreading communist values among the people of the earlier generation. The Young Pioneers is a body of the teen agers whose aim is to promote good social behaviour and loyalty to the party among the school children. All-China Students Federation does the same for College and University students. All-China Women's Federation represents the interests of the women exclusively. Apart from this, there are 'friendly societies', charitable foundations and national professional groups. The Chinese leaders call it as a step towards 'socialist corporatism' in which the CCP, rather than overtly suppressing the divergent social interests, co-opts them by allowing them some autonomy in exchange for their reconstitution of the ultimate authority of the party-state.

In fine, it may be pointed out that as China is moving from communism to consumerism, its economic and political systems are also moving in the liberal directions. The ruling party very cautiously acts in synthesising the ideology of communism with the trend of liberalisation whose growing force cannot be ignored by a developing country. The CCP is still in the

Centre and it has managed to establish a kind of constellation system in which minor parties and groups revolve around it. The satellites operate in a way as the centre permits, for they know that any organisation may be scorched by the heat of the central planet if it tries to have its own orbit. It is well observed: "The Communist Party is at the heart of the policy process in China. Party domination, however, does not mean that politics operates in a monolithic way; in fact, the system wriggles with politics of many kinds, formal and informal. In order to get a complete picture of policy-making in China, one must look at how various influences, including bureaucratic interests, personal connections, ideological differences, factional conflicts and social pressures, shape the decisions made by the Communist Party leadership."[4]

Obviously, the Chinese Communist Party "retains the power to decide all major political, social and economic policy issues and to appoint leaders to all public sector bodies, including government offices, public institutions and State-owned enterprises. It employs four basic models to achieve continuing control over the other bureaucratic nomenklatura-appointments and interlocking directorates, leadership small groups, party 'core groups', and party line. All four of these date back to the 1950s or before. These four practices in their totality lock government officials into such a powerful web of party interference and controls that one of the major issues confronting the Chinese political system today is how to establish a meaningful separation of party and government functions."[5]

The fact stands out that China does not have any design of a liberal democratic order. One-party rule can never be democratic. It is always associated with authoritarianism or totalitarianism in view of the fact that here only one political party monopolises politics and other parties are

4. Joseph, *op. cit.*, p. 67.

5. J. F. Kornberg and J. R. Faust: *China in World Politics: Politics, Processes, Prospects* (Boulder, Colorado: Lynne Rienner Publishers, 2005), p. 234. Also see Kenneth Lieberthal: *Governing China: From Revolution Through Reform* (New York: W. W. Norton Co., 2004).

banned or excluded from power. The ruling party serves several functions. A critic may hardly endorse the official view that the Communist "has no interests of its own and rules solely in the interests of the nation and the people. It follows that the rule by party's leaders is rule in the people's interest and by definition democratic."[6]

6. Andrew J. Nathan: *Chinese Democracy* (Berkeley; University of California Press, 1985), p.124.

Part - VI

French Constitution

The keystone of new regime is the new institution of a President of the Republic, designated by reason and feelings of the French people to be the head of State and the guide of France. Far from requiring that the President must, as was once the case, remain confined to the role of advisory and representative functions of the Constitution, confers on him the outstanding responsibility for the destiny of Frence and of the Republic. ***—Gen. Charles de Gaulle***

21

CONSTITUTION OF FRANCE

A study of the French political system in a work on modern political systems is governed by certain pertinent reasons. It is the country where the Great Revolution took place in 1789 for realising the boons of 'liberty, equality and fraternity' and where the Great Declaration of the Rights of Man and Citizen was adopted by the National Assembly that marked the inauguration of representative democracy. However, in the period following the Great Revolution, the people of this country made several important experiments with a republican system off and on tempered with the entry and exit of the remnants of an autocratic government like that of a Directory under Napoleon Bonaparte and the restoration of the Bourbon dynasty, until the notorious monarchy had its final termination in the revolution of 1848. Revolutionary trends continued with the result that one republic was replaced by another and the people continued their struggle to solve the problem of bringing about a workable reconciliation between the existence of an effectual parliament vis-s-vis the authority of a strong executive. As a result, since the Revolution of 1789, this country has had 16 constitutions under which many experiments took place all revealing the conviction of the people in this political axiom that "a parliamentary government is a representative government, whereas monarchical government is not. Democratic government must be both parliamentary and republican. The student of comparative government must, therefore, be prepared to assume that in France *political democracy*, the parliamentary system, and republicanism are, for practical purposes, three interchangeable concepts."[1]

1. R.K. Gooch: "France" in J.S. Shotwell (ed.): *Governments of Continental Europe*, p.36.

French Constitutionalism

The French people have their own notions about constitutionalism hinging on the touchstone of republicanism'- a term about which they have some general and well-understood outlines, though subtle differences persist among the leading political forces so far as the matter relating to essential details is concerned. It all begins from the Great Revolution when the people could establish their republican tradition that in a period of less than 10 years moved the country from a monarchy ruled virtually by the divine rights dogma of the Louis dynasty to a Republican Monarchy, and then to a Republic, thereon to a government by one party controlled in effect by a small directorate (under Robbespiere), known as the Committee of Public Safety, to a collegial dictatorship-the Directorate-and, finally, to a Consulate and an empire with the young Napoleon at its head.[2] And yet the movement did not stop. Once again monarchy had its termination paving way for the advent of a full-fledged republican system until France had the bitter lessons of a dictatorial system during the Second World War at the hands of the Vichy regime. Even this system of uncontrolled Bonapartism had its termination. A new model of republicanism witnessed its establishment that failed to live beyond a period of 12 years when in 1958 the people hailed the return of Gen. de Gaulle and then a new constitution came into force.

The French concept of constitutionalism may, however, be said to have been swinging between the traits of parliamentary sovereignty on the one hand and a strong one-man rule on the other. The result is that questions like Who rules France? Who speaks for France? How France should be ruled? and the like have been bedevilling the minds of the people. One may find that sometimes the absolute monarch, sometimes the legislature, sometimes one man with the gun have been trying to solve the crucial issues.

The history of French constitutional experiments begins with inauguration of the First Republic in 1792. We have already seen that the National Assembly adopted the 'Declaration of the Rights of Man and Citizen' in 1789 and then drafted a constitution on its basis. The form of government set up under the constitution was comparable with the traditional American system or with the British government before the

2. R.C. Macridis, "France" in Ward and Macridis (eds): *Major Political Systems: Europe*, p.164.

establishment of the present cabinet system. In other words, it was based on the twin principles of separation of powers and sovereignty of the people. The powers of the monarch were drastically cut so as to make him a constitutional monarch, while the law-making body took the form of a unicameral Legislative Assembly of 745 members chosen for two years and distributed amongst the 83 Departments according to territory, population and direct taxes.

A basic change took place in 1793 when the Convention succeeded the Legislative Assembly that abolished the monarchy. A new constitution (called the Girondin Constitution) was presented that could not be voted in the Convention. Rather another constitution (called the Montagnard Constitution) was adopted in 1793 after its ratification by the people. It vested power in an Assembly that was to be elected annually by direct universal manhood suffrage. It was empowered to issue decrees and pass laws, the latter being subject to the kind of optional referendum. The executive was to consist of a Council of 24 to be chosen one-half annually by a complicated process. The voters were to choose electors who in turn were to nominate candidates from amongst whom the legislative body was to select the actual members of the executive council.

This constitution was replaced in 1799 by the Constitution of the Consulate based on a plan framed by Abbe Sieyes considerably modified in a monarchical direction by Napoleon Bonaparte. Thus, Napoleon Bonaparte assumed all authority in his hands as the First Consul so much so that in 1804 he made a drastic change in the constitution so as to establish the First Empire. The constitutional charter of 1814, in a certain theoretical sense, marked the restoration of the *ancient regime* in view of the fact that the personal sovereignty of the king was definitely recognised. The king became the personal chief of the executive power and he alone possessed the initiative in law-making. The Monarchy of the Restoration (established after the military defeat of Napoleon) was succeeded by the Monarchy of July when Charles X was supplanted by Louis-Phillipe and the constitutional charter of 1830 came into being. It marked some change so far as the position of the monarch was concerned. No reference was made to his divine rights as was done under the charter of 1814. Though the king entertained definite ambitions of being himself able to direct the

Some Important Statements

France was the first European nation in which a revolution abolished the monarchy and established a republic based on the belief that all citizens, regardless of social background, were equal before the law. It is difficult to over-estimate the impact of the revolution on people's thinking in France and elsewhere.

—Mark Kesselman

The chief accomplishment of the French Revolution was the institution of a democratically new political culture... Revolution in France contributed little to economic growth or to political stabilisation. What it did establish, however, was the mobilising potential or democractic republicanism and the compelling intensity of revolutionary change. ***—Lynn Hunt***

The revolution was the moment when the masses had broken in on the stage of history... that is why, in a sense, everything indeed 'began' there. 1789 opened a period when history was set adrift. ***—Francois Furet***

policy of government, the principle of political responsibility of the ministers to the Chamber of Deputies became, in practice, clearly recognised and the general result was that the parliamentary system became better established in the French tradition.[3]

In a sense, the constitutional charter of 1830 established the system of limited monarchy. However, the 'Orleanist July Monarchy' met its end in the revolution of 1848 when the system of presidential government came into being. A new constitution came into force whereby the executive power was vested in the President elected directly by the people for a term of four years, while the legislative power was entrusted to the Assembly directly elected by the people for a term of three years.

Like its predecessor, the 'Second Empire' had its doom within a couple of years and once again return to the republican system took place in 1870 as a result of the military defeat of the king and the successful revolution of the people. It is called the Third Republic that lasted till 1940–the longest period in the history of the republics of France so far. Constitutionalism under the Third Republic witnessed certain features that could be described as real movements in the direction of a republican system. For the first time, there was established a parliamentary system.

The Third Republic officially came to an end in 1940 when President Petain secured the constituent powers by the use of amending process in a

3. Gooch, *op.cit.*. p. 51.

way that he became the virtual despot of the country. He shelved the requirement of a constitutional amendment measure's ratification by the people and adopted the way of promulgating 'constitutional acts' one after another. Shortly after July, 1940 he declared himself as the head of the French State, assumed plenary powers, adjourned until further order the two chambers, and repealed all provisions of the constitution of the Third Republic that were inconsistent with his authoritarian position.

The Fourth Republic came into being in 1946 that failed to have a life of more than 12 years. A new constitution was adopted that placed the President in a very weak and the Parliament in a very strong position. It paid utmost adherence to the principles of a parliamentary government by vesting supreme authority in the Parliament, notably in the Lower House. The Prime Minister and his Cabinet governed as long as they had majority support in the National Assembly. The President of the Republic was elected by the Parliament and, like the British monarch, was the titular head of the state. The system of proportional representation in the elections enabled even very small political parties to have some seats in the national legislature and thereby form groups to face the government with the problem of its survival. Since the ministry was made accountable to the Parliament and, more-over, no party could be in a position to have a comfortable majority behind it, the Prime Ministers came and went away with the disturbing frequency as the majorities shifted back and forth in the National Assembly.[4]

The result was that France earned the notorious distinction of having a system of political instability in view of the fact that 20 cabinets had their existence during a short period of 12 years. As such, the people came to understand the folly of cultivating a fanatic zeal for the parliamentary system. They could realise that the system under the previous constitution had the model of a 'paralysed republic' . The 'demand for reform' thus gathered more and more momentum in the direction of doing away with the system of an 'unmanageable legislature'. The crisis in Algeria provided a more calling force. The net result was that the nation reposed its faith in the leadership of Gen. de Gaulle who gave a new constitution that placed France under the Fifth Republic.

It is a well-known fact that Gen. de Gaulle was the most uncompromising critic of the constitution that had inaugurated the Fourth

4. Macridis, *op. cit.*, p. 167.

Republic and it was because of his stern attitude that he left the government and since then lived in retirement off and on revealing his forebodings about the erratic working of a constitution that had delivered an 'omnipotent' Parliament. However, the circumstances that helped to make his return possible was the transformation of the Algiers demonstration into a movement in which the settlers and the army leaders in Algeria combined to demand a 'Government of Public Safety' headed by a strong man like him–a trend which, as time went on, was gathering support in France.

The result was that power was entrusted to the man known for being capable of giving 'a government of public safety.' The Parliament endorsed his appointment as the Prime Minister keeping in view the conditions that he had already made public along with its five terms that he would keep in mind while drawing up the new constitution–the principle of universal suffrage, the responsibility of the government to the parliament, the separation of legislative and executive powers, the independence of judiciary, and the provision for the possibility 'of organising the relations between the Republic and the associated peoples'. In addition to observing these five principles, de Gaulle gave further assurance to the National Assembly in person that in the new constitution the offices of the President and the Prime Minister would remain distinct.

The way for the making of the new constitution was thus paved. A small group of ministers and experts headed by the then Minister for Justice and later Prime Minister (Michael Debre) prepared the text in a period of two months. A special consultative committee composed of 39 members (2/3 elected by the Parliament and 1/3 nominated by Gen. de Gaulle) endorsed the proposed text after suggesting certain minor amendments. It was approved by the Cabinet and then debated and passed by the Parliament. Finally, it was submitted to a popular referendum on Sept. 20, 1958 which the people ratified by an overwhelming majority. All the 90 Departments voted in favour with 17,688,790 against 4,624,511 votes. Out of 84.8% of the electors, 79.15 cast their votes in favour. In Algeria 80% voters went to the polls out of which 96% voted for the new constitution, though French Guinea voted for independence. Subsequently elections took place and Gen. de Gaulle assumed the office of the President.

Salient Features

The constitution of the Fifth Republic has been variously evaluated by the people of France ranging from those of its protagonists who have lauded it as a model of republicanism to those who have denounced it as 'a prelude to dictatorship'. Critics have coined words and phrases to highlight their reactions in this regard with the result that it has been described as 'a tailor-made constitution for Gen. de Gaulle', 'quasi-Presidential', 'a Parliamentary Empire', 'an unworkable document', 'the worst drafted in French constitutional history', 'ephemeral' and the like.[5] Its salient features are an follows:

1. A Written and an Enacted Constitution: The Constitution of the Fifth Republic is a written document. Originally it had 89 Articles grouped into XVI Titles, but now it has 92 Articles. It is a gift of the constitutional consultative committee that worked for a period of about two months in 1958 under the direction of Gen. Charles de Gaulle. It was endorsed by the Cabinet and then approved by the Parliament after much discussion in which the Gaullists managed to have their say. Finally, it was approved by the Departments and people with an overwhelming vote. Thus, like the constitution of a major country of the world as the United States or China, it is a brief document.

By all means, the new constitution is not only an enacted and a written instrument of government, it displays the fact of the triumph of Bonapartism-a trend, as advocated by a section of the republicans, of a strong executive headed by a powerful leader who may take effective action in the moments of crisis and who may resort to the device of referendum for having the acceptance or rejection of his regime or its achievements. It is due to this that the highest power of the state has been entrusted to the President elected by the people and armed with authority to deal with a crisis either inside the country or abroad, including the exercise of an effective popular sovereignty. It is evident from the fact that the new constitution has "strikingly enhanced the importance of the presidential office making the President the actual head of the government as well as the formal head of state."[6] In particular, some of the Ordinances providing for the institutions of the community were completed by the Presidential 'decisions', appearing from time to time in the Official Journal. Keeping all these points in view, a critic like Dorothy Pickles calls it an 'untidy Constitution."[7]

5. Dorothy Pickles: *The Fifth French Republic*, p. 26.

6. Harold Zink: *Modern Governments*, pp. 323-24.

7. Dorothy Pickles: *The Fifth French Republic*, pp. 27.

2. A Rigid Instrument of Government: Unlike the Constitution of England, the French constitution is rigid. Here a special process of amending the provisions of the Constitution has been provided. Art. 89 of the Constitution provides for its revisions. It says: "The initiative for amending the Constitution shall belong both to the President of the Republic on the proposal of the Premier and to the members of Parliament. The Government or Parliamentary bill for amendment must be passed by the two assemblies in identical terms. The amendment shall become definitive after approval by a referendum. Nevertheless, the proposed amendment shall not be submitted to a referendum when the President of the Republic decides to submit it to Parliament convened in Congress in this sense, the proposed amendment shall be approved if it is accepted by the three-fifth majority of the votes cast. The Secretariat of the Congress shall be that of the National Assembly. No amendment procedure may be undertaken or followed when the integrity of the territory is in jeopardy. The republican form of government shall not be subject to amendment."

From the above, following main impressions may be derived. First, the power of initiating a proposal of amendment lies only with the central government located at Paris. Since France is a unitary state, the questions of participation by the units as we find in the case of United States and Switzerland does not at all arise. Then, like the United States but unlike Switzerland, the people have no right tc initiate the proposal of constitutional amendment. Second, there is the provision for referendum. If the bill is passed by both the Houses of Parliament, it shall be referred to the people for approval. But the Constitution assigns a qualified accommodation to the provision of popular control in the sphere of its amendment. It is laid down that a proposal of amendment adopted by the national legislature shall not be referred to popular referendum in case the President of the Republic decides to submit it to Parliament convened in Congress and is accepted there by a majority of the three-fifths of the votes cast. Third, the work of amendment cannot be undertaken when the territorial integrity of France is in danger, or when the object of the proposal is to tamper with the republican form of government.

It appears that, like the constitution of Switzerland, the provision of popular control over constitutional amendment exists in France. But the very provision is not effective to check the growth of Presidential despotism. Not only under the existing Constitution the French Presidency is powerful, but the passage has not been closed for making it more powerful in time to come through the use of constitutional amendments.

The arrangement whereby the need for referendum may be set aside is really very pernicious and always keeps the way open for the murder of parliamentary democracy in France-a matter of pride for the French people.

3. Unitary System: Like England, France makes another leading example of a unitary system. The country is divided into territorial circumscriptions called 'departments' and these are subdivided into cantons, arrondissements, and communes, each having its own organs for certain purposes of local government, but the authority which they possess is very restricted; it is derived not from the Constitution but from the acts of Parliament. As a matter of fact, these local organisations are mere agents of the central government located at Paris and the exercise of powers left to them is subject to its wide control. However, unlike the unitary system of Britain, the unitary system of France is rooted both in history and sentiments of the people which justify that all French political systems 'always gravitate automatically and rapidly towards unity and homogeneity of powers.'

It is owing to this fact that after the First World War a movement of Regionalism (a movement that demanded the breaking up of the country into local units and giving them a real measure of local autonomy in order to relieve the Central government of some of its multifarious functions) could not gain success. Moreover, as a result of this, French unitary system is more rigid and centralised than that of Great Britain. Hence, the Constitution of the Fifth Republic retains the spirit of the earlier constitutions in this regard and indicates nothing more than the intention to vitalise French local government and to secure greater co-ordination of functions between the state departments and the units of local administration. Naturally the aspect of centralisation in the unitary system of France "is more significant also because the French state undertakes such a wide range of governmental activities"[8]

Although the unitary system of France is more centralised than that of Britain, the like fact remains that in a unitary state the powers of the central government know no division. The salient characteristic remains that while the units of local government are created for a certain essential purpose, they are the creatures of the central government and, as such, their functions, powers and even their very existence depends upon its

8. Herman Finer: *The Major Governments of Modern Europe*, p.339.

will. What Prof. Ogg says about English constitutional system holds true for every such system that central control "is both wide and deep; not only so, but it is steadily penetrating to new phases and levels."[9]

4. Rule of 'Incompatibility': The way the de Gaulle Constitution has managed to keep the legislative and executive departments apart and, at the same time, sought to establish the bond of conjunction between the two is really an innovation. It has led to the establishment of a peculiar model of government that may be termed both quasi-presidential and quasi-parliamentary, though the former appellation would be more appropriate. It provides for a Cabinet under a Prime Minister eventually led by the President whose members cannot be the members of the Parliament, but who are accountable to it. That is, France has a Cabinet without, what the English people call, a cabinet government.

Instances of the separation of the legislature from the executive organ can be found in various arrangements. Though the President is the real executive head, he is not accountable to national legislature; the Prime Minister and his ministers are responsible to the Parliament without being members of either house. It is provided that as a legislator joins the government, he shall forfeit his membership of the House that would be given to his 'substitute.' The legislature may show its no-confidence in the Government as a result of which it shall resign. The Prime Minister may himself table a resolution of confidence which, if not adopted, would amount to the defeat of the Government and thereupon its resignation would take place.

It shows that while the executive and legislative departments have been kept apart, they have also been bound by the doctrine of ministerial responsibility. What has acted as the motivating force behind this peculiar arrangement is the political philosophy of de Gaulle who wanted to arrest the erratic behaviour of the national legislature as demonstrated by it under the Fourth Republic. At the same time, de Gaulle wanted to implement the essential principle of republicanism whereby the popular sovereignty should be reposed in the national legislature. The result is that the doctrine of an omnipotent parliament has been modified in a Cromwellian fashion so as to keep a parliament with 'a role both quantitatively and qualitatively diminished'.[10]

9. F.A. Ogg : *English Government and Politics*, p. 366.

10. Pickles, *op. cit.*, p. 29.

5. Quasi-Presidential Government: As pointed out above, the French government under the present Constitution pertains more to a quasi-presidential than to a quasi-parliamentary model in view of the fact that the authority of the President is far more extensive than that of the Prime Minister. The President is not at all a titutar head of the state like the English monarch, rather he has his prototype in his American counterpart. Moreover in certain respects he is more powerful than the American head of the state. He appoints his Prime Minister and other ministers on the advice of the Prime Minister. He also administers to them the oaths of office and secrecy and accepts their resignations. He presides over the cabinet meetings and thereby sees to it that the decisions of the government are taken in accordance with his wishes. It all shows the traits of a presidential government. On the contrary, the fact that not the President but the Prime Minister and his ministers are responsible to the Parliament indicates the incorporation of a parliamentary system in the French Constitution. The heavier point should, however, be traced in the position of the President who is the real working head of the state and also of the government.

It is, therefore, obvious that the Constitution of the Fifth Republic maintains the irresponsibility of the President, and, at the same time, gives him personal powers that he can exercise as per his discretion. For instance, he may refer a bill of great importance to the verdict of the people in a referendum, or he may postpone the holding of the referendum on such a bill after it is passed by the Parliament with absolute majority, or he may exercise his veto power, or he may do many other important things. He also has powers to make decisions concerning all matters related to the Community (now abolished) or exercise a virtual veto power over a large, even ill-defined, area of policy-making.[11] A great Gaullist like Debre had no reservations when he expressed his thoughts in the National Assembly on the debate over the draft of the constitution. He said; "That keystone is the President of the Republic. Without a genuine chief of state, the cabinet, given the state of public opinion and other traditional quarrels, lacks the support which is normally essential for it."[12]

What, however, places the President in a far more important and powerful position is his long tenure of 5 years and his election with the mandate of the people. Moreover, the process of his removal is too difficult

11. R.C. Macridis and B.E. Brown: *The De Gaulle Republic: Quest for Unity*, p. 161.

12. Martin Harrison (ed.): *French Politics*, p. 144.

to be followed. The result is that de Gaulle could give shape to a strong and positive Presidency touching the verge of unlimited monarchy without a crown at the head of the real executive of the state. One may say that while the Constitution makes a distinction between the head of the state and that of the government, it all applies to the realm of theory. In practice, the former is both or either as he wills, the latter is neither. And this is the peculiar feature of the de Gaulle Constitution which "is so difficult to characterise, because it is essentially a monarchical constitution, though a monarchical constitution in a republican guise."[13]

6. Syncretisme: The Constitution of the Fifth Republic may be said to introduce a system of multiple principles what the French people call *syncretisme.* It can be visualised in the following institutional arrangements provided by it:

1. The Parliament is a bi-cameral organisation having Senate and the National Assembly in which the powers of the former are co-ordinate with that of the latter, except where the government decides to give the Assembly the last word.
2. Though the Prime Minister and his ministers cannot be the members of the Parliament, they are responsible to it.
3. The Prime Minister has both procedural and constitutional means of dominating the Parliament, including the National Assembly.
4. Though the Head of the State (President) and the Head of the Government (Prime Minister) remain distinct in theory, in practice the former is both or either as he wills, the latter is neither.
5. The Constitution recognises the existence of as many political parties as possible, it also rationalises their existence by making it binding that they adhere to the norms of democracy and national independence.
6. The government is in-charge of legislation and even effective criticism by Parliament is difficult, unless the National Assembly is prepared to go to the length of defeating it.
7. The President may refer a bill of great public importance to the verdict of the people in a national referendum, or that he may postpone a referendum even after such a bill is passed by the Parliament.

13. R.G. Neumann: *European and Comparative Government*, p. 243.

Three Important Characteristics of the French State

Despite frequent changes of constitutional regimes in France within the past several centuries, three important characteristics of the French state remained constant at least until recently. The fact that all the three have changed substantially in the past decade suggests the importance of the transition presently occurring in French politics.

First, for centuries there has been nearly universal agreement in the desirability of a unitary state.

Second, for generations, there has been a near consensus among French citizens that the state should play a central role in directing social affairs,

The third change involves limits that have developed on state action from within the state itself.

—*Mark Kesselman*

8. The President is both the judge and the jury in deciding about the proclamation of emergency under Art. 16 of the Constitution or its revocation.
9. The President may either remain in the background by entrusting his powers to the Prime Minister, or he may himself interpret his rights in such a way as may lead him to govern instead of reigning particularly in the areas where responsibility for policy belongs constitutionally to the Prime Minister.

7. Constitutional Council: It is a unique institution having advisory, adjudicating and controlling powers. It is neither a cabinet, nor a wing of the national legislature , nor a supreme judicial organ of the state. And yet it is a peculiar fusion of all. It has 9 members (three nominated by the President, three nominated by the President of the National Assembly, and three nominated by the President of the Senate) having a tenure of nine years, 1/3 retiring after every three years. Re-nomination is not permitted. Besides, all former presidents of the Republic are its *ex-officio* members. The head of this body (President) is appointed by the President of the Republic. It supervises the regularity of the election of the President and of the members of Parliament, and proclaims the results of a referendum. It may pronounce on the constitutional validity of an act of the executive or a law of the Parliament. It must be consulted by the President if he decides to declare state of emergency and the measure he takes to deal with it. It may give its view on the constitutional validity of an international treaty or agreement signed by the President or the Prime

Minister. It may also decide whether the post of the President of the Republic should be declared vacant in the event of his 'incapacity' for any reason. What particularly engages our attention here is that, in courses of time, it has widened its area of authority like the Senate and the Supreme Court of the United States. Virtually it has become like a source of restraint on the executive and the legislature of the French republic. So it is aptly observed: "Originally an obscure institution conceived to play a marginal role in the Fifth Republic, the Constitutional Council has gradually moved towards the centre stage of French politics and acquired the status of a major actor in the policy-making process."[14]

8. Economic and Social Council: The Constitution provides for the establishment of this body whose composition and the rules of procedure shall be determined by an Institutional Act. On a reference from the Government, it shall give its opinion on such official bills, draft ordinances or decrees, and Members' bills as have been submitted to it. A member of this body may be designated by it to present to the parliamentary assemblies its opinions on such bills and drafts. It may be consulted by the Government on any economic and social issue. Obviously, it is an advisory body to give its opinion on policies and programmes of the Government relating to issues of social and economic significance.

9. Rapport with Trans-Nationalism: France is an original member of the European Union (once European Economic Community formed in 1958 vide the Treaty of Rome of 1957 and then renamed as European Community) and thus the constitution of the Fifth Republic has provisions relating to European Communities and European Union. It signed the Treaty of European Union on 7 February, 1992. Vide Art. 88-1, the Republic shall participate in the European Communities and in the European Union constituted by States which have feely chosen to exercise some of their powers in common. Hence, France agrees to the transfer of powers necessary for the establishment of European economic and monetary union and for the determination of rules relating to the crossing of the external borders of the Member-States of the European Community. (Art. 88-2) Then, Art. 88-3 lays down that the right to vote and stand as a candidate in municipal elections shall be granted only to the citizens of

14. John T. Keeler and Alec Stone: "Judicial-Political Confrontation in Mitterand's France: The Emergence of the Constitutional Council as a Major Actor in the Policy-Making Process" in *The Mitterand Experiment*; *Continuity and Change in Modern France*, p.176.

the Union residing in France. Such citizens shall neither exercise the office of mayor or deputy mayor, nor participate in the designation of Senate electors or in the election of senators. Finally, Art. 88-4 lays down that the Government shall lay before the Parliament any proposal for community instruments which contain provisions which are matters for statute as soon as they have been transmitted to the council of the communities.

In fine, the Constitution of the Fifth Republic manages to accommodate much as advocated by the Gaullists as well as by the leftist elements of the country. It reflects conservative tendencies, it offers rationalised parliamentarism, it exudes a scent of 'historic mission' and dependence on popular consensus, it allows for arbitration to be exercised by an incumbent President who rejects the very notion of party itself and it enables the President to 'confiscate the ball' whenever the players in the game "prove themselves to be divided or inept."[15]

15. Lowell G. Noonam: *France: The Politics of Continuity and Change,* p.51.

22

NATIONAL EXECUTIVE

The French governmental system exhibits the abandonment of the traditional sanctity of both the parliamentary and the presidential models as found in Britain and the United States respectively; it is a half-way house between the two with greater weight in favour of the latter. The Constitution "greatly strengthens the executive and diminishes the role of Parliament."[1] The executive branch is still dual (as under the previous Republics) having a President and a Cabinet under the Prime Minister, but the astonishing difference finds place in the fact that "major emphasis is now placed on the President of the Republic,"[2] and not on the Prime Minister who acts like the nominee of the real head of the State. The real centre of the executive is the President and not the Prime Minister in view of the fact that the Constitution of 1958 has been designed "to vest substantial independence in the executive and to do this by the gift of a very considerable independent political power to the President of the Republic.'[3]

President

The President of the Fifth Republic of France, as already pointed out, is neither like a constitutional monarch of Britain, nor is he a replica of the American chief executive; he stands between the nominal sovereign of the United Kingdom (so far as his theoretical position is concerned) and the real executive of the United States with a considerably greater amount of tilt in favour of the latter. The reason for this may certainly be

---

1. Neumann: *European and Comparative Government*, p. 244.
2. *Ibid.*, p. 245.
3. R.C. Macridis: "France" in Macridis and Ward (ed.s): *Modern Political Systems: Europe*, p. 254.

traced in the serious problems with which the nation was confronted on the eve of the termination of the Fourth Republic. The framers "wished to give the President the prestige and the prerogatives that would enable him to provide for the continuity of the state, to cement the bonds between France and the former colonies of the French union, and to supervise the functioning of the Constitution. The President is the 'keystone of the arch of the new Republic'; he "is both the symbol and the instrument of reinforced executive authority."[4]

Election: The French Constitution provides that the President shall be elected by an electoral college for a period of seven years, which is now of 5 years vide an amendment of 2000. Another amendment of 2008 limits it to two consecutive terms at the most. The idea of direct election was rejected in view of the 'past mistakes' which had enabled Napoleon I and Napoleon III to overturn the then democratic governments. Hence, it was provided that the President shall be elected by an electoral college of approximately 80,000 electors. Though composed in a highly complicated manner, this electoral college consisted of (*a*) grand electors by right, being members of the Parliament, local government councils of the departments, mayors and deputy mayors of the municipal councils, and a number of municipal councillors in proportion to the population of each municipality, (*b*) additional delegates from municipalities of over 30,000 inhabitants, elected by the municipal councillors, and (*c*) members of the overseas territorial assemblies, the deputies and senators from there and representatives of overseas municipal councils. It was also provided that the mayors and deputies and municipal councillors who were also members of the Parliament must have substitutes, for the same man would be allowed to vote twice, It is aptly said: "It may be that, as a result, the Presidency will acquire some of the authority which de Gaulle certainly wished it had in the past, though the President clearly does not have the powers which he would certainly be granted in a presidential system."[5]

The constitutional reform of 1962 was implemented by ordinances that simplified the electoral process. The present position is that name of a candidate must be endorsed by 100 'notables', he is elected directly. The members of the Parliament or of the Social and Economic Council, or general departmental councillors and mayors (10 of whom would have

4. Herman Finer: *The Major Governments of Modern Europe*, p. 316.

5. Blondel and Godfrey, Jr.: *The Government of France.*, p. 48.

to be elected representatives of Overseas departments and territories) and by making a deposit of 2,000 dollars to be forfeited if he fails to receive at least 5% of the votes polled. It is also provided that every candidate shall be given equal time to speak on the radio and television for his canvassing. The candidates securing more than 5% of the votes polled shall also receive a grant of $ 20,000 in a lump sum to cover their election expenses. It is, however, required that the winner must secure absolute majority of the electoral college. If no candidate wins more than 50% of votes, the election shall take place again within next two weeks in which only two candidates having highest number of votes shall be allowed to take part. No candidate could secure absolute majority in the first ballot in the elections of 1974 and de Estaing was declared successful in the second ballot by defeating Mitterand.

The Constitution is, however, silent on many important points. For instance, it nowhere mentions the age and length of residence in France of a person holding this office. More so, an easy channel has been left for an ambitious national leader to exalt his power even by introducing an innovation in clear violation of the terms of the Constitution. For instance, the electoral reform of 1962 is nothing but a major constitutional innovation effected without the observance of the specified procedure. The bogey of 'over-representation of the rural areas' was a swindle to cover the ambition of the first President. And yet the position is not very clear. Many loopholes are there to be avoided which were highlighted in the previous election. It is true to say that the election of 1965–the first election under the revised arrangement "did not settle the future of the constitution, though while campaigning for the Presidency, both Lecanuet and Mitterand introduced many caveats and promised reforms for the great autonomy and initiative of the Parliament and a restriction on the powers and personal leadership of the President."[6]

The work of exercising supervision over the Presidential election and dealing with the allegations of irregularities and corrupt practices has been entrusted to the Constitutional Council. It is provided in the Constitution that the election of new President shall take place not less than 20 and not more than 35 days before the expiry of the term of the retiring President. If the office of the President falls vacant due to his death or resignation, the President of the Senate shall act in the officiating capacity until the next incumbent comes. If the Constitutional Council declares the President

6. Macridis, *op. cit.*, p. 236.

in office to be permanently incapacitated, the President of the Senate shall act as the President of the Republic until the election of a new President. This must take place within 20 to 35 days from the declaration made by the Constitutional Council in regard to the vacancy of office or incapacity of the office holder. It is clearly mentioned that the Acting President shall have powers of the office except some as relating to the dissolution of the National Assembly, reference of matter to the verdict of the people, conditions in which a government may be defeated and its obligations under circumstances, and the revision of the Constitution.

In 1976, Art. 7 of the Constitution was amended. It empowers the Constitutional Council to postpone Presidential election (*i*) if in the 7 days preceding final dates for the deposit of candidatures of person who had publicly announced his candidacy not more than 30 days before the date he died or was incapacitated, (*ii*) or if an officially accepted candidate died or was incapacitated before the first round of voting, in the event of death or incapacity, of one of the two most successful on the candidate's part for the second round, the Constitutional Council would declare that the whole election procedure must be gone through again, and the same would be the case in the event of the death or incapacity of one of the two candidates remaining in contention for the second round. In the light of the foregoing, the Constitutional Council would decide to extend for upto 35 days from the date of its decision the time limits for the holding of a presidential election as laid down in Art. 7 of the Constitution.

Functions and Powers: A look at the functions and powers of the President of the Fifth Republic brings home the fact that his authority "is formidable."[7] Apart form executive and legislative powers usually granted to the head of the state in other democratic countries of the world, the French President has 'emergency' powers as well which leave in his hands a loaded gun to save his nation or finish his opponents in the name of national unity and security. Says Dorothy Pickles: "Like his predecessors under the Third and Fourth Republics, the President is politically irresponsible for acts carried out by him in pursuance of his functions, except in the case of high treason, for which he can be tried before the High Court of Justice. This provision is comprehensible in the case of a President who presides but does not govern, but less so in that of a President of the Fifth Republic who, even in normal circumstances, can exercise

7. Neumann, *op. cit.*, p. 249.

some degree of real power, and who, in an emergency, has the right to exercise almost unlimited power."[8]

First, we discuss the executive powers of the President. The President is the head of the state as well as of the government, since all business of the government is conducted in his name and he presides over meetings of the cabinet which 'determines and directs the policy of the nation'. He appoints the Prime Minister and other ministers (on the recommendation of the Prime Minister) and terminates their functions when anyone of them tenders his resignation. He presides over the meetings of the Council of Ministers and signs ordinances and decrees as decided by this body. He also makes appointments of civil and military officers of the state, State Councillors, the Grand Chancellor of the Legion of Honour, ambassadors and envoys extra-ordinary, Master Councillors of the Audit Office, prefects, representatives of the Government in the Overseas Territories, general officers, rectors of academies (i.e., regional divisions of the public educational system) and directors of central administration. These appointments are made by the President in the meeting of the Council of Ministers. It is provided that an organic law shall determine other posts and their conditions of service under which the President shall make appointments or delegate his powers to his nominees.

As head of the state, the President accredits ambassadors to foreign countries and receives foreign ambassadors in his country. As Commodore of the armed forces, he presides over the high councils and committees of national defence. Whenever he has some doubts over the constitutional validity of an international treaty or agreement, he can refer the question for referendum over the decision of the State Council and can delay the ratification of the said treaty until the Constitution is amended in case the decision of the Council is favourable. In domestic sphere, he stands forth as the guarantor of national independence and protector of the territory and has been charged with the duty of ensuring respect for the Constitution. He speaks for the nation and incarnates the national will and he is the arbiter of national affairs. Finally, he has the prerogative of mercy and thus he can exercise his right to pardon a criminal or commute his punishment.

Then, the President has important legislative powers. He promulgates the laws within 15 days following the transmission to the Government of

8. Dorothy Pickles: *The Fifth French Republic*, p. 133.

the finally adopted law. Before the expiration of the time-limit, he may ask the Parliament for the reconsideration of the law or its certain parts and this recommendation cannot be refused. It is further provided that the President, on the proposal of the Government during the parliamentary session or on joint motion of the two Houses published in the Official Journal, may submit to a referendum any bill dealing with the organisation of governmental authorities, entailing approval of a Community agreement, or providing for authorisation to ratify a treaty that, without being contrary to the Constitution, might affect the functioning of existing institutions. When the referendum decides in favour of the bill, the President promulgates it within the time limit of 15 days. With the consultation of the Prime Minister and the Presidents of the National Assembly and the Senate, the President can declare the dissolution of the Assembly. Then, general elections shall take place at least 20 days before and at most 40 days after the dissolution. The National Assembly shall convene by right on the second Thursday following its election. However, if this meeting takes place between the period provided for ordinary sessions, a session shall by right be held for a duration of 15 days.

The Constitution empowers the President to send messages to the two Houses of the Parliament. He can call the Parliament for special sessions to hear his messages. This message is to be read in the Assembly and the Senate but not to be debated. He appoints the President of the State Council and its three members out of nine. He can seek the opinion of the Constitutional Council in regard to the constitutional validity of organic laws and regulations made by the Parliament before they come into operation. It is obvious that the President has no veto power like his American counterpart to reject a bill and he has no power of placing his signatures on the bill passed by the Parliament. According to a well-established convention, it may be pointed out that he has a suspensive veto in the sense that he may ask the Parliament for the reconsideration of a bill as a whole or in part and his request cannot be refused.

In addition to these executive and legislative powers, the President has emergency powers also. Art. 16 of the Constitution lays down: "When the institution of the Republic, the independence of the nation, the integrity of the territory, or the fulfilment of its international commitments are threatened in a grave and immediate manner and when the regular functioning of the constitutional governmental authorities is interrupted, the President of the Republic shall take the measures commanded by these

Vital Functions and Powers of the French President

1. To name the Prime Minister and other Cabinet Ministers as well as top-ranking civil, political, military and judicial officials,
2. To preside over the meetings of the Council of Ministers,
3. To ensure by his arbitration, regular functioning of the governmental authorities as well as the continuance of the State,
4. To act as the guarantor of national independence, of the territorial integrity of France, and to ensure respect for Community agreements and treaties,
5. To conduct foreign affairs through the power to negotiate treaties and for this sake to appoint ambassadors and accredit foreign envoys,
6. To direct and mobilise the armed forces,
7. To dissolve the National Assembly and call for new elections,
8. To appoint three members of the Constitutional Council and to designate its chief (President),
9. To propose constitutional amendments with the approval of the Prime Minister and to sponsor a referendum, and
10. To declare state of emergency and take necessary measures to defend independence and integrity of France or to execute some international treaty or agreement.

circumstances, after official consultation with the Premier, the Presidents of the Assemblies and the Constitutional Council. He shall inform the nation of these measures in message. These measures must be prompted by the desire to ensure to the constitutional governmental authorities, in the shortest possible time, the means of fulfilling their assigned functions. The Constitutional Council shall be consulted with regard to such measures. Parliament shall meet by right. The National Assembly may not be dissolved during the exercise of emergency powers by the President."

This provision places sweeping powers in the hands of the President by empowering him to take whatever steps he deems necessary and expedient to face the national crisis caused by a serious threat to the independence of the nation, the integrity of its territory or the fulfilment of international commitments, or when the regular functioning of the constitutional government is seriously interrupted. The actual use of authority under the provision of Art. 16 enables the President to secure more powers after their authorisation from the Parliament, or even delegate his emergency powers to the Cabinet if he is out of the country. For instance,

President de Gaulle left a decree with his Cabinet (when he had gone to the United States in May, 1960) to make use of this particular power in case a rebellion broke out. Justification of this particular action of the President finds place not in the words of the Constitution as such as in the precedents of history. While discarding a note of dissent in this regard, de Gaulle recollected the case of President Lebrun who had told him that he had not been able to leave France in 1940, and so the resistance was delayed.

An enumeration of the functions and powers of the President confirms the view that he is not at all a nominal executive like the English monarch. He is the 'master' of the national executive which has taken the Parliament under its subservience. The President is the virtual 'master' of both the executive and the legislature and the behaviour of de Gaulle well confirmed the fears of his critics. Herman Finer points out: "By these powers the executive branch has been immensely strengthened; the Assembly has been put in a subordinate place, in which it has reason truly to fear intimidation by a determined President of the Republic."[9] While taking the case of de Gaulle, Pickles holds that the Head of the Fifth Republic "regards both Government and Parliament as being, in their different ways, mere agents of the President. In fields which he considers vital, the President rules as well as reigns."[10]

Actual Position: The actual position of the French President is a matter of debate. To the defenders of the Constitution, he is meant to be the head of the state as, according to the letter and spirit of the fundamental law of the land, he should be no more than that particularly during normal times. The chief engineer of this Constitution, Michael Debre, designates his political system as 'parliamentary' and the 'only one suitable for France'. If France has a parliamentary system of government, the position of the President despite a formidable list of his powers and prerogatives, remains like the President of the Indian Republic. On the contrary, it is asserted that France has a peculiar 'Presidential' system of government in which real power is in the hands of the President who keeps the Prime Minister as his nominee and who reigns as well as rules. It is evident from these points:

9. Herman Finer, *op. cit.*, p. 329.

10. Pickles, *op., cit.* p.136.

Some Important Statements

As the Constitution stands, a President can either make himself effective Head of Government as well as Head of the State with the Prime Minister as little more than a senior member of his cabinet, or he can be content with nominal and advisory powers leaving the main work to the Prime Minister. —***Michael Stewart***

The President's influence will depend on the personality of the man and on what type of men Parliament will accept as Ministers. If the articles regarding the Cabinet and Parliament are applied, the President will neither be directing force once advocated by de Gaulle nor the directing force feared by some critics of the Constitution. —***Campbell and Chapman***

By allowing each person to choose at closer intervals the person who presides over the destiny of the nation, the reduction of Presidential mandates from seven to five years will give our country a more democratic pulse.

—***President Jacques Chirac***

1. The strong position of the President, not found in a cabinet system of government, becomes evident from various directions where he uses his authority independently or in his own discretion. Nothing save his personal judgement is the decisive factor. President is the 'arbiter'–the custodian of the constitutional government. The powers of the President are 'over-riding' in matters of war, foreign policy, defence, internal peace and, above all. the functioning of the governmental institutions.
2. The President is the virtual master of his Council of Ministers. He not only presides over the meetings of the cabinet, he can also veto a decision. The position of the Prime Minister is extremely delicate; he must support the President, or face his own downfall. The President does not 'designate' the Prime Minister (as under Third and Fourth Republics), he appoints him without mandate from the National Assembly. The Constitution nowhere makes it obligatory that the Prime Minister must secure mandate from the National Assembly prior to his becoming the Head of the Government, gathering ministers, and starting to work with full authority.
3. More astounding is the arrangement of 'counter-signatures'. It is stipulated in the Constitution that the acts of the President (excepting appointment and dismissal of the Prime Minister and other ministers, decision to hold a referendum, dissolution of the National Assembly, use of emergency powers, sending messages to the Parliament, referring certain matters to the Constitutional Council, appointment of the President and the three members of the Constitutional Council,

and referring organic laws and important matters of this body before promulgating them to test their constitutional validity) must be countersigned by the Prime Minister and other ministers if circumstances so require. But the astonishing feature of the French constitutional system is that the responsibility is of the Prime Minister and of his Cabinet and not that of the President. The National Assembly can pass a vote of censure against the Cabinet but not against the President.

4. The President has the power to dissolve the National Assembly in his discretion for no other reason than to impose his point of view. His consultation with the Prime Minister and the Presidents of the National Assembly and the Senate is a mere formality. The decree of the President in this direction does not need approval of any other agency. The only limitation on the power of the President in this regard is that the new Assembly cannot be dissolved before the expiry of one year. It is understandable that, like the British Prime Minister, the French President has a very effective power in his hands to compel 'rival' politicians to come to terms with him. It is also conceivable that the President might use this weapon not merely to bring an unruly Assembly in discipline but also to get rid of a government with which he finds it difficult to get along.
5. There is the provision of referendum where the President can act in his discretion or on the recommendation of the Government if he so pleases. Art. 3 of the Constitution vests national sovereignty in the people who exercise it through their representatives and by means of a referenda. The initiative for submitting a question to the people for their vote at a referendum rests with the Government or the Parliament. It is laid down in Art. 11 of the Constitution that on the proposal of the Government during the session of the Parliament, or when the two Houses propose that a referendum be held on a bill dealing with the organisation of public authorities, approving a Community agreement or proposing notification of a treaty which, without being contrary to the Constitution, affects the functioning of institutions, the President may submit it for a referendum.
6. The emergency powers of the President, as provided under Art. 16 of the Constitution, are hailed by the supporters of the framers as the essential instrument to prevent the recurrence of any catastrophe like that of 1940, these are also taken as a channel of legal dictatorship by those who may be called the critics of the Constitution. Although

the President is constitutionally required to consult four agencies (Prime Minister, President of the National Assembly, President of the Senate and President of the State Council), he is the sole judge to determine whether the circumstances so warrant or not. It is in his discretion to decide when the declaration should be made and what necessary steps should be taken to face that crisis.

7. The President is the 'guide' of the nation. He is the final source and holder of the power of the state and the only man to hold and delegate the authority of the State. Really speaking, he can hold in his hands all powers of the state, provided he holds the office by virtue of an election and as long as his reforms are approved by the people. In domestic as well as in foreign affairs, his office has become the real centre of policy- making. A strong leader like de Gaulle is capable of, according to the language of this Constitution, taking any measure even without the consultation of his Government and the no matter it pertains to the withdrawal of the country from North-Atlantic Treaty Organisation or instigation of the French people of Quebec in Canada to stage a demand for more autonomy. It is all due to the fact that he "is deeply involved in politics and can no longer be considered as an 'irresponsible head of the state' like the British Crown."[11]

In a word, the President occupies the most celebrated office in the French constitutional system. He is the President of the Republic as well as of the entire French community. As France has a unitary system of government and the model of government is quasi-Presidential, it is understandable to regard the President as the single-most powerful and important authority of the state. Pickles is right in her judgment that public interests "is focused on him and not on the Prime Minister, and the President takes great care to see that the spotlight remains on him."[12] It is well observed: "In France, the President is not only head of the state, the symbolic and ceremonial leader of the country, but also possesses substantial policy-making and executive power.......As long as a single party controls both the executive and the legislature, the powers of the French President are immense. The President combines the independent

11. Macridis, *op. cit.*, p. 257.

12. Pickles, *op.cit.*, p. 136. As Vincent Wright observes: The Presidency has apparently become omnipresent–a phenomenon which is all the more surprising, since it has little in the constitution." *The Government and Politics of France.* p. 48.

power of the U.S. President–notably, command of the executive establishment and independence from legislative control–with the powers that accrue to the government in a parliamentary regime–namely, control over Parliament's agenda and its day-to-day activity, and the ability to dissolve Parliament and force new general election. Moreover, the government–usually under the President's direction, controls Parliaments more tightly than other democratic regimes do. The result is a greater degree of executive dominance within the French political system than in virtually any other democratic nation. And the President occupies the office at the very top of this commanding edifice."[13]

Government

The Government of France under the Fifth Republic, in a wider sense, means the ,President, his Prime Minister and the Ministers. As already said, in the present French constitutional system, the executive is more powerful than the Parliament, the President is the 'master' of all. He is the head of the State. Prime Minister and his Ministers are subordinate to him and the Parliament is more or less like a deliberative forum. This arrangement has been made with a definite purpose. It is a fact that the chief objective of the architects of the present Constitution was to remove the serious flaw of the previous constitution which had made the National Assembly strong enough to try to govern and to legislate as well as to supervise and thwart the executive. A workable solution to this problem was discovered by the framers in strengthening the executive at the expense of the legislature.

Organisation: The Constitution makes an academic distinction between the President and the Government (ministers under the Prime Minister) by adding that while the business of the former is "to ensure the guardianship of the Constitution, the role of the government is to govern."[14] While the President, is elected for a 'safe' term of 5 years, the Prime Minister is appointed by the head of the State for the time he enjoys his pleasure as well as the confidence of the National Assembly. The President nominates the Prime Minister. It is hardly necessary to point out that the President has much greater amount of freedom in the choice of the Prime Minister than the British monarch for no other reason than the existence

13. Mark Kesselman: "France" in Kesselman, Joel Krieger and W.A. Joseph: (eds): *Comparative Politics at the Crossroads*, p. 129.
14. Blondel and Godfrey, Jr., *op. cit.*, p. 48.

of a number of political groups in the Assembly, none of them commanding absolute majority.

The ministers are appointed by the President on the recommendation of the Prime Minister. It appears that here French system pertains to the maxim of a parliamentary government as prevailing in Britain. However, the real position is quite different. It may be repeated that under the existing system the President is in a very strong position to materially influence the choice of the ministers even though the decree showing the appointment of ministers has to be countersigned by the Prime Minister. The provision of direct election of the President affords the most compelling reason for the real executive to induct some of his 'favourites' into the Government and the strong leadership of de Gaulle had confirmed this fact. This incidentally introduces an element of the Presidential system in the 'so-called' parliamentary system of France and is in keeping with the principle of the separation of powers.

The Prime Minister has the right to determine the size of the Cabinet, though its exercise depends upon his ability to please several coalescent groups by accommodating them with at least one major portfolio. The total number of Cabinet ministers has varied around twenty. Apart from the Cabinet ministers, there are some 'ministers of state' or ministers without portfolios. They donot hold the charge of any independent department in order that they concentrate their attention on general policy. However, it is required that they must invariably be the leading politicians of the country. There are some 'deputy' ministers as well to assist their principals. On some occasions, the post of Deputy Prime Minister has also been created.

A point of distinction exists between the Council of Ministers and the Cabinet in the present French constitutional system. The Constitution lays down that the President shall preside over the meetings of the Council of Ministers and the Prime Minister can do so only at the behest of the President. But the Prime Minister acts as the presiding officer of the Cabinet as a matter of right. It shows that there is a subtle difference between the two. The Council of Ministers is a smaller group consisting of the President, the Prime Minister and all the ministers of the Cabinet; while the Cabinet includes the Prime Minister and all other ministers whether of cabinet rank, or state ministers, or deputy ministers, if any. It implies that the Cabinet is a bigger body than the Council of Ministers–an arrangement quite different from that of Britain and India where the Cabinet is smaller than the Ministry or the Council of Ministers.

Another astonishing feature of the French system is that the Cabinet is less powerful than the Council of Ministers. The Council of Ministers is the group of leading statesmen who discuss major matters of national policy and who decide the issues of seeking vote of confidence, or the dissolution of National Assembly. As it meets under the chairmanship of the President, it is inferrable that the President of the Fifth Republic, unlike his predecessors, has a very important role in the administration of the country. It is a queer arrangement that while the President is the party to the decision of the Council of Ministers, the Prime Minister is accountable to the National Assembly and in case a vote of censure takes place, it is the latter who has to resign.

Functions and Powers: According to the language of the Constitution, the chief function of the Government is to determine and direct the policy of the nation. It has at its disposal the administration and the armed forces of the Republic. Although law-making is the business of the Parliament, the Government may obtain its permission from the Parliament to issue ordinances for regulating matters which normally come within the domain of law. These ordinances are made by the Council of Ministers in consultation with the Council of State and become null and void if the bill for their ratification is not submitted to Parliament before the date set by the enabling act. The Prime Minister has been given the power to initiate legislation.

Despite his weak position, the Prime Minister holds a key place in the Government. On his recommendation other ministers are appointed by the President. It is he who directs the work of administration and is responsible for national defence. He sees to it that laws made by the Parliament are carried out. Besides, he advises the President in making high civil and military appointments. He can also ask for convening a special session of the Parliament for the consideration of some important matter. He can also submit to the consideration of the President some proposals regarding amendment of the Constitution. He may call a joint meeting of the two Houses if there is a disagreement between them to pass a bill after its second reading, or when the matter is too urgent to be discussed without loss of time. He is consulted by the President before the decree of dissolution of the National Assembly is promulgated. It indicates that the Prime Minister is the chief spokesman of the government before the Parliament in making general discussion of policy.

The salient feature of the cabinet government is traceable in the arrangement that not the President but the Prime Minister and his ministers are responsible to the National Assembly. This arrangement has three dimensions. First, the Prime Minister may go to the National Assembly and put his policy for approval. If the matter is adopted by a simple majority of the members present and voting, the Government is said to enjoy the confidence of the Parliament. Second, the Prime Minister may put a motion of confidence in his government and get it passed by the National Assembly by simple majority of the members present and voting. Third, the Prime Minister may stake his position on the adoption of a bill. If such a bill is presented, the fate of the bill shall coincide with the fate of the Government. If such a resolution is passed by the simple majority of the members present and voting, the bill shall be taken as passed by the Assembly without debate implying confidence of the Parliament in the Government.

However, the last and most significant weapon is in the hands of the National Assembly. If at least 1/10 members sign a motion censuring the Government, a debate shall take place after the lapse of 48 hours and in case the motion is adopted by the Assembly by an absolute majority of the House, the Government must resign for want of confidence. It is further provided in the Constitution that the same signatories cannot table another motion of censure during the same session in case their first move fails. It, however, does not apply to the arrangement where the Prime Minister stakes the life of his Government with the passage of a bill. When such a step is taken by the Prime Minister, the burden is on the Assembly to outvote the Government by having a censure motion signed by at least 1/10 of its members and get it passed by the absolute majority. In case the censure motion fails, or in case the Government wins (in the absence of any such censure motion) by a simple majority, it amounts to a vote of confidence in it. It shows that the National Assembly may take the initiative of moving a vote of censure against the Government and throw it out if the motion is carried through by absolute majority.

It is striking to note that while simple majority is needed for the survival of the Government, absolute majority is required for causing its fall. In case a censure motion is lost, another censure motion may be brought forth by at least those 1/10 signatories who were no party to the previous motion. It is often for the Prime Minister to pledge his Government's responsibility, after deliberations of the Cabinet, with a specific bill, but the text of the bill shall not be tabled unless a motion of censure, moved within the next 24 hours, is voted and passed by the absolute majority of the House. This is, indeed, a better arrangement in view of the past political experiments. That the same 1/10 signatories cannot put forward another censure motion during the rest of the session is certainly a check on the extremist elements who may indulge in obstructionist practices recklessly. The members of the Assembly "have still considerable elbow room to defeat the Governments, since there is no restriction on the number of censure motions relating to the issue that the Government has made question of confidence. What the procedure does put a stop to is the possibility that a Government may see its Bill defeated while it retains, constitutionally speaking, the confidence of the Assembly."[15]

Special Features: It is understandable that the French governmental system represents a crude mixture of the traits of parliamentary and presidential models. In order to make the points intelligible, we may highlight some special features of the French executive and its relationship with the legislature. These are:

1. The Constitution accommodates the principle of 'incompatibility' whereby the ministers, like the Secretaries of the United States, are not allowed to enjoy the membership of the Parliament. It is provided that the Prime Minister and his ministers cannot serve in a double capacity and in case a parliamentarian is appointed as a minister, he will have to resign his seat in the Parliament. At the same time, a member of the Government is also deprived of holding any office at the national level in business, professional or labour organisation, and with any public employment or professional activity. This arrangement has been lauded by the supporters of the Constitution as the most effective way of keeping the 'greedy' politicians and 'wealthy' magnates away from the Parliament and ministerial assignments.
2. In addition to the advantage of implementing the system of separation of powers, the bar of inducting professional businessmen and seasoned politicians into the ministry at the cost of their parliamentary career is a very effective arrangement to discourage the ambitious political leaders to make or unmake the Government in a most reckless manner. It appears to act as a great check on the politicisation of the Government. It is hoped that the envisaged arrangement would reduce the temperature of politics in as much as only those leaders would like to join the Government who are prepared to sacrifice

15. Pickles: *The Fifth French Republic*, p. 112.

their parliamentary career. It is further said that this arrangement would compel the ministers to abandon the outlook of a rank politician and force them to take the air of a dedicated statesman.

3. The arrangement of asking a minister to first relinquish his membership of the Parliament in preference to his Government assignment opens the question of by-election which the present Constitution solves by the device of 'substitutes'. It is provided that in order to avoid the cascade of a bye-election at each ministerial reshuffle, all parliamentarians shall have their substitutes and when a member after his ministerial assignment leaves his membership of the Parliament, his seat shall go to his substitute automatically.
4. The line of a presidential government is markedly visible when one finds that the Government of France consists mainly of "President's men". The Prime Minister is the nominee of the President and in the selection of other ministers (though on the recommendation of the Prime Minister) the behaviour of the French President is not like that of the English monarch or Indian President. He is at the helm of national affairs to dictate his choice by many subtle means. It implies that when the Prime Minister is the nominee of the President himself, the entire Government is hardly anything more than a family of the head of the State. Even if the National Assembly outvotes a Prime Minister, the vacancy has to be filled by the President without any consultation with some other agency or institution.
5. Another weighty feature of a presidential system in the composition of the ministry and its working finds place in the fact that the Government works under the direction, superintendence and control of the President, not of the Prime Minister. A parliamentarian loses his autonomy to become a minister under the masterly control of the President who is not at all a *primus inter pares*. It is clear from the preceding account that the decision-making body is the Council of Ministers and the President is its chairman. It is also understandable that the President has many committees and commissions in his Palace to assist him in the running of administration. Thus, he has necessary expertise at his disposal to make use of his discretionary powers in matters of national administration.
6. The Government of France is still organised on the basis of coalition. As no single political party becomes capable of having absolute majority in the National Assembly, the portfolios are distributed in a way that different parties are properly accommodated. The result

is a coalition cabinet. It is noteworthy that, despite arrangements of coalitions, the government of France has stability in marked contrast to its its pre-1958 position.

7. Under the present arrangement, the Prime Minister has the most unusual weapon of staking the life of his Government with the passage of a bill in a way that the position of the popular chamber is in jeopardy. It is inequitable that while simple majority is needed by the Prime Minister to achieve his purpose, absolute majority is required by his opponents to mark their victory. It is inferrable that this provision arms the Government with a strong potential-capacity to arm a piece of legislation through the House without a debate or division.
8. The State Council, apart from being mainly an administrative court, is an agency to assist the Cabinet in its legislative business. It is required that this agency must be consulted by the Government with regard to all legislation originated by the Prime Minister or his ministers. At the behest of Government, the State Council may make investigations into any important matter or call attention of the President towards some reform in the sphere of administration. Then, the State Council also serves as an inspector over all authorities which exercise functions of administrative justice in metropolitan France and overseas.
9. The French Government now enjoys much control over financial matters. The Constitution has severely curtailed the right of the members of the Parliament to propose and increase expenditure. Art. 40 of the Constitution debars a member form proposing amendments which have the effect of either diminishing public financial resources or adding to public expenditure.
10. The Government of France operates under the strong control of the President and not under the effective leadership of the Prime Minister as we find in the United kingdom. In 1964 de Gaulle himself admitted that clearly it "is the President alone who holds and delegates the authority of the State. But the very nature, the extent and the duration of his task imply that he is not absorbed without remission or limit by political, parliamentary, economic and administrative contingencies. Further, it is the Prime Minister who deals with the 'contingencies' which are his lot, as complex and meritorious as it is essential.'[16]

16. Cited in Blondel and Godfrey, Jr. *op. cit.*, pp. 52-53.

Some Important Statements

Whereas the Constitution of the Fourth Republic established a government by the Parliament, the Constitution of the Fifth Republic establishes a government by the President. —*Dorothy Pickles*

The President has apparently become omnipresent–a phenomenon which is all the more surprising, since it has little in the Constitution. —*Vincent Wright*

The Constitution of the Fifth Republic is extremely confusing in regard to the division of responsibilities between the President and the Government. —*Mark Kesselman*

Whether the French President is a powerful head of the state elected by the people for a period of 5 years to rule over the country without the check of an effectual legislature or a supreme judiciary, or he is expected to run the administration of the realm with the real cooperation of his Prime Minister responsible to the National Assembly. The matter, apart from being an interesting issue of academic controversy, is to be settled by the events of time. Kesselman aptly remarks that the French Constitution "provide a brief catalogue of the government's powers that are shared with the President but these are important areas of overlap and, therefore, potential conflict."[17]

Bureaucracy

In France bureaucracy has a particularly important position for three reasons. First, the Constitution is extremely confusing in regard to the division of responsibilities between the President and the Government (implying Council of Ministers). It provides a brief list of Government's powers which are shared with the President. But there are many areas of 'overlap' which create situations of 'conflict'. Thus a sort of vacuum exists that naturally provides room for bureaucratic intervention. Second, the Constitution severely restricts the number of fields in which Parliament can make laws and thereby authorise the concerned departments to issue necessary direction or regulation. Thus, bureaucracy may overstretch its arms in the absence of the mechanism of 'delegated legislation'. Last, mention should be made of the ministerial cabinets and personal staffs. Such cabinets do not consist of the ministers as such. They are not, strictly speaking, part of the administration. Rather, they

17. Kesselman, *op. cit.*, p. 134.

advise cabinet ministers on policy and partisan matters, and informally supervise department of the minister in his name. Most of the members of such cabinets are recruited from the ranks of talented rising young administrators who often return to the regular administration when they leave the cabinet.

Obviously, in France bureaucracy unusually enjoys great authority and autonomy. It is well observed. "The French bureaucracy is generally regarded as one of the most competent and efficient in the world. Positions at the top of the administration are among the most powerful in France, given the country's dirigiste tradition."[18] The French bureaucracy intervenes more extensively and is more powerful than is true in most comparable nations. For example, despite the growth of European Union institutions and the new political economy, in which market forces play a prominent role, administrators continue to make many important choices regarding particular forms (even those formally within the private sector), industries and the entire economy."[19]

18. Dirigiste (or dirgisme) highlights importance of state in steering national economy. It implies neither socialism nor communism. The state has a relatively small role in the economic governance.

19. Kesselman, *op. cit.*, p. 135.

23

PARLIAMENT

A study of the political system of the Fifth Republic leaves an impression that the Parliament "is the 'step-child' under the new constitutional dispensation."[1] It is, indeed, a major departure from the old tradition that the legislature is no longer the sole embodiment of the sovereignty of the people. The Constitution establishes a fundamentally different system under which the lower house (National Assembly) and the upper one (Senate) "are more nearly co-equal than they were in the Fourth Republic, although both are diminished in stature compared with the power of the executive."[2] Whereas the organisation of the legislature under the old system was dubbed as "incomplete bicameralism" or modified unicameralism, the present system "may be considered as a strongly modified parliamentarism."[3]

Composition of National Assembly and Senate: Like British Parliament and American Congress, the French Parliament is bi-cameral having Senate and National Assembly as the upper and lower chambers respectively. However, the arrangement of two chambers is well in conformity with the old tradition of the Third and Fourth Republics with three exceptions. First, the upper chamber has a changed name; it is no longer the Council of the Republic as under the Fourth Republic, it is Senate as it was under the Third Republic. Second, the powers of the Senate have been increased in order to make it a more or less equally powerful chamber as compared with the powers of the National Assembly except in matters of passing money bills or censuring the government. Last, the 'principle of incompatibility' has been introduced to debar a

1. Blondel and Godfrey, Jr. : *The Government of France,* p, 56.
2. Neumann: *European and Comparative Government,* p. 268.
3. *Ibid.*

minister from retaining his seat in the Parliament for no other reason than to depoliticise the government or reduce the temperature of politics.

Like the House of Commons of Britain and the House of Representatives of the United States, the lower house of the French Parliament is organised on the basis of direct election. Its strength is 577—555 from Metropolitan France and 22 from the Overseas Possessions. The minimum age for voting is 21 years, while for being elected to the Assembly, it is 23 years. For the upper house the minimum age for being elected is 35 years. It is required that the candidates must have completed their military service and they must be French citizens of at least 10 years' standing. Convicts and persons declared undischarged bankrupts and others deprived of their civil rights are not eligible for the membership of either house. Besides, members of the boards of nationalised industries, directors of companies which receive state aid or hold Government contracts, and persons who hold any office (paid) on behalf of a member-state of the Community or any foreign power or an international organisation are not eligible for membership.

The total membership of the Senate has been fixed. It has 343 members out of which 311 represent Metropolitan France, 9 represent Overseas Departments and Overseas Territories and 12 represent Frenchmen living abroad. The metropolitan seats are distributed among the 'departments' each having 1 seat for the first 150,000 inhabitants and additional ones for each additional 250,000 or fraction thereof. Each electoral college is composed of (1) local parliamentary deputies, (2) members of the departmental councils, and (3) representatives of the municipalities according to the size of various municipal councils. All the members of the electoral colleges number about 115,000 in all. About 400 communes with over 9,000 inhabitants choose their delegates by proportional representation, while others with less than 37,000 inhabitants choose their delegates by absolute majority allowing three ballots to attain this.

A new law approved by the Parliament in July 2003 effected a number of reforms to the election of the Senators. Henceforth, the Senators are to be elected for a term of 6 years with one half of the seats renewable after three years (compared with a term of 9 years and one-third of seats renewable every three years previously). With effect from 2011, the number of Senators will be increased to 348 and the minimum age for the eligible candidate to the Senate be reduced from 35 to 30 years. The first stage of reforms whereby the number of Senators increased from 321 to 331 had taken place at the partial Senatorial elections held in September, 2001,

Some Important Statements

Within Parliament, the National Assembly is by far the more powerful chamber. Only the Assembly possesses the power to censure the government. And the National Assembly has the decisive role in passing legislation. —***Mark Kesselman***

One of the most important innovations of the Fifth Republic is the restriction on the scope of Parliamentary activities. This represents a break with the Republican traditions of Parliamentary Sovereignty. —***Dorothy Pickles***

Parliamentary sessions are now brief, its powers overshadowed by regulations and ordinances. Not only do the private members use their powers to make financial proposals, Parliament as a whole finds that the budget can be passed over its head. All this is to prevent irresponsible and secret intrigue against the Government, such as occurred under the Third and Fourth Republics. It may well be that Parliamentary Government has been not so much reformed as extinguished. —***Michael Stewart***

this number was subsequently increased to 343 at the partial Senatorial elections held in September, 2008.[4]

It is laid down in the Constitution that the matters relating to the qualifications, emoluments, terms, conditions of incompatibility *etc.* of the members of Parliament shall be determined by Organic Laws. Thus an organic law was passed to abolish the 'notorious' system of proportional representation in the elections of National Assembly and substituted in its place the single-member constituency system with a second ballot in case no candidate succeeds in obtaining absolute majority of the votes polled at the first ballot. It shall be determined by the organic law as to what shall be the conditions governing the replacement of deputies of the National Assembly and members of the Senate who are either appointed as ministers or resign their seats. A very innovatory arrangement in this regard is the election of the alternates or 'substitutes', that is 'dummy' candidates, who take seat in the Parliament when a member dies or resigns his seat particularly on being a minister.

Like the British House of Commons, the National Assembly is elected by the people for a period of 5 years. However, it may be dissolved earlier by the President. It is required that the President must 'seek the opinions' of the Prime Minister and the presiding officers of the two Houses before promulgating his decree, though the matter lies in his discretion. The Senate, like its American counterpart, is a permanent body with the difference that while the members of the latter are indirectly elected for a

4. *The Europa World Year-Book* (London: Routledge, 2010), Vol. I, p. 1783.

period of 6 years, 1/3 retiring every second year, the members of the former are elected by an electoral college for a period of 6 years, 1/2 retiring every third year. According to a law made in 2003, the Senators are to be elected through a combination of majority voting and proportional representation.

Sessions and Presiding Officers: The Constitution lays down that the Parliament shall convene by right in two ordinary sessions in a year. The first session begins on the first Tuesday of October and lasts till the third Friday of December. That is, it lasts for nearly 74 days and is mainly concerned with the passing of the budget. The second session begins on the last Tuesday of April and cannot continue for more than three months. It is concerned mainly with the passing of ordinary legislative matters. It is understandable that the President has no right to convene the ordinary session of the Parliament, for it is held as a matter of right. However, he may call an extra-ordinary session of the Parliament at any time to consider 'urgent' business. It shall usually be done on the advice of the Prime Minister, because the decree issued by the President in this regard must be countersigned by the Prime Minister. Parliament may itself hold its extraordinary session by right.

Each house of the Parliament has its presiding officers and a bureau. The chairman of the National Assembly is not called the Speaker as in other democratic countries, he is designated as the 'President' elected by the house for the duration of the chamber. The chairman of the Senate, called the President, is elected by the chamber for a term of three years. That is, his election is renewed after every partial organisation. The Presidents of both houses are elected by secret ballot with absolute majority of the membership of the house at the first and second ballots, but a relative majority is deemed sufficient at the third ballot. The presiding officers of both houses perform functions usually granted to the chairman of a democratic chamber like maintenance of order and discipline in the chamber, recognising and naming the members, allowing debates, giving ruling and counting votes to declare the result etc. In addition to these conventional functions, they are also consulted by the President when he wants to declare emergency or dissolve the National Assembly. Each house elects its own bureau consisting of the President, Vice-Presidents (6 for the Assembly and 4 for the Senate), secretaries (12 for the Assembly and 4 for the Senate) and 3 'questeurs' who are responsible for the administrative and financial arrangement of the house. The functions of the bureau as a body are related to the organisation and supervision of the different services in the house; they also pertain to the rendering of advice to the presiding officer in matters put before the house.

The powers and position of the presiding officers of the Assembly and of the Senate appear unusual to a student of comparative government and politics who keeps in his mind the cases of English and American representative systems. The presiding officer of the National Assembly is a partyman like the American Speaker, but his position is inferior to the President of the Senate in order of precedence. In case there is a dispute between the Government and the President of the National Assembly over the question of constitutional validity of a bill moved by a private member, the matter is to be settled by the Constitutional Council. It makes the French Speaker (President of the National Assembly) subservient to the control of a non-legislative agency. Finally, the election of the President of the Assembly for the full duration the house (though it has been devised as an improvement upon the situation of the pre-1958 period when he was elected for a year only) is still inherent with the serious lacuna that a longer and safer tenure has strengthened his position of staying in politics while being in the chair demanding non-partisanship.

Functions and Powers: We have seen that the framers of the new Constitution were successful in breaking the 'teeth' of the National Assembly by making it subservient to the will of the Government. It, however, does not imply that French Parliament is a prototype of the National People's Congress of China which is hardly anything more than a constitutional rubber-stamp in the hands of the arch-leadership of the ruling party. It is said that the de Gaulle Constitution establishes a 'rationalised' Parliament in view of the fact that its two ordinary sessions are allowed as a matter of right subject to the arrangement of extraordinary sessions either convened by the President (on the advice of the Prime Minister) or by its own members, that it can legislate only on 'matters defined in the Constitution', that the order of business is now fixed by the Government, that the President of National Assembly is elected for the full duration of the house and of the Senate for a period of three years, that the Parliament is no longer free to establish its own standing orders, that the number of parliamentary committees is reduced, that Government bills come before the house as a whole for discussion, and last, that the Government has the right to reject all amendments and to demand a single vote on its own text with only those amendments which it accepts-a procedure known as the 'blocked' vote.

The functions and powers of the Parliament may be discussed under three heads–(*i*) relating to law-making. (*ii*) control over Government, and (*iii*) supervision over the President. First we take up the legislative powers of the Parliament where it has a circumscribed authority. A very peculiar arrangement is provided by Art. 34 of the Constitution which divides the field of legislative competence into two parts. In the first category come the laws which shall establish the rules concerning:

1. Civil rights and the fundamental guarantees granted to the citizens for the exercise of their public liberties; the obligations imposed by the national defence upon the persons and property of citizens.
2. Nationality, status and legal capacity of persons, marriage contracts, inheritance and gifts.
3. Determination of crimes and misdemeanours as well as the penalties imposed therefor; criminal procedure, amnesty; the creation of new judicial systems, and the status of magistrates.
6. The establishment of categories of public institutions.
4. The basis, the rate and the methods of collecting taxes of all types, the issuance of currency.
5. The electoral system of the parliamentary assemblies and the local assemblies.
7. The fundamental guarantees granted to civil and military personnel employed by the state; and
8. The nationalisation of enterprises and the transfer of property of enterprises from the public to the private sector.

To the second category belong a number of items where the Parliament can make laws determining the general principles regarding their organisation. These are:

1. General organisation of the national defence.
2. Free administration of local communities, the extent of their jurisdiction and their resources.
3. Education.
4. Property rights, civil and commercial obligations.
5. Legislation pertaining to employment, unions and social security.
6. Laws pertaining to national planning determining the objectives of the economic and social action of the state.

The Constitution makes a distinction between the two types of laws by specifying that in regard to the first the Parliament lays down underlying 'general principles' and also determines the details of their application; in regard to the second category, it confines only to the enunciation of 'fundamental principles' without going into the details. It may be pointed out that the distinction between the 'law' and the 'rule-making', as designed here, is a very perplexing affair and the scope of one seems to overlap that of the other. It is also laid down in the Constitution that the enumeration of the legislative power can be enlarged by means of an organic law only.

Apart from legislative powers, the Parliament exercises control over the Government. Both houses may ask questions from the Ministers and may go to the length of accusing the Prime Minister of various 'crimes of commission and omission.' However, the right of censuring the Government is with the National Assembly alone. It is provided that at least 1/10 members of the Assembly may sign a notice of moving a censure motion. After the lapse of at least 48 hours of the tabling of the motion, the debate shall take place and in case the motion is carried through by absolute majority of the Assembly, the Government will have to resign. This is the most specific way of throwing out the Government. However, the Government must resign in case a vote of confidence (tabled by it) is not adopted by simple majority, or when the Bill staked with confidence in the Government at the initiative of the Prime Minister falls through after a motion signed by at least 1/10 members of the Assembly is adopted by the absolute majority of the house. In order to prevent the indignant members of the Assembly from misusing their weapon of control over the Government (as happened till 1958), it has been provided that the same signatories cannot introduce another censure motion against the Government during the rest of the session if their motion falls, though this restriction is not applicable to a situation where the Prime Minister stakes the life of his Government with the passage of a bill. To keep the Government safe from the hazards of responsibility to the Parliament, it has also been provided that while simple majority is required to save the Government, absolute majority is needed for causing its fall.

Finally, the Parliament has been given some power to exercise supervision over the President. It is laid down in the Constitution that the President, before making his declaration of the state of emergency or dissolution of the National Assembly, shall consult the Presidents of the two houses. It is also necessary that the President must send a message to the Parliament specifying conditions which motivated him to make use of his emergency powers. The President cannot dissolve the National Assembly during the state of emergency, nor can he dissolve it until it has enjoyed a life of at least one year. The Parliament can exercise control over the foreign policy of the President by the negative means of censuring the Government. Finally, it is provided that the Parliament shall authorise the declaration of war and the prorogation of martial law (though decreed in the meeting of the Council of Ministers) shall be authorised, by it alone after the period of 12 years.

It is easy to form an impression that the authority of the French Parliament is of a very attenuated kind. It appears that serious arrangements have been devised to keep the legislature in a position weaker than that of the executive

Special Features: An account of the functions and powers of the legislature highlights the fact that French Parliament is not a very strong organ of the national government if its authority is compared with that of the executive under the President. The Parliament is not at all a sovereign law-making body like its British counterpart, nor is it as powerful as the American Congress working within the legislative arena earmarked by the Constitution according to the system of separation of powers and checks and balances. Its authority neither resembles the legislature of a parliamentary government where the executive can be out-voted by the popular chamber by a resolution passed by simple majority, nor does it look akin to the powers of a legislature organised on the principle of presidential model where the law-making organ of the government has freedom to operate within its allotted 'legislative sphere,' what to say of a legislature modelled on the convention theory where the government runs according to the will of the deputies elected by the people.

That the new Constitution places the Parliament under the subservience of the executive (Government) is evident from following main points:

1. The Government does not depend upon the reckless behaviour of the legislature as it was in the past. Nothing but a censure motion passed by the National Assembly with its absolute majority (signed by at least 1/10 of its total membership) is required to throw out the Government. It is hardly conceivable that the Government would be thrown out by the simple majority of the House in case a motion of confidence initiated by the Prime Minister falls through. The system of 'interpellation' is no more in existence to facilitate the task of the indignant legislators to defeat a Government for no other

reason than to satisfy their political hunger for ministerial rewards. Moreover, the right to dissolve the National Assembly is the most formidable weapon in the hands of the President of the Republic to create fear in the minds of the ambitious and irresponsible deputies.

2. The enhancement of the powers of the Senate has gone to the benefit of the Government at the expense of the authority of the National Assembly. It is provided that a bill must be passed by both the houses and in the event of disagreement, it is the Government which shall take the initiative of either calling a joint meeting of the two houses through a conference committee in order to settle the dispute, or it may ask for the reconsideration of the bill by the National Assembly and thereby override the veto of the Senate in case the bill is passed by the Assembly. Every situation seems to go to the benefit of the executive when there is a difference of opinion between the two houses. It is the Government that alone can end a deadlock between the two houses either by calling them to reconsider the bill in question or by asking the National Assembly (if the difference persists) to pass the bill and thereby over-ride the veto of the Senate.
3. There is Constitutional Council-an extra-legislative body-to sit over the head of the legislature. Not only the sphere of legislation is restricted where the Parliament can operate, more serious is the provision that the Constitutional Council would (particularly at the initiative of the Government) prevent the Parliament from 'over-stepping' its powers. It is laid down in the Constitution that all organic laws, prior to their promulgation, must be deemed constitutional by this extra-legislative (mainly judicial) body. It is also stipulated that in the event of difference of opinion on the bill regarding its constitutional validity, the matter is to be settled neither by the Presidents of the two Houses nor by the Government but by the Constitutional Council.
4. What has put a great premium on the inherent power of the Parliament is the provision of delegated legislation in the new Constitution. The Constitution empowers the Government to take measures which may be necessary for the execution of its programme but which are normally in the domain of law. Such measures can be passed only by the authorisation of Parliament and hold good for a limited period only. Art. 37 of the Constitution empowers the Government to regulate matters which are not governed by laws but by means of official orders. Art. 38 says that the Government may

ask the Parliament to authorise it to promulgate ordinances on items coming under the domain of law.

5. The powers of the Parliament in regard to electoral disputes have been vested in the Constitutional Council. The Senate and the House of Representatives of the United States have a right to disqualify an elected member of their chamber on the charge of having indulged in corrupt practices. Likewise, the House of Commons is the sole judge of the eligibility of its members. But the Parliament of France has been deprived of this inherent power under the present Constitution. Any matter relating to the regularity of elections and referendum or use of corrupt means in the elections falls under the jurisdiction of the Constitutional Council and not under the authority of the Parliament.

It all makes the point clear that under the Fifth Republic the Parliament of France is neither a sovereign law-making body like its English counterpart, nor is it a powerful legislative organ as found in other democratic countries following the English model; more so it is not even as powerful as the American Congress where the national legislature has its earmarked area of law-making and, in addition to that, has some checks over the executive and the judiciary.

System of Commissions and Legislative Process: Now we turn to the study of the commissions (committee system) and legislative process to illustrate the fact that the Parliament of France works in a way which is quite different from the ways of the British Parliament and the American Congress. What is slightly similar to the American practice is that under the new Constitution, the powers of the committees have been cut to make the house powerful as has happened in the United States after the 'revolution of 1911' to finish the menace of Cannonism. But the study of legislative process leaves the same impression that the powers of the Parliament have been usurped by the written rules of the Constitution and not by the unwritten maxims of the fundamental law of the land which are called conventions of the constitution in Britain.

Commissions: The Parliament of France works with the help of its commissions or committees as known in other countries like Britain and the United States. Both houses have their own commissions and their staff; they are called 'permanent commissions' as they are formed for the whole session, while some temporary or *ad.hoc* commissions may also be set up for a specific purpose. The Constitution has fixed the number of commissions at six less to encourage departmental interconnections but more to discourage lobbying from outside forces. Each commission appoints from among its members its own bureau consisting of a President, 2 Vice-presidents, 2 secretaries in the smaller commission; I President, 4 Vice-presidents and 4 secretaries in the bigger ones. The meetings are arranged and convened by the President.

Like the American system, the commissions of the Parliament perform an important role as the bills are first discussed here before they are taken up by the house. On receiving a bill, the commission appoints a rapporteur, whereas the Finance Commission sets up a rapporteur-general per government department. If the commission so desires, it may be assisted by a civil servant. The commission may hold its meetings *in camera* or in public and examine witnesses and interested parties if so authorised by the Parliament in advance. A precis of proceedings is published weekly without record of voting and minutes are available to the members of Parliament, though special care is taken to maintain the secrecy of an 'important' matter.

The rapporteur of the commission is charged with the work of guiding the commission from the standpoint of legislative policy, while the President sees to it that the link between the Parliament and the commission is maintained. As the debates over the bill proceed, the rapporteur keeps the minutes. When finance is involved, the Commission on Finance must send its rapporteurs to the commission in-charge of the bill, where they have a consultative part. Representation on the commissions must be allowed to the Economic and Social Council in case a bill under discussion has a bearing on its life or working. The commissions submit their reports to the house after consideration, but the Government or 50 deputies may move the discharge of a bill to the National Assembly.

The commissions of the French Parliament resemble the committees of the English Parliament in the sense that their number is limited to 6 (Art. 43) and they are not 'specialised' groups. It is a different thing that an *ad hoc* commission may be set up for a specific work.

However, the large number of members in each committee is the result of a deliberate thinking: the new Constitution strives to make the strength of a committee rather 'unwieldy' so that each commission includes many others than the 'experts' who, as during the previous regimes, desired fighting private battles with the ministers.

Commissions	
Assembly	***Senate***
1. Church, Family and Social Affairs	1. Cultural Affairs
2. Foreign Affairs	2. Economic Affairs and Planning
3. National Defence and Armed Forces	3. Foreign Affairs, Defence and Armed Forces
4. Finance, Economy and Planning	4. Social Affairs
5. Constitutional Laws (Legislation and General Administration)	5. Finance, Budgetary Control and Nation's Economic Accounts
6. Production and Exchange	6. Constitutional Laws, Legislation, Universal Suffrage, Procedure and General Administration
7. Procedure of the Assembly	

What is, indeed, striking to note here is that the new arrangement has deprived the commissions to behave like the masters of their creators. It is the house which takes final decision on the adoption or rejection of a bill and the commission cannot go to the final length of changing the bill in question to the point of its 'derecognisability.' It seeks "to reduce drastically the power of the committees from one of complete control of the legislative process to that of advice given to the House on the line to take on the bill in general and on the various clauses.[5] However, the utility of the commission system is undeniable. As Herman Finer notes: "The commissions save the Assembly from being swamped by the deluge of private members' bills, the proposal of which is allowed without limit. Secondly, they are essential to the production of coherent and consistent laws, considering that the cabinets have not lived long enough to assure this."[6]

Legislative Process: The right to move a bill is available to a minister as well as to an ordinary member of both the houses with two differences- first a finance bill must originate in the National Assembly and, second, a bill moved by a minister is called a 'project', while a bill moved by an ordinary member is called a 'proposal' or 'proposition'. The mover has to draft his bill himself, but the minister may take the help of his secretariat.

5. See Blondel and Godfrey Jr., *op. cit.*, p. 70.

6. See Herman Finer, *The Major Governments of Modern Europe*, p. 302.

There is no office of the Parliamentary Counsel in France as it is in Britain to draft official bills according to the policy of the cabinet. It is provided in the Constitution (Art. 40) that bills and amendments introduced by the members of the Parliament shall not be considered when their adoption would result either in the diminution of public financial resources or in the creation or increase of certain public expenditures.

A bill is first sent to a bureau of the house in which it originates. It is immediately referred to the appropriate committee or commission in the printed form and consists of a brief explanation of what it expects to achieve. The Government may demand that the bill be sent to a special committee, to be established for that special purpose, rather than to one of the six permanent commissions and this request must be honoured vide Art. 43 of the Constitution. Then, the committee studies the bill and submits its report to the House within a period of 3 months unless otherwise suggested. In certain cases, the bills may be referred by the committee to the Economic and Social Council for an advisory opinion. The committee holds debate and then refers the bill back to the house with its report.

After this, the bill comes before the house as a whole. It depends upon the house to pass the bill or kill it, no matter what the report of the committee says. It is also possible that the bill may be referred back to the committee for reconsideration. No major amendment must be placed as the committee has already studied such a proposal before referring it to the house concerned. When the general discussion is over, the debate takes place article-wise. Decision is taken by vote. The old practice of 'proxy' voting has been abolished whereby a present member could cast as many votes as he liked for all who were absent. Art. 47 of the Constitution provides that the right to vote is a personal affair and one member may vote for another in absentia in case an organic law is made to authorise so, but no member may be delegated more than one vote.

After the bill crosses this stage (called first reading), it goes to the second house for concurrence. If the second house adopts it, it is referred to the President of the Republic for promulgation within 15 days except, of course, where he makes use of his suspensive veto to return the bill to the Parliament for reconsideration, or when the matter is disputed and the issue is referred to the Constitutional Council for examining whether the Parliament has gone beyond its enumerated powers or not. In this case the issue of constitutional validity of the bill shall be adjudicated by the Constitutional Council. In case the bill is returned to the Parliament for reconsideration by the President of the Republic, it is upto the Parliament to readopt it or not in accordance with the wishes of the President. However, as the President enjoys a very strong position and the bill comes to him after debates in the two houses where his own ministers take part, it is inferrable that the President's wishes must have been honoured by the two houses before the adoption of that bill.

It is quite possible that the two houses may disagree over the adoption of a bill. In the event of disagreement, the bill is returned to both the houses for reconsideration, what may be termed second reading, until the Government has declared the matter officially 'urgent'. In case there is no agreement either at the stage of first reading (when the Prime Minister has declared the bill 'urgent'), or when the difference of opinion persists after the reference of the bill for second reading, the Prime Minister has the right to demand the meeting of a conference committee consisting of equal number of members of both the houses and its resolution may be submitted by him for the approval of the Assembly and the Senate. When such a committee meets, it shall not discuss any proposal of amendment but resolve to pass or reject the bill in question.

Another contingency may arise when the report of the conference committee (in favour of the adoption of the bill) is not accepted by either house of the Parliament or when the disagreement persists to block the passage of the bill, then the Government may ask the National Assembly for the third and final reading of the bill. In this situation the decision of the Assembly shall be final and the bill passed by it shall go to the President of the Republic for its promulgation within 15 days without the concurrence of the Senate. It shows that in the event of irreconcilable differences between the two houses, the decision of the popular chamber is final which automatically implies favourable initiative of the Government in advance.

At various places the new Constitution authorises legislation by means of an organic law. The process of passing this type of law is almost identical as discussed above with the difference that such a bill may be deliberated and voted only after a period of 15 days following its introduction. In case, it is further provided, such a bill is passed by one house and rejected by the other, the National Assembly shall have second reading on such a bill and register its approval by absolute majority. Among other points of difference, it may be mentioned that a bill of this kind must be passed by both the houses in an identical manner when the text of the bill deals with the functions of the Senate and that the bill must be submitted to the Constitutional Council for examination with regard to the issue of its constitutional validity.

There is a different procedure for the adoption of a money bill. Such a bill may be initiated by any member of the National Assembly, but the budget is presented by the Minister for Finance. After the presentation of a money bill or budget, it is soon referred to the Finance Committee for consideration. This budget is reported out by the general rapporteur of this commission who, in his initial speech on the floor of the National Assembly, deals primarily with financial situation rather than with specific items. General discussion over the money bill or budget begins after the report of the Finance Committee. The budget is discussed ministry by ministry and chapter by chapter. Each chapter is voted separately. The deputies may propose amendments in the form of separate bills without proposing for a fresh taxation. In case a deputy desires strongly to see that his point is accommodated into the budget, he may transmit his proposal to the Finance Committee so that proper discussion may be had on it at the same time when the budget is under discussion.

The Constitution has made the Parliament very weak in financial matters. It is provided that if the National Assembly fails to reach a decision on a finance bill in its first reading within 40 days after the submission of the bill, the Government shall refer it to the Senate which must register its verdict within 15 days. In case the two houses have disagreement and fail to adopt it within 70 days, the provision of the bill may be put into operation by an executive decree. In case a finance bill (containing the revenues and expenditures for a given fiscal year) has been submitted to the National Assembly too late to be promulgated before the start of the first fiscal year, the Government shall urgently request the Parliament for authorisation to collect taxes and shall make available the funds necessary to meet government commitments already voted by means of an executive decree. This arrangement has been devised by the framers of the Constitution to prevent the National Assembly from demolishing fiscal policies of the Government.

Keeping it all in his view, Kesselman observes: "In the semi-presidential system of the Fifth Republic, the French Parliament is probably the weakest Parliament of any democratic regime. The Constitution apparently assumes that Parliament should be seen but not heard. Parliament lacks the autonomy and separation from executive that legislature enjoys in presidential systems; yet, because it cannot pass a motion of no-confidence in the President, it cannot hold the executive accountable as legislatures can in parliamentary systems. The French Parliament does not provide a forum for important national debates, adequately represent conflicting interests, or check governmental abuse of power."[7]

7. Kesselman, *op. cit.*, p. 139.

24

JUDICIAL SYSTEM AND ADVISORY BODIES

After making a study of the executive headed by the President assisted by the Prime Minister and the Council of Ministers and the Parliament having National Assembly and Senate as the lower and the upper chambers repectively, it shall be worthwhile to present a brief account of the judicial and advisory organs that have a rather less significant role in the political system of France. It is due to the fact that the French do not appreciate the 'trinity theory' whereby government is regarded as consisting of three separate and independent organs; instead they subscribe to 'duality theory' whereby executive and legislature are treated as separate and independent organs of the government, while judiciary is regarded as a subordinate branch of the former.

Judicial System

Special Features: The French judicial system may be said to have three main characteristics:

1. It ensures independence of judiciary. If justice is to operate efficiently, the judicial authority must be protected from the pressures of the legislature as well as of the executive; this independence is ensured by the creation of the Higher Council of Magistracy and a Special Statute for members of the judicial body. The method of the appointment of judges has been laid down so as to keep the incumbents free from outside pressures. Moreover, a Special Statute for judges and public prosecutors has been framed which guarantees the satisfactory unfolding of their careers. It has been devised to make the nature of judicial offices more attractive. The judges and public prosecutors have been assured of a more rapid promotion. No member of the Bench may receive a new posting without his

consent even if it is a matter of promotion. The principle of 'irremovability' of judges has also been incorporated.

2. There is the separation of administrative and judicial authorities. The rule forbids judicial tribunals to settle disputes of law involving administration. It is based on the law of 16-24 August, 1970 that (vide its Art. 13) says: "The judicial functions are distinct and will always remain separate from the administrative functions; judges shall not, without exceeding their powers, interfere in any way whatsoever with the operation of the administrative bodies, nor summon administrators before them by reason of their functions. The proper application of this principle requires, on the one hand, that the administration must have the means to resist encroachment by the judicial courts and, on the other that those involved may have at their disposal procedures enabling them to find the competent judge. The procedure of the conflict of competence comes into play only to guarantee the autonomy and independence of the administration vis-a-vis the judicial courts which can thus never lay claim to a field in which the administrative courts deem themselves competent."
3. There is the double degree of jurisdiction which makes it possible for any party to an action or trial to appeal to a superior court against a decision rendered by an inferior court; it is an old rule; but while under the *ancien regime* the appeal was a means for the king to assert his rights, it has now become a guarantee of good justice. That is why, an appeal is always brought before a court that is higher in the hierarchy than the one which made the first decision; litigants are thus assured that their case will be settled by the judges who are more competent and more experienced. A decree of 22nd December, 1958 introduced an all-important reform in the matter by superseding all special courts of the second degree; in all cases, the appeal is now brought before the Court of Appeal.

Organisation: The organisation of the judicial system of France has a hierarchical design of its own. First of all, we refer to the Supreme Council of Justice. The Constitution of the Fourth Republic set up the Supreme Council of the Magistracy (Higher Council of Judiciary) for the maintenance of the independence and impartiality of the judges. The new Constitution retains the old body though with reduced powers. It makes the President of the Republic the guarantor of independence of the judicial authority to be assisted by the Supreme Council of Justice in the discharge of this important function. The composition of the Supreme Council is to be determined by the organic law of the Parliament. It is provided in Art. 65 of the Constitution that the Supreme Council of Justice shall be presided over by the President of the Republic and the Minister for Justice shall be its *ex–officio* Vice-President to act as the presiding officer when the President of the Republic is not available.

This body now consists of 9 members appointed by the President of the Republic in accordance with the provisions of the organic law. It presents nominations for the judges of the Court of Causation and for First President of the Court of Appeal. It gives its opinion under the conditions to be determined by an organic law, on proposals of the Minister of Justice relating to the nomination of other judges. It may be consulted on the questions of pardon under conditions to be determined by an organic law. It also acts as a disciplinary council for judges. In such cases, it is presided over by the First President of the Court of Causation. It is noteworthy that while under the Fourth Republic, the Supreme Council appointed and promoted the judges, under the new Constitution it has been empowered to advise the Government in matters relating to the appointment of the judges of the Court of Causation and of the First President of the Court of Appeal.

Then, there is the High Court of Justice. Art. 67 of the Constitution lays down that it shall be composed of the elected members of Parliament in equal number by the National Assembly and the Senate after each general or partial election to these assemblies and it shall elect its own President from amongst its members. An organic law shall determine the composition of the High Court, its rules and also the procedure to be followed there. Art. 68 says that the President of the Republic shall not be accountable for actions performed in the exercise of his office except in the case of high treason. He may be indicted only by the two assemblies ruling by identical vote in open balloting and by an absolute majority of the members of the said assemblies. He shall be tried by this High Court of Justice. It further lays down that the members of the Government shall be liable for actions performed in the exercise of their office and deemed to be crimes and misdemeanours at the time they were committed. The procedure defined above shall be applied to them, as well as to their accomplices, in the case of conspiracy against the security of the state. In the cases provided for by the present paragraph, the High Court of Justice shall be bound by the definition of crimes and misdemeanour, as well as by the determination of penalties, as they are established by the criminal laws in force when the acts are committed.

According to the provisions of an organic law, the High Court of Justice consists of 24 members, 12 chosen by each house from among its members following a general election in the case of the National Assembly and partial renewal in the case of the Senate. Its most important function is to try the President of the Republic on charges of high treason and the ministers or their accomplices on the charge of plotting against the security of the State. However, three important points must be kept in view in this regard. First, the decision to bring a 'party' before the court must be taken by both the houses and not by the National Assembly alone as under the Fourth Republic. Second, the vote is no longer secret as it is by open ballot. Last, the sentence on a President of the Republic found guilty of high treason is no longer to be determined on the basis of rules laid down in the penal code. However, this requirement is retained in the case of other offenders dealt with by the High Court of Justice.

Different from the Anglo-Saxon system of law and justice, the judicial system of France is two-tiered–'ordinary' and 'administrative'. While the ordinary jurisdiction is concerned with private and criminal actions, all grievances of the citizens against the state (including units of local government but not nationalised corporations) go to the administrative courts. In both sections there are hierarchical judicial institutions and there is a Court of Conflicts (composed of the judges of both the hierarchies) to settle difficult cases of jurisdiction. While ordinary courts decide on the basis of codes, the administrative courts (while using the statute book) deliver case-law and general principles of considerable weight.

Administrative law is the unique contribution of France. As Dicey says, it covers no less than the whole realm of relationship between public authorities and the individual.[1] Strangely enough, this variety of law is based to a very large extent on judicial precedents with which the legislature does not ordinarily interfere and which the administrative courts themselves alter only gradually. And yet it remains to be commented that the entire system of administrative law is much complicated which, according to an observer, becomes comprehensible only when one remembers that it was designed to control the overly powerful and administrative staff.[2] More astounding is the point that the importance of administrative law outweighs the value of ordinary justice which is considered as an integral part of the democratic system.

---

1. A.V. Dicey: *An Introduction to the Study of the Law of the Constitution*, Ch. XII.
2. Carl J. Friedrich: *Constitutional Government and Democracy*, pp. 368 ff.

Other Constitutional Agencies

After studying French judicial system, we may refer to two important constitutional agencies which have a place of their own in the political system of this country.

Constitutional Council: The Constitutional Council replaces the Constitutional Committee of the Fourth Republic. However, it should not be taken as a mere substitution of the old body: its powers are much more important to form the view that it makes a striking innovation in the French constitutional system. The uniqueness of this institution lies in the fact that it is a quasi-judicial body designed to work under the influential leadership of the Government. According to the implications of the language of the Constitution, as contained in Articles from 56 to 63, it seems to have been designed "to guarantee the working of the new system, to protect the national interest against partisan passions, and to moralise politics."[3]

The Constitutional Council consists of 9 members whose term of office is of 9 years and who are not eligible for renomination. Three of them are appointed by the President of the Republic, three by the President of the Senate, and the rest three by the President of the National Assembly. Three of them retire after every third year. In addition to these 9 regular members, it is provided that all ex-Presidents of the Republic shall be the life members of this body. The President of this Council is appointed by the President of the Republic and has his casting vote to break the tie. It is further provided that no minister and member of the Parliament can have its membership.

The Constitutional Council has four main functions. First, it determines the constitutional validity of the standing orders and organic laws passed by the Parliament. It is laid down in the Constitution that such orders and laws must be referred to this body for examination with regard to their constitutional validity before they are put into force. Its verdict is final, but what should be done to regularise the impugned order or law after its judgment is a matter for the Parliament to decide and act upon. Second, the Prime Minister or the President of either house of the Parliament may seek its opinion whether or not an international agreement or a law which is going to be promulgated is in conformity with the Constitution. Its opinion may be taken on certain conflicts which may arise between the

3. Williams and Harrison: *De Gaulle's Republic,* p. 131.

Government and the Parliament regarding the delimitation of executive and legislative competence. Third, the Constitutional Council is charged with the duty of ensuring the regularity of election of President of the Republic, examining all complaints about it and declaring the result. Last, it advises the President of the Republic in matters relating to the exercise of his emergency powers.

However, there is a big difference between the power of judicial review exercised by this Council on the one hand and same by the Supreme Court of the United States on the other. The Supreme Court of the United States begins its work of judicial review after an executive order has been given by the President or a law passed by the Congress has come into effect, and when some aggrieved person challenges the same in it or in any federal court of the country. In marked contrast to it, the work of the Constitutional Council begins when the matter is brought before it prior to the promulgation of that order or law and the matter is referred to it by the Government alone. Another noteworthy point is that while the verdict of the American Supreme Court is final in all cases decided by it, the decision of the Constitutional Council is just like a recommendation whose enforcement depends upon the discretion of the President. In matters where this Council simply advises (as exercise of emergency powers by the President), the President and his Government are free to accept the view of the Council or not. This arrangement in the form of advisory jurisdiction has contributed to the weak position of the Constitutional Council by making it adjunct to the strong authority of the President.

It may be admitted that the Constitutional Council has been designed to work as the brains trust of the Fifth Republic or the custodian of the Constitution. However, two things may be pointed out to reveal the weak position of this quasi-judicial body. First, it cannot be compared with the strong judicial system of the United States and India, where the people move their highest judiciary to protect their fundamental rights and the Courts defend the people against official encroachments by directing the government to enforce their decisions. In France the Constitutional Council lacks necessary authority to enforce its judgments. Second, it meets *in camera* and decides an issue referred to it on the basis of documentary evidence supplied to it. That is, no personal hearing is allowed. Hence, it would not be incorrect to take it as a part of the executive agency brought into existence largely "to help the cabinet and the President resist Parliament's efforts to regain its lost rights."[4] No matter it has played an

4. Williams and Harrison, *op. cit.*, p. 132.

important role in the transformation of relationship between executive and legislature, "but when a strong leader like de Gaulle were at the helm of affairs, one does not know whether the Council buttresses the Constitution, or de Gaulle the Council."[5]

Economic and Social Council: The retention of this body in the Fifth Republic with the change of name (known as Economic Council under the Fourth Republic) illustrates that the spirit of the de Gaulle regime "very much favours technical solutions to economic and social problems by experts."[6] Representing the most important economic and social interests of the country, it "has consultative and advisory powers to give advice on proposed economic and social legislation and particularly on measures related to economic planning."[7] However, it is believed that the survival of this body, though with an improved title, is one of the minor surprises of the new Constitution. Despite the fact that the Economic Council of the Fourth Republic made useful contributions to the debates on many important issues as diverse as distributive costs, the National Plan and the Schuman Plan, its virtues "have never been recognised. Unknown to the public suspects to the Assembly who really heeded its opinions, its disappearance would have been little noticed or mourned."[8]

The Constitution says that the composition *of* this body shall be determined by an organic law passed by the Parliament. As such, this body has 189 members in this manner: 41 from the sector of Commerce and Industry, 40 from Agriculture, 10 from Overseas Departments, 15 from economic and social interests overseas, 45 from the representatives of the employees, 15 from housing co-operatives and family associations, and a few others to represent minor interests. The members of this body serve for a period of 5 years. Its sessions are not held in public and its main work is done in technical sections to which specialists from outside may be co-opted. The body is intended to be used primarily as a technical adviser to the Government.

The functions of this body have been defined in Articles 69, 70, 71 of the Constitution. Art. 69 says that whenever the Government calls upon it, this body shall give its opinion on the Government bills, ordinances

5. Blondel and Godfrey Jr., *The Government of France,* pp. 75-76.

6. Herman Finer: *The Major Governments of Modern Europe,* p. 313.

7. See Dicey: *Law of the Constitution,* Ch. XII.

8. Williams and Harrison, *op. cit.,* pp. 254-55.

and decrees, as well as on the Private Members' bills submitted to it. A member of the Economic and Social Council may be designated by the latter to be present before the Parliamentary Assemblies to know about the opinion of the Council on the Government or private members' bills which have been submitted to it. Art. 70 says that this body may, likewise, be consulted by the Government on any problem of an economic or social character of interest to the Republic. Any plan or any bill dealing with a plan of an economic or social character shall be submitted to it for its advice.

However, the Economic and Social Council has not been a very successful agency for the reason of its being a house divided against itself and also on account of inhospitable attitude of the National Assembly towards it. It is rare that the body takes a unanimous decision for the plain reason that its members represent diverse social and economic interests, often they pull in different directions. Moreover, the Parliament takes the benefit of this baleful situation. As Finer says: "The direct influence of the Council in modifying the proposals of the Assembly and cabinet is very small. It finds itself condemned to producing reports that Government may or may not affect the future and seldom affect the present. The members of the Council are not, as some people hoped they would be, experts, but employers and employees. This reduces their 'scientific' influence. The hope that the Council would be an arbiter has been vain; *inter arma, silet scientia*. Amid wars, laws are silent."[9]

---

9. Finer, *op. cit.*, p. 35.

25

POLITICAL PARTIES AND PRESSURE GROUPS

France is ill-known not for having a multi-party system as for leaving an observer baffled in drawing plausible conclusions from the drama of complication and simplification of political parties and groups, including 'clubs' and 'families', in which the rightists, the leftists, and the centrists have peculiar roles to play. One is perplexed at the spectacle of different organisations coming closer on one occasion and running far on another, merging with one today and splitting with another tomorrow, now presenting one configuration and then switching over to another with the result that a serious observer develops certain impressions that enthuse him to jump from one point to another without being capable of laying down certain definite rules of the political behaviour of different parties and groups.

Political Parties

Special Features: The French party system "is unique in the Western world, and probably in the world as well."[1] The reason for this should be traced in the special traits that the party system of this country possesses and which may be enumerated as under:

1. France is notoriously known for having a multiplicity of political parties. In a general election more than a dozen 'national' parties and, in addition to that, a varying number of less important formations take part with the result that quite a large number of organisations secure representation in the national legislature. The point of peculiarity, however, lies in the fact that this multiplicity is always in a fluid position. So loosely organised and so indisciplined are the political parties of France and, at the same time, they are so extremely

1. Blondel and Godfrey, *The Government of France*, p. 79.

volatile and so excessively resilient that they split and break with considerable ease and eagerness showing that the trends of complications and simplification run together. As a result, the drama of reunions and rearrangements has become a normal feature of the stasiological politics of France.

2. There is a lot of diversity in the organisation and attitudes of French political parties. They cover a range extending from communism on the extreme left to mild fascism (Gaullism) on the extreme right, while some attach great importance to political principles and doctrines and would expel members who stray openly or continuously from the orthodox path. Some parties appear to have no general principles at all, while others lack even a coherent policy. For instance, 'radicalism' has been described as a state of mind, while 'conservatism' as a collection of interests often in conflict with each other.
3. The element of ideological make-up is virtually missing in all parties excluding the communists. There is no party in France that 'may be treated like the Conservative or Labour parties of England in respect of its political commitment to the 'right' or to the 'left'. Likewise, there is no party that may be identified with the Republican or Democratic parties of the United States that are like 'vote mobilisation' machines. Even now the *Central national des Independents* is not a party as such as it is a loose federation of different units despite the fact that most of the members of this organisation profess the creed of conservatism. Nearly all parties, excluding the communists, advocate the elements of radicalism, individualism, conservatism, free trade, protestantism, and social reformism in varying degrees.
4. Apart from diversity in respect of organisation and attitude, the political parties of France make confusion still worse confounded by using terminologies that mean something to one and something else to another. The national mind of France is largely theoretical, not practical in politics. An average Frenchman is inclined to pursue an ideal striving to realise his conception of a perfect form of society and feels reluctant to give up any part of it for the sake of attaining so much as lies within his reach. The French people want to follow their own bent of mind than to imitate others. Thus, they do not appreciate the idea of subordinating their views in the name of party discipline.

Some Important Statements

Franch parties come and go in bewildering numbers sometimes within a very short time. —*Dorothy Pickles*

Multiplicity of parties is, in fact, inevitable in any country where the fundamentals are themselves matters of dispute, where social and economic conditions have brought political power within the reach of all social classes and where a highly developed and widely diffused education, coupled with a strong spirit of individualism, creates keenness of political thought and numerous political and social theories. —*Roger H. Soltau*

The formation of rival political coalitions has strengthened the legitimacy and stability of the Fifth Republic by making possible political alteration in office. Popular support and political stability increase when elections represent a choice between alternative political coalitions. —*Mark Kesselman*

5. The multiplicity of party system coupled with the diversity of organisation, and attitude draws sustenance not only from the factors of sociology and economics, it also derives its source from the geographical composition of the country. We have already noted the 'myth of two Frances', that is, division of France into northern and southern parts of the country divided by the river Loire. It may be visualised in the eastern and western regions of the country also. It is pointed out that both history and geography have to be linked, if one is to account for the permanence of certain traditions in some areas more than in the others. Right and Left, the anti-revolutionary right and the revolutionary left as well as other forms of right and left, are written in the countryside, as are geographically located, the areas of the deep religious areas of practice and the areas of de-Christianisation'.

It is owing to these reasons that the political atmosphere of France always remains at the fever pitch, being a characteristic of ever-growing number of interpellations, personal bickerings and perpetual strifes. Naturally this country is bedevilled by a multiplicity of political parties, passionate and internally fissiparous. The party members live in a state of constant flux often shifting their loyalty from one group to another and. success comes to those who are adept in the art of manipulation rather than being consistent supporters of a certain policy. From the above account, it is obvious that political parties in France are weak in their structure, loose in organisation, lacking in definite commitments and followed by heterogeneous and rather fickle clientels.

Leading Political Parties: As pointed out above, France under the Fifth Republic has a controlled multi-party system in which the tendencies of the 'right', the 'left' and the 'centre' may be visualised, though one may also notice the phenomenon of cross-infiltration of the three trends in different political organisations leaving aside the case of the Communist Party. Let us examine the cases of the following major political parties:

Union of New Republic: Gaullism is the most important movement of France which has been in existence particularly since 1946. First as the Rally of the French People (RPF), it started its political career under the inspiring leadership of Gen. de Gaulle. Feeling highly critical of the constitution of the Fourth Republic, de Gaulle resigned and went into forced retirement, while he allowed his trusted followers to play their part in the politics of the country. In the elections of 1956 the number of the Gaullists declined considerably with the result that a section organised itself into a new formation called the Social Republicans. However, with the return of de Gaulle to power in 1958, all Gaullists rallied under his leadership and the Union of New Republic (UNR) came into being.

Very curious is the story of the role of this party in the recent politics of France. Though formed after the triumph of de Gaulle, the great leader in 1958 refused to give his formal support to this party and even denied its members to associate his name with this organisation. The reason was that, as a shrewd leader, de Gaulle sought to use this organisation as per his political interests without aligning himself formally with it. He preferred to have it like a ready-made platform that he would make use of at his discretion instead of letting it grow into the form of a coherent party that might come with its own demands or emerge as a potential challenge to his authority. As a result, while de Gaulle could thrive at the almost unflinching allegiance of his supporters, the latter failed to get as much capital from the political personality of their supreme leader. It was due to the tailor-made support of the UNR that de Gaulle could emerge victorious in the first and second Presidential elections and that he could also win the referendum on the constitutional reform of 1962 with flying colours, though the Gaullists could not show a remarkable success in the parliamentary elections.

In certain respects, Gaullism is identified with Fascism in view of the fact that the RPF was inspired by the towering personality of a single leader (de Gaulle) and that it "combined demands for radical social change with intense nationalism. It was anti-parliamentary, anti-trade union and virulently anti-communist. Its most distinctive positive policy, apart from the constitutional reforms demanded by its leader, was the association of capital and labour in a way reminiscent of corporatism. Yet, with some Jewish traders, it never succumbed to anti-semitism that had earlier disfigured the Right in France and the real parallel are perhaps Bonapartism and Boulangism. Finally, de Gaulle's determination to come to power legally probably, prevented the RPF from developing further fascist characteristics."[2] The surprising part of the study is that after the establishment of the Fifth Republic, the UNR became a basically different organisation in the sense as it was formed to support de Gaulle in power, not to win power for him; it was formed by the supporters of de Gaulle without his being involved, not by de Gaulle to attract supporters.

Finally, it should also be taken note of that the trend of 'left Gaullism' developed and that too with the 'private' blessings of the great leader. A progressive section of the UNR took to a different line. The victory of Estaing as the President in the elections of 1974 is a clear indication of this trend. One is, however, not very sure that the movement of Gaullism would continue to save the country from relapsing into the morass of political instability. It cannot be ruled out that new leaders may emerge on the political scene not to let the UNR remain like the poodle of a single leader like de Gaulle, Pompidou or Estaing. If so happens, nothing would break the UNR more quickly than the setting up of factions inside the Party and the organisation of joint groups with other parties. However, if such leaders come smoothly without creating difficult succession problems, the UNR "can hope to survive and new style be imposed upon the Right and the Centre-Right of French politics and, indeed, indirectly on the Left as well."[3]

Communist Party: It is the most active political party of France which "provides an interesting picture of the role and tactics of a dictatorial Marxist party inside a democracy." It was formed in Dec., 1920 by a vote of many members of the Socialist Party who desired to join the Third International and although the Comintern was dissolved in 1943, the party "is still Bolshevised in spirit, principles and organisation."[4] Obviously, it used its vote to mainly negate whatever was proposed except when it suited the then Soviet Union. In other words, it is definitely anti-American

2. M. Stead: "France" in Henig and Pinder: *European Political Parties*, p. 122.
3. Blondel and Godfrey, *op. cit.*, p. 115.
4. Herman Finer; *The Major Governments of Modern Europe*, p. 265.

in denouncing France's servitude to the Wall Street for Marshall Aid, membership of the North Atlantic Treaty Organisation, and other military pacts. It has opposed the official policy of supporting German rearmament or aggressions in various parts of Africa and Asia. Its ultimate goal is social revolution. It calls for the reconstruction of France and its industry, the modernisation of agriculture, provision of food for the people, the restoration of a sound financial position, and protection of the health of the people. In 1950 it evolved a special programme for the benefit of the rural areas. Its tactics have been exceptionally opportunistic on many occasions and it has been condemned for inciting sabotage, riots and violence and sedition in the colonial areas.

Socialist Party: Founded in 1879 and though close to the Communist Party, the Socialist Party (PSU) "stands worlds apart, because it is rooted in the principle of responsible democracy and civil rights."[5] Originally it represented a fusion of two separate and antagonistic groups-the liberal reforming and parliamentary led by Jean James comprising the majority and working with the radicals and the second one of revolutionary Syndicalists and Marxists led by Jules Guesde. In 1920 there was a split when its 15,000 members and 13 deputies joined the Communist Party. It is referred to officially by the initials of S.F.LO. meaning *Section Francaise del Internationale Ouvriere* or the French Section of the Second International *i.e.*, the Socialist International founded in 1905.

This party is the defender of the Democratic Republic of France and stands for the programmes of nationalisation, welfare state, planned economic investment, public housing, industrialisation, educational opportunity, more equal tax structure, more municipal liberty and more local welfare services. It has also supported French membership of the Brussels Treaty, North Atlantic Treaty Pact, the Schuman Plan, the European Common Market and the Euratom. It is an advocate of extended self-government and economic development of the colonies, but not outright independence. In the elections of 1956 it captured 100 seats in the National Assembly and formed government under the Premiership of Guy Mollet. In the elections of 1958, it suffered heavy losses; its strength in the National Assembly decreased to 40 and so it refused to join the cabinet. The party remained in opposition but supported President de Gaulle on the question of crushing insurrection in Algeria.

---

5. *Ibid.*

Radical Party: It was founded in 1901. Its official name is the *Parti Radical or et Radical Socialiste.* It is organised around local notables, committees and provincial newspapers. It had a very strong influence under the Third Republic, but now it is nothing more than a congeries of departmental groups, a battle of the federations, and unblendable assemblage of interests and policies, highly personalised. Its members have always been detachable from the main body for the purpose of joining left, right and centre coalitions. It has stood for return to the constitution of the Third Republic, single-member districts, governmental economy, amnesty to tax-evaders and safeguards for the interests of the tenants. However, it has been divided on sliding scales for wages, welfare policies, tax increases, and the budgets. However, it is pro-West and thus insisted on French membership of the American military pacts. In the crisis of 1958 it was sadly split. The conservatives led by Andre Morice joined the right and Soustelle in voting for de Gaulle first as the Prime Minister and then as the President of the Republic.

This party has its nation-wide structure by electing delegates from the local *comites* up through cantonal and then departmental federations. But their federations are highly independent of Paris headquarters even in the choice of the candidates and electoral strategy. It has an annual National Congress consisting of the elected delegates. Editors of the Radical owned newspapers are its *ex-officio* delegates. Day-to-day decisions especially when the cabinets are in crisis, are made by the Executive Committee of 70 composed of the representatives of party members, members of party chambers, and a small contingent of party officials in consultation with the parliamentary group.

Small Parties: In the political process of France, some minor parties have a role of their own in view of the fact that they exploit regional and local issues so as to attract the sympathy of the voters. On certain crucial issues, the viewpoints of the major parties become analogous and so the voters prefer to cast their votes in favour of small parties which have a divergent stand that sometimes coincides with their wishes. The National Front is an organisation of those who want 'France for the French'. They find the cause of growing unemployment and increasing number of crimes in the immigration of the foreign people. Hence, they are branded as 'racists'. Its leader Jean Marie Le Pen contested the presidential election in 1995 and, though he was. defeated, the pro-Chirac voters hoped that his ideas would be taken seriously into account by the newly elected President.

Then, there is a party of the environmentalists called the 'Greens'. They are critical of nuclear experiments and of all measures that pollute the enviromnent. It has no commitment to any ideology and so it is neither rightist nor leftist. Its leaders as Waechter and Brice Lalonde have often laid stress on the prime need for maintaining a healthy and pollution-free environment. These parties have no chance to be in power, but they play a notable part by raising crucial issues and soliciting the sympathy of the people by exploiting their sentiments. Their voice has its effect on the working of the governing coalitions.

France is under the de Gaulle constitution. Despite de Gaulle's opposition to political parties on the ground that they nurture division, instablility, and paralysis, the emergence of powerful political parties has played a key role in buttressing cohesion, stability and leadership within the Fifth Republic. An important development has been the emergence of governing coalition of political parties. Moreover, there "has been a powerful tendency for parties to coalesce into two opposing coalitions facing each other across the left-right divide."[6]

Critical Appreciation: As a matter of fact, the party system of France defies characterisation on certain specific lines. Though it is a model of multi-partyism, it is not so in the strict sense of the term. It offers a unique case where several political parties and groups, including splinter and fringe organisations, called 'clubs' and 'families', play the part of actors in the stasiological drama of the country without having permanent commitments to certain social, economic or political norms that may make them identifiable with the political parties of other democratic countries. One is struck with the fact that there is no party in France that may be identified even with the Liberal Party of England known for its flexible political attitudes. And while one may appreciate the trend of integration after the electoral reform of 1961 resulting in the simplification or configuration of political parties, it cannot be said with confidence that this trend would last so as to become the normal feature of French party system.

A student of French politics is, however, beset not with the multiplicity of parties or groups, what really agitates his mind is that he cannot find himself safe in making precise, even general, statements about the policies and programmes of a party, excluding the Communists, showing its

6. Kesselman, "France" in Kesselman and others (ed.): *Comparative Politics at the Crossroads*, p. 143.

permanent commitments-something that constitutes the hallmark of a political party. It has become all the more important ever since Gaullism has dominated the scene. So loose is the movement of Gaullism that its frontiers or implications cannot be drawn with any degree of confidence. A leading French leader Charlot endeavours to place the doctrinaire Gaullists into three broad categories-a group whose ideas centre on the State, a group whose central idea is the 'common good' and the left-wing social Gaullists, each of them drawing on de\Gaulle, himself for their distinctive inspiration."[7]

Even in this too general a version of the dominant movement of France, its real implications cannot be traced out. In fine, a study of French party system presents both a matter of special interest and peculiar difficulties aggravated more since the inauguration of the reformed electoral system in 1962 the reason for which should be traced in the fact that all political forces of this country relate themselves to a certain concept of the French nation-state as well as to a particular attitude towards their history. All political parties, groups and their sub-parts, big or small, as Stead says, "like to claim themselves sound strand of French tradition."[8]. The result of all is that the analysis of French political parties "is a rich subject of study which has not ceased to fascinate the French; but the entry into the study is difficult and can be painful."[9]

Pressure Groups

A study of the role of pressure groups in the political system of France has an importance of its own despite the fact that here the term 'interest organisation' has for a long time been used in a pejorative sense. Formerly the term had essentially moral implications as the French people differentiated between altruistic groups and those working to further their personal ends. "They designated the latter as interest groups and placed those working towards the general welfare in another category."[10] However, this distinction failed to survive under the weight of changing conditions of politics. The traditional approach broke down after the development of modern political science in France that witnessed the

7. Cited by M. Stead in Henig and Pinder, *op. cit.*, p. 151.

8. *Ibid.*, p. 98.

9. Blondel and Godfrey, *The Government of France*, p. 80.

10. G.A. Almond: "Introduction" in Almond and Coleman (ed.s) *The Politics of Developing Areas*, p. 300.

devaluation of Rousseau's general will as well as other democratic myths with the result that today the leading political scholars of this discipline identify interest groups on none other than the criterion of whether they succeed or fail to establish compatibility of their ends with those of the general welfare.[11]

General Characteristics: Though France is a free and open society with a plural culture that manifests itself in the existence and operation of different political parties and groups, the existence and articulation of interest organisations in this country has its own characteristics that may be enumerated as under:

1. The culture of France has its salient trait in the absence of a stable consensus that has its definite impact on the existence and operation of both the political parties and the pressure groups. As there are several parties, so there are numerous groups, both deriving inspiration from the events of the past. It may be said that group divisions in this country are characterised by their multiplicity, their intense ideological character and, what may be termed, the tenacity of 'group memories'. The divisions may be seen on regional, social, economic. cultural and political lines, most of them are related to old quarrels on issues like economic freedom versus *dirgisme*, the perennial question *scolaire*, the vague but ever present conflict between Left and Right which reflects differences more in tendency and style than in substance.
2. The process of fragmentation of groups into sub-groups coupled with their further disintegration creates a very perplexing spectacle. One feels astonished at the fact that even social and economic groups whose objective interest appears to have a common denominator are divided and further split into smaller splinter organisations so much so that infiltration and cross-infiltration of one type of people into another has become a moral affair of the stasiological politics in France. The veterans, farmers, workers, artisans and middle classes, merchants, teachers, students and public servants are all spread out among a great number of organisations with conflicting political affiliations and ideological outlooks. "There is no other major political system where the multiplicity of professional and occupational groups is compounded to such an extent by the

11. See George Lavau : "Political Pressure by Interest Groups in France" in Ehrmann (ed.,): *Interest Groups in Four Continents*. pp. 60-65.

ideological element. The interest groups are 'politicised', that is, impregnated with political attitudes."[12]

3. The fact of diversity and multiplicity, as given above, is so outstanding that it prevents both the parties and the pressure groups to form an autonomous sub-system in the realm of politics. Sometimes, it appears that there is much of non-differentiation between the parties and groups. As such, either a blurred boundary line between the two exists, or it would be too tedious a job to draw such a line of demarcation. The features of division are so sharply set in the historical consciousness of the people that they do not forget the past with the result that the existing lines of cleavage are more sharpened and making of compromises becomes a still more difficult job.
4. Most of the people of France lack the tendency of rigid political commitments. They have a flexible temperament like the Americans with the result that no political party can claim its invariable support from a particular section or class of the society. Naturally, it enhances the position of the groups at the cost of the parties. Most of the people consider the party they vote for as only one of the groups that represent them and not znecessarily the one which represents them best, even politically. To many voting is a means of recording ideological preferences, more than a means of choosing a delegate. In normal times the citizenry aligns itself with political groupings identified with the traditional political ideologies.
5. Owing to the absence of a strong and disciplined party system, the politics of interest groups has a flourishing form in France. One of the commonest political illusions is the belief that the removal of the party whip would force the politician to search according to the dictates of his conscience for that nebulous ideal called the 'general will'. In the real world party discipline often constrains a member, but it protects him too. It helps to screen him against the demands of influential groups which claim to control marginal votes in his constituency. And it greatly reduces the danger of parliamentary corruption, since it is easier to enforce responsibilities upon a party than upon an individual. Political morality is low where authority is diffused. Responsibility in France is not enforced by a coherent opposition upon a government with undisputed power.[13]

12. Macridis and Brown. *The deGaulle Republic*, pp. 2–3.
13. Phillip Williams: *Politics in Post-War France*, p. 327.

Kinds of Pressure Groups As pointed out above, pressure groups exist in France in all walks of life-social, economic, political and the like. Almost every interest group is solidly organised with the result that one may hardly make a complete census of all such organisations. It is on account of this essential fact that while the political parties do not, and also cannot, represent all 'interests' of the society, the groups have to fill the void. The result is that pressure groups "represent all the forces at work in political life rather than political parties and groups."[14] An eminent student of this subject endorses that "for every conceivable interest group, there seems to be an association or a spokesman. If we look at the Paris telephone directory under 'association' or 'union' or 'syndicate' , we shall quickly realise that there is no possible interest that does not have an office or an organisation in France. What is more, for each single interest there are many associations."[15]

Organised groups in France vary from very large and representative entities like the National Council of French Employers to quite small ones giving sectional representation like the National Federation of Republic and the Veterans. Moreover, while there are some leading business organisations having a distinctly economic character like that of National Council of Small and Medium-Size Business, there are others having a purely academic character like that of the Confederation of Intellectual Workers of France. The workers have their own trade union organisations, the most important of which is the General Confederation of Labour. We may study the leading interest organisations of France grouped into some important categories in the following manner:

In the first place, we take up the case of business and employers' organisations. The name of CGPF (*Confederation Generale de la Production Francaise*) renamed as CNPF (*Counsel Nationale du Patronat Francaise*) in 1945 deserves mention here. This organisation is said to have been born in an unfriendly environment. Though the new Council was technically a federation covering all types of firms, small and medium-size enterprises were organised under Leon Gingembre into a semi-independent Confederation called the CGPME (*Confederation Generale des Petites at Moyennes Enterprises*) which because of the large

14. Maurice Duverger : *French Political System* (Eng. Trans. by Barbara and North), p. 112.

15. R.C. Macridis : "France" in Ward and Macridis (eds.) : *Modern Political Systems: Europe*, p.192.

number, smaller income of its members and the general cult of the 'petit', could afford to be more militant. When the employers of large firms felt somewhat uncertain of their rights, a section of the *Petronat* organised into a *Centre des Jeunes Patrons* aimed at more progressive attitudes and criticised typical bases for their conservatism.

Probably the most solidly organised professional group in France is that of the businessmen. It includes industrialists, corporation managers, bankers and merchants. It is the CNPF that, as claimed by its leaders, includes almost a million firms, which employ about 6 million wage earners and salaried personnel. Besides individual firms, it also includes other business associations, of which the CNPME (*Counsil Nationale des Petiteset Moyens Enterprises*) is one together with organisations representing particular industries such as chemicals, steel and shipbuilding. Its function are: (*a*) to establish a liaison between industry and commerce, (*b*) to represent business firms before the public authorities, (*c*) to undertake studies for the purpose of improving the economic and social conditions of the country; and (*d*) to provide information to its members.[16] The Council speaks on behalf of many powerful interests. Its representative character and its huge size "render it somewhat inflexible and immobile, and its highly diversified membership makes it difficult to arrive at a common attitude on particular issues.[17]

The class of wage-earners and salaried personnel has its own organised groups, the most important of which is the General Confederation of Labour–C.G.T. (*Confederation General du Travail*), It includes many industrial unions of craftsmen, steel workers, etc. Its directive medium is the National Confederation Committee that is elected by the delegates to the annual National Congress. The French Confederation of Democratic Labour-CFDT – is very much like the CGT in respect of its organisation. Most of its members desist from adopting the tactics of the communist leaders who have been in power in the CGT. A militant section of this organisation left it to form the National Confederation of Labour—CNT—that is said to be influenced with the philosophy of anarchism.

The interests of the farmers, particularly the richer ones, are represented by the National Federation of Farmers-FNSEA. It claims the membership of 700;000 farmers. As this organisation is largely dominated

16. Macridis in Ward and Macridis, *op. cit.*, p. 197.

17. *Ibid.*

by the richer sections of the peasantry, the socialists, communists and others have also formed their splinter groups. For instance, the socialists have their General Confederation of Workers, the communists run their General Confederation of Agriculture, Farm Workers, the Catholics and the MRP work through various Catholic Action Groups, while a dynamic and small group of agriculture experts, technicians and intellectuals has organised the National Council of Young Farmers.

While the business and labour-agrarian groups constitute the volatile element of pressure group of politics in France, a brief reference may be made to the organisation of the intellectuals and the veterans. The most important organisation of the 'intellectuals' is the Confederation of the Intellectual Workers of France. A very loose organisation of some 400,000 members representing about 80 association, it includes printers, painters, writers, journalists, teachers and like. A special point to be noted about this organisation is that the members have sharp differences on the merits of economic issues and the strategy of action to be adopted for protecting and promoting their interests. The League of the Rights of Man founded at the time of the Dreyfus Affair champions the cause of freedom of the press, maintenance of individual liberty and opposes all forms of authoritarianism. It is mostly dominated by the 'left'. The teachers have their FederatIon of National Education. The students have their own organisations like National Students Union of France that remain concerned with the advancement of their own status and well-being in the form of scholarships, loans, living quarters etc.

Finally, we refer to the associations of the army officers and the veterans that are dominated by different shades of political forces. The 'centrists' have their National Union of Veterans, the 'communist-minded' have their Republican Association of the Veterans, the 'radicals' have their National Federation of the Republican Veterans, while the 'socialist-minded' have their Federation of Workers and Peasant Veterans. All these organisations of officers, non-commissioned officers and graduates of the different military schools have their own groups that largely concentrate on obtaining pensions and other financial privileges. During the times of Algerian crisis and war in Indo-China, there came into being the French Union of the Associations of Veterans and War Victims.

Not the variety of organised groups but their role in the politics of the country is of real importance that places France in a category quite different from that of England and the United States. It can be visualised in the fact that interest groups play a very powerful and, at the same time, a very irresponsible role not because the political system of this country pertains to the hitherto parliamentary, now quasi-parliamentary system, but for the reason that the people have a different temperament and their sectional interests "tend to take precedence over the national interest."[18]

Lobbying is the main tactic of the business pressure groups. The owners of hotels, gas stations, liquor distillation centres, automobile productions, oil companies and the like have their powerful groups engaged in influencing the legislators and administrators. These 'lobbies' give financial support to the candidates at the time of elections, induct their own men into the high ranks of the bureaucratic administration, release their own journals and handouts in an attempt to sway the public opinion in their own favour and do a lot of other things that brings them close to their American counterparts so far as the method of action is concerned. Their agents are very much in the National Assembly and the Senate to support or oppose a bill as per their interest. In case their purpose in not served in the legislative world, they shift their attention to the world of administration where every interest "attempts to 'colonise' the government in a number of ways: by influencing administrators, by offering them important jobs in their own organisations, by representing them with facts and figures that appear to be convincing."[19]

Critical Appreciation: However, the political behaviour of the interest groups in France is much different from that of their Anglo-American counterparts in view of the fact that here pressure groups, like political parties, frequently take to the course of agitation and violence in which the part of the communists is too obvious. The multi-party system of this country with the tradition of violent revolutions is responsible for making the position of institutional and anomic groups more important than that of the situation obtaining in Britain. The Communist Party has its 'supporters' in the trade union organisations and certain institutional groups (like the Catholic Church) have their colonies in the political parties with the result that the parties and pressure groups interpenetrate each other.

Such a study of the existence and articulation of interest organisations in the politics of France shows that here political pluralism has a very fragmented character. Not the existence of so many political parties and

18. Bernard E. Brown: "Pressure Groups in France" in *Journal of Politics*, cited in Doughlas V. Verney: *An Analysis of Political Systems*, pp. 137-38.

19. Macridis, *op. cit.*, p. 193.

groups but the state of isolation and the process of disintegration engage our attention. The differences between different groups, even among the important figures of the same group, have been so deep that they have not been able to act in unison. Quite often the groups have failed to generate a common strategy with the result that no definite rule of political behaviour can be laid down after making a study of pressure group politics in this country. One is struck with the fact that even the groups of the workers and intellectuals have sharp differences so much so that one may suggest the existence of an isolative political culture in this country. Though at times of great national crisis, unity has been achieved around the 'myth of France' , yet the content of national symbols "has always given rise to disagreement-the interpretations of Jaures and Maurras, Renan and Daudet, being obviously incompatible. The. real France has never been able to produce a legal France in its image."[20]

It is due to this that while the 'bourgeois' interests have been in a position of advantage due to the practical application of their secret lobbying tactics, the 'proletarian' organisations have suffered. The political ineffectiveness of the labour organisations stems from a relatively late development of an organised working class movement and also from the tendency of French trade unionists to divide themselves between rivals, if not warring, ideological camps. Moreover, the failure of the movement of syndicalism had its own impact on the working class movement of France. A large section of the workers felt disillusioned when it found that the official policy of the Confederation (CGS) was wrong as it was based on the belief that working class victories could be won not piecemeal through parliamentary means but, in one major push, through the general strike. Moreover, a section of the ultra-leftists was taken aback when it found that most of the workers' unions took a pro-bourgeois stand during the days of the First World War. The result was that the ultra-Ieftists (communists) formed an organisation (CGTU) that was disbanded in 1936 when the Popular Front came into being and a large section of the 'leftists' rejoined the CGT dominated mostly by the socialists."[21]

The state of disintegration is still plaguing the politics of pressure groups to the extent that neither political parties nor pressure groups have been able to form an autonomous sub-system of their own. There is much

20. Macridis and Brown, *op. cit.*, p. 4.

21. Blondel and Godfrey, Jr.: *The Government of France*, pp. 152-53.

of anomism and Poujadism in the political behaviour of various interest groups that places the stasiological politics of France in a category different from its Anglo-American counterparts. In fact, the significance of many institutional and anomic interest groups "is directly related to the uneven effectiveness of associational interest groups, the absence of any effectively aggregative party system, and its fragmented or isolative political culture. Parties and interest groups in France do not constitute differentiated, autonomous political subsystems. They interpenetrate one another."[22]

22. Almond, *op. cit.*, pp. 37-38.

Part - VII
German Constitution

On 3 October, 1990, Germany achieved national unity. By virtue of a sovereign, conscious decision of the people, the Basic Law became the constitution for the whole nation. The successful democratic revolution in the former German Democratic Republic had achieved its goals: human dignity, civil rights, fundamental freedoms and democracy for the entire German people in a society based on the rule of law tempered by social justice.

—Roman Herzog

26

CONSTITUTION OF GERMANY

A study of the political system of Germany in an advanced study of the modern political systems of the world is governed by certain pertinent reasons. Like other prominent states of the world, it has its peculiar institutions the types of which are not available in other Western countries having a liberal-democratic order. Of course, the country has a federal system, but this pattern has some unique characteristics that ascribe to it the character of a quasi-centralised or vertical system. Though looking like a parliamentary model of government, its actual working is different from what we see in Britain, Italy, Canada, Australia and Japan. It may be traced in a unique arrangement known as the system of 'constructive vote of confidence'. Above all, the leaders and the people of this country prefer to call their constitution 'Basic Law' which "does not carry quite the same connotation of sovereignty in the German usage. Secondly, the Preamble to the Basic Law of 1949 desired 'to give a new order to political life for a transitional period' and called upon the entire German people "to accomplish by free self-determination the unity and freedom of Germany."[1]

German Constitutionalism

Modern state adheres to the principle of constitutionalism which implies that all state actions must be subject to the norms of law and justice. This makes state activity limited to a particular domain as well as to a particular way by virtue of which it becomes both predictable and examinable for the people. The legislature, the executive, the bureaucracy and even the courts have a defined area of activity and a specified procedure

1. R.G Neumann: *European and Comparative Government*. p.414. The ideal of national unity was accomplished on 3 October 1990 with the unification of the two parts of this country. The revised Preamble expresses determination of the German people "to promote world peace as an equal partner in a United Europe."

of conduct. But judiciary is invested with the power of 'judicial review' whereby it may examine the validity of any legislative and administrative measure and then hold it *ultra vires* of the constitution, in part or full, in case it transgresses the area of its well defined authority. This is the only way to keep the government in operation while implementing the principle of 'separation of powers' so as to maintain balance between the liberty of the individual and the authority of the state. The authors of the German Basic Law took it into their account that the state should be committed to the principle of real justice. Injustice remains injustice even if it is protected by the law of the land. A call against all forms of tyranny is contained in Art. 20 of the Basic Law which says: "Legislation shall be subject to the constitutional order; the executive and the judiciary shall be bound by law and justice. *All Germans shall have the right to resist any person or persons seeking to abolish that constitutional order, should no other remedy be possible.*"[2]

The promulgation of the 'Golden Bull' (imperial constitution) by King Charles IV in 1356 may be described as the first landmark in the history of constitutionalism in Germany. However, it is after the Vienna Congress of 1815 when its proper development finds its start. The Confederation of the Rhine came into being in 1815 as an imposed gift of the authors of the Vienna settlement. It was a loose organization governed by a federal assembly or Diet established at Frankfurt. Movement in the direction of German unification continued. In 1834 the German Customs Union (Zollverein) came into being that created a unitary inland market. But the important event is the revolution of 1848 when a 'democratic constitution' was drawn up which attempted to combine the old and the new ideas and designed a government responsible to parliament. But it could not be accomplished because of the opposition of Austria as well as the reservations of king Fredrick Wilhelm IV. With the rise of Bismarck (a Prussian) in 1862 the hold of Austria came to an end. It was replaced by the North German Federation whose constitution came into effect on 1 July, 1867.

The political system of Germany established under this constitution was neither democratic, nor anti-democratic; it was a peculiar fusion of the two. Imperial Germany remained like an oligarchical regime ruled by a combination of an Emperor, his court, bureaucracy, nobility, military,

2. The portion in italics was added to the Basic Law by a Federal Law on 24 June, 1968.

Some Important Statements

The Basic Law has proved its worth. It is the most liberal constitution the Germans have ever had and has served as a model for many other democratic constitutions. We Germans have every reason to be proud of our Basic Law and to defend it to the best of our ability.

—Roman Herzog

The organisation of the German state is similar to that of other western democracies in terms of its political institutions, organisation of participation, and rotation in office. The Federal Republic, even after the addition of five states from former East Germany, remains a parliamentary democracy anchored within the European Union.

—Christopher S. Allen

The Basic Law for the Federal Republic of Germany is a catalogue of fundamental norm setting out conditions under which the state derives authority, it contains rules organising and determining procedures for the exercise of that authority and recognises individual freedoms as limits to it..... The Basic Law was not explicitly called a constitution, as its normative content would have allowed, because it was conceived as an interim solution applicable until reunification becamae possible.

—Dr. Ilse Staff

and a weak parliament that was taken by the people as a 'gossip club'. The federal system established under this constitution was also defective in many respects. The States were treated unequally so far as the powers relinquished by them to the federal authority were concerned. The Reich (state) was much dependent for its revenues on the periodical contributions of the units or the States. The States managed the administration of federal legislation through their own civil servants, necessitating a kind of Reich diplomatic procedure to ensure the enforcement of laws of federal supervision. The States had unequal representation in the Federal Council.

The constitutional system of imperial Germany had its end in the First World War. The third Reich came into being as a republic under the Weimer Constitution of 1919. The office of the monarch was abolished and Germany had an elected President. The real authority was given to the Chancellor (Prime Minister) appointed by the President and responsible to the Parliament (Reichstag). The principle of universal adult suffrage was introduced with the result that all citizens, including women, were enfranchised on completing the age of 20 years. The system of proportional representation was adopted for parliamentary election. A better model of a federal system was established so that the units could enjoy autonomy. But the most obnoxious arrangement of the Weimer constitution was related to certain 'emergency powers' whereby the Centre could impose its decision on any 'recalcitrant' Land (State) of the German federation and, more than that, the President under Art. 48 had the right to suspend civil liberties of the people during the times of national crisis. The system of proportional representation also played its part in enabling minor parties and groups to secure seats in the Reichstag (Parliament) and then convert it into a theatre of petty political rivalries.

The result was that the Weimer republic started cracking after a life of some ten years. The great economic depression of 1929-30 added to the conditions of political and economic instability in Germany. The Nazis managed to secure many seats in the National Assembly in the elections of 1933 and they became a party to the coalition government. Then, Hitler became the Chancellor and by adopting the tactics of a power-maniac, he managed to force the President to dissolve the Assembly and hold fresh elections in 1934 in which the Nazis secured greater number of seats. Hitler became Chancellor again. All important leaders of other political parties were caught, tortured, humiliated and suppressed. After the death of President von Hindenberg. Hitler assumed the office of the head of the state as well and thereafter he acted like a 'dictator'. The result was the outbreak of the Second World War in which Germany not only saw her second defeat, but her occupation by four great powers of the world resulted in her division in 1949.

Germany came under the occupation of the Allied Powers in the summer of 1945. Already at the Yalta Conference of February, 1945 it was decided that the USA, Britain and the USSR should each occupy a zone in Germany and that the French government should be invited to accept a similar zone for administration. The Allied Powers took formal possession of Germany on 5 June and then four zones of occupation with the control of all the Four over Berlin came into being. In the months of July-August, 1945 the Potsdam Conference was held in which the Allied Powers resolved to extirpate Nazism and militarism but not to destroy the German people.

For some time the fate of Germany hung in the balance owing to the outbreak of the 'cold war' between the Soviet leaders on the one side and the three Allied powers on the other. The meaning of a democratic system of Germany was differently interpreted by the two camps opposing each other. In the summer of 1948 when all hopes of solving the problem of Germany had to be given up in the face of the opposition of the USSR, the three Allied Powers gave the signal for the establishment of a state of West Germany even at the expense of her virtual division. They proposed that a national assembly should work out a constitution. Since the people opposed this move under the fear of virtual partition of their country, the term 'Basic Law' had to be used in place of the term 'constitution' so as to underline the fact of a make-shift arrangement or a temporary solution of the constitutional problem. Thus came into being a Parliamentary Council of 65 delegates sent from the Lander parliaments. It started its work from 1 September, 1946 under the chairmanship of Konrad Adenauer. It worked for about seven months and adopted the Basic Law by 53 votes to 15 on 8 May, 1947. On 24 May, 1949 it came into force after getting approval of all the States (Lander) except Bavaria that did not appreciate the 'centralised control' of the Federal Government amounting to the abridgement of the powers of the States.[3]

With the annulment of the partition of Germany on 3 October, 1990, the Basic Law became the constitution of a unified nation–state. As a result, amendments were made, where necessary, so as to bring the whole country under a democratic and social welfare state. In November, 1994, Federal President Roman Herzog could proudly say: "We overcame the division of Germany within the wider framework of a redical transformation of Europe. The creation of the European Union entails new challenges and opportunities for us all. Both our country's increasing integration and the completion of its national unity were bound to have repercussions on our constitutional law. The fact that only adjustments were necessary attests to the Basic Law's excellent quality as the foundation of our polity from its inception. Its liberal, democratic, federal and welfare elements enabled our country to acquire economic prosperity and social security while maintaining internal stability."[4]

3. It may be pointed here that the people of Bavaria have strong sentiments of their freedom by virtue of historical traditions. They still feel pride in calling their Land (State) as Free State of Bavaria.
4. Herzog: "Foreword" to *The Basic Law for the Federal Republic of Germany,* published by the Press and Information Office of the Federal Government at Bonn, 1998, p. 3.

Salient Features

As taken by the German people with pride, this constitution has these important features:

1. **A Charter of Faith and Hope:** Every constitution is a charter of faith which the people repose in some form of political organisation. But the case of the German people is different. In order to dispel any wrong impression about their political culture and also in order to infuse the spirit of a liberal-democratic order, they have formulated the clauses of this constitution. The aim of the authors is to redefine the meaning of their nationalism and then to align it with the principle of internationalism. The goal of national and political integration is to be achieved. Hopefully, they looked forward to the nullification of the partition of their country. The Preamble says: "Conscious of their responsibilities before God and men, animated by their resolve to preserve their national and political unity and to serve the peace of the world as an equal partner in a united Europe, desiring to give a new order to political life for a transitional period, have enacted by virtue of their constituent power, this Basic Law for the Federal Republic of Germany. They have also acted on behalf of those Germans to whom participation was denied. The entire German people are called upon to achieve in free self-determination the unity and freedom of Germany."
2. **An Enacted, Written and Rigid Constitution:** Like the constitution of other countries of the world, excluding Britain, it is an enacted constitution. It is a creation of a body (Parliamentary Council) having 65 members who worked for about seven months at Bonn under the chairmanship of Adenauer. It has 146 Articles some portions of which have been added and some deleted in course of time. Then, it is a rigid constitution because its portions can be amended by two-thirds vote of the membership of the both the houses—Bundestag and Bundesrat. It is given that the form of government, membership of the Lander in the Federation and the fundamental rules of the participation of the Lander in federal legislation cannot be amended. In order to make the rule of law paramount, Art. I of the constitution has also been declared unamendable. It says: "The dignity of man is inviolable. To respect and protect it is the duty of all state authority. The German people, therefore, acknowledge inviolable and inalienable human rights as the basis of every human community, of peace, and of justice in the world." Obviously, the provision of

two-thirds majority makes the procedure of amendment difficult and that is enough to regard it as a rigid constitution. The rigidity of the constitution has been softened by abolishing the provisions of initiative and referendum that were given in the Weimer Constitution.

3. **A Document of Peace:** Like the constitution of Japan, this constitution should be described as a document of peace. It registers the resolve of the people in world peace and international law. Art. 25 says: "The general rules of public international law shall be an integral part of the federal law. They shall take precedence over the laws and shall directly create rights and duties for the inhabitants of the federal territory." Art. 26 says: "Acts tending to and undertaken with the intent to disturb the peaceful relations between nations, especially to prepare for aggressive war, shall be unconstitutional. They shall be made a punishable offence. Weapons designed for warfare may not be manufactured, transported or marketed except with the permission of the Federal Government. Details shall be regulated by a federal law."[5]
4. **Democratic and Social Welfare State:** Art. 20 declares Germany a democratic and social welfare state. The democratic principle means that the people are sovereign. The system of representative government is established whereby the people exercise their political powers through representatives elected by and accountable to them. Elections are general, direct, free, secret and equal in which all citizens above the age of 18 years take part. The elected members of the Bundestag elect the Federal Chancellor. The President is also elected. At the same time, the constitution declares Germany a social welfare state. It does not mean its commitment to a particular form of socialism. It is a modern supplement to the inherited concept of constitutionalism. It obliges the state to protect the socially weaker people and always to strive for social justice.
5. **Parliamentary Form of Government:** The constitution establishes parliamentary form of government which is slightly different from

---

5. Reference may also be made to Art. 24 of the Basic Law which says: "For the maintenance of peace, the Federation may enter a system of mutual collective security: in doing so it will consent to such limitations upon its rights of sovereignty as will bring about and secure a peaceful and lasting order in Europe and among the nations of the world. For the settlement of disputes between states the Federation will accede to agreements concerning international arbitration of a general, comprehensive and obligatory nature."

the English model. The President is the head of the state and he holds nominal authority. The real authority is vested in the Chancellor (Prime Minister) and his ministry. The President nominates the Chancellor and he has to seek confidence of the Bundestag. The Parliament (Bundestag) has the power to pass a vote of no-confidence and then the government must resign. There is no provision for passing a vote of no-confidence against any minister or ministers. But the constitution provides for 'constructive vote of no-confidence'. It means that while dismissing a Chancellor, the House shall immediately elect his successor.

6. **Basic Rights:** The incorporation of fundamental rights into the constitution of a state has become a matter of necessity in present times. The Weimer constitution had a list of civil basic rights, but the great mistake of its authors was that they made them only 'declaratory' and, as such, they did not constitute actual legal obligations. But the authors of the present constitution have rectified the mistake by declaring them 'directly valid law on legislation, administration and judiciary'. There is a long list of civil rights covering political, social, economic, cultural and moral spheres. They incorporate many important provisions as those relating to protection of human dignity, liberty of person, equality before law, freedom of faith and expression, marriage and family, education, freedom of assembly and association, privacy of post and telecommunications, freedom to move and choose any occupation, liability to military and other services, inviolability of home, property and its inheritance and expropriation, socialisation, deprivation of citizenship, asylum and extradition, and sending petition. The constitution also sanctions restrictions on basic rights for the members of the armed forces and their forfeiture in the event of their abuse by the citizens. The state may impose 'general restrictions' on these basic rights, but such restrictions are subject to judicial review by the Federal Constitutional Court. It is also important to note that the constitution makes one basic right (relating to protection of human dignity) unamendable.

7. **Judicial Review:** The constitution of a federal state must make provision for the existence of an independent and impartial judicial body to act as the guardian of the fundamental law of the land and a standing convention to interpret the meaning of the provisions of the constitution. In the United States, Canada, Japan and India, this

work is done by the Supreme Court, but in Germany it is given to the Federal Constitutional Court. It has the power to examine whether a particular law of the Federal or Land governments is consistent with the principles of the Basic Law or not, and whether a particular law of the States (Lander) is consistent with the law of the Federal Government or not. In case it finds it inconsistent, it may declare it null and void. This court alone has the power of judicial review and in case some point of constitutional validity of an impugned law or executive action comes up in any other court of the country, the matter shall be referred to the Federal Constitutional Court for adjudication.

8. **Federalism:** According to Art. 20 of the constitution, Germany is a federal state. The powers of administration have been divided between the Federal Government and the governments of the Lander (States). Art. 73 assigns exclusive powers to the Centre like foreign affairs, defence, migration and immigration, currency and coinage, federal citizenship, federal railroads and air transport, postal and telegraphic communication etc. Then, Art. 74 enumerates concurrent powers like civil and criminal law, birth and death, marriage and family, residence and establishment of aliens, weapons and explosives, public welfare, citizenship of the Lander, war damages and reparations, labour law, ocean and coastal shipping, regulation of hospitals, transfer of land and natural resources, prevention of the abuse of economic power, use of nuclear energy for peaceful purposes, regulation of education and training grants etc. It may be noted here that while the Federal government has its exclusive hold over the items of Art. 73, the concurrent items are under the jurisdiction of both governments with the over-riding authority of the Centre. The residuary powers are with the States (Lander). Then, there is the Federal Constitutional Court to interpret the meaning of the provisions of the Basic Law and also act as an umpire between the Federal and State governments in matters of constitutional dispute. As we shall see later, the model of the German federation has its own features in which the units are neither as powerful as the States of the USA nor as weak as the provinces of Canada.

Basic Rights of the Citizens

That the German Constitution attaches upper-most significance to the fundamental rights of the citizens becomes evident from this patent fact that its first 17 articles have their detailed enumeration. It well indicates that the state is there for the sake of the people and not *vice versa*, that it is not to rule but to serve. Every possible care has been taken to ensure that the present state would not permit the rise of ultraleftist and aggressive forces in the country. The first basic right relating to the protection of human dignity has been declared unamendable and any restriction on the use and enjoyment of any basic right, if any, imposed by the law of the state has been subjected to the power of judicial review of the Federal Constitutional Court. It is for this reason that the Court ruled dissolution of the neo-Nazi Socialist Reich Party in 1952 and of Communist Party in 1956. Another important point to be noted here is that a citizen may forfeit his basic rights in the event of their abuse, while the basic rights of the members of the armed forces may be restricted by the law of the State in the national interest.

The Basic Rights of the people of Germany are enumerated as under:

Art. 1 **(Human Dignity):** The dignity of man shall be inviolable. To respect and promote it shall be the duty of State authority. (2) The German people, therefore, acknowledge inviolable human rights as the basis of every community, of peace and justice in the world.

Art. 2 **(Liberty):** (1) Everyone shall have the right to free development of his personality in so far as as he does not violate the rights of others or offend against the constitutional order to the moral code. (2) Everyone shall have the right to life and inviolability of his person. The liberty of the individual shall be inviolable. These rights may only be encroached upon pursuant to a law.

Art. 3 **(Equality before Law):** (1) All persons shall be equal before law. (2) Men and women shall have equal rights. (3) No one may be prejudiced or favoured because of his sex, parentage, race, language, homeland and origin, faith, religious or political opinions.

Art. 4 **(Freedom of Faith and Creed):** (1) Freedom of faith, con science, creed, religious or ideological, shall be inviolable. (2) The undisturbed practice of religion is guaranteed. (3) No one may be compelled against his conscience to render war service involving the use of arms. Details shall be regulated by a federal law.

Art. 5 (Freedom of Expression): (1) Everyone shall have the right to freely express and disseminate his opinions by speech, writing and pictures and freely inform himself from generally accessible sources. Freedom of the press and freedom of reporting by means of broadcasts and films are guaranteed. There shall be no censorship. (2) These rights are limited by the provisions of the general laws, the provisions of law for the protection of the youth, and by the right to inviolability of personal honour. (3) Art and science, research and teaching shall be free. Freedom of teaching shall not absolve from loyalty to the constitution.

Art. 6 (Marriage, Family, Illegitimate Children): (1) Matters of family shall enjoy special protection of the State. (2) The care and upbringing of children are a natural right of and a duty primarily incumbent on the parents. The national community shall watch over their endeavours in this respect. (3) Children may not be separated from their families against the will of the persons entitled to bring them up except pursuant to a law, if those so entitled fail or the children are otherwise threatened with neglect. (4) Every mother shall be entitled to the protection and care of the community. (5) Illegitimate children shall be provided by legislation with the same opportunities for their physical and spiritual development and their place in society as are enjoyed by legitimate children.

Art. 7 (Education): (1) The entire educational system shall be under the supervision of the State. (2) The persons entitled to bring up a child shall have the right to decide whether he shall receive religious instructions. (3) Religious instruction shall form part of the ordinary curriculum in state and municipal schools, except in secular schools. Without prejudice to the state's right of supervision, religious instruction shall be given in accordance with the tenets of the religious communities. No teacher may be obliged against his will to give religious instruction. (4) The right to establish private schools, as a substitute for state or municipal schools, shall require the approval of the State and shall be subject to the laws of the Lander. Such approval must be given if private schools are not inferior to the state or municipal schools in their educational aims, their facilities and the professional training of their teaching staff, and if segregation of pupils according to the means of the parents is not promoted thereby. Approval must be withheld if the economic and legal position of the teaching staff is not sufficiently assured. (5) A private elementary school shall be permitted only if the education authority finds that it serves a 'special' pedagogic interest, or if on the application of persons entitled to bring up children, it is to be established as an inter-denominational or denominational or ideological school and a state or municipal elementary school of this type does not exist in the commune. (6) Preparatory schools shall remain abolished.

Art. 8 **(Freedom of Assembly):** (1) All Germans shall have the right to assemble peaceably and unarmed without prior notification or permission. (2) With regard to open air meetings this might be restricted by or pursuant to a law.

Art. 9 **(Freedom to Form Associations):** (1) All Germans shall have the right to form associations and societies. (2) Associations, the purposes or activities of which conflict with criminal laws or which are directed against the constitutional order of the concept of international understanding are prohibited. (3) The right to form associations to safeguard and improve working and economic conditions is guaranteed to everyone and to all trades, occupations and professions. Agreements which restrict or seek to impair this right shall be null and void; measures directed to this end shall be illegal. Measures taken pursuant to Art. 12 a, paras 2 and 3 of Art. 35, para 4 of Art. 37 a, or Art. 91 may not be directed against any industrial conflicts engaged in by associations within the meaning of the first sentence of this para in order to safeguard and improve working and economic conditions.

Art. 10 **(Privacy of Post and Telecommunications):** (1) Privacy of post and telecommunications shall be inviolable. (2) This right may be restricted only pursuant to a law. Such a law may lay down that the person affected shall not be informed of any such restriction if it serves to protect the free democratic basic order or the existence or security of the Federation or a Land, and that recourse to the courts shall be replaced by a review of the case by bodies and auxiliary bodies appointed by Parliament.

Art. 11 **(Freedom of Movement):** (1) All Germans shall enjoy freedom of movement throughout the federal territory. (2) This right may be restricted only by or pursuant to a law and only in cases

Some Important Statements

The Federal Republic has generally practised a procedural democracy, characterised by constitutional provisions for free elections, civil liberties and individual rights, and an independent judiciary. —***Christopher S. Allen***

Basic rights are rights of defence against the state. They guarantee the principle that individuals have no privacy, while all incursions by the state require justification. This is expressed by the inclusion in most basic rights of a statutory reservation. —***Dr. Ilse Staff***

In Germany capitalist industrialisation in the nineteenth century occurred under the guidance of a powerful authoritarian regime. Democracy came in the later part of the twentieth century. —***Patrick O'Neil***

in which an adequate basis of existence is lacking and special burden would arise to the community as a result thereof, or in which restriction is necessary to avert an imminent danger to the existence of the free democratic basic order of the Federation or a Land, to combat the danger of epidemics, to deal with natural disasters or particular grave accidents, to protect young people from neglect or to prevent crime.

Art. 12 **(Choice of Trade, Occupation or Profession):** (1) All Germans shall have the right freely to choose their trade, occupation or profession, their place of work and their place of training. The practice of trades, occupations and professions may be regulated by or pursuant to a law. (2) No specific occupation may be imposed on any person except within the framework of an additional compulsory public service that applies generally and equally to all. (3) Forced labour may be imposed only on persons deprived of their liberty by court sentence.

Art. 12 a **(Liability to Military and Other Services):** (1) Men who have attained the age of 18 years may be required to serve in the Armed Forces, in the Federal Border Guard, or in a Civil Defence Organisation: (2) A person who refuses, on grounds of conscience, to render war service involving the use of arms may be required to render a substitute service. The duration of such substitute service shall not exceed the duration of military service. Details shall be regulated by a law which shall not interfere with the freedom of conscience and must also provide for the possibility of a substitute service not connected with the units of the Armed Forces or of the Federal Border Guard.

(3) Persons liable to military service who are not required to render service pursuant to para (1) or (2) of this Art. may, when a state of defence exists, be assigned by or pursuant to a law to a specific occupation involving civilian services for defence purposes, including the protection of the civilian population; it shall, however, not be permissible to assign persons to an occupation subject to public law except for the purpose of charging police functions or such other functions of public administration as can only be discharged by persons employed under public law. Persons may be assigned to occupations within the Armed Forces including the supply and servicing of the latter, or with public administrative authorities; assignments to occupations can be acted with supplying and servicing the civilian population shall not be permissible except, in order to meet their vital requirements or to guarantee their safety. (4) If, while a state of defence exists, civilian service requirements in the civilian public health and medical system or in the stationary military hospital organisation cannot be met on a voluntary basis, women between 18 and 25 years of age may be assigned to such services by or pursuant to a law. They may on account render service involving the use of arms. (5) During the time prior to the existence of such a state of defence, assignments under para (3) of this Art. may be effected only if the requirements of para (1) of Art. 80 (a) are satisfied. It shall be admissible to require persons by or pursuant to law to attend training courses in order to prepare them for the performance of such services in accordance with para (3) of this Art. as presuppose special knowledge or skills. To this extent the first sentence of this para shall not apply. (6) If, while a state of defence exists, the labour requirements for the purpose referred to in the second sentence of para (3) of this Art., cannot be met on a voluntary basis, the right of a German to give up the practice of his trade or occupation or profession, or his place of work, may be restricted by or pursuant to a law in order to meet these requirements. The first sentence of para (5) of this Art. shall apply *mutatis mutandis* prior to the existence of a state of defence.

Art. 13 **(Inviolability of Home):** (1) The home shall be inviolable. (2) Searches may be ordered only by a judge or in the event of danger in delay, by other organs as provided by law and may be carried out only in the form prescribed by law. (3) In all other respects, this inviolability may not be encroached upon or restricted except to avert a common danger or a moral danger to individuals, or, pursuant to a law, to prevent imminent danger to public safety and order, especially to alleviate the housing shortage, to combat the danger of epidemics or to protect endangered juveniles.

Art. 14 **(Property, Right of Inheritance, Expropriation):** (1) Property and the right of inheritance are guaranteed. Their content and limits shall be determined by the laws. (2) Property imposes duties. Its use should also serve the public good. (3) Expropriation shall be permitted only in the public interest. It may be effected only by or pursuant to a law which shall provide for the nature and extent of the compensation. Such compensation shall be determined by establishing an equitable balance between the public interest and the interests of those affected. In case of dispute regarding the amount of compensation, recourse may be had to the ordinary courts.

Art. 15 **(Socialisation):** Land, natural resources and means of production may for the purpose of socialisation be transferred to public ownership or other forms of publicly controlled economy by a law which shall provide for the nature and extent of compensation in respect of such compensation the third and fourth sentences of para (3) of Art. 14 shall apply *mutatis mutandis*.

Art. 16 **(Deprivation of Citizenship, Extradition, Right of Asylum):** (1) No one may be deprived of his German citizenship. Loss of citizenship may arise only pursuant to a law, and against the will of the person affected only if such person does not thereby become stateless. (2) No German may be extradited to a foreign country. A person prosecuted on political grounds shall enjoy the right of asylum.

Art. 17 **(Right of Petition):** Everyone shall have the right individually or jointly with others to address written requests or complaints to the appropriate agencies and to parliamentary bodies.

Art. 17(a) **(Restriction of Basic Rights for the Members of the Armed Forces etc.):** (1) Laws concerning military service and substitute service may by provisions applying to members of the armed forces and of substitution services during this period of military or substitute service, restrict the basic right freely to express and disseminate opinions by speech, writing and pictures the basic right of assembly and the right of petition in so far as this right permits the submission of requests or complaints jointly with others. (2) Laws for defence purposes including protection of the civilian population may provide for the restriction of the basic rights of freedom of movement and inviolability of home.

Art. 18 **(Forefeiture of Basic Rights):** Whoever abuses freedom of expression of opinion, in particular freedom of the press, freedom of teaching, freedom of assembly, freedom of association, privacy of posts and tele-communications, property, or the right of asylum in order to combat the free democratic basic order, shall forfeit these basic rights. Such forfeiture and the extent thereof shall be pronounced by the Federal Constitutional Court.

Art. 19 **(Restriction on Basic Rights):** (1) In so far as basic rights may under this Basic Law be restricted by or pursuant to a law, such law must apply generally and not solely to an individual case. Further-more, such law must name the basic right, including the Article concerned. (2) In no case may the essential content of a basic right be encroached upon. (3) The basic rights shall apply also to domestic juristic persons to the extent that the nature of such rights permits. (4) Should any person's right be violated by public authority, recourse to the court shall be open to him. If jurisdiction is not specified, recourse shall be to the ordinary courts.

Mere enumeration of basic rights in the fundamental law of the land is not enough. Two more things are required. First, they should be protected by an independent and impartial judiciary. Second, they should be amplified by necessary legislative and administrative actions of the state. The German state has paid regard to both these requirements. The Federal Constitutional Court has played the desired role in this direction. Necessary follow-up action has also occurred as the state has made law to elaborate or amplify the scope of some of the basic rights.[6]

Federalism

Germany is a federal state like the USA, Canada, Australia, Switzerland, India etc., though it has some peculiar features of its own. The federative structure is as old as the German constitutional tradition, though it was seriously interrupted by the Nazis under Hitler. The Lander (States) were partly reconstituted and partly created anew after the Second World War and now they have their autonomous position. Each Land has its own constitution conforming to the Basic Law of Germany and it is free to amend it. Each Land has its citizenship laws. The notable point is that "German federalism has historic roots and in the past was often lamented as an expression of national fragmentation or even as a national misfortune. Today the federal structure is proving a great advantage. It makes it possible to a great extent to do justice to regional peculiarities, wishes and special problems."

The political system of Germany meets all the essential requirements of a federal system. In the first place, the constitution is written; its procedure of amendment is difficult because of the provision of two-thirds majority that requires support of both the Federal and State governments; and it is the supreme law of the land. Second, it specifies the distribution of powers between the Centre and the States. While Art. 73 specifies the powers of the Centre as those relating to foreign affairs, defence, currency and coinage, federal railways and transport, post and telecommunications, Federal citizenship, migration and immigration, industrial property rights etc., Art. 74 specifies concurrent powers given to both the Federal and State governments with an overriding authority of the former in the event

6. Besides, we should make reference to two more provisions of the Basic Law in this connection. Art. 33 says: "Every German shall have in every Land the same political rights and duties. Every German shall be equally eligible for any public office according to his aptitude, qualifications and professional achievements. The exercise of state authority as a permanent function shall as a rule be entrusted to members of the public service whose status, service and loyalty are governed by public law. The law of the pubic service shall be regulated with due regard to the traditional principles of the professional civil service." Then, Art. 34 says: "If any person, in the exercise of a public office, entrusted to him, violates his official obligations to a third party, liability shall rest in principle on the state or the public body which employs him. In the event of wilful intent or gross negligence the right of recourse shall be reserved. In respect of the claim for compensation or the right of recourse, the jurisdiction of the ordinary courts must not be excluded."

of any dispute or controversy. This category includes items like civil and criminal law, registration of births and deaths, public welfare, refugee and expellees matters, war damages and reparations, labour law, prevention of the abuse of economic power, agricultural and forest production, use of nuclear energy for peaceful purposes, ocean and coastal shipping etc. The residuary items are left to the Lander (States) as local government, parts of environmental protection, police administration, elementary and secondary education, cultural affairs etc. Finally, there is the Federal Constitutional Court to act as the interpreter of the meaning of the provisions of the constitution and to settle constitutional disputes between the Centre and the States. It has the power of judical review by virtue of which it may invalidate a law of the Federal or State governments if it is inconsistent with the Basic Law of Germany; it may also strike down a Land law if it is inconsistent with the law of the Centre. The federal system of Germany has its distinctive features mentioned as under:

1. Art. 29 says that the federal territory may be reorganised to ensure that the Lander by their size and capacity are able effectively to fulfil the functions incumbent upon them. Due regard shall be given to regional, historical and cultural ties, economic expediency, regional policy, and the requirement of town and country planning. Measures for the reorganisation of the federal territory shall be introduced by federal laws which shall be subject to confirmation by referendum. The Lander, thus affected, shall be consulted. Other modifications of the territory of the Lander may be affected by state agreements between the Lander concerned or by a federal law with the approval of the Bundesrat if the territory which is to be subject of reorg-anisation does not have more than 10,000 inhabitants.[7]
2. Art. 30 says that the exercise of governmental powers and the discharge of governmental functions shall be incumbent on the Lander in so far as this Basic Law does not otherwise prescribe or permit.
3. Art. 31 says that Federal Law shall override law of the Land.
4. Art. 32 says that relations with foreign states shall be conducted by the Federation. Before the conclusion of a treaty affecting the special circumstances of a Land, that Land must be consulted in sufficient time. In so far as the Lander have power to legislate, they may, with the consent of the Federal Government, conclude treaties with foreign states.

---

7. Since unification of Germany in 1990, the Federation has 16 States Baden-Wurttemberg, Bavaria, Berlin, Brandenburg, Bremen, Hamburg, Heasse, Lower Saxony, Mecklenburg-Western Pomerania, North Rhine-Westphalia, Rhineland-Palatinate, Saarrland, Saxony, Saxony-Anhalt, Schleswig-Holstein and Thuringia.

5. Art. 35 says that all Federal and Land authorities shall render each other legal and administrative assistance. In order to maintain or restore public security or order, a Land may in cases of particular importance call upon forces and facilities of the Federal Border Guard to assist its police, if without this assistance, the police could not, or only with considerable difficulty, fulfil a task. In order to deal with a natural disaster or an especially grave incident, a Land may request the assistance of the police forces of other Lander or of forces and facilities of other administrative authorities or of the Federal Border Guard or the Armed Forces. If the natural disaster or the accident endangers a region larger than a Land, the Federal Government may, in so far as this is necessary, effectively to deal with such a danger, instruct the Land governments to place their police force at the disposal of other Lander, and may commit units of the Federal Border Guard or the Armed Forces to support the police forces. Such measures taken by the Federal Government must be revoked at any time upon the request of the Bundesrat, and in any case upon the removal of the danger.
6. Art. 36 says that civil servants employed in the highest federal authorities shall be drawn from all Lander in appropriate proportion. Persons employed in other federal authorities should, as a rule, be drawn from the Land in which they serve. Military laws shall, *inter alia*, take into account both the division of the Federation into Lander and the regional ties of their population.
7. Art. 37 says that if a Land fails to comply with its obligations of a federal character imposed by this Basic Law or some other federal law, the Federal Government may, with the consent of the Bundesrat, take the necessary measures to enforce such compliance by the Land by way of federal enforcement. To carry out such federal enforcement of the Federal Government or its commission shall have the right to give instructions to all Lander and their authorities.
8. The strong hold of the States should be seen in the institution of the Bundesrat. Art. 50 says that the Lander shall participate through this body in the legislation and administration of the Federation. Art. 51 says that this body shall consist of the representatives of the Land governments; each Land shall have at least 3 votes; but a Land having more than two million inhabitants shall have 4 votes and a Land with more than six million inhabitants shall have 5 votes. The votes of a Land shall be cast as a bloc. Art. 52 says that all decisions of this body shall be taken by the majority of votes. Art. 53 says that this body must be currently kept informed by the Federal Government of the conduct of affairs.

9. Art. 72 says that in matters within the concurrent legislative powers, the Lander shall have power to legislate as long as and to the extent that the Federation does not exercise its right to legislate. The Federation shall have the right to legislate in these matters to the extent that the need for regulation by federal legislation exists because (*i*) a matter cannot be effectively regulated by the legislation of individual Lander, or (*ii*) the regulation of a matter by a Land law might prejudice the interests of other Lander or of the people as a whole, or (*iii*) the maintenance of legal or economic unity, especially the maintenance of uniformity of living conditions beyond the territory of any Land, necessitates such a regulation.
10. Art. 75 says that subject to the conditions laid down in Art. 72, the Federation shall have the right to enact skeleton provisions concerning the legal status of persons in the public services of the Lander communes, or other corporate bodies under public law, general principles governing higher education, general legal status of the press and film industry, national conservation and landscape management, hunting, land distribution, regional planning and water regime, and matters relating to the registration of changes of residence or domicile and to identity cards.
11. Art. 83 says that the Lander shall execute federal laws as matters of their own concern in so far as this Basic Law does not otherwise provide.
12. Art. 84 says that where the Lander execute federal laws as matters of their own concern, they shall provide for the establish-ment of the requisite authorities and the regulation of administrative procedures in so far as federal laws consented to by the Bundesrat do not otherwise provide. The Federal Government may with the consent of the Bundesrat, issue pertinent general administrative rules. Should any shortcoming which the Federal Government has found to exist in the execution of federal laws in the Lander not be corrected, the matter shall be decided by the Bundesrat.
13. Art. 85 says that all Land authorities shall be subject to the instructions of the appropriate highest federal authorities. Such instructions shall be addressed to the highest Land authorities unless the Federal Government considers the matter urgent. Execution of the instructions shall be ensured by the highest Land authorities. Federal supervision shall extend to the conformity with law and appropriateness of execution. The Federal Government may, for this

Some Important Statements

Although unification in 1871 reflected the growing might of Prussia, a federal structure helped to allay the fears of central control of the other 38 Germanic states that had long enjoyed political independence. The tradition of regional autonomy, briefly interrupted during the Nazi period, was formalised in the constitution of the Federal Republic of Germany, adopted in 1949, which granted each of the 11 *Lander* (provinces or states) its own constitution. Their number was increased to 16 as a result of the reunification of Germany in 1990. ***—Andrew Heywood***

The constitutional decision to opt for a federal state was taken in 1949 as a means of counteracting experience with state centralism under the national socialist dictatorship. One significant characteristic is that Art. 30 of the Basic Law, in allocating power to the Federation and the *Lander*, states that the exercise of governmental functions is incumbent on the *Lander*. ***—Dr. Ilsa Staff***

Under federalism, significant powers, such as taxation, law-making and security are develoved to regional bodies as States in the US and *Lander* in Germany that control a specific territory within the country. These powers are defined within the national constitution and, therefore, are not easily constricted or eliminated by the government. ***—Patrick O'Neil***

purpose, require the submission of reports and documents and send communications to all authorities.[8]

14. Since a federal system desires Centre-State cooperation in certain important matters, Art. 91 (*a*) says that the Federation shall participate in the discharge of the following responsibilities of the Lander provided that such responsibilities are important to society as a whole and that federal participation is necessary for the improvement of living conditions. The 'joint tasks' include: extension and construction of institutions of higher education including university clinics, improvement of regional economic structures, and development of the agrarian structure and of coast preservation. Joint tasks shall be defined in detail by federal legislation with the consent of the Bundesrat. Then, Art. 91 (*b*) says that the Federation and the

8. Carl J. Friedrich says: "In exercising its supervision, the Federal government may send commissioners to a Land government and if the Minister President of the Land government refuses access to the Land authorities concerned, the Federal Government can go to the Federal Council and seek authorisation for approaching the particular Land authorities directly. In general, this supervision which also involves the making of reports and the submission of documents, functions smoothly, the cases where conflict has resulted are relatively rare. *Trends of Federalism in Theory and Practice*, p. 130

Lander may, purusant to agreements, cooperate in educational planning and in the promotion of institutions and projects of scientific research of supra-regional importance. The apportionment of costs shall be regulated in the pertinent agreements.

15. In the end we may look into the sphere of finance (Articles 105 to 109) where the Centre (Bund) has an upper hand, though the role of the Bundesrat is still there. The Bund has exclusive right to raise revenues from customs and governmental enterprises (fiscal monopoly) like sale of matches and liquor and, if necessary concurrently with the Lander income, inheritance, property, donations, real estate and business property and excise taxes except on beer. The Lander too have substantial scope to finance their governments, for they have power to levy taxes in all fields in which the Bund does not have exclusive power, i.e., customs and fiscal monopolies. Some taxes accrue to the Lander, though the Federation legislates them as taxes on beer, business transactions (but not transportation or turnover) income, corporation profits, property, inheritance, real estate and business premises. The important thing to be noted here again is that the Bund cannot raise its money without the consent of the Bundesrat.

The critics have described the German federal system as 'centralised' due to some strong reasons. First, the law of the Centre shall prevail over the law of the States. Second, the States are bound to carry out all instructions of the Centre. Third, the Centre has the power to make a law for the preservation of uniformity of living conditions so as to maintain legal and economic unity extending beyond the territory of any Land. Fourth, in respect of concurrent matters, the overriding authority of the Centre is unmistakable. Fifth, the Federal Constitutional Court has power to strike down a law of the Land in case it is inconsistent with the law of the Centre. Last, while the Lander get no share of the revenue exclusively placed at the disposal of the federal government, the federation may take. a share of the revenues normally assigned exclusively to the States. Thus, Neumann says: "There can be little doubt that the text of the Bonn Constitution shows a decided centralist tendency. This is not so much in evidence in the exclusively federal powers, which comprise a bare minimum, but in the concurrent powers in which the federal government is supreme when it wishes to act."[9]

---

9. Neumann. *op. cit.* p. 420.

The view of the English and American writers on the subject of federalism in relation to the system of Germany may be correct in the light of the conditions of the 1950s and the 1960s. A startling change has occurred after great economic miracle. The States have discovered many areas where they may assert their position and behave like autonomous units of the American and Swiss federations. If judged solely by their legislative competence, the Lander appear to be in a weak position. This, however, is not the case. The strength of the Lander lies in administration and in participation in the law-making of the federation. They are responsible for all internal administration with which they also implement most of the federal laws and regulations. Accordingly the responsibilities of the administrative bodies of the Lander are: (*i*) They exercise administrative tasks for which the Land has exclusive power (as schools, planning, maintenance of law and order); (*ii*) They implement federal laws as matters of their own concern and responsibility (as building and trade regulations, protection of the environment); (*iii*) They implement federal laws as agents of the Federation (as federal roads and training promotion). In practice, Germany has thus evolved into a state with predominantly centralised legislation and on the whole federally structured administration.

The German writers examine the case of their federal system in the light of their national traditions and political culture of the people. For this, they dwell on these reasons. First, there has been barely any manifestation in Germany of the centrifugal tendencies often cited as drawbacks of federalism. Small in area in any case, it is well served by all means of transport and its population is more unitary than those of many other countries. The once very marked tribal differences have been blurred somewhat by the great post-war population movements and the great mobility modern economic life entails. Second, the Federal Council or Bundesrat is there to contribute to the balance of power. Its rôle is seen as so fundamental that both the federal structure and the States' participation in federal legislation are laid down as irremovable by the Basic Law. By all means, credit should be given to the Bundesrat that scrupulously seeks to maintain balance between the Central and State governments. It "does, in fact, act specifically to protect governmental integrity and freedom of action at the Land level and does, in fact, maintain a sensitive and protective attitude within the Federal Parliament towards Land governments' interests."[10]

10. E.L. Pinney: *Federalism, Bureaucracy and Party Politics in Western Germany,* p.173.

27

STATE STRUCTURE

We have taken note of the fact that Germany has a federal-democratic system with parliamentary form of government. In its federal set up she is bracketed with the United States, Switzerland, Canada, Australia, India etc., despite the fact that her federal set up has been described as 'vertical' or 'centralised'. But in respect of her parliamentary form of government, her set up looks like a curious blending of the English and French governments, though one may also discover some typical features of the German model of parliamentary democracy. Taking lessons from the role of presidency under the Weimer Constitution (first under von Hindenberg and then under Hitler), the authors of the Bonn Constitution have made the President the head of the state with titular position, while actual authority is given to the Chancellor (Prime Minister) acting with his ministers and civil servants. The Government (Chancellor) is accountable to the Bundestag (Parliament), but the Chancellor may advise the President to dissolve the Parliament and hold fresh elections. The position of the Parliament is not very strong, though not very weak too, vis-a-vis the strong position of the Chancellor.

Federal Executive

The Basic Law has assigned state power to the executive, the legislature and the judiciary and together they constitute the democratic structure of the Republic of Germany. The executive has a dual position—nominal authority vested in the President and real authority vested in the Chancellor (and his ministers) accountable to the Bundestag. However, this dual character of the executive should not be identified with the present French system in which the President is the real head of the state and by virtue of that he is more powerful than the Prime Minister. In Germany the President is the titular head of the state, the Chancellor is the real head of the government.

President: The head of the state of Germany is the President. According to Art. 54, he shall be elected without debate by the Federal Convention consisting of the members of the Bundestag and an equal number of members elected by the Diets of the Lander (States) in accordance with the principle of proportional representation. This body shall meet not later than 30 days before the expiration of the term of office of the President or, in the case of premature termination, not later than 30 days after that date. The meeting of this body shall be convened by the President of the Bundestag. After the expiration of a legislative term, this period shall begin from the first meeting of the Bundestag. The candidate receiving the votes of the majority of the members of the Federal Convention shall be declared elected. If such a majority is not obtained by any candidate in two ballots, the candidate receiving the largest number of votes in the next ballot shall be elected. For this election every German shall be eligible who is entitled to vote for the Bundestag elections and has attained the age of 40 years. The term of the office of the President shall be of five years. Re-election for a consecutive term shall be permitted only once.[1]

Some restrictions have been fixed on the office of the President. Art. 55 says that the President may not be a member of the government nor of a legislative body of the Federation or of a Land. He may not hold any other salaried office, nor engage in a trade or an occupation, nor practise a profession, nor belong to the management or the board of directors of an enterprise carried on for profit. He takes the oath of office (Art. 56) whereby he swears to dedicate his efforts to the well being of the German people, enhance its benefits, ward harm from it, uphold and defend the Basic Law and the laws of the Federation and fulfil duties conscientiously, and to do justice to all. Art. 57 says that if the President is prevented from acting, or if his office falls prematurely vacant, his powers shall be exercised by the President of the Bundestag.

The Constitution assigns to the President some representative and integrative functions. These are:

1. It should be noted that the Federal President, who has held two terms consecutively, is re-eligible for election after a break. It is different from the American system where a person cannot avail more than two terms.

1. According to Art. 59, he represents the Federation in its international relations. He concludes treaties with foreign states on behalf of the Federation. He accredits and receives foreign envoys.
2. According to Art. 60, he appoints and dismisses the federal judges, the Federal civil servants, the officers and non-commissioned officers, unless otherwise provided for by law. He exercises the right of pardon in individual cases on behalf of the Federation. He may also delegate these powers to other authorities.
3. When a government is formed, under Art. 63 the President nominates a candidate for the post of the Chancellor. He also appoints and dismisses Federal ministers on the proposals of the Chancellor. In certain cases, as when a candidate for the Chancellorship fails to get majority in the Bundestag, or if the Parliament carries a motion of no-confidence against the Chancellor and the name of his successor is not approved by absolute majority of the chamber, within seven days he can either appoint a new Chancellor, or he may dissolve the Bundestag as happened in 1972 and in 1983.
4. He confers Orders of Merit on persons who have served the country with distinction.
5. The declaration of war must be made by the Bundestag and signed by him, unless the Bundestag is prevented by pressure of time from meeting.
6. He examines legislation in the making to ensure that it is in conformity with the Constitution and finally promulgates laws in the Federal Law Gazette.
7. He has a sort of veto power over Federal and Land legislation. In case he objects to the passing of a bill in the legislature of the Centre or of any State, the matter would be referred to the Federal Constitutional Court. The view of the Court is final. In case the President differs from it, he may either keep quiet, or resign, or invite conditions of his impeachment.

It implies that, like the Presidents of other countries, the President of Germany may be removed by the process of impeachment. Art. 61 lays down that the Bundestag or the Bundesrat may impeach the Federal President before the Federal Constitutional Court for wilful violation of the Basic Law or any other Federal law. This motion of impeachment must be brought forward by at least 1/4 members of the Bundestag or 1/4 votes of the Bundesrat. The decision to impeach shall require a majority of 2/3 members of the Bundestag or of 2/3 members of the Bundesrat The impeachment shall be substantiated by a person commissioned by the impeaching body. If the Federal Constitutional Court finds the Federal President guilty of wilful violation of the Basic Law or of any other federal law, it may declare him to have forfeited his office. After impeachment it may issue an interim order preventing the Federal President from exercising his functions.

Keeping in view all these relevant constitutional provisions and the actual behaviour of the incumbents, it appears that the President of Germany is the head of the state and a symbol of the nation. "Like the Crown in England and the President of Fourth French Republic, he is a kind of 'moral magistrate.' In his own speech and acceptance in 1949, Heuss described the position as that of 'conciliating intermediary'; an office 'elbows' need not be used; one in which he would have friendships to right and left; which would stand above the necessary political battles, to be an arbitral, equilibrating force." According to Christopher S. Allen, the German President "is the head of state, a much weaker position than that of the Chancellor. Like constitutional monarchs in Britain, for example, German Presidents stand above the political fray, which means that their role is more ceremonial than political. However, if there were a political crisis affecting the Chancellor, the President would remain as an overseer of the political process, thus providing continuity in a time of national calamity."[2]

Chancellor and His Ministers: The Federal Government has Chancellor as its head and a number of ministers. According to Art. 63, the Chancellor shall be elected without debate by the Bundestag upon the proposal of the President. The person obtaining the votes of majority of the members of the Bundestag shall be elected and then he must be appointed as the Chancellor by the President. In case the person proposed by the President is not elected within 14 days, the Bundestag may elect a new Chancellor by the votes of more than 1/2 of its members. If no person is elected within this period, a new ballot shall take place without delay in which the person obtaining largest number of votes shall be elected. If the person elected has obtained absolute majority of the votes of the Bundestag, the President must appoint him within 7 days of the election. If the person is elected by simple majority the President may, within 7 days, either

2. C.S. Allen: "Germany" in Mark Kesselman, Joel Krieger and William A. Joseph (eds): *Comparative Politics at the Crossroads*, p.196.

Some Importance Statements

In most liberal democracies (having parliamentary government), the position of the head of the state (President) is largely ceremonial. The Japanese Emperor and the Presidents of Israel and Germany have little power, though each serves an important symbolic role, representing the nation and the regime.

—***Patrick O'Neil***

Unlike the Bundestag and Federal Government, the Federal President has no policy-making function. At home he plays the role of integrator, abroad he represents the Federal Republic of Germany. He also has individual powers conferred on him by the Basic Law. —***Dr. Ilse Staff***

As head of the state, the President represents Germany in international affairs, concluding treaties with other countries and receiving the credentials of foreign ambassadors and envoys. He or she formally appoints and dismisses federal civil servants, federal judges and officers of the Federal Armed Forces and may exercise the right of presidential clemency. He or she participates in the legislative process through the promulgation of laws, the dissolution of Bundestag, and the formal proposal, appointment and dismissal of the Federal Chancellor and the ministers. The political system of Germany assigns the President a non-partisan role, often of a ceremonial nature, with powers that rest largely on the moral authority of the office rather than on political power. An exception is the occurrence of a parliamentary crisis when no candidate can command the support of an absolute majority of Bundestag members. In this case, the President can decide whether the country is to be governed by a minority administration under a Chancellor elected by a plurality of deputies or whether new elections are to be called.

—***German Information Office, Bonn, May 20, 1994.***

appoint him as the Chancellor or dissolve the Bundestag. This arrangement looks similar to one obtaining in France. So it is well remarked: "The President's function, like that of his French counterpart, is, therefore, to employ his skill in finding a government which stands a fair chance of being elected by the Bundestag."[3]

Then, Art. 64 says that the Federal Ministers shall be appointed and dismissed by the Federal President upon the proposal of the Federal Chancellor. The Chancellor and his ministers after being appointed shall take oaths of office and secrecy. Art. 65 says that the Chancellor shall determine and be responsible for the general policy guidelines. Within the limits set by these guidelines, each minister shall conduct the affairs of his department autonomously and on his own responsibility. The Federal Government shall decide matters of differences of opinion among

3. R.G. Neumann; *European and Comparative Government.* p. 421.

ministers. The Chancellor shall conduct the affairs of his government in accordance with the rules of procedure adopted by it and approved by the President. But the power of command over defence forces shall be vested in the Defence Minister. Art. 66 lays down that the Chancellor and his ministers may not hold any other salaried office, nor engage in a trade or occupation, nor practise a profession, nor belong to the management or, without the consent of the Bundestag, to the board of directors of an enterprise carried on for profit.

The key characteristic of the parliamentary form of government is accountability of the executive to the legislature. The parliament may pass a vote of no-confidence and thereby remove the government. The principle of collective responsibility means that all ministers swim and sink together. But in Germany this key characteristic of parliamentary form of government has been modified by two peculiar provisions. First, not the ministers but the Chancellor can be removed by a vote of no-confidence. It is a different matter that in practice it is the head of the ministry who is censured by the parliament for any serious act of commission or omission. Second, the Bundestag may pass a 'constructive vote of no-confidence.'[4] It is a typical arrangement of the Basic Law (Art. 67). It says that the Bundestag can express its lack of confidence in the Chancellor after electing a successor with absolute majority of its members and at the same time requesting the President to dismiss the Chancellor and appoint the new one elected by it. Forty eight hours must elapse between the motion and the election. It is also given that in case a motion of confidence put by the Chancellor is not approved by a majority of the Bundestag, then the President may upon the proposal of the Chancellor dissolve the Bundestag within 21 days. The right to dissolve shall lapse as soon as the Bundestag with the majority of its members elects another Chancellor. Fortyeight hours must elapse between the motion and the vote thereon. The tenure of the Chancellor and of his ministers shall end in any event on the first meeting of a new Bundestag. The exit of the Chancellor would amount to the exit of all ministers. (Art. 69)

4. Perhaps the most significant source of the Chancellor's powers is a constitutional provision called the constructive vote of no-confidence. It means that a Chancellor cannot be removed unless the Bundestag simultaneously elects a new Chancellor. It strengthens the powers of the Chancellor in two ways. First, the Chancellors can more easily reconcile disputes among cabinet officials without threatening their own position. Second, the opposition must come up with concrete and specific alternatives to the existing government, thus preventing confrontation just for the sake of opposition." C.S. Allen, *op. cit.*, p. 196.

Another point of peculiarity about the German government is that its size is considerably smaller as compared to its British and French counterparts and, more than that, most of the ministers are confined to the supervision of the corresponding ministries of the States which actually perform their tasks under the provision of Art. 83 of the Basic Law. We have already made this point clear that in this country most of the work of the Centre is done by the States. At present there are 17 departments as those of foreign affairs, interior, justice, finance, economics, food and agriculture and forestry, intra-German relations, labour and social welfare, defence, youth and families and women and health, transportation, environment and natural protection and reactor safety, post and telecommunications, regional planning and urban development, research and technology, education and science, and economic cooperation. The Chancellor appoints one of his ministers as Deputy Chancellor.

A novel feature of the working of federal ministries may be traced in the fact that much of their work consists in determining the legal responsibility for the performance of certain acts and a great deal of the distribution of the work load is determined by administrative law. This fits in well with the insistence on the legal education of the top bureaucratic personnel. Within each ministry there are several divisions which, in turn, known as *Referate*, are headed by a *Referant* who has a small staff at his disposal and his principal job is the legal determination of who in the Lander administration should do the job. Each division chief is responsible for efficiency within his division. It is quite obvious that this system leaves the bulk of administrative problems to the Lander where the administrative set up is more elaborate and more centralised. It emphasises federal structure of the country, but it also makes tighter the degree of policy-making centralism.

It is clear that the real executive of Germany is the government of the Chancellor. The Constitution has made three special provisions to ensure strong position of the Chancellor. First, he is elected by the absolute majority of the Bundestag and, as such, he has the force of parliamentary support behind him. In case the Parliament desires to pass a vote of no-confidence against him, it must be supplemented with the passing of a confidence motion in favour of some other leader who may be appointed as the Chancellor by the President. Naturally, this peculiar arrangement of the adoption of a constructive vote of no-confidence strengthens the position of the Chancellor. Second, the Chancellor has the power to advise the President to dissolve the Bundestag in case it fails to elect his successor.

Third, in case the Chancellor fails to get confidence vote of the Bundestag, in stead of advising the President to dissolve it, he may request the President (with the consent of the Bundesrat) to declare a state of 'legislative emergency' under Art. 81 of the Basic Law. In this way, he may continue in office for a period of 6 months. Above all, much depends upon the personal qualities and capabilities of the incumbent. In this direction, we may refer to the contribution of the first Chancellor, Konrad Adenauer, who remained in office from 1949 to 1963.

It is now very clear that the Federal Chancellor has a strong position. That is why, the German system of government is referred to as 'Chancellor democracy.' The Chancellor is the only member of government elected by the Parliament and he alone is responsible to it. He determines the guidelines of the government policy. The ministers direct their departments within these guidelines, independently and under their own responsibility. He alone can choose and dismiss his ministers. In times of peace, the commander of the armed forces is his Defence Minister, but once war is declared by the Parliament or by the President, the power of command passes on to him. His office (Federal Chancellory) concerns itself with the general supervision of all policies, the coordination of departmental activities, the securing of necessary information, preparation of cabinet meetings *etc*. It all demonstrates the primacy of the Chancellor in the constitutional system of this country. He "is the master of the main lines of policy, and is entitled to exact conformity to them of his ministers."[5]

Federal Legisature (Diet)

Like other major countries of the world, Germany has a bi-cameral legislature having Bundestag as the popular national chamber and Bundesrat as a chamber of the ambassadors of the Lander (States). As we shall see, the composition and working of the Bundesrat are so peculiar that it becomes a kind of terminological inexactitude to place it in the category of a second chamber. Art. 20 declares that "all state authority emanates from the people. It shall be exercised by the people by means of elections and voting and specific legislative, executive and judicial organs." The Bundestag is the supreme democratic organ by virtue of the fact that it plays a key role in the structure of the state and in forming the political will. In other words, it is the national representative assembly. But the Bundesrat is the institution by means of which the 16 Germany States

5. Herman Finer: *Major Governments of Modern Europe*, p. 513.

participate in the legislative and administrative process of the federal government.

Bundestag: Art. 38 of the Basic Law says that deputies to this chamber shall be elected in general, direct, free, equal, and open elections. They shall be the representatives of the whole people, not bound by the orders and instructions and shall be subject only to their conscience. Any one who has attained the age of 18 years shall be entitled to vote. It is also required that he must have lived in that electoral area for at least three months and not been disqualified by a judicial decision. Anyone who has attained full legal age shall be eligible for election. Till 1969 the minimum age of a candidate for Bundestag elections was 25 years, it was reduced to 21 years in 1972 and then to 18 years in 1974. Thus eligible to stand for elections are persons who have been German subjects for at least one year, are above 18 years of age, and have not been disqualified on the basis of special statutory provisions. Details shall be regulated by a federal law. It is obvious that this chamber personifies the will of the people as expressed in the elections. This reflects the concept of the representative democracy which in a community of millions is regarded as the best means of implementing the principle of self-determination for the people.

The method of composition of the Bundestag is a little complicated. Since the leaders of Germany had the bitter taste of proportional representation system as provided under the Weimer constitution and, at the same time, they very much wanted to retain it, they could evolve some workable formula for their purpose. The electoral law of 10 May, 1949 came as a compromise formula known as the sixty-forty law. Under its terms, sixty per cent of the seats were filled through elections in the single-member constituencies and forty per cent by proportional representation of votes cast in each State. But a new law came into force in 1953 according to which the following arrangement has been made:

1. Fifty per cent of the seats in the Bundestag are filled by general, open, direct and free elections; and the candidate getting largest number of votes in a single-member constituency (*i.e.*, plurality of votes) shall be declared elected. It is first-past-the-post system or majority representation system the kind of which prevails in the parliamentary elections of other countries like United States, Canada, Britain etc.
2. Fifty per cent of the seats are filled by means of proportional representation with list system.

At present it has 663 members.

At the time of election a voter is given a ballot paper having two foils. On one foil he makes his choice and the vote goes to some candidate. On the second foil the list of the parties is given and here he has to mark his preference for a political party that has already notified a list of its candidates. When counting begins, the votes of the first foil are counted and results prepared on the basis of the plurality of votes. This is called upper or higher distribution. The counting of votes of the second foil is done according to Niemeyer method.[6] The names of the candidates finally elected by each party under the PR are simply taken from the top of each party list down in the sequence indicated by the party presenting the list. Thus, the strength of a party's representation in Parliament is determined by the PR and the only effect of the single-member district elections is the internal ratio between directly elected deputies and deputies elected by means of proportional representation with list system. This is called 'lower distribution.' Three important points should be noted here:

1. A party cannot have a seat in the Bundestag unless it either wins at least three seats in the single-member constituencies or secures at least 5% of the total second votes cast in the Federal Republic.
2. It is possible that for a party to have what are known 'overhung' seats when it wins more seats in the single-member constituencies on the first vote than it is entitled to according to the result of the

6. Now Niemeyer method is used, Its formula is that the number of second votes secured by a party should be multiplied by the total number of seats in that State and then that figure is to be divided by the total number of second votes of all parties having polled more than 5%, of all second votes, Percentage is to be drawn and seats are to be allocated to different parties on the basis of full percentage figures, In case some vacancies remain, they are to be filled up on the basis of merit list to be prepared according to rump percentage. In order to make it clear. we may take a hypothetical case. Suppose seats to be tilled are 31 and different parties secure second votes as:

Party	A	18,500 × 31 = 5,63,5007 ÷ 36,900 = 15,542 – 15 seats
Party	B	12,900 × 31 = 3,99,9007 ÷ 36,900 = 10,837 – 10 seats
Party	C	1,900 × 31 = 58,9007 ÷ 36,900 = 1,569 – 1 seat
Party	D	3,600 × 31 = 1,11,6007 ÷ 36,900 = 3,024 – 3 seats

In this calculation 29 seats are filled up and then 1 seat goes to B and the other to C according to their rank in subsumed digits. It is also possible that the rump percentage of a party is taken to some other Land or Lander and then a seat is given to it after lumping its rump percentages.

second-vote calculation. The Bundestag has a strength of 663 elected members, but this figure may be marginally revised. If a party wins more direct mandates in the single-member constituencies, then it would be entitled to them by its Land list share, it keeps those so-called additional seats.

Art. 39 of the Basic Law says that the Bundestag shall be elected for a term of four years. The new election shall be held at the earliest 45 and at the latest 47 months after the beginning of the legislative term. If the House is dissolved, the new election must be held within 60 days. It shall assemble at the latest on the thirteenth day after the election. It shall determine the termination and resumption of its meetings. Its president may convene it at an earlier date if there is a requisition by the President of the Federation or the Federal Chancellor or by 1/3 members of the House. Art. 40 says that it shall elect its president, vice-presidents and secretaries, it shall also draw up its rules of procedure. The president shall exercise the proprietary and police powers in the building of the House and no search or seizure of premises can be made without his prior permission. The president of the House is like the Speaker of other countries, though his position and powers are much more than them. There is a body of some vice-presidents (now four according to usage) who with him constitute a presidium. This is the highest body of the German parliament that is constituted after the election. It is another written rule that this body, while being non-partisan, should at the same time reflect the relative strength of the political parties represented in the Bundestag. It has thus become a tradition for a member of the largest parliamentary group to be elected as its President.

Both in terms of protocol and also politically, the high rank and status of the president are emphasised in a number of ways. As a representative of the legislature, he is next in rank to the Federal President in order of precedence. Of political significance is the fact that all bills and other items submitted to Parliament by the Federal Government (and the Bundesrat) are addressed to him. This stresses the precedence of legislative over the executive authority. He is the recipient of all submissions from the Bundestag itself or addressed to it. Last, he and his four vice-presidents are elected for the entire duration of the legislative term that normally lasts for four years and thus, in principle, cannot be removed. His three main functions are: First, he presides over the session of the House and implements the Rules of Procedure in order to conduct the session in a fair and orderly manner. Second, he is the head of the Bundestag administration in which capacity he takes important decisions on personnel matters together with his vice-presidents. Last, he has proprietary and police powers to protect the dignity of the House.

Apart from the 'presidium' there is another body called the Council of Elders. It includes the president, vice-presidents and 23 other members appointed by the parliamentary groups in proportion to their relative strengths in the chamber. In addition to a number of administrative responsibilities, this body performs three important functions. First, it draws up the work programme of the Bundestag and the agenda of its plenary meetings. Settling the question as to which subject is to be discussed when and at what length can be a preliminary political decision of great importance. Such a decision should be taken with the cooperation of the members of the House and so in the event of any dispute, the matter shall be settled by the House. Second, it works out an understanding at the beginning of each legislative term, among the parliamentary groups on the distribution of committee chairmanships and vice-chairmanships, to be affected in accordance with the principle of proportional representation and the relative strength of the parliamentary groups. Last, it discusses and, where possible, settles amicably points at issue with regard to the dignity and rights of the House or the interpretation of the Rules of Procedure. It should be added here that it has no power to replace the authority of the plenary session: it is a kind of steering committee that relieves the plenary session of many time-consuming formal decisions; at the same time, it serves as an effective channel of communication among the parliamentary groups and between them and the presidium.

In order to ensure that the Bundestag works in a democratic way, some important arrangements have been made. Art. 42 says that its meetings shall be public, but public audience may be prohibited by a decision of the House adopted by 2/3 majority on a motion put by the Federal Government or by 1/10 members of the House. Moreover such a decision shall be taken by the House in *camera*. All decisions are to be taken by simple majority unless provided otherwise. True and accurate reports on the public meetings of the House and its committees shall not give rise to any liability. Art. 43 of the Basic Law lays down that the House and its committees may demand the presence of the Chancellor or any of his ministers. The members of the Federal Government and of the Bundesrat as well as persons commissioned by them shall have access to the sessions of the House or its committees and have the chance to speak there.

The functions and powers of the Bundestag are as under:

1. According to Art. 54, it takes part in the election of the Federal President.
2. According to Art. 44, it has the right and upon a motion of 1/4 of its members the duty to set up a committee of investigation which shall take the requisite evidence at public hearings. The public may be excluded. The results of the criminal procedure shall apply *mutatis mutandis to* the taking of evidence. The privacy of post and telecommunications shall remain unaffected. Courts and administrative authorities shall be required to provide administrative assistance. The decisions of committees of investigation shall not be subject to judicial consideration. The courts shall be free to evaluate and judge the facts on which the investigation is based.
3. It has power to control the executive. The Federal Chancellor is responsible to it. As such, it may express lack of confidence in his government and then elect someone else to head the federal government. (Art. 67) The Federal President must appoint the newly elected person as the Chancellor (Prime Minister). If 1/4 members of the House put a motion to investigate defence matters, it can be done. (Art. 45) It is also given that a Defence Commissioner of the House shall be appointed to safeguard the basic rights and to assist it in exercising parliamentary control.
4. Under Art. 61, it may initiate impeachment proceedings against the Federal President in the Federal Constitutional Court.
5. It passes bills which become laws after they are passed by the Bundesrat.
6. It elects 8 judges of the Federal Constitutional Court and with Bundesrat sends a joint delegation to the North Atlantic Assembly, the unofficial association of the members of the NATO community.

The Basic Law also says about the indemnity and immunity of the members of the House. Art. 46 makes it clear that a deputy may not at any time be prosecuted in the courts or subjected to disciplinary action or otherwise called to account outside the Bundestag for a vote cast or a statement made by him in the House or any of its committees, though it shall not apply to defamatory insults. A deputy may not be called to account or arrested for a punishable offence except with the permission of the House unless he is apprehended in the commission of the offence or in the course of the following day. The permission of the House shall also be necessary for any other restriction on the personal liberty of a deputy or for the initiation of proceedings against a deputy under Art. 11 for the abuse of his basic freedoms. Any criminal proceedings or any other proceedings under Art. 18 against a deputy, any detention or any other restriction on his personal liberty shall be suspended upon the request of the House. Then, Art. 47 lays down that the deputies may refuse to give evidence concerning persons who have confided facts to them in their capacity as deputies, or to whom they have confided facts in such capacity as well as concerning these facts themselves. To the extent that this right to refuse to give evidence exists, no seizure of documents shall be permissible. Last, Art. 48 guarantees to each deputy leave necessary for his election campaign and entitlement to remuneration adequate to ensure their independence. We have already noted the fact that Art. 38 ensures freedom of the deputies to act according to their 'conscience'.

Bundesrat: It is an institution having no parallel in any other country of the world. To call it a second chamber would be either to make a superficial statement or to commit an error of judgment. Its existence owes to the adherence of the German people to their historical traditions. Since it is a body of the 'ambassadors' of the units of the German federation, it may be designated as a council of states, though its popular English equivalent is 'Federal Council.' According to Art. 51 of the Basic Law, it shall consist of the members of the governments of the Lander who have the power to appoint and recall them. Other members of such governments may act as substitutes. It is also given that each Land shall have at least three votes, but four votes if its population exceeds two million inhabitants, 5 votes in case its population exceeds six million inhabitants, and 6 votes if the population exceeds 7 million inhabitants. Each Land may delegate as many members as it has votes, but the votes of each Land may be cast as a bloc by members present or their substitutes. At present, it has 69 members.

Then, Art. 52 of the Basic Law says that the Bundesrat shall elect its president who shall convene its session. He would also convene session when it is so demanded either by the Federal Government or by at least two States. It shall take its decisions with the majority of its votes. It shall draw up its rules of procedure. Its meetings shall be open, though the public may be excluded. Other members or persons commissioned by the Land governments may serve on its committees. Finally, according to Art. 53, the members of the Federal Government shall have the right and on demand the duty to attend its committees' meetings. They must be heard at any time. It must be currently kept informed by the Federal Government of the conduct of affairs. The presidentship of this body rotates annually among the members on the basis of the demographic make up of the Lander.

The Basic Law ascribes to the President of the Bundesrat a special duty outside the sphere of his own office. He assumes the authority of the Federal President if the latter is prevented from conducting the affairs of his office. In this case, the president of this body is the Acting President of Germany and, as such, he is often referred to as the 'second man' of the State. He represents Germany in all Bundesrat matters. His main duty is to call and chair the plenary sessions of the chamber. He is assisted by a body of three vice-presidents who with him form the 'Presidium. It is responsible for drafting the budget of this body and to deal with internal matters that donot require a plenary decision. Adjunct to the 'presidium' is the Permanent Advisory Council consisting of the plenipotentiaries of all the States. As a rule, they are cabinet ministers in their State governments. It keeps itself in touch with the conduct of affairs as done by the Federal Ministers and then to inform their respective State governments.

The pecular features of the Bundesrat may be enumerated as under:

1. The function of this body is a manifestation of the distribution of powers as well as of the checks and balances contained in the German federal system. In general, it can be said that in the distribution of the tasks of government between the Federation on the one hand and its constituent States on the other, legislation is largely a federal responsibility and administration is generally a matter left for the States. Thus, this body gives the States a kind of compensation for the lack of their own legislative responsibility in many areas and a say in the formulation of administrative guidelines they themselves will have to implement.
2. As such, this body has three main functions. First, it incorporates the political idea and administrative experience of the States in federal legislation and administration. Second, it protects the interests of the States at the federal level. Third, like other federal institutions, it bears responsibility for the Republic of Germany as a whole. In the exercise of these functions, it helps to shape federal policies as a counterweight to the Bundestag and the Cabinet but, at the same time, also as a link between the Centre and the States.

Some Important Statements

In Germany, although the lower chamber (the Bundestag) is in most cases legislatively dominant, the upper chamber (the Bundesrat) enjoys considerable veto power in relation to constitutional questions and matters related to the *Lander*. When disputes occur, they are referred to the joint Bundestag-Bundesrat conciliation committee, the members of which are drawn from the two chambers in equal proportion. —***Andrew Heywood***

The Bundesrat is the constitutional institution of the Federation by which the *Lander* participate in the legislative process and administration of the Federation and in matters concerning the European Union. It is a significant feature of the federal system with the capacity to decentralise public authority; it highlights the political and other objectives of the *individual Lander*, which do not necessarily always concur with the interests of the Federation. —***Dr. Ilsa Staff***

As the upper chamber of the legislative branch, the Bundesrat occupies a position quite different than either the US Senate, or the British House of Lords. The Bundesrat is the mechanism that makes the federal system work. It is responsible for the distribution of powers between national and state levels and grants to the states the right to implement federal laws. It is the point of intersection for the National and State governments. —***Christopher S. Allen***

3.. Membership of the Bundesrat is not connected with parliamentary immunity or indemnity. In keeping with the German constitutional tradition, the members of the Bundesrat have a special right to attend the session of the Bundestag or of its committees and to speak there at any time. But this privilege is not available to the members of the Bundestag to attend the session of the Bundesrat or of its committees. One person cannot be a member of both the Houses at the same time. If a member of the Bundesrat is elected to the Bundestag, he must inform the president of this body within an appropriate time as to where he desires to be. The members of this body are not paid for their work in Bonn. They are given free facilities of travel and some fixed allowance to meet daily expenses.

4. In voting the members of this body are bound by the decisions of their State governments. It is not the position of the individual member of this body but rather that of the State represented in it. It is clear that the members of this body donot have a free mandate. As members of the State governments, they are themselves involved in determining how the State government would cast its vote. Each State casts its vote as a bloc. Voting is by show of hands and all decisions are taken by the majority of votes.

5. A characteristic of the meeting of this body is the lack of parliamentary bluster. No matter how different the standpoints may be, there is a strong emphasis on objective and business-like communication. Interruptions are rare; expressions of displeasure or applause are not customary. Members tend to work briskly. It meets for its public sessions on Fridays 'at intervals of at least three weeks.'
6. Since the members of this body are not elected, it does not have a legislative term as such. In constitutional parlance it is a permanent body that changes as State elections take place. It means that the State elections, which are held at different times, always have country-wide political significance since whenever a State electorate determines the composition of State government and State assembly, it indirectly determines as to who would represent the State in this body.
7. Like Bundestag, the Bundesrat may initiate impeachment proceedings against the Federal President in the Federal Constitutional Court.
8. Like Federal Cabinet and Bundestag, the Bundesrat has the right to initiate legislation. A resolution to this effect must be passed first in its plenary session. The chamber votes on a proposal submitted by one or a number of States. The bill is then submitted to the cabinet for assessment. The cabinet is required to send the proposed bill with its assessment to the Bundestag within three months.
9. Most of the bills are introduced by the Federal cabinet in the Bundestag. The Bundesrat has the 'first say' in the parliamentary treatment of the 'executive bills', since the government is required to submit its proposal directly to the Bundesrat for assessment. The experience the States have in the implementation of the laws is incorporated into the federal legislation in this 'initial run-through'. In this context the executive governments of the States conduct an intensive dialogue on specific issues with the executive government at the federal level. The Bundesrat's check-and-balance function in the federal system of government is clearly manifested here.
10. In its committees the Bundesrat assesses draft bills from every possible standpoint, *i.e.*, in terms of constitutionality, technical expertise, finances and political factors. Quite often changes, additions or alternatives are proposed. In many cases the result of the assessment is 'no objection'. In case the Bundesrat rejects a

draft bill, then the cabinet may introduce it in the Bundestag anyway after formulating its 'counter-statement'. In such a situation, the draft bill with Bundesrat's initial statement and cabinet's counter-statement shall come to the Bundestag. In case the Bundesrat is not in agreement with the stand of the Bundestag in passing that bill, it may apply for the Mediation Committee having members of both chambers within a period of three week.[7]

11. Bills may be divided into two categories keeping in view the veto power of the Bundesrat. It has absolute veto power in the case of legislation that has a special bearing on the interests of the States. Such a bill cannot become law unless it gives its express approval.[8] Even if the Mediation Committee reports in favour, the bill dies if it is not acceptable to the Bundesrat. In this category three kinds of bills may be put: (*i*) bills of constitutional amendment requiring approval by 2/3 majority of the chamber, (*ii*) bills affecting finances of the States as income tax, value-added tax, motor vehicles tax, and (*iii*) bills that affect the administrative sovereignty of the States. It applies where, for example, federal law prescribes certain jurisdictional arrangements, forms, time limits, administrative fees or types of mail delivery. All such bills are known as 'consent bills'. In the second category we may put 'objection bills'. Here the veto of the Bundesrat is qualified. After the conclusion of the mediation proceedings, the Bundesrat may file its objections within two weeks. Then, the Bundestag will have to subject that bill to another reading. If the Bundestag does not share the reservations of the Bundesrat, it can override the objection by the same kind of majority (absolute or two-thirds) as has been done in the Bundesrat. Thus, by over-riding

7. This committee is different from the Joint Committee having 2/3 members of the Bundestag and 2/3 members of the Bundesrat to deal with plans of Federal Government in respect of a state of defence under Art. 53 (*a*) of the Basic Law. The Mediation Committee may only make a proposal; it has no decision-making powers as regards the contents of bill. However, it has become an important body in the legislative process. It has been called upon to mediate in connection with about every eighth bill. It has called upon to think that in most of the controversial cases it is able to work out a compromise. *Facts about Germany*, p. 102.

8. The 'absolute veto power' of the Bundesrat covers bills seeking amendment of the Constitution, changes in the boundary lines of States, regulation of the execution of federal laws by the governments of the States, the enlargement of federal administration by the creation of new agencies of direct administration, fiscal legislation and for the disposition of property belonging to the former Reich.

the objection of the Bundesrat, the Bundestag may have that bill signed into law and then promulgated.

12. The role of the Bundesrat in federal administration is less conspicuous but often more immediately tangible. The Federal Ministers are empowered to issue ordinances or detailed regulations of considerable political importance. The approval of Bundesrat is required. In case it recommends some modification in that order or ordinance, the Federal Minister should honour it.
13. It performs some other important tasks also. For instance, half of the members of the Federal Constitutional Court are appointed by it and the other half by the Bundestag. A 2/3 majority in a plenary meet is required for a Bundesrat appointment. It can institute proceedings on questions regarding constitutionality and present its standpoint on the proceedings before the Federal Constitutional Court.
14. It has some controlling powers in the international sphere also. The German law ratifying the Treaties establishing the European Communities obliges the Cabinet to keep the Bundestag and the Bundesrat informed about developments in the European Economic Community (European Union). It attempts to promote international cooperation through contacts with foreign participants. It also maintains close contact with European Parliament. The Bundestag and the Bundesrat send a joint delegation to the North Atlantic Assembly.

After seeing this, we may form a strong impression that the Bundesrat "does not fall into any of the patterns of bi-cameral legislatures. It is not the equal of the Bundestag, but it has considerable power. It is both a legislative and an administrative body. It is a part of parliament, but it is also a council of ambassadors whose members represent other administrations."[9] It acts as a counterweight to executive and legislative power at the federal level and at the same time as a link between federal and state governments. So it is commented: "The key organ in adjusting and regulating relation between the Bund and the Lander, and at the same time of the distinctive mechanisms in the German federal structure-is the Bundesrat or Federal Council. It is not a simple second chamber. It has clearly defined constitutional rights and can effectively exert pressure on

9. Neumann, *op. cit.*, p. 437.

federal politics and policies. It is important to note that Bundesrat is completely independent of the federal government."[10]

Legislative Process

Art 76 of the Basic Law lays down that a bill shall be introduced in the Bundestag by the Federal Government (Chancellor and his Ministers), or by its members, or by the Bundesrat. We have already taken note of Art. 50 which says that the Lander shall participate through the Bundesrat in the legislation and administration of the Federation. It is also provided that a government bill must first be introduced in the Bundesrat which has to give its comments within three weeks and after that it must be introduced in the Bundestag. The Bundesrat may either approve the draft bill, or return it with its 'comments' and when the Federal government introduces it in the Bundestag, the copy of the bill must be accompanied by the 'statement' of the Bundesrat and of the 'counter-statement' of the Government. The purpose of this procedure is to involve the Lander in the process of legislation from the very outset as well as to draw the attention of the Bundestag to their suggestions and objections in good time.

As happens in other democratic countries, so here passage of a bill requires three readings and the provision of a joint conference committee is also there to sort out matters of difference between the Bundestag and the Bundesrat. We may describe different stages of legislation as follows:

First Reading: It begins with the introduction of the bill in the Bundestag. A discussion over the general principles of the bill is held. No serious discussion over the details of the bill takes place, nor any amendment is moved until the bill is of a crucial nature and the partes in the chamber have serious reservations about its provisions. After a favourable vote, the bill is referred to some 'committee' where it is subjected to a detailed and serious examination.

Second Reading: The fate of a bill is determined in the deliberations of the committee. At this stage amendments may be moved to the extent of rechanging the whole bill. Then, it comes to the chamber with the report of the committee. A vote in the house terminates the discussion of each general topic. The members of the opposition often put some alternative

10. David Childs and Jeffrey Johnson: *West Germany: Politics and Society.* pp. 41-42.

proposals so as to amend the bill which may be accepted or rejected by the majority of votes. It should be added here that only international treaties must be discussed and decided without amendment.

Third Reading: When a bill is cleared by the house, it comes up again for the last or third reading. It begins with the discussion of the general principles of the bill followed by a detailed discussion of its component parts. Even at this stage amendments may be considered if they are seconded by 10 members. A decision of the House then clears the passage of the bill. We may take note of the point here that this stage is different from one we have seen in the cases of British and American legislative processes where third reading is a formality.

However, in a study of the legislative process of this country, three important points should be noted. First, this process may be considerably speeded up by the unanimous vote of the house whereby all the three readings may be rushed through within a span of few hours. The debate may be curtailed by the decision of the Council of Elders or a member may not be allowed to speak for more than an hour unless so sanctioned by a resolution of the house. In such a case the rules of procedure of the house may be relaxed or adjusted upon as per the decision of the house. Second, in the event of differences between the two chambers, a mediation committee is to meet. As per Art 77 (*a*) of the Basic Law, it shall have equal members of both chambers. The rules of procedure of the Bundestag as approved by the Bundesrat shall apply when this committee meets. But at this stage the members of the Bundesrat would not be bound by any restrictions, though one may easily calculate the political consequences of a member of the Bundesrat going against the wishes of his State government. The discussion over the bill in this committee has been called 'fourth reading' in view of the fact that now any kind of change in the bill is a possibility. It is expected that the verdict of the committee shall be acceptable to both the houses and, as such, the controversy would come to an end. But it is not necessary that the Bundesrat in each and every case may concede. The Bundesrat may have its upper hand in the cases of certain bills signifying its absolute veto power.

Last and the most important situation is related to the declaration of the state of 'legislative emergency' under Art. 81 of the Basic Law. It is true that the authors of the Bonn Constitution have made no provision for emergency powers of the head of the state (as was done under the Weimer Constitution and whereby Hitler could go to any extent after making the

Enabling Act of 1934), a curious and involved residue of the situation still persists. If the Federal Chancellor has failed to secure confidence of the Bundestag, and if the Bundestag has failed to choose Chancellor's successor after passing a vote of no-confidence against him, and if the Bundestag has failed to pass a bill that the government has declared 'urgent', then the Federal Government (not the Chancellor alone) may advise the Federal President to declare a state of legislative emergency with the concurrence of the Bundesrat. This period would last six months. Now the Government may have a law (even if the bill is rejected by the Bundestag) in force with the consent of the Bundesrat. If the same bill moved by the Government is not passed within 28 days of its reintroduction, it shall be treated as passed by the house in case it is assented to by the Bundesrat.[11] Moreover, during this period any other bill rejected by the Bundestag may become a law in the same manner within a period of 6 months after the first declaration of the state of legislative emergency. But some safeguards have also been provided. First, the consent of the Bundesrat is essential for the making of any law. Second, the period of emergency cannot go beyond six months if the same Chancellor continues in office. Last, the bill must not deal with constitutional amendment, repeal or suspension of the Constitution, in part or full.

Committee System

Every legislature acts with the help of its committees for the sake of having a detailed and thorough discussion of the bills by the 'expert' members of the house as far as possible. It saves time of the house as well. These committees are formed in proportion to the party-wise strength of the house. At present Bundestag has 21 committees—on foreign affairs, internal affairs, petitions, sports, law, finance, scrutiny of elections and immunity and rules of procedure, budget, economic affairs, food and agriculture and forestry, labour affairs, defence, youth and family affairs and women and health, transport, post and tele-communications, regional planning and building and urban development, intra-German relations, research and technology, education and science, economic cooperation and environment, nature conservation and nuclear safety. There are 14

11. If there is a dispute over the question whether a bill or a treaty requires the express consent of the Bundesrat or not, it can be decided by the Federal Constitutional Court.

committees in the Bundesrat—on agriculture, labour and social policy, foreign affairs, European Community questions, finance, intra-German relations, domestic affairs, youth and family and health, cultural affairs, legal affairs, urban development and housing, transport and postal affairs, defence, and economic affairs.

It is a fact that participation in the activities of these committees accounts for the major part of the work of the members. It can, at any rate, be said that every item which reaches the plenary session for a final decision has already been discussed at length in some committees and, as such, the plenary sittings often appear to be routine exercises. Surprise decisions are rare. Statistics show that from 1949 to 1987, while the Bundestag had about 2,200 plenary sittings, its committees had about 26,100 sittings. Committee consultations have done a great deal to ensure that specialised issues are submitted to a careful and expert analysis in the Bundesrat, thus guaranteeing an effective check on the role of the federal executive.

Federal Judiciary

In Germany the administration of justice is divided between the federal and state governments. Judicial power is exercised by the judges who act independently in their area of activity. The system affords complete legal protection through independent branches of judiciary. Apart from the ordinary courts of civil and criminal law, there are also administrative, labour, social and taxation courts. At the head of each branch is a federal court, the lower courts being courts of the federal States. The main responsibility of the federal Supreme Court is to ensure uniform interpretation of law. But, for our purpose, the Federal Constitutional Court with its seat at Karlsruhe has a significance of its own by virtue of having the power of judicial review having no counterpart in German constitutional history.

This Court has two senates with 8 judges in each, half of whom are elected by the Bundestag and half by the Bundesrat for a term of 12 years. They cannot be re-elected. It has original jurisdiction to settle constitutional disputes between the Federation and the Lander or between the Land governments. It reviews Federal and Land laws and may declare them unconstitutional in case they are not compatible with the Basic Law of Germany. It may also invalidate a law of the Land in case it is inconsistent with the law of the Bund (Centre). The people may also move this Court for the protection of their fundamental rights. It may rule that a particular political party is undemocratic because of working against the constitutional system of the country. Besides, the Court may also look into the validity of other matters like impeachment of the Federal President or of a judge, loss of fundamental rights by a person in the event of their gross abuse, continued validity of an older law, compatibility of a Land law with Land constitution (if so provided), suppression of a political party in the case of its undemocratic behaviour, rights and duties of the Federation and the Lander pertaining to their mutual relationships in administrative matters. The Federal President may also seek advisory opinion of the Court before expressing his reservations in certifying a bill passed by the Bundestag.

Ever since its creation, the Federal Constitutional Court has achieved an excellent record that greatly exceeds its expectations. It has not hesitated in acting vigorously and courageously in spite of the fact that it has no identical historical precedent. In the much discussed South-West Case (1952), it did not hesitate in declaring an executive order unconstitutional, because in delegating this right to the executive, the Bundestag had failed to define the limits and purposes of such delegation precisely as required under Art. 80 of the Basic Law. In this way, the Court honoured the principle of American constitutional law that 'what is delegated cannot be further delegated'. It reminded the parliament of its constitutional obligations and helped to curtail sharply any possible return to a Weimer type of the rule by decree. In 1952 it ruled in favour of the unconstitutionality of the Socialist Reich Party (a neo-Nazi body) and so it ruled in the case of the Communist Party in 1956. In this way, its judgment could suppress two political parties of the country in the name of their undemocratic or unconstitutional character. It also ruled in favour of the constitutional validity of 5% debarring clause relating to the representation of political parties in the federal and state parliaments. It is well observed that the leading decisions of the Court "have revealed one of the brightest spots in the constitutional fabric of the new German state."[12]

12. Neumann, *op, cit.*, p. 452.

28

POLITICAL PARTIES AND PRESSURE GROUPS

The party system is one of the indispensable features of a democratic political system in modern times. In other words, it means that every democratic system has a party system of its own, though we may also take note of its peculiar distinctive features in each case. However, the noticeable point in this connection is that while in other countries party system is a result of conventional growth, in Germany it is a gift of the fundamental law of the land. This is the first instance of its kind the repetition of which may now be noted in the case of other countries like France under the constitution of 1958 and in South Africa under the constitution of 1996. It shows the commitment of the architects of the Constitution to a full-fledged democratic system along the lines of their country's historical traditions.

Political Parties

Though a country notorious for having the traditions of an authoritarian order, now democracy appears well established in Germany. It may be noticed in the high voter turn out, a stable and responsible multi-party political system, and a healthy civic culture.[1] Many observers "now believe that broad-based political participation is part of the fabric of German political life."[2] A German writer proudly declares that now this country "is primarily a representative democracy. Democratic formation of the political will of the people is the on-going process of reconciling individuals' ever-changing social interests so as to assist state institutions in taking decisions which are socially acceptable."[3] Participation is central

1. G.A. Almond and Sidney Verba (eds.): *The Civic Culture Revisted* (1989).
2. Christopher S. Allen: "Germany" in Kesselman, Krieger and Joseph (eds.) *Comparative Politics at the Crossroards*, p. 223.
3. Dr. Ilse Staff: "Introduction" in *the Basic Law for the Federal Republic of Germany*, Press and Information Office of the Federal Government, Bonn, 1998, p.17.

Some Important Statements

Germany has often been called a party democracy, because its parties are so important in shaping state policy. However, criticism of the major parties surfaced in the late 1980s and early 1990s due to several political and financial scandals involving members of all three of the major parties. Such developments have provided increased opportunities for the new parties and could possibly disturb the relatively 'tame' political party landscape. ***—Christopher S. Allen***

(1) Political parties shall participate in the formation of the political will of the people. They may be freely established. Their internal organisation must conform to democratic principles. They must publicly account for their assets and for the sources and use of their funds. (2) Parties that by reason of their aims or the behaviour of their adherents, seek to undermine or abolish the free democratic basic rights or to endanger the existence of the Federal Republic of Germany shall be unconstitutional. The Federal Constitutional Court shall rule on the question of unconstitutionality. ***—Art. 21 of the Basic Law for the Republic of Germany***

All liberal democracies uphold the rights of free speech and association. Yet in some countries, such as Germany, the democratic constitution outlaws anti-democratic activity, meaning that the state can ban political parties that are seen as hostile to democracy. ***—Patrick O'Neil***

to liberal democracy; it is hard to imagine a regime as democratic, if people have no say in politics. However, it does not mean that the process of political participation should not be regulated by laws and rules. It is for this resaon that the German constitution provides for "a ban on political parties that are hostile to democracy."[4]

The party system of Germany has its distinctive features that may be enumerated as under:

1. It is of recent origin. Although the history of party system in this country is fairly old, it demonstrates sudden breaks from the past. The Weimer constitution of 1919 permitted the role of many political parties, but with the assumption of power by the Nazis in 1933, democratic party system virtually came to an end.
2. The authors of the Bonn Basic Law very carefully made provisions for its regulated operation. Since a political party is an association of the people, though of a particular kind, Art. 9 of the Basic Law makes it very clear that all Germans shall have the right to form associations, but their activities should conform to the constitutional order or the concept of international understanding. In this

4. Patrick O' Neil: *Essentials of Comparative Politics*, p- 173.

connection, Art. 21 has its own importance which says: "The political parties shall participate in the forming of the political will of the people. They may be freely established. Their internal organisation must conform to democratic principles. They must publicly account for the sources and the use of their funds and for their assets."

3. The Constitution empowers the state to make necessary laws or issue decrees to regulate the working of political parties. Germany has a detailed law on political parties. Moreover, Art. 21 also empowers the Federal Constitutional Court to suppress a political party in case its aims and activities are undemocratic or unconstitutional. "Parties which by reason of their aims or the behaviour of their adherents, seek to impair or abolish the free democratic basic order or to endanger the existence of Germany shall be unconstitutional." It is in pursuance of this provision that in a judgement on 2 October, 1952 the Court ruled out the validity of the Socialist Reich Party (a Nazi-type party) and then in another judgment on 17 August, 1956, it did the same in the case of the Communist Party.
4. Though Germany looks like a multi-party state, it cannot have a multiplicity of parties whose notorious instances can be seen in other democratic countries of the world. The law on party system has made it mandatory that a party shall be entitled to have a seat in the national legislature in case it wins at least three seats in the direct elections of the Bundestag in single-member constituencies or at least 5% of the votes polled in the elections in the whole country. The result is that many 'splinter' organisations have gone out of existence and only four parties have been in the field since 1957—Christian Democratic Union/Christian Socialist Union, Social Democratic Party and Free Democratic Party. Recently a small party (The Greens) has also appeared. Moreover, the fact that the CDU/CSU act as 'sister parties' make a peerless case of the two-in-one. The Greens are a very small party. As such, it would not be wrong to say that Germany has a bi-party system of its own kind.
5. The 'iron law of oligarchy', as laid down by Robert Michels, has its application everywhere, but it has its outspoken form in Germany. The political parties like CDU/CSU, SDP and FDP are controlled by small groups of professional party bureaucrats or leaders of great influence. Moreover, the fact of 'influence' is not sustained by the element of wealth, political astuteness or charisma on the evidence of party regularity and seniority. It is for this reason that Adenauer

dominated the CDU and Schumacher had the same control over the SDP for a fairly long time.

6. The British political parties are known for having sharp differences on matters of policies and pragrammes. This is not so with the American party system where the two parties have differences over issues only. 'Ideological similarity but issue conflict' is the characteristic of the American party system. The party system of Germany stands somewhere between the two. Here the parties may be differentiated on the grounds of their policies and programmes, but the line of cleavage is not very sharp. It is a different thing that different parties are generally associated with different social classes as the CDU with business and agriculture and the SDP with labour, or the CSU has its operation in the region of Bavaria, or the Greens sustain their movement on the stress for environmental protection and natural conservation. The reason behind it is the pragmatism and dynamism of the German people. Instead of fighting over ideological premises, the leaders of German political parties show their concern with problems of immediate national importance.
7. Above all, the party system works according to the traditions of the German people. They regard political participation as a matter of civic obligations and not as a political luxury or rivalry. It is for this reason that they dislike both the extreme rightists and the extreme leftists. It may also be admitted that they welcome the role of political parties having a moderate character, as a matter of indispensability to their system under the obtaining conditions of modern democracy. Now we may have a brief study of the major political parties of Germany and their policies and programmes.

CDU/CSU: The Christian Democratic Union is the first interdenominational, middle-class, catch-all party in Germany. Right from the outset, it has regarded itself as a "people's party" with a programme aimed at the public weal, and representing no particular interests. The word 'union' in the name of this party is intended to outwardly emphasise the integrating factor-especially in regard to religious denomination.

The basic principles of Christianity, the idea of a free market economy and the firm integration of Germany in the Western world still constitute the basis of its policies and programmes. All drafts approved since that time are variations or modifications of these fundamental convictions. The 'Mannheim Declaration' of 1975, for example, reasserting its commitment to a free market economy was supplemented by the 'New Social Question'. It is based on the assumption that a changed conflict situation has arisen between organised and unorganised social interests resulting in an unbalanced distribution of social burdens. It objective is to concern itself in greater measure with those groups whose involvement in economic and social developments in Germany has not been sufficiently appreciated, *e.g.*, working women, pensioners, foreign workers and disabled persons. In this connection, it has appealed to the general public sense of responsibility and solidarity vis-a-vis fellow citizens, the dominance of the personal entitlement attitude must be done away with and state tutelage of individuals overcome. It has also laid stress on need to safeguard fundamental pattern of the democratic set up of the country with reinforcement of state security services and improving legal system. In the economic field, it desires that the state should boost private initiative, recreate optimum basic conditions for entrepreneurial activity and provide tax legislation that would stimulate investments.

The programme of this party in the international sphere is very attractive. It includes integration of the West whilst continuing to honour agreements concluded by Germany with the countries of Eastern Europe. Special emphasis is attached to the consolidation of world peace by intensifying East-West dialogue and a committed attitude favouring developing countries in the North-South dialogue. In order to realise detente in Europe, a balance of military power must be achieved between the East and the West.

The Christian Socialist Union is the Bavarian wing of the CDU. It is an autonomous state party of Bavaria. It has an agreement with the CDU whereby the latter should restrict itself organisation-wise to the other federal States and that the CSU, in return, fields all candidates in Bavaria. It has consented to the combined parliamentary group (CDU/CSU) on the condition that the CDU must stick to the 'Federalism Clause' and, as such, the parliamentary group would not consent to any change in the Basic Law which the CSU regards as violative of the federal structure. It desires a 'restructured economy'—a global state-owned economy on the basis of property ownership committed to Christian social ideals. The fundamental concept of social reform, however, was rapidly replaced by a liberal economic concept, supplemented by domestic and legal ideas of a conservative nature. It attaches particular importance to the Christian system of values as the basis of all politics, representing an accentuated counter programme to communist and socialist ideology. One central component of its foreign policy programme is the demand for a European confederation which conforms with its demand to reinforce the federalistic principle at all levels. The most striking point is that the two parties act in combination and never permit any iota of difference to reach the point of split.

SDP: The second place is occupied by the Social Democratic Party that emerged on the scene in Germany under the leadership of Kurt Schumacher and had the chance to be in power during 1969-82. In the period before 1959 it was a reformist, anti-capitalist and anti-communist workers party. But, thereafter, it was transformed into a public weal-oriented, social reformist people's party. It categorically rejected any form of collaboration with communist and bourgeois parties. It assumed that the post-war Germany would provide socialism with an opportunity to win through, allowing democracy to be consolidated on a permanent basis. Its socialism meant the socialisation of major industries, expansion of state planning with the inclusion of the free market elements of competition and the setting up of regularised management by the employees. It presses for the realisation of democratic socialism as an alternative both to capitalism and communism. It called for reflection on national policy and efforts to achieve a break-through in the right to national self-assertion. In quite unmistakable terms, it stood for a united Germany and rejected Adenauer's West-oriented policy.

But the SDP realised the shortcomings of its policies and programmes after the elections of 1953. It adopted the 'Godesberg Programme' that it still follows. Though it still subscribes to the way of democratic socialism, it lays greater emphasis on free market elements rather than on the possibilities of state planning and intervention. Its new slogan is: 'As much competition as possible, as much planning as necessary'. Privately-owned means of transport are to remain untouched; private property is entitled to protection and promotion provided it does not impede the development of a just social pattern. One of the main points is the demand for effective parity-co-management rights to provide the basis for a democratic company constitution. It also made a change in the items of its foreign policy programme after 1960. It accepted the Atlantic alliance and efforts towards the reunification of Europe. It also committed itself unequivocally to national defence. At the same time, it stressed that it would do all in its power to oppose the nuclear arms race and to promote detente. Now its old programmes are being supplemented by declarations on ecological problems, technical-scientific development, equal status of men and women, and the problem of North-South discrepancy. It has also stressed dispensing with nuclear energy over the medium-term.

Free Democratic Party: It was founded in Happenheim in 1948 and it captured the presidency twice (under Heuss during 1949-59 and under Scheel during 1974-79). It is a party of the liberals divided into right and left wings. While the right-wingers regard the boosting of private enterprise and a free market as the central aims of their policy, the left-wingers place heavy emphasis on extending and safeguarding the rights of the individuals. In 1971, it approved its 'Freiburg Theses' on social policy with the aim of democratisation of the society and strengthening of the civil rights. Basically, it represented a rejection of the classical liberalism of the nineteenth century. It desired that the unequal distribution of power in the economic sector was to be rectified. The 'Kiel Theses' of 1977 brought about a further change. Here the champions of the free market concept were able to win through once more. Now this party lays more emphasis on its commitment to a free economy market and its development and placement of curbs on trade union influence. It also seeks tax relief for private enterprise. In the domestic and legal sectors, it calls for as much individual freedom as possible. The policy of detente *vis-a-vis* the East bloc should be based on a balance of power. It also desires recognition of human rights and entitlement of all people to self-determination.

The Greens: It is a new party established at the federal level in 1980. The Greens want that professional politics should be replaced by grass-roots politics. They base their views on the assumption that the destruction of living and working conditions in the developed world has reached dimensions requiring a radical change of course. It desires an ecologically and socially structured economy of a strictly decentralised nature. Environmental conservation should have priority over economic interests in profit. Nuclear energy is rejected by them. Direct democracy should be promoted. The system of democracy given by the Basic Law of Germany is a hindrance to the 'democratisation of society'. The systems of initiative, referendum and plebiscite should be introduced so as to have popular participation in the political process of the country. Equality of sex should be recognised. The system of 'rotation' should be adopted so that the members of the Bundestag have to vacate their seats for other members of the party halfway through the legislative period. Their main foreign policy demand is immediate withdrawal of Germany from the NATO. They reject all forms of rearmament and have called for uniform unilateral disarmament measures. A serious development in the ranks of this party is that its 'fundamentalists' are totally opposed to established party system, while others stand for cooperation with other parties to manage the affairs of the state.

It all shows that although the people of Germany donot have a very soft opinion about the party system and its role in the operation of a democratic system, its indispensability has, in general, been accepted. The central role of political parties in the formation of 'political will' is acknowledged; it is also widely believed that the parties are the decisive 'transmission belts' between the political objectives in the social sector and the binding decisions within the Government. It has shown itself to be extremely stable and, in turn, represented a basic factor in the stability of the political system as a whole.

Pressure Groups

Apart from the three major political parties, some interest groups also play their part in the political process of Germany. However, the politics of the pressure groups in this country has its own characteristics. First, because of the use of proportional representation system, many groups attach more importance to the leaders of State governments sitting in the Bundesrat who may, or may not, belong to a party in power at the Centre. It seems rather pointless to try to influence individual members of the Bundestag. Instead, the groups work directly upon the party leadership and seek direct representation in parliament.[5] Second, the political parties of this country prefer the course of consensus rather than conflict. The pressure groups have to act on their own for protecting and promoting their specific interests. Last, by temperament the people of this country shun the ideology of Marxian socialism. They believe in work and not in terms of the war between the haves and the have-nots. Naturally, the business groups have a better and safer role to play in the politics of the country. "Regardless of which party forms or parties form the government, the interests and claims of the German business will receive a thorough hearing. Indeed, the frequent charge of the Left is that even the Social Democrats are too receptive and accommodative to the interests of business."

We may now have a brief look at various leading interest groups. Among the leading business groups, we may refer to the Federation of

5. Gerhard Loewenberg says that the pressure groups "have their members through parties in Parliament." *Parliament in the German Political System*, p. 113.

German Industry (BDI), Federation of German Employees Association (BDA) and German Industrial and Trade Conference (DIHT). The BDA tends to specialise in wage policies, while the DIHT concentrates most of its efforts on maintaining economic viability of small independent businessmen and craftsmen. Thus, neither organisation is politically active or visible on as broad a front as the BDI which focuses its activity on national or international economic policies of the government and is clearly the most influential and effective voice of business in national politics. The BDI is a federation made up of 39 individual industrial associations which have a membership of over 90,000 firms.

Then, there are labour organisations. When the German labour unions were revived after the II World War, considerable pressure was brought to bear upon them to amalgamate. In October, 1949 this amalgamation could occur and then came into being the German Trade Union Federation (DGB). It consists of 16 separate trade unions with a combined strength of more than 7 unions. Although, officially it is non-party organisation, the overwhelming majority of its leaders and members are Social Democrats. The rest belong to the left-wing of the Christian Democratic Union. It is virtually free from the influence of the Communists.

Among the organisations of the farmers, we may refer to the German Farmers Agriculture League, Greens Front, and the Association of Agricultural Chambers. The Christian Socialist Union (CSU) also fights for the interest of the Bavarian agriculturists. An entirely different type of pressure group has appeared in the form of the various German veterans' organisations having a nationalistic as well as a conservative outlook.

We may repeat the point that in the political process of Germany the organised groups prefer to follow the course of consensus and cooperation and, as such, a change in the government from one party to another is not a source of either inconvenience or embarrassment to them. At the federal level, the CDU/CSU combination has been in power since 1949 with the exception of thirteen years (1969-82) when the SDP had the chance to be in power, but it did not affect the political behaviour of many interest organisations. As a German writer comments, the business interests "discovered that they could flourish under a socialist government as they did under the CDU rule. Agricultural interests, more pragmatic than during the Weimer Republic, have seen the subsidies and protectionist policies so vital to their survival continued under socialist-liberal governments. In short, there has been a high degree of consensus and cooperation between major interest alignments and all three system parties."[6]

6. David P. Cowradt: *The German Polity*, p. 101

Part - VIII

Canadian Constitution

The process and the reformed Constitution (1982) itself will undoubtedly play a central role in reshaping Confederation in decades to come. The new provisions of the reformed Constitution include many which will change the working of Canada's federation: the expansion of provincial powers with respect to resource taxation and management; the entrenchment of language rights, particularly with regard to schooling; the Charter of Rights and Freedoms, which will certainly afford better legal protection of individual rights than Canadian Bill of Rights; and the increased importance of the Courts, especially the Supreme Court of Canada, in the interpretation and protection of individual rights. ***—Paul Davenport***

29

CONSTITUTION OF CANADA

A study of the Canadian constitutional system in a work on major modern political systems has its own relevance in view of the fact that here is the case of a Dominion where we find the peculiar fusion of parliamentary democracy coupled with the system of federalism having no parallel in the political system of the mother of the British Commonwealth of Nations. In this sense, like Australia, Canada falls in the same category where parliamentary system of the United Kingdom has been harmonised with the federal system of the United States in a way conducive to the public interest. The historic decision taken at the Imperial Conference of 1926 declaring every Dominion a fully sovereign and independent entity and the incorporation of this fact into the Statute of Westminster of 1931 assigns to each Dominion the status of a full-fledged nation-state. But the Constitution Act of 1982 (superseding some of the provisions of the British North America Act of 1867 and now terming it as the Constitution Act of 1867) is a grand step in this direction.

Canadian Constitutionalism

The constitution is "the frame or chassis in which the working engine of government is set."[1] If the basic function of any constitution is to determine or define relationship between the citizen and the state, and to the extent that relationship can be determined and defined, then every country can be said to have some form of constitution. This celebrated norm has its relevance in every democratic country of the world. Slightly different, however, is the case of Canada. Once a colony under British control, then a Dominion governed by the constitution of 1867 framed by the British Parliament involving some formal elements of 'dependence',

1. J.A. Corry and J.E. Hodgetts: *Democratic Government and Politics*. p. 85.

and, finally, a fully sovereign nation-state after the 'patriation' of the constitution in 1982, Canada offers a unique example of its people's 'constitution-consciousness'. The story of constitutionalism in this country ever since the adoption of the Quebec Resolutions of 1866 finding its incorporation into the British North America Act of 1867 and then witnessing its historic culmination in the Constitution Act of 1982 reveals the significant fact that to the people of this country, a constitution is, or should be, "a source of pride and unifying influence within a political community."[2] Representing the general view of his countrymen in this regard, a learned Canadian writer describes the constitution of his country as "a mirror reflecting the national soul."[3]

The constitution of 1867 underwent some changes as a result of 13 Acts made by the British Parliament, 7 Acts made by the Parliament of Canada, and 4 Orders-in-Council promulgated by the British Government till 1981. Thus, the constitution of Canada before its historic 'patriation' in 1982 should be treated as something supplemented with 24 other important documents providing these important arrangements:

1. A federation comprising provinces, territories, national and provincial legislatures and executives;
2. A Parliament with power to create new provinces out of the territories or redrawing political map of the country with the consent of the provinces going to be affected;
3. Determination and definition of the powers and jurisdiction of the national and provincial governments;
4. Vesting formal executive power in the Queen to be exercised in her name by the Governor-General and a Privy Council having highly distinguished figures, in practice all executive powers with a cabinet headed by the Prime Minister as per conventions of the British parliamentary system;
5. Establishment of the Supreme Court of Canada according to the law made by the national Parliament;
6. Guarantee of certain limited rights equally to English and French languages in the national legislature and courts as well as in the legislatures and courts of Quebec and Manitoba;

---

2. Van Loon and Whittington: *The Canadian Political System: Environment. Structure and Process*, p. 104.

3. R.L. Cheffins: *The Constitutional Process in Canada*, p. 5.

7. Guarantee of Quebec's distinctive civil law;
8. Prohibition of provincial tariffs;
9. Guarantee of separate schools for the Protestant and Roman Catholic minorities in Quebec and Ontario and of separate schools in any other provinces where they existed by law in 1867 or thereafter;
10. Parliament's power to assume jurisdiction over property and civil rights or any part of such jurisdiction in other provinces with the consent of the provinces;
11. Power with the provincial legislature to amend their constitutions barring the office of the Lt.-Governor; and
12. Special powers to the federal government to appoint and dismiss Lt.-Governors, disallow a provincial law within one year after its enactment, Governor-Gerneral's veto power over some kinds of bills passed by the provincial legislatures.

From 1867 to 1981 Canada was ruled according to the BNA Act as amended in 1871,1886,1907; 1915, 1930, 1940,1964,1965, 1974, and 1975. The Constitution Act of 1982 makes four important changes in the BNA Act or the Constitution Act of 1867:

1. It provides four processes of constitutional amendment covering different provisions of the constitution with the co-operation of federal and provincial governments in most of the cases. The noticeable point at this stage is that a work of constitutional amendment is to be done by the Canadians themselves without any involvement or intervention of the British government at any stage and that, in cases of some very important provisions, the provincial governments have absolute veto power.
2. Allied with the above point is the change that certain parts of the constitution are 'entrenched' implying that neither the federal nor the provincial government has exclusive power to touch them in a way not conducive to the pleasure of the other.
3. It gives wider powers to the provinces over their natural resources. Now each province has power to export primary production from its mines, oil wells, gas wells, forests, electrical power plants on the condition that it does not discriminate against other parts of Canada in prices or supplies. It is further provided that in the event of any clash between federal and provincial laws on this score, the law of the former shall prevail. Moreover, the provinces shall also be able

Some Important Statements

The BNA provided the legal framework within which we could, and did, adopt, adjust, manoeuvre, innovate, compromise, arrange, by what Prime Minister Robert Braden called, the exercise of the commonplace equality of commonsense.

—Eugene A. Forsey

After fifty years of discussion, we have finally decided to retrieve what is properly ours. It is with happy hearts, and with gratitude for the patience displayed by Great Britain, that we are preparing to acquire today our complete national sovereignty.

—Pierre E. Trudeau

The difference between formal constitutional change and the forms of change that have marked the development of the Canadian constitution is the difference between doing a crossword puzzle in ink, which is not erasible, and doing it in pencil, which is. If a mistake is made, it can be remedied quickly and easily with the constitutional style that we enjoy in this country. In this way, the constitution can more closely reflect the current values and needs of the Canadian society.

—R.J. Van Loon and M.S. Whittington

to levy indirect taxes on their mines, oil wells, gas wells, forests and electric power plants and primary production from these sources. It is given that such taxes must be the same for products exported to other parts of Canada and products not so exported.

4. The most notable change is the incorporation of a very comprehensive charter of fundamental rights and freedoms that neither the Parliament of the Dominion nor any provincial legislature can alter on its own. It protects fundamental rights of the people of the country.

It may now be added that the fundamental law of Canada is contained in the BNA Act (Constitution Act) of 1867 as modified from time to time and in the Constitution Act of 1982 that supersedes some and instead inserts some of the important provisions as given above. In other words, it implies that the Constitution Act of 1982 is not a new Canadian Constitution; the BNA as well as other important laws that touch constitutional matters remain in existence and are incorporated into the Constitution Act of 1982.

Salient Features

Following important features of the Canadian constitution may be enumerated:

1. **An Enacted and a Written Constitution:** Like the American, Swiss and Australian constitutions, the Constitution of Canada is enacted and written. It is a creation of the British Parliament in the form of the British North America Act of 1867. From time to time, it has been amended, the latest being in 1982 that terminated the provision of final sanction of the British government in matters of constitutional amendment and thereby made the federal and provincial governments final authority in this important regard. Moreover, it is written. It has 147 sections (as given in the BNA Act, 1867) as modified by the Constitution Act of 1982. In addition to this, it incorporates two more Schedules. Schedule B with VII Parts has its outstanding significance in view of the fact that it embodies a charter of fundamental rights and freedoms. Since it all happened in the face of opposition demonstrated by the French-majority provinces, particularly of Quebec, the whole achievement of Prime Minister Trudeau is treated with mixed feelings. Paul Davenport says that the constitutional reform of 1982 "represented the culmination of a century of constitutional wrangling and will likely be the prelude to another century of legal and political infighting in Canada."[4]
2. **A Rigid Constitution:** The Constitution Act of 1982 supersedes the former procedure of amendment (when final authority was vested in the British government) and makes the Canadian federal and provincial governments sovereign in this important respect. This event is hailed as the 'patriation' of the Constitution. The Act of 1982 spells out four categories for the purpose of constitutional amendments. The first category covers amendments of certain provisions (concerning the monarch, Governor-General, Lt.-Governors of the provinces, allocation of seats for the provinces in the Parliament, use of English and French languages for official purposes, composition and jurisdiction of the Supreme Court of Canada, and the process of amendment itself) where it is required that a bill must be passed by both the Houses of the Parliament (by the House of Commons only if the Senate does not adopt it within 180 days) and then by all the provincial legislatures. It gives every province a veto power over constitutional amendment in certain very important matters. The second category covers some provisions (like proportionate representation of the provinces in the House of

4. Davenport: "Introduction" in Davenport and Leach (eds): *Reshaping Confederation: The 1982 Reform of the Canadian Constitution.* p. 2.

Commons, powers of the Senate and the method of selecting the Senators, number of Senators for each province and their residential qualifications, extension of existing provinces into the territories, creation of new provinces, curtailment of the powers and privileges of the provincial government, constitutional position of the Supreme Court of Canada, and the charter of fundamental rights and freedoms) where amendment may be made if a bill is first passed by the Canadian Parliament. (Here the same point should be repeated that in case the Senate does not pass the bill within 180 days, after it is adopted by the House of Commons, it shall be taken as passed by the Dominion Parliament.) Then, it must be passed by the legislatures of at least 2/3 provinces and at also by least half of the population of all provinces (population of the country excluding territories).[5] It is also given that any provincial legislature may pass a resolution to opt out of any amendment made under this category that takes away any of its rights, powers privileges; and if the amendment it opts out or transfers powers over education or other cultural matters to the federal Parliament, then the Parliament must pay 'reasonable compensation' to that province.

These two categories cover almost all important parts of the constitution. However, two minor categories may also be mentioned. The third category covers amendments dealing with matters that apply only to one province, or to several but not to all provinces. Such amendments must be passed by both the Houses of the federal Parliament (by the House of Commons alone in case the Senate does not pass it within 180 days) and then by the legistature or legislatures of the particular province or provinces concerned. This category includes provisions relating to the boundaries of a province and the use of English or French language there for official purposes. The last category covers changes in the executive government of Canada or in the Senate and the House of Commons (other than those covered under the first and second categories). These amendments may be made by an act of the Parliament of Canada. It makes rigid nature of the Canadian constitution.

3. **Federal System:** Like the United States, Canadian Constitution establishes a federal system. However, unlike the former, here the

5. It implies that any four provinces taken together (for example, the four Atlantic provinces, or the four Western provinces) may veto any such amendment. So may be done by Ontario and Quebec taken together. The seven provinces seeking such an amendment would have to include either Quebec or Ontario.

federal government is very powerful that, as Dawson says, places the provincial governments in a position of 'inflated municipalities'. The federal and the provincial governments have their allotted areas of jurisdiction and yet the former has an over-riding authority in several important directions. There is a Supreme Court to interpret the provisions of the Constitution and also to act as an umpire between federal and provincial governments. A marked change done by the Constitution Act of 1982 is that it has widened the powers of the provinces to a certain extent. For instance, it gives them wider powers over their natural resources. Now each province has the authority to control its natural resources and export to any other part of Canada its primary production goods from its mines, oil wells, gas wells, forest and electric power plants, provided it does not discriminate against other parts of the country in terms of prices or supplies.

It, however, does not diminish the overriding jurisdiction of the federal government. Still the federal Parliament may legislate on these matters and the law of the federal government shall prevail if there is conflict with a provincial law on this score. The provinces may levy indirect taxes on their mines, oil wells, gas wells, forests and electric power plants, and primary production from these sources. But such taxes must be the same for products exported to other parts of Canada as well as products not so exported. A distinguished writer on the subject of federalism, therefore, hesitates in designating Canada as a truly federal state 'in view of this country's constitution standing as a powerful weapon of centralising and unifying the government."[6]

4. **Dominion Status:** Like Australia, Canada has the status of a Dominion. It implies that it is a fully sovereign state paying final allegiance to the British Queen. She is the titular head of the Canadian state and the Governor-General appointed by her on the advice of the Canadian cabinet acts as her nominee. It is for this reason that as the Queen still has some prerogatives, these are naturally possessed by the Governor-General by virtue of being her nominee. The appointment of the Prime Minister and other Ministers, including their dismissal, and the summoning, proroguing and dissolving the Parliament may be especially referred to at this stage. It is a different

6. See K.C. Wheare : *Federal Government.* p. 20.

matter that with the entrenchment of a cabinet government in this country, all powers have been usurped by the cabinet headed by the Prime Minister as a result of which the Queen as well as her nominee have been reduced to the status of a ceremonial head of, what Walter Bagehot calls, the 'dignified executive'. And yet we may appreciate the view that it "would be a great error to assume that while the Governor-General's powers are limited, he has no power at all. In his public speeches, he must walk, what Earl Grey called, 'the tight rope of platitudinous generalities'. But while in some respects, the position of the Governor-General resembles that of a Merovingian king, the parallel is far from complete."[7]

5. **Cabinet Government:** While the Queen (and her nominee in the form of the Governor-General) is mere constitutional head of the state, the real executive authority is in the hands of the cabinet headed by the Prime Minister. The leader of the party having clear majority in the House of Commons is invited by the Governor-General to form the government; it is on his advice that other ministers are appointed. All ministers must belong to the party of the Prime Minister. The cabinet is collectively responsible to the House of Commons. It implies that the government can live in office so long as it enjoys the confidence or pleasure of the Parliament. As Dawson observes: "The most striking feature of the Canadian form of government is undoubtedly the superficial absurdity of the dual nature of the executive power. In the absence of the Queen, the Governor-General as her representative, is the official head of the state; but the active and puissant head of the government of the state is the Prime Minister. Appointments are made, acts of Parliament are proclaimed, mails are carried, criminal prosecutions are instituted, war is declared, treaties are negotiated and ratified in the name of the Queen or of the Governor-General, although the Prime Minister and the cabinet are, in fact, ones who make the selections and decide the policies which lie behind all these activities."[8]

6. **Judicial Review:** As Canada has a written constitution and a federal polity, the Supreme Court has been given the power to act as an umpire between the federal and provincial governments. Since 1949, it is country's final court for the reason that an important act made

7. George Hambleton: *The Parliament of Canada.* p. 50.

8. R.M. Dawson: *The Government of Canada* (rev. by N. Ward), p. 167.

by the Canadian Parliament terminated the system of appeals over and against its judgments preferred in the Privy Council of England. The Court has acted as the guardian of the Constitution and, by virtue of exercising its power of judicial review, sought to maintain a harmonious balance between the federal and provincial governments.[9] For instance, in the case of *Attorney-General of Ontario* v. *Attorney-General of Canada* (1896), it ruled that while the federal government could make a law in the name of 'peace, order and good government' of the country, it could not exercise this power so as to encroach on any subject enumerated in the list of provincial subjects as given in Sec. 92 of the BNA Act. It led to the evolution of the 'watertight compartments theory'. In due course. the Court took a positive view and softened its ruling in *Cooperative Committee on Japanese Canadians* v. *Attorney-General of Canada* (1947) so as to imply that the federal government could encroach upon any subject of the provincial list in the name of 'order, peace and good government' of the country when conditions of grave emergency prevailed. We may refer to a host of leading cases in this important direction when the Court looked into the constitutional validity of an impugned federal or provincial legislative or executive measure and pronounced upon its *intra* or *ultra vires* and then came to the conclusion that the students of Canadian constitutional law appreciate it all despite their divergent contentions on the value of the system of judicial review as prevailing in their country.

7. **Bi-Cameralism:** As in Britain and other liberal-democratic countries of the world, Canada has a Parliament with two chambers. While the Senate is the upper chamber, the House of Commons is the lower one. The House is like the popular chamber of other democratic countries of the world. It has 282 members directly elected by the people for a specified term (five years) and the cabinet, headed by the Prime Minister, is collectively responsible to it. It may be dissolved by the Governor-General at any time before the expiry of its term on the recommendation of the Prime Minister. During the

9. As J.R. Mallory remarks: "While the relations between the federal government and the provinces of the Confederation were essentially the 'colonial' model of superior and subordinate, it was clear that the courts saw the relationship in a more 'federal' form in which the provinces were, within their jurisdiction, the equals of the Dominion." *The Structure of the Canadian Government*, p. 341.

conditions of war, real or apprehended, its term may be extended. The Senate is the upper chamber without being a prototype of the American and Australian models in view of the fact that it is a body of members appointed for life but who may now seek retirement on completing the age of 75 years. Thus, like the British House of Lords, it is criticised for being anachronistic. It is also condemned as a refuge for the discredited and burnt out politicians playing to the tune of their mentor (Prime Minister) and thereby giving a bold proof of their partisan orientations. Hence, we often hear about a movement for its reform, nay its abolition. However, a protagonist of the existing system has his own assessment when he says: "The Senate is a chamber of infinite appeal. It has an air not of this world, a dignity, a repose, a charm all its own. The House of Commons hurries and scurries... The Senate is gentlemanly. It is discreet. It is refined. It excites no sordid passions. Members of the House always have a fearful eye on the polling booth. The Senator rejoices in permanence. He need not descend to the soap box and the mob. He is there for life. He is responsible to nobody."[10]

8. **Charter of Fundamental Rights and Freedoms:** The incorporation of a bill of fundamental rights is regarded as an essential part of modern constitutionalism. It finds place in the great charters signed by the monarchs (like Magna Carta and Bill of Rights) which protect the fundamental rights of the English people. The First Ten Amendments of the American constitution serve the same purpose for the people of the United States. Since the people of Canada belong to different ethnic stocks and as they have their own cultural differentiations, the need for having a bill of fundamental rights was felt strongly. Thus occurred the enactment of the Bill of Rights in 1960. It protected essential freedoms as those of speech, expression, press, association, religion, life and security of the person, enjoyment of property, legal equality, due process of law etc. But more important is the Constitution Act of 1982 that incorporates a detailed charter of fundamental rights and freedoms so as to remove all lurking fears and misgivings in the minds of the people in minority and establishment of a full-fledged liberal-democratic order.

10. Hambleton, *op. cit.*, p. 56.

Charter of Fundamental Rights and Freedoms

Schedule B of the Constitution Act of 1982 incorporates a very comprehensive catalogue of fundamental rights and freedoms of the people. It says that whereas this country is founded upon the principles recognising supremacy of God and the rule of law, it guarantees some important rights and freedoms set out in its subject only to such reasonable limits prescribed by law as can be demonstrably justified in a free and democratic society. It has these rights and freedoms:

1. **Fundamental Freedoms:** Everyone has the following fundamental freedoms:
   (*i*) freedom of conscience and religion,
   (*ii*) freedom of thought, belief. opinion and expression, including freedom of the press and other media of communication,
   (*iii*) freedom of peaceful assembly, and
   (*iv*) freedom of association.
2. **Democratic Rights**
   (*i*) Every citizen of Canada has the right to vote in an election of the members of the House of Commons or of a legislative assembly and to be qualified for membership therein.
   (*ii*) In time of real or apprehended war, invasion or insurrection, the House of Commons may be continued by the Parliament and a provincial legislative assembly may be continued by the legislature beyond five years if such continuance is not opposed by the votes of more than one-third of the members of House of Commons or the legislative assembly, as the case may be.
   (*iii*) No House of Commons and no legislative assembly shall continue for longer than five years from the date fixed for the return of the writs at a general election of its members.
   (*iv*) There shall be a sitting of Parliament and of each legislature once every 12 months.
3. **Mobility Rights**
   (*i*) Every citizen of Canada has the right to enter, remain in, and leave Canada.
   (*ii*) Every citizen of Canada and every person who has the status of a permanent resident of Canada has the right (*a*) to move to and take up residence in any province; and (*b*) to pursue the gaining of a livelihood in any province. But these rights are subject to (*i*) any laws or practices of general application in

force in a province other than those that discriminate among persons primarily on the basis of province or present or previous residence; and (*ii*) any laws providing for reasonable residency requirements as a qualification for the receipt of publicly provided social services. These provisions do not preclude any law, programme or activity that has as its object the amelioration in a province of conditions of individuals in that province who are socially or economically disadvantaged if the rate of employment in that province is below the rate of employment in Canada.

4. Legal Rights

(*i*) Everyone has the right to life, liberty and security of the person and the right not to be deprived thereof except in accordance with the principles of fundamental justice.

(*ii*) Everyone has the right to be secure against unreasonable search or seizure.

(*iii*) Everyone has the right not to be arbitrarily detained or imprisoned.

(*iv*) Everyone has the right on arrest or detention: (*a*) to be informed promptly of the reasons thereof; (*b*) to retain and instruct counsel without delay and to be informed of that right; and (*c*) to have the validity of the detention determined by way of *habeas corpus* and to be released if the detention is not lawful.

(*v*) Any person charged with an offence has the right: (*a*) to be informed without unreasonable delay of the specific offence, (*b*) to be tried within a reasonable time, (*c*) not to be compelled to be a witness in proceedings against that person in respect of the offence (*d*) to be presumed innocent until proved guilty according to law in a fair and public hearing by an independent and impartial tribunal, (*e*) not to be denied reasonable bail without just cause, (*f*) except in the case of an offence under military law tried before a military tribunal, to the benefit of trial by jury where the maximum punishment for the offence is imprisonment for five years or more severe punishment, (*g*) not to be found guilty on account of any act or omission unless, at the time of omission, it constituted an offence under Canadian or international law, or was a criminal according to the general principles of law recognised by the community of nations, (*h*) if finally acquitted of the offence, not to be tried for it again and, finally found guilty, and punished for the offence, not to be tried or punished for it again, and (*i*) if found guilty of the offence and if the punishment for the offence has been varied between the time of commission and the time of sentencing, to the benefit of the lesser punishment.

(*vi*) Everyone has the right not to be subjected to any cruel and unusual treatment or punishment.

(*vii*) A witness who testifies in any proceedings has the right not to have any incriminating evidence so given used to incriminate that witness in any other proceedings, except in a prosecution for perjury or for the giving of contradictory evidence.

(*vii*) A party or witness in any proceedings who does not understand or speak the language in which the proceedings are conducted or who is deaf has the right to the assistance of an interpreter.

5. Equality Rights

(*i*) Every individual is equal before and under the law and has the right to the equal protection and equal benefit of the law without discrimination and, in particular, without discrimination based on race, national or ethnic origin, colour, religion, sex, age or mental or physical disability. It does not preclude any law, programme or activity that has as its object the amelioration of conditions of disadvantaged individuals or groups including those that are disadvantanged because of race, national or ethnic origin, colour, religion, sex, age or mental or physical disability.

6. Official Languages

(*i*) English and French are the official languages of Canada and have equality of status and equal rights and privileges as to their use in all institutions of the Parliament and Government of Canada. These are the official languages of the New Brunswick and have equality of status and equal rights and privileges as their use in all institutions of legislative and executive departments. No legislature, whether Dominion or Provincial, can change the status of one language over or against another.

(*ii*) Everyone has the right to use English or French in any debates or proceedings of the Parliament. The statutes, records and journals of the Parliament shall be published in both the languages and be equally authoritative. It shall apply to the province of New Brunswick.

(*iii*) Either English or French may be used by any person in, or in any pleading in or process issuing from, any court established by Parliament. It shall be applicable to the province of New Brunswick also.

(*iv*) Any member of the public in Canada has the right to communicate with, and receive available services from, any head or central office or an institution of the Parliament or Government of Canada in English or French and has the same right with respect to any other office of such information where (*a*) there is a significant demand for communications with and services from that office in such language, (*b*) or due to the nature of office, it is reasonable that communication with and services from that office be available in both languages. It also applies to the province of New Brunswick.

(*v*) Nothing in the above sections abrogates or derogates from any right, privilege or abrogation with respect to the two languages or either of them that exists or is continued by virtue of any other provision of the Constitution of Canada. Moreover, nothing in the above sections abrogates or derogates from any legal or customary right or privilege required or enjoyed either before or after the coming into force of this charter with respect to any language that is neither English nor French.

7. Minority Educational Rights

(*i*) Citizens of Canada whose first language learned and still understood is that, of the English or French linguistic minority population of the province in which they reside, or (*b*) who have received their primary school instruction in Canada in English or French and reside in a province where the language in which they received that instruction is the language of the English or French linguistic minority population of the province, have the right to have their children receive primary and secondary school instruction in that language in that province.

(*ii*) Citizens of Canada of whom any child has received or is receiving primary or secondary school instruction in English or French in Canada, have the right to have all their children receive primary and secondary school instruction in the same language.

(*iii*) The right of citizens of Canada under the above sections applies:

(*a*) wherever in the province the number of children of citizens who have such a right is sufficient to warrant the provision to them out of public funds of minority language instruction;

(*b*) and includes where the number of those children so warrants, the right to have them receive that instruction in minority language educational facilities provided out of public funds.

8. Enforcement

Any person who feels that his rights and freedoms guaranteed in this charter are infringed or denied may apply to a court of competent jurisdiction to obtain such remedy as the court considers appropriate and just in the circumstances. But while in the course of proceedings, the court concludes that evidence was obtained in a manner that infringed or denied any rights or freedoms guaranteed by the charter, the evidence shall be excluded, if it is established that having regard to all the circumstances, such an admission in the proceedings would bring the administration of justice into disrepute.

9. General

(*i*) The guarantee in this charter of certain rights and freedoms shall not be construed so as to abrogate or derogate from any aboriginal treaty or other rights of freedoms that pertain to the aboriginal peoples of Canada including (*a*) any rights or freedoms that have been recognised by the Royal Proclamation of 7 October, 1763; and (*b*) any rights or freedoms that may be acquired by the aboriginal peoples of Canada by way of land claims settlement.

(*ii*) The guarantee in this charter of certain rights and freedoms shall not be construed as denying the existence of any other rights of freedoms that exist in Canada.

(*iii*) This charter shall be interpreted in a manner consistent with the preservation and enhancement of the multicultural heritage of the Canadians.

(*iv*) Notwithstanding anything in this charter, the rights and freedoms referred to in it are guaranteed equally to all male and female persons.

(*v*) Nothing in this charter abrogates or derogates from any rights or privileges guaranteed by or under the Constitution of

Some Important Statements

The economic and social conditions of this country are generally similar to those of the United States. The political institutions have been framed upon English models and political habits, traditions and usages have retained an English character.

—Lord James Bryce

The Charter has radically changed the situation—Parliament and the legislatures will, of course, still not be allowed to jump the fence into each other's gardens. But both federal and provincial laws can now be challenged and thrown out by the courts on the ground that they violate the Charter. This is something the Americans, with their Bill of Rights entrenched in their constitution, have been familiar for almost 200 years.

—Eugene A. Forsey

I speak of a country where every person is free to fulfil himself or herself to the utmost unhindered by the arbitrary action of the Government.

—Pierre E. Trudeau

Canada in respect of denominational, separate or dissentient schools.

(*vi*) A reference in this charter to a province or to the legislative assembly or legislature of a province shall be deemed to include a reference to the Yukon Territory and the North West Territories, or to the appropriate legislative authority thereof, as the case may be.

(*vii*) Nothing in this charter extends the legislative powers of any body or authority.

It is quite obvious that the charter of fundamental right and freedoms not only protects the essential liberties of the people, particularly those in minority, and dispels all sorts of lurking apprehensions, it widens as well as circumscribes the powers of both the federal and provincial governments in many important directions and, on that score, goes to have its definite effect on the systems of federalism and judicial review. Keeping this in his view, an eminent Canadian writer asserts: "For us, it is almost completely new, indeed revolutionary."[11]

Federalism

The leaders and statesmen of the eighteenth and nineteenth centuries happily identified the term 'confederation' with 'federation' as a result of which the constitutions of the United States, Switzerland and Australia

11. Eugene A. Forsey: *The Canadian Political System*, p. 16.

became the classic examples of a 'confederal' model.[12] Important developments took place in due course that demonstrated conversion of a confederation into a federation. Matters brought about a clear distinction between the two terms as a result of which the political theorists and statesmen of the twentieth century prefered the term 'federal' as against 'confederal' with a view to make things precise and incontrovertible. However, different is the case of Canada where the framers used the term 'federal' that surprisingly looked identical with the term 'colonial' for the reason of prevailing political conditions of the country. The Preamble to the BNA Act of 1867 said that "whereas the provinces of Canada, Nova Scotia and New Brunswick have expressed their desire to be federally united into one Dominion—and whereas such a union would conduce to the welfare of the Provinces."

As already defined in the study of the American, Swiss, Russian and German political systems, a federal system stands on the principle of distribution of powers between two co-ordinate governments. The Constitution is written and it specifies the jurisdiction of the central and regional governments as clearly as possible so that there is almost no scope for controversy or litigation. Powers are distributed in a way that while all major items of national importance are given to the federal government, those of local importance are assigned to the governments of the units. Some items of common importance are enumerated in the concurrent category and their administration is assigned to both with this note that, in the event of any conflict, the law or decree of the federal government shall prevail and that of the provincial governments shall become inoperative to the extent it is inconsistent with that of the Centre. Residuary items are given to the units. Finally, an independent and impartial judiciary is set up to act as the guardian of the constitution endowed with the power of judicial power. It looks into the constitutional validity of an impugned legislative or executive measure and then may pronounce upon its *intra* or *ultra vires* so as to maintain the desired balance between the central and provincial governments.

Keeping in view the three essential marks of a federal system, we are definitely led to conclude that Canada belongs to the category of a 'federation'. A distinguished student of this subject like P.M. Kennedy

12. See J.R. Mallory: "The Five Faces of Federalism" in P.A Crepeau and C.B. Macpherson (ed.s): *The Future of Canadian Federalism*, pp. 3-15.

confidently asserts that Canada is 'a federation in essence' on the basis of these forceful arguments:[13]

1. The Dominion Parliament is not a delegation from the British Parliament, nor is its authority derived from the provinces. It has its defined area of authority as given in Sec. 91 of the BNA Act of 1867.
2. Likewise, the provincial governments have their own area of authority as given in Sec. 92 of the BNA Act, 1867 (now supplemented with Sec. 92A of the Constitution Act of 1982). In this sense, the governments of the units are neither a delegation from the British Parliament nor from the Dominion government.
3. Both the governments have autonomous existence and their allotted areas of authority are protected by the judiciary. As a result of this, both "exercise co-ordinate authority and are severally sovereign within the sphere specifically or generally or by implication constitutionally granted to them." In support of the same contention, we may refer to the observation of a learned English writer who says: 'Canada is politically federal and that no Dominion government which attempted to stress the unitary elements in the Canadian constitution at the expense of the federal elements would survive."[14] Again: "It seems justifiable to conclude that although the Canadian Constitution is quasi-federal in law, it is predominantly federal in practice. Or to put it in another way, although Canada has not a federal constitution, it has a federal government."[15]

The federal system of Canada, however,. has its peculiar features, the most important of which is the existence of a 'strong' centre. It is evident from these important provisions:

1. A comparative study of the distribution of powers shows that all important powers have been allotted to the federal government, while items of minor importance have been given to the provinces. Thus, a critic may add that while the American constitution assigns some items as criminal law, marriage and divorce to the States, these are given to the Dominion Government in Canada. Residuary powers are with the Centre.

---

13. Kennedy: *The Constitution of Canada.* p. 408.
14. K.C. Wheare : *Federal Government.* p. 21.
15. *Ibid.*

Some Important Statements

Caught between centripetal and centrifugal forces, Canada's future, like its past, may continue to oscillate between times of federal and times of provincial predominance, depending upon the immediate needs of the people and the temper of their various politicians. Or–more likely–the political future of Canada will lie in the direction of greater centralisation in some areas and greater decentralisation in some others. But at all times, cooperation and interchange between the two levels of government will be, as they have been, an absolute necessity.

—Pierre E. Trudeau

Federalism, of all the forms of government, is the most difficult to work. The fact that we have been able to work it at all for nearly a century should be a matter of pride and sustain our belief that will continue to work. The fact that the Canadian federal system has materialised in so many forms is a proof of its essential vitality, but the surviving of any system depends on a consensus that is worth while and worth paying.

—J.R. Mallory

Federalism today is a very tightly integrated network of federal-provincial consultative bodies at various governmental levels. There is a constantly moving relationship between the actors in the federal system, as each of the provinces and the federal government attempt to maximise their bargaining advantages vis-a-vis others.

—R.J. Van Loon and M.S. Whittington

2. The Dominion government has the power to make a law for 'order, peace and good government of the country' and on this plea it may encroach upon the authority of the provinces. The Supreme Court has given a ruling that it is permissible during the times of national crisis or emergency.
3. The Dominion government has the power to disallow a law of the provincial government within a year of its enactment.
4. It is given that in the event of a conflict on an item of the concurrent jurisdiction, the law of the Dominion government shall prevail and that of the provinces become inoperative to the extent of being repugnant to it.
5. The Governor-General appoints Lt-Governors of the provinces. He may issue necessary instructions that they must follow and he may also remove them in certain conditions. He may advise a Lt. Governor to veto a bill passed by the provincial legislature, or reserve it for his own signification. In such a case he might use his absolute veto power over provincial legislation.
6. All important judicial appointments in the provinces are made by the Governor-General.

7. The Senate is the upper chamber of the Canadian Parliament and yet it does not have representatives of the units the kind of which is seen in the federal systems of the world. It has members appointed for life (now may be retired at the age of 75 years) by the Governor-General on the recommendation of the Prime Minister. Thus, the upper chamber of the Canadian Parliament does not protect the interests of the provincial governments.
8. The provinces have no right to initiate a bill of constitutional amendment. They may veto a move by not ratifying a bill already passed by the Canadian Parliament. It applies to all important provisions of the Constitution relating to the offices of the Queen, Governor-General, Lt-Governors, representation of the provinces in the House of Commons and Senate, use of English and French languages, composition and jurisdiction of the Supreme Court, rights and privileges of the provincial governments, charter of fundamental rights and freedoms and the process of constitutional amendment itself. But this arrangement does not cover some other provisions of the Constitution (like alteration of the provincial boundaries, use of English or French language in a particular province, pattern of the executive government of Canada) where the federal Parliament has all authority, the only exception being that while altering the boundary line of a province, it must obtain the consent of the province going to be so affected.
9. It is true that the Constitution Act of 1982 has widened the powers of the provincial government by adding Sec. 92 A and thereby giving them control over their mines, oil wells, gas wells, forests, electric power plants etc., but it may be taken into account (particularly in view of the ruling already given by the Supreme Court in some leading cases) that in the event of any conflict, the law of the Dominion government shall prevail and that of the provinces become ineffective to the extent of repugnancy.
10. The Constitution Act of 1982 empowers the provincial governments to make and amend their constitutions, but in doing so they cannot touch provisions relating to the office of the Lt.-Governor, voting rights of the people, and qualifications of their legislators, nor can

they make a change adversely affecting the jurisdiction of the Dominion government.

On 30 April, 1987, Meech Lake Accord came into being. It sought o give these powers to the provinces:

1. to nominate candidates for appointment to the Senate and Supreme Court of Canada, though the Central government would maintain its right of veto;
2. to exercise veto over changes affecting the House of Commons, Senate, Supreme Court and the creation of new provinces;
3. to regulate immigration,
4. to opt out of new national shared cost programmes and to receive compensation from the Federal Treasury provided they had their own programmes to meet national objectives; in addition, there would be annual constitutional and economic conferences between the heads of the central and provincial governments; and
5. to ratify constitutional amendments.

This accord proved a failure. The 'integrationists' condemned it as an attempt in the direction of dividing the Union, and the 'disruptionists' took it as short of their demand for full autonomy for the provinces. With a view to resolve the crisis, Prime Minister Maulroney presented a new plan on 24 September, 1991 that desired to keep the province of Quebec within the federation without alienating other provinces. Its main points were:

(*i*) the granting within 10 years of self-government to the country's Indian peoples for Ontario's recognition of Indian rights.

(*ii*) the recognition of Quebec as a distinct society empowered to control such areas as employment training, immigration, cultural programmes, broadcasting and tourism, but with the proviso that similar powers would be granted to other provinces,

(*iii*) the creation of an elected Senate,

(*iv*) the prohibition by mid-1995 of any laws or practices which restricted the mobility of people, capital, services and goods across the country, and

(v) greater regional representation on the Bank of the Board of Canada. It also failed to satisfy the two sides. Most of such points incorporated into a 'reform package' had been agreed upon at a constitutional conference of federal, provincial and native leaders and which required their ratification by the federal and provincial legislatures. Known as the Pearson Accord or Charlottetown Agreement, it had the same fate. It was rejected by the people in a referendum held on 20 October, 1992.[16]

16. Taking the case of Quebec in particular, it may be observed that "national identity can create nationalism, a pride in one's people and the belief that thay have their own unique political destiny that is separate from those of others. In Quebec, for example, we find a people uncertain of whether they are just an ethnic group or also a nation—a group that desires self-government through an independent state." Patrick O'Neil: *Essentials of Comparative Politics* (New York: W.W. Norton and Company, 2004), p. 50.

30

STATE STRUCTURE

Canada is a liberal democracy on the pattern of English constitutional monarchy coupled with the American federal polity the kind of which we may see in the case of Australia. The head of the Canadian state is the Queen of Britain and every official act is done in her name, but the authority for every act flows from the people of the country. When the Fathers of the Confederation designed the basic law of 1867, they freely, deliberately and unanimously chose to vest the formal executive authority in the Queen to be administered according to the well-established and well-understood principles of the British Constitution. It implied a parliamentary system with a Cabinet responsible to Parliament, and a Parliament ultimately answerable to the people. Except when the Queen is in Canada, all her powers are exercised by her representative-the Governor-General. The Governor-General, sometimes inaptly described as 'the nominated President' of this country, is always a Canadian, appointed by the British monarch on the advice of the Canadian Prime Minister. Barring very extraordinary circumstances, he exercises his powers on the advice of the cabinet having support of the majority of the members of the popularly elected House of Commons. The people are well satisfied with the system. As a Canadian writer puts: "And government is our creature. We make it, we are ultimately responsible for it, and, taking the broad view, in Canada, we have considerable reason to be proud of it."[1]

Formal Executive

The executive organ of the Canadian State has its dignified' and 'efficient' parts. While the former has its place in the offices of the monarch, the Governor-General and the Privy Council, the latter is contained in the

1. Eugene A. Forsey: *The Canadian Political System,* p. 2.

offices of the Prime Minister, Ministers of the Cabinet and the bureaucrats. For these reasons, like Britain, Canada is said to have constitutional monarchy or parliamentary system of government. The head of the state is the Queen who delegates her authority on the advice of the Canadian Cabinet to her nominee (Governor-General) who, in reality, exercises very few powers in his own right as a person. As we shall see, his principal function "is to represent the Crown, the institution which embodies the executive authority; and in this capacity he rarely takes the initiative himself or follows his own inclinations, but rather speaks and acts in accordance with the counsels given to him by his constitutional advisers, the cabinet."[2]

The Crown: Like Australia, Canada is a Dominion having cultural links with the mother imperial country. Sec. 9 of the Constitution Act of 1867 says that "the executive government and authority of and over Canada is hereby declared to continue and be vested in the Queen." Sec. 17 says that there "shall be one Parliament for Canada consisting of the Queen, the Upper House styled the Senate, and the House of Commons." All federal acts begin: "Her Majesty, by and with the advice and consent of the Senate and the House of Commons, enacts as follows." Same is the case with provincial legislation. Then, the Dominion Parliament as well as provincial legislatures meet at the royal summons and no bill passed by them can become an act without the consent of the Crown. In practice, however, it means that, as in other Dominions, the Queen acts through her Governor-General unless she happens to be present there on a royal visit.

It implies that the English Queen has different capacities. She is not only the reigning monarch of the United Kingdom, she is also the Queen of Canada separately. One may, however, take note of the fact of changing nature of the authority of the Queen in this regard. At each step of the evolutionary process of constitutional development, the relationship of Canada with the English Crown has altered so as to meet the aspirations of a growing nation. So the Canadians take it all as the case of a Canadian and not of an imperial Crown. The office of the monarch symbolises a wonderful synthesis of the executive and the legislature working in the name of Her Majesty.' The Canadians take pride in the fact of their cultural association with the United Kingdom for which the Preamble to the Constitution Act of 1867 *inter alia* stated: "Whereas the Provinces of Canada, Nova Scotia, and New Brunswick have expressed their desire to be federally united into One Dominion under the Crown of the United

2. R.M. Dawson: *Democratic Government in Canada* (revised by N. Ward), p. 37.

Kingdom of Great Britain and Ireland, with a Constitution similar in principle to that of the United Kingdom."

In practical terms, the British monarch is simply a symbol of Canada's free association with Britain and other Commonwealth nations, and a symbol of the history and traditions which majority of the Canadian people revere by virtue of a very long and well-established tradition. All acts are done in her name and the Governor-General is there to represent the highest office. But there are some prerogatives still with the Queen. These are:

1. Appointment of the Governor-General,
2. Appointment of ambassadors, ministers, or plenipotentiaries accredited to foreign states, and the issue of letters of credence for them,
3. Declaration of War (for reasons of urgency the actual proclamation would probably, as in 1939, be submitted to and signed by the Governor-General but thc approval of the Queen would first be obtained),
4. Change in the royal style and titles (since these affect the Queen personally, her approval would be obtained even if the changes were not implemented by any royal instrument; in fact, in 1953, the change was brought about by the royal proclamation signed by the Queen),
5. Changes in the Table of Precedence within Canada,
6. Honours and awards, and
7. Appointment of additional Senators pursuant to Sec. 26 of the British North America Act (or the Constitution Act) of 1867.

It may, however, be added at this stage that as the Queen is the symbolic head, she has no reserve powers enabling her to act independently of the aid and advice of the Canadian ministers. As Mallory says: "The Queen no longer serves as a symbol of an imperial connection and of uncritical colonial loyalty to the British Empire. By all means, the Crown is the model of a formal executive in which the Queen, as in the case of the United Kingdom, despite having certain prerogatives, can do no wrong. In practical terms, it implies that by no proceeding known to the law can the monarch be made personally responsible for any act done by her and that no one can plead orders of the Crown in defence of any act not otherwise justifiable by law.[3]

3. A.V. Dicey, *An Introduction to the Study of the Law of Constitution.*, pp. 424-25.

Governor-General: While the Queen of England may be called the 'Queen of Canada' most of the monarchical functions are performed in her name by the Governor-General. Originally the appointment of the Governor-General was the responsibility of the Queen acting on the advice of the British government. Obviously, it had made him effectively independent of the control of the Canadian cabinet, but since the important decisions taken at the imperial conferences of 1926 and 1930, this office has become independent of the British imperial control but subservient to the will of the cabinet headed by the Prime Minister of Canada. He is appointed by the Queen on the advice of the same body. Moreover, the normal term of the office of the Governor-General (five-years) may be stretched or shortened by the Queen on the advice of the Canadian cabinet. Thus, the term of the Governor-General may be simply, if somewhat ambiguously, stated as being officially recognised "as six years, customarily treated as five years, while on occasion it has been seven years."[4]

First, let us examine the 'prerogative' powers of the Governor-General where he acts like the monarch of Britain. These are:

1. He appoints the Prime Minister. For this purpose, he. 'commissions a public man (to use Sir John Bourinot's phrase) who is the recognised leader of the party having clear majority in the House of Commons. Here he is not required to act on anybody's aid and advice and in some exceptional situations (as the death of the Prime Minister or electoral stalemate) he may take a momentous decision as per his discretion.
2. He appoints Ministers on the advice of the Prime Minister. Here he has power to exercise some influence subject to the pleasure of the real working head of the State (Prime Minister). For instance, Lord Grey objected unsuccessfully to the appointment of Sir Sam Hughes as Minister of Militia in the government of Prime Minister Borden.
3. He may dissolve the House of Commons in a way that conforms to the advice of the Prime Minister or not. For instance, in 1926 Lord Byng did not accept the advice of Prime Minister Mackenzie King and instead appointed Arthur Meighen as the new Prime Minister. It is a different matter that the new Prime Minister could not run the government and shortly afterwards the Governor-General had to order the dissolution of the House of Commons that, in very clear terms, vindicated the stand of Mackenzie King.

4. R.M. Dawson, *op. cit.*, p. 163.

4. Above all, the Governor-General is expected to play the role of a friend, a philosopher and a guide of his government. In the words of Bagehot, he must encourage and warn the Prime Minister in the interest of the nation. "There are often problems which can be partly eased just by talking about them to a sympathetic listener. A Prime Minister may upon occasion find it a solace and an aid to unburden himself to a listener who is both above political interest and a proper recipient of the most intimate secrets of the government. Thus, a Prime Minister may seek an interview with the Governor-General as Mackenzie King occasionally did with the Earl of Athlone, simply because "expounding a difficult problem some-times helped him to clear his mind on it."

Then, we may enumerate 'statutory' powers of the Governor-General where he acts as the head of the state. These are:

1. He is the commander-in-chief of the land, naval and air forces of the Dominion.
2. He appoints representatives of Canada to the United Nations and other international bodies and signs treaties that are not signed directly by the Crown.
3. He appoints Lt.-Governors of the Provinces and may remove them from office on the advice of the Dominion cabinet.
4. He appoints the Speaker of the Senate, Senators, judges of the Supreme Court and Provincial Courts, Commissioners, Justices of Peace *etc.*
5. He summons and prorogues the sessions of the Parliament and may dissolve the House of Commons.
6. He has veto power over Dominion and Provincial legislation. He may also reserve a bill for the signification of the Queen.
7. As the head of the state, he performs certain ceremonial functions like receiving foreign dignitaries, inaugurating the Parliament and representing his country abroad.

Despite this all, the fact stands out that Canada has cabinet government in which the Governor-General has the office of a constitutional head. "The relevance of the Crown to the Government of Canada appears to be everything or nothing. The monarchical language of the BNA Act makes it appear as though the Governor-General runs the country. In fact, most of these powers have atrophied and his relevance is now almost completely nominal in the field of policy-making."[5] In reality, he "is a viceroy representing the king personally and performing all the royal functions relating to legislative matters. The forms and ceremonies of viceregal participation in parliamentary processes at Ottawa are a reflection of those observed at Westminster, but if the monarchial principle introduces any personal influence in legislation, it is not that of this king but of his Governor-General."[6]

Privy Council: Sec. 11 of the Constitution Act of 1867 says that "there shall be a council to aid and advise the Government of Canada, to be styled the Queen's Privy Council for Canada; and the persons who are to be Members of that Council shall be, from time to time, chosen and summoned by the Governor-General and sworn in as Privy Councillors, and Members thereof from time to time be removed by the Governor-General." This is a very large body consisting of about 113 members. Apart from the Prime Minister and his Cabinet Ministers, it includes all important dignitaries such as the Prince of Wales, British Prime Minister, ex-Prime Ministers of the country, Canadian High Commissioner in England, Speakers of the Senate and the House of Commons, the Chief Justice of the Supreme Court, Leader of the Opposition in the Parliament, Provincial Premiers *etc.*

The Privy Council as a whole body meets very rarely as on the occasion of taking part in the coronation ceremony in England. For instance, it met in 1947 to receive the formal announcement by the British monarch of his consent to the marriage of Princess Elizabeth and then in 1952 to hear the proclamation of the succession of Queen Elizabeth II on the death of her father. In fact, it has fallen into desuetude and its place has been taken over by the Cabinet. Practice shows that formal actions which require to be actions of the Governor-General-in-council are dealt with by the ministers acting as committees of the Privy Council and the draft minutes or orders are then transmitted to the Governor-General for him to signify his approval in his office. The most common of these actions is for the cabinet to resolve itself into the committee of the council for the purpose of approving submissions of draft orders and minutes to the Governor-General.

5. T.A Hockin: *Government in Canada.* p. 172.

6. H.M Clokie : *Canadian Government and Politics,* p.116.

Some Important Statements

The most important characteristic of the Canadian constitution is nowhere written down, nowhere guaranteed. It is that Canada is a constitutional democracy. The essence of constitutional order is that it provides effective means of preventing abuses of power, and ensures that those in authority cannot take away the ultimate right of the governed to remove them or reject their policies. —***J.R. Mallory***

And government is our creature. We make it, and we are ultimately responsible for it, and taking the broad view, in Canada, we have considerable reason to be proud of it. —***Eugene A. Forsey***

The powers of the Prime Minister are very great. The functions and duties of the Prime Minister in Parliament are not only important, they are supreme in their importance. —***Prime Minister Meighen***

Real Executive

The development of the parliamentary system in Canada over the last one hundred and fifty years shows an irresistible decline of the authority of the Governor-General and instead the emergence of the authority of the cabinet under the headship of the Prime Minister. It is rightly pointed out: "The Governor-Gerneral, like the king in Britain, has always been the central figure in the Government of Canada. His history, like that of his illustrious prototype, has been a steady, unsensational, rather reluctant progress from virtual dictatorship to virtual impotence." [7] The remarkable point in this direction is that it all has changed in practice without touching the text of the Constitution Act of 1867.

Prime Minister: It is true that formally all executive acts are performed by the Governor-General-in-Council, in reality all administrative matters are taken up by the Prime Minister (named as First Minister in the Salaries Act) and his cabinet and then rubber-stamped by the constitutional head of the Dominion. "To say that the Governor-General would never dare to oppose the will of the Prime Minister is pure speculation, but the fact remains that the norm of popular sovereignty which is the core of the Canadian constitution imposes severe political limitations on the actual powers of the Queen's representative."[8]

The Prime Minister is appointed by the Governor-General. In doing so, the recognised leader of party having clear majority in the House of

7. *Constitutional Issues in Canada.* p.65.

8. Van Loon and Whittington. *The Canadian Political System*, p. 130.

Commons is naturally picked up and, as such, the Governor-General has hardly any chance in this matter to exercise his will or discretion. However, he may use a sort of negative discretion in such an important matter. It is possible only in a situation of electoral stalemate. In the appointment of a Prime Minister no one-not even a retiring Prime Minister—has the right to tender advice. And if ever such an advice is sought, it may be given, but it need not be sought form the retiring Prime Minister. The fact that the appointment of a Prime Minister does not require the issuing of any documents or instruments simplifies the problem, since it does not even indirectly involve the reponsibility of ministers whose participation might otherwise be necessary for the use of seals or to make up a quorum for the issuing of a minute of Council. The advice tendered in such a situation is not 'advice' in the strict constitutional sense, "since the giver is not held politically accountable for."[9]

The functions and powers of the Prime Minister may be enumerated as under:

1. He makes his government, recommends the names of his colleagues for appointment as ministers to the Governor-Gerneral and may make changes in their portfolios.
2. He presides over the meetings of the cabinet. All important matters are decided in his presence. He may ask a minister to resign if he is not in agreement with his policy or line of action.
3. He acts as the link between the Governor-Gerneral and his ministers on all matters of public concern and, in a special sense, is the chief adviser of the former.
4. His power of patronage is vast. He recommends all important appointments as those of ambassadors, cabinet ministers, provincial Lt.-Governors, judges etc. and then the action is taken by the Governor-General.
5. As the leader of the parliamentary majority party, he guides all legislative deliberations. He acts as the leader of the House of Commons, makes all important announcements of policy and business, answers all questions on departmental affairs and upon critical issues, initiates or intervenes in debates of general importance and corrects the errors of omission and commission of his colleagues. He apportions the time of the House of Commons and submits the measures and proposals of his Government for its discussion and approval.

9. Mallory, *The Structure of the Canadian Government*, pp. 73-74.

Since the Prime Minister is the real working head of the state, his office cannot be identified with the classical phrase of 'first among equals' or with 'a moon among the lesser stars'. As has occurred in other democratic countries of the world having parliamentary or cabinet form of government so here, the Prime Minister "is now incomparably more powerful than any of his colleagues. Not only does he choose them in the first place, but he can also ask any minister to resign, and if the minister refuses, the Prime Minister can advise the Governor-General to remove him and the advice would invariably be followed. Cabinet decisions do not necessarily go by majority vote. A strong Prime Minister having listened to the opinions of all his colleagues, and finding most or even all, opposed to his own view, may simply announce that his view is the policy of the government, and, unless his dissenting colleagues are prepared to resign, they must bow to his decision."[10]

Finally, when we come to examine the real position of the Prime Minister vis-a-vis his ministers, we form an impression that he is the head of the cabinet and he far surpasses his colleagues in importance and power. His authority over his cabinet "is potentially enormous, although the degree and manner in which it is used will depend in large measure on the leader himself."[11] But as the Canadians follow the English pattern of cabinet government, they are not in favour of rechristening their system as Prime Ministerial government. The accepted point of view is that the Prime Minister "may have enormous powers, but the basic condition under which he governs compels him to wield his authority strictly on sufferance; he moves in an atmosphere of friendliness, tolerance, and suspended judgment in his own party, in one of constant criticism, suspicion, and outspoken condemnation elsewhere."[12]

Cabinet: We have already noted that not the unwieldy Privy Council but the compact team of the Prime Minister called the cabinet, and identifiable with the 'committee of the Privy Council', is the operative body in the political structure of Canada. Being the mainspring of the Government, it "exists outside the law, though not of course, contrary to it. It is a team chosen by the Prime Minister himself."[13] It is seldom that the Governor-General seeks to influence the decision of the Prime Minister

10. Eugene A. Forsey, *op. cit.*, p. 26.

11. Dawson, *op. cit.*, p. 45.

12. *Ibid.*, p. 192.

13. Dawson, *op. cit.*, p. 41.

in regard to the selection of his colleagues. He commissions the job of choosing ministers to one who is commissioned by him to form the government. However, some important conventions are observed in this important direction:

1. All ministers must belong to the party having clear majority in the House of Commons. If a person chosen as a minister is not a member of the House at the time of his appointment, he must be a member within a very short but reasonable time. Since the inauguration of the Constitution Act of 1867, there have been 70 cases, but they had to secure a seat in the House or resign from the cabinet.
2. Ministers must generally belong to the House of Commons, but at least one must be from the Senate. After the inauguration of the Constitution, there was no such practice with the result that as many as 5 Senators could have the offices of the Ministers in a cabinet of 13 persons in all, but since 1911 usually there has been only one cabinet minister from the Senate and that too without portfolio, the leader of the government in the upper house of the Dominion Parliament.
3. No Minister having his seat in the Senate can sit in the House of Commons and so no minister having his seat in the House may sit in the Senate. But after getting an invitation, a minister belonging to the House may sit in the Senate, speak there, but not vote.
4. There must be one cabinet minister from each Province, particularly from a bigger one. The Prime Minister may fulfil this conventional requirement by picking up a Senator from that province. It is also required that most of the ministers must come from the major provinces of Quebec and Ontario. At least one minister from Quebec must be an English-speaking Protestant, and there must be at least one minister from the French-speaking minorities outside Quebec, normally from Ontario or New Brunswick or both. It obviously reflects Canada's multicultural social set up.

There are three kinds of ministers in the cabinet. First, there are very important ministers working as political heads of the departments of administration. The President of the Privy Council, Secretary of State for Canada, Secretary of State for External Affairs, Post Master General, Attorney-General or the Minister of Justice, President of the Treasury Board, and Registrar-General may be put in this category. The second group includes ministers without portfolio who donot draw full ministerial salaries. However, if these ministers are charged with special responsiblities, a ministerial salary is usually provided as in the case of a Government Leader in the Senate. Last, there is the category of associate ministers who donot have full responsibility for a department.

Viewed in a practical perspective, the cabinet is, above all, a committee to negotiate. It is the supreme policy-making organ of the government. Thus, its main function is to reach agreement on what the policy of the government is to be. It coordinates separate departments into which administration is divided. Finally, it sees to the implementation of the decisions taken by it. If so, it automatically implies that it must not be a large body. As in Britain so here the practice of having an 'inner cabinet' has had its own invisible growth.

The cabinet performs very important functions. According to Dawson, its executive functions are as under:[14]

1. Its outstanding duty is to furnish initiative and leadership, to provide the country and Parliament with a national policy and to devise means for coping with present emergencies and future needs.
2. Each member of the cabinet is individually charged with the responsibility of exercising a general supervision over the work of his particular department.
3. While the minister is almost always technically ignorant of the special activity of his department, he need not and should not for that reason be nothing more than a useless ornament at the top of the administrative pyramid.
4. It is not only a planning and executing body but also a coordinating body. When two or more departments are involved in a particular piece of work, they may create ad hoc or permanent committees at suitable levels to eliminate overlapping, friction and wasted efforts.
5. It usually performs a wide variety of executive acts as
   (*i*) making of appointments of high commissioners, ambassadors, privy councillors, Senators, judges *etc.*,
   (*ii*) removal or dismissal of some public servants,
   (*iii*) summoning, proroguing and dissolving Parliament,
   (*iv*) participating in international affairs through plenipotentiaries and sending instructions for the ratification of international treaties, agreements and conventions,

14. Dawson, *op., cit.,* pp. 197-217.

(*v*) exercising power of clemency, issuing of a reprieve or a pardon to offenders against the law of the land,

(*vi*) deciding on certain matters relating to provinces like disallowance of provincial legislation and on provincial bills reserved for the consideration of the Governor-General, appointing Lt.-Governors in the provinces and sending them instructions from time to time.

(*vii*) hearing appeals on decisions against those given by Canadian Transport Commission in transportation rates and other allied matters.

Then, in the legislative field, its functions are like controlling the House of Commons, writing text of the Speech from the Throne, selecting Speaker framing parliamentary programmes, controlling finance, making legislation and enacting subordinate legislation.

The cabinet is responsible to the Governor-General as well as to the Parliament. It is responsible to the former in view of the fact that he chooses the Prime Minister and, on his recommendation, appoints ministers and also accepts their resignations. Then, it is responsible to the latter in view of the fact that the ministers remain in office so long as they enjoy the pleasure or confidence of the House of Commons. The responsibility of the ministers is of two kinds-individual and collective. While every minister is responsible for his own acts of commission and omission, he is also linked to his colleagues by the celebrated principle that 'all ministers sink and swim together'.

Parliament

Sec. 17 of the Constitution Act of 1867 says that there "shall be one Parliament for Canada, consisting of the Queen, the upper house styled the Senate, and the House of Commons." It shows that the Canadian Constitution follows the model of the 'mother of Parliaments'. The Senate, borrowing its nomenclature from the United States, in respects of its composition and powers, is more or less a replica of the British House of Lords. The lower chamber is organised on the lines of British and American models, but again it is a replica of the British House of Commons and not that of the American House of Representatives when we study its real functions and powers as well as its actual position in the Canadian political system.

Senate: The Senate is the upper chamber of the Canadian Parliament. Its total strength has been fixed at 112 (Sec. 28 of the BNA Act as revised in 1982). At present, it has a strength of 105 members with highest number of seats given to the provinces of Quebec and Ontario. It is obvious that here the American or the Swiss or the Australian practice does not prevail whereby each unit of the federation is given equal representation in the upper chamber of the federal legislature irrespective of its geographical or demographic composition.[15] The Senators are appointed by the Governor-General on a regional basis on the advice of the Prime Minister and now they retire at the age of 75 years. (Those appointed prior to the law of 1965 enjoy life tenure.) They must reside in the province or territory for which they are appointed. Different is the rule of Quebec where they must reside or have property in the particular Senatorial district for which they are appointed.[16]

A Senator must be above 30 years of age; he must be a natural born or a naturalised citizen of Canada; and he must have real estate worth 4,000 dollars net and total net assets of at least 4,000 dollars. He may be disqualified from the membership of the chamber if he fails to give his attendance in the two consecutive sessions of the chamber; or if he is adjudged bankrupt or insolvent or a public defaulter; or if he is attained of treason or convicted of felony or of any infamous crime; or if he takes an oath or makes a declaration of allegiance to a foreign power amounting to the loss of his citizenship; or if he ceases to be qualified in respect of his residential or property qualifications. Whenever a dispute arises on the matter of disqualifications incurred by a member, it shall be decided by the Senate itself. A Senator may resign whenever he likes.

The Senate is presided over by the Speaker appointed by the Governor-General and is removable by him on some special ground. The Speaker has a right to vote in the chamber, but in the event of a tie the decision of the House shall be taken in negative. The presence of at least 15

15. Vide Sec. 26 of the Constitution Act of 1867 the Governor-General may appoint 4 or 8 additional Senators on the recommendation of the Prime Minister in a way that all the four divisions of the country are given equal representation.

16. Appointments of the Senators are, of course, really decided by the Prime Minister and party service has, in practice, been by far the most important qualification for a seat. The relative insignificance of the Senate as a legislative body "gives it little appeal, however, for an active and ambitious man, so that the appointments are most attractive to those whose political life is almost over and who are looking for a sinecure for their declining years." Dawson, *op.cit.*, pp. 63-64.

members (including the Speaker) is required to constitute the quorum of the Senate.

The Senate has equal powers with the House of Representatives except in financial matters. A non-money bill may originate in any House of the Parliament and it shall not be treated as passed unless it is passed by both Houses. In the case of money bill it is given that a bill shall be initiated in the House of Commons and then it shall go to the Senate. Thus, the Senate may initiate a non-money bill ; it may amend or reject a bill passed by the House. There is no provision for joint sitting of the Parliament (as in India) or the settlement of the issue through conciliation conference (as in United States).[17] Its main work is done in the committees where discussion takes place clause by clause and public hearing is allowed to interest groups. The committee work is especially effective, because the Senate has many members with specialised knowledge and long experience of legal, financial and administrative work. In recent times the Senate has taken a new task of investigating important problems as those of poverty, unemployment, inflation, old age, land use, science policy, Indian affairs, relations with the United States, efficiency of public services and the like. These investigations have produced valuable reports, having their effect on the policies and programmes of the government.

Undoubtedly, the Canadian Senate is no match to its American counterpart regarded as the most powerful upper chamber in the world. It cannot over-ride a stand taken by the House of Common. But it is more powerful than the British House of Lords in view of the fact that it may investigate important matters of public concern and thereby affect the

17. Both the Houses may appoint 'managers' to meet in a conference upon any subject which, by parliamentary usage, is considered appropriate for such a proceeding. A special category of such conference, called the Free Conference System, is preserved for resolving legislative deadlocks between the two chambers over a particular piece of legislation. It is in the absence of any effective constitutional provisions enabling the House of Commons to resolve a legislative deadlock and impose its will upon an intransigent upper chamber that lies a further source of the legal powers of the Senate. It is not only that the Senate can reject a measure outright; there is no machinery by which it can be compelled to yield its position or change its stand on a particular piece of legislation. To ensure the superiority of lower house, the constitutions of parliamentary systems invariably provide some kind of swamping technique, ranging from the ancient prerogative of British monarch to create enough new peers to outnumber the Government's antagonists in the upper house to joint votes of the two houses, which secures the preponderance of the lower house. F.A. Kunz : *The Modern Senate of Canada, 1925-1963, A Reappraisal,* pp. 356-57.

Some Important Statements

Here we have adopted a different system. We have expressly declared that all subjects of general interest, not distinctly and exclusively conferred upon the local governments and legislatures, shall be conferred upon the general government. We thereby strengthen the central Parliament and make the Confederation one people and one government instead of five peoples and five governments, with merely a point of authority connecting us to a limited and insufficient extent.

—Prime Minister Sir John A. MacDonald

Except for the primacy of the House of Commons in financial legislation, the powers of the chambers are declared to be equal, but in fact it is the House of Commons which is the heart and centre of Parliament. ***—J.R. Mallory***

The purpose of Parliament is to keep the Cabinet (Ministers) in touch with the public opinion, and to keep public opinion in touch with the problems of Government. ***—Ivor Jennings***

working of the government. And yet it cannot be denied that the Senate of Canada is a model of a weak and undemocratic chamber for these reasons:

1. It has members (once appointed for life but now retiring at the age of 75 if appointed after the implementation of the law of 1965) nominated by the Governor-General on the recommendation of the Prime Minister. There is no system of direct or indirect election. The people have no democratic control over the Senators. It is obvious that the Senatorship has become a victim of 'party spoils'. In most of the cases, these posts go to persons who have already crossed the age of 60 years with the result that the people in general take every such appointment as the conferment of a booty on a 'dark horse' than a honour done to a really deserving son of the soil. The result of all this is that most of the members donot take active interest in the working of the house. It leads to the general impression that the Senate "plays the role of a senior but minor partner in the parliamentary government."[18]
2. The property qualification of the Senate membership makes it a citadel of wealth. As in the case of the English House of Lords, so here we find that the upper chamber of the Canadian Parliament is a fortress for men of wealth. As a conservative body, it protects the economic interests of the aristocratic class. It frankly opposes proposals for economic and social reforms.

18. Mallory, *op. cit.*, p. 223.

3. The cabinet headed by the Prime Minister is responsible to the House of Commons and the Prime Ministers have stuck to the tradition of giving least possible representation to the Senators in their team of ministers. Not only this, some Prime Ministers like Mackenzie King recommended certain names to the Governor-General for nominations to the Senate with this prior instruction to them that they would certainly support his plan of reforming the chamber.
4. Though Canada is a federation, the Senate is not constituted in a way so as to protect the interests of the units as we find in other federal systems of the world. The members of the Senate are not elected by the provinces, they are nominated by the Governor-General on the advice of the federal Prime Minister. Obviously, they act like the nominees of the Dominion Government and not like the representatives of the regional governments. The only constitutional requirement is that they come form different provinces. Thus, it is the federal cabinet that is supposed to protect provincial interests.

The weaknesses in the organisation and working of the Senate have been thus summed up by Clokie: "As a delaying body, therefore, the Senate represents entrenched interests capable of delaying constitutional or social reform but probably incapable of continuous resistance. The Canadian Senate cannot be compared at all to the American Senate in functions. It is more comparable to the British House of Lords but with this difference that while the House of Lords is permanently biased in favour of conservatism as interpreted by the Conservatives, the Senate is permanently conservative under the slowly changing labels of partisan liberalism and Conservatism. At its worst, the Senate may be considered as parliamentary anachronism inherited from pre-democratic days of the early nineteenth century; at its best, the Senate institutionalised the political manoeuvring which was required in 1867 in order to reconcile provincial politicians especially the legislative councillors who were promised appointment to the Confederation movement. Its primary use, now as then, is to provide a dignified seclusion for retired politicians who have deserved well of their party leader."[19]

House of Commons: This is the lower and popular chamber of the Canadian Parliament. It has 282 members directly elected by the people. Each Province and Territory has its own quota in this regard as determined by the Redistribution Act.

19. H.M. Clokie: *Canadian Government and Politics*, p. 127.

But sweeping changes have been made by the Constitution Act of 1982 in regard to the composition of the House. The revised Sec. 51 provides that the number of the members of the House and the Representation of the Provinces therein after the enforcement of the new Constitution and thereafter every decennial census shall be readjusted by an authority and in such a manner and from such time by the Parliament subject to following rules:

1. Quebec shall have 75 members, but it shall have 4 additional members after every decennial census;
2. A large province[20] shall be assigned a number of members equal to the numbers obtained by dividing the population of the large province by the electoral quotient of Quebec.[21]
3. A small province[22] shall be assigned a number of members equal to the numbers obtained by dividing:
   (*i*) the sum of the populations determined according to the results of the previous decennial census of the provinces (other than Quebec) having population of less than one and a half million, determined according to the results of that census, by the sum of the number of members assigned to these provinces in the readjustment following the completion of that census; and
   (*ii*) the population of the small provinces by the quotient obtained.
4. An intermediate province[23] shall be assigned a number of members equal to the numbers obtained;

(*i*) by dividing the sum of the populations of the provinces (other than Quebec) having populations of less than a half million by the sum

20. A 'large province' means a province (other than Quebec) having a population of more than two and a half million.
21. 'Electoral quotient' means, in respect of a province, the quotient by dividing its population, determined according to the results of the latest decennial census by the number of members assigned to it.
22. A 'small province' means a province (other than Quebec) having a population greater than its population determined according to the results of the last census but less than one and a half million.
23. 'An intermediate province' means a province (other than Quebec) having a population greater than its population determined according to the results of the last decennial census but not more than two and a half million and not less than one and a half million.

of the numbers assigned to those provinces.

(*ii*) by dividing the population of the intermediate province by the quotient obtained, and

(*iii*) by adding to the number of members assigned to these intermediate provinces in the redistribution following the completion of the preceding census one half of the difference resulting from the subtraction of that number from the quotient.

At present it has a strength of 308 members.

Sec. 51 says that each province shall be entitled to a number of members in the House of Commons not less than the number of Senators representing each province. Then, Sec. 52 says that the strength of the House may be increased by the Parliament without disturbing the proportionate representation of the provinces. The Revised Statutes of 1970 further lay down that the Yukon Territory shall be entitled to one representation in the House and two seats shall be given to the North West Territories.

The Constitution Act of 1867 says nothing about the qualifications of the representatives. It has been done by statutes made and amended from time to time. It is required that a member of this House must be a citizen of Canada above 21 years of age. Right to vote is given to every citizen above 18 years of age irrespective of his religion, creed, residence, language, sex, economic status and the like. The normal term of the House is of 5 years, but it may be enhanced in times of real or apprehended war, invasion or insurrection. It can be effected if the Parliament passes a resolution by its 2/3 majority. A peculiar usage has developed in this connection. It is that no Prime Minister desires to let the House have a full term of five years. Premature dissolution is sought a little earlier with the result that the House may be said to have a tenure of about 4 years.

The presiding officer of the House is called the Speaker. He is elected by the House soon after its first assembling. If the office falls vacant on account of the death, resignation or some other reason, the House with all practicable speed proceeds to fill up the post. In case the Speaker remains absent for a period of 48 consecutive hours, the House may elect another person in his place to work during the period of his absence. At least 20 members (including the Speaker) must be present in the House to constitute its quorum. The session is presided over by the Speaker. He exercises control over the House and its staff. All decisions are taken by the majority of votes. The Speaker has a right to vote, but a situation of tie amounts to the negative vote of the House. He is expected to be impartial, non-partisan, and as firm in enforcing the rules against the Prime Minister as against the humblest opposition back bencher.

Unlike his British counterpart, the Canadian Speaker is a partyman. He is elected by the House on a proposal made by the Prime Minister seconded by some leading minister or a backbencher. Since the Prime Minister is the leader of the House, his proposal must invariably be accepted. Thus, he may accommodate one of his trusted friends here after he fails to include his name in his cabinet. For instance, Prime Minister Mackenzie King persuaded Rudolph Lemieux to accept Speakership after he could not be accommodated in his cabinet in 1926. Because of this tradition, the Speakers have a sort of ambition to switch over to some ministerial assignment in time to come. Moreover, they are quite interested in enhancing the scope of their authority. An example of this type may be seen in the developments of 1965 when the House abolished the rule whereby the ruling of the Speaker on some crucial point could be challenged in the House and its decision was to be final.[24]

A comparative study of the functions and powers of the two chambers of the Canadian Parliament shows that the House of Commons is more powerful than the Senate. All financial business can be initiated in it with the prior recommendation of the Governor-General and then it is referred to the Senate for confirmation. The Senate may suggest some changes in a bill already passed by the House which it may, or may not, accept. The cabinet headed by the Prime Minister is responsible to the House of Commons. It is well remarked: "The key part of Parliament then is the House of Commons. Its power comes from its position as the directly elected House of Parliament and from its principle of representation."[25]

Supreme Court and Judicial Review

"Responsible government and federalism are two cornerstones of our system of government There is a third, without which neither of the first two would be safe: the rule of law. It means everyone is subject to the law; that no one, no matter how important or powerful, is above the law; not the government: not the Prime Minister, or any other minister; not the

24. See J.H. Aitchison: "The Speakership of the Canadian House of Commons" in R.M. Clark (ed.): *Canadian Issues: Essays in Honour of Henry F Angus*. p. 24.

25. Hocking, *Government in Canada*, p. 171.

Queen or the Governor-General or any Lt.-Governor; not the most powerful bureaucrat; not the armed forces; not Parliament itself, or any provincial legislature."[26] It is true that the Canadians have imbibed the well-established principles of the judiciary (established in England since the Act of Settlement of 1701), they have gone ahead in engrafting upon it some celebrated principles of American constitutional law as well.

The Supreme Court of Canada (established by an Act of the Dominion Parliament in 1875) stands at the apex of the judicial structure. It has a Chief Justice and 8 puisne judges who are appointed by the Governor-General and who retire at the age of 75 years. Three of the judges must come from Quebec. The Governor-General may dismiss a judge after an inquiry into his 'wrong doings' is conducted and then both Houses of Parliament pass a resolution of impeachment. Thus, it is said that the judges remain in office during 'good behaviour'. No judge of the Court has been removed so far. The only change effected in 1962 is that the judges (who held life tenure so far) are now retired at the age of 75 years. A judge may tender his resignation whenever he so likes.

The Supreme Court is the highest court of appeal. It deals with appeals against decisions of the provincial courts of appeal. It has the final decision not only on constitutional questions but also on defined clauses of important cases of civil and criminal law. It is also required to render advisory opinions on questions referred to it by Governor-General-in-Council. An important change was effected in 1949 whereby the practice of challenging the decisions of the Supreme Court of Canada in the Judicial Committee of the Privy Council was terminated. However for our purpose, the most significant part of the study is the power of judicial review that takes it very close to its American counterpart on account of the existence of a federal system. Instead of exercising this power in an indirect way and that too in respect of delegated legislation, the Canadian Supreme Court exercises this power in a direct way. It may be attributed to pragmatic considerations flowing implicitly from the principle of federalism entrenched as one of its critical dimensions into the BNA Act. Thus, direct judicial review of legislation in Canada "has occurred almost exclusively with respect to the distribution of powers between the federal parliament and the provincial legislatures, and never has it functioned to place matters beyond the competence of government generally."[27]

26. Forsey, *op. cit.*, p. 21.

It is true that neither the English Common Law nor the Constitution Act of 1867 specifically lays down the system of judicial review, yet its historical origin and growth can be traced in the decisions of the Court and of the Privy Council in the pre-1949 period. One may refer to numerous cases taken up by the Supreme Court and the Privy Council in which the power of judicial review was exercised and important maxims like those of Centre's paramount power over federal legislation during times of 'emergency' and Dominion Government's supreme power after the enforcement of the Westminster Statute of 1931 were laid down. For instance, in 1940 the Dominion Government referred to the Supreme Court the issue whether the Canadian Parliament had the power to make a law so as to amend the Supreme Court Act of 1875 in a way that the provision of appeal to the Privy Council be abolished. The Supreme Court had earlier given its view in favour in the case of *Attorney-General of Ontario* v. *Attorney-General of Canada* (1896). The case went up to the Judicial Committee of the Privy Council that upheld the judgement of the Supreme Court. It enabled the Dominion Parliament to make a law in 1949 whereby the system of appealing to the Privy Council over the judgement of the Supreme Court was terminated.

The Supreme Court has appreciated the provision that the Dominion Parliament may make a law for the order, peace and good government of the country amounting to the encroachment of provincial authority in this regard. But it has emphasised this point that the central or provincial government cannot delegate its inherent power in favour of the other. In the *Attorney General of Nova Scotia* v. *Attorney-General of Conada* (1951) the Court ruled that since the Dominion and Provincial legislatures were sovereign entities in th r own fields, neither had the power to transmit its inherent powers to the other in violation of the letter and spirit of the Constitution. In doing so the Court has recognised the fact that the Constitution was written in terms expressive of the ideas and desiderata of an age long gone and the Courts must face the task of reading the words so as to encompass developments unforeseen by their authors."[28]

The protagonists of the existing constitutional system appreciate the flexible and sensible stand of their national judiciary. They are of the view that the Court, as the final guardian of the Constitution, has begun to develop a more generous interpretation of the federal power than has

27. Van Loon and Whittington, *op. cit.*, p. 134.

28. MacDonald; *Legislative Power and the Supreme Court*, pp. 26-27.

existed, except in war times and thereby a proof of its adherence to the norm of judicial self-restraint instead of being accused of treading the path of judicial activism like its American counterpart. In this respect, the Canadian Supreme Court is no match to its American counterpart; it may be taken as a protoype of the Australian model. That is, it is not as powerful as the Supreme Court of the United States and India, it is not as weak as the Supreme Court of Japan and the the Russian Federation. Its parallel may perhaps be seen in the Supreme Court of Australia.

31

POLITICAL PARTIES AND PRESSURE GROUPS

As a country subscribing to the liberal-democratic order, Canada is known for having its own model of political pluralism. Some political parties and numerous interest groups play their role in the political process at the national and provincial levels. Once again, the striking fact stands out that these organisations operate in the midst of ethnic, religious and regional-economic diversities without ever trying to create condition leading to the 'political decay' of the country. The political system looks like a curious blending of the English and the American models, but the working of political parties and interest groups may hardly find its true parallel in the world of Anglo-American politics.

Political Parties

An attempt should be made to discuss the role of political parties and pressure groups in the political process of Canada so as to highlight their peculiar characteristics. First, we take up the case of the party system whose peculiar features may be enumerated as under:

1. Apparently, Canada has a multi-party system like that of France. There are several parties, big and small, operating at the national and regional levels. For instance, while the Progressive Conservative Party and Liberal Party are the two big parties, the National Democratic Party and Social Credit Party may be ranked among the smaller ones. A critical study of the party system shows that only two major parties (Conservatives and Liberals) dominate the national scene and, for this reason, Canada may also be placed in the rank of a bi-party system as prevailing in Great Britain.
2. The Canadians happily designate their party system not as a model of bi-partyism but that of 'one-party domination.' An eminent writer

in this field like F.H. Underhill says that what Mackenzie King established was a one-party domination at Ottawa with two or three splinter parties posing as opponents of the leviathan in office. The party of king, that called itself 'liberal' , not only blanketed the centre in politics but spread out so far both to the right and to the left that the opposition groups seemed to become more and more ineffective. This party remained in a predominant position until the PCP could challenge its position in 1958 with the force "still more overwhelmingly blanketing the centre and spreading out to left and right." This kind of party system has no resemblance with that of Britain and the United States where two parties have their distinct and stable identities and whose functioning cannot be disturbed or vitiated by the role of third or 'minor' parties.

3. It is true that the Canadian party system does not pertain to bi-partyism the type of which we find in two leading democracies of the world-Britain and the United States-and yet it is true that it is a bi-party system in its own right. The national political scene is dominated either by the Liberals or by the Conservatives. When one forms the government on the basis of its own strength or with the cooperation of a minor party, the other major party forms the opposition. It is not necessary that the party forming the government must be having absolute majority in the House of Commons.
4. This peculiar feature of the Canadian party system is interpreted in a different way as well. Sometimes, it is designated as the one party dominance. The element of ideology or rigid commitments to certain political values has been thoroughly absent. Whether it is the Liberal or the Conservative party, the leaders and their followers never take obdurate stands smacking of their convictions in a particular brand of political religion. It is in conformity with the political culture of the people. For this reason, Canada has almost no place for a communist, even a socialist, party. Its party system has been designated as 'accordion' implying that the party structure is extremely flexible, even loose, inviting a person of liberal disposition as an avenue of upward mobility.
5. The structure and working of the two major parties of Canada further shows their character of, what Maurice Duverger calls, a 'cadre' organisation. A cadre party is characterised by the fact that a relatively small group of leaders overtly holds power in the party. The small, well-organised elite which controls the party is usually centred in

the parliamentary wing. Moreover, the historical origin of the two parties may be traced in the legislature.

6. Barring the case of the FLQ (that has its marked existence in the province of Quebec), political parties of Canada aspire to maintain their 'mass' character. They desire to be ranked in the category of 'mass legitimate' organisations. It implies that they aspire to live and grow on the basis of people's support without sharpening religious, ethnic and cultural cleavages. They also desire to work on the basis of 'consensus'. The reason of the two parties being cohesive and broad-based lies in the fact that they have a remarkable ability to act as 'brokers'.[1]
7. Last, pragmatism is the hallmark of Canadian party politics. It may be seen in the untheoretical character of the politicians of this country. A French writer like Dorothy Pickles comments that 'over-indulgence in a national predilection for argument about ideas rather than about practical policies' is characteristic of French political party politics, but in clear contradistinction to it, is the case of Canada where the attraction for theories, doctrines and distinctions of principle is foreign to the world of political parties. The tradition of this country is heavily empirical, cautious about offering general explanations and well-known for its suspicion of almost all broad theories.

Now it shall be worthwhile to have a bird's eye view of the history and role of some leading political parties of Canada as under:

Conservative Party: Also known by the name of the Progressive Conservative Party since 1942, it is the oldest party of this country. Its origin may be traced to the days of the mid-nineteenth century when its leaders played a very instrumental role in the establishment of the Canadian Union and then remained in power for a fairly long time under the towering leadership of John MacDonald. In the beginning it looked like a motley gathering of extreme Tories, moderate Liberals from upper Canada and from the areas of Quebec as well as some English-speaking elements from the Lower Canada. They stood for centralisation of power, identified

1. The politics of moderation or brokerage politics is one which minimises differences, restrains fissiparous tendencies and thus, over time, helps knit together the diverse interests of a polity weak in integration A. Cairns: The Electoral System and the Party System in Canada, 1921-65" in *Canadian Journal of Political Science*, Vol. I, No. I, 1963.

themselves with the propertied class, defended commercial and industrial interests and, to the pleasure and satisfaction of the people in general succeeded in achieving the goal of nation-building. Their centralising influences and the policy of unifying people of diverse interests, origins and beliefs into one single whole found its expression in the national policy of protective tariff, in the construction of trans-continental railways, and in many other directions towards that end. Economic nationalism was, therefore, considered the best means of welding the people in a community of diverse interests and aspirations.

On account of being notorious for its conservative orientation, this party has its natural opponents in the French-Canadians of Quebec. For this reason, it sometimes tries hard to woo the Quebecans or forming alliance with groups of the French Canadians. The reason behind the prefixing of the word' Progressive' in 1946 should be traced here. It paid dividends to some extent, but it had its cost in another way. When under Diefenbaker the Conservatives sought to become the party of other ethnic groups of the country, they alienated as many Canadians as they gained by over-emphasising the 'different' nature of people who much preferred to integrate themselves with the Canadian culture. Keeping it in view, it is remarked that perhaps the structure of this party over the last fifty years or so "could best be described as a broken concerting, rather than an open accordian."[2]

Liberal Pary: While the roots of the Conservative Party lay embedded in the policies and convictions of the confederalists, those of the Liberals must be traced in the convictions of the provincialists. That is, while the Conservatives pursued, what the Americans call, the Hamiltonian line in establishing a federal union of the country under a new constitutional dispensation, the Liberals adopted, again what the Americans call, the Jeffersonian line of action. That is, while the former preferred the policy of centralisation and urban industrialisation, the latter adhered to the policy of decentralisation with special stress on the interest of the provinces and agricultural section of the people. Above all, this party adheres to the principle of flexibility as a result of which it does not incur the natural opposition of the French Canadians particularly those living in the province of Quebec and professing the creed of Roman Catholicism.

2. Alexander Brady: *Canada*, p. 263.

Some Important Statements

Canadian parties do not try to exploit such advantages as they enjoy among particular groups in the population at the exclusion of more general appeals to a larger constituency. Nor does one or the other of the two groups comprising the various cleavages try to press. But some groups identify with given priorities more than with others and this is of course reflected in and, no doubt, related to, the predispositions the parties bring to national problems. ***—John Meisel***

As far as we Canadians are concerned, the two-party system in this classical sense is only a sort of political Garden of Eden towards which our newspaper editors and our university political scientists yearn nostalgically. But an angry God drove us out of the Garden after 1918, and it is mostly wishful thinking that sees us now being readmitted to it. ***—Frank H. Underhill***

With respect to the most familiar items, the number of parties, Canada has to be described as a two-plus party system rather than as a two-party system in the clear-cut American national sense, or in the less clear cut British sense. 'Multi-party', however, would not be the appropriate label, since regularly not more than two parties have had broad enough voting support to win national power and since much—though by no means—all of the time, one of these two parties has been able to win national power on its own. ***—L.P. Epstein***

As its name suggests, the Liberal Party does not appreciate increasing interference of state activity in the social and economic life of the people. It stands for low tariffs. It champions the rights of the provinces and essential freedoms of the people. It is for this salient fact that while accomplishing the mission of 'patriation' of the constitution in 1982, the Liberal Prime Minister (Trudeau) also included a charter of fundamental rights and freedoms and specific rights of the provinces in matters of amendment in the Constitution Act of 1982. It also supports the plea of making trade agreements not only with the countries of the Commonwealth of Nations but also with other countries of the world. Its thesis of political nationalism accommodates the case of regional autonomy. It is due to this that it, under the leadership of Pearson, allowed its Quebec unit in the 1960s to act like a completely separate unit in its fight against the Centre on the issue of more autonomy for the provinces in the Canadian federation.

Third Parties: Apart from these two major parties, a passing reference may be made to third or minor parties of Canada that have some significance in the stasiological politics of this country. The wave of socialism led to the creation of a Cooperative Commonwealth Federation (CCF) in 1933. It was a definite result of the conditions of great economic depression that had engulfed all capitalist countries of the world in the early 1930s. Under the leadership of J.S. Woodsworth it could embrace within its fold the critics of the capitalist system. At its first annual convention held at Regina in 1933, it adopted a manifesto declaring: "We aim to replace the present capitalist system, with its inherent injustice and inhumanity, by a social order from which the domination and exploitation of one class by another will be eliminated, in which economic planning will supersede unregulated private enterprise and competition and in which genuine democratic self-government based upon economic equality will be possible."

The sharp socialist stance of this party failed to win wide appreciation. Thus, in 1961 the CCF changed its name to become National Democratic Party. The rank and file preferred the course of 'pragmatism' in stead of blind faith in the line of 'socialism'. Thus, Woodsworth claimed its more egalitarian character than any other political party of the country and launched a campaign against Canada's joining the second World War. In the post-war phase, it opposed heavy expenditure of the country on defence etablishments singly or in collaboration with the United States. These facts, however, confirm its leftist character. The protagonists have, for this reason, described it as a 'party of innovation in Canadian politics', though a critic keeping in view 'rightist' slant of the political culture of this country, may contend that the role of this party as an innovator "may derive not so much from the radical nature of the positions which were adopted by its predecessors some forty years ago."[3]

The NDP is said to have its effective ground in the provinces of Manitoba and Saskatchewan, but Union Nationale and Partai Quebecois are the two leading parties of the province of Quebec. A passing reference to these two parties shall be in the natural fitness of things in view of the fact that among all provinces of Canada, Quebec has politics of its own. It is the place of French Canadians subscribing to the creed of Roman Catholicism and often creating problems for the federal government. Union Nationale was formed in 1935 as a stern reaction against the then corrupt Liberal government of the province. It emerged in the form of a nationalistic reform party under Maurice Duplessis and remained in power in Quebec from 1936 to 1939. It lost much of its influence after the death of Duplessis in 1958. In the 1960s separatist trend developed and then a party called Partai Quebecois was formed in 1967 under the leadership of Levesque.

3. Van Loon and Whittington, *The Canadian Political System*, p. 275.

It could make some success in 1970 when, in the parliamentary elections of this province, it captured about 24% of seats banking on the support of the youth and other separatist elements.

Critical Estimate: A study of party politics in Canada leaves an impression that it suffers from three main weaknesses:

1. The political parties of Canada are like loose organisations tied with social and economic bonds and not with distinct political principles. Moreover, regional and local bonds play 'a more important part than national or confederal attachment. It is true that the two major parties play a significant role at the national level and yet this country cannot be placed in the category of bi-partyism. Sartori describes Canada's case of a bi-party state as 'debatable'. The Liberal and the Conservative parties "donot appear to be clear ideological enemies, yet party competition remains intense. The most frequent explanation in most analysis of the Canadian party system and of Canadian voting behaviour has been to emphasise the impact of regionalism on voting behaviour.
2. The functioning of the Canadian political parties is not regular, it is intermittent. The activity of different parties is quite visible on the eve of elections, otherwise it is almost non-existent. Even links between the national and provincial units of the same party remain apart during the intervening period.
3. Finally, all political parties suffer from the paucity of funds. The law of 1969 provides for state finance for the parties in opposition. But this help is too meagre. The result is that political parties donot remain active in the field of politics. They have limited staff just for dealing with routine activities. On the eve of elections, the parties depend upon the help of 'fund collectors'. Since big business houses provide financial assistance by way of donations, the party in power remains bound to be loyal towards its financiers. It is due to this that big industrial houses and commercial centres have power of changing the government in their hands. To them the source of attraction is the personality of a great leader like King, Pearson, Diefenbaker, Trudeau, Maulroney and the like.

Pressure Groups

A study of the organised interest groups in the political process of a country forms an integral part of the study of its party politics. The reason behind it is that while the groups articulate interests, the parties aggregate them. The former are the vehicles through which the demands emanating from the various subsystems of the society are carried to the political system. They make these demands in order to secure favourable policies and acts of administration. As they do so on behalf of interests in various subsystems—economic, ethnic, social, cultural and the like-they are engaged in, what Almond calls, 'interest articulation'. Political parties are the medium through which different interest groups operate, or they prefer so on account of pretending to maintain their apolitical character. A sort of two-way traffic prevails whereby both support each other for the sake of protecting and promoting some specific interest.

Some important features of politics played by the pressure groups of Canada in the political process of their country may be enumerated as under:

1. Since major political parties (the Conservative and the Liberal) have an amorphous character in respect of their 'ideological' commitments, the pressure groups also avoid firm partisan orientations. There is no such thing as rigid convictions or commitments on their part the kind of which we find in Great Britain where business groups invariably support the Conservative party and labour groups have the same attitude towards the Labour party. A minor party like the NDP may be an exception here that always counts on the support of labour unions. Interest groups look towards the personality of the great leaders of political parties and the prospects of their political advantages by acting under their leadership.
2. As Canada is a federation, most of the groups not only maintain their units at the central and provincial levels, they rather prefer to have their federated organisations. It is logical in important fields like business, agriculture, labour and the like. For instance, the Canadian Chamber of Commerce is the national roof organisation of about 850 local chambers in the country with their own large and small commercial centres. In order to be in close touch with the levels of administration at the federal and provincial levels, they have their hierarchical organisation with requisite staff. They follow rules and regulations of the central and provincial governments and maintain their headquarters mostly at the Centre, also in some cases in the provinces, as per their strategy for the protection and promotion of their specific interests.

3. All political parties suffer from the paucity of funds. Though the state provides financial assistance to the opposition parties under the law of 1969, it is all too meagre. The result is that political parties have to bank upon financial support available from the big industrial and agricultural houses of the country. Naturally, the role of money assumes an importance of its own in the politics of Canada.
4. Interest groups endeavour to operate through the medium of political parties. As Canadian parties have faith in the utilisation of democratic and constitutional means, so the groups eschew the ways of violence and extremism. We seldom hear about the activities and incidents of arson, sabotage, riots, assassinations and the like in this country the kind of which may be frequently noticed in other countries of the world. The case of some extremist groups of French Canadians in the province of Quebec may be regarded as an exception.
5. In most of the cases interest groups prefer to play an independent and autonomous role. They donot want mediation of a political party for their purpose what they call 'going into politics'. In several important cases political parties may, or may not, be found involved in carrying demands to the governmental structure. The civil service, most regulatory boards and Royal Commissions are approached by interest groups without the interposition of political parties, tendency among many interest groups is to transmit their demands directly to the governmental structure and not to parties. The reason behind it is their fear of identifying themselves with a particular political party and thereby facing opposition or isolation by the other or others.

When we come to study the role of pressure groups in the political process of Canada, we find that they try to influence the real decision-makers (Prime Minister and his Cabinet) by supplying necessary information and expertise, off and on, with much attendant fanfare. They submit briefs to highlight their interest in the name of the 'climate of the country.' They see to it that some of their seasoned members manage to be in the federal or provincial ministry. For instance, Drury and Sharp were leading members of the Canadian Manufacturers Association before they joined the Pearson cabinet, and Gardiner (a minister in the cabinet of Mackenzie King) had very close relations with the Canadian Federation of Agriculture. They also indulge in lobbying activities to bring a minister or a set of legislators under their influence. They depute their experts to the time of meetings of the standing committees to the Parliament to discuss a particular bill already passed by the House in its first reading. Royal

Commissions, especially the 'road-show' variety which holds hearings all across the country, provide an opportunity for great numbers to be heard. However, the most effective presentations of interest groups views are the kind that the public never hears about, for they "involve direct and informal contact between bureaucracy and interest groups during the process of policy formulation."[4]

In other words, it may be added that principal interest groups maintain close liaison with federal bureaucracy that affects them most directly. In the case of the Canadian Labour Federation, it is the Department of Labour. In the case of the Canadian Federation of Agriculture, it is the Department of Agriculture, and in the case of Canadian Manufacturers Association, it is the Department of Industry, or Finance, or Labour, or Trade and Commerce. The Consumers Association of Canada, whose interest spans many departments of government, at one point claimed relations of mutual trust and friendship with the civil service in six of these departments. In his discussion of pressure group activity on the Ottawa scene, Don McGillivray points to the 'continuous two-way consultation' between group representatives and civil servants. He testifies to this fact in these words: "If a decision is going to be made by five civil servants the lobbyist's special knowledge can pick out the man who will dominate the meeting and any persuasive efforts can be focused on him. It's no use lobbying people who won't stay lobbied."[5]

In short, as interest groups play a very significant part in the political process of every state of the world, Canada has its own interesting record in this direction. It is all the more relevant in view of the fact that it is both a democratic and an administrative state: though Hockin prefers to designate it as a 'modified administrative state."[6] Despite the fact that the relationship between the government and the interest groups is not as close as it is either in Great Britain or in the United States, it should not warrant us to minimise the importance of pressure group politics in this country. The fact stands out that the interest group structure "laces together the higher socio-economic levels of Canadian society and the political decision-makers."[7]

4. Van Loon and Whittington, *op. cit.*, p. 311.

5. Englemann and Schwartz, *Political Parties and the Canadian Social Structure*, p. 99.

6. Hocking, *op. cit.*, p. 135.

7. Van Loon and Whittington, *op. cit.*, p. 321.

Part - IX

Australian Constitution

There is no such thing as Typical Democracy, for in every country physical conditions and inherited institutions so affect the political development of a nation as to give its government a distinctive character. But if any country and its government were to be selected as showing the course which a self-governing people pursue freely from all external influences and little trammelled by intellectual influences descending from the past, Australia would be that country. It is the newest of all democracies. It is that which has travelled farthest and fastest along the road which leads to the unlimited rule of the multitude. In it, better than anywhere else, may be studied the tendencies that rule displays as it worked itself out in practice.

—Lord James Bryce

32

CONSTITUTION OF AUSTRALIA

A study of the Australian political system in a work on major constitutional systems of the world is informed by certain pertinent reasons. Like Britain, here parliamentary system of government prevails, though it has some distinctive features which have no resemblance with the English system. Here federal system prevails in which the units are neither as powerful as the States of America and the Cantons of Switzerland, nor are they weak like the provinces of Canada. This country is known for evolving the model of cooperative federalism. The High Court has the power of judicial review as in America and Canada. Regional and local interests have their impact on the operation of political parties and pressure groups. One may find a sort of mixture of the British, Canadian and American constitutional systems in the political system of Australia.

Australian Constitutionalism

The story of constitutionalism in Australia is neither very old, nor chequered in any sense of the term. The reason behind it is that it began as a British colony founded in 1788 at Sydney. The immigrants not only settled in an unknown place, they also looked towards their home country as the brilliant source of inspiration. They had a nostalgic appreciation for the legal and political institutions of their home country. The movement of Sir Henry Parkes triumphed in the inauguration of the Australian commonwealth in 1901. The establishment of a centralised administration at Sydney in the first colonised area of New South Wales could not remain at standstill. The pace of increasing population necessitated the separation of Tasmania (Van Diemen's Land) that was soon followed by Western Australia, South Australia and Queensland. In 1850 the British Parliament made a law that separated Victoria from the mother colony of New South Wales.

Accordingly, in 1883 the British Parliament passed the 'Federal Council of Australasia Act' whereby a Federal Council was set-up two years after with legislative powers over relations of Australia with the islands of the Pacific, prevention of the influence of criminals, fisheries in Australian waters beyond territorial limits, service of process, and enforcement of judgements beyond the limits of a colony. In addition, it had derivative powers over defence, quarantine, patent law, copyright, bills of exchange, marriage and divorce, naturalisation and other matters which any two or more colonies might agree to refer to it. This experiment proved a failure.

The conference of the colonial premiers held at Hobart in 1897 in the wake of great financial crisis took a historic decision. It was the setting up of a Convention that, at its Adelaide meeting in 1897, drew up a draft constitution. It was put to a referendum. It was endorsed by all colonies except that of New South Wales. But the mission of Parkes was now taken up by George Reid. His concerted efforts in his own ways led to the drafting of some amendments that were approved at the premiers conference held at Melbourne on 21 January, 1899. The revised draft was put to second referendum and fortunately this time it was ratified by all the colonies in June, 1899.[1] Queensland joined the movement in September 1889 and Western Australia followed suit about two years after. Then, it became possible for the premiers of all colonies to make a demand for the making of a federal constitution in the country. With this purpose, a delegation visited England in 1900.

The move of the Australian representatives was appreciated by the British Government. In his speech, while introducing the Commonwealth of Australia Bill on 14 March, 1900, the then Secretary of State for Colonial Affairs (Joseph Chamberlain) said in the Parliament that it "is the result of the careful and prolonged labours of the ablest statesmen in Australia. it enables that great island Continent to enter at once the widening circle of English-speaking nations. No longer will she be a congeries of states, each of them separate from and entirely independent of the others, a position which anyone will see might possibly in the future, through the natural consequences of competition, become a source of danger and lead, at any rate, to friction and to weakness."[2] Then, after discussing the result

1. A. F. Davies observes that "in drafting the clauses finally dealing with the executive, the founding fathers of the federal constitution showed an astonishing openmindedness." *Australian Democracy,* p. 19.

2. Cited in A. P., Newton: *Federal and Unified Constitutions,* pp. 311-12.

Some Important Statements

The Commonwealth of Australia was no phoenix arising from the ashes of a revolution or disaster; it was begotten of no great surge of political idealism; it was, in fact, the child of as hard-headed a marriage of convenience as was ever arranged in the salons of France. —***Ross Anderson***

The Constitution sweeps aside the difficulties which might be thought to arise in a federation from the traditional distinction between, on the one hand, the position of the sovereign as the representative of the State in a monarchy, and, on the other hand, the State as a legal person in other forms of government.... and goes directly to the conceptions of ordinary life. From beginning to end, it treats the Commonwealth and the States as organisations or institutions of government, possessing distinct individualities. —***Justice Owen Dixon***

We should seek to erect a constitutional edifice which shall be a guarantee of liberty and union for all time to come, to the whole people of this continent and the adjacent islands, to which they shall learn to look with reverence and regard, which shall stand strong as a fortress and be held sacred as a shrine.—***Alfred Deakin***

of a common Australian policy embodied in this important bill, he went on to add: "We believe that it is in the interest of Australia, and that has always been with us the first consideration. But we recognise that it is also in our interest as well; we believe that relations between ourselves and these colonies will be simplified, will be more frequent and unrestricted and, if it be possible, though I hardly think it will be more cordial when we have to deal with a single central authority instead of having severally to consult six independent Governments. Whatever is good for Australia is good for the whole British Empire."[3] In this way, the Commonwealth of Australia Act (9 July, 1900) came into existence.

Salient Features

The Constitution of Australia (being the Commonwealth of Australia Constitution Act, 63 and 64 Vict., Chapter 12 and as amended from time to time) has these important features:

1. **An Enacted, Written and Rigid Constitution:** This Constitution is a creation of the British Parliament. It shows its enacted nature. Then, its written character is evident from the fact that, in addition to a lengthy Preamble, it has 128 sections grouped into VIII Chapters followed by a Schedule and a Royal Proclamation. The detailed

3. *Ibid.*, pp. 312-13.

provisions of the Constitution cover the Parliament, Governor-General and his Federal Executive Council (including Prime Minister and his Cabinet), Judiciary, Finance and Trade, and the States, including New States. Finally, it is rigid in the sense that it has a special procedure of its amendment. Sec. 128 says that a bill of constitutional amendment must first be passed by absolute majority in each House of Parliament and then after two but before six months be submitted to the people for final ratification. In other words, a referendum shall take place in which all persons qualified to take part in the elections of the House of. Representatives, whether in a state or in a territory shall take part. In such a case 'double majority' (absolute majority of the electorate as a whole and absolute majority of the voters in at least four States) is required before that bill is presented to the Governor-General for the assent of the Queen.

The Constitution also takes into account the contingency of difference of opinion between the two Houses of Parliament. Hence, it is given that if such a bill is adopted in one House and rejected by another, or returned by the other with some recommendations or modifications not acceptable to the first House, and then in the same or in the next session but within a period of three months, the same House re-adopts it by an absolute majority with or without any amendment that has been made or agreed to by the other House, and once again the next House either rejects it or returns it with some recommendations or alterations that are not acceptable to the first House, then the Governor-General may submit the proposed law, as last proposed by the first House, and either with or without any amendment subsequently agreed to by both Houses, to the electors in each State and Territory qualified to vote for the election of the House of Representatives.

It is further given that when a proposed law is submitted to the electors, the vote shall be taken in such a manner as the Parliament prescribes. But until the qualification of electors of members of the House of Representatives becomes uniform throughout the Commonwealth, only one-half of the electors voting for and against the proposed law shall be counted in any state in which adult suffrage prevails. And if in a majority of the states a majority of the electors voting also approve the proposed law, it shall be presented to the Governor-General for the Queen's assent. No alteration diminishing the proportionate representation of any State in either House of

Parliament, or the minimum number of representatives of a State in the House of Representatives, or increasing, diminishing, or otherwise altering the limits of the State, or in any manner affecting the provisions of the Constitution in relation thereto, shall become law unless the majority of the electors voting in that State approve the proposed law. For the sake of clarification, it is given in the end that here 'Territory' means any territory referred to in Sec. 125 of this Constitution in respect of which there is in force a law allowing its representation in the House of Representatives.

2. **Cooperative Federalism:** Australia is ranked among the leading federal states of the world like the United States, Switzerland and Canada. Its constitution specifies distribution of powers between the Federal and State governments. While the powers of the Federal government have been specified in Sec. 51, the residuary powers are with the States. The High Court has been given the power under its original jurisdiction to settle Centre-State disputes and interpret the terms of the Constitution. The novelty of the Australian federal system lies in its 'cooperative nature'. There are certain concurrent spheres like those relating to taxation and borrowing. Some agencies of Centre-State coordination like Australian Agriculture Council, Coal Board, Premiers Conference and Loan Council may be referred to in this connection.

   Slight changes occurred during the Second World War when the Centre introduced uniform taxation and retained the power of taxation till 1975. It was called 'coercive federalism'. But again matters took a turn in 1975 when income tax was shared between the Centre and the States and the latter were restored the right to impose income tax surcharge or allow income tax rebate to their own taxpayers. The dissatisfaction of the people was removed to a great extent and they called it 'new federalism'. At the same time, the Australian government upheld the principle of States' rights and undertook to review its administrative relations with the States (manifested in the establishment of the Advisory Council for Inter-Governmental Relations) and to seek ways of avoiding duplication, overlap and interference with the affairs of the States. An intrinsic part of the 'new federalism' is that there should be greater coordination between the Federal and State governments in major areas of social and economic policy with coordination to be achieved by cooperation rather than by coercion.

3. **Parliamentary Form of Government:** The Australian Constitution has adopted the Westminster model of government. The Governor-

General is the nominal head of the state, while the Prime Minister and his cabinet wield real excecutive authority. It is given that each member of the Federal Executive Council must be a member of the Parliament. In case a minister is not an MP, he must be a member of either House within three months. The Governor-General acts on the advice of his ministers. His 'reserve' powers are very few like appointment and dismissal of the government, but their extent is legally and constitutionally uncertain. The Prime Minister is the leader of the party having majority in the House of Representatives. The ministry is collectively responsible to this House and through it to electorate. Since the trend of executive dominance is universal, this country has also witnessed the growing position of the cabinet at the expense of the inherent powers of the Parliament. For this reason, it shall not be inappropriate to call this system by the name of 'Cabinet government', though one may go steps ahead in christening it as 'Prime Ministerial Government'. Unmistakable is the fact that the authority of Prime Minister's office has increased many times over the recent years. In verification of it, Sir Ronald Munro-Ferguson says: "In this course of Mr. Hughes' struggle after efficiency the Prime Minister's Department became greatly enlarged, and (became) something of a maelstrom into which business for all departments is sucked and continues to swirl round and round, seldom getting back again into ordinary channels, where presumably it might be carried further."[4]

4. **Bicameral Parliament:** Like the United Kingdom, Australia has the system of bicameralism. It is the Governor-General-in-Parliament. Though not a member of any House of Parliament, the Governor-General is its integral part. He summons the sessions of Parliament, prorogues them, and may dissolve the House of Representatives. A peculiar feature of the Constitution is that of 'double dissolution'. It implies that the Governor-General may dissolve both the Houses simultaneously to remove the situation of deadlock. The Senate is the upper chamber having 12 representatives elected from each State and 2 from each of the two principal Territories. Its total strength is 76. The Senators are elected for a term of 6 years, half of whom are retired after every 3 years. But Senators coming from the Union Territories of North and Australian Capital are elected for a term of 3 years. When a new Senate is composed, it is decided by lot as to which half shall retire at the end of 3 years and then this process is set in motion. In Senatorial

4. Sir Ernest Scott; *Australia During the War,* p. 175.

elections, the voters of each State and Territory vote as a single electorate under system of proportional representation.

The House of Representatives is the lower or popular chamber of the Australian Parliament. The Constitution requires that the membership of this House must be about twice of the Senate. It has 148 members (51 from New South Wales, 39 from Victoria, 24 from Queensland, 13 from South Australia, 13 from Western Australia, 5 from Tasmania, 2 from Australian Capital Territory and 1 from the Northern Territory. Members are elected in a single-member constituency under a system of preferential voting for a term of three years. It shows that the term of the Representatives and of the 4 Senators representing the two Territories coincides, but it does not apply to a situation when the House is dissolved earlier on the recommendation of the Prime Minister.

5. **Dominion Status:** Like Canada, Australia is a dominion enjoying complete independence in internal and external spheres and yet recognising the British monarch as her highest constitutional authority. She retains close institutional links with Great Britain and pays final allegiance to the British Queen. She is formally the Queen of Australia. The Governor-General at the Centre and 6 Governors of the States are appointed by Her Majesty and they act on her behalf. The Governor-General is the head of the state and formally its Chief Executive. His functions and powers include appointing and dismissing the Ministers summoning and proroguing the Parliament, dissolving the house of Representatives (and the Senate also in some exceptional situation), assenting to bills passed by the Parliament or reserving any bill of great significance for the consideration of the Queen, setting up departments of State, appointing the judges and commanding armed forces of the Commonwealth. He presides over the meetings of the Federal Executive Council which ratifies or confirms the decisions taken by the cabinet. By convention, he acts on the advice of his ministers in virtually all matters and he is selected by the British Queen on the advice of the Australian Government. But State Governors are appointed by the British monarch on the advice of her ministers and cases decided by State Supreme Courts can be taken to the Privy Council of England in appeal.
6. **Independent Judiciary and Judicial Review:** Like the American constitutional system, the High Court of this country possesses the power of judicial review. It stands at the apex of the judicial system

and may deal with matters arising under Federal and State laws. It may exercise original jurisdiction in a number of cases like those involving interpretation of the Constitution and determination of legal disputes between the Federal and State governments, litigation between State governments, and claims between citizens from different States. In most of the cases it is the final court of appeal. In some cases litigants may still appeal to the Privy Council of England instead of appealing to the High Court. These situations relate to the cases decided by the Supreme Courts of the States in which the matters arise solely from the State law. But now a decision of the High Court can be challenged in the Privy Council after it (High Court) gives leave to do so. It is almost rare and so the High Court has become the highest court of the country for all practical purposes.

The High Court has a Chief Justice and 6 other judges appointed by the Governor-General. They retire at the age of 70 years. The Governor- General may remove a judge after an impeachment motion is passed by the Parliament against him on the ground of 'proved misbehaviour' or 'incapacity'. This Court exercises power of judicial review and, therefore, may pronounce judgment upon the constitutional validity of a law or administrative action in question. The Constitution says that no State law can prevail that is inconsistent with the law of the Commonwealth. In this way, the High Court may declare any state law void and make it inoperative to the extent it is repugnant to the law of the Federal Government. At the same time, it may act like the custodian of the Constitution. It may invalidate a law of the Centre on the plea of encroaching upon the legitimate domain of the State governments. It may be pointed out here that the Australian High Court, in this direction, is not as powerful as the Supreme Courts of the United States and India.

Federal System

As already pointed out, Australian federal system is a definite result of search of the colonies for unity and security in the midst of diversity created by their contacting economic interests. "There was no Damascus Road miracle about Australia's federal conversion. It took sixty years of spasmodic official effort and fluctuating public interest to bring the Commonwealth into being. British Colonial Secretaries and Governors, Colonial political leaders and public petitioners, intercolonial conferences, Royal Commissions and Parliamentary Select Committees, local

Some Important Statements

For the proper construction of the Australian Constitution, it is essential to bear in mind the principle of responsible government interwoven in its texture. It is, in the words of a distinguished lawyer (Lord Haldane) 'permeated through and through with the spirit of greatest institution which exists in the Empire'... I mean the institution of responsible government. ***—Sir Isaac Isaacs***

It was pointed out that his highest function would be of a dummy and that although he was the only link between us and the crown, in being that link he was less than the least in the whole of the colonies a useless image and a bauble.

—John Cockburn

The executive power is conferred upon the Queen represented by the Governor-General, and is actually exercised by a ministry formed by the party or parties having a majority in the House of Representatives in accordance with the Westminster practices of responsible government.

—A.R. Browning

demagogues and factions all, by 1890, had at one time or another been concerned with the issue of closer union."[5] Though the anti-federalists expressed their serious misgivings and showed a stiff resistance, ultimately the federalists had their victory after a good deal of wrangling. The draft of the Constitution prepared by the Convention and ratified in the second referendum assumed the form of the Commonwealth of Australia Constitution Act. It vested a limited and enumerated set of powers in the Commonwealth, the remainder lying undisturbed within States. No doubt, there has been, in fact, a fairly continuous development in the balance of power within the federal system of this country, but as Baker and others had foretold, "most of it has not sprung from nor entailed formal changes in document over which he and his colleagues so long and sharply contended. In this development, popular expectations, financial necessity, and judicial interpretations have played major parts."[6]

A federal system has three important features. In the first place, there must be a written and rigid constitution as the supreme law of the land. Then, powers of administration must be divided between central and regional governments in a way that both are autonomous in their respective spheres and thereby co-ordinate in relation to each other. Finally, there

5. The Australian federation has 6 States, namely, New South Wales, Victoria, Queensland, South Australia, West Australia. and Tasmania. It has two 2 units (Northern Territory and Canberra) under the Central Government. Crisp: *Australian National Government* pp. 1-2.

6. *Ibid.*, p. 39.

.must be an independent and impartial judiciary to settle constitutional disputes between the two governments and also act as the final interpreter of the provisions of the Constitution. Since Australia is counted among the federal states of the world, it is obvious that her Constitution meets all the essential requirements of a federal system:

1. The Constitution is written and also rigid so far as its process of amendment is concerned.
2. It specifies distribution of powers between the federal and regional governments. Sec. 51 gives 39 important powers to the Commonwealth as those of trade and commerce between the units of the federation as well as with foreign States, taxation, borrowing money on public credit, post and telegraph, telephone and wireless, defence, currency and coinage, census and statistics, state insurance, naturalisation and aliens, marriage and divorce, immigration and emigration, external affairs, acquisition of property, control over railways, patents and copyright, quarantine, fisheries in Australian waters, astronomical and meteorological observations *etc.*
3. There is the High Court to adjudicate constitutional disputes. It has the power of judicial review whereby it can invalidate any Federal or State law or decree to the extent it is repugnant to the provisions of the Constitution.

The Australian federal system has its own distinctive features which may be put as under:

1. It presents the model of a 'natural' or 'unofficial' federalism. It is like a gift of the British government to the people of another country without having marked diversities in social, cultural and economic spheres as is the case with other countries like USA, Switzerland and India. Behind all this in Australia is an inclination to preserve separate State and Federal personalities that let them adjust to one another by controversy and compromise. There are no sharp cleavages in the spheres of religion, language, culture and the like and yet the life of the people of this country "tends to arrange itself in a federal pattern: voluntary bodies such as political parties, churches, sporting and philanthropic bodies are organised on a federal basis and especially in the less populous States the sense of locality is strong."[7]
2. Australian system is appreciated for being a model of co-operative

7. J.D.B. Miller: *Australian Government and Politics*, pp. 138-39.

federalism. There are some useful institutions for maintaining Centre-State co-ordination. For instance, there is Joint Coal Board. Most of the country's black coal is mined in New South Wales, but the Board (having collaboration of State and Federal governments) takes important decisions relating to the supply, distribution and export of coal. Besides this, the Federal Government negotiates with the State governments for advancing money to them for house-building purposes and, in return, the State governments follow directions of the Centre in matters of design and use of such buildings. Most important of all is the annual conference of the Premiers. It is the occasion when Federal and State Prime Ministers discuss matters of mutual interest, though debates over distribution of the receipts under uniform tax or over tax reimbursement grants given by the Federal government highlight mutual suspicion and rivalry. "The result is a process of compromise, sometimes friendly, more often bitter and grudging."[8]

3. The people and the statesmen of Australia do not attach much importance to the issue of 'autonomy of the States' that often becomes a source of tension and conflict between the two sets of government in other countries of the world. They look like endorsing the view of Laski that federalism is an obsolescent form of government, an impediment to effective administration rather than a topic for dispassionate investigation."[9] Federalism, Australian style, is often seen as little more than an invention of politicians, without roots in social sub-structures, an impediment to effective government which leads only to obsolescent and unduly legalistic governing processes."[10] One may gather facts to highlight Centre-State conflicts on the occasion of annual Premiers Conferences, but a defender of the distinctive trait of the Australian federal system would say that those "who defend States' rights have done so more out of a common dislike of centralist policy than a shared political philosophy."[11]

8. *Ibid.*, p. 155.
9. H. J. Laski: "The Obsolescence of Federalism" in *New Republic*, 3 May, 1939.
10. Jean Holmes and Campbell Sharman: *The Australian Federal System*, p. 12.
11. *Ibid.* p. 20. It is also said that 'the Father of the Federation', Parkes himself appears at one time to have favoured unification and in his memoirs he recalls that in 1889 he had urged union on the model of Canada rather than the United States. See. L. F. Crisp, *op. cit.*, p. 31.

A critical evaluation of the Australian federal system, however, leads to some important conclusions. First, the enumeration of the powers of the Centre under Sec. 51 "looks more like a collection of odds and evens than a coherent plan of those matters."[12] Second, the trend of centralisation of authority has become universal now. If it has its unmistakable manifestation in other federal systems, Australia is no exception. The judicial review power of the High Court has gone to the advantage of the Centre to a very large extent in view of the fact that when a law is challenged in the High Court and its invalidation is feared, the federal government with a view to avert or forestall such an unpleasant situation "may enter an agreement with one or more of the States, whereby the constitutional power which the States possess is married to federal financial power, to produce a result which both regard as worthwhile."[13]

A study of the development of Australian federalism shows that since its inception it has passed through four distinct phases of 'coordination', 'cooperation,' 'coercion' and 'new cooperation', it is nevertheless certain that it has witnessed the trend of centralization as has happened in other leading federal systems of the world. This can be taken note of in the following important directions:

1. **Growing Authority of the Centre:** The irresistible growth of the powers of the Federal Government has its adverse effect on the autonomous position of the States. The state has lost its 'police' character in the period following the first World War and in stead taken upon itself numerous tasks of public welfare. The people, in general, have seen it with favour. The scope of government activity has increased considerably, Taking due note of this development, a defender of this trend holds the view that in the case of this country, the reasons for entrusting greater powers to the Commonwealth "are probably more compelling than in any other federation, simply because the hindrances to unity do not exist to the same extent. It would seem, therefore, that the factors enunciated by Wheare as making federalism an appropriate form of government either do not apply at all to Australian conditions or are of far less importance today than they were in 1900. The case for greater commonwealth powers could hardly be more conclusive."[14]

12. Miller, *op. cit.*, p. 140.
13. *Ibid.*, p. 153.
14. Gordon Greenwood: "The Case for Extended Commonwealth Powers" in Geoffery Sawer (ed.) : *Federalism in Australia*, p. 47.

2. **Control over Finance and Economy:** It is true that the States are autonomous in carrying on their administration in the allotted area of authority, but the power of the purse is tending to subject them in their positive activities to policies initiated by the Federal authorities. Through the formation of the Reserve Bank in particular, the Federal Government has assumed the role of a centralised authority in fiscal sectors. The emphasis on funding specific purpose financial assistance programme in recent years has shifted from capital grants and loans to current grants. In State areas in which the Federal Government continues to be involved, it has retained its dominant role where it considers national priority involved and over the general planning objectives and strategies adopted. Although the general feeling is that there is changing inter-relationship so far as the character of federalism is concerned.
3. **Judicial Interpretations:** The interpretations of the Constitution as made by the High Court from time to time have contributed to the same development. As in the United States so here, the general trend of judicial interpretations has been to increase the powers of the Federal Government by reading into the words of the founders a width of meaning which many of them did not contemplate. Reference may be made to Sec. 109 specifically saying that no State law can prevail that is inconsistent with the law of the Federal Government. Through its operation, the Centre "has ousted the States *pro tanto.*" In the *Forty Four Hours Case* of 1926, Justice Isaac laid down 'covering the field' doctrine that, for all practical purposes, is another way of expressing the principle that it "is the intention of the Federal legislature which is to be ascertained in every case."[15]
4. **Centre's Dominance in Federal-State Bodies:** Same development may be seen in the role of some bodies of Federal-State coordination like the Premiers Conference and the Australian Loan Council (another name for the Premier's Conference) entrusted with the task of coordinating public borrowing of Commonwealth and State governments. The Premiers Conference has no formal rules of organisation of debate, no separate secretariat, and is nowhere regulated by the Constitution or statutes. It is purely a conventional body laying down uniform policies on such matters as public health,

15. W. Anstey Wynes: *Legislative, Executive and Judicial Powers in Australia*, p. 96.

railways, motor car registration and driving licenses for inter-States visitors and the like. In the pre-War period, its annual conferences rotated around the State capitals and were dominated by State premiers. The representatives of the Commonwealth were invited only when the agenda so required. But the situation changed fundamentally after 1920 with the growth of Centre's powers. Now the meetings are held in Canberra, are summoned by the Federal Prime Minister and he occupies the position of its head. A meeting of the Premiers' Conference may be called by the Federal Prime Minister at the request of the State Premiers as well.

Undoubtedly, State governments may be found grumbling about Federal intervention on several occasions. But the fact stands out that the persons having a pragmatic view of the political developments of their country take it all in good spirit. As an advocate of this new trend testifies: "Australian federation was supremely a matter of convenience—first proposed in the late forties by way of official tidy-mindedness, it was only effected fifty years later when the predictable consequences of the 'barbarism of borderism' had made themselves painfully clear... The 'barbarism of borderism' lay not merely in the foolishness of present restrictions, but also in the reasonable expectation that misfortune would set them to spiral up in a species of ruinous competition. Only a single national political authority could assure the economic unity on which prosperity should be based."[16]

16. A. F. Davis: *Australian Democracy: An Introduction to the Political System*, p. 65.

33

STATE STRUCTURE

Australian political system is both federal and parliamentary. It is federal in the sense that the subjects of administration have been divided between the Centre, called the Commonwealth,[1] and the States, and the High Court has been given the authority to act like an umpire between the two. At the same time, it is parliamentary in the sense that the head of the state (Governor-General) has been endowed with formal authority, while real authority is with the executive (Federal Executive Council) headed by the Prime Minister responsible to the Parliament. However, as the parliamentary system has changed so as to signify the dominant position of the executive, it may be termed, what Sir Ivor Jennings, calls the 'cabinet government', although a follower of Crossman's doctrine may go to extent of designating it as 'Prime Ministerial Government'. It all shows that the Australian political system has its own form whose foundations are British, but on which some institutions of the American model have

---

1. It may be pointed out at this stage that the word 'Commonwealth', though often identifiable with the terms 'Union', 'Centre', 'Central' and 'Federal' as used in other federations of the world, has its own significance in the case of Australia. "In some Australian States and also in official documents, the adjective common-wealth' is habitually used to describe federal institutions and powers as 'Commonwealth Parliament', but in some documents and in common speech the noun 'Commonwealth' is often used to describe the whole complex of State and federal institutions, the economic and social life, the emerging culture and everything else which makes up the Australian nation. Federal politicians, sometimes in the heat of argument, speak as if Australian nationalism was an appendage of the federal government and fostered only from federal capital (Canberra). Such an appropriation of the national implications in the noun 'Commonwealth' is constitutionally unjustifiable and is unfair to the States, whose educational systems instil national sentiment." Geoffery Sawer: *Australian Government Today,* p. 2.

been engrafted. In this way, it finds its close parallel in the political system of Canada.

The Crown and the Governor-General

Since Australia has parliamentary form of government, the Governor-General is the constitutional head of the state. He is appointed by the monarch of the United Kingdom on the advice of the ministers of this country. In this way, Australia enjoys 'dominion status'. Sec. 61 of the Constitution says that the executive power of the Commonwealth is vested in the Queen and is exercisable by the Governor-General as Queen's representative and it extends to the execution and maintenance of the Constitution and the laws of the country. Though the Constitution says nothing about his term, as per usage it is of five years. The notable point at this stage is that since 1930 the Governor-General has become a model of the English monarch in the political system of his country without being an 'Agent' of the English Crown. His functions and powers are:

1. He represents the Crown in its Australian national aspect and symbolizes the executive authority of the Commonwealth internally and before the world.
2. He presides over the meetings of the Federal Executive Council and signs minutes of the Executive Council and other instruments approved by it.
3. He is nominal Commander-in-Chief of the armed forces of the Commonwealth.
4. He appoints the Prime Minister and other ministers and administers to them the oaths of office and secrecy.
5. He summons, prorogues and dissolves the House of Representatives. He may also dissolve the two Houses simultaneously in the event of an irreconcilable deadlock between them. Moreover, he may call a joint session of the Parliament in case fresh elections fail to resolve the deadlock.
6. He recommends appropriations to the Parliament.
7. He has veto power. As such, he gives assent to the bills passed by the Parliament. He may also return a bill with his suggestions for reconsideration in the Parliament and may even refer a bill for Queen's 'pleasure.'

8. He appoints judges of the High Court and of other Federal courts and may remove them from office upon receipt of an address from both the Houses of Parliament.
9. He appoints ministers. He also appoints officers to administer departments of State as the Governor-General-in-Council may establish. They hold office during his 'pleasure'.

The Governor-General is by all means the constitutional head of the state. His position is well comparable to the office of the English monarch with this line of difference that while the latter acts on the advice of his ministers, the former has some discretionary area of authority as well which can be seen in his power to reserve a bill for the consideration of the latter and also order dissolution of both the Houses of Parliament simultaneously on or against the advice of the Prime Minister. Keeping this in view, two eminent writers observe that the principal functions and powers of the Governor-General may be put in two groups. "The first group includes powers which properly or historically belong to the prerogatives of the Crown, and survive as parts of the prerogative: hence they are vested in the Governor-General as the Queen's representative. The second group includes powers either of purely statutory origin, or which have, by statute or custom, been detached from the prerogative; and they can, therefore, without any constitutional impropriety, be declared to be vested in the Governor-General-in-Council. But all these powers which involve the performance of executive acts, whether parts of the prerogative or the creatures of statutes, will in accordance with constitutional practice, as developed by the system known as responsible government, be performed by the Governor-General by and with the advice of the Federal Executive Council."[2] In short, the "Governor-General occupies a position of titular head of the state that 'appears to the active politician to be little better than a glittering and gaudy toy' (Alfred Deakin), or 'a dummy with a useless image and a bauble' (John Cockburn). However, appreciable is the view of George Gray that this great office shall be open at all times to that man in Australia who is deemed the greatest and worthiest and fittest to hold so noble a post."[3]

2. Quick and Garran, *Annotated Constitution of the Australian Commonwealth,* p. 406.
3. J.D.B. Miller: *Australian Government and Politics*, pp. 111-112.

Prime Minister and Cabinet

Whereas the Governor-General is the nominal head of the Commonwealth, the real executive authority is in the hands of the Federal Executive Council accountable to the Parliament. Its members (ministers with Prime Minister as their leader) are appointed by the Governor-General and they remain in office during his 'pleasure'. To ensure the principle of ministerial responsibility, it is laid down that after the first general election no Minister of State shall hold office for a longer period than three months unless he becomes a member of any House of Parliament. (Sec. 64). It is also given that until the Parliament otherwise provides, the Ministers of State shall not exceed seven in number. Moreover, they shall hold such offices as the Parliament prescribes, or in the absence of such a provision, as the Governor-General directs. (Sec. 65)

A notable feature of the Australian political system is that here Federal Executive Council is a formal organisation like the British Privy Council with this important difference that its members do not enjoy a dignified life-tenure. The reals centre of authority is a small body, called the Cabinet, consisting of some very important ministers. It is largely informal and often meets in secret in accordance with British tradition. Where necessary, legal effect is given to the decisions of the Cabinet by the Federal Executive Council. But the Australian tradition "has been to make no distinction between Cabinet and Ministry, but to have all ministers as members of the Cabinet. In all essentials, the formal part played by the Cabinet in an Australian Parliament is much the same as at Westminster. It is the government of the day; it decides the orders of parliamentary business; it prepares legislation; it is regarded as collectively responsible for government policy, and each minister is individually responsible for the administration of his department."[4]

In view of the fact that the Australian system of government is of the English model, it is quite obvious that the essential nature of this system emanates not as much from the words of the Constitution as from a whole set of constitutional conventions of responsible government. In this direction, the noted authorities on the Australian Constitution well endorse: "The cabinet is an informal body having no definite legal status; it is, in

4. *Australian National Government,* p. 396. In theory, the powers of the Governor-General of Australia are very great like the royal prerogative from which they have emanated, but their retention depends upon their non-employment. S. Encel: *Cabinet Government in Australia,* p. 39.

Some Important Statements

It is misleading to think of Australia striding remorsely towards unification because of the growth in federal power. The States no longer have the full independence within their spheres that the Constitution envisages, but they are vigorous agencies of government, deeply rooted in their own regions and charged with the task of seeing that their regions are not left behind in the race for development and expansion.

—*J.D.B. Miller*

During the courseof the sessions of the Conventions, there were cross currents and divisions of every kind. Sometimes, the divisions would be between free traders and protectionists, sometimes between conservatives and liberals; sometimes large states against small states. Any two members might feel themselves one day in agreement and the next day in opposition. They thus got to know and appreciate one another's point of view and a federal spirit developed continuously.

—*R.R. Garran*

The anti-federalists flamed the jealousies which naturally exist between small and large communities, telling the former that they would be over-borne in voting, and the latter that they would suffer in purse; and they wound up with the usual and often legitimate appeals to the local sentiment.

—*Lord James Bryce*

fact, an institution unknown to the law, it exists by custom alone, and yet it is the dominant force in the Executive government of every British country. It may be described as the select committee of... the Executive Council... and a parliamentary committee whose composition and policy are determined by the party commanding majority in the national chamber.... The proceedings of the cabinet are conducted in secret and apart from the Crown.... Resolutions and matters of administrative policy requiring the concurrence of the Crown, decided at meetings of the cabinet are formally and officially submitted to the Executive Council where they are recorded and confirmed. The principle of the corporate unity and solidarity of the cabinet requires that the Cabinet should have one harmonious policy, both in administration and in legislation and that the advice tendered by the Cabinet to the Crown should be unanimous and consistent; that the Cabinet should stand or fall together. The Cabinet as a whole is responsible for the advice and conduct of each of its members. If any member of the Cabinet seriously dissents from the opinion and policy approved by the majority of his colleagues, it is his duty as a man of honour to resign. Advice is generally communicated to the Crown by the Prime Minister either personally or by Cabinet minute. Through the Prime Minister, the Cabinet speaks with a united voice."[5]

5. Quick and Garran, *op. cit.*, pp. 705-06.

If Cabinet is the principal machinery of national administration, the Prime Minister by virtue of being its head is its central figure. "The leader and pivot—and, in an increasing degree, it would seem, normally the master–of the Cabinet is the Prime Minister."[6] He chooses the team of his ministers and may demand resignation from one who differs from him in policy matters. He is the leader of the party commanding clear majority in the House of Representatives or a common leader chosen by parties forming the coalition government. He may take special steps during abnormal times for smooth and efficient running of his government. For instance, Prime Minister Menzies announced the formation of his 'Economic Cabinet' in 1939, under his chairmanship consisting of some very important ministers of his Cabinet. In his long later period, he also developed a useful practice of appointing some younger ministers holding relatively light portfolios to assist those heading important departments.

Finally, we may take note of the fact that the growing trend of executive authority has been having its own form in the Australian political system. The authority of the executive is constantly increasing at the expense of the inherent powers of the Parliament.

Parliament

Like the system of King-in-Parliament of the United Kingdom, there is the system of Governor-General-in-Parliament in Australia. The Governor-General is the constitutional head of the state and he is an integral part of the Parliament having Senate as the upper and House of Representatives as the lower chambers respectively. Though not a member of either House, he is its integral part in view of the fact that he summons the sessions of the Parliament, prorogues them, dissolves the Lower House, and in an exceptional situation of deadlock may order 'double dissolution'. Here the powers of the Governor-General are more sweeping than those of the English monarch. Moreover, it is a case having no parallel in its English counterpart. Some other points of distinction shall also come to our notice in due course of our study. Miller is, therefore, right in holding that though the Australian Parliament stems from the common root at Westminster, it "has developed its own characteristics over the years that makes it possible to say that there is such a thing as an Australian style."[7]

6. Crisp, *op. cit.*, p. 357.

7. Miller, *op. cit.*, p. 96.

Senate: The Senate is composed of the representatives directly elected by the people of each State on the principle of universal adult franchise. The States have equality of representation in the sense that 12 Senators are taken from each of the six States and two Senators each from Australian Capital Territory and the Northern Territory. The Parliament may enhance this number without violating the principle of equality of representation. The tenure of the Senators is of 6 years. However, as the double dissolution system is a peculiar feature of the Australian Constitution, it is provided that as soon as possible after the first meeting, and after each first meeting following the dissolution thereof, the Senate shall divide its members chosen for each State into two classes as nearly equal in numbers as practicable. Thus, the seats of the Senators of the first lot shall become vacant at the expiration of three years, and the places of those of the second one at the expiration of six years from the beginning of their term of service. Afterwards, the places of the Senators shall become vacant at the expiration of six years, from the beginning of their term of service. The election to fill vacant places shall be held within one year before the seats are to fall vacant. Moreover, for the purpose of this section the term of service of a Senator shall be taken to begin on the first day of July following the day of his election, except in the cases of the first election and of the election next after any dissolution of the Senate, when it shall be taken to begin on the first day of July preceding the day of election.

The Parliament may make laws for the election of the Senators and the filling up of their vacancies. When the number of the Senators is increased (or decreased), it may make such provision for vacating of the seats of the Senators for the State as it deems necessary to maintain regularity in the rotation. If the seat of a Senator becomes vacant before the expiration of his term of service, the House of Parliament of that State for which he was chosen, sitting and voting together, or, if there is only one house of the Parliament, that House shall choose a person to hold the seat until the expiration of the term. But if the Parliament of the State is not in session when the vacancy is notified, the Governor of the State on the advice of the Executive Council thereof, may appoint a person to hold the seat until the expiration of 14 days from the beginning of the next session of the Parliament of the State or the expiration of the term, whichever earlier. It is also to be noted that each State may make its own laws for the election of the Senators within the framework of the central law in force. In elections each elector has one vote. The State legislature may also make a law to determine the time and places of the election of the Senators for its State. The Governor of the State shall certify the names of the chosen Senators to the Governor-General. It is also given that the Senate may proceed to dispatch its business notwithstanding the failure of any State to provide for its representation in this chamber of the federal legislature.

The qualifications of a Senator shall be the same as that of a Representative. The Senators elect a President from amongst themselves before the chamber starts its proceedings and they may replace him as well. The President may submit his resignation to the Governor-General. During the absence of the President, the Senate may choose another President to discharge the duties of the office. A Senator may submit his resignation to the President or to the Governor-General, if the President of the Senate is not in the country. The seat of a Senator shall be deemed vacant if he remains absent for two consecutive months without the permission of the President. Whenever a vacancy occurs, the President (or the Governor-General during his absence) shall notify this fact to the Governor of that State. At least 1/3 members of the Senate should be present to conduct the session of the Senate. Questions arising in the Senate are determined by a majority of votes in which each Senator has one vote. Here the noteworthy point is that the President takes part in voting in all cases and that a situation of the is taken as a negative decision of the House.

Upper chambers in modern democratic systems have lost much of their relevance on account of the ever-increasing significance of the lower chambers. It has happened in this country also. What has really affected the status of the Australian Senate is the factor of party politics and the peculiar provisions of the Constitution. The hopes of the founding fathers have been belied in this important respect.

Then, the provision of 'double dissolution' has had its own effect in this important regard. Either the Senators must ditto the line of the Prime Minister, or face their doom. Obviously, the Australian Senate cannot enjoy the status that is with its American counterpart. Whenever the Senate opposes the Government firmly, it is then the subject of very considerable and anxious thought on the part of Cabinet and of noticeably more interest in the House of Representatives. For there is likely to be in a Senate hostile to the Government none of what Shane Leslie described as 'the languid and dignified indignations peculiar to opposition in the House of Lords'. The Senate majority is in a strong position to snipe at and obstruct every measure of Government business and, if it is prepared to invite a double dissolution, to reject items of that business. The constitutional experts have desired that the provision of double dissolution should be done away with in view of the fact that it is contrary to the Westminster model of government.

Such developments have taken place in view of the obdurate role of the Senate in defeating bills passed by the House of Representatives particularly in the 1970s and early 1980s as a result of which double dissolution took place in 1974, 1975 and 1983. The men of disposition took it all as highly undesirable on the part of the Senate. The general view was that it "is impossible to reconcile sound democratic principles with the power of a Second Chamber constituted as is the Australian Senate to hold to ransom a government with a clear House of Representatives majority and mandate to govern from the latest House general election."[8] Thus, some proposals for reform, short of its abolition, have been suggested as removal of the 2:1 ratio between the numerical strengths of the two chambers, provision for a synchronised House and Senate polls and hence variable rather than 6 year terms for the Senators, requirement for each Senate casual vacancy to be filled for the balance of its term by a person of the same party. However, none of these proposals could be adopted on account of stiff opposition.

A critical study of the Australian Senate shows that its character has been vitiated by rampant party politics. It cannot be treated as a replica of the American Senate. In this regard, Bryce says: "All the expectations and aims wherewith the Senate was created have been falsified by the events. It has not protected State interests, for these interests have come very little into question... Neither has it become the house of sages, for the best political talent of the nation flows to the House of Representatives, where office is to be won in strenuous conflict... Not having any special functions, such as the control of appointments and of foreign policy which gives authority to the American Senate, its Australian copy has proved a mere replica, and an inferior replica of the House."[9] It may not amend proposed laws imposing taxation, or proposed laws appropriating revenue or money for the ordinary annual service of Government. It may not amend any proposed law so as to increase any proposed charge or burden on the people. In contrast, the significance of the House has increased. The House "is the vital centre of political life, but its vitality was impaired when the

8. Crisp, *op. cit.*, p. 348.

9. Bryce: *Modern Democracies*. Vol. II, p. 204.

Labour caucus was established, for the centre of gravity shifted to that caucus in which the Labour Senators sit alongwith their comrades of the House."[10]

House of Representatives: It is composed of the members directly elected by the people of the Commonwealth of Australia. According to Sec. 24, the total strength of this House shall be twice the number of the Senators as far as practicable. The number of the members chosen in different States shall be in proportion to the respective numbers of their people. Until the Parliament decides otherwise, it shall be determined, whenever necessary, in the following manner: (*i*) a quota shall be ascertained by dividing the number of the people of the Commonwealth, as shown in the latest statistics of the Commonwealth, by twice the number of the Senators; (*ii*) the number of members to be chosen in each State shall be determined by dividing the number of the people of the State, as shown by the latest statistics of the Commonwealth, by the quota; and if on such division there is a remainder greater than one-half of the quota, one more member shall be chosen in the State. However, at least 5 members must be chosen in each Original State of the Commonwealth. The Parliament has the power to increase or decrease the number of seats allotted to each State. The term of the House is of 3 years, but it may be dissolved earlier by the Governor-General. It lies within the powers of the States to demarcate constituencies for electing the Representatives. But the Parliament of the Commonwealth has the power to make rules for the qualifications of the Representatives. The Governor-General-in-Council may issue writs for holding new general election in the country. The minimum age of a voter is fixed at 18 years.

The Representatives elect a Speaker from amongst themselves and they may remove him also by a majority vote. He may tender his resignation to the Governor-General. During his absence, the House may elect someone else to discharge the duties of his office. The Speaker (or during his absence the Governor-General) shall issue writs for the election of a member for a

10. *Ibid.* The former Clerk of the House of Representatives of Australia observes: "Today, among so many functions, the Senate serves as an important check in the federal system of government. It acts as house of review, it checks the administration of the laws including the Executive's regulation-making power, and it helps protect the personal rights and liberties of the citizens, a feature of Senate consideration of legislation." A.R. Browning: "The Parliament of the Commonwealth of Australia" in S.C. Kashyap (ed.): *Parliaments of the Commonwealth* (New Delhi: National Publishing House, 1989), p. 6.

Some Important Statements

The House was intended to protect the States generally, and in particular to protect less populous States from any unfair use of the majority representation which the more populous States have in the Lower House. The working of party politics has largely defeated this object. Senators have come to be the members of one of the great parties first State representatives second; in fact, they represent their States no more and no less than do the representatives from various States in the Lower House. When feeling between the Federation and a State is tense (as in 1934 when Western Australia attempted to secede from the Federation), then all State representatives in the federal Parliament reflect that feeling. The normal relation between the States and the federal authorities varies from uneasy truce to amicable cooperation, and in such circumstances, the activities of the Senators follow ordinary party lines.

—Geoffery Sawer

It would be a falsification of democracy if, on any matter of government policy approved by the House of Representatives possibly by a large majority, the Senate, representing the States, and not the people, could reverse the decision.

—Prime Minister Robert Menzies

There is the growing necessity of Parliament's exercising not less but greater and more contant vigilance and greator care to maintian in its own hands the power to fulfil the trust of the nation that the Constitution contemplates, traditions and commonsense alike dictate, and every elected Member impliedly undertakes.

—Justice Isaac Isaacs

vacant post and it shall be referred to the Governor of that State. A Representative may submit his resignation to the Speaker or to the Governor-General in case the Speaker is out of the country. In case a Representative does not attend session of the House for two consecutive months without the permission of the Speaker, his seat shall be taken as vacant. The presence of 1/3 members of the House is required to constitute a quorum. Questions arising in the House are determined by a majority of votes in which the Speaker takes no part. He has his casting vote to break a tie.

The Constitution has some special provisions relating to both the Houses of the Federal Parliament. It says that no adult person who has or acquires a right to vote at elections for the more numerous House of Parliament, shall, while the right continues, be prevented by any law of the Commonwealth from voting at elections for either House of the Parliament of the Commonwealth. Every Senator and Representative shall have to subscribe to an oath of office before the Governor-General or some other person appointed by him in this behalf before taking his seat in the House. A person is not qualified to be a member of either House in case he:

(*i*) is under an acknowledgement of allegiance, obedience, or adherence to a foreign power, or is a subject or a citizen or entitled to the rights or privileges of a subject or a citizen of a foreign power; or

(*ii*) is attained of treason, or has been convicted and is under sentence, or subject to be sentenced, for any offence punishable under the law of the Commonwealth or of a State by imprisonment for one year or longer; or

(*iii*) is an undischarged bankrupt or insolvent, or

(*iv*) holds any office of profit under the Crown, or any pension payable during the pleasure of the Crown out of any of the revenues of the Commonwealth, or

(*v*) has any direct or indirect pecuniary interest in any agreement with the Public Services of the Commonwealth, otherwise than as a member and in common with other members of an incorporated company consisting of more than 25 members.

Powers of Parliament: The Parliament has the power to fix and revise the salaries and allowances of its members. In case a person is declared illegible for the membership of either House, he will pay a sum of one hundred pounds (equivalent to his daily allowance) for everyday on which he attends the session to a person who sues for it in any court of competent jurisdiction. Any matter relating to the qualifications of any member of Parliament or respecting a vacancy and any question of disputed election to either House shall be determined by the House in which the question arises. The powers, privileges and immunities of a member of Parliament, including those of different committees, shall be such as codified by the Parliament itself and pending that those of the House of Commons of the United Kingdom. Each House of the Parliament may make rules and orders with respect to the mode in which its powers, privileges and immunities may be exercised and upheld, including the order and conduct of its business and proceedings either separately or jointly with the other House.

Sec. 51. of the Constitution enumerates 39 'exclusive' powers of the Parliament. These are: foreign and inter-State commerce, uniform taxation, uniform bounties throughout the Commonwealth, borrowing money on public credit, post and telegraph, telephone and like service, lighthouses, astronomical lighthouses, observatoues, quarantine, fisheries, census and statistics, currency and coinage, national banking, insurance, weights and measures, copyrights, naturalisation, foreign corporations, marriage and divorce, civil and criminal law; emigration and immigration, external affairs, acquisition of property, control of railway, settlement of industrial disputes etc. Sec. 52 says that the Parliament shall have 'exclusive' power to make laws for the peace, order and good government of the Commonwealth with respect to (*i*) the seat of the government of the Commonwealth and all places required by the Commonwealth for public purposes, (*ii*) matters relating to any department of the public service the control of which is by the Constitution transferred to the executive government of the Commonwealth, and (*iii*) other matters declared by this Constitution to be within the exclusive power of the Parliament.

Financial legistation (relating to the imposition or remission of a tax and appropriation of revenues) shall not originate in the Senate. Such a bill shall be introduced in the House and then sent to the Senate which may return it for reconsideration with its recommendations. It shall, however, be within the power of the House to accept any of the recommendations of the Senate or not. A vote, resolution or proposed law for the appropriation of money or revenues shall not be passed unless the purpose of the appropriation has in the same session been recommended by message of the Governor-General to the House in which the proposal had originated.

Apart from these enumerated powers of the Parliament, reference should be made to its enhanced powers as a result of the interpretation of the Constitution by the High Court. Most of the powers of the Parliament are of a concurrent nature in the sense that the States retain the power to legislate on the same subject matter. But Sec. 109 specifically lays down that no State law shall prevail that is inconsistent with a Federal law and the High Court has the power to invalidate a State law to the extent it is repugnant to the law of the Commonwealth. The extended interpretation given to most of the powers by the High Court and the dominance of the Parliament in financial matters have served to increase substantially the scope of the powers of the Centre. The Federal Government's constitutional power over defence is sufficient in wartime for it to control many of the activities of the Australian citizens in a way it could do in peace time. Its constitutional power over external affairs includes matters necessary to give effect to international treaties. This power also enables the Government to secure benefits for Australia under international conventions.

Under the banking power, the Australian Government has created a central bank, a trading bank, a savings bank and a development bank and has provided for the regulation of the activities of private banks. Another important source of actual or potential legislative power exists in relation to foreign corporations and trading or financial corporations formed within the limits of the country. In the name of this power, the Federal Government has made some laws for restricting trade practices. By a law the Australian Conciliation and Arbitration Commission has been set-up that may issue orders and make awards governing the conditions of employment of the parties to the dispute. The Federal Parliament could have a more extended area of authority, but the interpretations of the High Court relating to Sec. 92 came into the way. It says: "On the imposition of uniform duties of customs, trade, commerce, and intercourse among the States, whether by means of internal carriage or ocean navigation, shall be absolutely free."

Sec. 57 of the Constitution has an importance of its own in the study of Australian Parliament. It says that in case a bill is passed by the House of Representatives and then Senate rejects or returns it with some recommendations that are not acceptable to the House and after an interval of three months tne House readopts it, whether in the same or in the next session, but again the Senate either rejects it or returns it with some recommendations that are not acceptable to the House, it shall be taken as a situation of deadlock and then the Governor-General shall have the power to order simultaneous dissolution of both the Houses. Besides, in case after fresh elections the newly constituted House again passes that bill and once again the newly constituted Senate either rejects it or returns it with some recommendations not acceptable to the House, then the Governor-General shall call a joint session to remove the deadlock.[11] Now the members may deliberate and vote together upon the proposed law (as last proposed by the House) and the adoption of that bill alongwith the adoption of any amendment to that bill, shall be effected by an absolute majority of the total membership of the House as well as of the Senate. Finally, we come to the veto power of the Governor-General. He may either give his assent to a bill passed by the Parliament, or return it for reconsideration by the Parliament alongwith his recommendations, or reserve the bill for the approval of the Queen.

11. Sec. 57 can be invoked when a deadlock between the two Houses is not removed within a period of 3 months, but it cannot occur within 6 months of the normal date of expiry of the House of Representatives.

Role and Position: However, the most significant part of our study relates to the declining position of the Australian Parliament. No doubt, each Parliament performs some functions and so is the case with the Australian Parliament; equally incontrovertible fact is the 'demise', nay 'decline', of the authority of the parliamentary institutions that is once again a universal phenomenon. The formal functions of the Commonwealth Parliament may be enumerated as under:

1. Making and maintaining a responsible government and, in addition, an alternative government;
2. Developing and winnowing leaders for government;
3. Seeking information on and clarification of Government's policy and debating it in a public forum designed for that purpose;
4. Appraising and criticizing Government's administration;
5. Ventilating grievances and requirements of individuals or interests in respect either of policy or the administration of the Government and pressing for redress or fulfilment;
6. Granting of supply and authorising the raising and expenditure of revenue together with the making of reasonable checks upon Government expenditure and accounts; and
7. Consideration, debate and passing of legislation.

But the authority of the Australian Parliament has been circumscribed by the following institutional arrangements:

1. The federal system has defined its exclusive jurisdiction over certain items and at the same time allotted separate field of activity for the States normally beyond its encroachment.
2. The High Court has been given the power to act as a constitutional umpire between the Centre and the States and while it has enhanced the authority of the Commonwealth Parliament by sticking to the doctrine of 'covering the field', it has also invalidated some laws and executive orders of the Centre in the name of being an unjust encroachment upon the power of the States.
3. There is the provision of referendum on bills of constitutional amendment. A bill passed by the Parliament seeking alteration in any provision of the Constitution must be approved by the people in a referendum. It means that the final veto power is in the hands of the electorate.

4. The nature of parliamentary business has changed. So technical has become the field of public administration that the ministers banking on the support of the bureaucrats have usurped the inherent powers of the Parliament in the name of their 'expert' knowledge.
5. Above all, the lethargic behaviour of the members and the acute paucity of time for debates has crippled the position of the members of the Parliament with the result that it has now become like a registering body.

Keeping all these points in view, Crisp has pointed out: "It is now-a-days a commonplace in British countries that Parliament is in eclipse, a pale, even sickly pale, moon reflecting but a little of shining sunlight of Executive power."[12]

However, Browning throws light on the relevance of the Parliament in these words: "National sovereignty lies in the people. The government is answerable to the people at elections and to the Parliament, which consists of the people's representatives between elections. It is this latter feature which characterises our system as one of the responsible government–the executive is drawn from the Parliament and is constitutionally responsible to it. In order to carry out its accountability functions, the Parliament needs opportunities; opportunities to influence, advise, criticise, and scrutinise."[13]

Judiciary

The judicial power of the Commonwealth is vested in a Federal Supreme Court, called the High Court, and in such other federal courts as the Parliament may create from time to time. At present the High Court consists of a Chief Justice and 6 other judges who are appointed by the Governor-General-in-Council and who can be removed by the Governor-General after an address for the removal of a judge on the ground of proved misbehaviour or incapacity is passed by the Parliament in the same session. The remuneration of the judges shall be fixed by a law of the Parliament and it cannot be varied to the disadvantage of an incumbent during his term of office. The retirement age of the judges has been fixed at 70 years. It shall apply to the judges of all other courts set up according to a law of the Parliament. A judge may submit his resignation to the Governor-General.

12. Crisp, *op. cit.*. p. 267

13. A.R. Browning, *op. cit.*, p. 14.

The High Court has original as well as appellate jurisdictions. Its original jurisdiction (vide Sec. 75) covers matters (*i*) arising under any treaty, (*ii*) affecting consuls or other representatives of other countries, or where the Commonwealth or a person suing or being sued on behalf of the Commonwealth is a party, (*iii*) between States or between residents of different States, (*iv*) between a State and a resident of another State, (*v*) in which a writ of *mandamus* or prohibition or injunction is sought against an officer of the Commonwealth. Besides, according to Sec. 76, the Parliament may make laws conferring original jurisdiction on the High Court in any matter arising under this Constitution or involving its interpretation, or arising under any laws made by the Parliament, or of admiralty and maritime jurisdiction. Vide Sec. 77, the Parliament, with respect to any of the matters mentioned in the last two sections, may make laws (*i*) defining the jurisdiction of any Federal Court other than the High Court, (*ii*) defining the extent to which the jurisdiction of any Federal Court shall be exclusive of that which belongs to or is invested in the Courts of the States, (*iii*) investing any Court of a State with federal jurisdiction.

The appellate jurisdiction of the High Court (under Sec. 73) is related to the hearing and determination of appeals from all judgements, decrees, orders and sentences of a Justice or Justices exercising original jurisdiction of the High Court, (*ii*) of any other Federal Court or Courts exercising federal jurisdiction, or the Supreme Court of any State, or of any other Court of any State from which at the establishment of the Commonwealth an appeal lies to the Queen-in-Council (Privy Council of England), (*iii*) of the Inter-State Commission but as to questions of law. The Parliament has the power to make regulations and exceptions in this regard. However, no exception or regulation prescribed by the Parliament shall prevent the High Court from hearing and determining any appeal from the Supreme Court of a State in any matter in which at the establishment of the Commonwealth an appeal lies from the Supreme Court to the Queen-in-Council. The Parliament may make laws conferring rights to proceed against the Commonwealth or a State in respect of matters within the limits of judicial power. The federal jurisdiction of any Court may be exercised by such number of judges as the Parliament prescribes. The trial on indictment of any offence against any law of the Commonwealth shall be by jury, and every such trial shall be held in the State where the. offence was committed, and if the offence was not committed within any State the trial shall be held at such place or places as the Parliament prescribes. In all judicial cases the judgement of the High Court shall be final and binding.

The High Court stands at the apex of the Australian federal judicial system. The notable point at this stage is that while it "operates within the English legal tradition, but owes much in conception and function to the Supreme Court of the United States."[14] It is on account of the fact that it has power of judicial review whereby it may interpret the terms of the Constitution and then declare a State law unconstitutional and hence inoperative to the extent it is repugnant to the law of the Centre. It is true that the power of judicial review is given to all courts, but the judgement of the High Court, as we have already seen, is final. Moreover, this principle of judicial review "does not apply only to the federal constitution or to the statutes of the Federal Parliament; it applies equally to the State constitutions, and to the validity of State legislation under both the State and federal constitutions."[15]

The Australian Constitution, like its American counterpart, nowhere confers this power specifically upon the federal judiciary. It is, however, contained in the text of Sec. 109 that the law of the Centre shall prevail and the law of a State shall be inoperative to the extent it is inconsistent with the law of the Commonwealth. In other words, the Constitution does not expressly establish judicial review, but it was always contemplated that the Courts would police its provisions and the special provisions made for the hearing of the constitutional cases are inconsistent with its assumption. Thus, what Chief Justice Marshall did in the United States was done by Sir Isaac Isaacs in Australia. He is said to be chiefly responsible for establishing in this period a characteristic doctrine concerning supremacy of the law of the Commonwealth. According to this view, Commonwealth law renders State law inoperative not only when there is direct collision between the two laws, but also when the Commonwealth law seems intended to provide a complete code on the relevant matter. This is known by the name of 'covering the field doctrine'.

In order to describe briefly the system of judicial review in Australia we may refer to some leading cases. In 1936 the Privy Council held that the Dried Fruits Act, 1928-35 of the Commonwealth Parliament, was *ultra vires* of Sec. 92 of the Australian Constitution.[16] In 1948 in the case of

14. Miller, *op. cit.*, p. 141.

15. Geoffery Sawer: *Australian Government Today*, pp. 43-44.

16. See Wade and Phillips: *Constitutional Law*, Ed. 1957, p. 456.

Bank of New South Wales v. *Commonwealth of Australia,* the High Court ruled that the nationalisation of banks violated Sec. 92 of the Constitution and the Privy Council confirmed the decision in appeal. The plea was that it amounted to the creation of a monopoly. In this case Lord Porter observed: "Sec. 92 does give to the citizen and the Commonwealth the right to ignore and, if necessary to call on, the judicial power to help him to resist legislative or executive action which offends against this section".

A pertinent question at this stage may be asked as to how the system of judicial review has acquired legitimacy in this country. Miller has given three main reasons for this.

1. It is accepted by everyone as final and no one indicts the judgements as other than strictly legal in character, although governments spend much time in trying to evade that effects of the Court's judgements. It is not subject to anything like the same degree of criticism and controversy as the US Supreme Court.
2. The Court does not give 'advisory opinions' on proposed legislation, and delivers no judgement until an actual case is brought before it; consequently a government never knows for certain when it passes legislation through Parliament that legislation will prove valid.
3. One should not proceed on the assumption that in all the cases before the Court the Federal Government is ranged against the States. The situation is usually that a Federal law is challenged in the Court by some individual citizens or corporation anxious that the law should not be passed at all, either at the State or Federal level, and who wants the Commonwealth law disallowed, in the confident expectation that, even if the States have power to pass it, they will not do so. Sometimes, in such cases a State will range itself alongside the litigant, because it is of a different political complexion from the Federal government which passed the law in question or because it considered State rights in danger: but in most such cases the issue is not between State and Federal Governments, but whether a particular law is to be enacted at all.

Therefore, the process of judicial review has become a part and parcel of the Australian constitutional system. Judicial supremacy was written in its interpretation firmly into the Constitution despite the fact that some protagonists of the English constitutional system ridiculed it as 'a creation of the lawyers looking for fat fees'. The fact stands out that the Constitution of Australia was written by the men of law and justice and a learned figure like Justice Griffith in the case of *D 'Emden* v. *Pedder* (1904) frankly confessed that the framers "had received definite and settled interpretation of certain provisions of the American constitution." The process of judicial review has now national recognition in the light of new urges and aspirations of the people as well as new conditions and circumstances of the age. Crisp is justified in saying: "Whether one agrees with their 'judicial statesmanship' or admires their 'strict and complete legalism', they have succeeded, with varying degrees of zeal and wisdom, in imparting a necessary measure of flexibility and an adaptability and a capacity for 'growth' to the constitutional text."[17]

17. Crisp, *op. cit.*, pp. 81-82

34

POLITICAL PARTIES AND PRESSURE GROUPS

Every democratic country has a party system of its own and every party system operates with the visible as well as invisible support of numerous organised groups. In the language of 'comparative politics', as given by G. A. Almond of the United States, while the groups articulate specific interests, the parties aggregate them. There happens a two-way traffic: while the political parties need cooperation of interest groups for requisitioning man-power and money-power, the organised groups have an alliance with the parties for seeking political guidance as well as influencing the role of decision-makers as per their specific interest to the best possible extent. This phenomenon has its manifestation in all democratic countries of the world. Hence, Australia can be no exception. Rather the peculiar feature of the politics of this country is that here groups dominate parties, as in the United States, in view of the fact that no political party has a unified and centralised apex structure the kind of which we find in Britain. All political parties have local and regional branches controlled by their State units with the result that their top units stationed in the Federal Capital Territory of Canberra exercise nothing more than formal control. The fact stands out that each political party "is supported by easily identifiable syndicates, *i.e.*, organisations of people whose economic and vocational interests have induced them to band together for action to their common advantage..."[1]

Political Parties

Party system has become indispensable in every democratic polity of the world. For this reason, Australia can be no exception. In defence it is said that the main interest of political parties lies in their anti-bureaucratic

1. J.D.B. Miller: *Australian Government and Politics*, p. 65.

role in the political system. Their main functions "are to collect and absorb the chaotic and irrational demands of a wide section of primary political groups, to order them, and on gaining office, to impose them as an authoritative pattern of policy on the administration. There are, of course, other groups and institutions of an anti-bureaucratic setup, but none rivaling the parties in sheer bravado."[2] One may say that such a broad generalisation in favour of the party system is applicable to any democratic country of the world. As such, it applies to Australia as well. But the significance of political parties in the political system of Australia is further strengthened with the fact that here these "are the first bodies which occur to the Australian when he thinks of 'politics', and they are inextricably woven into the fabric of government. The Australian is inclined to rebel periodically against 'party politics' as something which prevents the true achievement of the common good, but his solution to a problem is either to apply to one of the existing parties or form a new one."[3]

The party system of Australia has its essential characteristics that may be enumerated as under:

1. **Three-Party System**: Australia is generally ranked among the multi-party states of the world. Four parties are represented in the Federal Parliament. These are: Liberal Party, Australian Labour Party, National Party of Australia and Australian Democrats. Among smaller ones are Country Party, Communist Party, Progress Party and Call to Australia Party. But in practical terms, two major parties (Liberal and Labour) dominate the scene at the Federal and State levels, though Tasmania and South Australia may be excepted. And yet Australia cannot be likened with the British or American bi-party system. Here Country Party and National Party, though very small, sometimes hold veto in their hands and compel one of the two major parties to join hands in the formation of government. Thus, Australia is occasionally described as two-and-a-half party state. However, taking into account the strong position of the Country Party particularly in the State of Victoria, it shall be in the natural fitness of things to describe Australia as a three-party state.
2. **Moderate Character:** Moderatism is another feature of the Australian party system. All parties have faith in the system of

2. A.F. Davis: *Australian Democracy: An Introduction to the Political System*, p. 137.
3. Miller, *op. cit.*, p. 63.

parliamentary democracy and there are no sharp ideological dissensions among them. All desire maintenance of the liberties of the individual (including freedom of speech, religion, association) and rule of law. The Communist Party is an exception in this regard and, for this reason, it has no place of significance. A change in the rule of the party, therefore, fails to bring about a sudden and major 'change in the character of administration. The general view is that all major parties act according to some 'settled policies'.

3. **Predominance of Economic Issues:** Not political but economic issues have more effective say in the working of party system in this country. The parties do not bother for the form of government or pattern of public administration that should be retained or changed as may be seen in many countries of the world; they remain concerned more with the protection and promotion of their specific economic interests. Moreover, as this is the specialized field of interest groups, naturally relationship between political parties and pressure groups becomes very strong in the country.
4. **Weight of Regional Forces:** All parties have similarity in organisation; they are federal in character, with State divisions or branches and federal executive conferences. The reason is that this country has become a nation-state for the colonies. Parties have their primary and effective organisations in the States and they have spread out their network to the national level in order to operate effectively in the Federal Parliament. There is nothing like centralised command over the lower branches of the parties the kind of which we find in Britain and India. In this respect, Australian party system has its parallel in that of the United States. The State bodies count most and the Federal organisation comes into picture at the time of elections to the Federal Parliament or some national crisis.
5. **Parties of Government:** If the term 'party' involves participation in power, it has its best reflection in Australia. Each party gets chance to be in power on some as well as in opposition on some other occasions. The result is that each party is accustomed to behave responsibly. The National Party and Country Party are a case by themselves. Sometimes, either of the two forms coalition with some other party, at others it sits in opposition. The notable point is that while some parties always live in political wilderness in other countries of the world, as in India, it does not happen in this country. Serious clashes between the government and the opposition do not

take place and with the change of party rule, a major reversal of policy is not possible unless there is some exceptional situation of national or international crisis.

Since Australian party system is constituted by the role of three major parties, it shall now be in the natural fitness of things to discuss their organisation, policies and programmes in the following manner:

Liberal Party: This party looks like a fusion of some organisations ranging from the pole of mellowed conservatism to soft progressivism. Called National Party in 1917 and United Australia Party in 1931, it restored its original name in 1945 as a result of the efforts of R.G. Menzies. The change of nomenclature by no means affects its political traditions. Its leaders interpret it as a definite consequence of the infusion of 'new blood' in the organisation. It operates as a loose federation with strong roots at the State levels. The local branches are controlled by the State units and its annual conference or convention held at Canberra hardly exercises an effective control on subordinate units. It adheres to British traditions of parliamentary democracy. Its broad aims and objectives cover its stress on the maintenance of an intelligent, free and liberal democracy, rule of law, protection against exploitation and the like.

It has no affiliate syndicates in an outward form, though it depends upon the support of business houses. In this way, it can be likened with the British Conservative Party. In this sense, it is the anti-socialist party of Australia, the party of low taxation and economic freedom. Whenever the big business class is put to difficulty by the Labour government, this party immediately gains its support. "The position may be summed up by saying that the Liberal Party is likely to be well supplied with funds at times when a Labour Government has passed legislation, especially damaging to business, such as an attempt at bank nationalisation or the 40-hour week, but that it may find its funds falling if there is disagreement among its syndicates over the policy it should pursue in office (such as new tariffs or a change in the external exchange rate, or if manufacturers in particular have come to terms with a Labour government which they regard as benevolent or harmless. Manufacturers, traders, commercial firms and the higher professions constitute the syndicates which normally support the Liberal Party, but they have no formal connection with it and so cannot be held responsible for its actions in the same way as the trade unions can, at times, be held responsible for the Labour Party'. They are not 'solid' with one another as groups, or even within each group.

In fine, Liberal party is anti-labour. Since the National and Country Parties may be treated as its counterparts, often they may be seen very close to each other. The general impression is that it is 'anti-Labour party' or the 'big business party' whose advocates claim having held important ideals helping to preserve and nourish the best aspects of Australian life. It may be termed the party of capital for the obvious reason that it stands for the protection of the interests of the affluent class. A defender may, however, argue that it does not subscribe to the full *laissez faire* philosophy of classical individualists, and yet it cannot be denied that it prefers to set limits on the area of state activity.

Country Party: It is the rural counterpart of the Liberal Party in its own right. Formed in 1914 by the Farmers' and Settlers' Association and developed after 1919, it is known for holding veto in its hands. Whenever Liberal Party needs its cooperation in view of its slender majority or to keep itself in power, it dictates its own terms and manages to have a Prime Minister of its choice in the coalition government. Though it is very close to the Liberal Party in terms of its economic philosophy, it may be taken note of that it creates problems for the Liberals when they try to woo rural votes. It plays a unique kind of politics by supporting the Liberal Party and yet criticising its policies and programmes so as to retain the position of a powerful minority group compelling the Liberal Party to bow head before requisitioning its cooperation. Its leaders frequently borrow the invectives of the Labour Party to condemn its capitalist orientation just to see Liberal leaders unsuccessful in rural constituencies and instead its own representatives sitting in the Federal and State legislatures for protecting and promoting specifically rural interests. This kind of politics becomes successful in South Australia where the two parties are combined to make a Liberal-Country League.

The rural orientation of this party is evident in its call that 'the man on the land is the backbone of the country.' By all means, it is a 'country' party. But to offset the notorious appellation of its strictly country character, it lays stress on the interest of the 'country as a whole'. It fights for the interests of the farmers, dairyists, and small manufacturers. In the States of Victoria and Western Australia it has an alliance with the Liberals with the result that the two become one with the name of Liberal (or Town) and Country Party. However, its sternly anti-socialist posture is unmistakable. On some occasions, the two make open 'election pacts' and also exchange preferences in situations where both are in competition. The overall purpose is to keep labour at bay. It may be described as a federation of rural syndicates like Graziers' Association, and Farmers' Associations *etc.* in spite of the fact that these groups have their separate identity.

Labour Party: It is the oldest organisation. Founded over a hundred years ago as the champion of the 'masses' against the 'classes', it grew out of numerous labour unions of the country. As a result of this, unlike the Liberal and Country Parties, it has its open alliances and affiliations with the trade unions of the country. Organic ties between the two may be seen in this affirmation that while the party is the 'political wing', the trade unions are the 'industrial wing' of the 'labour movement' striving towards the power to reorder society. Thus, it may be labelled as the socialist party of Australia with this note of caution that the word 'socialism' is not to be identified with Marxism; it may be treated as the prototype of English Fabianism in view of the fact that its spokesmen "have given a thousand and one variant of nineteenth and twentieth century expositions, and its opponents-especially during election campaigns as many horrific and misleading caricatures."[4]

The ALP is by all means a 'trade union party' and so a 'left' party or a 'party of resistance'. Its funds come from the trade unions and it has its safe constituencies in the labour-dominated areas like New Castle and Kalgoorlie. Persons having name in the field of trade union activity are its leaders. It is distinctly anti-monopolist. For instance, in 1906 one of its leaders hailing from New South Wales contended: "Where these monopolies have reached the stage of the complete centralisation of an industry, where all the articles of a certain kind within a given community are made under a single control, then we say we have arrived at a stage of things which is absolutely incompatible with the continued freedom, happiness and development of the individual citizens of that country. If any man or group of men is permitted to establish a monopoly in a single necessity of life, to that extent that man is the monarch of the community, and as free, independent citizens of Australia we deny that we. . .established self-government and constitutional institutions here in order to subject ourselves again to unrestricted and unfettered tyranny of an economic mastership such as monopolists would be able to impose upon us."[5]

The working of the ALP has remained beset with two important factors. First, as it is a federation of numerous trade unions, it has most of the problems which are inherent in the chequered labour movement of every

4. Crisp, *Australian National Government*, p. 180.

5. *Ibid.*, p. 181

democratic country of the world. Numerous trade unions fight for their respective interests and try to pull things in their desired direction. Seldom matters are decided in a way that all or even most of the parties involved in the controversy are satisfied. Second, the federal system of the country has its effect on this party.

Critical Appreciation: Australian party system has the merits of stability as well as flexibility. The three major parties may be grouped into two-Labour and anti-Labour-each avoiding extremes and operating within the parameters of a liberal-democratic order. The 'rightist' organisations often work in coalition as if linked in a marriage of convenience and bound by the force of tradition. They are federated entities with the result that there is nothing like a 'High Command' to control and regulate the working of subordinate units. It is owing to the fact that the people, in general, have faith in the weight of traditions that make their parliamentary democracy successful. They avoid rigid political commitments and, for this reason, the 'floating vote' plays the part of a deciding factor. "There are the people, who attracted by the promises of one party or disgusted by the performance of another, or merely because they think that it is time the other gang had a fair go, create the political pendulum; the object of all parties at each election is to woo the swinging vote as much as to satisfy regular supporters."[6]

So significant is the role of these parties that the people generally cast their vote in favour of anyone of them; they generally detest the role of the 'independents' in spite of their criticism of the party system. In verification of this Geoffery Sawer affirms: "The Australian man in the street from time to time grumbles about the defects of party politics, and looks wistfully backward or forward to a time when none were a party and all were for the state. For this reason, independents frequently secure election to Parliament and have often held a balance in the Federal and State houses. Opinions differ as to the merits of such a political balance, much depends upon the ability and integrity of the independents. Sometimes, their 'discriminating support' compels the party in power to show more care and intelligence in policy and administration than it would otherwise exhibit. At other times, the necessity for appeasing the independents leads to irresolute government, or even to the promise of favours. The long-term trend is for the electors to return to

6. Sawer, *Australian Government Today*, p. 32.

the support of one of the major parties. No electorate consistently returns independents."[7]

Pressure Groups

We have already pointed out that in this country party politics is very much influenced by the role of numerous organised interest groups. Hence, it shall now be in the natural fitness of things to have a brief study of the interest groups that have their own part in the domain of political pluralism. The parties take part in the political process of the country, but behind them can be seen the role of many groups, big and small, involving very many people "ignoring for the moment constitutional theory on one side, and a little crackle of arbitrariness at the pinnacles on the other."[8]

A noted writer on the subject of Australian government and politics like L.F. Crisp has put interest groups of his country into three varieties. First, there are cause groups which are concerned with the protection and promotion of a particular cause from which their members cannot themselves derive personal, assessable, and material benefits. The Family Planning Association and Council for Civil Liberties may be included in this category. Then, there are the hybrid groups whose purpose would seem to align with but also remain distinguishable with the groups belonging to the above category. The Returned Servicemen's League, Parents and Citizens' Association and a host of other denominational bodies belong to this category. Last, there are associations with specifically vocational and economic interests situated at the Federal and State levels. The Australian Chamber of Commerce, Australian Farmers Federation, Australian Bankers' Association and a host of such bodies may be ranked in this category.

However, a study of these organizations in the political process of this country leaving aside the case of trade unions (that invariably support the Labour Party), interest groups maintain a sufficiently independent stance in their role in order to do their 'business' with the government of the day irrespective of its party composition. They prefer to stick to the course of expediency and thus they may break their long-standing bonds of affiliation with a particular party as certain rural interest groups in the State of New South Wales did during the second Great War. This fact has

7. *Ibid.*, p. 33.

8. See A.F. Bentley: *The Process of Government*. p. 210.

Some Important Statements

Formally, Australian elections provide only for geographically-based representation of all by individuals, though the imposition of modern parties on the electoral processes has incidentally added various interests and ideological dimensions to parliamentary representation. —***L.F. Crisp***

The special characteristic of Australia is that economic and social developments have made the syndicates specially powerful, especially well-organised, especially comprehensive, and especially political in operation; trade union in Australia, for example, accept political action in a way that American unions do not, and assume a greater right of interference in the affairs of the Australian Labour Party than the British unions in those of the British Labour Party. —***J.D.B. Miller***

The Australian Labour Party, whether in or out of power, has been the magnetic pole by which all political ships must set their course. —***J.A. McCallum***

its parallelism in the behaviour of the pressure groups of Britain to the extent that the labour unions are invariably tied to the Labour Party, though it may not apply to the case of other associations living in their vulnerable association with the Liberal, National and Country Parties.

Like Britain, the working of Australian pressure groups remains within bounds on account of these institutional and extra-institutional arrangements:

1. There is party discipline. Lobbying is prohibited and the role of the MPs in the form of lobbyists is not appreciated the kind of which we find in the United States. There are no open public hearings in the Committees of the Parliament. Most of the important bills are discussed in the House as a whole that constitutes the Committee of the whole House and the members have to speak and vote according to the commands and directives issued by the leader of the party.
2. There are a number of extra-parliamentary institutions (from the Conciliation Commission to the Grants Commission, from the Tariff Board to the Film Censorship Boards) that act like 'buffers' between group pressure on the one hand and Government departments on the other.
3. Interest groups make use of the techniques of press advertisements and news 'plants', broadcasts and telecasts, posters, pamphlets, petitions, public meetings, demonstrations, picketing, boycotts, mass lobbying etc.; they cannot take recourse to means of violence as often happens in poor and undeveloped countries of the Third World. The level of political understanding and the norms of political culture

stand as a powerful barrier that prevent them from resorting to the ways of violence and extremism.

That is, groups have to play their part in the political process of their country within these clear-cut limitations. And they do. Since economics dominates politics in the most unmistakable manner in the case of Australia, the groups invariably force the leaders to fight for their specific interests. It has its indelible impact upon the politics of the country as a whole. National leaders have to draw sustenance from their supporters at the State level and as the latter are inextricably bound by their regional interests, the leaders living in Canberra cannot be oblivious to the weight of these economic interests. Every leader of some standing has to keep in his mind two outstanding facts of his country's politics. First, his country's politics in the main "is overwhelmingly concerned with such economic matters as land, jobs, immigration, taxation, industrial disputes, marketing, water and social services."[9] Second, to an average Australian, "State is a vast public utility whose duty it is to provide the greatest happiness of the greatest number."[10]

9. Miller, *op. cit.*, p. 65.

10. W.K. Hancock: *Australia*, p 61. For a deeper study see P.B. Westerway: "Pressure Groups" in J.Wilkes (ed.): *Forces in Australian Politics* (1963).

Part - X

Japanese Constitution

The MacArthur Constitution relegated the Emperor to a purely symbolic and ritual role while making the Japanese people the sovereign of the nation. It made all members of both chambers of the Diet directly elected by the people and elevated the Diet to the status of the state's highest and sole law-making organ. In a provision unprecedented and unique in the history of constitution, the Japanese constitution forbids Japan to maintain any form of military power or to engage in acts of war in order to settle international disputes. ......The spirit of pacifism that the provision represents, however, lives on in the minds of the majority of Japanese half a century after the document was written by the Americans.

—*Shigeko N. Fukai*

35

CONSTITUTION OF JAPAN

A study of the political system of Japan in a work on major modern constitutional systems of the world is not without certain pertinent reasons. Japan is the most industrialized country of Asia and has the potential of becoming a great power of the world. Within the span of less than a hundred years, she has given ample proof of her modernisation. However, for our purpose, the most astounding feature of Japanese politics is the pace with which this country has adopted the values of a liberal- democratic order. It informs some of its critics to doubt whether this country, once so ill-known for the traditions of authoritarianism and militarism, would really switch over to the traditions of democracy and rule of law. Such a criticism is all the more strengthened with this fear whether the new Constitution of 1946, called 'Peace Constitution' , being an 'imposed gift' of the American military leaders, would work well in a country which has had no democratic traditions. However, the Japanese leaders and intellectuals do not bother about such apprehensions cultivated mainly by the Americans and they confidently endorse that the emergence of democracy in their country is one of the 'most significant political developments of the mid-twentieth century.[1]

Japan's Constitutionalism

The history of constitutionalism in Japan begins with the restoration of the Meiji monarchy in the later part of the nineteenth century. It is from this that the pace of modernisation finds place and the political system operates according to certain rules contained in a formal document known by the name of the 'Meiji Constitution'. It is claimed by the Japanese themselves that with the Meiji restoration of 1867, their country had turned

1 G M Maki: *Government and Politics in Japan*

from two and a half centuries of self-imposed isolation and embarked on the building of a modern state. The return of direct rule of the Throne (for centuries the Emperors had merely reigned as figure-heads in Kyoto), the overthrow of the feudal establishments with its feudal domains and its rigid class distinctions such as *samurai* (warriors), and *heimin* (commoners) *etc*. and the opening of the country to foreign intercourse were all marks of the dramatic turning points towards modernisation. Thus, with the introduction of the Meiji constitution, Japan "emerged as Asia's first constitutional state, and the nation has maintained its constitutional polity ever since, notwithstanding the full and radical revision of the Meiji Constitution as a result of the promulgation on May 3, 1947 of the Peace Constitution of Japan."[2]

The Meiji Constitution was burnt in the fire of the Second World War. The authoritarianism of Japan was a result of this very constitution that resisted the growth of parliamentary democracy in the country with the occupation of American military forces under Gen. MacArthur, the way was opened for the promulgation of a new constitution that would displace the traditions of militarism and authoritarianism and thereby open the way for the democratisation of the country. Gen. MacArthur minced no words when he set forth these two primary objectives of the Occupation:

1. To ensure that Japan will not again become a menace to the United States or to the peace and security of the world.
2. To bring about the eventual establishment of a peaceful and responsible government which.... should conform as closely as may be to the principles of democratic self-government, but it is not the responsibility of the Allied powers to impose upon Japan any form of government not supported by the freely expressed will of the people.

In practice, the two goals so frankly put forth by the American military Commander "were commonly called demilitarisation and democratisation."[3]

It shows that the present Constitution of Japan is a forced gift of the American military leaders. Though it is said to have been accepted by the Cabinet, the Emperor and also by the Diet, it was all a formality done so

2. Koichi Kishimoto: *Politics in Modern Japan*: *Development and Organisation*, p. 9.
3. R. E. Ward: "Japan" in Ward and Macridis (eds.): *Major Political Systems: Asia*, p. 33.

Some Important Statements

I believe that the enforcement of the constitution meant a renaissance in Japan. Its significance is immensely great, for it clearly defines the people as the sovereign of the state and guarantees peaceful life; by the basic principles stipulated in the constitution, all political and social institutions have been reformed in a democratic manner. ***—Prime Minister Katayama Tetsu***

It may be safely said that the existing constitution and parliamentary system of government have come to stay in Japanese society. However, there is no denying the fact that the weak points of both the conservative and progressive camps are a major factor in creating the feeling of apathy towards politics seen in some segments of the population today. ***—Koichi Kishimoto***

The choice was alien military government or autonomous civil government. My fixed determination and purpose was to avoid such violent discrimination and to reconstruct Japan's sovereignty along modern and liberal lines as soon as practicable.

—Gen. Doughlas MacArthur

as to put the formal stamp of its enactment by the people themselves. Hence, it was not appreciated by most of the Japanese writers. For instance, Maki says: "It was the Occupation that originated, directed, and obviously controlled the drafting, the content and the process of approval of the new Constitution."[4]

Likewise, Ike says: "Normally a constitution results from the interplay of historical, legal and political forces, and seeks to give expression to shared ideals and values. The present constitution enacted as an amendment to the 1889 Meiji constitution in late 1947 does not fit this pattern, because it was written rather hurriedly by the American Occupation authorities and in effect imposed on the Japanese government, which after a desultory debate in the Parliament accepted it as the basic law of the land. It is not surprising, given its origins, that the constitution should stress liberal-democratic values. If the Japanese had been given a free hand in writing their constitution, they would undoubtedly have stressed traditional Japanese values and produced a more authoritarian and paternalistic document."[5]

4. John M. Maki: *op. cit.*, p. 80.

5. Nobutaka Ike: *Japanese Politics*, p. 21.

Salient Features

The present Constitution of Japan, also known as the MacArthur Constitution, looks like basically different from the old one, though it contains much of its former self. For this reason, it may be said to be rather a continuation of the old one in certain important respects. Its outstanding characteristic lies in its nomenclature that makes it a 'peace document'—a title given to no other constitution of the world. As such, it affords a new direction in the sphere of constitutionalism and the Japanese people "feel pride over the fact that, though an imposed gift of the American military genius, it contains safeguards to boldly stem or check any move towards remilitarization and de-democratisation."[6] The salient features of this Constitution may be thus enumerated:

1. **A Document of Peace:** The most outstanding feature of the Japanese Constitution, as already said, is its open declaration of the renunciation of war. Art. 9 is very important which says: "Aspiring sincerely to an international peace based on justice and order, the Japanese people for ever renounce war as a sovereign right of the nation and the threat of the use of force as a means of settling international disputes. In order to accomplish the aim of the preceding paragraph, land, sea, and air forces, as well as other war potential, will never be maintained. The right of belligerency of the state will not be recognised." This provision is a clear elaboration of the desire for peace contained in the preamble which say: "We, the Japanese people, desire peace for all time and are deeply conscious of the high ideals controlling human relationship and we have determined to preserve our security and existence, trusting in justice and faith of the peace-loving peoples of the world. We desire to occupy an honoured place in an international society striving for the preservation of peace, and the banishment of tyranny and slavery, oppression and intolerance for all time from the earth. We recognise that all people of the world have the right to live in peace, free from fear and want."

   It is said that such a novel provision goes against the tradition of Japan. It not only proclaims the renunciation of war as an instrument of national policy but also provides for the supremacy of the civilian control over military command. It may, however, be pointed out

6. Koichi Kishimoto: *Politics in Modern Japan.*, p. 35.

that the provision of Art. 9 does not mean that Japan cannot have armed personnel for national defence. The leftist parties make such interpretations and oppose Government's any move towards militarisation of the country. On this ground they vehemently denounced the Peace Treaty with the United States. The result is that the provision of Art. 9 has become the 'most unusual and controversial feature'[7] of the Constitution and even the Supreme Court in the Sunakawa Case of 1959 has not been able to offer an authoritative interpretation of the terms 'self-defence' and the 'war potential' needed for this purpose. It is for this reason that, as Matsumotu Shigeharu says, even a section of the sober people of Japan feels that this provision "has been brought about against the sentiment of a large segment of the Japanese population."[8]

2. **Sovereignty of the People:** The new Constitution makes another departure from the classical tradition by vesting sovereignty in the people. If the old tradition signified appreciation of the aristocratic system, emphasis on loyalty and discipline rather than individual self-expression and militarism, the new Constitution makes a radical change by destroying the principle of imperial sovereignty. The Preamble affirms: "We, the Japanese people, acting through our duly elected representatives in the National Diet, determined that we shall secure for ourselves and our posterity the fruits of peaceful co-operation with all nations and the blessings of liberty throughout this land, and resolved that never again shall we be visited with the horrors of war through the action of government, do proclaim that sovereign power resides with the people and do firmly establish this Constitution. Government is a sacred trust of the people, the authority for which is derived from the people, the powers of which are exercised by the representatives of the people, and the benefits of which are enjoyed by the people. This is a universal principle of mankind upon which this constitution is founded. We rejected and revoke all constitutions, laws, ordinances and rescripts in conflict herewith." Art. I supplements the doctrine of popular sovereignty by laying down: "The Emperor shall be the symbol of the State and

7. A. W. Burks. *The Government of Japan*, p. 21.

8. *Ibid.*, p. 32.

of the unity of the people, deriving his position from the will of the people in whom resides sovereign power."

3. **Unitary System:** Like Britain and France, Japan is a unitary state. The Constitution provides nothing like distribution of powers as obtaining in the United States or Switzerland. It vests all powers in the Central government. Although there are administrative units like provinces and prefectures, they are subordinate to the government of the Centre situated at Tokyo. The provinces have powers given to them by an act of the Diet. Art. 92 says: "Regulations concerning organisations and operations of local public entities shall be fixed by law in accordance with the principle of local autonomy." Art. 93 says: "The local public entities shall establish assemblies as their deliberative organs in accordance with law." It may, however, be pointed out that the organisation and working of the units of local government is subject to the laws made by the national legislature.
4. **Rigidity of the Constitution:** Like the American and Swiss constitutions, the Constitution of Japan is rigid in view of the fact that a special method of its amendment is provided. Art. 96 says: "Amendment to this constitution shall be initiated by the Diet, through a concurring vote of the two-thirds or more of all the members of each House and shall thereupon be submitted to the people for ratification, which shall require the affirmative vote of the majority of all votes cast there at a special referendum or at such election as the Diet shall specify." It shows that the Constitution prescribes a separate method for its amendment. The bill must be passed by 2/3 majority in both the houses of the national legislature and then approved by the people in a referendum. The noticeable thing, in this direction, is that the Japanese Constitution has not been amended even once ever since its promulgation, inspite of the fact that the Conservatives have often desired so. It, however, does not imply that no addition has been made to the stock of the provisions whereby the government of Japan has been operating. The laws made by the Diet have done a lot to supplement the existing provisions. We may refer to the Imperial House Law, Finance Law, Cabinet Law, Public Autonomy Law and the National Diet Law in this regard. Mention may also be made to the Commission on Constitution set up under a law of the Diet in 1955 for the purpose of studying the Constitution, investigating and deliberating on

problems relating to it and reporting the results to the Cabinet and through it to the Diet. However, nothing has come out of it so far in the form of constitutional amendment.

5. **Limited Judicial Review:** The Constitution specifically provides for the system of judicial review. Art. 98 says: "This constitution shall be the supreme law of the nation, and no law, ordinance, imperial rescript or other act of government, or part thereof, contrary to the provisions hereof, shall have legal force or validity." Besides, Art. 81 says: "The Supreme Court is the court of last resort with power to determine the constitutionality of any law, order, regulation or official act." It may, however, be pointed out here that the Japanese Supreme Court has not followed the line of its American counterpart perhaps in view of the fact that the conduct of the judges is itself subject to review by the people after every ten years. In particular, in the Sunakawa Case of 1959, the Supreme Court gave its judgement in favour of the Government by ruling that the stationing of American troops in any part of the country was not a violation of the Art. 9. The point of satisfaction is that the new Constitution makes a clear provision for the protection of the rights and liberties of the people and thereby frankly subscribes to the principle of a liberal-democratic order.

6. **Parliamentary Form of Government:** The Constitution has adopted the British pattern of government by making the Emperor a mere symbol of the State and vesting all executive authority in the Council of Ministers headed by the Prime Minister collectively responsible to the Diet. The Diet designates the Prime Minister and the Emperor formally appoints him. The resignation of the Prime Minister would mean the exit of the Cabinet as a whole. The House of Representatives may throw out the Cabinet by passing a vote of no-confidence. This is a major improvement upon the old position when, under the Meiji constitution the principle of ministerial responsibility was not spelt out clearly. However, as the Japanese had a sort of quasi-parliamentary system under the old arrangement, the establishment of a full-fledged cabinet form of government now looks like keeping with country's political tradition.

7. **Fundamental Rights and Duties:** Indisputable is the fact that the incorporation of a detailed bill of rights is the most important feature of this Constitution. It is quite comprehensive so much so that it

covers social, economic and political rights of the people. Besides, the bill also covers the duties of the citizens. One may marvel at the fact that about 1/3 of the provision of the constitution contained in Chapter III of the Constitution relate to the fundamental rights and duties of the people. Elsewhere judicial protection is also provided. It shows that Japan is a democratic state in view of the fact that all the freedoms guaranteed to the people in a democracy are provided.[9]

We may enumerate the fundamental rights and duties of the people of Japan in the following manner:

1. The conditions necessary for being a Japanese national shall be determined by law. (Art. 10).
2. The people shall not be prevented from enjoying any of the fundamental human rights which shall be conferred on them and the future generations as eternal and inviolate. (Art. 11).
3. These freedoms and rights guaranteed to the people shall be maintained by their constant endeavour who shall refrain from making their abuse and always be responsible for utilizing them for public welfare. (Art. 12)
4. All people shall be respected as citizens and their right to life, liberty and pursuit of happiness shall, to the extent that it does not interfere with public welfare, be the supreme consideration in legislation and other governmental affairs. (Art. 13)
5. All people are equal under law and there shall be no discrimination in political, economic or special relations because of race, creed, sex, social status or family origin. (Art. 14)
6. Peers and peerage shall not be recognised. No privilege shall accompany any award of honour, decoration or any distinction, nor shall any such award be valid beyond the life time of the individual who now holds or hereafter may receive it. (Art. 14)
7. The people have the inalienable right to choose their public officials and to dismiss them. All public officials are the servants of the whole community and not of any group thereof. Universal

9. Chitoshi Yanaga: *Japanese People and Politics*, p. 352.

adult suffrage is guaranteed with regard to the election of public officials. In all elections, secrecy of the ballot shall not be violated. A voter shall not be answerable, publicly or private for the choice he has made. (Art. 15)

8. Every person shall have the right of peaceful petition for the redress of damage, for the removal of public officials, for the enactment, repeal, or amendment of laws, ordinances, or regulations and for other matters, nor shall any person in any way be discriminated against for sponsoring such a petition. (Art. 16)
9. Every person may sue for redress as provided by law from the State or public entity, in case he has suffered damage through illegal act of any public official. (Art. 17)
10. No person shall be held in bondage of any kind. Involuntary servitude, except as punishment for crime, is prohibited. (Art. 18)
11. Freedom of thought and conscience shall not be violated. (Art. 19)
12. Freedom of religion is guaranted to all. No religious organisation shall receive any privileges from the State, nor exercise any political authority. (Art. 20)
13. No person shall be compelled to take any part in any religious act, celebration, rite or practice. The state and its organs shall refrain from religious education or any other religious activity. (Art. 20)
14. Freedom of assembly and association as well as speech, press and all other forms of expression are guaranteed. No censorship shall be maintained, nor shall the secrecy of any means of communication be violated. (Art. 21)
15. Every person shall have freedom to choose and change his residence and to choose the occupation to the extent that it does not interfere with the public welfare. Freedom of all persons to move to a foreign country and to divest themselves of their nationality shall be inviolate. (Art. 22)
16. Academic freedom is guaranteed. (Art. 23)

17. Marriages shall be based only on the mutual consent of both sexes and it shall be maintained through mutual cooperation with equal rights of husband and wife as a basis. With regard to choice of spouse, property rights, inheritance, choice of domicile, divorce and other matters pertaining to marriage and the family, laws shall be enacted from the standpoint of individual dignity and essential equality of the sexes. (Art. 24)
18. All people shall have the right to maintain the minimum standards of wholesome and cultural living. In all spheres of life the State shall use its endeavours for the promotion and extension of social welfare and security, and of public health. (Art. 25)
19. All people shall have the right to receive equal education correspondent to their ability, as provided by law. All people shall be obligated to have all boys and girls under their protection, receive ordinary education as provided by law. Such compulsory education shall be free. (Art. 26)
20. All people shall have the right and the obligation to work. Standards for wages, hours, rest and other working conditions shall be fixed by law. Children shall not be exploited. (Art. 27)
21. The right of workers to organise and to bargain and act collectively is guaranteed. (Art. 28)
22. The right to own or to hold property is inviolable. Property rights shall be defined by law in conformity with the public welfare. Private property may be taken for public use upon just compensation therefor. (Art. 29)
23. The people shall be liable to taxation as provided by law. (Art. 30)
24. No person shall be deprived of life or liberty, nor shall any other criminal penalty be imposed, except according to procedure established by law. (Art. 31)
25. No person shall be denied the right of access to the courts. (Art. 32)
26. No person shall be apprehended except upon a warrant issued by a competent judicial officer which specifies the offence with

which the person is charged, unless he is apprehended, the offence being committed. (Art. 33)

27. No person shall be arrested or detained without being at once informed of the charges against him or without the immediate privilege of counsel, nor shall he be detained without adequate cause; and upon demand of any person such cause must be immediately shown in open court in his presence and in the presence of the counsel. (Art 34)

28. The right of all persons to be secure in their homes, papers and effects against entries, searches and seizures shall not be impaired except upon a warrant issued for adequate cause and particularly describing the place to be searched and the things to be seized, or except as provided by Art. 33. Each search or seizure shall be made upon a separate warrant issued by a competent judicial officer. (Art. 35)

29. The infliction of torture by any public officer or cruel punishment are absolutely forbidden. (Art. 36)

30. In all criminal cases the accused shall enjoy the right to a speedy and public trial by an impartial tribunal. He shall be permitted full opportunity to examine all witnesses, and he shall have the right of compulsory process for obtaining witnesses on his behalf at public expense. At all times the accused shall have the assistance of competent counsel who shall, if the accused is unable to secure the same by his own efforts, be assigned to his use by the State. (Art. 37)

31. No person shall be compelled to testify against himself. Confession made under compulsion, torture or threat, or after prolonged arrest or detention shall not be admitted in evidence., No person shall be convicted or punished in cases where the only proof against him is his own confession. (Art. 38)

32. No person shall be held criminally liable for any act which was lawful at the time it was committed, or of which he has been acquitted, nor shall he be placed in double jeopardy. (Art. 39)

33. Any person in case he has been acquitted after he has been arrested may sue the State for redress as provided by law. (Art. 40)

Some Important Statements

Labelled, 'uncommon democracy' by some scholars, because democracy is more commonly identified as a political system in which the voters 'throw the rascals out' fairly regularly and frequently, the long rule by single party has given rise to a lively debate among scholars over the democratic character of government and politics in post-war Japan. While uncommon, however, Japan is by no means the only democracy that has experienced a long rule by the same party.

—*Shigeko N. Fukai*

To the foreign observer, democracy appears to flourish in Japan. Advocates of totalitarianism either of the left or of the right, are unable to degenerate mass support for the establishment of dictatorship. —*Theodre McNelly*

Japan is a late democratiser and industrialiser. Its economic changes were directly in large part by the state, and its democratic system was imposed from the outside—by the US occupation after World War II. Since the War, Japan has become a major power in the international system, a fact that many attribute to its mercantilist political-economic system. This system was forged in large part by the Liberal Democratic Party, which has dominated the Japanese government and state almost continuously since 1955. —*Patrick O'Neil*

The merit of the Japanese Constitution is that, apart from containing such a comprehensive bill of rights in Chapter III, it also makes provisions for their due protection by the Courts. The importance of Chapter X should be understood here which declares Constitution as 'Supreme Law'. Art. 97 says: "The fundamental human rights as guaranteed here are fruits of the age old struggle of man to be free; they have survived the many exacting tests for durability and are conferred upon this and future generations in trust, to be held for all time inviolate." Art. 98 says that the Constitution "shall be the supreme law of the nation and no law, ordinance, imperial rescript or other act of government or part thereof, contrary to its provisions shall have legal force or validity. The treaties concluded by Japan and established laws of nations shall be faithfully observed." Finally, Art. 99 says that the "Emperor or the Regent as well as Ministers of State, members of Diet, judges and all other public officials have the obligation to respect and uphold this constitution". We may, therefore, well endorse the view of Chitoshi Yanaga that "never before has the individual citizen enjoyed such extensive rights and freedoms which have been made an integral part of the legal system to protect and enhance his position in society."[10]

10. Yanaga, *op. cit.*, p. 352.

8. **Separation of Powers and Checks and Balances:** It is rather unusual to talk about the system of separation of powers and checks and balances in a country having parliamentary form of government in view of the fact that it prevails in a country having presidential form of government. Its study, however, in a country like Japan is important, because it implies that the era of concentration of power is over. Under the Meiji constitution, the Emperor had absolute power. Different from this, under the present Constitution, sovereignty has been vested in the people and the Emperor has been reduced to the status of a constitutional head of the state. The legislative power has been given to the Diet that designates the Prime Minister who is appointed by the Emperor. The Cabinet has been made responsible to the Diet. Finally, the judicial power has been given to the Supreme Court and subordinate courts established by law. It shows separation of powers. Moreover, the system of checks and balances is also there. For instance, the Emperor may dissolve the House of Representatives on the advice of the Prime Minister and the Supreme Court has been given the power of judicial review. In this way, dispersion of power has been made a fact. Such a study of the nature of the new constitution should, however be made with this impression in mind that "the transition from theoretical absolute monarchy to the parliamentary-cabinet system has not meant that fusion of powers has given way to thorough-going separation of powers. Instead, fusion of powers has continued, but important changes in the distribution of powers among the branches have occurred."[11]

The constitutional system of Japan established under the present constitution is basically different from what it was before. The trends of monarchical absolutism and militarism have become a relic of the past. Now democracy "has become fully accepted both ideologically and institutionally."[12]

11. T. McNelly, *Contemporary Government of Japan*, pp. 68-69.
12. Haruhiro Fukui and Shigeko N. Fukai: "Japan" in Mark Kesselman, J. Krieger and W.A. Joseph (eds): *Democracies at the Crossroads* (Lexington: D.C. Heath and Company, 1996), p. 238.

36

STATE STRUCTURE

The most outstanding characteristic of the new Constitution of Japan should be traced in the fact that it replaced the superficial model of parliamentary government, as established under the Meiji Constitution, by a real one more or less analogous to its British counterpart. Thus, its novelty lies in shattering the myth of Kokutai—national polity signifying the faith of the Japanese people that their nation is like a large family ruled by an emperor who is its patriarchal head and, for this reason, the relationship between the Emperor and his people is governed by the ties of filial affection and noticed obligation. As we shall see, the real law-making authority has been vested in the Diet and the Cabinet has been made accountable to it. Obviously, it represents a vast improvement upon the old system.

Formal and Real Executive

Like Britain, Japan is a constitutional monarchy and a parliamentary democracy. The head of the state is a person holding hereditary office with mystic aura of royalty with nominal authority, while real power is vested in the body of elected ministers under the Prime Minister who are responsible to the Diet. However, the point of dissimilarity may be traced in the fact that while in Britain the people clipped the wings of absolute monarchy in a series of fights, in Japan the powers of the emperor could be circumscribed by the American military authorities who foisted a liberal-democratic order on the people ridden with the tradition of taking their emperor as the 'son the sun god'. Thus, in theory the people are sovereign, the real authority is with a limited and accountable government, and the "emperor is the symbol of the nation and the unity of the people."[1]

1. Shigeko N. Fukai: "Japan" in Mark Kesselman, Joel Krieger and W.A. Joseph (eds.): *Comparative Politics at the Crossroads*, p. 138.

Some Important Statements

The constitutional position of the Emperor has changed considerably in the post-War period. He is no longer the source of authority, political and moral; he has been reduced to a symbol and sovereignty is now deemed to lie in the people. He has certain ceremonial functions under the constitution, but he has no powers related to Government. ***—Nobutaka Ike***

What the constitution-makers could not take away were the emperor's moral assests—his symbolical position as titular head of the state, his prestige rooted in centuries of tradition, his hold upon the affections and instinctive loyalties of the people. ***—F.A. Ogg and Harold Zink***

Under the new post-war constitution which became effective in 1947, the Emperor is no longer the chief of the state or the representative of the nation. He has become merely the symbol of the state and the unity of the people in whom sovereignty now resides. This means in effect that legally if the majority of the people so desire, the institution of the Emperor can be abolished. He no longer possesses any power of Government, for he has ceased to be the fountain-head of power which he was formerly. He performs only such acts in matters of state as are provided for in the constitution, but he must secure the advice and approval of the Cabinet. For these acts which he performs neither the Cabinet nor he is responsible.

—Chitoshi Yanaga

The Emperor: The Emperor stands at the apex of the constitutional structure as a symbol of the state and the unity of the people. His office is dynastic and succession is governed by the Imperial House Law passed by the national parliament, the Diet. The advice and approval of the Cabinet is required for all acts of the Emperor in matters of the state and the Cabinet is accountable for them to the Diet. The Imperial House Law is executed by an Imperial House Council often, only two of whom are members of the Imperial family. Of the remaining eight, seven serve as *ex officio* members during their own terms of office—the Prime Minister, the Presidents and the Vice-Presidents of the Houses of the Diet, the Chief Justice of the Supreme Court, and the Head of the Imperial Household Agency.

In addition, it may be noted that the Supreme Court elects one other justice to serve on the Council and his term, as well as of the two family representatives, is of four years. The Prime Minister presides over the meetings of the Imperial House Council, in which only six members constitute a quorum and the decisions are taken by a majority of votes. The expenses of the imperial household are managed according to an Imperial House Economy Law which is passed by the Diet. Finally, there is one more agency Kullaicha, an external organ of the Prime Minister's office, to administer the affairs of the Imperial household.

Under the Constitution, the Emperor is 'the symbol of the state and the unity of the people', deriving his position from the will of the people in whom resides the sovereign power. Art. 7 provides that on the advice and approval of the Cabinet, the Emperor shall perform the following functions in matters of state on behalf of the people:

(*i*) Promulgation of amendments of the Constitution, laws, Cabinet orders and treaties;

(*ii*) Convocation of the Diet;

(*iii*) Dissolution of the House of Representatives;

(*iv*) Proclamation of the General Elections;

(*v*) Attestation of the appointment and dismissal of the Ministers of state and other officials as provided by law and of full powers and credentials of ambassadors and ministers;

(*vi*) Attestation of general and specific amnesty, commutation of punishment, reprieve and restoration of rights;

(*vii*) Awarding of honours;

(*viii*) Attestation of the instruments of ratification and other diplomatic documents as provided by law;

(*ix*) Receiving foreign ambassadors and ministers; and

(*x*) Performance of other ceremonial functions.

The precise role of the Emperor within the executive power under the Constitution is still a matter of legal dispute. It is undeniable that under the Meiji Constitution, the Emperor was absolute whose exalted position was buttressed by the myth of Kokutai. The Japanese used the throne as a counterpoise to the decentralising tendencies and in so doing they developed a kind of Emperor cult. The great office was adorned as divine, sacred, all-wise and virtuous, above public discussion and immune from any derogatory comment. This myth was carefully fostered by a process of indoctrination for which it "is hard to find a close parallel in modern times, though the mass propaganda methods of authoritarian states in recent years resemble it in some respects."[2]

But the new constitution replaces the old theory of imperial sovereignty by the doctrine of popular sovereignty. Now the people are sovereign and

2. G.B. Sansom: *The Western World and Japan*, p. 356.

the Emperor derives his position from their will. Even in practical terms, the life and conduct of the Emperor has changed so much so that the fears of the conservatives have been perfectly belied and no disintegration has taken place in the social and political structure of Japan with the 'humanising' personality of the Emperor. A considerable portion of the taboos which once shrouded the imperial institution have gone and it has become possible to discuss and even critically examine the conduct of the Emperor both as a person and an institution. Besides, the daily life of the Emperor has changed so much so that he makes personal appearances, visits farms, factories, schools and theatres and thus the people have become free from the hazards of imperial superstitions.

Thus, the constitutional position of the Emperor has changed. No longer he is the source of all authority—political or moral; nor is he the real executive of the land. Hence, his position is not at all analogous to the American President, though he may be said to have become the prototype of the British monarch. Of course, under the new Constitution, the Emperor undertakes a good number of responsibilities with the advice and approval of the Cabinet, which most often represents the majority party in the Diet; yet all of these are governmental acts undertaken on behalf of the people. There are specific examples to show that from the functional point of view, the Emperor, in modem times, "has served as a symbol of national and cultural unity."[3]

Prime Minister and Cabinet: In Japan the cabinet system was established by an imperial ordinance in 1885, clearly four years before the promulgation of the Meiji Constitution. Its name was not mentioned in the old constitution and thus it was an extra-constitutional body. The Constitution simply provided that the Ministers of State "shall give their advice to the Emperor and be responsible for it." In fact, the ministers were made responsible not to the Prime Minister but to the Emperor. The Prime Minister selected his ministers taking into account various factors like factions within the party, strong wishes of the oligarchy and the usage that the ministers of war and navy should be career officers of great military ranks. Moreover, there was another powerful executive agency like the Privy Council to circumscribe the role of the cabinet. As a result, the old

3. Ike, *Japanese Politics*, p. 186.

cabinet "became the major battleground for contending aristocrats, militarists, financier-industrialists, party leaders and bureaucrats."[4]

However, the post-war cabinet system is markedly different. It is distinctly specified in the new Constitution that the executive power is vested in the Cabinet which consists of the Prime Minister as its head and other ministers of state as provided by law. All members of the Cabinet should be the civilians. The expression clearly reveals the care taken by the framers to keep the military element aloof from the highest authority of national administration. As we shall see, the post-war Prime Minister has attained a superior executive status both in law and in fact.

The Prime Minister is designated from among the members of the Diet by its resolution. In case, the House of Representatives and the House of Councillors disagree, and in case a joint committee of both houses, as provided by law, fails to reach an agreement, or in case the House of Councillors fails to make designation within ten days, excluding the period of recess after the House of Representatives has made its designation, the decision of the House of Representatives shall be final. In other words, it means that the Prime Minister is elected by the Diet by simple majority, each House voting separately; and if they fail to agree, the election is thrown open to a joint committee; and if the disagreement still persists, the vote of the House of Representatives is decisive. It clearly shows that normally, though not necessarily, the Prime Minister is the head of the party with the largest number of seats in the House of Representatives.

The Prime Minister appoints the ministers of state. However, it is required that a majority of the ministers must be chosen from among the members of the Diet. The Prime Minister may also remove any member from his Cabinet in the event of disagreement of view. Thus appointed by the Emperor, after being elected by the Diet, the Prime Minister becomes the head of the Cabinet. Moreover, he lives in an enviable political position within the Cabinet, for he appoints and removes all other ministers. He presides over the Cabinet meetings, declares a consensus of opinion of the Cabinet and represents his colleagues in parliamentary debates.

The Prime Minister and his Cabinet are entrusted with the responsibility of general administration. They manage foreign affairs, negotiate and conclude treaties with foreign states, submit bills before the Diet and work for their faithful execution, prepare national budget and get it passed by the Diet, decide on general and special amnesty including

4. Burks, *The Government of Japan*, p. 101.

commutation of punishment, reprieve and restoration of rights, administer civil service in accordance with standards established by law, exercise control over the executive branches of the government, designate the Chief Justice of the Supreme Court and appoint other judges, and issue Cabinet orders to carry out the Constitution and other laws. (Art 73).

Then, there is a Secretariat of the Prime .Minister headed by a Director assisted by the deputy directors. It arranges the agenda of the Cabinet meetings, prepares documents, and handles other business matters. The meetings of the Cabinet are generally held on Tuesday and Friday mornings at the official residence of the Prime Minister whose minutes are kept secret. There is no quorum and even if the decisions are made by a minority of the members, the absent members may be asked to sign the documents later on. If the Prime Minister is not available, the Cabinet meetings are presided by the Vice-Premier.

The Cabinet is responsible to the Diet for its policies and actions. The responsibility is collective which is interpreted to mean that the cabinet decisions must be unanimous. The Cabinet is required to report to the Diet on the state of national affairs, national finance and foreign affairs, and submit final accounts of income and expenditure. The Cabinet has the power to dissolve the House of Representatives and to call the House of Councillors in emergency session. Thus, the Cabinet can stay in power so long as it has the support of the majority of members in the lower house of the Diet. However, when the support is lost, or when a vote of no-confidence is passed, it must resign as a body or dissolve the house within ten days. In the former case, the presiding officers of both the houses are notified in writing by the Cabinet, whereupon the Diet begins the process of choosing the new Prime Minister.

It may be noted that the Prime Ministership in Japan has become a focus for intense political pressure. He is elected by the Diet, and after the general election or after his resignation, the Speaker of the lower house takes the initiative in finding out a new leader by seeking party agreement. Once the Prime Minister is identified, the formation of the Cabinet proves to be slow, difficult and often a painful process, because party factions now come into the play. The struggle revolves around the office of the party secretary-general. Hence, what happens inside the Diet at the time of designating the Prime Minister is a matter of formality and the party pressure through the Diet "is too fierce to be ignored."[5]

5. *Ibid*, p. 105.

It may, however, be added here that what makes the powers of the Prime Minister so conspicuous, is not simply his role as the head of the administration. Under the existing system of parliamentary democracy, at the same time, he is normally the head of the majority party, casting his substantive influence over the legislative branch of government. Thus, through consultation with other party leaders, he "can exercise leadership in such aspects of Diet business as the selection of presiding officers of the two Houses and the submission of and deliberation over legislation and other matters. Present day Prime Ministers, moreover, are restricted neither by the Privy Council nor by unofficial aides close to the Emperor, like the Lord Keeper of the Privy Seal or the *genro* (elder statesmen), such as existed under the Meiji constitution. In short, his power—and his responsibility—is far reaching."[6]

We may also take note of this fact that from time to time the Diet, by virtue of possessing the power of investigating or censuring the role of the Cabinet, can drive the Prime Minister and his Ministers into a tight corner. In such cases, the Prime Minister may exercise his most straightforward and potent right under the system of parliamentary democracy, namely that of dissolving the House of Representatives. By such means he brings whatever may be the issue before the people and thus seeks a popular mandate. Moreover, under Art. 7 of the Constitution, he may take either on his own or at the instance of his colleagues an important decision to advise the Emperor to dissolve the House of Representatives. Thus, this power is like Prime Minister's trump card popularly referred to by the Japanese as his *denka no hoto* or 'the sword treasured as family heirloom.[7] Obviously, like his English counterpart, the Prime Minister is the central figure in the political system of Japan.

Parliament (Diet)

The national legislature of Japan is the Diet. True to say that Japan has the longest history of parliamentary government and its Diet is the oldest and most experienced legislature of the non-western world. Under the present Constitution, the Diet has been rendered a very powerful position. Being the sole law-making organ of the state, it is the highest organ of the state power. It is no more like a mere talking workshop and

6. Koichi Kishimoto, *Politics in Modern Japan*, p. 82.

7. *Ibid*, p. 83.

its influence and power have effectively developed owing to the system of universal adult franchise, freedom from executive domination, plenary legislative authority with a decisive vote and responsibility of the legislators to the electorate. As we shall see, the powers of the Diet are extensive and go beyond purely legislative matters which is sufficient to know that the intent of the framers of the Constitution was to make it "the core of the government."[8]

The Diet is bicameral. The House of Representativests having 480 members in the lower chamber. (300 members are elected from single member constituencies and 180 are elected by proportional representation system.) It consists of the members elected from 130 electoral districts. Each district is represented by 3 to 5 members, but each voter casts his ballot for only one candidate. The upper chamber is the House of Councillors. It consists of 252 members, 152 are elected from the prefectures and 100 from the nation at large. Each voter casts two votes, one for the prefectural candidate and another for the national one. Thus, both the houses consist of the elected members. However, the mode of election, qualifications of the electors, their term *etc.*, are governed by the law passed by the Diet, and no discrimination on the grounds of family status, property, sex, religion, creed, education, *etc.* is allowed.

The term of the lower house is of four years. But it may be dissolved earlier and in such a case new elections must be held within a period of 40 days. But the upper house is a permanent wing of the national legislature whose members are elected for a term of six years, with one-half retiring every third year. The term of the two houses is subject to a law passed by the Diet. No person can enjoy the membership of both the houses simultaneously. The members receive their annual payments from national treasury according to a law passed by the Diet.

Much of the work of the Diet is handled by the committees which deliberate on legislative proposals and the fate of these proposals is determined by their action. Sometimes, the committees hold public hearings to which witnesses and other interested individuals are summoned. The Diet has 16 standing committees, one for each major field of legislation, e.g. foreign affairs, education, budget, labour, agriculture, commerce, transportation etc. Each member of the Diet must be appointed to at least one committee but not more than three. The chairmanship and the

8. Nobutaka Ike. "Japan" in G. McT. Kahin (ed.): *Major Governments of Asia*, p, 190.

> **Some Important Statements**
>
> Even during the period of the LDP-dominated Diet, from the mid-1950s through to early 1990s, the national legislature played a central, indispensable role in the operation of democratic government in Japan as the most authoritative arena of public debates on important policy issues between the government and opposition. After all, the Constitution declares that the Diet is the highest organ of state and that it decides the government budget, approves international treaties, elects the prime minister, and oversees the conduct of the cabinet. ***—Shigeko N. Fukai***
>
> Even though Diet operations are organised along the lines of a parliamentary system, in actual practice, it is not infrequent that the system does not function as smoothly as might be expected. ***—Koichi Kishimoto***
>
> But after more than four decades of the working of the Constitution, the House of Councillors is not greatly different from the House of Representatives either in terms of age or in politics. ***—Theodore McNelly***

membership of the standing committees are allocated on the basis of party strength. However, from time to time, special committees are appointed to deal with the problems that cannot be resolved effectively by the standing committees.

The powers and functions of the Diet may be thus summarised:

1. It designates the Prime Minister and can force the Cabinet to resign by passing a vote of censure. It may investigate the activities of the executive branch. On various occasions, its committees have examined the charges of corruption levelled against governmental agencies.
2. The Diet controls the purse of the nation. The national budget prepared by the Cabinet is passed by the Diet. It sanctions the imposition of taxes and ratifies the measures of national appropriations. The estimates of various departments are gathered together by the Budget Bureau of Finance Ministry and then presented to the House of Representatives. The Ministers make administrative speeches which are followed by their appearance before the standing committees. Public hearings on the budget are mandatory. Consequently, on the report of the committees, the parties begin their interpellations and it depends upon the plenary sessions to pass the budget.
3. The Diet exercises control over the conduct of foreign affairs through its power of ratifying or rejecting any treaty or agreement concluded by the government with a foreign state. Any amendment adopted by

the Diet becomes binding and the Cabinet has to change its stand in its light.

4. The Diet has the authority of judging the conduct of the judges by establishing a court of impeachment. In a court of impeachment, both houses should be equally represented and the proceedings of impeachment against any member of the judiciary shall be conducted according to the Diet law.
5. The Diet passes the bills which take the shape of law. A bill (other than a money bill) must be passed by both the houses. In the event of any disagreement, a joint committee may be set up to resolve the tangle. However, if the upper house does not concur with the wishes of the lower house, the bill may be re-passed by the lower house by its at least two-thirds majority and in that case the concurrence of the upper house is not needed. If the upper house fails to take any action on the bill already passed by the House of Representatives within 60 days of its receipt (period of recess excluded), it may be interpreted by the lower house as its rejection.
6. Each house elects its presiding officers and other officials and makes rules for the transaction of its business. For the sake of discipline, it may punish any member for disorderly conduct and by a majority of two-thirds, may pass a resolution expelling him. So each house has the power of judging dispute relating to the qualification of its member. Curiously, the quorum in each house is two-thirds of the entire members. The members enjoy privileges of speech and expression. Except in a particular situation provided by law, they cannot be arrested during the days of session.

From the above, it may be inferred that the constitutional position of the House of Representatives is stronger than that of the House of Councillors. A money bill and other financial business can originate in the lower house and the wishes of the upper house may be overridden by the lower house in various cases through the application of special majority. The composition of the lower house is fully democratic. Moreover, the upper house has lost much of its former prestige and influence by witnessing riots even on its floor.

An over-all picture of the Diet's constitutional position reveals that although its authority is much more effective than that of its predecessor under the Meiji constitution, the practical role of the Cabinet has usurped much of its actual authority which is quite natural in the system of present-day parliamentary system of government. Only in terms of legal structure, the cabinet is inferior to the Diet. But, in practice, the character of party politics has brought about a considerable change. The growing power of the executive has sometimes been studied apprehensively for the reason that voices "are being heard which propose the reinstitution of executive power, with the Emperor at the top of the pyramid; permission for the Cabinet to dissolve the Diet and suspend sessions; and even subsequent Diet approval of emergency (cabinet) budget decrees."[9]

From a critical standpoint, it may be said that though the present Diet is the 'backbone of Japan's parliamentary democratic politics,"[10] its weaknesses have also come into limelight. Not the party politics as such as the element of political corruption has adversely affected its authority. Mention in this connection may be made of the debate over an amendment to the Political Funds Control Law in July, 1975 when the two sides were evenly divided in the House of Councillors and the presiding officer had to cast his vote in favour of the amendment (as desired by the then government) to break the tie. It may also be pointed out here that the strong position of the national legislature has been adversely affected by the hitherto dominant position of the Conservatives for the last 30 years or so that has compelled the progressive and socialist forces to live in a state of 'perennial opposition' and even take to the use of extremist tactics. As a result, there has been lack of proper understanding between the government and the opposition. "Such matters tend to become issues of bitter rivalry between the two camps, with the ruling party vowing to see the legislation approved and the opposition equally adamant in its resolution to obstruct the passage."[11]

Supreme Court

As in other spheres of executive and legislature, so here, important innovations have been made under the present Constitution so as to place judiciary in a position of independence and impartiality. For instance, Art 76 says that the whole judicial power is vested in the Supreme Court and in other inferior courts established by law. The Supreme Court is also vested with the rule-making power under which it determines the rules of procedure and of practice, and of matters relating to attorneys, internal

9. Burks, *op. cit*, p. 133.

10. Kishimoto, *op. cit.*, p. 49

11. *Ibid*, p. 63

discipline of the courts and the administration of judicial affairs. Public procurators shall be subject to the rule-making power of this Court. However, it may also delegate some of its powers to the inferior courts. It is provided that the Supreme Court shall consist of one Chief Justice and other judges as determined by a law of the Diet. (At present, it consists of Chief Justice and 14 subordinate judges). The Chief Justice is appointed by the Emperor on the recommendation of the Cabinet, while all subordinate judges are appointed by the Cabinet. However, one very astounding provisions is that all these appointments are reviewed by the people at first general election of the members of the House of Representatives after a lapse of every 10 years and in the same manner thereafter. In such a case, if a majority of the voters prefers the dismissal of a judge, he shall be removed. The judges retire at the age specified in a law of the Diet. (Art. 79)

Adequate safeguards have been made in the Constitution for the independence of the judiciary. For instance, it is laid down that no extra-ordinary tribunal shall be established, nor shall any organ or agency of the executive be given judicial power. All judges shall be independent in the exercise of their conscience and shall be bound only by the Constitution and the laws. (Art. 76) It is further said that the judges shall not be removed except by public impeachment unless judicially declared mentally or physically incompetent to perform official duties. No disciplinary action against judges shall be administered by any executive organ or agency. (Art. 78) It is also given that matters pertaining to the review of the conduct of the judges at the time of elections shall be prescribed by law. All judges shall receive at regular intervals, adequate compensation which shall not be decreased during the term of office. (Art. 79) Finally, it is given that trials shall be conducted and judgments declared publicly. Where a court unanimously determines publicly to be dangerous to public order or morals, a trial may be conducted privately, but trials of political offences, offences involving the press or cases wherein the fundamental rights of the people are in question, shall always be conducted publicly. (Art. 81)

Curiously, the present Constitution confers upon the Supreme Court the power of judicial review and thereby seeks to make it a prototype of the American federal judiciary. Art 81 says: 'The Supreme Court is the Court of last resort with power to determine the constitutionality of any law, order, regulation or official act." At infrequent intervals, the Supreme Court has made use of this power. For instance, in October, 1952, it turned down a law suit instituted by Chairman Mosaburo Suzuki of the left-wing

Socialist Party over the unconstitutionality of the establishment in August 1950 of the Police Reserve Force, forerunner of today's Self-Defence Forces. At the same time, the Court ruled that it had no right to inquire into an abstract constitutionality case in which no dispute over specific rights was involved. In December, 1959, it reversed the judgement in a case passed at the first court trial holding the American military presence in Japan to be unconstitutional. In this way, the Court put an end to constitutionality law suit concerning Art 2 of the Criminal Special Act (carrying penalities for trespassing on U.S. military facilities and zones), which had been instituted following a forcible land survey for a projected expansion of an American air base in the Sunakawa Town situated in the west of Tokyo.

In the *Sunakawa Case*, the Supreme Court based its decision on the point that Art. 9 of the Constitution does not in any way deny Japan the right of self-defence of a sovereign nation and that Japan may take all measures necessary to defend itself as a nation. Moreover, the Court ruled that what para 2 of Art. 9 prohibits is the maintenance of war potential in the form of military forces under Japanese command and control, and not the stationing of foreign armed forces. Subsequently, the Supreme Court upheld its stand in the *Eniwa Case*, the *Nagamuna Case*, and the *Hayakuri Case*. Yet in all such cases, the Court avoided ruling directly on the constitutionality of self-defence forces (SDF) on the ground that the question was a particular one that must be decided by the government.

As regards, the Supreme Court's power of judicial review, there have been few occasions on which the Grand Bench of the Supreme Court has ruled a legislative act unconstitutional, and only two of these rulings have involved political issues. Both were concerned with the apportionment of seats in the lower house of Parliament among electoral constituencies as specified by the Public Office Election Law. On 14 April, 1976 while ruling on 1972 December general election, the Supreme Court declared that the 499 : 1 discrepancy in the value of a vote between certain electoral districts contravened the constitutional guarantee under the Constitution (Art. 14, para 1). In a similar ruling on 17 July, 1985 it declared the apportionment of seats at the time of December, 1983 election unconstitutional. In neither of the above cases, however, were the election results themselves declared invalid.[12]

A critical study of the Japanese judicial system, however, leads to

12. Koichi Kishimoto *op. cit.*, pp. 48-49.

these points of attack. First, the provision of the confirmation of judicial appointments at the polls every 10 years is a very unwholesome affair. It may be said that it puts a heavy premium on the independence of the judges. It certainly leaves ample scope for the infiltration of politics into the appointments and tenures of the judges. Second, the system of judicial review as obtaining in Japan is basically different from what we find in other democratic countries of the world like the United States and India. The provision of the review of the conduct by the people takes away the entire spirit of judicial power. The result is that the judges are virtually bound to toe the line of the party in power particularly one having bright future in political spectrum of the country. It is, for this reason, that the Supreme Court has not yet given even a single judgement against the government. In the light of the unimpressive record of the performance of the Court, it "would seem highly improbable that the Supreme Court "will ever make significant use of the power of judicial review."[13]

Above all, what keeps the Japanese judicial system in a relatively less significant position is the culture of the people. Not only the system of judicial review is alien to Japanese culture, the people are so tradition bound that, in stead of going to the courts of law, they prefer to settle their disputes with the help of local arbitrators. They are rather remarkably non-litigous people. In spite of all the progress made in the sphere of modernisation, the people adopt the course of conciliation and mediation and prefer, though reluctantly, to go to the courts only when the issue at stake is very critical and when the traditional methods of settlement of disputes have failed. In this way, although in a technical sense, the Courts though seem to be functioning reasonably well, do not play as important a role as might be expected.[14]

13. Ward, *op. cit.*, p. 104

14. *Ibid.*

37

POLITICAL PARTIES AND PRESSURE GROUPS

Every modern political system, whether democratic or totalitarian, has some form of party system. Moreover, every political system has a party system of its own that may be compared and contrasted with its counterpart in other countries of the world on this basis. What we have seen in the preceding chapters shows that Japan, being a democratic country, has an open party system. Not only this, the system is plural in view of the fact that, apart form leading political parties, numerous organised groups play their part in the political process of the country. Thus, the political parties, in the words of G.A. Almond, do the work of aggregation of diverse specific interests, while the interest groups articulate them. A study of the Japanese political system as such, would not be complete unless we make a study of the leading political parties and organized interest groups so as to arrive at this important conclusion that, though a country having parliamentary democracy, has a peculiar model of political pluralism. However, the surprising thing here is that the party system does not have strong grassroots on account of which it is often detested by the people who frankly denounce their leaders as "corrupt, self-seeking and uninterested in the welfare of the people."[1]

1. Theodre McNelly: *Contemporary Government of Japan*, pp. 148-49. Japan is labelled as 'uncommon democracy', because it is more commonly identified as a political system in which 'voters throw the rascals out' fairly, regularly and frequently. The long rule by a single party (Liberal Democratic Party) has given rise to a lively debate among scholars over the democratic character of government and politics in this country. Haruhiro Fukui and Shigeko N. Fukai: "Japan" in Mark Kesselman, Joel Krieger and W.A. Joseph (eds.): *Democracies at the Crossroads*, p, 252.

Political Parties

Like other countries of the world, the Japanese party system has its special characteristics which may be pointed out as under:

1. Japan is a multi-party state. Here about half a dozen political parties operate in the political field like Liberal Democratic Party, Japan Socialist Party, Democratic Socialist Party, Japan Communist Party, Komeito, New Liberal Club *etc*. However, such an affirmation is misleading in view of the fact that the Liberal-Democratic Party alone has been in power for the last many years and thus Japan has been characterized as a 'pre-dominant party system.' Some writers on the subject of party politics have denied even this title and instead preferred to treat Japan as a peculiar variety of the two-party system in view of the fact that while one party remains in power, all other parties are reduced to the status of a 'perennial opposition'.
2. The party system of Japan accords much significance to the factor of ideology. Ideological issues project themselves into every area of conflict. For instance, while the conservatives (having their place in the Liberal Democratic Party) pay deference to the office of the Emperor and appreciate close diplomatic relations with the United States, the progressive and the radicals (having their place in the Socialist and Communist parties) fear the growth of fascism and militarism by imparting significance to the authority of the Emperor and close diplomatic relations with an imperialist power like the United States. Basic differences over such matters "colour their attitudes towards educational reform, rearmament, political demonstrations, labour struggles, constitutional revision, foreign relations and parliamentary procedures."[2]
3. Japanese party system is ridden with factionalism that is admired by the people. To a foreign observer, it seems that internal, personal and ideological factionalism has been a constant threat to the unity of the party and the stability of the political system. But the Japanese people look at it with a basically different standpoint. In their view, factions and factionalism constitute their share to making Japanese politics more open and competitive. In the context of Japan's party political system, factionalism is not only advantageous but also eminently rational.

2. McNelly, *op.cit.*, p. 149.

Some Important Statments

After years of stability, the Japanese party system is now in such a great flux that it is hard to have any long-term confidence in it. Several new parties have been formed since 1993, most by groups that splintered from some other parties and then merged with each other and older parties. —*Shigeko N. Fukai*

In practice, it is the political parties that operate democratic parliamentary politics. Viewed in this light, the existence of political parties is indispensable to parliamentary politics, and the fate of parliamentary politics hinges entirely on course the political parties follow. —*Koichi Kishimoto*

But when we look more closely, we soon see that the Liberal Democratic Party really has no single leader. In fact, it is, in some way, more accurate to view it as a loose coalition of factions united for purposes of camping and legislative strategy than as a unified national party. —*Ward and R.C. Macridis*

4. The behaviour of most of the political parties demonstrates lack of the sense of democratic responsibility. Quite often there are events of violence and the threat of extremist methods in which the leaders of opposition parties have no reservations. Sometimes, mass urination campaigns take place so as to destroy the sanctity of a public place like one happened in 1960 when the radicals opposed the continuation of Peace Treaty of Japan with America and uncleaned the boundary walls of the Diet. It may also be taken note of that the leftist parties, feeling no chance of ever being in power, have lost hope of getting accustomed to gain power and for that reason they adopt an attitude of irresponsibility.
5. Last, the Japanese party system is both centralised and fractional. It is centralised in the sense that although different parties have their branches in all prefectures, towns and villages, they are centralised. Their headquarters are located in Tokyo and all important work of the party is handled by the organisations having their offices in the capital. And yet the party system is fractional in the sense that even after the 'fusion' of 1955, there are different groups and organisations into the fold of a single party, different layers continue to have their existence. The current party system pattern results from the developments of 1955 "and yet the prior and primordial units of Japanese politics were what are today its fractions. Hence, the genesis of the current party system can be described as a double layer of super-impositions, or as a two-step confederative process, originating

from the units that remain, despite their coalescence, the real protagonists of the game.[3]

Let us now look into the organisation, ideology and programmes of the major political parties of Japan:

Liberal Democratic Party: It came into being on November 15, 1955 as a result of the merger of two conservative parties then in existence—the Japan Democratic Party (with lchiro Hatoyama as president) which was the ruling party at that time and the Liberal Party (with Taketora Ogata as president) which having been in power until the resignation of the fifth Yoshida cabinet was in the opposition. Thus, it marked the union of major conservative elements. The leaders announced their ideology in these terms: "In forming the party, our political ideals are, first, to earnestly proceed along the road of parliamentary democracy. For this reason, we shall to the end denounce all forces and ideologies that condone as political means the use of violence or destruction, revolution or dictatorship. Second, we support freedom of and respect for the individual as the fundamental conditions of social order. We oppose, accordingly, absolutism and class-ism that depend on the use of power."

It is obvious that this party stands for observing the norms of parliamentary democracy. Its ideology is said to aim at threefold consummations-of a cultured and democratic nation, of autonomy and independence, and of social stability and welfare state. For this purpose, it gave its six-policy objectives—(*i*) to secure national morality and reform education, (*ii*) to reform the political and administrative system and practices, (*iii*) to achieve economic autonomy, (*iv*) to build a welfare community, (*v*) to take positive steps to evolve peace diplomacy, and (*vi*) to consolidate national sovereignty."

This party has been in power ever since the formation of a conglomerate alliance of all conservative groups and factions in 1955. It may be likened with Conservative Party of England and, for that very reason, it may be designated as an organisation of the plutocrats. As such, is has been denounced by the progressive sections for playing 'plutocratic politics'. Moreover, it is infested with factionalism. In 1963 Prime Minister Takee Miki made an appeal for the disbandment of all factions unconditionally. Thereupon, Prime Minister Tanaka issued a plan specifying:

3. Giovani Sartori, *Parties and Party System*, Vol.I, p. 92.

1. Factions are disruptive of party unity in that their members organise separate groups each of which raises political funds for itself and forcefully attempts to secure the election of its faction members at each Diet election.
2. On the occasion of nominating Cabinet ministers, the party officials as well as the factions apply group pressure to gain the selection of their members.
3. Government and the party machinery are susceptible to each faction's attempts to have them revised or relinquished to its advantage.

And yet nothing could happen with the result that the LDP is regarded as 'a federation of factions'.

This party is led by a president who is chosen by a party conference made up of party members elected to the two Houses of the Diet plus delegates from the prefectural branches of the party. Under the president, there are a good number of party officials like the secretary-general, the chairman of the executive board, and the chairman of committees dealing with the problems of discipline, national organisation and political research. In terms of organisation the staff is divided into a number of sections and divisions as youth, women, industry, labour, agriculture, publications etc. The organisation of the party is extremely weak and, in spite of its efforts to build a mass base, nothing remarkable has happened so far.

New Liberal Club: As a result of rampant factionalism, a section of the LDP broke away in 1976 and formed a separate organisation called the New Liberal Club. It is by all means a small group of the conservatives who, however, denounce the LDP for being a party of the plutocrats. Its arch-leader was Yohei Kono who tried to make some capital out of the involvement of the LDP ministers in the Lockheed scandal. This group desires to have a second conservative party in Japan pledged to shun corruption, establish new liberalism and extricate people from the political pattern of those who govern by imposing their will on the governed. Surprisingly, it has been able to influence a big section of the electorate as is evident from the election results.

Komeito: It is also a small political party formed on November 17, 1964 with Sokka Gakkai, a layman's organisation of the Nichiren Shoshu sect of Buddhism as the parent body. Obviously, it is another variety of the rightist political parties because it seeks to push religious values into politics. Its aim is to make politics 'clean' and, as its name suggests, it wants a 'Clean Government.' That is, it may be described as a religious party desiring unity of national religion with national politics. It talks of humanitarian socialism implying respect for humanism and Buddhist democracy. Its supreme leader is Koji Harajima who has often placed emphasis on a peace-oriented diplomacy for safeguarding the Constitution and the protection of basic human rights as well as for the establishment of parliamentary democracy.

Though a party of the right, it tries to maintain a very cautions attitude in its relationship with the Communist Party of Japan in view of the fact that it is doubtful about the commitment of the Communists in three directions—absolute pacifism as guaranteed by the Constitution, safeguarding basic human rights and keeping parliamentary democracy. It is for these reasons that, though a party in the opposition, it has not appreciated the proposals coming from the side of the communists for making a united front against the government of the LDP. And yet the party is plagued with the problem of maintaining cohesion in its ranks, because a section of the former Sokka Gakkai is interested in having some understanding with the communists.

Japan Socialist Party: On the side of the 'left', three political parties are important, the most important of which is the JSP which is also regarded as number-one opposition party. Like the LDP, it a came into being in 1955 as a result of the fusion of different elements and, soon after its formation, it was characterised as 'a class mass party'. Its ideology is contained in an important document titled 'Road to socialism in Japan' issued in 1962 and adopted by the party in December, 1964. Some revisions were made in it in January. 1966. This document says that the "JSP is a political party which believes in the inevitability of a socialist revolution in Japan and is convinced that it is possible and proper for a socialist revolution to be carried out democratically, peacefully and through the Diet." It pledges to strive for:

1. Socialist democracy,
2. Socialisation of key industries, organisation of cooperatives among small and medium enterprises in the agricultural sector and planned production in all sectors.
3. Land reforms and improvement of the living environment,
4. Development of education, culture and science,
5. Construction of a society bounded by solidarity and cooperation, and

6. Foreign policy contributory to the cause of peace and prosperity of mankind.

In this way, the JSP defines itself as the leading political force for realising such a socialist revolution.

As it is a party of the left, its opposition to the hold of the Americans is natural. It wants that Japan should follow a policy of peace and neutrality after abrogating the Peace Treaty with the United States. Moreover, she should conclude non-aggression treaties with the socialist countries like China. For this sake, it is also necessary that American defence bases in Japan should be liquidated. However, the real problem with this party is that, like the LDP, it is also ridden with intra-party dissensions. Some of its factions have a pro-China stance, while others have a favourable orientation towards other socialist countries. Moreover, there is a powerful section which desires a sort of compromise with the ruling Liberal Democratic Party so as to have a sort of coalition. That is, "intra-party contention has been continuing over a variety of the issues, the latest being the question of what concept should be formulated for gaining power." Another difficulty about this party is that while its leaders are committed to a peaceful revolution to overthrow capitalism and establish socialism, they have not unequivocally renounced the use of extra-parliamentary methods to achieve their goals.

Democratic Socialist Party: It came into being on January 14, 1960 as a political party upholding the precepts of democratic socialism. It was founded by the former members of the two factions of the JSP-Suehiro Nishio's group of Sharnin (Socialist People's Party) origin, and the Nichiro (Japan Labour-Peasant Party) faction. That is, it was formed by a splinter group of right-wingers who were dissatisfied with the hold of the ultra-conservatives as well as extreme left-wingers. Thus, it seeks to adopt a middle course between bourgeois 'rightism' and Marxist 'leftism'. It defines itself as "a political association of those people who believe in the principles of democratic socialism that would confront capitalism and totalitarianism whether of the left or of the right.

Like the JSP, this party also desires a sort of coalition government of all progressive elements so as to rid the capitalist system of all its contradictions and establish a really democratic system free from the shackles of any form of totalitarianism whether of the right or of the left. However, the coalition should be based on the recognition of three fundamental principles-defending all aspects of the present Constitution, establishing a welfare state, and realising parliamentary democracy. Some Japanese writers are of the view that whenever the LDP has a fall, the DSP would fill the void. However, one may not safely depend upon such optimism and endorse the view of a foreign critic: "In Japan's bi-polarised politics, the Democratic-socialists seem to have fallen between two poles. They have managed to exert a slight mediatory influence between the Liberal-Democratic and Socialist parties, but on the whole their lot stands as a warning to those who would blithely form splinter groups."[4]

Japan Communist Party: It was in 1921 that a minor Communist organisation was setup in Japan, though it could not survive owing to the repressive policy of the government. Strangely, it was reborn in October, 1945 when Gen. MacArthur forced the government to release all political prisoners unconditionally. In not much time, the party rose from the ashes and became the most powerful communist party in the free world after its Italian counterpart. It reiterated its resolve in the ideology of Marxism-Leninism. However, in July, 1955, it frankly abandoned its violence-oriented line.

By this time, leading lights like Miyamoto and Nosaka could establish their hold over the organisation and express their stern determination to fight the two enemies-American imperialism and Japanese monopolistic capitalism. However, this party could not save itself from the impact of ideological rift between the Soviet Union and China. The pro-Soviet faction dominated and in October, 1966 Miyamoto removed Ryuji Nishzawa from the Central Committee of the JCP. As such, the JCP has a three-pronged strategy:

1. Neutralising Japan by abolishing the military alliance with the United States.
2. Breaking down big monopoly politics and implementing policies geared to the defence of the people's lives and livelihood, and
3. Opposing an all-out revival and intensification of militarism and seeking democratic management of the Diet and the establishment of democracy in Japan.

In recent years what made the policies and strategies of the JCP a matter of general discussion was the 'soft line' approach adopted by its leadership which suggested the formation of a coalition government that could 'reduce' rather than 'disband' the Japanese self-defence forces and

4. Mc Nelly, *op. cit.*, p. 132

restrict public ownership of industry to the energy-related sectors only. It publicly set forth, for the first time, the party's new official policy to respect and defend the Constitution. It also came out with the old familiar definition of school teachers as 'members of a sacred profession' instead of the extremists' view of regarding them simply as employed workers. It is in this context that a section of the JCP came very close to the Sokka Gokkai in 1974 with a view to put an end to their past history of mutual animosity.

Pressure Groups

Since Japan is an 'open' country with a 'plural' society, the role of organised interest groups is a natural affair. As we have seen in other democratic countries like Britain, United States, Switzerland and France, so here various interest groups play their part in the political system. These groups fight for the interests of their own. Moreover, like other democratic countries, the Japanese interest groups also "provide a second level of representation and more precisely focused means of representing the views and interests of particular groups-political parties, legislators, administrators, and the public."[5] If so, let us first point out the special characteristics of pressure group politics in Japan as under:

In the first place, the role of pressure groups in Japan is backed by the social tradition of parent-child (*oyabun-kobum*) relationship. The people prefer one who can confer tangible benefits on them. As such, the organised groups manage to win favour of the people which can confer tangible benefits. Since political parties need the support of the common people, naturally they try to requisition the support of different groups. In return, the groups manage to secure favours from the government. In this way, the social tradition like that of parent-child relationship gets sustenance. Second, all leading political parties of this country are ridden with factionalism. In spite of the great fusions of 1955, splits often take place in the ranks of major political parties. Thus, different factions bank upon the support of different interest groups. Naturally, it makes the position of interest groups stronger. Above all, since money plays a very important role in the politics of Japan, business groups manage to have the biggest slice of the cake. The result is that the financially weak parties and groups try to make capital out of exposing the activities of political corruption. Hence, much focus was laid on the Lockheed scandal in 1976 when it was

---

5. Ward: "Japan" in Ward and Macridis (ed.s): *Modern Political Systems*: *Asia*, p. 80.

found that some ministers, including the Prime Minister, had taken secret financial help from a multi-national corporation dominated by the Americans and thereby made certain undue favours for it.

A look at the major interest organisations of Japan shows that they range from business to labour and agriculture, while some mention may be made of the humanitarian and social service groups also. The most important of all are the business groups in view of the fact that they have enormous financial sinews with them and their support to the rightist parties, particularly the Liberal Democratic Party, is a matter of faith. The leftist parties like Japan Socialist Party, Democratic Socialist Party and the Japan Communist Party manage to requisition the support of labour and agricultural groups. But the role of the business organisations is highly important in the political process of this country. It is admitted by all that so long as big business exists in this country, the *zaikai* (financial organisations) will remain with a collective group of *zaikai-jin* at its head and its position as a powerful political pressure group is not likely to change.

Another important point that engages our attention here is that most of the pressure groups fix their attention less on the national legislature but more on the organs of administration. We have already seen that bureaucracy constitutes the pool of leadership in this country, Most of the organised groups place their main reliance on the organisation and working of the permanent executive of the country. The leaders of the pressure groups know it well that the ministers and the bureaucrats, rather than the legislators, make most of the important decisions in the field of administration and it is virtually they who implement them, so their stress remains heavily on the higher bureaucracy.[6]

However, the most objectionable feature of the role of pressure groups in the political process of the country is that the heavy reliance on the higher echelons of bureaucracy leads to the growth of political corruption. It is alleged that a good deal of corruption results from the malpractices in which big and powerful groups are involved and they manage to influence the top decision-makers of the country. The press is largely convinced that in many cases the lobbies depend heavily on corrupt and illegal techniques, Quite obviously, the minor corruptions represented by geisha parties, elegant meals, and expensive entertainment for strategically placed individuals flourish in Tokyo. Equally obvious, and perhaps more serious,

6. *Ibid.* p. 83.

is the practice of providing positions for retired bureaucrats. There does seem to be a tendency, however, for some of the major interest groups to place increasing emphasis on 'educational materials' and appeals for broad popular support.[7]

Thus, different interest groups play an important role in the politics of Japan and since the country is on the path of modernisation, their role is becoming more and more important. Traditional forces are losing their weight and the country is taking more and more to the path of western democracies where articulation of diverse interests by organised groups and their aggregation by political parties is a natural affair. It has definitely contributed to the success of parliamentary democracy established on a rather uncongenial soil. It is a different matter that as left movement is very weak in this country, socialist parties and the labour groups rendering them their support have not been in a position of strength. Intra-party and intra-group dissensions among the leftist elements are equally responsible for this. Above all, the extremist methods adopted by the rightist forces to suppress the socialist elements and their condonation by the conservatives in power is also responsible for the same. Cases of stabbing and badly torturing the leftist leaders are not rare in Japan. Thus, it appears that the rightist elements have not yet given up their ultra-nationalistic and militant postures even under the aegis of the 'Peace Constitution'. It enables a foreign critic to say: "In contemporary Japan, the extreme right is remarkably similar in spirit to what it was in the pre-war era."[8]

7. *Ibid.*, p. 83.

8. McNelly, *op. cit.*, p. 139.

Part - XI

South African Constitution

The Republic of South Africa is a sovereign democratic state founded on the following values:

(*a*) Human dignity, achievement of equality and advancement of human rights and freedoms

(*b*) Non-racialism and non-sexism

(*c*) Supremacy of the Constitution and the rule of law

(*d*) Universal adult suffrage, a national common voters roll, regular elections, and a multi-party system of democratic government, to ensure accountability, responsiveness and openness.

Chapter 1: Founding Provisions of the Constitution

38

CONSTITUTION OF SOUTH AFRICA

The political systems of the Third World countries are not included in the major constitutional systems of the world by the Western writers, for their attention remains confined to the few countries of the First World, though they include the Communist systems of the Second World as a matter of academic compulsion. In the domain of comparative government and politics, this bias now seems to be loose and imbecile for the simple reason that the focus is now laid more and more on the developing countries of the world. If so, the developing countries of Africa like Egypt, Nigeria and South Africa have a natural claim for their inclusion in the major constitutional systems of the world. Political institutions of the advanced democratic countries have been implanted in these countries and attempts are being made to offset the situation, in the words of David Apter, of their 'institutional indigestion'. Hence, the South African constitutional system has been included in this study where the black people waged a long struggle to displace the rule of the white people and ultimately became successful in terminating the inhuman system of racial segregation (apartheid) and taking power in their hands by peaceful and democratic means.

Constitution and Constitutionalism

On 31 May, 1910 four British dependencies were merged to form the Union of South Africa, a dominion under the British Crown. In 1931 the British Parliament recognised the Union as an independent country within the British Commonwealth of Nations. But until 1984, the national administration remained the exclusive preserve of the white population. On 31 May 1961 following a referendum (held in October, 1960) among the white voters of this country, this country became a republic and it left the Commonwealth of Nations. Struggle of the black people against the white rule continued as a result of which a new Constitution came into effect in September, 1984. Legislative power was vested in the President with a trilateral parliament. It consisted of House of Assembly having 178 members for representing the white people, a 85-member House of Representatives of the coloured people, and a 45-member House of Delegates for the representation of the Indians. The office of the Prime Minister was abolished and then Botha became the President of the Republic.

And yet the fight of the 'coloured' people continued. The leaders of the African National Congress were not satisfied with this arrangement. They became more vocal after the release of Nelson Mandela from jail on 11 February, 1990 who was officially elected as the President by the National Assembly on 9 May, 1994. The new government adopted a Reconstruction and Development Programme which comprised extensive measures for social and economic development, including the reformation of the education and public health services. Now an interim Constitution was adopted. Accordingly, a 11-member Constitutional Court was installed in February, 1995 to ensure that the executive, legislative and judicial organs of government adhered to the principles entrenched in the interim Constitution and to endorse a final constitutional text. with respect to these principles.

Thus came into being the new Constitution of South Africa which was adopted on 8 May, 1996 and entered into force on 4 February, 1997. According to its preamble, it invokes the sacrifices of the people done in the past and expresses its resolve to establish a democratic and open system so as to improve the quality of life of all its citizens and thereby be able to take its rightful place as a sovereign State in the family of nations. The Constitution imbibes the values of a liberal-democratic order as prevailing in the Western countries and, at the same time, in its Chapter 12 has provisions for traditional leaders whose status and role at national, provincial and local levels is recognised subject to the terms of the Constitution which is the supreme law of the land.

Salient Features

Like any other Constitution of the world, this Constitution has its salient features which may be enumerated as under:

1. **An Enacted, Written and Rigid Document:** As pointed out above, it is an enacted Constitution. It has 243 articles grouped into 14

Chapters. Then, 7 Schedules follow. Art.2 says that it is the Supreme Law of the Republic. As such, any law or conduct inconsistent with it is invalid and the obligations imposed by it must be fulfilled.

Like the Indian Constitution it is very lengthy, for its provisions cover central, provincial and local governments. Not only this, it has provisions relating to State institutions supporting constitutional democracy, public administration, security services, traditional leaders, election procedure, languages, bill of rights etc. The Constitution is rigid because the process of its amendment is difficult. A bill of constitutional amendment must be passed by the majority of the lower house and at least by 6 affirmative votes of the provinces in the National Council of the Provinces.

2. **Founding Provisions:** The Republic of South Africa is a sovereign democratic State based on certain values as human dignity and freedoms, supremacy of the Constitution and the laws, no discrimination on the artificial grounds of sex, race, religion, language and the like, universal adult suffrage, popular elections, multi-party system, responsible government, equality before law and its protection, an open society and enlightened citizenship. It shows that the Constitution embodies the values of liberal-democratic order as prevailing in advanced countries of the world.
3. **Bill of Rights:** Chapter 2 of the Constitution has a detailed bill of rights. The provisions ensure equality before law and prohibition of discrimination among the citizens on any artificial ground as that of race, gender, sex, pregnancy, marital status, religion, creed and the like. It prohibits arbitrary detention of a person and ensures free and fair trial of the accused. It also guarantees freedom of conscience and expression, peaceful assembly and free movement throughout the country, formation of unions and associations, privacy and private property etc. It protects right to information and access to courts as well. These may be described as the fundamental rights of the people of this Republic.
4. **Cooperative Federal System:** A federal system stands for the division of powers between the Centre and the States or Provinces. The powers of both the governments are distinctly remarked and a supreme court is also established to interpret the provisions of the Constitution from time to time and to settle constitutional disputes between the two governments. The Constitution meets all the requirements of a federal system. But the unique feature is that what

prevails in Australia as a matter of extra-constitutional development, that makes it a model of cooperative federalism, is contained in the provisions of Chapter 3 of the Constitution. It contains a long list of the principles of co-operative government and inter-governmental relations. This is a unique arrangement not found in the constitutions of other federal countries. All the three levels of government—central, provincial and local—are distinctive, inter-dependent and inter-related. All spheres of government and all organ of State within each sphere must preserve peace, national unity and individuality of the Republic.

5. **Presidential Form of Government:** Like America, South Africa has presidential form of government. The President is elected by the National Assembly for a term of five years and he cannot hold more than two terms. He appoints his ministers and administers to them the oaths of office and secrecy. He presides over the meetings of the Cabinet. But in some respects his position is different from his American counterpart. He has to pick up ministers from various political parties, as each party having at least 20 seats in the National Assembly (equal to 5% of the national vote) is entitled to a proportional number of ministerial portfolios. The cabinet comprises at the most 27 members. Besides each party having at least 80 seats in the National Assembly (equal to 20% of the national vote) is entitled to nominate an Executive Deputy President. If only one party secures 80 or more seats, then it and the party holding largest number of seats in the National Assembly, each is entitled to designate the Executive Deputy President from among the members of the Assembly. The President may be removed by the National Assembly.
6. **Bi-cameralism:** Like other advanced countries of the world, South Africa has a bi-cameral national legislature (Parliament). The National Assembly is its lower house having at least 350 and at most 400 members who are elected in general by proportional representation system for a term of five years. The National Council of the Provinces is its upper house having 90 seats. There are 9 provinces and each province has 10 seats. Each provincial legislature appoints 6 permanent delegates and 4 special delegates to this chamber. Its terms is of five years. The notable point is that the national and provincial legislatures are elected separately under a 'double ballot electoral system'. It means that the elections are held

simultaneously for national and provincial legislatures in which a voter casts one vote for the National Assembly and the other one for the assembly of the province. The bills are passed in the Parliament by simple majority of votes, but for Constitutional amendment bills 2/3 majority of the members of the house is required.

7. **Judicial System:** The judicial authority of the Republic is vested in the courts which comprise the Constitutional Court, the Supreme Court of Appeal, the High Courts, the Magistrates' Courts and any other court established or recognised by a law of Parliament. The independence of judiciary is recognised as no person or organ of state may interfere with the functioning of the courts. At the apex is the Constitutional Court consisting of the President, a Deputy President and 9 other judges. But a matter before the court is heard by at least 8 judges. It is the highest court in all constitutional matters. It has the jurisdiction to settle a legal dispute between the Centre and the provinces, or between the provinces, and may pronounce its judgement on the constitutional validity of an impugned law or executive action. Its decision is final.

8. **Traditional Leaders:** Chapter 12 of the Constitution has provisions relating to the institution, status and role of the traditional leadership according to customary law subject to the provisions of the Constitution. A traditional authority that observes a system of customary law may function subject to any applicable legislation and customs, which includes amendments to or repeal of that legislation or those customs. The courts may apply customary law when that law is applicable subject to the Constitution and any legislation that specifically deals with customary law. National legislation may provide for role of traditional leadership as institution at local level on matters affecting local communities. It shows that the founding fathers have sought to reconcile the traditional tribal system with the paraphernalia of a modern democratic state.

9. **Internationalism:** Like the German and Russian constitutions, the Constitution of South Africa honours the principles of internationalism and international law. The State is required to honour its international treaties and commitments and the courts have been instructed to interpret law in a way that is consistent with the implications of the Constitution as well as with the principles of international law. In order to deepen the culture of democracy established by the Constitution, the Parliament may adopt an

international Charter of Rights consistent with the provisions of this Constitution. Surprisingly, it recognises right to self-determination for any community sharing a common cultural and language heritage within the territorial entity of the republic or in any other way as determined by a law of Parliament.

10. **Institutions Supporting Constitutional Democracy:** It is really a surprising feature of this Constitution that it has provisions for the creation and functioning of certain institutions which support and strengthen the system of constitutional democracy. The offices of the Public Protector and the Auditor-General and the Commission for Gender Equality, Human Rights Commission, Commission for the Promotion and Protection of the Rights of the Cultural, Religious and Linguistic Communities, and Electoral Commission may be referred to here. Provision has been made for an Independent Authority to Regulate Broadcasting. The offices can be given to the citizens of the Republic and have constitutional sanction.

Process of Amendment

Art 74 of the Constitution describes the process of its amendment. Chapter 1 having' Founding Provisions' may be amended by a bill passed by the National Assembly with a supporting vote of at least 75% of its members and by the National Council of the Provinces with a supporting vote of at least six Provinces. Chapter 2 having 'Bill of Rights' may be amended by a bill passed by the National Assembly with a supporting vote of at least two-thirds of its members and by the National Council of the Provinces with a supporting vote of at least six provinces. But any other provision of the Constitution may be amended by a bill passed by the National Assembly with a supporting vote of at least two-thirds of its members and also by the National Council of the Provinces with a supporting vote of at least six provinces if that matter (*a*) affects the Council, (*b*) alters provincial boundaries, powers, functions or institutions, or (*c*) amends a provision that deals specifically with a provincial matter.

A bill of amendment must be published in the National Government Gazette after at least 30 days it is introduced in the house by a person or a committee so that the people may know about it and may send their reactions and critical comments to the presiding officers of the two Houses of Parliament. In case the bill concerns a specific province or provinces, the National Council of the Provinces may not pass it, unless it has been approved by the legislature or legislatures of the Province or Provinces concerned. If such a bill is passed by both the houses of Parliament, then it is sent to the President. He may give his assent to it, or may return it for reconsideration by the National Assembly, or he may take action on it after obtaining the view of the Constitutional Court. It is clear that the process of amending the Constitution is quite tedious and so it may be called a rigid Constitution like the Constitutions of America, Switzerland and France.

Bill of Rights

Chapter 2 of the Constitution has its special significance. It contains a very long list of fundamental rights which constitute the 'cornerstone of democracy' in this country. The rights are available to all people of the country and boldly affirm the democratic value of human dignity, equality and freedom. The State is enjoined upon to respect, protect and promote them, but they are subject to reasonable limitations as well. The rights enshrined herein have a mandatory character, but they are not of a transcendental nature. Each right has a corresponding duty and, as such, these provisions bind a juristic person to the extent that is applicable taking into account the nature of the right and the nature of duty imposed by it. These rights may be enumerated as under:

1. **Equality:** Everyone is equal before law and has the right to equal protection and benefit of law. Equality includes full and equal enjoyment of all rights and freedoms. The State may not unfairly discriminate directly or indirectly against anyone on any ground as religion, race, gender, sex, ethnicity, marital status, culture, language, place of birth and the like.
2. **Human Dignity and Personal Freedom:** Everyone has the right to have his dignity respected and protected. Everyone has the right to life. Nobody can be subjected to slavery, servitude or forced labour. Everyone has the right to privacy in respect of his person, home, and communications. No person can be deprived of his freedom in an arbitrary manner; he cannot be detained without trial and cannot be tortured or punished in inhuman ways.
3. **Freedom of Faith and Expression:** Religious freedom is guaranteed to all. Religious observance may be conducted in State or State-aided institutions, but attendance therein is free and voluntary. Freedom of expression, including freedom of press, are secured, but nobody

can incite inhuman violence or propagate war or preach hatred by his words or actions. People have the right to form their associations and hold peaceful assembly without arms.

4. **Political Rights:** Freedom to make political choices is ensured. Every citizens has the right to form a political party and to take part in political affairs of the country. Every adult citizen has the right to vote in any election for any legislative body. No person may be deprived of his citizenship. Everyone may move throughout the country and reside or settle anywhere in the country. He has the right to leave the Republic.
5. **Economic Rights:** Everyone has the right to fair labour practices, to form and join a trade union, to strike, or to join his employer's organisation. No one may be deprived of his property except by the authority of law, but private property may be nationalised in the public interest on the payment of just compensation.
6. **Social and Cultural Rights:** Everyone has the right to protect environment for leading a healthy life. He has the right to adequate housing, health care, food, water and social insurance. Every child has the right to family care, to be protected from maltreatment and to be protected from exploitative labour. Everyone has the right to education in the official language or in a language of his choice. He may adopt the culture of his choice. The people may form their cultural and linguistic associations and other organs of a civil society.
7. **Right to Information and Judicial Remedies:** Everyone has the right to seek information held by the State or some other person. He has the right to administrative action that is lawful, reasonable and procedurally fair. He has the right to move the court for the redressal of his grievances. No one can be arrested without cause and, if arrested, he must be produced before a court within 48 hours. The trial must be fair and open.

The list of fundamental rights is quite exhaustive, but the point may be stressed again that during emergency they may be restricted by a law of Parliament. More than this, the proclamation of the President in this regard is subject to judicial scrutiny. The citizens may move the courts if their rights are infringed and only the courts may interpret the provisions of the Constitution to promote the spirit, purport and object of the Bill.

Federal System

Australia is known for having a cooperative federal system for the reason that it has some institutions to maintain good relations between the Centre and the States the best example of which is the Annual Premiers Conference in which matters of common interest are discussed and decisions are taken by the majority of votes which are binding on all. The Indian Constitution has made some such arrangements in the form of Inter-State Council, Finance Commission and Zonal Councils, while reference may be made to some other institutions devised for this purpose as National Development Council and annual meets of the Governors and Chief Ministers in New Delhi. However, credit goes to the Union of South Africa for having a chapter on this subject (Chapter 3) with the title of 'Cooperative Government'. The governments at the Centre, in the provinces and then at the local levels are 'distinctive, inter-dependent and inter-related.'[1] It is enjoined that all spheres of government must observe and adhere to the principles enshrined here and conduct their activities within the specified parameters as given below:

(*a*) to preserve peace, national unity and indivisibility of the Republic,

(*b*) to secure the well-being of the people of the Republic,

(*c*) to provide effective, transparent, coherent and accountable government for the republic as a whole,

(*d*) to be loyal to the Constitution, the Republic and its people,

(*e*) to respect the constitutional status, institutions, powers and functions of government in the other spheres,

(*f*) not to assume any power or function except those conferred on them by the Constitution,

(*g*) to exercise their powers and perform their functions in a manner that does not encroach on the geographical, functional or institutional integrity of government in any other sphere, and

(*h*) to cooperate with one another in mutual trust and good faith by fostering friendly relations, assisting and supporting one another, informing one another of, and consulting one another on, matters of common interest, coordinating their actions and legislation with one

1. The Republic of South Africa has 9 provinces, namely, Eastern Cape, Free State, Gauteng, Kwazulu-Natal, Mpumalanga, Northern Cape, Northern Province, North West, and Western Cape.

another, agreeing to adhered procedures, and avoiding legal proceedings against one another.

It is further provided that the Parliament shall make a law to establish or provide for structures and institutions to promote and facilitate inter-governmental relations, and make appropriate mechanisms and procedures to facilitate settlement of inter-governmental disputes. It is desired that all organs of State involved in an inter-governmental dispute must make every reasonable effort to settle the dispute by means of mechanisms and procedures provided for that purpose, and must exhaust all other remedies before it reaches a court to resolve the dispute. Not only this, the court may refer a matter back to the organs of the State involved in a dispute if it finds that all remedies available to them for this purpose are not exhausted.

The main problem of a federal system is related to its maintenance in a way that secessionist forces and tendencies are kept within checks. Such tendencies may lead to the breakdown of the federal system as happened in Congo and Pakistan. Ethnic nationalism may also play its devastating role as we may see in the case of erstwhile communist States like the USSR, Yugoslavia and Czechoslovakia. The Constitution of South Africa permits right to leave the Union and, at the same time, it has a workable mechanism to keep the country intact so that in course of time, like the United States, it becomes an indestructible Union of indestructible States. The provisions of Chapter 3 have this object in view.

39

STATE STRUCTURE

The Constitution of South Africa establishes a federal and presidential form of government. The model of the national executive is unique. It is neither like that of the United States where the President is the real executive and has no responsible ministry under his stewardship, nor is it like that of France where the cabinet (having a Prime Minister and Ministers) functions under the control of the President vested with real powers. The President and his ministers are responsible to the Parliament without being its members. The executive authority of the Republic is vested in the President who exercises it with other members of the cabinet by (*a*) implementing national legislation except where the Constitution provides otherwise, (*b*) developing and implementing national policy, (*c*) coordinating the functions of State departments and administrations, (*d*) preparing and initiating the legislation, and (*e*) performing any other executive functions as provided in the Constitution or in a law made by the Parliament.

National Executive—President and Cabinet

The President is elected by the National Assembly from amongst its members. The President of the Constitutional Court or his nominee presides over the election. The election to fill a vacancy must be held 30 days after the vacancy occurs, on a date and time as determined by the President of the Constitutional Court. After his election, he ceases to be a member of the National Assembly and within five days he assumes his office after taking the oath of faithfulness to the Republic and obedience to the Constitution. The term of the President is of five years and, like the President of the USA, he cannot have more that two terms. In case a person is elected to fill a vacancy in the office of the President, the period between that election and the next election of a President is not counted as one term.

The President may be removed by the process of impeachment on the basis of some charge as serious violation of the Constitution or the law, serious misconduct, or inability to perform the functions of the office. A resolution to this effect must be passed by 2/3 majority of the National Assembly. After his removal, he cannot receive any benefit of the office and may not hold any public post. In case the President is absent from the country, or is unable to perform his functions for any reason, then someone shall officiate in this order-Deputy President, a Minister designated by the President, a Minister designated by the members of the Cabinet, the Speaker until the National Assembly designates one of its other members. Before entering upon this office, the Acting President shall take the oath and have all the powers, functions and responsibilities of the President.

As head of the State as well as of the national executive, the President has important functions and powers. In the legislative sphere, he may summon an extraordinary session of the National Assembly or of the National Council of the Provinces, may refer a bill to the Constitutional Court for ascertaining its view on its constitutional validity, may refer a bill back to the National Assembly for reconsideration, and may assent to a bill passed by the Parliament. In the executive sphere, he has important functions to perform. He appoints Commissions of Inquiry. To maintain foreign relations, he appoints his ambassadors and diplomatic representatives to other countries and receives and recognises the ambassadors and diplomatic representives of other countries. He may make any appointments as required by the Constitution or the law of the Parliament. He may call a national referendum in terms of a law of the Parliament. As head of the State, he confers honours and may exercise his prerogative of mercy by pardoning or reprieving an offender or commuting his punishment.

The Cabinet consists of the President, who is its head, a Deputy President and some Ministers appointed by him. The Deputy President must be a member of the National Assembly at the time of his appointment. There is a limit on the strength of the Ministry. It can have at the most 27 members. The President may select any member from amongst the members of the National Assembly. He may also appoint at the most two Ministers who are not the members of the National Assembly. Besides, he may appoint any number of Deputy Ministers from among the members of the National Assembly. He may dismiss the Deputy President, the Ministers and the Deputy Ministers as they are individually responsible to him. At the same time, they are individually as well as collectively responsible to the Parliament for the exercise of their powers and performance of their functions. The President appoints a member of the

Cabinet to be the leader of the government business in the National Assembly.

The members of the Cabinet, before entering upon their office, take the oath of faithfulness to the Republic and obedience to the Constitution. Even after the dissolution of the National Assembly, the members of the Cabinet continue to function until the new Cabinet is formed. The President allocates work among the Ministers and he may make alterations in it. If a Minister is absent for some reason, or is incapable of performing his functions, or if there is a vacancy, the President may transfer his functions to some other Minister. Here two important points engage our attention. First, a Cabinet member may assign any power or function to a member of the Provincial Executive Councillor of a Municipal Council by mutual agreement in accordance with a law of Parliament and a Presidential proclamation is issued to this effect. Second, all the Cabinet members are bound by the code of ethics prescribed by the national legislation. As such, they cannot undertake any other paid work, they cannot act in a way that is inconsistent with their office, or expose themselves to any situation involving the risk of conflict between their official responsibilities and private interests. They cannot use their powers or any information entrusted to them so as to enrich themselves or improperly benefit any other person.

A decision of the President must be in writing if it is taken in terms of legislation or has legal consequences. It must be countersigned by another member of the Cabinet if it concerns a function assigned to him. All proclamations, regulations and other instruments of subordinate legislation must be accessible to the public. The Parliament may specify the manner in which and the extent to which such instruments are to be tabled in and approved by it.

The National Assembly may pass a resolution by the majority of its members to express its no-confidence in the Cabinet. Then the President shall reconstitute it. In case such a resolution is passed against the President, then he and all members of the Cabinet must resign.

Since the Union of South Africa has a federal system, its Constitution has some provisions whereby the Centre may exercise its control over the units. Art. 100 has its own significance in this regard. When a province cannot, or does not, fulfil its executive obligations in accordance with the terms of the Constitution or the laws of the Parliament, the national executive may intervene by taking any appropriate steps to ensure fulfilment of their obligations, including (*a*) issuing a directive to the provincial executive, describing the extent of the failure to fulfil its obligations and staying any steps required to meet its obligations, and (*b*) assuming responsibility for the relevant obligation in that province to the extent necessary to (*i*) maintain essential national standards or meet established minimum standards for the rendering of a service, (*ii*) maintain economic unity, (*iii*) maintain national security, or (*iv*) prevent that province from taking unreasonable action that is prejudicial to the interests of another province or to the country as a whole. In order to meet the requirement of natural justice, it is further provided that the notice of intervention must be tabled in the National Council of the Provinces within 14 days of its sitting after the commencement of the intervention, and the intervention must end unless it is approved by the Council within 30 days of its first sitting after the commencement of the intervention. The Council must review the intervention regularly and make any appropriate recommendations to the national executive. The entire process must be regulated by a law of the Parliament.

It is clear that South Africa has the presidential form of government that looks like a peculiar mixture of the American and French presidential systems. The President and his ministers cannot be the members of the Parliament as in America and France, but the National Assembly may remove them by the vote of no-confidence. A resolution to this effect is to be passed by simple majority of the members present and voting. A peculiar point to be noted here is that the National Assembly may throw out both the Cabinet and the President. In case the Cabinet is outvoted, the President shall reconstitute it, but if the no-confidence motion is passed against the President, then he and all the members of the Cabinet must resign. This arrangement has no place in the American and the French systems. The position of the President is weak in three respects. First, he has to choose his ministers in proportion to the strength of the parties in the National Assembly. Second, he can neither form a very big ministry, nor can he pick up the minister of his choice as there is a ceiling on the size of the Cabinet. Third, he can be removed by the National Assembly by a vote of no-confidence. And yet by virtue of having special powers, he is the real head of the State.

Parliament

The national legislature is known by the name of the Parliament. It is a bi-cameral body with the National Council of the Provinces and the National Assembly as its upper and lower chambers respectively. By virtue of being the upper chamber, the National Council of the Provinces, represents the units of the federation to ensure that their interests are taken into account in the national sphere of government. It does this mainly by participating in the national legislative process and by providing a national forum for public consideration of issues affecting the provinces. By virtue of being the lower chamber, the National Assembly represents the people. Its elected members ensure 'government by the people'. It does this by choosing the President of the republic, by scrutinising and overseeing executive actions, by passing legislation and, above all, by providing a national forum for public consideration of issues. Its seat is in Cape Town, but it may take a decision to have its seat elsewhere in the country on the grounds of public interest, security or convenience as provided in its rules and orders.

National Council of the Provinces: It is composed of a single delegation from each province consisting of 10 delegates who are taken in this manner: (*a*) Four special delegates consisting of (*i*) the Premier of the province or in his non-availability any member of the provincial legislature designated by the Premier either generally or for any specific business before the National Council of Provinces, and (*ii*) three other special delegates appointed in terms of sec. 61 (2) of the Constitution; (*b*) the Premier of a province, or if the Premier is not available, member of the province's delegation designated by the Premier heads the delegation. The Constitution has peculiar provisions for the allocation of delegates in this chamber.[1] Political parties having their seats in the provincial legislatures are entitled to include their delegates in the provincial delegation according to the formula set out in part B of Schedule 3.

This provision has a significance of its own as its purpose is to ensure that minor parties have their representation in the category of both permanent and special delegates in a manner consistent with democracy. The legislature of a province with the concurrence of its Premier and the leaders of the parties entitled to special delegates in the province's delegation must designate special delegates, as required from time to time, from amongst its members. A person nominated as a permanent delegate must be eligible to be a member of the provincial legislature. If a member of the legislature is picked up for this post, he ceases to be its member.

1. It provides that within 30 days after the result of an election of a provincial legislature is declared, its legislature must make a law to determine the number of its permanent and special delegates. It shall appoint its permanent delegates according to their nomination by parties. It is done according to a formula to determine party participation in provincial delegations to this House. It provides that the number of delegates must be determined by multiplying the number of seats the party holds in the provincial legislature by 10 and then dividing the result by the number of seats in the legislature plus one. If a calculation yields a surplus not absorbed by the delegates allocated to a party, the surplus must compete with similar surpluses accruing to any other party or parties and any undistributed delegates in the delegation must be allocated to the party or parties in the sequence of the highest surplus.

The permanent delegates are appointed for a term that expires immediately before the first sitting of the provincial legislature after its next session. But he ceases to be a permanent delegate in case he (*i*) ceases to be eligible to be a member of the provincial legislature for any reason other than being appointed as a permanent delegate, (*ii*) becomes a member of the Cabinet, (*iii*) has lost the confidence of the provincial legislature and is recalled by the party that had nominated him, (*iv*) ceases to be a member of the party that had nominated him and is recalled by it, and (*v*) is absent from the House without permission in circumstances for which the rules and orders of the Council prescribe loss of office as a permanent delegate. Vacancies among the permanent delegates must be filled in terms of the law of the Parliament. Each permanent delegate must swear or affirm faithfulness to the Republic and to the Constitution before performing his functions in the House.

The National Council has its presiding officers. It has a chairperson and two deputy chairpersons who are elected from amongst the delegates. The Chairperson and one Deputy Chairperson are elected from among the permanent delegates for five years unless their terms as delegates expire earlier. The other deputy chairperson is elected for a term of one year and must be succeeded by delegate from another province, so that every province is represented in turn. At the time of the election of the chairperson, the House is presided by the President of Constitutional Court, or by a any other judge in his absence, but the chairperson presides at the time of the election of the Deputy Chairpersons. The House may remove its presiding officers. It may elect from among the delegates other presiding officers to assist the Chairperson and Deputy Chairpersons. The House determines the time and the duration of its sessions, but the President of the Republic may summon its special sitting at any time to conduct a special business.

The ministers, deputy ministers and any official of the national executive may take part in the deliberations of the House and its committees without right to vote. Besides, not more than 10 part-time representatives designated by an organised local government to represent the different categories of municipalities may participate in deliberations of the House or its Committees when necessary without right to vote. Each province has one vote which is cast on behalf of it by the head of its delegation, and all questions before the House are agreed when at least 5 provinces vote in favour of the question. The Parliament may make a law for a uniform procedure in terms of which provincial legislatures confer authority on their delegations to cast votes on their behalf. Its sittings are open. The House may facilitate public involvement in its legislative and other processes but reasonable measures may be taken to regulate public access, including the media, and to provide for the searching of any person, or the refusal of entry to any person if so necessary.

National Assembly: It is the popular chamber of the national legislature having at least 350 and at the most 400 members, the number to be determined by a law of the Parliament. The electoral system shall be prescribed by national legislation, based on the national common voters roll. The minimum voting age is 18 years and any citizen who is qualified to vote for this House is eligible for its membership. But certain categories of the office holders are ineligible for its membership as the President, the Deputy President, Ministers and Deputy Ministers, permanent delegates to the National Council of the provinces or members of the provincial legislatures or municipal councils, unrehabilitated insolvent, anyone declared of unsound mind by the courts etc. The members have to subscribe to an oath before performing their functions.

The term of the National Assembly is of five years, but it may be dissolved by the President of the Republic earlier. If so, new elections must be held within next 90 days. The President may dissolve it, if it has passed a resolution to this effect by the majority of its members and the House has completed a term of three years. The Acting President must dissolve it if the office of the President is lying vacant and the Assembly fails to elect a new President within 30 days after the vacancy had occurred. More than 50% of the members must be present at the time of passing a bill, and at least 33% of the members must be present at the time when the house takes up any other matter. The Assembly elects a Speaker and a Deputy Speaker from among its members. The President of the Constitutional Court presides at the time of election of the Speaker, but the Speaker presides when the Deputy Speaker is elected. The House may pass a resolution by the majority of its members to remove the Speaker or Deputy Speaker. The presiding officer has the right of casting vote to break the tie which is known as the 'deliberative vote'.

The Constitution also specifies the powers of the National Assembly. In the exercise of its legislative powers, it may consider, pass, amend or reject any bill before it and it may initiate or prepare a bill except a money bill. It must provide for mechanisms to ensure that all executive organs of State in the national sphere of government are accountable to it, and to maintain oversight of the exercise of national executive authority including the implementation of legislation by any organ of State. It may determine and control its internal arrangements, proceedings and procedures, and make rules and orders concerning its business with due regard to the representative and participatory democracy, accountability, transparency and public involvement. Its rules and orders must provide for the establishment, composition, powers, functions, procedures and duration of its committees the participation in its proceedings and its committees of minority parties represented in it. It should be done in a manner consistent with democracy, financial and administrative assistance to each party represented in it in proportion to its size so as to enable it and its leaders to perform their functions effectively.

The Assembly allows public access to and involvement of the people in its deliberations. The business is conducted in an open manner and it is open to the press and information channels. Reasonable restrictions may be imposed in the case of urgency. Cabinet members and all other members of the Assembly have the right to express their views in its Assembly or its committees subject to rules and regulations. Their salaries and allowances are a charge on the National Revenue Fund. Civil and criminal proceedings cannot be initiated against a person for speaking in the House or its committees. The privileges of the members may be determined by a law of Parliament.

The Constitution has provisions relating to legislative process. Only a Cabinet Minister, or a Deputy Minister, or a member, or the committee of the National Assembly may move a bill in the House, but a money bill may be introduced by a Cabinet member holding the portfolio of Finance. A money bill may be introduced in the National Assembly, but a non-money bill may be introduced in either House of Parliament. Only a member or a committee of the National Council of the Provinces may introduce a non-money bill in the House. It is required that a bill must be passed by both the Houses. If there is a disagreement between the two Houses, it is sorted out by a Mediation Committee consisting of 9 members elected by the National Assembly in proportion to the strength of the parties in the House and 9 members nominated by the National Council of the Provinces, one representing one province. The National Assembly may seek the view of the Constitutional Court if the constitutional validity of a bill before it is contested.

It shows that the Parliament of South Africa is a democratic body in respect of its composition and working. It meets the requirement of a federal system by allotting seats to the provinces in the national upper chamber. It exercises check over the government as it may remove the President or the Cabinet by passing a vote of no-confidence or impeachment. It recommends the names for the posts of the Public Protector and Auditor-General as well of the Chairpersons and members of the Human Rights Commission, Electoral Commission and Commission for Gender Equality who are formally appointed by the President. On the basis of its resolution, the President may remove such office holders from office on the charge of misconduct, incapacity or incompetence. In this way, the President and the Parliament have been invested with the power of appointing high officers and commissions to establish and sustain the institutions of constitutional democracy.

Judicial System

The Constitution has made elaborate arrangements for the independent functioning of the judiciary. The courts must apply impartially and without favour or prejudice the law of the land. No person or organ of State may interfere with the functioning of the courts. The courts are Constitutional Court, Supreme Court of Appeal, High Courts, Magistrates' Courts, and any other court established by law of the land. At the apex is the Constitutional Court having a President, a Deputy President and 9 other judges. A matter before the Court must be heard by at least 8 judges. It interprets the provisions of the Constitution and may settle legal disputes between the Centre and the Provinces or between the Provinces, and may pronounce its judgement on the constitutional validity of an impugned law or executive action of the President and the National Assembly. Thus, like the Supreme Courts of America, Canada and India, it has the power of judicial review. Its decision is final.

The Supreme Court of Appeal is a different body. It consists of a Chief Justice, a Deputy Chief Justice and some judges of appeal determined by a law of Parliament. It hears and decides an appeal when a decision of the High Court is challenged. However, a notable feature of the judicial system of this country is the establishment of a Judicial Service Commission consisting of the Chief Justice of the Supreme Court, the President of the Constitutional Court, the Cabinet member holding the portfolio of law, two representatives of the bar, 6 members designated by the National Assembly, four members so designated by the National Council of the Provinces, four members nominated by the President of the Republic, one reputed teacher of law designated by the University Teachers Union, two practising attorneys etc. Certainly it is a very large body. It may advise the national government on any matter relating to the judicial system or administration of justice in the country. If a judge is found to be guilty of misconduct or inefficiency or gross incompetence by this Commission, the President may remove him from office.

Judiciary cannot function properly unless it is independent and has the cooperation of the people and other organs of the state. So it is given that no person or organ of state can interfere with the functioning of the courts. Organs of state, through legislative and other measures, must assist and protect the courts to ensure independence, impartiality, dignity, accessibility and effectiveness of the courts. A judicial decision or order is binding on all persons and organs of state to which it applies. A judge may commit a wrong for which he must be suitably punished after proper investigation. This important function has been assigned to the Judicial Service Commission which is a very large body as it includes professional jurists as well as legislators belonging to the ruling and opposition parties. In a word, the judiciary plays its important role in sustaining the democratic system of the country.

Political Parties and Pressure Groups

Like other democratic countries of the world, South Africa has its own party system. There are many political parties as African National Party, Inkatha Freedom Party, New National Party, United Democratic Movement, African Christian Democratic Party, Freedom Front, United Christian Democratic Party, Pan-African Congress of Azania, Federal Alliances, Minority Front, Afrikaner Enheid Sheweging Azanian People's Organisation, Abolition of Income Tax and Usury Party, Socialist Party of Azania, and People's Green Party. It shows that, like France and Switzerland, South Africa is a multi-party State. It may also be pointed out that some of the parties (as Abolition of Income Tax and Usury Party and People's Green Party) are like pressure groups because of their small numerical strength and their limited range of interest and activity.

Since the Constitution provides for proportional representation with single transferable vote system in the parliamentary elections and since ministers are inducted on the basis of their strength in the National Assembly, the party system, in a sense, has its sanction in the fundamental law of intellectuals. There are the groups of businessmen, workers, peasants, artists, intellectuals and the like which play the role of pressure groups to protect and promote their specific interests. But the government is faced with the problem of acting autonomously in the midst of growing demands of the people putting a heavy premium on its capacity to convert inputs into outputs. So it is observed by a critic: "Since the end of the racist apartheid regime in South Africa in 1994, that country has confronted limits in both autonomy and capacity, as a newly mobilised and active public has sought to expand its political demands on a state with limited resources that were once largely preserved for a small white elite."[2]

2. Patrick O' Neil: *Essentials of Comparative Politics* (New York: W.W. Norton & Co., 2004), pp. 42-43.

Part - XII

Bhutanese Constitution

Our Constitution is to strengthen the security, safegaurd our sovereignty, liberty, freedom, progress of the nation, prosperity of the country, happiness of the people and good governance.

—Chairman of the Drafting Committee
Lynopo Sonam Togbye

40

CONSTITUTION OF BHUTAN

Bhutan, known as Shangri-la and Drukul (Land of the Thunder Dragon) in history, is situated in the heart of the Himalayas. Its political history is not very old. It begins from 17 December, 1917 when the chiefs and principal lamas (religious teachers) unanimously chose Ugyen Wangchuk as their hereditary ruler (Maharaja) with the title of Druk Gyalpo (previous Ruler of the Dragon people). He ruled till August 1926. He was succeded by Jigme Wangchuk who ruled till 1952. Then came Jigme Dorji Wangchuk who ruled for 20 years. In 1972 Jigme Singhe Wangchuk, the fourth herditary monarch ascended the throne, though he was formally coronated in June, 1974. He brought about religions and social consolidation and endowed the country with political unity[1]. During his reign Bhutan emerged as a modern nation. Credit goes to him for launching social, economic, political and constitutional reforms. He abdicated the throne in 2005 in favour of his elder son Jigme Khesar Namgyel Wangchuk who inaugurated the constitution in 2008.

Bhutanese Constitutionalism

The history of Bhutanese constitutionalism is neither very old nor very dramatic. It was ruled by the dictates of the monarch who never acted like a despot. King Jigme Dorji Wangchuk was a man of clear vision and foresight. He introduced many constitutional reforms the most important of which was the establishment of Tashogdu (National Assembly)

---

1. For instance, while dispelling the fears of the Nepalis, the monarch made it clear that they "should never regard themselves as aliens, because your forbears were also born and reared in Bhutan and, as such, all of you are Bhutanese.... All of us must remain united as one people and as one nation and forge ahead together." *Speeches of Our Beloved King*, published by the Royal Government of Bhutan, Department of Information, Thimpu, 1979, p. 13.

in 1953 which converted the political system into constitutional monarchy. The assembly had members elected by the people and by the monastic order, and some official nominees. He also created Lodoe Tshogdu (Royal Advisory Council) to aid and advise him in day-to-day administration. It consisted of 8 members-5 representing the people, 2 representing the monastic order and 1 nominated by the king who would be its chief as well.

The main task of this body was to supervise the implementation of the policies and programmes made by the National Assembly. However, the most significant and ever-memorable step taken by this ruler was the making of monarchy accountable to the people. In May 1963 he announced that he would seek vote of confidence of the Assembly once in every three years. In case such a motion was adopted by two-thirds majority, he would abdicate and the throne would pass on to a person next in the hereditary line of succession. In May 1971 the Assembly adopted rules relating to the appointment, removal and privileges of the members of the Royal Advisory Council.

In 1972 was created Lhengye Shungtsog (Council of Ministers). It consisted of a chairman (King or Speaker of the Assembly), representatives of the king in the ministries of Finance and Development, all Ministers and deputy Ministers, a representative of the army, and all members of the Royal Advisory Council representing the National Assembly. The secretaries of various Ministries and the heads of important departments, though not members of the Council of Ministers, could be permitted to attend its meetings. Its decisions were to be ratified by the National Assembly. At the judicial apex was the High Court established in 1968 consisting of five judges appointed by the King[2]. No doubt, after the achievement of independence on 8 August, 1949, the rulers of Bhutan made commendable efforts for her social and political modernisation[3].

A special committee was convened in late 2001 to prepare a draft constitution. A complete first draft was submitted formally to the king (Jigme Singyh Wangchuk) in December, 2002. Then, the National Assembly and the Royal Advisory Councils were dissolved. First general

2. See Prakash Chander; "Bhutan" in J.C. Johari (ed.): *Governments and Politics of South Asia* (Delhi: Sterling Publishers, 1991), pp. 582-84.

3. Before independence Bhutan was a British protectorate. The Treaty of 1910 placed this country under the supervision of the Government of British India. This treaty was replaced in August, 1949 whereby Bhutan agreed to seek the advice of the Government of India with regard to its foreign relations which could be accepted by it or not. By all means now Bhutan is a sovereign state.

elections took place in March 2008 and then was installed a new Council of Ministers and a bi-cameral legislature composed of the National Council having 20 elected and 5 nominated members and the National Assembly having 47 elected members. The final version of the draft constitution was adopted by the new Parliament in July, 2008.[4] The slow but steady progress in the direction of constitutionalism had its culmination in the promulgation of the Constitution in 2008 that makes this country a Sovereign Kingdom.

Salient Features

The salient features of this Constitution may be enumerated as under:

1. **An Enacted, Written and Rigid Constitution:** Like the constitution of USA, Switzerland, France and other countries of the world excluding Britain, it is an enacted constitution. It was framed by the Grand National Assembly and King Jigme Singye Wanchuk made an announcement about it on 26 March, 2005. Elections to the National Council were held in December, 2007; elections to the National Assembly were held in March, 2008 and so this Constitution came into effect. It is a written document having a preamble and 34 Articles followed by four schedules. Each article has a number of sections. Then, it is a rigid constitution, because the process of its amendment is very difficult. A bill to this effect must be initiated in a joint session by a simple majority of the total number of members and then passed by three fourths of the total number of the members of Parliament. The Parliament may also call for a national referendum to have it finally passed.
2. **Enlightened Theocracy:** Unlike India and Nepal, but like Pakistan and Bangladesgh, Bhutan has a theocratic system. Buddhism is the official religion. The king must be a Buddhist. Buddhism is the spiritual heritage of this country which promotes among others the principles and values of peace, non-violence, compassion and tolerance. However, Bhutan offers the case of enlightened theocracy. The Monarch is the protector of all religions and holds supreme spiritual as well as temporal authority in his hands. All persons, whether citizens or not, enjoy equality before law and discrimination among them on the basis of religion or race is prohibited. It is also mentioned that it shall be the responsibility of religious institutions

4. *The Europa World Year-Book* (London: Routledge, 2010), Vol. I, p.899

and personalities to promote spiritual heritage of the country while ensuring that religion remains separate from politics.

3. **Unitary System:** Like Britain, France, China and Bangladesh. Bhutan has a unitary system. All powers are with the central government situated at Thimpu. There are District Councils as the units of local government, but they donot enjoy autonomy. They are under the control of the Central Government. There is no division of powers and, for this reason, the Parliament can make a law on any item of national, regional or local importance. The Parliament may make a law to create new districts or to alter the boundaries or areas of the existing districts. The only requirement is that a bill to this effect must be passed by three-fourths of the total number of the members of Parliament.

4. **Democratic Constitutional Monarchy:** Art 1 of the Constitution declares Bhutan as a democratic constitutional monarchy. Any other form of government is prohibited. It shows that like the British monarch, the king of Bhutan (Druk Gyalpo) is the titular head of the State, while real authority is vested in the Council of Ministers, headed by the Prime Minister, collectively responsible to the Parliament. The Monarch reigns, he does not govern. The entire administration is carried in his name, but it is done according to the will of the people embodied in the decisions of the Parliament and the Council of Ministers. The sovereign power belongs to the people of Bhutan.

5. **Parliamentary Form of Government:** Like Britain and India, Bhutan has parliamentary form of Government. Here the executive and the legislative organs of the state are combined. All Ministers must be the members of Parliament, but the Prime Minister must be a member of the National Assembly. The king appoints the leader of the party having majority in the National Assembly as the Prime Minister. He appoints Ministers on his advice. As the government is responsible to the National Assembly, it may be removed by a vote of no-confidence. The Council of Ministers aids and advises the King who acts accordingly. As the ceremonial head of the State, he may accept the advice or refer a matter for the reconsideration of the Ministers. In case the government loses confidence of the National Assembly and the formation of alternative government is not possible, he may make an appeal to the electorate.

Some Important Statements

The highest achievement of 100 years of monarchy has been the constant nurturing of democracy. This has culminated today with the first sitting of Parliament and the start of democracy, whereby, my father, the fourth Druk Gyalpo and I hereby return to our people the powers that had been vested in our kings by our forefathers hundred years ago. We do so with absolute faith and confidence, offer our complete support and our prayers for the success of democracy.

—King Jigme Khesar Wangchuk,

Address of Druk Gyalpo to the First Session of Parliament on 10 May, 2008.

How a democratic culture is developed and sustained is now an endeavour we must share for our own sake and that of posterity under the rule of our benevolent monarchs. Our collective effort must be to make politics a noble word.

—Prime Minister Jigme Thinley

Time has, however, moved on, and so have our two countries. As we enter a new era in our ties and a new century, I come to seek and reinforce the same meeting of minds, the same depth of understanding, and the same confluence of thoughts and aspirations that have characterised our relations thus far to guide us in the future.

—Indian Prime Minister Manmohan Singh

Address to the joint session of the Parliament of Bhutan on 17 May, 2008.

6. **Bi-Cameralism:** Bhutan has adopted the system of King-in-Parliament. Parliament means the Monarch, the National Council and the National Assembly. The upper house may have 25 seats at the most, while the lower house may house 75 seats at the most (At present it has 47 seats.) The members of both the houses are directly elected by the voters for a term of five years. The upper house is a permanent body, but the lower house may be prematurely dissolved. The members of National Council cannot belong to any political party. The Council of Ministers is responsible to the National Assembly. Like Britain and India, the lower house is more powerful than the upper house of Parliament.
7. **Fundamental Rights and Duties:** Like the constitutions of India, China and the Russian Federation, the constitution of Bhutan has a long list of fundamental Rights and Duties. People have right to equality before law. They may follow any religion according to their choice. Each citizen has the right to vote and contest elections. Freedom of speech and expression has been guaranteed. Right to property has been ensured, but the state may acquire private property

for a public purpose by the authority of law on the payment of reasonable compensation. Arbitrary arrest or detention is prohibted. An aggrieved party may move the courts for the protection of its rights. Besides, there is a long list of fundamental duties. Each citizen is bound to protect the sovereignty and unity of the country, to abide by the constitution, to respect the culture and heritage of the nation, to safeguard public property, to respect national flag and anthem, and to uphold justice and act against corruption.

8. **Principles of State Policy:** The makers of the Constitution have taken inspiration from the list of Directive Principles of State Policy as contained in Part IV of the Indian Constitution. It is expected that by applying these principles, the state shall ensure good quality of life for the people, protect human rights and dignity, minimise economic inequality, protect people against all forms of discrimination, provide justice through a fair and transparent process, prevent concentration of wealth among citizens, and strive to create conditions to enable the true and sustainable development of a good and compassionate society. However, the notable point is that these principles are of a mandatory character and the state is required to implement them.
9. **Emergency Provisions:** Like the Constitution of India, the Constitution of Bhutan has provisions which may be invoked by the Monarch on the written advice of the Prime Minister. A declaration to this effect may be made if the sovereignty, security and territorial integrity of the country or a part thereof is threatened by an act of external aggression or armed rebellion. A declaration to this effect may also be made by the Monarch on the written advice of the Prime Minister in case financial stability or credit of Bhutan or any part thereof is in danger. The duration of emergency may remain for a period of 21 days from the date of the first sitting of Parliament. The Parliament may extend the duration by passing a resolution to this effect by two-thirds majority of the total number of its members. These are abnormal provisions of the Constitution of Bhutan to deal with abnormal situations.
10. **Party System:** Art. 15 of the Constitution has detailed provisions relating to political parties. The purpose is to regulate the working of political parties without which representative government cannot function properly. The political parties are required to ensure that national interests prevail over sectional

interests and for this purpose provide choice based on the values and aspirations of the people for responsible and good governance. It is also required that political parties promote national unity and progressive economic development and well-being of the nation. The candidates of the parties should not resort to regionalism, ethnicity and communalism to incite voters for electoral gains. Each party must be registered the with the Election Commission. The important point to be noted here is that representation in the National Assembly shall be by two political parties established through a primary round of election in which all registered parties may take part.

11. **Environmental Protection and Development:** This issues became very important after the Stockolm Conference held in 1972 when it was resolved that all nations should protect environment and take to the path of sustainable development. This is the reason that this item saw its incorporation into the provisions of the constitutions of the Russian Federation of 1993 and of South Africa of 1996. Art. 5 of the Bhutanese Constitution says that the Royal Government shall protect, conserve and improve the pristine environment and safeguard the biodiversity of the country, prevent pollution and ecological degradation, secure ecologically balanced sustainable development while promoting justifiable economic and social development, and ensure a safe and healthy environment.

12. **Anti-Corruption Commission:** Corruption is the most serious problem with which every state of the world is afflicted. Hence, provisions to prevent it have their place in the constitutions of the Russian Federation and South Africa. Art. 26. of the Bhutanese Constitution says about the establishment of the Anti-Corruption Commisision having a chairman and two members appointed by the King. It shall be an independent authority to take necessary steps for preventing and combating corruption in the country. On the basis of its findings or reports, the office of the Attorney General shall initiate legal proceedings in accordance with the anti-corruption law made by the Parliament

A brief look at these significant features of the Bhutanese Constitution leaves an impression that its makers have borrowed much from the constitutions of other democratice countries like Britain and India. However, the peculiarity of this Constitution may be seen in a number of innovations like retention of enlightened theocracy, creation of accountable constitutional monarchy, establishment of an interim government, and regulation of party system. Its authors have taken "a solemn pledge to secure the blessings of liberty, to ensure justice and tranquillity, and to enhance the unity, happiness and well-being of the people for all time."

Fundamental Rights and Duties

Art. 7 of the Constitution guarantees fundamental rights to the citizens as well as to other persons residing in the country. The following rights have been guaranteed to the citizens.

1. Right to life, liberty and security of person and a citizen cannot be deprived of it except in accordance with due process of law,
2. Right to freedom of speech, opinion and expression,
3. Right to freedom of thought, conscience and religion, prohibition of conversion of faith by coercion or inducement,
4. Right to information,
5. Right to vote and its exercise,
6. Right to freedom of movement and residence in the country,
7. Right to equal access and opportunity to join public services,
8. Right to own property may be taken away by the state for a public purpose by the authority of law made by the Parliament and on the payment of fair compensation.
9. Right to material interests resulting from any scientific, literary or artistic production of which he/she is the author or creator.
10. Right to practise any lawful trade, profession or vocation,
11. Right to equal pay for equal work of equal value,
12. Right to freedom of peaceful assembly and freedom of association other than membership of associations harmful to the peace and unity of the country, and right not to be compelled to belong to any association.

Some fundamental rights are ensured to all persons living in the country. These are:

1. Freedom of press, radio and television and other forms of electronics, dissemination of information,

2. Equality before law and entitlement to equal and effective protection of the law and no discrimination against the people on the grounds of race, sex, language, religion, politics, or status,
3. Not to be subjected to torture or to cruel, inhuman or degrading treatment or punishment,
4. Not to be subjected to arbitrary or unlawful interference with his privacy, family, home, or correspondence, nor to unlawful attacks on his honour or reputation,
5. Not to be subjected to arbitrary arrest or detention.

However, these right are not of an absolute or transcendental character. Reasonable restrictions may be imposed by the state on their exercise or enjoyment on the following grounds:

(a) Interest of sovereignty, security, unity and integrity of the country,
(b) Interest of peace, stability and well-being of the nation,
(c) Interest of friendly relations with foreign states,
(d) Incitement to an offence,
(e) Disclosure of information received in regard to the affairs of the state or in discharge of official duties, or
(f) Rights and freedoms of others.

The supremacy of law has been established. Hence, a citizen or any person may be deprived of these rights in accordance with the due process of law. The right to initiate appropriate proceedings in the Supreme Court or High Court against the state for the enforcement of rights conferred by the Constitution has been guaranteed. The exercise or enjoyment of these rights may be restricted or suspended during times of emergency.

Art. 8 of the Constitution enumerates fundamental duties of the citizens as well as of other persons. The duties of the citizens shall be:

1. To preserve, protect and defend the sovereignty, security, integrity and unity of the country and render national service when called upon to do so,
2. To preserve, protect and respect the culture and heritage of the nation, and
3. To foster tolerance, mutual respect and spirit of brotherhood amongst all people transcending religious, linguistic, regional or sectional diversities.

Besides, the duties of all persons shall be:

1. To respect National Flag and National Anthem,
2. Not to tolerate or participate in acts of injury, torture or killing of another person, terrorism, abuse of women, children or any other person and to take necessary steps to prevent such acts,
3. To have the responsibility to provide help, to the greatest possible extent, to the victims of accidents and in times of natural calamity,
4. To have the responsibility to safeguard public property,
5. To pay taxes in accordance with law,
6. To uphold justice and to act against corruption,
7. To act in aid of the law.
8. To respect and abide by the provisions of this Constitution.

Principles of State Policy

Bhutan is a liberal-democratic state. The Constitution has provisions which make it a social welfare state as well. Art. 9 enumerates the principles of state policy which enjoin that the state shall endeavour to apply them so as to:

1. ensure a good quality of life for the people in a progressive and prosperous country committed to peace and amity in the world,
2. promote circumstances that would enable successful pursuit of Gross National Happiness,
3. create a civil society free of oppression, discrimination and violence based on the rule of law, protection of human rights and dignity, and to ensure the fundamental rights and freedom of the people,
4. protect a person from being unlawfully intercepted in telephonic, mail or any other mode of communication,
5. provide justice through a fair, transparent and expeditious process,
6. provide legal aid to secure justice that shall not be denied to any person by reason of economic or other disabilities,
7. develop and execute policies to minimise inequalities of income, concentration of wealth among citizens, and promote equitable distribution of public facilities along individuals and people living in different parts of the kingdom,
8. ensure that all districts are treated with equity on the basis of different needs so that allocation of national resources shall result in comparable socio-economic development,

9. achieve economic self-reliance within an open and progressive economy,
10. encourage and foster private sector development through fair market competition and prevent the growth of commercial monopolies,
11. promote those circumstances that would enable the citizens to secure adequate livelihood,
12. provide the right to work, vocational guidance and training and just and favourable conditions of work,
13. provide the right to rest and leisure, including reasonable limitation of working hours and periodic holidays with pay,
14. provide the right to fair and reasonable remuneration for one's work,
15. provide education for the purpose of improving and increasing knowledge, value and skills of the entire population with education being directed towards the full development of human personality,
16. provide for free education to all children of school going age upto tenth standard and ensure that technical and professional education shall be made generally available and that higher education shall be equally accessible to all on the basis of merit,
17. take all appropriate measures to eliminate all forms of discrimination and exploitation against women, including trafficking, prostitution, abuse, violence, degrading treatment and economic exploitation,
18. promote those circumstances that are conducive to cooperation in community life and the integrity of the extended family structure,
19. create conditions that will enable the true and sustainable development of a good and compassionate society rooted in Buddhist ethos and universal human values.
20. provide free access to basic public health services in both modern and traditional medicines,
21. provide security in the event of sickness and disability or lack of adequate means of livelihood for reasons beyond one's control,
22. encourage free participation in the cultural life of the community, promote arts and sciences and to foster technological innovation, and
23. promote goodwill and cooperation with nations, foster respect for international law and treaty obligations, and encourage settlement of international disputes by peaceful means in order to promote international peace and security.

Such a long list of directive principles of state policy may be appreciated as the charter or the declaration of social and economic democracy in the country. Most of the principles look like lofty ideals that the State is committed to realise. They look like a repetition of what is contained in the Indian Constitution with an important line of distinction. While these principles have a recommendatory character in the case of the Indian Constitution, they have a mandatory character in the case of the Constitution of Bhutan.

Obviously, under the present Constitution, Bhutan is a liberal democratic as well as a social welfare state, Like Britain, it is a 'crowned republic' in view of the fact that the head of the state has nominal authority, while real power is vested in the representatives elected by and accountable to the people. Such a momentous change in the political system of this tiny Himalayan state is nothing short of a miracle. The credit for this should be given to the sagacious personality of the King as well as the role of judicious national leaders.

41

STATE STRUCTURE

As already seen, Bhutan is a Constitutional Monarchy like Britain and Japan. The Monarch is the symbolic head of the state. The real power is vested in the Prime Minister and his Council of Ministers. The ministers work during the 'pleasure' of the Monarch, but they are responsible to the National Assembly. The Parliament is a bi-cameral body. Its upper chamber (National Council) is a unique institution by virtue of being a small body of educated persons who are required to remain aloof from party politics. On the pattern of the United States and India, the Supreme Court has been set up to act as the custodian of the supreme law of the land. Another important feature to be taken note of at this stage is that the Constitution establishes some autonomous institutions like National Judical Commission, Royal Civil Service Commission, Pay Commission and Election Commission. In a word, Bhutan may be proud of having the entire paraphernalia of a liberal-democratic order embodying the ideals of a social welfare state.

Monarchy

The Constitution recognises the institution of Monarchy which resembles as well as differs from the model of British Monarchy. In both the cases the Monarch is the Head of the State belonging to a particular religious order. The British Monarch must be a Protestant Christian, the Monarch of Bhutan is required to be a Buddhist. The rule of hereditary succession applies to both. Both are the symbols of the unity of the realm and of the people of their country. The line of difference, however, may be noted in the fact that while the British Monarch acts on the advice of the Ministers as a matter of well established conventions, the Monarch of Bhutan is bound to do so according to the written provisions of the fundamental law of the land. The British Monarch may abdicate the Throne according to the terms of a law made by the Parliament in 1936, the Bhutanese Monarch "shall abdicate the Throne for wilful violations of the Constitution or being subject to permanent mental disability, on a motion passed by the Parliament in a joint session presided over by the Chief Justice of the Supreme Court."

It implies that the King may be removed by the process of impeachment. A resolution to this effect must be moved by at least two-thirds of the total number of the members and after discussion must be passed by three-fourths of the total number of the members of Parliament. After its passage by the Parliament, the motion must be approved by the simple majority of the voters in a referendum. When the motion is under discussion, the King shall be given the opportunity to defend himself in person or through his representative in the Parliament. The abdication of the Throne shall be in favour of the heir apparent.

The functions and powers of the King have been specified in the Constitution. His executive powers may be enumerated as under:

1. On the advice of National Judical Commission, he appoints the Chief Justice and Judges of the Supreme Court and the High Court.
2. On the joint advice of the Prime Minister, the Chief Justice of the Supreme Court, the Speaker of the National Assembly, the Chairman of the National Council and the Leader of the Opposition Party, he appoints the Chief Election Commissioner and other Members of the Election Commission, the Auditor-General, the Chairman and Members of the Royal Civil Service Commission, and the Chairman and Members of the Anti-Corruption Commission.
3. On the advice of the Prime Minister, he appoints the Ministers, the Attorney-General, the Governor of the Central Bank or Bhutan, the Chairman of the Pay Commission, Cabinet Secretary, ambassadors and consuls, and the District Adminstrators subject to their nomination by the Royal Civil Service Commission.
4. On the advice of the Service Promotion Board, he appoints the heads of the Defence Forces. He is the supreme commander of the defence forces.
5. On the joint advice of the Speaker of the National Assembly and Chairperson of the National Council, he appoints Secretary-General of the respective houses of Parliament.

He has legislative powers which may be enumerated as under:

1. Though not a member of any house of Parliament, he is its integral part. It is like the King-in-Parliament.
2. He nominates 5 members to the National Council.
3. He designates the Speaker and the Chairman of the National Council after they are elected by the house.
4. A bill passed by the Parliament becomes an act after receiving his assent. He may return a bill for reconsideration with his recommendations. In case such a bill is passed by the Parliament again in a joint session, he shall assent to it.
5. He may send his message or messages to the Parliament that must be promptly attended to.
6. He may address any house of Parliament or both in a joint session.
7. He summons the first session of the Parliament after the general election. Each session of Parliament begins with his inaugural address.

In addition to this, the King has a number of other functions and powers which may be enumerated as under:

1. He is the protector of all religions and has supreme spiritual and temporal authority.
2. If the National Assembly is dissolved, within 15 days he shall appoint an interim government to look after the day-to-day administration whose term would not exceed 90 days. Such a government shall have one Chief Advisor and some other Advisors as he may deem expedient. The Chief Justice of the Supreme Court shall act as the Chief Advisor.
3. He may refer a matter for national referendum if an appeal is made by at least one-third of the total number of members of all District Councils, or a bill is not passed by the Parliament in a joint session which is of national importance in his view.
4. He may withdraw money from the relief fund established by a law of Parliament for urgent and humanitarian unforeseen relief works.
5. On the written advice of the Prime Minister, he may declare a state of emergency or calamity which threatens or affects the nation as a whole or a part thereof as a result of external aggression or armed rebellion in the country. He may also declare a state of financial emergency if there is a threat to the financial stability or credit of the country or any part thereof.

6. He may refuse to give assent to a bill of constitutional amendment passed by the Parliament. In such a case, the Parliament may call for a national referendum if the bill is of national importance in its view.
7. The grant of citizenship by naturalisation shall take place after he issues a written order to this effect.
8. On the recommendation of the National Judical Commission, he may establish other Courts and tribunals from time to time.
9. He may refer any matter of great public importance or a question of law to take the opinion of the Supreme Court.

Government—Prime Minister and Council of Ministers or Cabinet

As Bhutan has parliamentary form of government, the Monarch is the ceremonial head of the State, while real authority is vested in the Council of Ministers headed by the Prime Minister. The leader of the party having majority in the National Assembly shall be invited by the Monarch to form the government. That is, the Monarch appoints the Prime Minister. He may dismiss the Prime Minister. It is laid down that the Prime Minister should be a natural-born citizen of Bhutan and that a person can not have more than two terms. The Prime Minister must be an elected member of the National Assembly. It is also laid down that the number of the Ministers shall be determined by the number of the ministries and that not more than two members elected from the electoral constituencies of the same District shall be entitled to be appointed as Ministers[1].

The functions and powers of the Council of Ministers may be thus enumerated:

1. It shall protect and strengthen the sovereignty of the Kingdom, provide good governance and ensure peace, security, well-being and happiness of the people.
2. It shall aid and advise the Monarch in the exercise of his functions, including international affairs, but the Monarch may refer a matter for the reconsideration of his Ministers.

---

1. An important point to be noted here is that the number of ministries shall be determined by the requirement of efficient and good governance. Ministres shall not be created for the purpose of appointing Ministers. Thus, Section 2 of Art. 20 indirectly puts a ceiling on the size of the Council of Ministers.

3. The Prime Minister shall keep the Monarch informed about the affairs of the state, including international affairs, and shall supply such information to him as called for.
4. It shall promote an efficient civil administration based on democratic values and principles enshrined in the Constitution.
5. It shall assess the state of affairs arising from developments in the state and society and from events at home and abroad; define the goals of State action and determine the resources required to achieve them; plan and coordinate government policies and ensure their implementation; and represent the kingdom at home and abroad.

The Council of Ministers works during the pleasure of the Monarch and the National Assembly. A vote of no-confidence against the government may be passed. Such a motion must be initiated by at least one-third of the total number of the members of the National Assembly and be passed by at least by two-thirds majority of the total number of its members. If such a motion is passed, the Monarch shall dismiss the Government. After that the parties shall be called upon to demonstrate their strength to form the alternative government, failing which general election shall be conducted.

A caretaker government is formed after the dissolution of the popular chamber of Parliament in the countries having parliamentary form of government. The Prime Minister and the Ministers continue to function. It is done according to the established practice or convention. But the Bhutanese Constitution has a specific provision in this regard which should be lauded as an innovation. Art. 19 says about the installation of an Interim Government that would be set up by the Monarch just within 15 days of the dissolution of the National Assembly under the headship of the Chief Justice of the Supreme Court who would act as the Chief Advisor. It may have some advisors as well as desired by the Monarch. It shall carry out the routine functions of the government. It shall not be entitled to take any policy decision or enter into any agreement with foreign governments or organisations. It shall have a life of 90 days at the most and have its end after the constitution of the new National Assembly and the appointment of the new Prime Minister. An important point to be noted here is that it shall not include any outgoing Minister and that it shall enable the Election Commission to hold free and fair elections.

Parliament

The Bhutanese Constitution has embraced the celebrated principle of bi-cameralism. Parliament means the Monarch and the two chambers. The National Council is the second or the upper chamber, while National Assembly is the first or lower or popular chamber. The National Council has a strength of 25 members—20 members to be elected by the voters of each of the 20 districts and 5 members to be nominated by the Monarch from amongst eminent figures of the country. It is laid down that the members of this chamber cannot belong to any political party and that they must have a degree of graduation from any recognised university. It is noteworthy that besides its legislative functions, it shall act as a body to review matters affecting the security and sovereignty of the country and the interest of the nation as well as any other matter brought to the notice of the Monarch or the Prime Minister or the National Assembly. It shall elect its chairperson from amongst its members and shall meet twice a year at least[2].

The National Assembly is the lower chamber having a strength of at the most 75 members directly elected by the voters of the districts in proportion to their population, provided that no district shall have less than two and more than seven members. For this purpose, Parliament shall by its law provide for each district to be divided into constituencies through appropriate delimitation. The number of elected members from each district shall be reapportioned to reflect the changing population after every ten years, after the census for that year has been taken subject to the limitation of a maximum of seven and a minimum of two members from each district. It shall elect its Speaker from amongst its members and meet at least twice a year.

The functions and powers of the Parliament may be enumerated as under:

1. Its principal function is legislation. A bill must be passed by both the chambers and then assented to by the Monarch. In the event of disagreement or difference of views, if a bill passed by one house is not passed by the other house, the Monarch may call a joint session.

2. Elections to the National Council were held on 31 December, 2007. Elections to the National Assembly were held on 24 March, 2008. The Druk Phuensum Tshogpa led by Jigme Thinley secured 44 out of 47 seats, while People's Democratic Party led by Sangay Ngedup could secure only 3 seats. Thus, Thinley became the Prime Minister.

In each chamber the bill is to be passed by simple majority of votes, but in a joint sitting it must be passed by 2/3 majority of the total number of members present and voting.

2. Money bills and financial bills shall be moved in the National Assembly and shall be referred to the National Council within 30 days of their passing. In the case of a budget or an urgent bill, it must be passed by the National Council in the same session of Parliament.
3. Non-money bills may be introduced in any chamber and may be passed by them in the same session or in the next one, because such bills donot lapse with the prorogation of the session.
4. In case a bill passed by both the chambers is not assented to by the Monarch, or it is returned by him with some recommendations, it may be repassed in a joint session of Parliament by two-thirds majority of the members present and voting. Thereupon the bill shall be assented to by the Monarch.
5. The Council of Ministers is collectively responsible to the Parliament. The National Assembly may remove it by a vote of no-confidence.
6. Each house frames its rules of procedure for the conduct of its business and the presiding officer acts accordingly.
7. It considers the report submitted by the Prime Minister on the state of the nation which shall include legislative plans and annual plans and priorities of the government. It considers the annual report submitted by the Anti-Corruption Commission.
8. It ensures that the government safeguard the interests of the nation and fulfil the aspirations of the people through public review of policies and issues etc.
9. It can impeach constitutional authorities like Chief Justice and other judges of the Supreme Court and High Court, Chief Election Commissioner, Auditor-General, Chairman of the Royal Civil Service Commission and Chairman of the Anti-Corruption Commission on the charge of misbehaviour. The resolution must be passed by the two-thirds majority of the total number of members of Parliament in a joint sitting.
10. The Parliament has its control over the emergency powers of the Monarch to be exercised by him on the written advice of the Prime Minister. A declaration to this effect may remain in force for

21 days at the most from the date of the first sitting of Parliament. The Parliament may extend its duration by passing a resolution in a joint sitting by 2/3 majority of the total number of its members. At least 1/4 member of the National Assembly may make a request to the Speaker (if the House is in session) or to the Monarch to convene a special session to take a decision about the continuance of emergency.

11. A motion to amend the Constitution shall be initiated by a simple majority of the total number of the members of Parliament at a joint sitting and it must be passed by at least 3/4 majority of the total number of its members. In case the Monarch does not give his assent to such a bill, the Parliament may call for a national referendum.

In addition to this, some other points should be taken note of:

1. Both the Houses of Parliament have a tenure of five years. The National Council is a permanent chamber, but the National Assembly may be prematurely dissolved by the Monarch on the advice of the Prime Minister. The duration is to be counted from the date of the first sitting of each house.
2. One person cannot be a member of both the Houses at the same time.
3. The presence of not less than two-thirds of the total number of its members shall be required to constitute quorum for the sitting of each house.
4. A joint session of the Parliament shall be presided by the Speaker of the National Assembly.
5. The election of the members of Parliament shall be in accordance with the provisions of the election law of Bhutan.
6. The Monarch summons the first sitting of Parliament after each general election. Subsequent sittings are summoned by the presiding officer of each house. At the instance of the Monarch, the presiding officers may call an extra-ordinary session if the exigencies of the situation so demand.
7. The proceedings of the Parliament shall be conducted in public. However, the presiding officer may exclude the press and the public from any proceedings in the event of a compelling need in the interest of public order, national security and the like.

8. The members of Parliament shall take an oath of affirmation of office as provided in the Third Schedule of the Constitution before assuming their responsibilities.
9. The members of Parliament shall subscribe to maintaining decorum and dignity of the House and shall desist from acts of defamation and use of physical force.
10. All members of Parliament enjoy privileges and immunities as freedom from arbitrary arrest or detention, but these immunities shall not cover the acts of corruption and defamation.

It shows that Bhutan has a bicameral legislature like other democratic countries of the world. The Parliament is the repository of significant powers. However, it has some unique features. First, its upper house allows no room for party politics. It may be appreciated for presenting a brief model of partyless democracy. Second, both the chambers have a tenure of five years. But the upper chamber cannot be prematurely dissolved. In Australia both the chambers (Senate and House of Representatives) may be dissolved simultaneously and then reconstituted by the Governor-General, but in Bhutan the upper chamber is a permanent body. Third, for making quorum, the presence of at least two-thirds of the total number of members is required. It is a fine arrangement that puts a check on the number of unscrupulous absentees. Fourth, a motion of no-confidence against the government must be initiated by at least 1/3 members and passed by at least 2/3 members of the total number of the members of Parliament. It is another fine device to put a check on the reckless exercise of the opposition parties to create the situation of political instability. Last, the privileges and immunities granted to the members of Parliament donot cover acts of corruption and defamation.

Judiciary

The provisions of the Constitution establish an independent and impartial judiciary in the country. Art. 21 says that the judiciary "shall safeguard, uphold and administer justice fairly and independently without fear, favour, or undue delay in accordance with the Rule of Law to inspire trust and confidence and to enhance access to justice." The judicial authority of the Kingdom is vested in the Supreme Court at the top with a High Court and District Courts below it. On the recommendation of the National Judicial Commission, the King may establish subordinate Courts as sub-District Courts, and other Courts and tribunals. For our purpose, the Supreme Court is important which consists of a Chief Justice and four judges.

The Chief Justice of the Supreme Court shall be appointed by the King on the recommendation of the National Judicial Commission for a term of five years, or shall remain in office until he attains the age of 65 years, whichever earlier. He shall be promoted from amongst the judges of the Supreme Court, be chosen from amongst eminent jurists of the country. The King shall appoint the judges of the Supreme Court from amongst the judges of the High Court, or from amongst eminent jurists of the country on the recommendation of the National Judicial Commission. They shall remain in office for a period of 10 years or until they attain the age of 65 years, whichever earlier. On the charge of 'misbehaviour', and on the basis of a report submitted by the Attorney-General, a judge may be removed by the process of impeachment. A motion to this effect must be passed by the Parliament in a joint session by two-thirds members of the total number of the members of Parliament. The sitting shall be presided by the Chief Justice and by the senior most judge in case the motion is against the Chief Justice himself.

The jurisdiction of the Supreme Court is of three kinds—original, appellate and advisory. Vide its original jurisdiction, it may issue orders for the protection of fundamental rights of the citizens and other persons. The decision of the High Court may be challenged in the Supreme Court. So an appeal may be filed. The Supreme Court may uphold, reverse or quash the verdict of the High Court. The, Monarch may refer a matter of urgent public importance or an important question of law to the Supreme Court for seeking its opinion. From time to time, the Supreme Court may make rules to regulate the general practice and procedures of the Courts as required to enhance efficiency and effectiveness of the judicial process and system of the country.

Other Constitutional Bodies

National Judicial Commission: The Constitution makes provision for the establishment of a National Judicial Commission having four members The Chief Justice of the Supreme Court shall be its chairman. It shall include a senior-most judge of the Supreme Court, the Chairperson of the Legislative Committee, and the Attorney General. All the members shall be appointed by the King. This body shall recommend the names of the Chief Justice and other members of the Supreme Court and High Court for their appointments by the King. On the basis of its report, impeachment proceedings may be initiated in the Parliament against a judge of the Supreme Court and High Court.

Anti-Corruption Commission: It shall have a chairperson and two members to be appointed by the King on the joint recommendation of the Prime Minister, the Chief Justice of the Supreme Court, the Speaker of the National Assembly, the Chairperson of the National Council, and the Leader of the Opposition party. Its members shall remain in office for a term of five year or until they attain the age of 65 years, whichever earlier. It shall be an independent authority and take all necessary steps to prevent and combat corruption in the country. It shall exercise such functions and powers as may be prescribed by a law of Parliament. On the basis of its report, the office of the Attorney-General shall initiate proceedings in a Court of law against the guilty persons or organisations. It shall submit its annual report to the King, the Prime Minister and the Parliament.

Royal Civil Service Commission: The authors of the Constitution have made elaborate arrangements for having efficient and uncommitted public services. For this purpose, Royal Civil Service Commission has been provided. It shall consist of a chairperson and four members appointed by the King on the joint recommendation of the Prime Minister, Chief Justice of the Supreme Court, Speaker of the National Assembly, Chairperson of the National Council, and the Leader of the Opposition party. They shall remain in office for a term of five years or until they attain a specific age, sixty five years for the chairperson and 60 years for the members, whichever earlier. It is expected that the Commission shall ensure independent and apolitical civil services that will discharge the public duties in an efficient, transparent and equitable manner. It shall endeavour to ensure that civil servants render professional service, guided by the highest standards of ethics and integrity to promote good governance and social justice in implementing the policies and programmes of the government. Its chairperson may be removed on the charge of 'misbehaviour' in a manner prescribed for the Chief Justice of the Supreme Court.

Pay Commission: Headed by a chairperson, this body shall be autonomous and shall be constituted, from time to time, on the recommendation of the Prime Minister. It shall recommend to the Government revisions in the structures of the salaries, allowances, benefits and other emoluments of the Royal Civil Service, the judiciary, the Armed Forces, the Members of Parliament and local government, the monastic body, and all other public servants with due regard to the economy of the kingdom and other provisions of the Constitution. Its recommendations shall be implemented on the approval of the Council of Ministers and be subject to such conditions and modifications as made by the Parliament.

Election Commission: Art. 23 says that the "general will of the people shall be the basis of government and it shall be expressed through periodic elections." For this sake, Election Commission shall be set up having a chairperson and two members. The King shall appoint them on the joint recommendation of the Prime Minister, the Chief Justice of the Supreme Court, the Speaker of the National Assembly, the Chairperson of the National Assembly, the Chairperson the National Council, and the Leader of the Opposition party. They shall remain in office for a period of five years, or until they attain the age of sixty-five years, whichever earlier. On the charge of 'misbehaviour, the Chief Election Commissioner may be removed by the process of impeachment as prescribed for the Chief Justice of the Supreme Court. The function of the Commission is to superintend, direct and control elections to Parliament and local governments, including referendums.

Party System

Provisions relating to political parties in Bhutan should be admired for adding a new element to the subject of constitutionalism. The authors of the Constitution have really done a great job by incorporating provisions to regulate the working of political parties. Art. 15 enjoins that political parties shall ensure that national interests prevail over all other interests and, for this purpose, provide choices based on the values and aspirations of the people for responsible and good governance. The candidate of political parties shall not resort to regionalism, ethnicity and communalism to incite voters for electoral gains. Rather they shall promote national unity and progressive economic development and strive for well being of the nation. Political parties must be registered with the Election Commission. For registration it is required that a party must meet these requirements:

(a) Its membership is not based on sex, religion, language, region or social origin.

(b) It is broad-based with cross-national membership and support and is committed to national cohesion and stability.

(c) It does not receive any money or assistance from foreign sources, be it governmental, non-governmental, private organisations or private parties or individuals.
(d) Its members shall bear true faith and allegiance to this Constitution and uphold the sovereignty, security, unity and integrity of the kingdom.
(e) It is established for the advancement of democracy and for social, economic and political growth of the country.
(f) It has not been dissolved earlier by an order of the Supreme Court on the charge of violation of the above requirements or of a law of the Parliament.

The Constitution ensures the existence of a bi-party system. Before the general election, primary election shall take place. Only two parties shall have the right to contest Parliamentary elections which have secured highest number of votes in the primary election. Thus, only two parties shall have their entry into the National Assembly. The party securing more votes shall form the government, the other one shall be the Opposition party. Political defection is prohibited. It is laid down that the Parliament shall make a law to regulate the formation, function, ethical standards, and intra-party organisations of political parties and shall ensure the transparency of party funds through regular auditing of their accounts. It is another notable point that the Parliament shall make a law to establish public campaigning fund. The Election Commission shall fix ceiling on the amount of expenditure by a candidate or a party. It shall make payments after the general election in a non-discriminatory manner to the parties registered with the Election Commission.

Then, Art. 18 has a significance of its own which ensures that political party in opposition shall play a constructive role. Its duty shall be to ensure that the Government and the ruling party function in accordance with the provisions of this Constitution, provide good governance and strive to promote national interest and fulfil the aspirations of the people. It shall promote national integrity, unity and harmony and cooperation among all sections of society. It shall also endeavour to promote and engage in constructive and responsible debate in Parliament while providing healthy support to the Government in times of national calamities and crises.

Part - XIII

Indian Constitution

While we want this Constitution to be as solid and permanent as we can make it, there is no permanence in the Constitution. There should be a certain flexibility. If you make anything rigid or permanent, you stop the nation's growth, the growth of a living, organic, vital people.

—***Jawaharlal Nehru***

42

CONSTITUTION OF INDIA

To the students of Indian history, politics and constitutional law, the most important event of the twentieth century was the framing of our Fundamental Law by a grand assembly that worked for a period of about three years for this purpose. It was by all means the most stupendous task before our founding fathers who, after a lot of political wrangling, managed to start their monumental work on 9th December, 1946 in the midst of many gigantic constraints and difficulties and completed it on 26th November, 1949. The grand Con'sembly became the sovereign body after the advent of independence on 15th August, 1947 and henceforth it also assumed the status of the interim or provisional Parliament of the Dominion of India. As such, it came to have a dual capacity. As Con'sembly, it discussed and adopted the provisions of the draft constitution; as provisional Parliament, it performed the work of legislation, including making of the First Constitution Amendment Act in 1951.

Making of the Constitution

A historical survey of our freedom struggle bears testimony to the fact that the demand that India's political destiny should be determined by the Indians themselves had been put forward by Mahatma Gandhi as early as in 1922 when he said: "Swaraj will not be a free gift of the British Parliament. It will be a declaration of India's full self-expression. That it will be expressed through an Act of Parliament is true, but it will be merely a courteous ratification of the declared will of the people of India even as it was in the case of Union of South Africa." The demand for the setting up of a constituent assembly in very clear terms, however, assumed a shape of its own after the failure of the Indian Statutory (Simon) Commission (1928-29) and the three Round Table Conferences held at London (1930, 1931, 1932) that led Jawaharlal Nehru to say in early 1934:

"Politically and nationally, if it is granted, as it must be that the people of India are to be the sole arbiters of India's fate and must, therefore, have full freedom to draw up their Constitution, it follows that this can alone be done by means of a Constituent Assembly elected on the widest franchise. Those who believe in independence have no other choice."

Henceforth, the demand for a constituent assembly to frame a 'home-spun' constitution became a part of official Congress policy. It had its concrete from in the manifesto of the Congress Party issued on the eve of elections on 29th July, 1936. In 1938 Jawaharlal Nehru gave a definitive formulation to this demand in these words: "The Indian National Congress stands for independence and a democratic state. It has proposed that the Constitution of free India must be framed, without outside interference, by a Constituent Assembly elected on the basis of adult franchise."

However, the way for the creation of the grand Con'sembly was cleared by the recommendations of the Cabinet Mission released on 16 May, 1946, that provided:

1. Each Province and each Indian State or a group of States were to have a total number of seats proportional to their respective population roughly in the ratio of one to a million. As a result, the then Provinces were to elect 292 members, while the Princely States were allotted a maximum of 93 seats.
2. Seats in each Province were distributed among three main communities—Muslims, Sikhs and General—in proportion to their respective populations.
3. The members of each community in the Provincial Legislative Assemblies were to elect their own representatives by the method of proportional representation with single transferable vote.
4. The method of selection in the case of the representatives of the Princely States was to be determined by consultation.

Thus, the Con'sembly had 292 members elected by the Legislative Assemblies of the then 11 British Indian Provinces; 93 members were nominated by the rulers of the Indian Princely States; while 4 members represented the Chief Commissioners' Provinces of Delhi, Coorg, Ajmer-Merwara, and Andaman and Nicobar Islands.

As a result of the partition according to the Mountbatten Plan of 3rd June, 1947, a separate constituent assembly was set up for Pakistan. The

Some Important Statements

The Constituent Assembly alone can produce a constitution indigenous to the country and truly representing the will of the people.

—***Mahatma Gandhi***

It was no mean achievement that within a period of less than three years, the founding fathers succeeded in evolving a Constitution acceptable throughout the length and breadth of this vast and populous country and one capable of salvaging and strengthening the threads of national unity in the midst of the multiplicity of religions , races, languages, and all the variants of diversity.

—***Dr. S.C. Kashyap***

With the adoption of the Constitution by the members of the Constituent Assembly on 26 November, 1949, India became the largest democracy in the world. By this act of strength and will, Assembly members began what was perhaps the greatest political venture since that originated in Philadelphia in 1787.

—***Granville Austin***

representatives of East Bengal, West Punjab, Sind and Baluchristan, North-West Frontier Province and the Sylhet District of Assam, which joined Pakistan, ceased to be the members of the Con'sembly after the advent of independence. Fresh elections were held for the seats in the new Provinces of East Punjab and West Bengal. Consequently, when the Con'sembly reassembled on 31st October, 1947, its membership was reduced to 299 of which 284 appended their signatures to the constitution as finally adopted on 26th November, 1949.

On 29th August, 1947 it set up the Drafting Committee under the chairmanship of Dr. B.R. Ambedkar. It embodied the decisions of the Assembly with alternative and additional proposals in the form of the Draft Constitution of India that was published in February, 1948. The Con'sembly next met in November, 1948 to consider the provisions of the Draft Constitution clause by clause. The whole work was over on 17th October, 1949 and the coping stone was placed on 26th November, 1949 when the Preamble was adopted to complete the structure of the edifice of the Basic Law of the land. The President of the Con'sembly (Dr. Rajendra Prasad) placed his signatures and declared it as finally passed. Some of the provisions of this Constitution (as those relating to citizenship, elections, provisional Parliament, temporary and transitional measures) were given immediate effect. But the rest of the provisions came into effect on the 26th of January, 1950 to perpetuate the memory of the First Complete Independence Day observed in 1930.

No doubt, the grand Con'sembly did an immortal work by giving to us a Constitution in the form of as good and as workable a document that could have been made and that too as much democratically as possible under the prevailing conditions. It is nothing like 'imposed'; it is everything like 'adopted, enacted, and given to ourselves' by 'We, the People of India' for 'We, the People of India'. It is well observed: "It is as much democratically made as circumstances permitted.[1] Hence, if there remains the dream of social and economic democracy unrealised, the fault shall be ours, not that of the founding fathers who rendered their best services in the midst of worst circumstances. As the President of the Con'sembly (Prasad) in his concluding speech emphatically said: "The Constitution has provisions in it which appear to be objectionable from one point or another. We must admit that the defects are inherent in the situation in the country and in the people at large."[2]

Every constitution is based on certain definite principles of social, political and economic significance which constitute its philosophy that may also be termed as its 'ideology'. For this we must, look into the Preamble that reads:

"WE, THE PEOPLE OF INDIA having solemnly resolved to constitute India into a SOVEREIGN *SOCIALIST SECULAR* DEMOCRATIC REPUBLIC and to secure to all its citizens:

JUSTICE, social, economic and political;

LIBERTY of thought, expression, belief, faith and worship;

EQUALITY of status and of opportunity;

and to promote among them all

FRATERNITY assuring the dignity of the individual and the unity *and integrity* of the Nation.

IN OUR CONSTITUENT ASSEMBLY, this twenty-sixth day of November, 1949, do HEREBY ADOPT, ENACT AND GIVE TO OURSELVES THIS CONSTITUTION.[3]

---

1. K.V. Rao: *Parliamentary Democracy of India*, p. 26.
2. *Constituent Assembly Debates*. Vol. XI, p.993.
3. The italicised words were added vide 42nd Constitutional Amendment Act of 1976.

Salient Features

The salient features of the Indian Constitution may be enumerated as under:

1. **An Enacted, Written and Partly Rigid Constitution:** It is the creation of the Constitent Assembly that worked for a period of about three years. It is known as the lengthiest constitution of the world. It has 395 Articles grouped into XXII parts followed by 12 schedules (originally 8 schedules). Many articles are loaded with clauses and sub-clauses which make it a quite lengthy document. Its process of amendment is partly flexible and partly rigid. While most of its provisions are amendable by the unilateral action of the Parliament, some provisions relating to federal set up can be amended by the Parliament with the concurrence of at least half of the states. Most of the provisions can be amended if a bill to this effect is passed by both the Houses of Parliament by simple majority of the members present and voting and then assented to by the President. Some important provisions (like Fundamental Rights and Directive Principles of State Policy) are amendable if a bill to this effect is passed by both the Houses of Parliament by special majority (absolute majority of the whole House coupled with two-thirds majority of then members present and voting) and then assented to by the President. However, some provisions affecting our federal set up are amendable if a bill to this effect is passed by both the Houses of Parliament by special majority and then ratified by the legislatures of at least half of the States by simple majority of votes and then assented to by the President. The procedure is really unique on account of being a mixture of flexibility and rigidity.

2. **Derivations:** The framers of the Constitution intelligently borrowed material for their purpose from diverse sources as the Nehru Report of 1928 and the Government of India Act of 1935. They preferred the British parliamentary system in view of its experiment in our country since the inauguration of the Montford Reforms in 1920. They borrowed the system of judicial review from the American Constitution. The idea of incorporating Directive Principles of State Policy was taken from the Irish Constitution. The inclusion of Concurrent List was informed by the Constitution of Australia. From the Japanese Constitution they borrowed the phrase 'procedure established by law' and commitment to the cause of international

peace and security. It shows that our Constitution is like a splendid mixture of diverse institutional arrangements. It should not be debunked as 'a rag bag of borrowings'. The makers preferred to borrow material from diverse sources keeping in view the requirements of the time and their suitability to the country. Despite derivations from diverse sources, the design framed by the architects has its originality that cannot be found in any other Constitution of the world.

3. **Sovereign, Socialist, Secular, Democratic Republic:** The Constitution in its original form declared India a Sovereign Democratic Republic. But the forty-second amendment of 1976 inserted the words Socialist and Secular into the text of the Preamble. India is a sovereign country. It implies that she is not under the domination or control of any alien power. The word 'socialism' should not be taken in a rigid sense. It may be identified with a flexible variety of socialism that is called 'democratic socialism'. India is a secular country. It means that there is no state religion. All religions have equal respect and discrimination cannot be made among the people on the basis of religion. No religion can interfere in the affairs of the state, but the state may control and regulate the affairs of any religion for the sake of social reform. India has a democratic set up. It means that power is vested in the people which is delegated to their chosen representatives who are accountable to their electors. The rule of law prevails in the country that makes the government limited and responsible. Finally, India is a republic. It means that the head of the state (President) is elected for a definite period and he can be removed by the process of impeachment on the charge of violation of the Constitution. He does not hold his office by the rule of hereditary succession.

4. **Parliamentary Form of Government:** At the Centre as well as in the States, parliamentary model of government has been established. At the Centre, the President is the nominal head who acts on the aid and advice of the Council of Ministers, headed by the Prime Minister, that is collectively responsible to the Lok Sabha. At the State level, the Governor is the head who acts on the aid and advice of his Council of Ministers, headed by the Chief Minister, that is collectively responsible to the Vidhan Sabha. Similar pattern prevails in a Union Territory if the Parliament by its law provides for a Legislative

Assembly and a Council of Ministers there as we have in Pondicherry and Delhi.

5. **Federal System:** The Constitution establishes federal polity in the country. It is the supreme law of the land and the Central and State governments derive their powers from it. It is written. It is partly rigid as well in view of the fact that provisions relating to federal set up can be amended by the Parliament with the concurrence of at least half of the States. Powers have been distributed between the Centre and the States. The items of national importance (contained in the Union list) have been assigned to the Centre. The items of local importance (contained in the State List) have been assigned to the States. The items of common importance (contained in the Concurrent List) have been assigned to both with this provision that in the event of any conflict, the Centre has the over-riding authority. Last, there is the Supreme Court to interpret the provisions of the Constitution and to settle any legal dispute between the Centre and the States. Its decision or interpretation is final.
6. **Judicial Review:** The Supreme Court and the High Courts have the power to examine the constitutional validity of any law, regulation, or order of the state. The aggrieved party, or any public-spirited person on its behalf, may challenge the law, regulation or order of the state. The Court examines the case and then may declare the impugned law or regulation or order of the state constitutionally valid, or it may declare it void and therefore unenforceable to the extent it is repugnant to the provisions of the Constitution. The forty-second amendment of 1976 had a provision that an act of Constitutional Amendment could not be struck down by the Courts, but the Supreme Court in the Minerva Textile Mills Case (1980) struck it down. In the Waman Rao Case (1981) the Court ruled that it could strike down a law or regulation or order of the state even though it was incorporated into the Ninth Schedule, if it altered or destroyed the basic structure of the Constitution. The Court reiterated its view in the Ninth Schedule Case (2007) with this clarification that it could look into the constitutional validity of an impugned law or regulation or order of the state incorporated into the Ninth Schedule after the delivery of its verdict in the Kesavanand Bharati Case on 24th April, 1973.
7. **Fundamental Rights:** Part III of the Constitution has a long list of fundamental rights guaranteed to the people living in the country,

while some of them are available only to the citizens of India. These rights cover the spheres of Equality, Freedom, Non-exploitation, Religion, Culture and Education, and Constitutional Remedies. Art. 14 guarantees equality before law and its equal protection. Art. 15 prohibits discrimination on the grounds of religion, race, caste, sex and place of birth. It also empowers the state to make discrimination in favour of women, children, Scheduled Castes, Scheduled Tribes, and other socially and educationally backward castes or classes. Art. 16 prohibits discrimination in public services. It also makes provision for adequate representation of the Scheduled Castes, Scheduled Tribes and Other Backward Castes or Classes in public services for the sake of social justice. Art. 19 guarantees essential freedoms of the citizens relating to speech and expression, peaceful assembly, formation of unions, free movement throughout the country, residence or settlement in any part of the country, and doing of any trade or vocation. Art. 20 prohibits making of ex-post facto laws and double jeopardy. Art. 21 secures right to life and personal liberty. Art. 22 prohibits arbitrary arrest or detention of a person. Art 23 prohibits traffic in human beings and taking of forced labour. Art 25 ensures freedom of conscience or religion. Art. 29 guarantees right to conserve and preserve distinct language, script and culture. Above all, Art 32 guarantees right to move the Supreme Court for the protection and enforcement of these rights. This part is so important that Prime Minister Nehru called it the 'conscience of the Constitution'.

8. **Directive Principles of State Policy:** Part IV of the Constitution has a long list of principles whose aim is to establish a social welfare state in the country. Art. 38 enjoins that the state shall create, as effectively as possible, a social order in which justice—social, economic and political—shall inform all institutions of national life. Hence, the state should undertake steps to create adequate means of livelihood for all, prevent concentration of wealth in the hands of few people, ensure equal pay for equal work for men and women, establish village panchayats to make them units of rural self-government, create humane conditions of work, provide social security and improve cottage industries, implement uniform civil code throughout the country, adopt measures for the welfare of Scheduled Castes, Scheduled Tribes and, other weaker sections of the society, prohibit cow slaughter, modernise system of agriculture,

protect national monuments, separate judiciary from the executive and follow policy of international peace and security. These principles are not judicially enforceable, but it is expected that the state shall take them as nevertheless fundamental in the governance of the country. According to Dr. B.R. Ambedkar, these principles constitute the charter of social and economic democracy in our country.

9. **Fundamental Duties:** The forty-second amendment of 1976 has inserted Part IV A with Art. 51 A that contains a long list of the fundamental duties of the citizens. It is enjoined that they should respect national flag, national anthem and abide by the provisions of the Constitution; they should cherish and follow the ideals of the leaders of the freedom movement; they should defend the motherland and protect the sovereignty, unity and integrity of the country; they should promote harmony and spirit of common brotherhood and not do anything derogatory to the dignity of women; they should value and preserve our composite culture; they should protect and improve environmental conditions; they should safeguard public property and abjure violence; they should strive to achieve excellence in all walks of like; and the parents and the guardians should provide education to their children from 6 to 14' years of age. It is true that, like Directive Principles of State Policy, these duties do not form part of the justiciable provisions of the Constitution, yet it is expected that, as conscientious and enlightened citizens of the country, they should observe them in their daily life.

10. **Democratic Decentralisation:** In a democratic system, power should be decentralised so that people living at the lower level manage their affairs themselves. Local people may understand their problems and they may solve them in their own way. The seventy-third amendment of 1992 makes provisions for village Panchayats whose 29 functions are specified in the Eleventh Schedule. The seventy-fourth amendment of 1992 has similar provisions for the municipalities whose 18 functions are specified in the Twelfth Schedule of the Constitution. It is really appreciable that the provisions of local self-government have constitutional sanction in our country.

11. **Emergency Provisions:** Part XVIII of the Constitution has special provisions to deal with an abnormal situation affecting the country as a whole or any of its parts. The President may declare a state of

emergency covering country as a whole or some of its parts under Art. 352 in the event of war, or external aggression, or armed revolt in the country. Under Art. 356 emergency may be declared in a State (excluding Jammu-Kashmir) in the event of breakdown of constitutional machinery there. Last, under Art. 360, emergency may be declared by the President incase the financial stability or credit of India or any of its parts is in danger. These are extra-ordinary powers of the President which can be exercised by him on the advice of the Council of Ministers that is collectively responsible to the Lok Sabha. Thus, these provisions donot enable the President to act in an autocratic manner.

Our Constitution is the cornerstone of our nation. It has been in existence since its inauguration in 1950. Unfortunately, its working has now seen the trend of deterioration. President Nárayanan was right when he said: "The Constitution has not failed us, rather we have failed the Constitution." On the basis of such an observation, he gave a hint of the futility of setting up a National Constitution Review Commission in 2000. We should remember the glorious words of Ambedkar: "However good a Constitution may be, it is sure to turn out bad, because those who are called to work it, happen to be a bad lot. However bad a Constitution may be, it may turn out to be good if those who are called to work it, happen to be a good lot."[4]

4. *Constituent Assembly Debates*, Vol. XI, p.975.

43

FUNDAMENTAL RIGHTS, DIRECTIVE PRINCIPLES AND FUNDAMENTAL DUTIES

A study of Part III, Part IV and Part IVA of the Constitution in one chapter has its own significance. All the three constitute an integrated whole. The philosophy of the Constitution is embodied herein. The Fundamental Rights are like a charter of essential liberties of the citizens; the Directive Principles, though judicially unenforceable, constitute the charter of social and economic democracy in the country. Fundamental Duties, also judicially unenforceable, make the citizens conscious of their solemn obligations of diverse kinds.

Fundamental Rights

Part III of the Constitution incorporating 'fundamental rights' constitutes the Magna Carta of the essential rights of the Indian people. It contains a very comprehensive list of the rights that have 'a justiciable character inspite of the fact that the State may impose 'reasonable restrictions' on certain grounds on their use and enjoyment and that their enforcement can be suspended by the President during the days of national emergency excluding those relating to life and personal liberty enshrined in Articles 20 and 21. The 24th Constitution Amendment Act of 1971 has laid down that the Parliament may make any change in Part III of the Constitution in the public interest amounting to the extension or abridgement of the scope of the fundamental rights. The words of Nehru ring true: "No Supreme Court and no judiciary can stand in judgment over the sovereign will of the entire community."[1] And as Chief Justice S.M. Sikri observed: "Applied to Fundamental Rights, it would mean that while fundamental rights can be abrogated, reasonable abridgement of fundamental rights can be effected in the public interest."[2]

1. *Constituent Assembly Debates*, Vol. IX, pp. 1895-96.
2. *Kesavanand Bharati* v. *The State of Kerala*, AIR 1973, SC 1461.

Part III contains six categories of fundamental rights along with qualifying provisions hedged around them with the more formidable provisions enabling the Parliament to make necessary amendments in the Constitution in the name of placing 'reasonable restrictions' on the use and enjoyment of these rights. These are:

Right to Equality: First of all, there is right to equality. Art 14 says that the States shall not deny to any person equality before law or equal protection of laws within its territory. Art. 15 prohibits discrimination on the grounds of religion, race caste, sex or place of birth; nor can any person on any of these grounds be held able or unable for access to shops, hotels, public restaurants and places of public entertainment; use of wells, tanks, bathing *ghats*, roads and places of public resort maintained wholly or partly by the State funds or dedicated to the use of general public. Art. 16 says about the equality of opportunity in matters of public employment. It is further provided that in respect of public employment, the State can make no discrimination on the grounds of religion, race, caste, sex, descent, place of birth or residence. Art. 17 provides for the abolition of untouchability and forbids its practice in any form. Finally, Art. 18 says that the State shall confer no title on any person save that of a military or academic distinction.

The Constitution also specifies that these rights are subject to certain restraints. Thus, Article 15(3) and (4) lays down that though there can be no discrimination against persons on several grounds, it shall be open for the State to make any provision for the welfare of the women and children, or for the advancement of socially and educationally backward classes of the society. Similarly, in the case of Art. 16 providing for non-discrimination in matters of public employment, it is further given that the State can make special reservations and safeguards for adequate representation of the weaker sections of the society in public institutions, or that it shall be open for the State to lay down qualifications of residence (domicile) in respect of public employments in any part of the country. Likewise, Art. 18 deding with the abolition of titles, save those of military and academic distinctions, further says hat no citizen shall receive a title from a foreign State without the permission of the President of India.

As amended till now, Art. 16 deserves a full study. Its clause (3) allows the State to impose residential qualifications in public services. Its clause (4) allows the State to make discrimination in public services in favour of Scheduled Castes, Scheduled Tribes and backward classes of citizens in

> ### Some Important Statements
>
> The Declaration of the Rights of Man has become part and parcel of our mental make-up. These principles have become the silent, immaculate premise of our outlook.
>
> —***Dr. B.R. Ambedkar***
>
> A fundamental right should be looked upon, not from the point of view of any particular difficulty of that moment, but as something that you want to make permanent in this Constitution.
>
> —***Jawaharlal Nehru***
>
> The fundamental rights represent the basic values cherished by the people of this country since the Vedic times and they are calculated to protect and create conditions in which every human being can develop his personality to the fullest extent.
>
> —***Justice P.N. Bhagwati***

order to give them adequate representation in the services under the State. Its clause (5) exempts appointments to an office of a religious or denominational institution. The 77th Amendment of 1995 inserts clause (4A) which allows the State to make reservations in favour of Scheduled Castes and Scheduled Tribes at the time of promotions in public services. The 81st Amendment of 2000 says that the vacancies of the Scheduled Castes and Scheduled Tribes shall not be counted in the fresh vacancies, if taken over to next year, in determining the limit of 50 per cent reservations as laid down by the Supreme Court. The 82nd Amendment of 2000 inserts a proviso in Art. 335 that allows the State to make relaxation in qualifying marks or evaluation standards for Scheduled Castes and Scheduled Tribes in promotional examinfltions. Finally, the 85th Amendment of 2002 says about 'consequential seniority' in public services at the time of promotion for persons belonging to the Scheduled Castes and Scheduled Tribes.

Right to Freedom: The next place has been given to right to freedom. Art. 19 guarantees six kinds of essential freedoms relating to speech and expression, peaceful assembly without arms, forming associations or unions, free movement throughout the territory of India, residence and settlement in any part or territory of India, and practice of any profession, trade or business. Art. 20 provides for protection in respect of conviction for certain offences. It prohibits the promulgation of ex-post facto laws-laws with retrospective effect going to the disadvantage of the accused. It says that no person shall be convicted of any offence except for the violation of law in force at the time of the commission of the act charged as an offence, nor be subjected to a penalty greater than that which might have been inflicted under the law in force at the time of the commission of the offence; that no person shall be prosecuted and punished for the same offence more than once; and that no person accused of any offence shall be compelled to be a witness against himself. Art. 21 says that no person shall be deprived of his life or personal liberty except according to the procedure established by law. Art. 21 A (inserted by the 86th Amendment of 2002) says that the State shall provide free and compulsory education for all children of the age of 6 to 14 years in a manner determined by its law. Finally, Art., 22 guarantees protection against arbitrary arrest and detention. The man in custody will be informed, as soon as possible, of the grounds of such arrest. Moreover, an arrested person shall not be denied the right to engage or consult a legal practitioner of his choice for the sake of his defence. It is also provided that a person who is arrested and placed under police custody shall be produced before the nearest magistrate within 24 hours of such arrest (excluding the time necessary for the journey from the place of his arrest to the court of the magistrate) and that no such person shall be kept in custody beyond the said period without the order of the magistrate.

All these rights are subject to reasonable restrictions. Art. 19 (I) ensuring six kinds of essential freedoms has qualifying provisions which enable the State to lay down reasonable restrictions in the interest of the sovereignty and territorial integrity of India, security of the state, friendly relations with foreign states, public order, decency, morality, contempt of court, defamation, incitement to an offence etc. The State may also lay down special rules for technical and professional services, or for carrying on any trade or profession in general or public interest; similar arrangements can be made for the protection of the interest of the weaker sections of the community. Then, Art. 22 provides for the preventive detention that makes a distinction between a citizen and an alien, particularly one belonging to an enemy country, and it also provides for a special procedure in case of persons rounded up under the law of preventive detention as made by the government of the Centre or of any State.[3]

3. No law providing for preventive detention shall authorise the detention of a person for a longer period than three months, unless an advisory board consisting of persons who are, or have been, or are qualified to be appointed as Judges of a High Court have reported before the expiration of the said period of three months that there is in its opinion sufficient cause for such detention. But the Parliament may by law prescribe the circumstances under which and the class or classes of cases in which a person may be detained for a period longer than three months under any law providing for preventive detention without obtaining the opinion of an advisory board.

Rights Against Exploitation: The third category includes rights against exploitation. Art. 23 prohibits traffic in human beings and taking af forced labour like *begar*. A qualifying clause says that nothing shall prevent the State from imposing compulsory service for a public purpose, and in imposing such a service, the State shall not make any discrimination on various grounds like those of religion, race, class and the like. This provision specifically prohibits slavery or 'bonded labour' and traffic in human beings for immoral purposes. Art. 24 prohibits employment of children below 14 years of age in hazardous jobs.

Right to Religion: Then comes right to religion that constitutes the sheet-anchor of our secular state. Art 25 ensures freedom of conscience and free profession and propagation of any faith or religion. Art. 26 guarantees freedom to every religious denomination or to any section thereof to establish and maintain institutions for religious and charitable purposes to manage its own affairs in matters of religion, to own and acquire movable and immovable property and to administer such property in accordance with law. Art. 27 says that no person shall be compelled to pay any tax the proceeds of which are specifically appropriated in payment of expenses for the promotion or maintenance of any particular religion or religious denomination. Finally, Art. 28 prohibits compulsory attendance at religious instructions imparted in an institution wholly or partly maintained by the State.

Like other fundamental rights, this right is also subject to certain qualifying restrictions as norms of public order, morality and health. It is also provided that the State shall have the right to regulate or restrict any economic, financial, political or other activity that may be associated with a religious practice, or to provide for social welfare and reform or the throwing open of Hindu religious institutions of public character to all classes and sections of the Hindus. While defining the word " Hindu', it is said that it shall be construed to cover the Sikhs, Buddhists and Jains, and the wearing and carrying of *kirpans* shall be deemed to be included in the profession of Sikh religion. The provision of attendance at religious instructions in educational institutions, either wholly or partly maintained by the State, shall not apply to an institution which is administered by the State but has been established under some endowment or trust enjoining that religious instruction of that variety be imparted in the institution.

Cultural and Eduational Rights: The fifth category covers to cultural and educational rights. Art. 29 lays down that any section of the citizens residing in the teritory of India having its distinct language, script or culture shall have the right to conserve the same. No citizen shall be denied admission to any educational institution maintained by the State or receiving aid out of the State funds on the grounds of religion, race, caste, language or any of them. Art. 30 says that all minorities, whether based on religion or language, shall have the right to establish and administer educational institutions of their choice. The State shall not, while granting aid to educational institutions, discriminate against any educational institution on the ground that it is under the management of a minority whether based on religion or language. In making any law for the compulsory acquisition of the property of an educational institution established and administered by a minority, the State shall ensure that the amount fixed by or determined under such law for the acquisition of such property is such as would not restrict or abrogate the right guaranteed under that clause.

Right to Constitutional Remedies: Last, there is right to constitutional remedies. Since Part III of the Constitution is justiciable, an aggrieved person may move the appropriate High Court (under Art. 226) or the Supreme Court (under Art. 32) for the protection of his fundamental rights. Art 13(2) clearly lays down that no law (including executive action) of the Centre, or of the States, or of any subordinate government can prevail that is inconsistent with Part III of the Constitution. Thus, the Courts may look into the matter and then hold that law invalid, either fully or in part, so as to enforce the provisions of this part of the Constitution. For this sake, they may issue prerogative writs in the nature of *habeas corpus*, *mandamus*, prohibition, *quo warranto* and *certiorari*. In the words of a former Chief Justice of India, this provision is 'a very distinguishing feature of the Indian Constitution' and 'a cornerstone of the democratic edifice raised by the Constitution."[4]

The Constitution empowers the Supreme Court and the High Courts to issue five kinds of writs for the protection and enforcement of fundamental rights. These are:

1. **Writ of Habeas Corpus:** The Court may ask the detaining authority to produce the person before it and justify the cause of his detention there. If the Court feels that the reason of detention is not sufficient, it may ask the detaining authority to release the person.

4. P.B. Gajendragadkar: The *Constitution of India: Its Philosophy and Basic Postulates*, pp. 60 and 62.

2. **Writ of Mandamus:** The Court may order any inferior court or authority to perform some public or quasi-public legal duty which it has refused to perform and the performance of which cannot be enforced by any other adequate legal remedy.
3. **Writ of Prohibition:** The Court may order any inferior court or tribunal not to do what is not within its jurisdiction. It is different from mandamus in the sense that while the latter commands activity, it commands inactivity. Moreover, while the writ of mandamus can be issued to command any judicial or quasi-judicial or non-judicial authority, the writ of prohibition is issued only against a judicial or quasi-judicial authority.
4. **Writ of Certiorari:** While the writ of prohibition is available at an earlier stage, the writ of certiorari is available at a later stage only. The two resemble as well as differ. The object of both is to secure that the jurisdiction of an inferior court or tribunal is properly exercised and that it does not usurp the jurisdiction which it does not possess. Thus, the Court may ask any inferior court or tribunal not to proceed ahead with the case before it but to transfer it to some other court or tribunal.
5. **Writ of Quo Warranto:** The Court may inquire into the legality of the claim which a person asserts to a public office and to oust him from its exercise if the claim be not well founded. Thus the Court may quash a wrong appointment. But here three conditions must be satisfied. First, the office must be public and it must be created by a statute or by the Constitution itself. Second, the office must be a substantive one and not merely the function or employment of a servant at the will and during the pleasure of another. Last, there must be a contravention of the Constitution or of a statute or of a statutory instrument in appointing such person to that office.

Critical Appreciation: Fundamental Rights, as enshrined in Part III of our Constitution, have been lauded as the 'bedrock of Indian democracy'; on the other hand, they have been attacked on the ground of being given by one hand and taken away by another due to the qualifying provisions which circumscribe the scope of their exercise and enjoyment. By some critical members it was suggested in the Constituent Assembly that the title of Fundamental Rights should be substituted by the title of 'Limitations on Fundamental Rights and Limitations Thereon'. We may enumerate some of the points of criticism as under:

1. Part III of the Constitution has a number of very key terms without offering their precise or standard definition. In particular, we may refer to such terms as 'weaker sections of the community', 'socially and educationally backward classes of citizens', 'minorities', 'hazardous jobs', 'public purpose', 'amount' etc. as a result of which scope for litigation is widened more and more. It substantiates the argument of Sir Ivor Jennings that Indian Constitution is a 'lawyers' paradise'. The aggrieved persons rush to the Courts. More perplexing is the fact that the Courts give different meanings to the same terms from time to time with the result that the problem remains unsolved. What is given in one case is changed by the Court in another. The sensitivity of the Courts may be traced in this fact that they do not appreciate a situation where any part of the Constitution is immunised from judicial scrutiny.

2. The beautiful picture of our fundamental rights, as given in the original Constitution, has been vitiated by a series of amendments made by the rulers of the country just for political considerations. The First Amendment inserted clause (4) into Art. 15 and thereby introduced the system of reservations in favour of Scheduled Castes and Scheduled Tribes and other socially and educationally backward classes of citizens in clear violation of the principle of equality. It also introduced Schedule IX in the form of a protected area so as to keep any law of the Union or of the States immune from judicial scrutiny. The Fourth Amendment of 1955 deleted the requirement of compensation being just or adequate or reasonable. The Twenty-fifth Amendment of 1971 put the word 'amount' in place of 'compensation' and also introduced Art. 31 C so as to keep a law of the Union or of the States immune from judicial scrutiny if it was made to implement a directive principle contained in Article 39 (*b*) and (*c*) of the Constitution. The Forty-fourth Amendment of 1978 deleted right to property from Part III and inserted it into Part XII in the form of Art. 300A and thus created a confusion worst confounded in matters of a right relating to property.

3. The enforcement of our fundamental rights may be suspended during 'emergency' declared by the President. In such a situation the President would have the power to suspend the right to move the Courts for the enforcement of fundamental rights. The Forty-fourth Amendment of 1978 has made a little change that only two fundamental rights relating to protection in respect of conviction for offences (Art. 20) and protection of life and personal liberty (Art. 21) cannot be suspended. The fear remains

that as soon as the proclamation of emergency is made by the President, the State "shall be freed from the limitations imposed by Art. 19. This means that the Legistature shall be competent to make any law and the Executive shall be at liberty to take any action, even though it contravenes or restricts the right freedom of speech and expression, assembly, association, movement, residence, profession or occupation.[5]

4. Last, worst has happened with right to property. The provision of Art. 31, as enshrined in the original Constitution, honoured the maxim of 'eminent domain', but the requirement of compensation's being just or adequate was interpreted by the Supreme Court as equivalent to the market value thereof, otherwise it would be a fraud on the Constitution. The Fourth Amendment of 1955 deleted the rquirement of compensation's being just or adequate. Thus occurred confrontation between the Judiciary and the Executive. Ultimately came the Forty-fourth Amendment of 1978 that deleted the right to property from Art. (19)(1)(f) and Art. 31 and shifted it to a distant part of the Constitution by keeping it as a constitutional right but not as a fundamental right. The result is that while the body is still in Part III, the head has been taken away to Part XII of the Constitution and, surprisingly, the body is more important than the head now. The position has become all the more curious with the insertion of Art. (30)(I A) which says that in making a law providing for the compulsory acquisition of the property of an educational institution established and administered by a minority community, the State shall ensure that the amount fixed by or determined under such law for the acquisition of such property is such as would not restrict or abrogate the right guaranteed under the clause. "Legally speaking, the new provision is a tail which has lost its head by the repeal of Art. 31(2)."[6]

However, such points of criticism cannot efface the real significance of fundamental rights. "Despite the fact that some of the rights have been substantially modified in scope as a result of Constitutional amendments, the chapter on fundamental rights taken as a whole remains a formidable bulwark of individual liberty, a code of public conduct and a strong and sustaining basis of Indian democracy."[7]

---

5. D.D. Basu: *Introduction to the Constitution of India*, XII ed. 1989, p. 130.

6. *Ibid*, p. 120.

7. M.V. Pylee: *Constitutional Government in India*, p. 235.

Directive Principles of State Policy

The Directive Principles of State Policy, contained in Part IV of the Constitution, covering Articles from 36 to 51, underline the philosophy of democratic socialism with a touch of Gandhian idealism as incorporated into the fundamental law of our country. Though the direct source of inspiration is not the Instrument of Instructions issued under the Government of India Act of 1935 but the Irish Constitution of 1937 that has placed the two—Fundamental Rights and Directive Principles—as distinct entities by making the former enforceable and the latter non-enforceable through the Courts, this Part of our Constitution has assumed the form of a very novel as well as a very controversial feature. While the element of novelty should be traced in its being a catalogue of specific directions that the State must regard as 'nevertheless fundamental in the governance of the country', the element of controversy should be noted in the judicial interpretations that have somehow become the cause of contention between the administrators and the adjudicators of the country. But the fact stands out that this Part of the Constitution "constitutes a very comprehensive political, social and economic programme for a modern democratic State."[8]

Enumeration of Directive Principles: 1. The most important item of this chapter is contained in Art. 39 that imbibes the content of democratic socialism. It lays down that the State shall, in particular, direct its policy towards securing.

(*a*) that the citizens, men and women equally, have the right to an adequate means of livelihood;

(*b*) that the ownership and control of the material resources of the community are so distributed as best to subserve the common good;

(*c*) that the operation of the economic system does not result in the concentration of wealth to the common detriment;

(*d*) that there is equal pay for equal work for both men and women;

(*e*) that the health and strength of workers, men and women, and the tender age of children are not abused and that the citizens are not forced by economic necessity to enter avocation unsuited to their age or strength;

8. G.N. Joshi: *The Constitution of India*, p. 112.

> **Some Important Statements**
>
> The Directive Principles of State Policy represent a dynamic move towards a certain objective. The Fundamental Rights represent something static, to preserve certain rights which exist. Both are right. But somehow and sometime it might so happen that dynamic movement and that static standstill do not quite fit into each other.
>
> —***Jawaharlal Nehru***
>
> It is the intention of the Constituent Assembly that in future both the legislature and the executive should not merely pay lip service to these principles enacted in this Part, but that they should be made the basis of all executive and legislative action that may be taken here after in the matter of the governance of the country.
>
> —***Dr. B.R. Ambedkar***
>
> The purpose of the fundamental rights is to create an egalitarian society, to free all citizens from coercion or restriction by society and to make liberty available for all. The purpose of the Directive Principles is to fix certain social and economic goals for immediate attainment by bringing about a non-violent social revolution.
>
> —***Justice K. S. Hegde***

(*f*) that children are given opportunitities and facilities to develop in a healthy manner and in conditions of freedom and dignity and that childhood and youth are protected against exploitation and against moral and material abandonment.

2. The State shall secure that the operation of the legal system promotes justice on the basis of equal opportunity, and shall, in particular provide free legal aid, by suitable legislation or schemes or in any other way to ensure that opportunities for securing justice are not denied to any citizen by reason of economic or other disabilities.
3. The State shall take steps to organise village panchayats and endow them with such powers and authority as may be necessary to enable them to function as units of self-government.
4. The State shall, within the limits of its economic capacity and development, make effective provision for securing the right to work, to education and to public assistance in cases of unemployment, old age, sickness and disablement, and in other cases of undeserved want.
5. The State shall make provision for securing just and humane conditions of work and for maternity relief.
6. The State shall endeavour to secure, by suitable legislation or economic organisation or in any other way, to all workers, agricultural, industrial or otherwise, work, a living wage, conditions

of work ensuring a decent standard of life and full enjoyment of leisure and social and cultural opportunities and, in particular, the State shall endeavour to promote cottage industries on an individual or cooperative basis in rural areas.

7. The State shall take steps, by suitable legislation or in any other way, to secure the participation of workers in the management of undertakings, establishments or other organisations engaged in any industry.
8. The State shall endeavour to secure for the citizen, a uniform civil code throughout the territory of India.
9. The State shall endeavour to provide early childhood care and education for all children until they complete the age of six years.
10. The State shall promote with special care the educational and economic interests of the weaker sections of the people and, in particular, of the Scheduled Castes and the Scheduled Tribes, and shall protect them from social injustice and all forms of exploitation.
11. The State shall regulate the raising of the level of nutrition and the standard of living of its people and the improvement of public health as among its primary duties and, in particular, the State shall endeavour to bring about prohibition of the consumption, except for medicinal purposes of intoxicating drinks and of drugs which are injurious to health.
12. The State shall endeavour to organise agriculture and animal husbandry on modern and scientific lines and shall, in particular, take steps for preserving and improving the breeds, and prohibiting the sluaghter of cows, calves and other milch and draught cattle.
13. The State shall endeavour to protect and improve the environment and to safeguard the forests and wild life of the country.
14. It shall be the obligation of the State to protect every monument or place or object of artistic interest declared by or under a law made by the Parliament to be of national importance, from spoilation, disfigurement, destruction, removal, disposal or export as the case may be.
15. The State shall take steps to separate the judiciary from the executive in the public services of the State.

16. The State shall endeavour to (*a*) promote international peace and security, (*b*) maintain just and honourable relations between nations, (*c*) foster respect for international law and treaty obligations in the dealings of organise peoples with one another; and (*d*) encourage settlement of international disputes by arbitration.

Though the list of the Directive Principles well indicates that they are like the ideals, particularly of a socio-economic character, that the State should strive for, or they are like directions which the legislature and the executive should follow while making laws or issuing orders, the fact remains to be stressed that their underlying spirit "is to make India not a Police State but a Welfare State. Herein lies a standard presentation of what may be called a 'plastic state' in the sense that it can serve any party with any ideology unlike the fixed Constitutions of America and Russia."[8]

Critical Appreciation: Since the Directive Principles are of a non-justiciable nature, they have been identified with ideal aspirations or 'pious superfluities' or something comparable with a cheque payable by a concerned bank as per its convenience, as said by Prof. K.T. Shah[10]. An English writer says that the ghosts of the Fabians 'stalk through the pages of the text'[11]. The main point of attack is that these principles are nothing more than a manifesto of high aims and aspirations. However, such a view is cynical and pessimistic. The critics have certainly failed to understand the organic nature of relationship between Part III and Part IV of the Constitution.

A long list of the measures taken by the Government at the Centre as well as in the States shows that these principles have been well honoured over the years since the inauguration of the Constitution in 1950. Reference in this connection may be made to land reforms laws relating to the abolition of the system of landlordism. These statutory measures have given to the tillers of the soil security of tenure and prevented concentration of land holdings by imposing ceiling on land that a person may keep under his own cultivation. Several States have made laws to implement the system of democratic decentralisation and to provide for free and compulsory education of the children. While pursuing the policy of prohibition, according to the recommendations of the National Prohibition Enquiry Committee set up by the Planning Commission, severe restrictions have

9. K.V. Rao: *Parliamentary Democracy of India*, p. 353
10. *Constituent Assembly Debates*, Vol. VIII, p. 470.
11. Ivor Jennings: *Some Characteristics of the Indian Constitution*, p. 31.

been imposed on the production and consumption of intoxicating goods. The Criminal Procedure Amendment Act of 1973 has gone a long way in realising the aim of separating judiciary from the executive.

The most appreciable point of discussion, in this direction, is that the judiciary has judiciously interpreted the real value of the Directive Principles particularly in cases involving their Constitutional relationship with Fundamental Rights. Justices Hedge and Mukherjee in the *Kesavanand Bharati Case* (1973) observed: "The Fundamental Rights and Directive Principles constitute the 'conscience of our Constitution". In the same case Justice Chandrachud observed: "Our Constitution aims at bringing about a synthesis between 'Fundamental Rights' and the "Directive Principles of State Policy' by giving to the former a place of pride and to the latter a place of permanence. Together, not individually, they form the core of the Constitution."

Fundamental Duties

The Forty-second Constitution Amendment Act has inserted Part IV A with Art. 51 A having a set of Fundamental Duties. It says that it shall be the duty of every citizen of India.

(*a*) to abide by the Constitution and respect its ideals and institutions, the National Flag and the National Anthem;

(*b*) to cherish and follow the noble ideals which inspired our national struggle for freedom;

(*c*) to uphold and protect the sovereignty, unity and integrity of India;

(*d*) to defend the country and render national service when called upon to do so;

(*e*) to promote harmony and the spirit of common brotherhood amongst all the people of India transcending religious, linguistic and regional or sectional diversities; to renounce practices derogatory to the dignity of women;

(*f*) to value and preserve the rich heritage of our composite culture;

(*g*) to protect and improve the natural environment including forests, lakes, rivers and wild life and to have compassion for living creatures;

(*h*) to develop scientific temper, humanism and the spirit of inquiry and reform;

(*i*) to safeguard public property and to abjure violence;

(*j*) to strive for excellence in all spheres of individual and collective activity so that the nation constantly rises to higher levels of endeavour and achievement.

(*k*) to provide as a parent or guardian to his/her child or ward opportunities for education from the age of 6 to 14 years.

Since these Fundamental Duties are included in Part IV-A of the Constitution, it is obvious that they have a non-justiciable character. As such, a critic may say that they are hardly of any significance. However, their real value cannot be minimised. As Basu says: "The citizen, it is expected, should be his own monitor, while exercising and enforcing his fundamental rights remembering that he owes the duties to the State and that if he does not care for the duties, he should not deserve the rights... Of course, the duty as such is not legally enforceable in the Court, but if the State makes a law to prohibit any act or conduct in violation of any of the duties, the Courts would uphold that as a reasonable restriction or the relevant fundamental right just as they did uphold any law implementing the Directive Principles."[11]

12. D.D. Basu: *Constitutional Law of India*. II. ed., 1980, pp. 128-29

44

FEDERALISM

The political systems of the world have been classified into federal and unitary models keeping in view the point of concentration versus distribution of powers. While the unitary system signifies concentration of the powers of the state in the hands of one visible sovereign power, a federal system "means the distribution of the force of the state among a number of coordinate bodies each originating in and controlled by the Constitution."[1] This important point should, however, be kept in mind at this stage that the classical case of federalism has now undergone a serious transformation owing to significant changes in social, economic and political spheres. The powers of the central government have increased more and more, and that too at the expense of the powers of the provincial governments, that has led to the emergence of unmistakable trends of centralism in every federal system of the world. What is equally important in this connection is that in all federal systems some devices have also developed so as to ensure cooperation and coordination between the federal and regional governments. The result is that now a federal system has developed a difference of kind with a confederal model; it has developed a difference of degree with a unitary system.

Federal System

Despite the fact that the word 'Federation' has nowhere been used in the Constitution, it has all the features of a federal system. On the pattern of the Canadian Constitution, the word 'Union' has been used which implies federal system with very strong centre. In the *Keshavanand Bharati Case* (1973) the Supreme Court has defined federal system as one of the elements of the basic structures of the Constitution.

---

1. A.V. Dicey: *An Introduction to the Study of the Law of Constitution*, p. 15.

Essential Features: The Indian Constitution fulfils all the requirements of a federal system. In the first place, we have a Constitution that is the supreme law of the land. Both the Central and the State governments derive their powers from this Constitution. It is a written document having 395 articles grouped into XXII Parts followed by 12 Schedules. The process of amending articles relating to the federal structure of the country, as given in Art. 368, is also quite difficult and thus it is a rigid Constitution as well. Second, it frankly declares that 'India, that is Bharat, shall be a Union of States'. (Art. I) Schedule VII specifies distribution of powers in this manner:

1. The Union List has 97 items of national importance as defence of India, defence forces and their deployment, arms and ammunitions, atomic energy and mineral resources, central bureau of investigation, preventive detention for the security of India, foreign affairs, United Nations, war and peace, citizenship, extradition, railways, Election Commission, Supreme Court and High Courts, post and telegraph, telephone and wireless, currency and coinage, banking, insurance, mines and mineral development, Union public services, industries of national importance, inter-State migration, survey of India, foreign pilgrimage, international crimes, airways, waterways, national highways, etc.
2. The State List has 66 (now 61) items of regional importance as public order, police, jails, local self-government, libraries and museums, agriculture, irrigation, land and land tenure, sanitation and public health, pilgrimage inside the State, cremations and burials, transport, fisheries, State industries, markets and fairs, cooperative societies and corporations, State public services, veterinary training and practice, ponds and cattle trespass, production and sale of intoxicating liquor etc.
3. The Concurrent List has 47 items of common importance as criminal law and procedure, civil law and procedure, preventive detention for security of the State, marriage and divorce, succession and adoption, contracts and partnership, transfer of property other than agricultural, registration of deeds and documents, trusts and trustees, forests, protection of wild life, population control and family planning, factories, electricity, education, newspapers, printing of books, price control etc.

It has been made clear that the Union Government has full and exclusive control over the items of the Union List. The items of the State

List are given to the States. The items of the Concurrent List are given to both the governments with this provision that, in the event of any conflict, the Centre's authority would be overriding. The residuary items have been left to the Centre.

In a federal system an independent and impartial judiciary is also required to play the role of an umpire in Constitutional disputes between the Centre and the States. It acts like a permanent Constitutional convention at work and its decision is final as well as binding. This requirement is fulfilled by the Supreme Court. Thus, all the three requirements of a federal system have been met in our constitutional system. The 'federal principle' has been accepted which suggests the method of dividing powers "so that the Central and regional governments are each, within a sphere, coordinate and independent."[2]

It is, therefore, clear that as the Indian Constitutional system meets all the three requirements of a federal system, it cannot be designated as unitary. It also implies that though there are certain serious elements making the position of the Centre very strong at the expense of the area 'of' provincial autonomy; it does not at all render the character of the very Constitutional system unitary like that of England or France. Thus a conscientious student of the Indian Constitutional system says that India "is undoubtedly a federation in which the attributes of sovereignty are shared between the Centre and the States."[3]

A federal system stands for the decentralisation of powers and diversity in administration. Let us now examine the points which highlight the features of centralisation and uniformity in the following manner:

Centralisation: First, we take up the features of the centralisation of powers in the hands of the Union Government so much so that the autonony of the States has become of a highly attenuated kind. In this connection, following important points may be enumerated:

(*i*) This distribution of powers is highly unfair from the federal point of view. While the Centre has exclusive control over the Union List consisting of 97 items of national importance and an over-riding control over 47 items of common importance given in the Concurrent List, the States have control over 61 items of local importance contained in the State List. Moreover, even here as, we shall see, the

2. K.C. Wheare: *Federal Government*, p. 28.

3. C.H. Alexandrowicz: *Constitutional Development in India*, p. 169.

Centre has been endowed with the power to exercise paramount control in an indirect manner. The residuary powers have also been given to the Centre.

(*ii*) The distribution of revenues between the Centre and the States is of such a nature that the States have to depend largely upon the charitable assistance of the Centre.

(*iii*) There is no perpetual guarantee regarding the existence of any State as such. The Centre may redraw the political map of the country.

(*iv*) When we look at the process of Constitutional amendment, we find that the States have a very limited say. It is only with regard to certain provisions having their connection with the federal framework of the Constitution where the ratification by half of the States, and that too by simple majority of votes in the Legislative Assembly, is required.

(*v*) In a federal system, as we find in the case of American, Swiss and Australian models, there is the principle of the equality of representation given to the States in the upper chamber of the national legislature irrespective of the size and population of the component units. Contrary to this, in our country the number of the members elected to the Rajya Sabha varies according to the population of the States.

(*vi*) The Union Government has the power to issue directions to the State Governments which they must invariably follow. Its implication is that the failure of the State Government in this regard shall be treated as the breakdown of Constitutional machinery and that shall enable the President to take over the administration of that State under Art. 356 of the Constitution.

(*vii*) Apart from giving directions to the States, the Centre may delegate some of its functions to them in relation to any matter coextensive with their executive authority. No State law can prevail which is repugnant to the law of the Centre. The States cannot exercise their executive power in a way that goes to impede or prejudice the executive power of the Union Government.

(*viii*) It is provided that certain types of bills (like those seeking compulsory acquisition of private property, derogating the power of the High Courts, imposing tax on an item declared essential by the Centre, or likely to be in conflict with a law or policy of the Union government) shall be reserved by the Governor for the consideration of the President. Here President's veto power is absolute.

(*ix*) The Centre may make a law on any item of the State List in case a resolution to this effect is passed by the Rajya Sabha, or there is emergency in the country, or when the Centre desires to implement some international treaty or agreement.

(*x*) The emergency powers of the President are so sweeping in their effect that the very nature of the Indian political system can be transformed from an incidentally federal into a purely unitary system of government.

Uniformity: The elements of uniformity, which are treated as the hallmarks of a unitary system, are traceable in our federal system and may be thus enumerated

(*i*) There is single Constitution wherefrom the Centre as well as the State Governments derive their powers. That is, the States have no Constitution of their own. The State of Jammu-Kashmir is an exception in this regard, but it cannot have anything repugnant to the Constitution of India.

(*ii*) Despite ours being a federal state, we have single citizenship—the citizenship of India—so as to realise the ideal of 'one people, one country'. That is, there is nothing like the citizenship of States in our country.

(*iii*) This singleness is further visible in the legal institutional framework. There is uniformity in respect of civil and criminal laws and their procedure throughout the country.

(*iv*) There is integrated judiciary with Supreme Court at the apex. The High Courts are under the Supreme Court and their composition and jurisdiction is a subject of the Union List.

(*v*) This line of singleness may be seen in higher public services as well. The officers of the Indian Administrative Service and Indian Police Service are employees of the Union Government, but they serve State Governments.

Union-State Relations

The Constitution has elaborate provisions to specify relations between the Union and the States in three important directions. While Part XI specifies legislative and administrative relations, Part XII specifies financial

> **Some Important Statements**
>
> In India there has been a steady evolution in the direction of regional differentiation, and prophets of doom predict an eventual break-up of the Indian political order. One need not agree with such counsels of despair to recognise that the last word has not yet been spoken about the clash of centrifugal and centripetal forces.
>
> — ***Carl J. Friedrich***
>
> The Union is not a league of States, united in a loose relationship; nor are the states the agencies of the Union deriving powers from it. Both the Union and the States are created by the Constitution. Both derive respective authority from the Constitution. The one is not the subordinate to the other in its own field; the autonony of one is coordinate with that of the other.
>
> —***Dr. B.R. Ambedkar***
>
> India has been characterised by a dual process of centralisation and decentralisation, centralisation in response to the exigencies of national planning, and decentralisation as a result of the Centre's dependence on the States for administration, the increased solidarity of linguistic States, and the emergence of new regionally based State leadership.
>
> —***R.L. Hardgrave***

relations between the Centre and the States. We may have a brief study of the Union-State relations in the following manner:

Legislative Relations: Both the Centre and the States have been given power to make laws. The Centre can make a law on any item of the Union List. The States can take up any item of the State List. Both the Centre and the States can make a law on an item of the Concurrent List with this provision that in the event of any conflict between the Central and State laws, the law of the Centre shall prevail and the law of the State shall be void to the extent of being repugnant to that. It shows that while the Centre has direct control over the items of the Union List, it has the same kind of control over the items of the Concurrent List as well. However, the important point to be noted here is that under some conditions, the Centre can make a law on an item of the State List as well under these conditions:

1. Art, 249 says that the Rajya Sabha may adopt a special resolution by two-thirds majority of its members, present and voting, and thereby shift an item of the State List to the Union List or to the Concurrent List on the ground that it has become expedient in the national interest. Such a resolution shall remain in force for a period of one year, but the Rajya Sabha may readopt this resolution again and again. So long as this resolution stands, the Centre shall have

the power to make a law on that item of the State List. Such a law of the Centre shall remah in force and the law of the State or States shall remain 'suspended' to the extent of being repugnant to the Central law, but it shall come into effect when the law of the Centre is revoked. Such a law of the Centre, unless revoked earlier, shall remain in force at the most for a period of 6 months after the lapsing of that resolution.

2. Art 250 says that the Centre shall have the power to make a law on an item of the State List during the period of 'emergency'. It should be noted here that Parliament's power in this regard shall cover the whole country in case of emergency under Art. 352 and to some State in the case of emergency under Art. 356 in force. It should be repeated here that the State law shall remain 'suspended' to the extent it is repugnant to the Union law. However, the Union law, unless revoked earlier, shall remain in operation at the most for six months after the termination of emergency.
3. Art. 252 says that the Parliament shall have the power to make a law on an item of the State List if there is a request to this effect by two or more States. Such a law shall apply to the States that make such a request, or it may apply to some other State if it becomes a party to the request afterwards. It has also been made clear that such a law can be amended or repealed only by the Parliament at the request of the concerned State legislatures.
4. Art. 253 says that the Parliament can make law on any item of the State List to implement some international treaty, agreement or convention.

A student of the Indian Constitutional system may thus form an impression that the Centre has exclusive control over the items of the Union List and overriding control over the items of the Concurrent List, but there are some inroads through which it may exercise its control over the items of the State List as well in normal as well as abnormal times.

Administrative Relations: The strong and overriding position of the Centre may be noted in the administrative sphere as well. Here following points should be noted:

1. Art. 256 says that the executive power of every State shall be so exercised as to ensure compliance with the laws made by the Parliament and any existing laws which apply in that State, and the

executive power of the Union shall extend to the giving of such directions to a State as may appear to the Government of India necessary for that purpose.

2. Art. 257 says that the executive power of every State shall be so exercised as not to impede or prejudice the executive power of the Union, and the executive power of the Union shall extend to the giving of such directions to a State as may appear to the Government of India necessary for that purpose. The executive power of the Union shall also extend to the giving of directions to a State as to the construction and maintenance of the means of communication declared in this direction to be of national and military importance.
3. Art. 258 says that the President may, with the consent of the government of a State, entrust either conditionally or unconditionally to it or to its officers functions in respect of any matter to which the executive power of the Union extends. A law made by the Parliament which applies in any State may, notwithstanding that it relates to a matter with respect to which the legislature of the State has no power to make law, confer powers and impose duties, or authorise the conferment of powers and the imposition of duties, upon the State or officers and authoritie; thereof. Likewise, the Governor of a State may, with the consent of the Government of India, entrust either conditionally or unconditionally to that government or its officers functions in relation to any matter to which the executive power of the State extends.
4. Art. 260 lays down that the Government of India may by agreement with the government of any territory not being a part of the territory of India, undertake any executive, legislative or judicial functions vested in the government of such territory, but every such agreement shall be subject to, and governed by, a law relating to the exercise of foreign jurisdiction for the time being in force.
5. Art. 261 says that full faith and credit shall be given throughout the territory of India to public acts, records and judicial proceedings of the Union and of every State.
6. Art. 262 says that the Parliament may by law provide for the adjudication of any dispute or complaint with respect to the use, distribution and control of the waters or in any inter-State river or river valley.

7. Art. 263 says about the establishment of an Inter-State Council. If at any time it appears to the President of India that the public interest would be served by the establishment of an Inter-State Council charged with the duty of (*a*) inquiring into and advising upon disputes which may have arisen between States, (*b*) investigating and discussing subjects in which some or all of the States, or the Union and one or more of the States have a common interest, or (*c*) making recommendations upon any such subject, and in particular, recommendations for the better coordination of policy and action with respect to that subject, it shall be lawful for the President to establish by order such a Council and to define the nature and duties to be performed by it and its organisation and procedure.[4]

A look at these provisions of the Constitution confirms the same critical impression that, as in the legislative sphere so here, the position of the Centre is very strong and compared to that the position of the State Governments is very weak.

Financial Relations: Finally, we come to financial relations between the Union and the States. Here following points should be noted:

1. Art. 268 says about duties to be levied by the Union but collected and appropriated by the States. It includes duties on medicinal and toilet preparations, excise on tobacco, corporation tax, customs and import duties, estate duty, terminal taxes on goods and passengers, tax on goods for inter-State trade etc.
2. Art. 269 says about taxes to be levied and collected by the Union but assigned to the States. It includes duties in respect of succession to property other than agricultural land, estate duty in respect of property other than agricultural, terminal taxes on goods and passengers carried by rail, sea or air, taxes on railway fares and freights, taxes on the sale and purchase of newspapers and advertisements given therein etc.
3. Art. 270 says about taxes to be levied and collected by the Union and distributed between the Union and the States. It includes tax on income other than agricultural.
4. Art. 272 says about the taxes to be levied and collected by the Union and which may be distributed between the Union and the States. It

4. In1990 the Inter-State Council was set up under the chairmanship of the Prime Minister with the Chief Ministers of States and the Lt.-Governors or Chief Ministers of Union Territories.

includes many items given in the Union List as railways, post and telegraph, telephones, wireless, foreign exchange, foreign loans, customrs and export duties etc.

5. Art. 275 says about the grants-in-aid given by the Union to the States for implementing its planning programmes as well as for the development of the Scheduled Castes, Scheduled Tribes and other weaker sections of the community. It is provided that the President shall determine special grants to some States like Assam. Bihar, Orissa and West Bengal in lieu of export duty on jute and jute products.
6. Above all, Art. 280 says about the setting up of a Finance Commission by the President of India after every five years, or whenever he so deems necessary, having a chairman and four other members which shall make recommendations as to the distribution between the Union and the States of the net proceeds of taxes which are to be or may be divided between them and the allocation between the States of the respective shares of such proceeds and the principles which should govern the grants-in-aid of the revenues of the States out of the Consolidated Fund of India.

Critical Appreciation

A critical study of the provisions of the Constitution relating to Union-State relations in legislative, administrative and financial spheres leaves this impression that India has a federal system 'with strong centralising tendency.' The distribution of powers between the Centre and the States is hardly equitable in view of the fact that all important items are included in the Union List that is under the exclusive authority of the Centre. "Since all items of the Concurrent List are subject to the overriding authority of the Centre, same can be said about this List as well. Even the items of the State List are indirectly under the control of the Centre. Residuary items are also with the Centre. Moreover, under Art 200 the Governor of a State may reserve a bill passed by the State legislature for the 'consideration' of the President of India if it seeks to abolish private property, or imposes tax on an item already declared 'essential' by a law of the Parliament, or derogates the jurisdiction of the High Court, or may create a situation of conflict with some law or administrative action or policy of the Centre. It should be noted here that in such matters the veto power of the President is absolute. There is no time limit within which the President has to return a bill after his 'consideration'. Facts show that some bills passed by the State Legislatures became defunct because of pending in the office of the Union Law Ministry for a period of more than thirty years.

Similarly, in the administrative sphere, the Centre may issue directives to the States which they must carry out in order to avoid the invocation of Art. 356. The States cannot initiate a bill of Constitutional amendment, nor can they take disciplinary action against the IAS and IPS officers in spite of the fact that they draw salaries and allowances from the State exchequer for being in service there. The Governors and the High Court judges serve State Governments and draw their salaries and allowances from the State exchequer, but the States cannot initiate impeachment proceedings against them. The Centre can make alterations in the boundary lines of the States as per its own policy after taking the opinion of the concerned State. or States just for the sake of courtesy. The States have no power to frame their own Constitution. (Jammu-Kashmir is an exception due to political reasons.) There is single citizenship in the country. This feature of singleness may also be noted in the system of integrated judiciary and application of civil and criminal law and procedure throughout the country. Financially, the States are too weak and they are bound to exist on the assistance of the Centre. Keeping all this in his view, an English writer says that India "is a unitary state with some subsidiary federal features rather than a federal state with some subsidiary unitary features."[5]

5. K.C. Wheare: *Federal Government*, p. 28.

45

UNION EXECUTIVE

The Government at the Centre is called the Union Government. The President is the Head of the State. There is a Vice-President to assist the President and to act as the President during the absence of the latter for any reason. The Council of Ministers with the Prime Minister at the head is collectively responsible to the Lok Sabha. The indubitable fact that the Indian Constitution has adopted the Westminster model of government places the Head of the State (President) and the Head of the Government (Prime Minister) in the categories of, what Walter Bagehot said about his English system of government, the 'dignified' and the 'efficient' executives respectively.

President

Election: The President is the head of the Indian republic. He is elected for a term of five years and he may be re-elected any number of times. In order to be elected, he must possess three qualifications. First, he must be a citizen of India, Second, he must have completed the age of 35 years. Last, he must possess all other qualifications prescribed for an elected member of the Lok Sabha and that he must not be holding an office of profit. He is elected by an electoral college consisting of the elected members of the Parliament and State legislatures including the Legislative Assemblies of Puducherry and of the National Capital Territory of Delhi. In this election the value of votes is counted that is drawn according to a formula. In the States, the value of the votes of one MLA is drawn by dividing the population of the State (as given in census report of 1971) by the total number of elected MLAs and the quotient is further divided by 1,000. In case the remainder is more than 500, then I added to the value of votes. The total value of the votes of all elected MLAs of the country is divided by the total number of elected MPs in order to determine the value of the votes of an MP. Again, in case the remainder is more than half of the denominator, then I is added to the value of votes. It is also provided that the election of the President shall be held in accordance with proportional representation with single transferable vote system. The ballot shall be secret.

The makers of the Constitution made a mistake here. The proportional representation system cannot apply where only one seat is to be contested. The question arises as to proportion between whom or what? As a matter of fact, alternative or preferential vote system is used. The voter is given a ballot paper having names and symbols of the contestants with blank columns on the right side where he has to show his preference by writing the figures of 1, 2, 3, 4, 5 etc. At the time of counting, first preference votes are counted. The winner must secure more than 50 per cent of the votes polled. In case a candidate manages to secure votes upto the figure of electoral quota, he is declared elected. In case no candidate is able to get votes equal to or more than the figure of electoral quota (as happened in the election of 1969), the candidate having least number of votes is eliminated and his votes are transferred to other candidates according to second preferences shown on the ballot papers. Naturally, the votes of other candidates are enhanced. If this step fails to enable a candidate to get votes upto the electoral quota, then a candidate having least number of votes is eliminated and his votes are transferred to other candidates according to second preference shown on his ballot papers, while the votes already transferred according to second preference are now transferred to other candidates according to third preferences shown on the ballot papers. If a ballot paper does not indicate subsequent preference, it becomes invalid. This process goes on until one candidate manages to get votes upto the electoral quota or only one candidate remains after eliminating all other candidates.

Term: The President holds office for a period of five years from the date he takes the oath in the presence of the Chief Justice of India whereby he swears in the name of God, or solemnly affirms, that he will faithfully execute his office or discharge his function in a way so as to preserve, protect and defend the Constitution with the best of his ability and devote himself to the service and well-being of the people of India. He may resign his office before the expiry of his term for any reason. The letter of resignation must be addressed to the Vice-President. In the event of vacancy, the Vice-President shall act as the President and in case he is not available, then this office shall be given to the Chief Justice of India and, in the event of his not being available, to any other judge of the Supreme

> **Some Important Statements**
>
> Even if the President chooses to exercise some of the powers independently of the Council of Ministers, he will not be guilty of the violation of the Constitution.
>
> —***B.M. Sharma***
>
> Without violating the Constitution, the President can establish his authoritarian government. —***Allen Gledhill***
>
> After weighing the pros and cons of the Parliamentary Executives as they obtain in Great Britain and in some continental countries, and the presidential type of Government as it obtains in the United States of America, the Indian Constitution has adopted the institution of Parliamentry Executive.
>
> —***Sir Alladi Krishnaswamy Ayyar***

Court according to the principle of seniority. Within next six months the election of the new President must be held.

The Pesident may be removed by the process of impeachment for 'violation of the Constitution'. Any House of Parliament may initiate the proceedings of impeachment. A resolution to this effect must be signed by at least one-fourth members of the whole House and the matter may be taken up for discussion after at least 14 days' notice in writing. After debate such a resolution must be passed by two-thirds majority of the total membership of the House. If so happens, then the same matter shall be taken up by other House of Parliament which may investigate the charges, or may cause them investigated by some other authority. It is at this stage that the President shall have the right to appear personally or through his nominee for presenting his defence. In case the motion is passed by the House by two-thirds majority of its total membership, the President shall be removed forthwith from his office.

Functions and Powers: The normal functions and powers of the President may be discussed under five heads—executive, legislative, judicial, financial and others. Art. 52 says that the executive power of the Union shall be vested in the President and shall be exercised by him either directly or through officers subordinate to him. His executive functions and powers may be put as under:

1. All administration is conducted in his name; he makes rules for the conduct of government business and allocation of work among the Ministers.
2. He receives information of all important decisions of the cabinet relating to the affairs of administration and proposals for legislation

and he may refer any matter for the consideration or reconsideration of the Council of Ministers.

3. He appoints the Prime Minister; he appoints ministers on the advice of the Prime Minister. Besides, he makes a very large number of appointments as those of the Governors, ambassadors, Chief Justice and judges of the Supreme Court and High Courts, Chairman and members of the Union Public Service Commission, Attorney-General of India, Chief Election Commissioner and Election Commissioners, Comptroller and Auditor-General of India etc. He accepts resignation of the Prime Minister, ministers and other important functionaries.
4. The administration of the Union Territories and of Scheduled and Tribal Areas is also conducted in his name.
5. He maintains foreign relations. For this purpose he appoints ambassadors and envoys to foreign countries and accepts the credentials of the ambassadors and envoys of foreign countries.
6. He is the Supreme Commander of the Defence Forces.
7. He makes rules and regulations for the working of the Supreme Court and other autonomous agencies like the Union Public Service Commission.
8. He sends directions and instructions to the State Governments that must be complied with.

Then, in the *legislative sphere*, he performs a number of important functions as under:

1. He summons and prorogues the session of Parliament and may dissolve the Lok Sabha.
2. He nominates 12 members of the Rajya Sabha who are distinguished in the fields of art, literature, science and social service. He may nominate two members of the Anglo-Indian community in case it does not have its adequate representation in the Lok Sabha.
3. The first session of Parliament in a new year and a session held after the general election begins with his inaugural address.
4. A bill passed by the Parliament requires his assent. In case it is a non-money bill or it is not a constitution amendment bill, then he may either give his assent, or withhold it, or return the bill for re-consideration of the Parliament.
5. Certain bills (as seeking alteration of the boundary lines of a State) may be introduced in any House with his recommendation.

6. In case the Parliament is not in session and some law is to be made without any more loss of time, he may promulgate an ordinance having the force of law.
7. In case any House of Parliament is without a presiding officer, he may appoint a *pro tem* Speaker/Chairman.
8. He causes presentation of the reports of various commissions to the Parliament for consideration.
9. He may allow extension, modification or abrogation of any law in the case of ports and aerodromes.
10. Certain kinds of bills passed by the State legislatures are subject to his absolute veto power.

The President has some *financial powers* which may be put as under:

1. A money bill can be introduced in the Lok Sabha with his recommendation.
2. He keeps control over the Contingency Fund of India. He may make advances out of it to meet an unforeseen expenditure pending its authorisation by the Parliament.
3. He causes presentation of the annual financial statement of the government (budget) in the Parliament.
4. From time to time he sets up a Finance Commission for the distribution of the net proceeds of taxes between the Centre and the States and the principles which should govern the grants-in-aid of the revenue of the States out of the Consolidated Fund of India.
5. He may allow determination of the shares of States in the proceeds of income tax and of the amounts of grants-in-aid in lieu of jute export duty to some States as Assam, West Bengal, Bihar and Orissa.

The *judicial power* of the President constitutes his 'prerogative of mercy. He may grant commutation of sentence, reprieve or pardon to a person held guilty by the highest court of the land in a matter where it comes under the executive authority of the Centre, or where it is a sentence of death.

Some other functions and powers of the President may be put as under:

1. He may refer any matter of public importance involving a question of law or a fact of public importance to the Supreme Court for seeking its opinion.

2. He may make rules for the composition and working of the Union Public Service Commission.
3. He may issue directions for the progressive use of Hindi in response to the recommendations of the Official Languages Commission.
4. He may make rules for the administration and control of the Scheduled and Tribal Areas.
5. He may issue notification relating to the control of the Union Governement over the administrative of Jammu-Kashmir.

Emergency Powers: Now we may have a brief study of the abnormal functions and powers of the President. These are his 'emergency powers' specified in Part XVIII of the Constitution. These powers of the President have, indeed, a very sweeping effect and, for that reason, critical comments about their nature range from one of a protagonist like Sir Alladi Krishnaswami Ayyar who held it as 'the very life-breath of the Constitution' to that of a critic like H.V. Kamath to called it 'a charter of reaction and retrogression.' This part of the Constitution stipulates three kinds of 'emergency' with different effects.

Art. 352 empwers the President to declare national emergency whenever he is 'satisfied' that a serious situation has arisen or is likely to arise threatening the security of the country or any of its part by war, or external aggression or armed rebellion. Here the satisfaction of the President implies the satisfaction of his Council of Ministers. The President also has the power to issue another notification so as to vary or revoke his earlier proclamation to this effect. Such a proclamation can be made on the written advice of the Cabinet. It shall remain in operation for one month. But the duration can be extended in case a resolution to this effect is passed by both the Houses of Parliament by special majority (absolute majority of the whole House and two-thirds majority of the members, present and voting). Such an extension may not go beyond six months, but the Parliament may go on extending the duration for any length of time. In case the Lok Sabha is dissolved, the Rajya Sabha shall have the power to grant extension, but the time extended by it shall not go beyond 30 days of the commencement of the first session of the new Lok Sabha unless it is approved by the new House. Moreover, at least one-tenth members of the Lok Sabha may sign a resolution requesting the Speaker (if the House is in session) or to the President (if the House is not in session) to hold a special session wihin 14 days for reconsidering the continuance of such an emergency. A resolution to this effect shall be passed in the Lok Sabha by simple majority of the members present and voting.

In case Art. 352 is invoked, it shall have these effects: (*i*) The Parliament shall have the power to make a law on any item of the State List. Such a law made by the Parliament shall prevail and a law of the State, if already made, shall remain 'suspended' to the extent of being repugnant to the law of the Centre. The law of the Centre shall prevail at the most for six months after the revocation of this emergency and then the 'suspended' part of the State law would again be operative. (*ii*) The Parliament shall have the power to make laws so as to entrust more duties to the officers or public servants of the Union in order to implement such laws made in pursuance of its extended jurisdiction. (*iii*) The Parliament shall have the power to make a law so as to enhance its term beyond five years. It may also do the same for extending the tenure of the State legislatures. Thus, elections may be postponed. Such a law shall remain in force for one year at a time, but the Parliament may renew this law again and again. Elections must take place within six months of the revocation of such an emergency. (*vi*) The executive power of the Union shall extend to the issuing of any directions or instructions to the State Governments as it deems necessary. (*v*) The President shall have the power to issue a notification so as to suspend fundamental freedoms enshrined in Art. 19 and their enforcement provided in Articles 32 and 226 of the Constitution. He shall also have the power to suspend the enforcement of Fundamental Rights except those of life and personal-liberty provided in Articles 20 and 21 of the Constitution. (*vi*) The President shall have the power to make necessary alterations in the distribution of revenues between the Union and the States.

Such an emergency was proclaimed in October, 1962 when China treacherously attacked India. It continued till January 1968 with the result that its invocation could not be done in 1965 when we had a war with Pakistan in August-September 1965. It was invoked for the second time in December 1971 Pakistan attacked India. In June 1975 this provision was invoked again in the name of grave danger to the internal security of India. Both proclamations ended in March, 1977.

Then there is the provision of emergency in a State vide Art. 356 in the event of 'breakdown of constitutional machinery' there. Either on the recommendation of the Governor of that State or on the basis of his own 'satisfaction' (that really means the satisfaction of the Union Council of Ministers), the President may take over the administration of that State.

He may dismiss the government of that State and may either dissolve the Vidhan Sabha or place it under 'suspended animation'. In case the Vidhan Sabha is dissolved, fresh elections shall take place after the revocation of emergency; in case it is placed under 'suspended animation', the Vidhan Sabha may be revived or dissoived after some time. This arrangement is also known as the 'President's rule'.

A proclamation of emergency made under Art. 356 may remain in force for a period of two months. In case the Centre desires to extent this period, it may by done by a resolution of the Parliament passed in each House by simple majority. It is also provided that he period cannot be extended beyond six months in one instance and beyond three years in all. Besides, after giving two extensions, it is also required that further extension can be granted only when Art. 352 is in force, or the Election Commission has given its view that elections cannot be held there due to uncontrollable circumstances. This point may be repeated here that in case the Lok Sabha stands dissolved, the Rajya Sabha shall pass a resolution for the extension of duration of emergency. But the extension so granted by the Rajya Sabha shall not go beyond 30 days of the commencement of the session of new Lok Sabha, unless the new House has passed a resolution to the same effect.

If Art. 356 is put into effect, it shall have these effects. (*i*) The President shall assume all functions of the State Government and conduct its administration through his Governor or administrator who may be assisted by some advisers. (*ii*) Since the Vidhan Sabha is non-existent, the Parliament of India may make a law on any item of the State List for that State and also pass its budget. As we have already seen, it should be repeated here that a law made by the Centre shall remain in force for six months at the most after the revocation of energency. Moreover, any part of the State law being repugnant to such a law of the Centre shall remain suspended so long as the law of the Centre is in force. (*iii*) The President may make necessary or incidental or consequential changes in the provisions of the Constitution relating to the administration of the State so as to give a desirable effect to the object of his proclamation. This provision was, for the first time, invoked in 1951 in order to deal with the problem of Punjab and since then it has been invoked on a very large number of occasions in the States of the Indian Union.

Finally, there is the provision of financial emergency under Art. 360 of the Constitution. If the President is satisfied that a situation has arisen whereby the financial stability or credit of India or any part thereof has fallen in danger, he can issue a proclamation to this effect that may be varied or revoked by a subsequent proclamation. It is to remain in force for a period of two months. In case the President desires to extend its duration, it may be done by passing a resolution by both the Houses of Parliament by simple majority. Once approval is given by the Parliament, it continues until the Union Government desires to revoke it. The same point should be repeated here that in case the Lok Sabha stands dissolved, the Rajya Sabha may grant extension of time. But the time so granted by the Rajya Sabha shall not go beyond 30 days of the commencement of the session of the now Lok Sabha, unless the new House concurs with the decision of the Rajya Sabha. The proclamation of this kind of emergency shall have three effects. (*i*) The President shall have the power to lay down canons of financial propriety (to be approved by the Parliament after some time) and to issue necessary directions to the States. (*ii*) The Pesident shall have the power to lay down principles in the light of which salaries and allowances of all public servants, including the judges of the Supreme Court and High Courts, may be reduced. (*iii*) The money bills of the State governments shall be under the veto power of the President of India.

These emergency powers of the President have been criticised in vehement terms. It is said that these provisions "enable the federal government to acquire the strength of a unitary system, whenever the exigencies of the situation so demand."[1] Recalling the horrors of Hitler's Germany, it is feared that these arrangements may create an opening whereby some power-drunk leader may do what was done by the Nazi dictator before the Second World War. Art. 356 is an instrument in the hands of the Centre whereby the existence of any State Government can be finished as per the pleasure of the Union Government. If the Janata government of Morarji Desai finished 9 Congress (I) governments in 1977 in a single stroke, the Congress (I) government of Indira Gandhi did the same just three years after.

It shows that Art. 356 may be abused in a very reckless manner for political reasons. The term 'breakdown of the constitutional machinery' has nowhere been precisely defined and it may mean anything to the Union Government bent upon sacking a State Government by hook or by crook. In other words, the use of such powers makes the President like a dictator and lays down the foundations of a 'totalitarian state' in the country. While

1. K.V. Rao: *Parliamentary Democracy of India*, p. 259

speaking in the Constituent Assembl), a vocal member (H. V Kamath) said that "it will be a day of shame and sorrow when the President will make use of these powers having no parallel in any constitution of the democratic countries of the world."[2] But the defenders of these provisions have expressed their own views. For instance, while contradicting the fears of critics like Kamath, Mahavir Tyagi held this part of the Constitution as a 'safety valve.'[3] As eternal vigilance is the price of freedom, he continued, it "becomes the essential responsibility of the people also to see whether the President is really behaving like the highest symbol of democracy."[4] The Fact stands out that, as B.R. Ambedkar said, the President "is the head of the State, not of the Executive."[5]

The Indian President is neither a rubber stamp nor a quiescent volcano. Like the British monarch, he is expected to act as a friend, philosopher and guide of his government. "Instead of hardly remaining insensitive for long to the mysterious sense of authority and power emanating from the massive structure of the Rashtrapati Bhavan giving like that of a halo around the head of a god, and thus feeding his vanity and also an incipient hostility towards the real seat of power, he should invariably act in a way that he does not look like a magnificent cypher."[6] As the president of the Constituent Assembly, Dr. Rajendra Prasad hopefully visualised that "in our country healthy conventions will grow that will make him a constitutional President in all matters."[7]

Vice-President

The Constitution provides for a Vice-President. He is elected by an electoral college consisting of the members of both Houses of Parliament in accordance with proportional representation with single transferable vote system. A candidate for this office must possess three qualifications. First, he must be the citizen of India. Second, he must have completed the age of 35 years. Last, he must be eligible for election to the Rajya Sabha and that he must not be holding an office of profit under the Union or

2. *Constituent Assembly Debates*, Vol. IX, p. 105.

3. *Ibid*, p. 547.

4. *Ibid*, p. 120.

5. *Constituent Assembly Debates*, Vol. VII, p. 32

6. H.N. Pandit: *The PM's President*, p. 26.

7. *Constituent Assembly Debates*, Vol. X, p. 988.

State Government or any other government subject to their control. The term of the Vice-President is of five years. He may tender his resignation to the President. He may be removed from office on some charge if a resolution to his effect is, after 14 days' notice, passed by the Rajya Sabha by absolute majority and then agreed to by the Lok Sabha. He is the *ex-officio* Chairman of the Rajya Sabha. As such, he presidets over the session of the House and by virtue of that capacity receives salary and allowances equal to that of the Speaker of the Lok Sabha. In case the office of the President becomes vacant by any reason (like death, resignation, removal, long illness, foreign visit etc.) he acts as the Officiating President. He is expected to render cooperation to the President in matters so referred to him. It is true that the office of the Vice-President is not endowed with politically meaningful authority. But this office cannot be identified with the oftice of the American Vice-President nicknamed as 'His Superfluous Highness'. Indeed, the Vice-President occupies a position of considerable dignity ranking next to the President in the warrant of precedence.

Prime Minister and Council of Ministers

The Constituent Assembly came to the conclusion that the British system of government would be more suitable for our country in view of our familiarity with it. But one may feel surprise at the fact that while our Constitution has detailed provisions about many things, the principles of the cabinet system of goverment have been inexhaustively specified in articles 74, 75 and 78.[8] It shows that while some essential features have been reduced to writing, many things have been left to the established conventions. Art. 74 says: "(1) There shall be a Council of Ministers with the Prime Minister at the head to aid and advise the President who shall, in the exercise of his functions, act in accordance with such advice. Provided that the President may require the Council of Ministers to reconsider such advice, either generally or otherwise, and the President shall act in accordance with the advice tendered after such reconsideration. (2) The question whether any, and if so what, advice was tendered by Ministers to the President shall not be inquired into any court."

8. It may be pointed out here that the Constitution uses the term 'Council of Ministers'. The word 'Cabinet' has been used in the 44th Constitution Amendment Act, 1978. It means a body consisting of the Prime Minister and Ministers of the Cabinet rank according to Art 352 (3).

Then, Art. 75 says: "(1) The Prime Minister shall be appointed by the President and the other Ministers shall be appointed by the President on the advice of the Prime Minister. The number of the Ministers, including the Prime Minister, must not exceed 15 per cent of the total number of the members of the Lok Sabha and that a political defector cannot be appointed as a minister. (2) The Ministers shall hold office during the pleasure of the President. (3) The Council of Ministers shall be collectively responsible to the House of People. (4) Before a Minister enters upon his office, the President shall administer to him the oaths of office and secrecy according to the forms set out for the purpose in the Third Schedule. (5) A Minister who for any period of six consecutive months is not a member of either House of Parliament shall at the expiration of that period cease to be a Minister. (6) The salaries and allowances of Ministers shall be such as Parliament may from time to time by law determine and, until Parliament so determines, shall be as specified in the Second Schedule."

Finally, Art. 78 says: "It shall be the duty of the Prime Minister—(*a*) to communicate to the President all decisions of the Council of Ministers relating to the administration of the affairs of the Union and proposals for legislation; (*b*) to furnish such information relating to the administration of the affairs of the Union and proposals for legislation as the President may call for, and (*c*) If the President so requires, to submit for the consideration of the Council of Ministers any matter on which a decision has been taken by a Minister but which has not been considered by the Council."

Appointment of Prime Minister: We may well take note of the fact that the provisions of our Constitution in regard to the system of parliamentary government are sketchy. All possible situations have not been covered by the written words of the Constitution. Obviously, much has been left to the well-established conventions. The Prime Minister is the head of the Council of Ministers. He is appointed by the President by virtue of being the leader of the party having clear majority in the Lok Sabha. In case no party has absolute majority in the Lok Sabha, the President may invite the leader of the majority party to form the government. Nehru was appointed as the Prime Minister in 1952, 1957 and 1962 for being the leader of the Congress party having clear majority in the Lok Sabha. So was the case with Mrs. Gandhi who was the leader of the Congress party after the general elections of 1967, 1971 and 1980. Since the Congress (I) secured absolute majority in the elections of 1984, its leader (Rajiv Gandhi) was appointed as the Prime Minister. In case no

Some Important Statements

Prime Minister is central to the life and death of the Cabinet. —*H.J. Laski*

A Prime Minister is a Prime Minister and he can lay down the policy of the Government. To say that the Prime Minister cannot make a statement is itself a monstrous statement. —*Jawaharlal Nehru*

It is the Prime Minister's prerogative to change the portfolios of her colleagues or decide the composition of the Cabinet. —*Indira Gandhi*

party is in clear majority in the Lok Sabha, the President may study the situation and then invite the leader of the largest party banking upon the support of other parties so as to be in a position of majority in the Lok Sabha.[9]

The appointment of Prime Minister pertains to the discretionary power of the President, but this discretion must be used with great caution so that his action does not invite the stigma of partisanship. It should not become a matter of public controversy. The President must wait and watch the situation very carefully and then take a decision that wins the confidence of the nation. After the death of Nehru in May 1964, the President (Radhakrishnan) appointed Gulzarilal Nanda as the acting Prime Minister, but he invited Shastri to form the government after his name was cleared by the Congress Parliamentary Party. Similarly, in January 1966, he appointed Nanda as the acting Prime Minister after the death of Shastri and invited Indira Gandhi to form the government after her name was cleared by the CPP. But in August 1979, President Reddy did not invite Jagjivan Ram to form the government and instead dissolved the Lok Sabha on the advice of the outgoing Prime Minister (Charan Singh) and thereby faced the criticism of the leaders of the then Janata Party.

Functions and Position: The first and foremost function of the Prime Minister is to prepare the list of his ministers. He meets the President with his list and then the Council of Ministers is formed. Very important ministers are designated as Ministers of the Cabinet rank, others are called the Ministers of State, while ministers belonging to third rank are known as Deputy Ministers. The President has hardly any say in the selection of

9. So the President appointed P.V. Narshima Rao as Prime Minister in 1991 as he was the leader of the largest party and he accepted the offer. He was not a member of Parliament at the time of appointment, but he became a member of the Lok Sabha within next six months. In 1996 President Sharma appointed Vajpayee on the similar ground. On the same basis, Deve-Gowda was appointed in 1996, Gujral in 1997, Vajpayee in 1998 and 1999 and Manmohan Singh in 2004 and 2009.

the ministers. It is a different matter that a wise and sagacious President may gently advise the Prime Minister to include or not to exclude a particular name in his list of ministers. For instance, Prime Minister Nehru obliged President Prasad by keeping Jagjivan Ram in 1952, 1957 and 1962 and Prime Minister Indira Gandhi honoured the advice of President Radhakrishnan in not omitting the name of Nanda in 1966.

The President allocates portfolios among the Ministers on the advice of the Prime Minister. The Prime Minister may keep any department or departments under his control; he may also advise the President to reshuffle the portfolios of his ministers from time to time; he may bifurcate or trifurcate a department or have different departments amalgamated into one department. The Cabinet is the policy-making body and all ministers have to swim and sink together. In case a minister disagrees with the policy of the cabinet or with the views of the Prime Minister, he should resign. For instance, ministers like C.D. Deshmukh, Asoka Mehta and Morarji Desai resigned. It is also possible that the Prime Minister may ask a minister to resign or may advise the President to dismiss a member of his ministry. So Devi Lal was dismissed in August 1990.

The decisions of the Cabinet are virtually the decisions of the Prime Minister. The proposals about appointments of persons to high posts, the determination of home and foreign policies of the government, preparation of budget and introduction of bills in the Parliament, summoning and proroguing the session of the Parliament, and a host of other decisions are taken by the Prime Minister in consultation with his close confidants having important position in the Council of Ministers. In short, in the words of Ramsay Muir, the Cabinet is the steering wheel of the ship of the state and the Prime Minister is its steersman. However, the astonishing feature of the cabinet government in our country is that the Prime Minister has 'Presidentialised' his office. Once the Cabinet Secretariat and now the Prime Minister's Office (PMO) has become the real centre of power with the result that the phrase of Prime Minister's being first among equals has lost its relevance.

Theoretically, the Prime Minister is *primus inter pares* (first among equals); in practice, the case is quite different. His pre-eminent position, like his British counterpart, is evident from these facts:

1. While the resignation of other Ministers merely creates a vacancy, the resignation or death of the Prime Minister dissolves the Cabinet.

2. The Prime Minister stands between the President and the Cabinet. Though individual Ministers have the right of access to the Crown on matters concerning their-own Departments, any important communication, particularly relating to policy, can be made only through the Prime Minister.
3. He is in-charge of coordinating the policy of the Government and has accordingly the right of supervision over all the Departments.

In Indi,a all these special powers belong to the Prime Minister in as much as, apart from statutory provisions, the conventions relating to Cabinet Government are, in general, applicable here.

46

PARLIAMENT

Art. 79 of Chapter II headlined 'Parliament' contained in Part V titled 'The Union' provides for the constitution of the Union legislature called Parliament (Samsad) consisting of the President, the Rajya Sabha (Council of States) and the Lok Sabha (House of People) respectively as the upper and lower chambers. The President is an integral part of the Parliament, though he is not a member of any House, for the reason that he summons and prorogues the sessions, may dissolve Lok Sabha, delivers inaugural address and may send messages and, finally places his signatures to authenticate the bills passed by the Parliament. However, the peculiar thing about our Parliament is that while its general pattern is like that of the English Parliament, it is a non-sovereign law-making body like the American Congress. Its legislative power is circumscribed by the written provisions of the Constitution that provide for a federal system of government with power of judicial review vested in the Supreme Court and the High Courts to strike down any law or executive action, in part or full, if it is inconsistent with the Fundamental Rights given in Part III or with the basic framework of the Constitution.

Rajya Sabha

Composition and Term: The Indian Parliament is a bicameral body. Its upper chamber is the Rajya Sabha. It consists of 250 members at the most. Out bf this 12 members are nominated by the President from amongst persons distinguished in the field of art, literature, science and social service. The remaining members are the representatives of the States and Union Territories. The number of representatives, as determined by a law of Parliament and specified in Schedule IV of the Constitution, varies from State to State as the number of seats allocated to them is based on the factor of population. It is due to this that while a small State like

Some Important Statements

The principal point of distinction between the British Palliament and the Indian Parliament remains and that is that the Indian Parliament is the crtature of the Constitution of India and its powers, rights and privileges and obligations have to be found in the relevant Articles of the Constitution of India. It is not a sovereign body uncontrolled with unlimited powers. ***—Chief Justice H.L. Kania***

Where the Constitution is supreme and the legislaturt is a creature of the Constitution with limitations on its competence, its laws being liable to be struck down as ultra vires if they breach the constitutional controls, it may be called a 'controlled constitution.' ***—Nani A. Palkhivala***

As is natural in a system of parliamentary democracy, the Parliament of India occupies a place of primacy in the governance of the country. ***—S.C. Kashyap***

Nagaland has only one seat, a very big State like the UP has 31 seats. The members are elected by the members of the State Legislative Assemblies in accordance with proportional representation with single transferable vote system. The Parliament may make some other arrangement for the representation of Union Territories.[1] It is due to this that the party-wise composition of the Rajya Sabha reflects the party-wise composition of the Vidhan Sabhas in the country.

A member of the Rajya Sabha must possess three qualifications. First, he must be a citizen of India. Second, he must have completed the age of 30 years. Last, he must possess all other qualifications laid down in an act of Parliament. The Representation of the People Act, 1951 says that a person to be chosen as a member of this House from any State, excluding Jammu-Kashmir, must be an elector for a Parliamentary constituency in tht State. The disqualifications for the membership of this House are: holding an office of profit under the Government of India or any State except that of a minister or any other exempted by law of Parliament, being of unsound mind or an undischarged insolvent as declared by a competent court, being an alien or a non-citizen, and being disqualified under any law of the Parliament.

The Rajya Sabha is a continuing chamber. Its one-third members retire after every second year and elections are held for the vacant seats. Thus, a member of the Rajya Sabha has six years to serve, but he may be

1. For instance, the three members of the National Capital Territory of Delhi are elected by its Legislative Assembly according to plurality of votes system.

re-elected any number of times. (It applies to the nominated members as well). A member of the Rajya Sabha may tender his resignation or cease to be its member in case he incurs some disqualification as provided in Art. 101 of the Constitution. That is, a member of this House shall forfeit his membership in case he become a member of the Lok Sabha or of any State legislature, or has voluntarily acquired the citizenship of a foreign State, or is under any acknowledegment of allegiance or adherence to a foreign State, or remains absent from all meetings of the House or its committees for a period of 60 days without any reason communicated to the House, or he is expelled from the membership of the House, or is held a political defector by the Chairman of the House.

Functions and Position: Though a House of the Elders, the Rajya Sabha is regarded as a weak chamber in comparison to the Lok Sabha. A money bill cannot be introduced in the Rajya Sabha and when such a bill is referred to it after it is passed by the Lok Sabha, it has to pass it within a period of 14 days. The Rajya Sabha may return a money bill with some recommendations, but the Lok Sabha may accept them or not while reconsidering the same bill. A non-money bill may be introduced in any House of Parliament and here the Rajya Sabha is again a weak, though not very weak (as in the case of passing a money bill) chamber. In case there is disagreement between the two chambers, the President may convene a joint session of Parliament. Such a session (as occurred in 1961 in the case of Dowry Prohibition Bill, in 1978 in the case of Banking Service Commission Repeal) Bill and in 2002 in the case of Prevention of Terrorist Activities Bill) shall be held under the chairmanship of the presiding officer of the Lok Sabha (Speaker) and the matter shall be decided by majority of votes. The Speaker alone has the power to decide whether a bill is money bill or not. It is also provided that the Rajya Sabha must pass a bill already passed by the Lok Sabha or return it to Lok Sabha for consideration within six months. There is no such limitation in the case of a bill first passed by the Rajya Sabha and then referred to the Lok Sabha. Then, the Rajya Sabha cannot pass a motion of no-confidence against the government. Its members cannot move adjournment motion which, indeed, amounts to censure motion. At the most, they may criticise and thereby embarrass the government.

But in some other directions, the Rajya Sabha has powers equal to those of the Lok Sabha and, in that respect, it cannot be termed as a weak chamber. For instance, a bill of constitutional amendment requiring special majority (absolute majority of the whole House coupled with two-thirds majority of the members, present and voting) for its adoption must be passed by both the Houses. If there is disagreement between the two chambers in passing such a bill, joint session of the Parliament cannot be held. Thus the Rajya Sabha could show its 'teeth' by rejecting the 24th Constitution Amendment Bill (seeking abolition of the privy purses and privileges of the former rulers of princely States) in 1970 and the 64th Constitution Amendment Bill (seeking reorganisation of Panchayati Raj) and the 65th Constitution Amendment Bill (seeking restructuring of urban municipal boards) in 1989. The Rajya Sabha has equal powers with Lok Sabha in matters like electing the President and Vice-President, impeaching the President, judges of the Supreme Court and High Courts and other high officers, approving a proclamation of emergency and extending its duration, considering the reports of various commissions and autonomous bodies, setting up martial law courts during national emergency for dealing with the offences committed by the civilians and indemnifying officers for their acts done in good faith, taking away an item from the purview of the Union Public Service Commission, and exercising control over delegated legislation.

But there are some areas in which the Rajya Sabha has special powers and thereby appears more important than the Lok Sabha. For instance, vide Art. 249, it may pass a resolution by its two-thirds majority so as to shift an item of the State List to the Union List or the Concurrent List on the plea of its 'expediency in the national interest.' Such a resolution shall remain in force for one year, but it may renew it again and again. Vide Art. 312, it may pass a resolution by its two-thirds majority so as to propose the creation of an all-India public service to be regularised by a law of Parliament in time to come. Then, it may initiate a move for the removal of the Vice-President. Such a resolution is to be passed by the Rajya Sabha by its absolute majority and then agreed to by the Lok Sabha. Last, in case the Lok Sabha stands dissolved, the Rajya Sabha may allows extension of time in the case of 'emergency' declared by the President.

Allocation of Seats in Parliament

States and Union Territories	*Rajya Sabha*	*Lok Subha*
States		
1. Andhra Pradesh	18	42
2. Arunachal Pradesh	1	2
3. Assam	7	14
4. Bihar	16	40
5. Chhattisgarh	5	11
6. Goa	1	2
7. Gujarat	11	26
8. Haryana	5	10
9. Himachal Pradesh	3	4
10. Jammu and Kashmir	4	6
11. Jharkhand	6	14
12. Karnataka	12	28
13. Kerala	9	20
14. Madhya Pradesh	11	29
15. Maharashtra	19	48
16. Manipur	I	2
17. Meghalaya	1	2
18. Mizoram	1	1
19. Nagaland	1	1
20. Orissa	10	21
21. Punjab	7	13
22. Rajasthan	10	25
23. Sikkim	1	1
24. Tamil Nadu	18	39
25. Tripura	1	2
26. Uttar Pradesh	31	80
27. Uttarakhand	3	5
28. West Bengal	16	42
1. Andaman and Nicobar Islands	—	1
2. Chandigarh	—	1
3. Dadra and Nagar Haveli	—	1
4. Daman and Diu	—	1
5. Delhi	3	7
6. Lakshadweep	—	1
7. Pudducherry	1	1
Nominated	12	2
Total	245	545

It shows that the Rajya Sabha is neither a weak chamber like the British House of Lords, nor is it a powerful chamber like the American Senate. It is expected to be a house of the seasoned and elderly leaders. It is true that the Rajya Sabha has failed in living like a 'house of angels', it has certainly not been a gathering of reactionary and raw elements. Though its members are drawn by indirect election in which State Legislative Assemblies play their part, it "does not seem to have made the floor of the Council a battleground between Centre and States; a defence of States' rights, an expression of the regional demands, that is just likely to be heard in the other House."[2]

Lok Sabha

Composition and Term: The Lok Sabha is the popular chamber having at the most 550 elected members (530 from the States and 20 from the Union Territories). The President may nominate at the most two members of the Anglo-Indian community in case he finds it not adequately represented therein. The members of this chamber are elected directly by the voters. The whole country is divided into territorial constituencies in a manner that the ratio between the number of the representatives and the size of the population is, as far as practicable, the same throughout the State. Moreover under the Delimitation Commission Act of 1952, the Election Commission is authorised to determine forthwith the number of seats in the Lok Sabha on the basis of the latest census figures having regard to the constitutional provisions on the subject. Some seats are reserved for Scheduled Castes and Scheduled Tribes.[3]

A member of the Lok Sabha must be a citizen of India and that he must be above 25 years age. He must not be holding an office of profit, nor must he meet any disqualification as already pointed out in the case of

2. W.H. Morris-Jones: *The Parliament in India*. p. 256.

3. The Eighty Fourth Amendment of 2001 provides that until the relevant figures for the first census taken after the year 2026 have been published, it shall not be necessary to readjust the allocation of seats in the House to the States and the division of each State into territorial constituencies under this provision.

a member of the Rajya Sabha.[4] The normal term of the House is of five years to be computed from the date of its first sitting. The President may dissolve this House at any time. In case emergency is in force, the Parliament may make a law to extend the life of the Lok Sabha (as happened in 1976). Such a law shall remain in force for one year in one instance, but it may be extended again and again.

Speaker: The Speaker occupies a very dignified position in the order of precedence.[5] He is the presiding officer of the Lok Sabha. He is elected by the House and may be removed by it on some charge if a resolution, after 14 days' notice, is passed by its absolute majority. The House also elects a Deputy Speaker who, according to a practice, must belong to a party in the Opposition. " The Speaker conducts the session of the House, recognises the members and permits them to speak in the House. He puts matters to vote and then declares the result. He does not vote, but he may exercise his casting vote in order to break the tie. He may give his ruling to settle a dispute. He may admit a question or a motion or reject it if found out of order. In the event of grave disorder, he may adjourn the sitting of the House. He may ask a member to withdraw an unparliamentary

---

4. The office of the Minister is excluded from the office of profit. On 30 September, 1982 the President disqualified a member of the Rajya Sabha (M.R. Mohanrangam) as he was holding the post of special representative of the government of Tamil Nadu in Delhi. It was taken as an office of profit. So Mrs. Jaya Bachchan was disqualified in March. 2006. The Representation of the People Act 1951 lays down certain conditions for disqualification which are applicable to the members of Parliament and State legislatures. These are:

   (*a*) He must not have been found guilty by a Court or an election tribunal of certain election offences or corrupt practices in the elections.

   (*b*) He must not have been convicted by a Court of any offence and sentenced to imprisonment for a period of more than two years.

   (*c*) He must have not failed to lodge an account of his election expenses within the time and in a manner prescribed by law.

   (*d*) He must not have been dismissed for corruption or for disloyalty from Government service.

   (*e*) He must not be a director or a managing agent, nor hold an office of profit under any Corporation in which the Government has any financial interest.

   (*f*) He must not have any interest in Government contracts, execution of Government work or services.

5. The order of precedence is: (1) President, (2) Vice-President, (3) Prime Minister. (4) Governor. (5) Ex-Presidents and Ex-Governors, (5a) Deputy Prime Minister. (6) Lt-Governor. (7) Chief Justice of India and the Speaker of Lok Sabha.

expression or may expunge any objectionable portion from the proceedings of the House. He may also 'name' a member and order his police staff to take him out of the House in the event of his serious misbehaviour. He may accept the resignation of any member or may reject it on the ground of its submission under 'duress'. He certifies that a bill is passed by the House. He may correct a patent error in a bill after it is passed by the House. He may disqualify a member in the event of his political defection. Indeed, the Speaker occupies a position of great prestige and authority.

Functions and Powers: The Constitution provides that the sessions of the Parliament should be held in a way that the intervening period is of not more than six months. It means that the Parliament must meet at least twice a year. Both the Houses hold their session normally thrice a year known as the budget session, monsoon session, and winter session. In each House the quorum is one-tenth of its total membership. Any member may raise the issue of quorum. If there is no quorum, the Chairman/Speaker may ring the quorum bell to ensure minimum attendance of the members or adjourn the sitting for some time.

The functions and powers of the Lok Sabha must be understood in the light of what we have already said about the functions and powers of the Rajya Sabha. The Lok Sabha is known as the powerful chamber of the Indian Parliament for these reasons. First, it has control over the government. The Council of Ministers is collectively responsible to the Lok Sabha. As such, the ministry may be thrown out in case this House passes a motion of censure or no-confidence or makes a cut in the budget, or disapproves of the policy of the government. For instance, on 7 November 1990, the Lok Sabha created history by rejecting confidence motion put by Prime Minister V.P. Singh. The members may put the ministers to gruelling tests by asking questions, tabling motions (calling attention and adjournment), demanding half-hour discussion etc. Second, the Lok Sabha has a better position in the joint session by virtue of its numerical strength. Third, the Lok Sabha has control over the purse of the nation. A money bill (and so a budget) can be introduced in the Lok Sabha with the recommendation of the President and, when passed by it, it has to be passed by the Rajya Sabha within 14 days.

Position: However, a comparative study of the functions and powers of the two Houses leads to this unmistakable impression that the Lok Sabha is a powerful chamber as compared to the Rajya Sabha. There should be no doubt about Rajya Sabha being the upper chamber and Lok Sabha being the lower chamber of the Parliament. However, the two chambers should not be designated as such with a mind to exalt one and denigrate the ether that goes to intensify the bitter tradition of rivalry. What should prevail is the convention of harmony and cooperation between the two. Prime Minister Nehru well counselled on 6 May 1953 that we must not blindly follow the English practice in every way. As he said: "Our guide must, therefore, be our own Constitution which has clearly specified the functions of the Council of States (Rajya Sabha) and the House of the People (Lok Sabha). To call either of these Houses an upper house or a lower house is not correct. Each House has full authority to regulate its own procedure within the limits of the Constitution.That the Constitution treats the two Houses equally except in certain financial matters which are to be within the sole purview of the House of People."

No doubt, the Parliament is the pivot around which the whole structure of democratic government revolves. It may be lauded as our nation in miniature. As a learned writer comments: "Parliament of India, representing as it does all constitutionally organised shades of public opinion at the national level, occupies a pre-eminent and central position in Indian polity. It embodies and epitomises the sovereign will of the people; it is the mirror and voice of the nation. The Preamble to the Constitution makes it abundantly clear that the ultimate source of all power are the people of India in whom sovereignty vests. The Constitution, which is the fundamental law of the land, has been 'adopted, enacted and given to ourselves' by 'We, the People of India'. It is, therefore, one of the overriding concerns of the Parliament to see that the will and the aspirations of the people as reflected in its chambers are best fulfilled in the best manner possible. Members of Parliament, as elected representatives of the people. ventilate the people's grievances and opinions on various issues, scrutinise the functioning of the government on the floor of the Houses of Parliament and enact laws. Parliament functions as the grand inquest and watchdog of the nation."[6]

6. S.C. Kashyap: *Our Parliament*, pp. 33-34

47

UNIFIED JUDICIARY

As already pointed out, we have a unified judiciary with Supreme Court at the apex, the High Courts just below it, and district courts at the base. The ruling, and directions of the Supreme Court must be honoured by all the courts of the country. The decisions of the district courts can be challenged in the High Courts. The decisions of the High Courts can be taken to the Supreme Court in appeal and its decision is final. The jurisdiction of the Supreme Court is India-wide. While the composition of the district courts is a subject of the State List and as such, it falls under the purview of the State governments, the composition and jurisdiction of the High Courts is a matter of the Union List and, as such, it comes under the domain of the Union Government. The High Courts do not have autonomous position as they should have in a federal system. The power of 'judicial review' has been given to the Supreme Court as well as to the High Courts.

Supreme Court

Composition: The Supreme Court stands at the apex of the Indian judicial system. It consists of a Chief Justice and 30 other judges. The President appoints the Chief Justice of India after 'consulting' the judges of the Supreme Court. He appoints other judges with the 'consultation' of the Chief Justice of India. The President may appoint *ad hoc* judge or judges at the request of the Chief Justice of India. Only a working judge of some High court or a retired judge of the Supreme Court can be appointed on *ad hoc* basis. It should be noted that matters relating to the appointment of the judges of the Supreme Court relate to the discretionary power of the President and the provision that he should consult judges of the Supreme Court or of the High Courts, as he may deem necessary, in the event of selection for the post of the Chief Justice of India is of a recommendatory and not of a mandatory character. A person to be

Some Important Statements

As an independent judiciary under the scheme of the Constitution, the Supreme Court has played the role effectively in acting as a watch dog through judicial review under the acts of the legislature and the executive. The major contribution of the Supreme Court has been to uphold the Constitution by delineating the role of the three organs of the State. ***—Former Chief Justice A.S. Anand***

For the entire republic of India, there is one unified judicial system, one hierarchy of courts with the Supreme Court as the highest or the apex court and as the only arbiter in matter of relations between the Union and the States and the States *inter se*. ***—S.C. Kashyap***

The notion of an independent judiciary is also exposed to grave strain when sitting judges of the Supreme Court (and also of the High Courts) associate themselves with commissions, which are established often not on any well thought out course of policy to eliminate systematically the abuse of power, but merely on the ground of political expediency, or gain, or political necessity. ***—Prof. Upendra Baxi***

appointed as a Judge of the Supreme Court must possess two qualifications. First, he must be a citizen of India. Second, he must have served as a judge in a High Court or High Courts for at least five years, or practised in a High Court or High Courts as an advocate for at least ten years, or must be a distinguished jurist in the view of the President. As a matter of practice, one of the judges must be a Muslim so as to ensure secular character of the supreme judiciary.

The judges of the Supreme Court retire on completing the age of 65 years. A judge may resign his post by addressing a letter to the President of India. It is also provided that a judge of the Supreme Court may be removed by the process of impeachment. For this purpose the Parliament may pass a special address by its absolute majority coupled with two-thirds majority of the members, present and voting, on charging a judge with 'proved misbehaviour' or 'incapacity'. As per the Judges Inquiry Act, 1968 it is necessary that before the matter is taken up for discussion in any House of Parliament, it must be looked into by an inquiry committee consisting of the Chief Justice or a senior judge of the Supreme Court, Chief Justice or a senior Judge of a High Court, and a distinguished jurist of the country.

Jurisdiction: The jurisdiction of the Supreme Court is of three kinds—original, appellate, and advisory. Its original jurisdiction covers cases of constitutional law or fact between the Centre and the States or between the States. Here it acts as an umpire between the Union and the States. The matters relating to election disputes of the President and Vice-President may be tried in the Supreme Court alone. Art. 139A inserted by the Forty-fourth Amendment of 1978 adds two more points to it. First, where cases involving the same or substantially the same questions of law are pending before the Supreme Court and one or more High Courts or before two or more High Courts, it may withdraw the case or cases pending in the High Courts and dispose them of. It may be done on its own motion, or on the application of the Attorney-General of India, or at the request of the parties concerned. It is also possible that after determining the said question, the Supreme Court may refer that case back to the High Court or High Courts with its judgment. Second, the Supreme Court may transfer a case, appeal or other proceedings from one High Court to some other High Court for meeting the ends of justice.

The appellate jurisdiction of the Supreme Court covers cases already decided by the High Courts. The judgment of a High Court can be taken to the Supreme Court in an appeal in case the High Court itself certifies that the 'case is fit for appeal', or the Supreme Court gives its leave for this purpose. In civil and in constitutional cases, an appeal shall lie to the Supreme Court against the judgment of a High Court if it is satisfied that the case involves a substantial point of law as to the interpretation of the Constitution. In criminal cases it has to be seen whether the High Court has in appeal reversed the order of acquittal of an accused person delivered by a district court and sentenced him to death, or has withdrawn for trial before itself any case from any court subordinate to its authority and has in such a trial convicted the accused person and sentenced him to death. It shows that a person cannot move the Supreme Court in appeal as a matter of right. The Court may issue prerogative writs for the protection and enforcement of fundamental rights. Under Art. 136 the Supreme Court can allow special leave to appeal against the judgment of any court or tribunal in the territory of India.

Under Art. 143 the President may refer any matter of law or a fact of considerable public importance for taking the opinion of the Court that is not binding, though it has great persuasive value. This is known as advisory jurisdiction of the Supreme Court.

High Courts

Composition: The Constitution provides for a High Court for each State; there may be a common High Court for two or more States as well as for a Union Territory. A High Court consists of a Chief Justice and some other judges as the President may determine their number from time to time. The judges retire at the age of 62 years. It is also provided that the President may appoint additional judges to clear the arrears of work for a term of two years subject to the age limit of 62 years. The President may also appoint temporary judges to fill casual vacancies in the cadre of permanent judges caused by the reason of absence or any other factor. While appointing the Chief Justice or a judge of a High Court, the President may consult the Chief Justice of India, the judges of the Supreme Court, the Chief Justice of the High Court and the Governor of the concerned State. A judge of a High Court must possess two qualifications. First, he must be a citizen of India. Second, he must have held a judicial office in the country, or practised as an advocate in some High Court for at least 10 years. A judge may resign his post by writing a letter to the President of India; he may be transferred from one High Court to another; he may be appointed as a judge of the Supreme Court; he may be removed by the process of impeachment as applicable to a judge of the Supreme Court discussed above.

Jusrisdiction: The jurisdictional competence of the High Courts still remains as it was before the commencement of the Constitution. As a result, while the High Courts of Calcutta, Bombay and Madras have both original and appellate jurisdictions (in civil cases of the value of more than Rs. 2000 and in criminal cases referred to them by the Presidency magistrates and other cases of revenue), all have limited original jurisdiction in cases relating to admiralty, will, divorce, marriage, company law and contempt of court. All High Courts have appellate jurisdiction in civil and criminal cases.

Like the Supreme Court, the High Courts have the power to issue prerogative writs for the protection and enforcement of fundamental rights in the nature of *habeas corpus, mandamus.* prohibition, *certiorari*, and *quo warranto*. Unlike the Supreme Court, they may also issue such writs 'for any other purpose'. The original jurisdiction of the High Courts also covers election disputes of the members of Parliament and State legislatures. Like Supreme Court, each High Court is a court of record.

The decisions of the district courts can be challenged in the High Court. The High Court can call from the subordinate courts returns, issue general rules and forms to regulate their proceedings, prescribe for them account forms and books, and settle the table of fees allowed to the clerks and officers of such courts and to the pleaders practising therein. It has the power of superintendence and control over the lower courts within their areas except military courts. If a High Court is satisfied that a case pending before any subordinate court involves a substantial question of constitutional law it can take up the case and decide it itself or may send it back to the subordinate court, in question, after deciding the question of law involved therein.

Judicial Review

It may be defined as the power of a court to look into the constitutional validity of an impugned law or executive action and hold it unconstitutional and, for that reason, unenforceable to the extent it is inconsistent with the fundamental law of the land. It is an invention of Chief Justice Marshall of the American Supreme Court and now it has been adopted in the constitutional systems of many countries like Canada, Australia, Switzerland, Germany, Nigeria, Japan and India. The reason behind it is that in a country having a written constitution, the ordinary law must be subordinate to the higher (constitutional) law of the land. No organ of government can transgress its area of authority and in case it occurs in the form of a law made by the legislature or some other organ having authority delegated to it, or if some administrative action is taken in violation of the doctrine of 'competence,' it may be challenged in the Court and then the Court may declare it null and void to the extent of its being repugnant to the Constitution. Such a unique function of the judiciary stems from a feeling that a system based on a written constitution can hardly be effective in practice without an authoritative, independent and impartial arbiter of constitutions issues and also that it is necessary to restrain governmental organs from exercising powers which may not be sanctioned by the Constitution."[1]

The source of the power of the judicial review is contained in Art. 13 (2) of the Constitution. It says that "all laws in force in the territory of India immediately before the commencement of this Constitution, in so far as they are inconsistent with the provisions of Part III shall, to the extent of such inconsistency, be void. The State shall not make any law which takes away or abridges the rights conferred by this Part and any law made in contravention of this clause, shall to the extent of the

1. M.P. Jain; *Indian Constitutional Law*, III Ed., 1978, p. 669.

contravention, be void. Unless the context otherwise requires, the word 'law' includes any ordinance, order, by-law, rule, regulation, modification, custom or usage having in the territory of India the force of law. It also includes 'laws in force' or laws made by a Legislature or a competent authority in the territory of India before the commencement of this Constitution and not previously repealed, notwithstanding that any such law or any part thereof may not be then in operation either at all or in particular areas.[2]

The power of judicial review is vested in the High Courts and the Supreme Court. As such, an aggrieved party may challenge a law or any executive order on the ground of its being inconsistent with the provisions or the basic structure of the Constitution. It is true that our Courts cannot invoke the plea of 'due process of law' as it is invoked by the American Supreme Court for the reason that they are specifically bound to follow 'procedure established by law'. It appears that the judiciary is virtually under the sway of the legislature. However, this point should not be understood in a way to minimize the position of the judiciary. The Courts may also look into the fact that the procedure established by law is not a fraud on the Constitution. In the case of *Kesavanand Bharati* v. *The State of Kerala* or *Fundamental Rights Case* (1973) the Supreme Court laid down the doctrine of the 'basic structure of the Constitution.' It is true that the Court did not clearly define the term 'basic framework or structure', but it is very clear that it could establish its powerful position vis-a-vis the power of the legislature. The judgment of the Court in this case may be regarded as our Republic's greatest contribution to jurisprudence, and its underlying philosophy as of momentous significance for the survival of democracy in our country.

While exercising the power of judicial review, the Courts are guided by certain maxims. For instance, the point of 'competence' is taken into consideration. The Court examines whether the law-making or order-issuing authority has acted within its jurisdiction or not. It is known as the doctrine of pith and substance. The Court distinguishes between the good and the bad parts of an impugned law and, as such, it may declare only its bad part void. The Court may declare a law void in case it transgresses the

2. In a case the Supreme Court observed: "An order which the Court can make under Art. 142 of the Constitution in order to do complete justice between the parties must not only be consistent with the fundamental rights guaranteed by the Constitution but also with the substantive provision of the relevant statutory laws." *K.M Nanavati* v. *State of Bombay*, AIR 1961 SC 112.

authority of the legislature or of the executive. For instance, the Supreme Court invalidated a decree of the President (1970) that derecognised all former rulers of the princely States and thereby made them ineligible for privy purses and privileges. The Court may also see whether a law or decree is had in part and may then strike it down as it invalidated some parts of the law whereby 14 banks were nationalised in 1969. In case the Parliament makes an amendment in the Constitution, or it makes a change in a law in rectification of a mistake for which the Court had invalidated a particular law, then the Court will not strike down an impugned law or administrative action. However, the Court may change its view from time to time in the light of new conditions or circumstances.

The position of the Courts with regard to the exercise of the power of judicial review, as it obtains our country, is well evident from the observation of Justice S.K. Das in the case of *A.K. Gapalan v. The State of Madras* (1950): "In India the function of the judiciary is somewhat between the Courts in England and the United States. While, in the main, leaving our Parliament and State legislatures supreme in their respective legislative fields, our Constitution has, by some of its Articles, put upon the Legislature certain specified limitations. The point to be noted, however, is that in so far as there is any limitation on the legislative power, the Court must on a complaint being made to it, scrutinise and ascertain whether such limitation has been transgressed and if there has been any transgression the Court will courageously declare the law unconstitutional, nor the Court is bound by its oath to uphold the Constitution. But outside the limitation imposed on the legislative powers, our Parliament and State legislatures are supreme in their respective legislative fields and the Court has no authority to question the wisdom or policy of the law duly made by appropriate legislature. Our Constitution, unlike the English Constitution, recognises the Court's supremacy over legislative authority, but such supremacy is a limited one, for it is confined to the field where the legislative power is circumscribed by limitations upon it by the Constitution itself."[3]

3. No doubt, the power of judicial review must be exercised by the Courts with caution. As Justice H.R. Khanna has observed: "In exercising the power of judicial review, the Courts cannot be oblivious of the practical needs of the government, the door has to be left open for trial and error. Constitutional law, like other mortal contrivances, has to take some chances. Opportunity must be allowed for vindicating reasonable belief by experience. Judicial review is not intended to create what is sometimes called judicial oligarchy, the aristocracy of the robe, covert legislation, or judge-made law," *Kesavanand Bharati* v. *State of Kerala.* AIR 1973, paras 1901-2.

The power of judicial review, as exercised by the Supreme Court and the High Courts, has been criticised as well as defended by the writers on constitutional law and politics. It is said that judicial review opens the flood-gates for more and more judicial debate signifying a "lawyers' paradise". It leads to judicial despotism that virtually results in a hostile confrontation between the executive and the judicial departments of the state. It is also commented that judicial review becomes an effective instrument in the hands of the vested interests owing to the highly conservative attitude of the Courts. Further, the Courts, instead of giving stability to judicial thought, tamper it with their shifty stands as a result of which uncertainty prevails in the realm of law and justice. Above all, it elevates the position of the Courts to act like the 'powerful third chambers' or the 'super-master of the legislature.' As a learned writer remarks: "What is distinctive to the Indian experiment... is the fact that the Indian Supreme Court has functioned largely in an inapposite Westminster model of Parliamentary democracy."[4]

However, viewed in a correct perspective, judicial review looks like an essential instrument in the hands of the judges to work as the protectors of our democratic system as enshrined in the provisions of the Constitution. It is by virtue of this power that the judiciary can save the ordinary people from the onslaught of executive or legislative despotism. What is really needed is that the custodians of the Constitution must not exercise their power in a way that would lead to the intrusion of their personal philosophy into the social philosophy of the nation and thereby cause a sort of hostile confrontation between the two organs of the political system.

4. Upendra Baxi: *The Indian Supreme Court and Politics*, p. 12

48

STATE AND LOCAL GOVERNMENTS

The framework of the State governments is almost the same as we have seen in the case of the government at the Centre. Some minor points of difference may, however, be noted. For instance, he Governor is the constitutional head of the State government, but he is not elected; he is appointed by the President and may be recalled or reappointed or transferred by him from one State to another. The Governor performs the same functions what the President does at the Centre with this difference that he has no 'emergency' powers. Each State has a Vidhan Sabha, but in some States the legislature is bicameral having Vidhan Parishad and Vidhan Sabha respectively as upper and lower chambers. All Vidhan Sabhas have a normal term of five years, but the Vidhan Sabha of Jammu-Kashmir has a term of six years. Since we have a unified judiciary, the High Courts are not the third organ of the State governments in the correct sense of the term, they constitute the sub-part of the Union judiciary. Above all, since we have a federal system with a strong Centre, the State governments do not have autonomy that is enjoyed by the states of the USA or the cantons of Switzerland due to the overriding and over-arching control and interference of the Centre in many areas of the administration of the States.

Governor

Appointment: Each State has a Governor. There may be a common Governor for two or more States. He is appointed by the President on the advice of the Union Council of Ministers for five years. A person to be appointed for this post must be a citizen of India; he must be above 35 years of age; and he must not be holding an office of profit. Two usages have developed in this direction. First, the person to be chosen for this post must not be a domicile of that State. For instance, a Maharashtrian should not be appointed as the Governor of Maharashtra. Second, before making this appointment, the Union government must consult the Chief

Some Important Statements

Situated as he is today, appointed and removed by the Centre, the Governor is what the Centre makes him to be; practically there is nothing that the Governor could do by himself. *—Prof. K.V. Rao*

In order to give true meaning to the office of the Governor, the first essential thing is to choose proper persons for filling the office. It should not be treated as the last refuge of a retired politician or a civil servant, or as a place for the distribution of patronage. Outstanding men in the political, social or educational life of the country, who are not controversial figures, must obviously, be the proper choice.

—Dr. L.M. Singhvi

For the fear of losing his office, or of not getting another State on the expiry of his current term, the Governor may heed to the promptings of the Union more carefully than what is offered to him under Art. 163 of the Constitution. It is, therefore, reasonable to hold that the Governor is more an agent of the Union than the Head of the State over whose destiny he presides. *—Prof. S.C. Dash*

Minister of the concerned State just for the sake of courtesy. It does not mean that the Chief Minister may dictate his will in this matter; it is simply a gesture of goodwill that the Centre should show to the real head of the State government. Unfortunately, the second usage has not been observed scrupulously on several occasions. Not only that, the Centre has failed to evolve a clear-cut-policy about the selection of persons for this post. Facts illustrate that this post has been given to persons ranging from eminent public figures and seasoned bureaucrats to burnt out politicians and fallen horses. A noted jurist like M.C. Setalvad regretted that since the advent of independence, many of those selected for the post "have fallen short of the required standard, largely due to the lowly place given to the office which has come to be treated as a sinecure for mediocrities or as a consolation prize for burnt out politicians."[1]

1. The Setalvad Committee of the Administrative Reforms Commission in 1967 recommended that persons known for their integrity and eminence should be appointed as the Governors of States. So the Sarkaria Commission Report (1987) recommended that eminent publicmen having impeccable character should be selected for the post of the Governors of the States. The National Commission to Review the Working of the Constitution in its Report (2002) recommended that only eminent and detached persons from outside the State should be appointed as the Governors after consultation with the concerned Chief Ministers.

Functions and Powers: The functions and powers of the Governor cover executive, legislative, judicial, financial and other spheres. In the *executive sphere,* his functions are as under:

1. He is the executive head of the State government. The executive power of the State is vested in him that he has to exercise directly or through officers subordinate to him. All executive actions of the State government are taken in his name. He makes rules for the transaction of business of the government and for the allocation of work among his ministers.
2. He appoints the Chief Minister and on his advice appoints other ministers. He administers to them the oaths of office and secrecy. He accepts their resignations. He may dismiss the Chief Minister or any minister on the advice of the Chief Minister. He makes appointment of high officers of the State like Advocate-General, Chairman and members of the State Public Service Commission, Election Commissioner of State, Chairman and members of State Finance Commission etc. and is consulted by the President in the appointment of the judges and Chief Justice of the High Court of his State.
3. He may call for information from the Chief Minister relating to the affairs of administration and proposals for legislation.
4. He may refer any important matter for the consideration of the Council of Ministers.
5. He acts as the Chancellor of State universities.
6. In case he is satisfied that constitutional machinery in his State has broken down, he may write to the President recommending invocation of Art. 356 of the Constitution. If it happens, he acts as the 'agent' of the President in running the administration of the State.

Then, he performs important functions in the *legislative sphere* which may be put as under:

1. He is an integral part of the State legislature without being its member. He summons the session of the legislature and prorogues it. He may dissolve the Vidhan Sabha at any time on or against the advice of the Chief Minister.
2. He may nominate one member of the Anglo-Indian community to the Vidhan Sabha in case he finds it not adequately represented in it. If the State legislature is bicameral, he nominates about one-sixth

of its members from amongst persons distinguished in the fields of art, literature, science, social service and cooperative movement.

3. On the advice of the Election Commission, he can decide a matter relating to the disqualification of a legislator of his State.
4. The first session of the legislature of a new year and a session after a general election begins with his inaugural address.
5. He may send messages to the legislature for consideration.
6. In case the legislature is not in session and some law is necessarily to be put into force, he may promulgate an ordinance having the force of law. It may be withdrawn at any time by him, but it can remain in force at the most for six weeks after the reassembling of the State legislature.
7. The annual reports of various bodies like State Public Service Commission and Auditor-General are submitted to him that he causes of be laid before the legislature for consideration.
8. He has veto power. As such he may give assent to a non-money bill, or withhold his assent, or return it for the reconsideration of the legislature.
9. In case he finds that a bill passed by the State legislature seeks abolition of private property, or derogates the jurisdiction of the High Court, or seeks to impose tax on an item declared 'essential' by a law of the Parliament, or is likely to be in conflict with any law or policy of the Union government, he may 'reserve' it for the consideration of the President of India.

Like the President, in the *judicial sphere,* he has 'prerogative of mercy'. He may grant pardon to a person convicted by the Court or may remit or commute the sentence, provided all judicial remedies have been exhausted and the matter falls within the executive authority of the State government. He can decide matters relating to the appointments, posting and promotions of district judges and other judicial officers. He enjoys personal immunity from all civil and criminal proceedings during his term of office.

In *the financial sphere*, he has these powers. A money bill can be introduced in the Vidhan Sabha with his recommendation. He causes the annual financial statement or budget of the State government laid before the Vidhan Sabha. The Contingency Fund of the State is at his disposal and he can make advances out of it to meet an unforeseen expenditure pending its authorisation by the State legislature.

Besides, the Governor has some *discretionary* powers. He may study the situation prevailing in his State and on the basis of his 'satisfaction' may advise the President to invoke Art. 356 of the Constitution. The Governors of Assam, Arunachal Pradesh and Nagaland have special powers to deal with anti-national elements. In case a Governor is entrusted with the charge of an adjoining Union Territory, there he may act independently in the capacity of its Lt.-Governor or Administrator. He may permit initiation of legal proceedings against the serving or ex-Chief Minister or Minister involved in some alleged scandal or criminal wrong. In case he is satisfied that the Chief Minister has lost majority in the Vidhan Sabha, he may either dismiss him or ask him to prove majority in the House at an early date.

Position: The Governor acts in a dual capacity. On the one hand, he acts as the constitutional head of the State government. As such, he is expected to act on the advice of the Chief Minister. Here his position may be identified with the British monarch. But a critic may go to the extent of calling this post as a sinecure job or a gubernatorial assignment. Since the Governor has to act invariably on the advice of the Chief Minister, his position may be compared, in the words of a former Governor of UP (Mrs. Sarojini Naidu), with 'a bird in the golden cage'. On the other hand, the Governor acts like the agent or the eyes and the ears of the Centre. Since he can live in office during the 'pleasure' of the President, he must look towards the Centre in each and every delicate or sensitive situation. Whenever a critical situation arises, the Governor rushes to New Delhi to deal with it in a way appreciable to the Central leaders.

It is for this reason that the office of the Governor becomes the subject of criticism particularly when State government is run by a party which is not in power at the Centre. It is a fact that a person may live as a Governor only when he manages to keep both the Prime Minister and the Chief Minister in good humour. A Governor has to go in case he forfeits the pleasure of the Prime Minister as happened with Prabhu Das Patwari of Tamil Nadu, Raghukul Tilak of Rajasthan and Jagmohan of Jammu-Kashmir. It is also possible that sensing the mood of the Council of Ministers, the President may tacitly or indirectly advise the Governor to resign instead of facing premature exit. It is also a fact that a person in the good books of the Prime Minister may continue as a Governor either in a particular State or be shifted to another State with every prospect of reappointment.[2]

Chief Minister and Council of Ministers

Appointment: The Chief Minister is the real head of the State government. He is appointed by the Governor in accordance with the principle of parliamentary government. He must be the leader of the party having majority in the Vidhan Sabha. In case a political party manages to secure clear majority in the Vidhan Sabha, its leader is invited by the Governor to form the government. In case no party gets absolute majority in the Vidhan Sabha, then a coalition government is formed. Two or more parties may form a coalition and then their chosen leader is invited by the Governor to form the government. If no party gets clear majority and there is no chance of the formation of a coalition government either, the Governor may advise the President to invoke Art. 356. The Governor appoints ministers on the advice of the Chief Minister. Since the ministry lives in office during the 'pleasure' of the Governor, he may dismiss Chief Minister in case he forfeits the claim of being the leader of the party having majority in the Vidhan Sabha, or when there is a serious split in the ranks of the party having clear majority there.

Functions and Powers: Like the Prime Minister at the Centre, the Chief Minister is the real head of the State government. He advises the Governor to appoint ministers and deputy ministers and distributes portfolios among them. He may advise the Governor to dismiss a minister in case he differs from the policy and working of the Council of Ministers. He acts as the channel of communication between the Governor and the Council of Ministers and also between the Council of Ministers and the State legislature. He advises the Governor to make high appointments, to summon the session of the State legislature, and to dissolve the Vidhan Sabha. However, his actual position depends upon three situational

2. Throwing light on the present state of affairs, Soli J. Sorabjee in a press statement said. "No institution has seen greater debasement than the office of the Governor. It has declined into a cheap political post. There have been many instances when ministers dismissed from the government for strictures passed on them, have got promotion to the office of the Governor." *The Times of India,* New Delhi, 19 January, 1995.

variables. In case he is a powerful leader of the party having comfortable majority in the Vidhan Sabha and is also in the good books of the Prime Minister, he behaves like a 'showman' of his government. All ministers work under his leadership and the Vidhan Sabha cannot present to him a formidable challenge. In case he is a strong leader of the party having comfortable majority in the Vidhan Sabha but in opposition at the Centre, his position becomes weak owing to the hostile attitude of the Central government. In such a situation, he manages to act like a 'spokesman' of his party. With tact as well as with worldly wisdom he may prove his strong hold over the government of the State. But in case he is the leader of a coalition government with different constituents pulling in different directions coupled with the hostile attitude of the Centre, his position is quite vulnerable on every front and thus he plays, in the words of Jyoti Basu, the role of a 'postman'. The experiences of the days of Congress hegemony show that most of the Chief Ministers happily devalued themselves as 'chief messengers' of the supreme leader of their party and the Prime Minister of the country.

The Council of Ministers is the team headed by the Chief Minister to aid and advise the Governor in the exercise of his functions, except where he has the power to act in his discretion, and is collectively responsible to the Vidhan Sabha. The number of Minister, including the Chief Minister must not exceed 15 per cent of the total number of the numbers of the Vidhan Sabha. A political defector cannot be appointed as a Minister. The Council of Ministers must have atleast 12 numbrs including the Chief Minister. It is necessary that all ministers must be the members of the State legislature. In case the Chief Minister or any of the ministers is not a member of the legislature, he must secure its membership within a period of 6 months.

The following important points should be noted in this regard:

1. The Chief Minister should be the leader of the party having clear majority in the Vidhan Sabha, or a common leader of parties making a coalition having clear majority in the Vidhan Sabha.
2. The State Council of Ministers, including the Chief Minister, shall have not less than 12 ministers and not more than 15 per cent of the total strength of the Vidhan Sabha.
3. A political defector cannot be appointed as a minister. The stigma may be removed if he is re-elected, or the House of which he was a member is dissolved.

4. There shall be a minister in charge of tribal affairs having additional charge of the welfare of Scheduled Castes, and Backward Classes in the States of Jharkhand, Orissa, Chhattigarh and Madhya Pradesh.
5. The Council of Ministers shall be collectively responsible to the Vidhan Sabha.

The Council of Ministers is the policy-making body. The Chief Minister presides over the meetings of the cabinet and every member is bound to honour the decisions taken therein. In the event of difference of views, the minister should resign. The Governor may refer any important matter for the consideration of the Council of Ministers. If a question arises whether there is any matter in respect of which he Governor is required to act in his discretion, the decision of the Governor shall be final and the validity of anything done by the Governor shall not be called in question on the ground that he ought to or not have acted in his discretion. The question whether any, and if so what, advice was tendered by the ministers to the Governor shall not be inquired into any court. In case the Governor asks for any information relating to the affairs of administration or proposals for legislation, the Chief Minister is duty bound to supply it to him. However, the 'pleasure' of the Governor does not involve the element of arbitrariness or anything like subjective assessment, because it is for the Legislative Assembly to enforce the principle of collective responsibility.

Legislature

Each State of the Indian Union has a Vidhan Sabha, but seven States (Bihar, UP, Karnataka, Maharashtra, Andhra Pradesh, Jammu-Kashmir and Tamilnadu) have the upper chamber (Vidhan Parishad) as well. As per Art. 169, the Centre has the power to create or abolish Vidhan Parishad in case a resolution to this effect is passed by the Vidhan Sabha of that State by special majority (absolute majority of the whole House as well as 2/3 majority of the members, present and voting). Hence, the Parliament made laws to abolish the Vidhan Parishads of West Bengal, Punjab, Andhra Pradesh and Tamil Nadu. It is also possible that the Centre may adopt a dilatory attitude and in the meantime a newly constituted Vidhan Sabha may rescind the earlier resolution and thereby save the Vidhan Prishad as happened in the cases of UP and Bihar. It is also possible that a Vidhan Parishad may not be created in a State in spite of its provision in the Constitution as we may note in the case of Madhya Pradesh.

Vidhan Prishad: The strength of a Vidhan Parishad varies from State to State. It is provided that the strength of the Vidhan Parishad may be at least 40 and at the most not more than one-third strength of the Vidhan Sabha of the State. The composition of this chamber is determined by a formula involving the method of indirect election in some and direct election in some other categories, leaving the case of some members nominated by the Governor. It is as under:

1. About one-third members are elected by the Vidhan Sabha from amongst persons who are not its members.
2. About one-third members are elected by the local bodies of the State (like municipal boards, zila parishads or any other authority as specified in a law of Parliament).
3. About one-twelfth members are elected by persons of at least 3 years' standing as teachers in educational institutions not lower in standard than that of a secondary school.
4. About one-twelfth members are elected by the university graduates of at least 3 years' standing in the State.
5. About one-sixth members are nominated by the Governor from amongst persons possessing special knowledge of or experience in the fields of art, literature, science, social service and cooperative movement.

A member of the Vidhan Parishad must have three qualifications. First, he must be a citizen of India. Second, he must be above 30 years of age. Last, he must possess all other qualifications as laid down in a law of Parliament. A person cannot be a member of both the Houses of Parliament, or of both the Houses of State legislature, or of a House of a State legislature and a House of Parliament at one and the same time. The Vidhan Parishad is a permanent chamber. Its one-third members retire after every second year. As such a member enjoys a tenure of six years. He may be re-elected any number of times. The Parishad elects its Chairman and Deputy Chairman.

The Vidhan Parishad has no effective powers. It has to pass a money bill passed by the Vidhan Sabha within 14 days and a non-money bill passed by the Vidhan Sabha within 3 months. In case the Vidhan Parishad rejects or returns a non-money bill, the Vidhan Sabha may readopt it and then the Vidhan Parishad has to pass it within one month. There is no provision for joint sitting in such a matter. A money bill cannot be introduced in the Vidhan Parishad and in case it returns a money bill to the Vidhan Sabha, the latter may pass it again after accepting or rejecting the recommendations of the former. The Council of Ministers is collectively responsible to the Vidhan Sabha. As such, it may put the government to some inconvenience at the most by throwing critical light on its acts of commission and omission. The members of this House do not take part in the election of the President and of the members of the Rajya Sabha. In short, the Vidhan Parishad cannot override the will of the Vidhan Sabha. Keeping in view its insignificant position and condemning it as a rendezvous of retired and burnt-out politicians, it is said that the Vidhan Parishads are not even like an ornamental chamber. "Should they prove inoffensive, they might be retained. If not, they can be abolished without much trouble."[3]

Vidban Sabha: The Vidhan Sabha is the popular and powerful chamber of the State legislature. The Vidhan Sabha of a State may have at the most 500 members and at the least 60 members depending upon the demographic composition of the State. (The strength of a Vidhan Sabha is specified in a law of the Parliament that may fix a strength of even less than 60.) The members are elected directly by the voters of the State, but the Governor may nominate one Anglo-Indian as a member in order to give representation to this community. Some seats are reserved for Scheduled Castes and Scheduled Tribes except in the State of Assam where special provisions have been made for the sake of Scheduled Tribes. After each census the total number of seats in each State and the division of seats into territorial constituencies is readjusted by the Election Commission in accordance with the law of Parliament. It is essential that the ratio between the population of each constituency and the number of seats allotted to it must be, as far as practicable, same throughout the State.

3. M.P. Sharma: *The Government of the Indian Republic.* V ed, p. 256.

Allocation of Seats in State Legislative Assemblies

	States	*Seats*		*States*	*Seats*
1.	Andhra Pradesh	294	2.	Arunachal Pradesh	60
3.	Assam	126	4.	Bihar	243
5.	Goa	40	6.	Gujarat	182
7.	Haryana	90	8.	Himachal Pradesh	68
9.	Jammu-Kashmir	89	10.	Karnataka	224
11.	Kerala	140	12.	Madhya Pradesh	230
13.	Maharashtra	288	14.	Manipur	60
15.	Meghalaya	60	16.	Mizoram	40
17.	Nagaland	60	18.	Orissa	147
19.	Punjab	117	20.	Rajasthan	200
21.	Sikkim	32	22.	Tamil Nadu	234
23.	Tripura	60	24.	Uttar Pradesh	403
25.	West Bengal	294	26.	Chhattisgarh	90
27.	Jharkhand	81	28.	Uttarakhand	70

A member of the Vidhan Sabha must be a citizen of India; he must be above 25 years of age; and that he must fulfil all other qualifications as laid down in an act of Parliament. No person can be a member of the two Houses, including the Parliament, or some other State legislature at the same time. The normal term of the Vidhan Sabha is of five years. It begins from the date of its first meeting. In case national emergency (under Art. 352) is in force, the Parliament may extend the life of Vidhan Sabha by one year by making a law in this regard. Such a law may be renewed again and again. But within 6 months of the termination of emergency, elections must take place. The Governor has the power to dissolve the Vidhan Sabha at any time. In case Art. 356 of the Constitution is invoked, it depends upon the text of the proclamation of emergency to place the Vidhan Sabha under 'suspended animation' or to effect its dissolution. The House elects its Speaker and Deputy Speaker who are accountable to it. That, is, the Vidhan Sabha may remove its presiding officer by passing a vote of no-confidence against him by its absolute majority.

As already pointed out, the Vidhan Sabha is a powerful chamber. A money bill and a budget are introduced in it. Its members take part in the election of the President of India and of the members of the Rajya Sabha and Vidhan Parishad (if it is there) in accordance with proportional representation with single transferable vote system. Since the ministry is accountable to the Vidhan Sabha, it may throw out the government by passing a vote if no-confidence against it. It may express its lack of confidence in the government by rejecting an official bill, or by making a cut in the budget, or by disapproving the policy of the cabinet, or by passing the motion of no-confidence. It considers reports submitted by the State Public Service Commission, Auditor-General etc. In case the Centre desires to make alteration in the name, area or boundary lines of a State, the President shall refer that proposal to know its view before recommending its introduction in the Parliament. He may also fix a time lim it within which the Vidhan Sabha has to give its view. The Vidhan Sabha gives its view on such a proposal, but the Centre is not bound to honour it. In the case of a constitutional amendment bill referred to it for ratification under Art. 368, it passes a resolution by simple majority to endorse it or not.

On the whole, the position of the State legislatures is very weak. They can make a law on a subject of the State List. They can make a law on a subject of the Concurrent List also. In case a law on a subject of the Concurrent List has already been made by he Centre, then the bill passed by the State legislature shall be 'reserved' by the Governor for the consideration of the President of India. Moreover, in the event of any conflict between the Central law and the State law on a matter of Concurrent List, the former shall prevail and the latter shall remain inoperative to the extent of being repugnant to the former. We have also seen conditions in which the Centre can make a law on a subject of the State List and here in the event of any conflict between the Central law and the State law, the latter shall remain 'suspended' to the extent of being repugnant to the former and be effective again after the revocation of the former. It may also be kept in view that the Governor is duty bound to keep any bill passed by the State legislature 'reserved' for the consideration of the President in case he finds it likely to be in conflict with any law or policy of the Centre. Thus the operation of the legislative process at the Central as well as at the State levels reinforces the Union predominance in the legislative field.

Critical Appreciation: Though the component units of a federal system, the State governments do not have the type of autonomy that is enjoyed by the states of America or the cantons of Switzerland. There are many inroads through which the Centre may exercise its dominance over the States in normal as well as abnormal times. Not only this, the States must carry out the directives sent to them by the Centre, otherwise it would be taken as the 'breakdown of constitutional machinery' there and then the Centre shall have the power to dismiss a State government under Art. 356. The President is the head of the Indian Republic and the Governor, while being the constitutional head of the State government, acts as the 'eyes and the ears' of the Centre. Despite this all, our State governments cannot be identified with the provinces of Canada which, in the words of Dawson, 'are like glorified municipalities'. It is true that such a statement has now become outdated as the Canadian provinces have gained more powers, still they have no autonomy as is available to the states of America, Australia and Germany. In short, the position of the States of the Indian Union falls somewhere between the states of America on the one side and of the provinces of Canada on the other.

Democratic Decentralisation

A democratic polity involves decentralisation or deconcentration of power in a way that the local affairs of the people are managed by means of their positive participation. Known by the popular name of democratic decentralisation, it implies extension of democracy at the grass-roots level in view of the fact that people's participation signifies the constitution of a democratic government not merely at the top but also at the foundation-level of the political system. It signifies marked devolution of power from the higher to the lower levels in a way that the units of local government exercise their power with the participation of the people of that area with occasional control and supervision of the provincial and central governments. Thus, Panchayati Raj was introduced in our country in the light of the recommendations of the Balwantray Mehta Committee Report (1957). It failed to achieve the desired result. Hence, the government of Rajiv Gandhi introduced the 64th and the 65th Constitution Amendment Bills in the Lok Sabha in 1989 which, though passed by it, could not be adopted in the Rajya Sabha. The effort failed. The government of P.V. Narsimha Rao took up the issue with the same motive and the two bills moved in the Parliament could be adopted which became the 73rd and the 74th Constitution Amendment Acts of 1992 now placed in Parts IX and IX A of the Constitution.

Village Panchayats: The 73rd Constitution Amendment Act inserts Part IX into the Constitution. It empowers the State Legislatures to make laws for the organisation of Panchayats at the village level as well as at the higher levels of a district. Such laws shall define the mode of composition, strength of the members including reservation of seats for Scheduled Castes, Scheduled Tribes and other weaker sections of the community. The members shall be elected directly by the voters of the territorial constituencies, but the law of the State shall lay down the method of the inclusion of the MPs and M.L.A.s of that area in such bodies and the representation of the chairpersons of such bodies at the intermediate or higher levels of Panchayati Raj in a district. The chairperson of a village panchayat shall be elected directly by the voters of a constituency, but the law of the State government shall determine the method of the election of the chairpersons of higher units of Panchayati Raj in a district. The law of the State government shall also provide for reservation of seats for Scheduled Castes and Scheduled Tribes in proportion to their population, but 1/3 seats shall be reserved for women under such a category. The reservation system shall come to an end if the provision for such reservations, as given in Art. 334 of the Constitution, comes to an end.

The normal duration of a Panchayat has been fixed at 5 years from the date of its first meeting. But the State government shall have the power to dissolve it earlier. If so happens, next elections shall take place within 6 months, provided that where the remainder of the period for which the dissolved Panchayat would have continued is less than 6 months, it shall not be necessary to hold any election under this clause for constituting it. But a new Panchayat constituted upon the dissolution before the expiration of its duration shall continue only for the remainder of the period for which the dissolved Panchayat would have continued, had it not been dissolved. A person shall be disqualified for being a member of the Panchayat if he holds any office of profit under the Central or State government, or is declared by a competent court to be a man of unsound mind, or is an undischarged insolvent, or is not a citizen of India, or is disqualified under any law in force. Any dispute of this kind shall be referred to the Governor and his decision shall be final.

However, the most important feature of this arrangement is related to financial autonomy granted to such bodies. Within one year of the commencement of this Amendment Act and thereafter at the expiration of every fifth year, the Governor shall have the power to set up a Finance Commission to review the financial position of the Panchayats and to make recommendations for the Governor as (*a*) to the principles which shall govern (*i*) the distribution between the State and the Panchayats of the net proceeds of the taxes, duties, tolls and fees leviable by the State, which may be divided between them under this part and the allocation between the Panchayats of all levels of their respective shares of such proceeds, (*ii*) the determination of the taxes, duties, tolls and fees which may be assigned to or appropriated by the Panchayats, (*iii*) the grants-in-aid to the Panchayats from the Consolidated Fund of the State; (*b*) any other matter referred to the Finance Commission by the Governor in the interests of sound finance of the Panchayats. The composition, jurisdiction and the procedure of working of the Finance Commission shall be determined by the law of the State. It shall submit its report to the Governor who shall cause it to be laid before the State legislature together with an explanatory memorandum as to the action taken thereon. The State legislature shall also make law for the maintenance of accounts of these bodies and their auditing. It shall also make laws for the election to such bodies under the superintendence, direction and control of the Chief Electoral Officer of the State.

The provisions of this Constitution Amendment Act shall apply to the Union Territories as well with any number of exceptions and notification made by the President of India in it. But these provisions shall not be applicable to the States of Nagaland, Meghalaya, Mizoram, the Hill Areas in the State of Manipur and the Hill Areas of the District of Darjeeling in West Bengal. But the Legislatures of these five States may empower the District Councils with such facilities for the sake of decentralisation of power after passing a resolution by absolute majority of the whole House and 2/3 majority of the members, present and voting. The State Legislatures shall also provide by law for the settlement of electoral disputes, but the delimitation of constituencies and the allotment of seats in these bodies shall not be questioned in any court of law.

This Act introduces XI Schedule into the Constitution conferring 29 functions on Panchayats as agriculture and agricultural extension, land improvement and soil conservation, minor irrigation and water management, animal husbandry, fisheries, social and farm forestry, minor forest produce, small-scale industries, khadi and cottage industries, rural housing, drinking water, fuel and fodder, roads and other means of communication (like bridges, ferries, waterways etc.), rural electrification, non-conventional energy sources, poverty alleviation programmes, primary and secondary education, technical training and vocational education, adult and non-formal education, libraries, cultural activities, markets and fairs, health and sanitation including primary dispensaries and health centres, family welfare, women and child development, social welfare, welfare of the weaker sections, public distribution system, and maintenance of community assets.

Some Important Statements

When Panchayati Raj is established, public opinion will do what violence can never do. In Panchayati Raj only the panchayats will be obeyed and the panchayats can only work through the laws of their making. —*Mahatma Gandhi*

Panchayati Raj institutions should act as the units of self-government at the Village, Block and District levels. In acting as the units of self-government they will undertake responsibilities which they can discharge within the framework of their resources and requirements. —*Jayaprakash Narayan*

Municipalities The 74th Constitution Amendment Act inserts Part IXA so as to define the organisation and working of local self-government in the urban areas known by the name of Nagar Panchayats or municipalities/boards/councils/corporations. The State legislatures shall by law determine the strength of these bodies, the number of seats reserved for Scheduled Castes, Scheduled Tribes and other weaker sections of the community in proportion to their population in the State, including women. These members shall be elected directly by the voters of the territorial constituencies including the chairperson of such bodies. The State Legislatures may by law also provide for the making of committees at the ward level or other levels within the territorial area of the Municipality including their powers and the election of their chairpersons.

The accounts of the Municipal Corporations or boards shall be subject to auditing according to the rules framed by the Governor after consulting the Comptroller and Auditor-General of India. The Comptroller and Auditor-General of India shall cause the accounts of the said Municipal Corporation or board to be audited in such a manner as he may deem fit and the report of the Comptroller and Auditor-General shall be submitted to the Governor of the State who shall cause it to be laid before the Legislature of his State and the Municipal Corporation concerned.

The normal tenure of these bodies shall be of five years from the date of their first meeting. In case a body is dissolved earlier, election shall be held within next six months from the date of dissolution. Provided where the remainder of the period for which the dissolved body would have continued is less than six months, it shall not be necessary to hold any election under the clause for constituting it. But such a body constituted upon its dissolution before the expiration of its duration shall continue only for the remainder of th[illegible] period for which the dissolved body would have continued. A person [illegible]l be disqualified from the membership of this body if he holds any office of profit under the Central or State government, is declared of unsound mind by a competent court, is an undischarged insolvent, is not a citizen of India, or is disqualified under any law in force. Any dispute of this kind shall be referred to the Governor whose decision shall be final.

Within one year of the commencement of this Act and thereafter at the expiration of every fifth year, the Governor shall set up a Finance Commission to review the financial position of these bodies and to make recommendations as to (*a*) the principles which should govern (*i*) the distribution between the State and the Municiplities of the net proceeds of the taxes, duties, tolls and fees leviable by the States, which may be divided between them under this part and the allocation between the Municipalities at all levels of their respective shares of such proceeds, (*ii*) the determination of the taxes, duties, tolls and fees which may be assigned or appropriated by the Municipalities, (*iii*) the grants-in-aid to the Municipalities from the Consolidated Fund of the State, (*b*) any other matter referred to the Finance Commission by the Governor in the interests of sound finance of these bodies. Moreover, the State Legislature shall by law define the composition, strength and procedure of working of the Finance Commission. It shall submit its report to the Governor who shall cause it to be laid before the State Legislature with an explanatory memorandum as to the action taken thereon.

It inserts Schedule XII into the Constitution which assigns 18 functions to Municipalities as urban or town planning, regulation of land use and building construction, planning for economic and social development, roads and bridges, water supply for domestic and commercial purposes, public health and sanitation including conservancy and solid waste management, fire service, urban forestry and promotion of ecological aspects, safeguarding the interests of weaker sections of society including physically handicapped and mentally retarded, slum improvement and upgradation, urban poverty alleviation, urban recreational facilities, promotion of cultural and educational activities, burial and cremation grounds, cattle pounds and prevention of cruelty to animals, and vital statistics including registration of births and deaths.

No doubt, the provisions of Part IX and Part IXA have their own significance in the sphere of democratic decentralisation in our country. For the first time, the units of local self-government in the rural and urban areas have been accorded a constitutional status. Now their existence is not dependent on the whims and caprices of the rulers of the States. Obviously, it would strengthen democracy at the grass-roots level. And yet a critic may throw light on certain weak points. It may be feared that the innocent people living in the rural and urban areas would suffer from the hazards of struggle for power in which violence would have its own part in vitiating the peaceful atmosphere of the rural and underdeveloped areas of country. It may also be feared that these institutions of local self-government would be grabbed by crafty and mischievous politicians who would abuse their powers recklessly by committing acts of impropriety like misappropriation of public funds. The judiciary would not appreciate the provision that any law made by a State Legislature for the delimitation of territorial constituencies or the allotment of seats in the rural and urban bodies shall be immune from its scrutiny.

49

POLITICAL PARTIES AND PRESSURE GROUPS

A study of the political parties and the pressure groups in one chapter is informed by a certain reason. A modern democratic system cannot operate without the role of political parties. A pluralistic social order has a number of organised interest groups that play a part of their own in the political process of the country in alliance, open or secret, with political parties. A two-way traffic can be noted in that while the political parties need followers and resources which groups provide, the groups require leadership and direction which is provided by the parties. The groups articulate their interests and the parties aggregate them. Thus, interaction takes place that has its visible term in the role of political parties and its invisible form in the role of organised (catalyst) groups. Since India has a pluralistic society and a democratic welfare state, the role of political parties and pressure groups deserves a particular study.

Party System

The critics of the Indian political system comment that India has parties but no party system. The crux of their argument is that while there are several political parties, big and small, in the country, there is nothing like emotional or psychological attachment of the people with a particular party or some parties on the basis of which some concrete rules of political behaviour may be formulated. Moreover, frequent fragmentation of political parties and, at the same time, movement for the polarisation of like-minded parties creates another baffling problem. Facts indicate that many political parties come into being as a result of either splits in their ranks or an alliance of various contending factions. The 'charismatic' personality of a particular leader has its own place. A leader of national or regional importance may carry with him a large number of followers and float his private political party that loses its identity with the death or eclipse of the leader or its merger with some party. The panorama of Indian

Some Important Statements

Political Scientists all over the world are divided in their opinions on the importance of parties in a democracy, but the fact remains that the parties do exist, and play vital roles in all modern democratic states, and indeed in most states, whatever their ideological orientation. If India is to survive as a state moving generally in the democratic direction, it must evolve a healthier party system or develop some effective alternatives to parties. ***—Norman D. Palmer***

This is all the more necessary, because the functioning core of the system—the political parties—is fast disintegrating. There are hardly any parties left. The Congress has been reduced from a movement to a family that is aggressively claiming to be the sole depository of it and flaunting the whole lineage over five generations as the legitimate inheritors of its mantle. ***—Rajni Kothari***

The fact is that no party has a programme to solve people's problems. Their only aim is to win power. One has often heard from party leaders that the manifestos may be good only for research scholar. ***—Kuldip Nayyar***

party system is also vitiated by rampant factionalism operating in every political party. For all these reasons, a neat picture of the Indian stasiological scenario cannot be drawn.

Characteristics Features: In order to make an empirical study of the Indian party system, we may enumerate its characteristics as under:

1. India has neither a single party system as prevailing in a communist or a fascist country, nor does it have a bi-party system as prevailing in Britain and the United States. Here operates multi-party system as prevailing in many countries of the world. If a complete catalogue of Indian political parties is prepared, the number many exceed the astonishing figure of 50. At the national level, we may mention the names of Indian National Congress, Janata Dal, Bharatiya Janata Party, Communist Party of India and Communist Party of India-Marxist. At the regional level we may refer to National Conference in Jammu-Kashmir, Shiromani Akali Dal in Punjab, Telugu Desam in Andhra Pradesh, Dravida Munnetra Kazhagam and Anna-DMK in Tamilnadu, Assom Gana Parishad in Assam, Samajvadi Party and Bahujan Samaj Party in U.P., Shiv Sena in Maharshtra, etc.
2. Multi-partyism is taken as one of the patent features of Indian party system, but it does not cover the case of country as a whole. A stable party system may be noticed in some parts of the country. Power

alternates between the DMK and the A-DMK in the State of Tamilnadu, and between the Congress and the BJP in the State of Rajasthan and in the Union Territory of Delhi. Despite efforts, no other political party has been able to set its foot in Tamilnadu, Rajasthan and Delhi.

3. Ideology plays an important part in the organisation and working of the political parties. But the element of ideology cannot be traced in many political parties of India. Leaving aside the BJP on the right and the two Communist parties on the left, all parties are like ideologically neutral organisations. Their commitments to the principles of social, economic and political significance are so flexible that they may be termed non-ideological organisations. It is a different matter that someone may characterise it as a typical case of ideology and therefore coin a term like 'Congress ideology.'
4. The factor of 'personality' has a place of its own in the operation of Indian party system. The Indian National Congress lived like an organisation of Mahatma Gandhi, then of Nehru, then of Indira Gandhi and then it was identified with the name of Rajiv Gandhi and Sonia Gandhi. An influential leader of U.P. like Chaudhry Charan Singh left the Congress in 1967 and then floated his own political parties like Bharatiya Kranti Dal, Janata (S) and Lok Dal. In Tamil Nadu M.G. Ramachandran left the DMK and floated his Anna-DMK; in Andhra Pradesh Telugu Desam was the party of N.T. Rama Rao; for many years the National Conference of Jammu and Kashmir worked like an organisation of Sheikh Abdullah.
5. One perplexing feature of the Indian party system is that, in many cases the distinction between a political party and a pressure group is blurred. For instance, Majlis-i-Ittehad-ul-Musalmeen of Andhra Pradesh and Indian Union Muslim League of Kerala were like pressure grounds each having one seat in the Lok Sabha and became constituent partners of the coalition government formed by Manmohan Singh in 2004. Not only this, all major parties have factions within themselves which play the role of pressure groups in their own right.
6. Above all, we may take note of the perplexing fact of frequent disintegration and polarisation of political parties. There are two Congresses, two Communist parties, two Janata Dals, two DMKs, three Akali Dals, three Muslim Leagues, about half a dozen socialist parties etc. Most of these parties are sustained by the factor of

anti-Congressism or anti-BJPism. Politics means struggle for power and struggle for power requires combination of strange partners. Thus, *ad hoc* alliances are formed.

Major Political Parties: We may have a brief look at the policies and programmes of some leading parties.

Indian National Congress: It is the oldest party of India. It was founded in 1885 to organise constructive and sane nationalism in the country. It became the vehicle of national movement under the leadership of Mahatma Gandhi who converted it into a mass organisation of all 'hues' of people. The Congress became like a huge umbrella under whose cover people of diverse backgrounds and different 'ideologies' could come to play their part in the freedom struggle of the country.

What is the ideology of the Congress party? We may say that it is an ideologically neutral organisation. It subscribes to certain policies and programmes of social, economic and political significance. It displays a curious blending of three different currents—Gandhism with its emphasis on rural reconstruction on the lines of decentralisation of power and economic self-sufficiency; Liberalism recognising the right of free enterprise in a mixed economy; and Socialism with its emphasis on State ownership and control of the means of production and distribution. It is the radicalism of the Congress that has had its manifestation in the nationalisation of some major private establishments and that attributed to this party the label of a left-of-centre organisation.

The Congress leaders have been of the view that the strength of this party lies in its lack of ideological clarity.[1] Jagjivan Ram preferred to call it 'Congress culture' and Sadiq Ali cautioned that the Congress ideology 'must not be interpreted as any rigid and unaltered system of ideas whose acceptance is obligatory on all Congressmen.' Thus, the leaders of the Congress make use of the term 'ideology' in a particular sense so that the amorphous character of the organisation is maintained. Its ideology stands on the pillars of parliamentary democracy, democratic socialism and enlightened secularism. The Election Manifesto issued on the eve of the general elections in 1989 revealed four ingredients of the Congress ideology—(1) Independence of thought and action in the face of external challenge to our freedom and internal subversion of our integrity; (2) Democracy, to translae independence for the nation into the freedom of the individual; (3) National integration, to preserve the emotional integrity

1. Shriman Narayan: *An Idea for Ideological Clarity,* p.1.

of the country while celebrating its glorious diversity; and (4) Equal respect for all religions.

Congress is like a very old and strong banyan tree. Its leaves wither away during autumn, it has new leaves during spring. Its fall means its autumn when opposition parties thrive on the slogan of anti-Congress-ism. The fall of such anti-Congress alliances harbinges its spring. The BJP arose at the fall of the Congress, the Congress in turn had its resurgence under the leadership of Sonia Gandhi at the fall of the BJP. On the occasion of the 125th anniversary of her party on 28th December, 2009, Sonia Gandhi said: "Doubt were raised about our party's very existence after the death of Rajiv Gandhi. Nevertheless, we soldiered on, anchored in our core values and overcame many seemingly insurmountable odds."

Janata Dal: We may have a brief study of other national and secular political parties as well. On 11 October, 1988 (birthday of Jayaprakash Narayan) a new party came into being with the merger of three parties (Janata Party, Jan Morcha and Lok Dal) under the leadership of V.P. Singh. Its name is Janata Dal. Shortly before the ninth general election (1989), it had an alliance with Congress (S), Telugu Desam, Dravida Munnetra Kazhagam and Assom Gana Parishad that assumed the name of 'National Front' under the chairmanship of N.T. Rama Rao. The policies and programmes of this party cover social, economic and political spheres and they look like based on the foundations of democracy, secularism and socialism. In the political sphere, it desires restoration of civil liberties and extension of the rights on the people, eradication of corruption, revitalisation of parliamentary institutions, reversal of over-centralisation process, more autonomy to the States, and decentralisation of powers, solution of national problems through the process of national consensus and reconciliation, social justice to the weaker sections of the community, incorporation of right to work in the list of Fundamental Rights, curbs on the use of Art. 356 sanctioning President's rule in the States, reorganisation of Panchayati Raj, establishment of a responsive administrative structure etc.

In the economic sphere, it desires prevention of concentration of wealth in the hands of the few, encouragement to small-scale and cottage industries, more production of basic consumer goods, land reforms, crop insurance system, maximisation of employment opportunities, alleviation of poverty and indebtedness, rationalisation of tax system etc. In the social sphere it desires preferential opportunities and concessions to Scheduled

Castes and Scheduled Tribes, improvement of the status of women, social security for the physically handicapped people, vocation-oriented education etc. This party had the chance to be in power when Deve-Gowda led the coalition government in 1996. His successor I.K. Gujral formed another coalition government in 1997 which had its fall in 1998. In 1999 its dissidents formed Janata Dal (United) under the leadership of Sharad Yadav. Deve-Gowda became the head of the Janata Dal (Secular).

Bharatiya Janata Party: The Bharatiya Jana Sangh founded by Shyama Prasad Mukherji in 1951 lost its identity when it merged with the Janata Party in 1977. But after the failure of the Janata experiment it had its revival in 1979 under the leadership of Atal Behari Vajpayee with the name of Bharatiya Janata Party. It expresses its commitment to five ideals—nationalism and national integration, democracy, positive secularism, Gandhian socialism, and value-based politics. It shows its faith in democratic norms with the hope that it would attempt to create a consensus on all major issues and compete with others where situations of conflict arise. However, as national consensus cannot be built on mere struggle for power, it must be based on certain principles and national objectives. The people of different faiths and ideologies should be able to coexist in peace and harmony, but those who have extra-territorial loyalties or engage in anti-national activities cannot be expected to contribute to national consensus and, for this reason, would have to be kept out.

As a believer in democracy, the BJP would fight against all trends of fascism and authoritarianism. Its commitment to positive secularism implies a rejection of what the Congress has been advocating so far. It rejects the case of appeasement towards any community and instead supports the idea of full protection to the life and property of the minorities. It desires distillation of common moral values whether derived from different religions or from other historical and civilisational experiences and approaches, which always remained integral to Indian nationalism. While accepting the doctrine of Gandhian socialism, it seeks to replace both capitalism and statism by the principle of a cooperative system and a form of trusteeship in all fields of economic activity. Finally, it desires value-based politics. It means that social and political life should be guided by a set of norms and values the abridgement of which should bring forth social sanctions and punishment. It successfully contested the elections of 1989 and 1990. Under the presidentship of L.K. Advani it managed to secure 117 seats in the Lok Sabha in 1990. Its performance became more spectacular in the Assembly elections of 1990, 1991, 1993 and 1995 as a result of which it could have is governments in the States of U.P. Himachal Pradesh. Madhya Pradesh and Rajasthan. In 1995 it formed its government in Gujarat and with Shiv Sena in Maharashtra. It improved its position in the elections of 1998 and 1999 as a result of which Vajpayee led the coalition government at the Centre till 2004.

Communist Parties: Both Communist Parties claim Marxism-Leninism as the foundation of their ideology. According to its constitution, the Communist Party of India "is the political party of the Indian working class, its vanguard, its highest form of class organisation. It is a voluntary organisation of workers, peasants and toiling people in general, devoted to the cause of socialism and communism." The policies and programmes of the CPI cover political, economic and social spheres. In the political sphere, it desires restructuring of the federal system in a way so as to ensure autonomy of the States, abrogation of Art. 356 sanctioning President's rule, abolition of the office of Governor, introduction of proportional representation with list system, enlargement of democratic rights of the people, making justice inexpensive and easily available, ensuring freedom of the press and repeal of all 'black' laws, pursuance of the policy of peace and friendship with socialist countries.

In the economic sphere, the CPI desires curbs on monopolies and transnational giants, nationalisation of major industries (sugar, textile, steel, jute and vanaspati) and foreign trade, State take-over of trade in foodgrains, strengthening the network of public distribution system, need-based minimum wage for low paid factory workers, encouragement to cottage and small-scale industries, protection of the trade union rights of the workers, participation of workers in the management of industry, employment programme for rural workers and educated youth including unemployment allowance etc. Finally, in the social sphere, it desires free education of all children upto secondary stage, economic assistance in matters of education for low income groups, security of the person and honour of the people belonging to weaker sections, social insurance in the event of accident or disability, ban on communal and obscurantist organisations, secularisation of the polity etc.

The Communist Party of India-Marxist (CPM) claims itself as the genuine leftist party based on the ideology of Marxism-Leninism. It frankly accuses the CPI of being a gathering of opportunists and class collaborationists working in alliance with the feudal-bourgeois elements having their place in the Indian National Congress. As such, it desires end of the Congress rule and instead establishment of 'people's democracy.' Its social, economic and political commitments are more or less the same as espoused by the CPI. However, what is striking about the CPM's ideology is that it denounces the CPI as a body of Dangeite revisionists and seeks to keep itself in equidistance from the 'rightism' of the BJP, 'centrism of the Congress' and the so-called 'leftism' of the CPI. When formed in 1964, it adopted a frankly pro-China line and lauded Mao as the real source of revolutionary inspiration. Thus, it could be described as a pro-China and anti-USSR communist party, but after some time it left its pro-China stance and thereby could improve its relations with the CPSU. Under the leadership of Jyoti Basu and E.M.S. Namboodiripad, it adopted an independent line and thereby followed the course of equidistance from the Communist Parties of China and the USSR. It is for this reason that the CPM was critical of the *glasnost* and *perestroika* policies of the USSR under the leadership of Gorbachev; so it criticised the action of the Chinese government in suppressing the movement for democracy by means of force in June, 1989.

As a result of the disintegration of the Soviet Union and China's patent moves towards the system of 'state capitalism,' the movement of the leftist parties has declined all over the world. It would not be wrong to say that now the left is in an unprecedented state of quandary. So is the case with the two Communist Parties of our country. While both are still critical of each other on account of smarting under the shadow of the past, the way out of the present impasse has been found out by them in supporting any national or regional organisation, or any alliance of this sort, that declares its resolve to improve the lot of the poor and backward sections of the people. The trend of globalisation of economy has overtaken them. It is a fact which they cannot deny. The Marxist Chief Ministers of West Bengal had desired investment of foreign capital in their State so as to solve the problem of economic development. The communists hold the view that the Nehruvian strategy of development has lost its relevance. And since the Centre has frankly taken to the course of 'privatisation,' it is now better to remould their ideology than to curse and look at the boons of a capitalist system with a coloured eye.

Criticism: A critical study of the Indian party system shows that it suffers from certain weaknesses.

1. The fact of ideological orientation is missing in most of the parties operating at the national and regional levels. Leaving aside the BJP

on the rightist and the two Communist parties on the leftist spectrums, all other parties are ideologically neutral organisations more concerned with their attitude towards 'personalities' than with a clear-cut commitment to some particular type of social and economic philosophy. The requirement of the amended Representation of the People Act (that every political party seeking its registration with the Election Commission must have a constitution of its own expressing its commitment to Democracy, Secularism and Socialism) has made the line of distinction between parties further blurred.

2. Frequent events of fragmentation of parties and then moves for polarisation of like-minded parties disturb the stasiological map of the country from time to time. One faces difficulty in preparing a list of all kinds of 'socialist' parties in the country, for instance.
3. Each party is ridden with rampant factionalism and even the Indian National Congress has failed to manage its internal dissensions. Consequently, the opportunists and the careerists have been able to establish their hold over the organisation. In recent years a more pernicious trend may be noted in the growing nexus between the politicians and the criminals. The sanctity of elections has been vitiated by the criminalisation of politics to a great extent.

The present position is that all political parties have become power-hungry and they have thrown all norms to the wind. They are haunted by mad craze for power and so all sorts of tactics are adopted to win the game. It has prepared a fertile ground for increasing political corruption, maladministration and criminalisation. These developments stand as powerful barriers in the growth of a healthy party system in the country.

Pressure Groups

A number of organised groups play their own part in the political process of the country. Since these groups are organised on the basis of some 'interest,' they are known as 'interest groups' and since they adopt pressure tactics to protect and promote their specific interests, they are generally taken as 'pressure groups.' Here we have to see the role of numerous associations of the businessmen, industrialists, workers, peasants, engineers, technicians, lawyers, teachers etc. Arthur Bentley of the United States discovered this field in his work *The Process of*

Government (1908) and since then a number of leading writers (as D.B. Truman, V.O. Key, Jr., G.A. Almond. Harry S. Eckstein, Joseph la Palombara, Myron Weiner, S.A. Kochanek etc.) have made their own contributions to highlight the role of these groups in the political process of various countries of the world. In view of the importance of the role of these groups, they have been nicknamed as 'invisible government' and 'unofficial government.' S.E. Finer has coined the meaningful title of 'anonymous empire.'

General Characteristic: Though some broad features of the nature of pressure group politics having its universal application may be enumerated, it should be done in the light of typical conditions of each country. As such, we may enumerate these characteristics of pressure group politics in our political system:

1. As we have a loose, disorganised and fragmented multi-party system, we have numerous groups, big and small, with long as well as ephemeral durations, living in conflict with one another, appearing and disappearing in response to the prevailing conditions and, above all, riven with shifting political allegiances. It presents a very confusing as well as a perplexing spectacle. Though we may make a list of such groups for the sake of a convenient study, it is quite a tedious job to prepare their taxonomic illustration as most of them may be found cutting across the boundaries of their real political character. In addition to that, the shifting affiliations of the groups with political parties and the penetration of the influence of the political leaders into the functioning of these groups further adds to our difficulty.
2. The organised groups, like political parties, lack definite political commitments. Their political loyalties are shifting and that contributes to their unstable political culture. Their attitudes towards political parties as well as their faith in the strategies and techniques lack definite commitments in respect of which rigid norms cannot be laid down. For instance if we take up the case of the business groups, we may take note of the fact that they "are divided politically and have conflicting views about strategy towards particular parties and also about the potential consequences of the support that they give to any of the major parties."[2]

2. Stanley A. Kochanek: *Business and Politics in India*, p. 4.

3. Owing to the absence of clear-cut ideological commitments, most of the groups feel interested in creating conditions of anarchy and lawlessness. They have less, rather very little, faith in the use of constitutional methods as adopted in democratic countries. It appears that they have no hesitation in indulging in activities of an extra-constitutional and uncostitutional nature. Strike is a favourite weapon in their hand that sometimes assumes the form of *bandh* (complete closure); demonstrations and long marches are undertaken. The groups may unhesitatingly take to the ways of arson and violence causing great damage to people's life and property. More than this, the path of frank militancy may display overtones of anti-nationalism. It may, therefore, be admitted that violence has come to occupy a special place in the political process of our country.[3]
4. The point of 'bi-culturalism' may also be discovered in the political behaviour of the groups. That is, while they try to operate on modern lines, they cannot give up their traditional mores or primordial loyalties. They may have their registered offices; they may openly or clandestinely finance political parties and try to induct men of their favour into the legislative and executive organs of the government, or they may adopt the way of keeping the bureaucrats in good humour by paying them in cash or kind. And yet they may not make themselves totally free from religious, communal, communitarian, regional, sub-regional or parochial attachments. Thus, the elements of tradition as well as modernity may be traced in the political behaviour of most of the groups playing their part in the political process of the country.
5. Above all, the role of the groups can be termed non-autonomous. They prefer to work under the leadership of some political party and be guided by its directions. The fear psychosis has its indelible effect so much so that while playing their definite role in the politics of the country they not only pretend to be neutral in political matters, they try to change the label of their political affiliations in response to the requirements of a rank opportunistic policy. It enables the ruling party to set the parameters within which the groups loyal to the parties in opposition have to operate.

---

3. Myron Weiner says that "economic outburst is unplanned and is analogous to the temper tantrum of a child whose violence is directed at all objects within reach." *The Politics of Scarcity*, p. 204.

Leading Interest Groups: As already pointed out, organised groups may be horizontally classified as business groups, labour groups, peasant groups, professional groups and the like. Almond has classified them as associational, non-associational, institutional and anomic groups. Some groups may also be termed as religious, communal, tribal, ethnic, linguistic, cultural and the like. For the sake of a convenient study, we may put them under these broad heads:

First of all, we may refer to a number of business groups or the organisations of the industrialists and capitalists. In the post-independence period we have three great organisations of the business class—Federation of the Indian Chambers of Commerce and Industry with its major constituents like Indian Merchants Chamber of Bombay, Indian Merchants Chamber of Calcutta and Southern Indian Chamber of Commerce of Madras; Associated Chamber of Commerce having its major constituents in Bengal Chamber of Commerce of Calcutta and its lobby (Central Commercial Organisation in Delhi), and All-India Manufacturers Organisation with its headquarters in Delhi and branches in Calcutta and Bombay.

The business groups contribute to the funds of the political parties with the hope of getting their support when they are in power. Pragmatism may be termed as the ideology of the Indian business groups. Most of the business groups support the party in power as their policy is to salute the rising sun. They also try to have good relations with important ministers and bureaucrats with obvious motives. They have their lobbies for this purpose in the Central and State legislatures. They also use press as an instrument for protecting and promoting their interests. In the last resort, they prefer to move the judiciary for this purpose. Any law or executive order going to harm their interests is challenged in the courts and then best legal brains are engaged to have it struck down in the name of being unconstitutional. In the main, they rely upon the support of the influential members of the ministry and bureaucracy.

The trade unions play the part of pressure groups of the working class. Here two points are noticeable. First, such organisations act like the labour wings of different political parties and, for this reason, the relationship between a trade union and a political party is invariably static. For instance, the Indian National Trade Union Congress is the labour wing of the Indian National Congress; the All-India Trade Union Congress is the labour wing of the CPI; the United Trade Union Congress is the labour wing of the

CPM; the Hind Mazdoor Parishad is the labour wing of the BJP; and the Socialists have their Hind Mazdoor Sabha. Second, the labour groups adopt the methods of strike, *gherao* (encirclement of the officer concerned for compelling him to meet their demands), *bandh* (complete strike), demonstrations, marches etc. and may go to the extreme of damaging public property by violent means. They fight for the security of employment, better emoluments, more bonus, housing and medical facilities, adequate compensation in the event of death or physical disability of a worker etc.

Then, we may look at the role of peasant groups or farmers' organisations. The Indian National Congress established its peasant wing (All-India Kisan Congress) that after some time became All-India Kisan Sabha. The Socialists set up their Hind Kisan Panchayat and the Communists have their United Kisan Sabha. All-India Kisan Sammelan was organised under the leadership of Chaudhry Charan Singh in 1978. Recently some more organisations have come up as Shetkari Sanghathan under Sharad Joshi and Bharatiya Kisan Union under Mahendra Singh Tikait. These peasant groups fight for their own interests like availability of seeds and fertiliser at a cheap rate, remunerative price for agricultural products, development of irrigation and agriculture, rural credit scheme, insurance of crops, supply of electricity at cheaper rates, representation of the farmers in all decision-making bodies of the government, waiver of loans given to small farmers, implementation of the scheme of land reforms etc. However, like the groups of workers, these groups of the farmers have not been able to assert effectively due to mass ignorance, casteist rivalries, inadequate financial resources, rampant factionalism etc.

Finally, we may refer to a very large number of professional and anomic groups. The lawyers have their bar associations. The medical practitioners have their Indian Medical Association and, also a large number of subsidiary organisations. The teachers have their own groups. So is the case with other professionals like engineers, technicians, artists etc. The students unions may also be included in this category. The Hindus have their religious organisations like Arya Samaj and Vishwa Hindu Parishad, the Muslims have their Jamaat-i-Islami; the Christians have their Roman Catholic Association; the Parsis have their Anjumun; the Shiromani Gurdwara Prabandhak Committee protects the interests of the Sikhs; the Republican Party of India fights for the interests of the depressed classes; the Jharkhand Mukti Morcha is an organisation of the tribals of Jharkhand.

In brief, Indian political system provides considerable freedom to different sectors of society to make demands upon its operators. The groups articulate their 'specific' interests and the political parties manage to aggregate them so that the process of accommodation of diverse interests remains undisturbed. But the unfortunate thing is that the decision-makers do not understand the gravity of the situation until the groups take matters to the streets and public peace is disturbed. A noted Indian sociologist. M.N. Srinivas, has correctly evaluated that in India a grievance has to mature into a street riot in order to attract the attention of those in power. It would not be an exaggeration to say that all classes of Indians everywhere have come to realise that the only way they can convince their rulers about the strength of their feeling is by resorting to the politics of street violence. However, it is the role of political elites whereby the problem of crisis management is solved. It is well said by Y.K. Malik: "Indeed, agitational methods have become an accepted part of the political process. Tension generated by the use of such agitational methods is often diffused by the politics of accommodation practised by the Indian elites."[4]

4. Malik: "Groups in Indian Politics: Interest Articulation" in Craig Baxter, Yogendra K. Malik. C.H. Kennedy and R.C. Oberst: *Government and Politics in South Asia*, p. 131.

Part - XIV

Bangladeshi Constitution

Power must be won by the people, whether it be through elections, or if elections are aborted, through the strength of an awakened people. The urge of the people of Bangladesh for autonomy cannot be denied. Bangladesh is now awake; it will give its verdict at the polls, if the polls are not frustrated. If the polls are frustrated, the people of Bangladesh will owe it to the millions who have died to make the supreme sacrifice of another million lives, if need be, so that we can live as a free people and so that Bangladesh can be the master of its own destiny.

—*Banglabandhu Sheikh Mujibur Rahman*

50

CONSTITUTION OF BANGLADESH

Pakistan came into being as a result of India's partition in August, 1947 with its two wings—West Pakistan and East Pakistan. The government of Pakistan with its capital at Karachi (later at Islamabad) committed a series of wrongs to annoy the people of East Pakistan. For instanoe, in 1952 Urdu was imposed on them as the national language. The Bengali people resented it and the problem could be solved two years after when Urdu and Bangla were declared as the joint national languages of the State of Pakistan. Apparently a federation, the rulers of West Pakistan virtually converted it into a unitary system and they flagrantly violated all norms, values and traditions of parliamentary democracy. Thus, the people of East Pakistan raised their demand for 'autonomy'. The crisis reached the final point when President Yahya Khan declined to appoint Sheikh Mujibur Rahman as the Prime Minister in spite of the fact that his Awami League had secured 162 out of 300 seats in the elections to the National Assembly held in December, 1970. He shocked the people by postponing the session of the National Assembly scheduled to be held on 1 March, 1971. His dilatory tactics in the form of prolonged negotiations with the Sheikh failed. On 25 March, Gen. Tikka Khan ordered his army units to arrest the Sheikh and suppress the movement by force. Thus, the leaders of the Awami League declared independence on 26 March, 1971. It "plunged the country into a bloody civil war. After about nine months of continuous armed struggle, the East Pakistanis, at the cost of millions of lives, liberated their motherland from the clutches of the forces of Pakistan. Thus, emerged the new nation-state of Bangladesh in December, 1971."[1]

1. M. Nazrul Islam: "Bangladesh" in J.C. Johari (ed.): *Governments and Politics of South Asia* (New Delhi: Sterling Publishers, 1991), p. 373.

Constitutionalism

From the Declaration of Independence on 26 March till the defeat of the army of Pakistan on 16 December, 1971, Bangladesh remained under the administration of a government-in-exile[2] run by the colleagues of the Sheikh like Syed Nazrul Islam as the Vice-President and Tajuddin Ahmed as the Prime Minister. As per the terms of the Declaration of Independence, the Constituent Assembly was formed consisting of 160 members of the then National Assembly of Pakistan and 288 members of the then Provincial Assembly of East Pakistan. It empowered the government of Bangladesh-in-exile to form a provisional government with Sheikh Mujibur Rahman as the President. However, as Sheikh was detained in the Lahore jail, Syed Nazrul Islam became the officiating President. After his release from the jail, the Sheikh came back to his country on 10 January, 1972 and then the seat of the government-in-exile was shifted to Dhaka. The next day he promulgated provisional Constitutional Order which replaced the presidential system by the parliamentary form of government. The Constituent Assembly took 10 months to frame the Constitution which was adopted on 16 December, 1972. However, the unfortunate part of the story is that the rulers of this country recklessly tampered with the provisions of this Constitution as a result of which the drama of switching over from presidential to parliamentary system and back occurred intermittently. Amendments after amendments "have not only destroyed the pristine qualities of the original 1972 Constitution but also posed a great threat to the spirit and stability and, above all, the future of democracy in Bangladesh."[3].

---

2. It was situated at Meherpur bordering Indian state of West Bengal and is now renamed as Mujibnagar.

3. Nazrul Islam, *op. cit.*, p. 385. He well observes: "Paradoxically, the framers of the 1972 Constitution were the members of the then Pakistan National Assembly who received no mandate from the electorate to frame a Constitution for an independent state of Bangladesh. On the other hand, these members of the Constituent Assembly of Bangladesh were entirely the supporters of only one party. *i.e.*, the Awami League who even did not desire to test popularity of their proposed Constitution at a referendum, and thereby obviously failed to reflect the national consensus on a most vital issue as the Constitution, the Basic Law of the Land." *Ibid.*, p. 384.

Some Important Statements

Jinnah and his followers did not seem to realise that geography was against them. These two regions (West Pakistan and East Pakistan) have no point of physical contact. People in these two countries are completely different from one another in every respect except only in religion. It is one of the greatest frauds on the people who suggest that religious affinity can unite areas which are geographically, economically, linguistically and culturally different.

—Maulana Abul Kalam Azad

(1) All powers in the Republic belong to the people, and their exercise on behalf of the people shall be effected only under, and by the authority of, this Constitution. (2) This Constitution is the solemn expression of the will of the people, the supreme law of the Republic, and if any other law is inconsistent with this Constitution and any other law, shall, to the extent of inconsistency be void.

—Art. 7 of the Constitution

The Constitution is not a document of fastidious dialectus, but a means of ordering the life of a people. It is an organic growth. ***—Justice Oliver Wendell Holmes***

Salient Features

The Constitution of Bangladesh adopted in 1972 and amended or modified from time to time has these salient features:

1. **An Enacted, Written and Rigid Constitution:** Like other countries of the world except Britain, this Constitution is the creation of a Constituent Assembly having representatives duly elected in December, 1970 for the then National Assembly of Pakistan and the then Provincial Assembly of East Pakistan. It is a long document having 153 Articles grouped into XI parts followed by Four Schedules. Moreover, by nature it is rigid, for the process of its amendment is very tough. A bill of Constitutional amendment must be passed by the Parliament by two-thirds majority of the whole house and then assented to by the President. In case such a bill covers the Preamble and the provisions of Articles 8, 48 and 56, the bill shall be presented to the President who shall give his assent to it in case it is approved by the people in a referendum by the majority of the total votes cast.[4]

4. Art. 8 contains Fundamental Principles of State Policy as absolute faith in the Almighty Allah, nationalism, democracy and socialism. Art. 48 is related to the election of the President. Art. 56 is related to the appointment of the Prime Minister and other Ministers.

2. **Enlightened Theocracy:** Like Pakistan, Bangladesh is a theocratic state. Islam is the official religion. It is specifically given that absolute trust and faith in the Almighty Allah shall be the basis of all actions of the State. At the same time, this Constitution pays deference to the principles of a secular order. It ensures freedom of conscience or faith and prohibits discrimination among the citizens on the basis of religion, caste and race. It is also given that a citizen cannot be forced to attend religious instructions or ceremonies in educational institutions if these are related to a religion other than his own. Nowhere it is mentioned that the President, the Prime Minister and his Ministers and other high functionaries of State must be Muslim despite the fact that Islam is the official religion. Art. 2 A says that in this Islamic republic, other religions may be practised in peace and harmony.
3. **Unitary System:** Like Britain and France, Bangladesh has unitary system. It means that all powers are vested in the Central Government. Art. 59 says that local government in every administrative unit of the country shall be entrusted to bodies consisting of persons elected according to the law of Parliament. The law of Parliament may empower such bodies to manage affairs relating to administration and work of public officers, maintenance of public order, preparation and implementation of plans relating to public services and economic development, including power to impose taxes for local purposes, to prepare their budgets and maintain their funds. The units of local government operate under the control of the Central Government. Hence, they do not enjoy autonomy that is given to the units of a federation.[5]
4. **Parliamentary Form of Government:** Like Britain and India, Bangladesh has parliamentary form of government. The President is the Head of the Republic who holds nominal authority. The real authority is vested in the Prime Minister and his Council of Ministers collectively responsible to the Parliament. Thus, while the President is the 'dignified executive', Prime Minister is the head of the 'efficient executive'. All executive actions of the Government are done in the name of the President and he makes rules for the

5. At present the country is divided into seven administrative divisions (each named after their divisional headquarters) which are themselves subdivided into 64 administrative districts, each of which is further sub-divided into sub-districts.

allocation and transaction of the business of the Government. However, the installation of a non-party care-taker government is a peculiar feature. After the dissolution of the Parliament, the administration of the country shall be in the hands of a care-taker government with Chief Justice as the Chief Adviser and at the most ten Advisers appointed by the President who shall be non-partymen and who shall be collectively responsible to the President. It shall function till the new Prime Minister enters upon his office after the constitution of Parliament.

5. **Fundamental Rights:** Part III of the Constitution has a long list of fundamental rights having a mandatory character. It may be appreciated as the spirit or conscience of the fundamental law of the land. Equality before law has been ensured and discrimination among the citizens on the grounds of religion, race, caste, sex and place of birth has been prohibited. In matters of public employments, equality of opportunity has been guaranteed and here again discrimination among the citizens on various grounds has been prohibited. Personal liberty has been secured. Thus, nobody can be arrested or detained without a cause and that his case shall be tried openly in a competent court. All citizens enjoy freedoms of speech and expression, movement throughout the country, holding peaceful assembly, and carrying on any trade or profession. However, all liberties are subject to reasonable restrictions imposed by the state in the name of national security, public morality, contempt of court and the like. Right to property has been guaranteed, but the state may nationalise anybody's property by the authority of law for a public purpose and on the payment of fair compensation. Right to constitutional remedies has also been guaranteed. Hence, the aggrieved person may move the High Court Division of the Supreme Court for the protection of his or its fundamental rights.

6. **Fundamental Principles of State Policy:** Part II of the Constitution has a long list of guiding or directive principles which, though judicially non-enforceable, are to be treated by the state as nevertheless fundamental in the governance of the country. The principles of absolute trust and faith in the Almighty Allah, nationalism, democracy and socialism meaning economic and social justice together with their implications are set out in this chapter. It is expected that the state shall implement these principles to achieve the ideals of social and economic justice. Effective arrangements

shall be made by the state for the establishment of democracy, protection of human rights, participation of women in national life, emancipation of workers and peasants, rural development and agricultural revolution, free and compulsory education, public health and morality, dignity of labour, separation of executive and judiciary, preservation of national culture, protection of the monuments of national and historical importance, and promotion of international peace, security and solidarity. A comparative study of Part II and Part III of the Constitution leaves an impression that while fundamental rights establish a liberal-democratic order, the aim of the fundamental principles is to establish social and economic democracy in the country.

7. **Unicameralism:** Like China, Bangladesh has a unicameral national legislature. The Parliament or the House of the Nation (Jatiyo Sangsad) has 300 members elected directly by the voters of the country and 45 women members elected by the members of the House on the basis of proportional representation. It has a tenure of five years, but the President may dissolve it prematurely. The legislative powers of the Republic are vested in it. The President summons its sessions; he prorogues the session and may dissolve the House. It elects its Speaker and Deputy Speaker. Apart from performing legislative functions, it exercises its control over the Council of Ministers. It may make a law for the appointment of Ombudsman to check corruption and abuse of authority by any public servant.

8. **Judicial Review:** Like the United States and India, Bangladesh has a Supreme Court with Appellate Division and High Court Division. It has a Chief Justice and some judges appointed by the President. It is the highest Court of the country and has the power of judicial review. An aggrived person may move the High Court Division for the protection of his or its fundamental rights. Any law or action of the state may be challenged on the ground of unconstitutionality. The Court shall hear the petition and then may strike down the impugned law or order of the state, in part or full, on the ground of being inconsistent with the provisions of the Constitution. The Appellate Division may review a judgment or order pronounced by the High Court Division.

9. **Emergency Provisions:** If the President is satisfied that a grave emergency exists in which the security or economic life of the country

is threatened by war, or external aggression, or internal disturbances, he may issue a proclamation of emergency. It can be done on the recommendation of the Prime Minister and may continue for 120 days. The period may be extended by a resolution of Parliament. In case the Parliament is already dissolved, or it is dissolved during the period of 120 days, the emergency may continue till 30 days after the session of the new Parliament begins. Such a proclamation may be made when the actual situation exists or there is imminent danger thereof. During the period of emergency the fundamental rights of the citizens, including right to move the Court, may be suspended. Even the proceedings pending in any Court for the enforcement of such rights shall remain suspended during the period of emergency. These abnormal provisions have been incorporated to deal with a critical situation. As the President shall act on the written advice of the Prime Minister, there is nothing to feel afraid of for the obvious reason that the Cabinet is responsible to the Parliament.

10. **Ombudsman:** Every country is ridden with the problem of corruption or abuse of office by the functionaries of the state. So the institution of Ombudsman is established. The Constitution of Bangladesh has such a provision (Art. 77). The Ombudsman shall be appointed by the President and shall act according to the law of Parliament. He shall investigate any action taken by a Ministry, a public officer, or a statutory public authority. He shall also prepare an annual report concerning the dischage of his functions that shall be laid before the Parliament.

A look at the salient features of this Constitution leaves an impression that all arrangements have been made to establish liberal-democratic order in the country whose people valiantly fought against the 'internal colonialism' of Pakistan and could achieve emancipation at the cost of great sacrifices.[6] Now a notable development as taken place. The XV amendment (2011) resrors secular features of this constitution.

6. The term 'internal colonialism' generally refers to the process of exploitation and domination of one ethnic group by another within the same country. Z.R. Khan: "Leadership, Parties and Politics in Bangladesh" in *Western. Political Quarterly*, Vol. 29, No. 2, 1976, p. 102.

Fundamental Principles of State Policy

Some lofty principles of state policy, first enshrined in the Irish Constitution of 1937 and then in the Indian Constitution of 1949, have their significance place in the Constitution of Bangladesh of 1972. These principles are of a non-justiciable nature, though it is expected that the state shall regard them as fundamental in the governance of the country. As far as possible, such principles shall be honoured by the state in the making of laws, implementation of executive decrees and the interpretation of the Constitution. These principles may be enumerated as under:

1. Absolute trust and faith in the Almighty Allah, nationalism, democracy and socialism signifying economic and social justice together with their implications,
2. Promotion of the institutions of local government composed of the representatives of the areas concerned and with special representation to peasants, workers and women,
3. Participation of women in all spheres of national life,
4. A democratic setup guaranteeing human rights and freedoms, with effective participation of the people through their elected representatives in administration at all levels,
5. Ownership and control of the instruments and the means of production and distribution in the form of nationalised public sector, cooperative sector and private sector,
6. Emancipation of the toiling masses, the peasants, the workers and backward sections of the people from all forms of exploitation,
7. Attainment of a constant increase of productive forces and a steady improvement in the material and cultural standards of living of the people through planning so as to meet the basic necessities of life, right to work at a reasonable wage, and right to social security,
8. Radical transformation in the rural areas through the promotion of agricultural revolution, rural electrification, development or cottage industries and public health,
9. Free and compulsory education to all children catering to the needs of the society,
10. Improvement of public health, prohibition of alcoholic drinks and prevention of prostitution and gambling,
11. Equality of opportunity to all citizens so as to ensure equitable, distribution of wealth and uniform level of economic development,
12. Dignity of physical and intellectual labour, prohibition of enjoying

unearned incomes, and creation of humane conditions of work for the expression of creative endeavour and of human personality,

13. Duty of every citizen to abide by the Constitution and observe law to maintain discipline, to perform public duties and to protect public property,
14. Separation of judiciary from the executive organs of the state,
15. Adoption of measures to conserve the cultural traditions and heritage of the people, to foster and improve the national language, literature and arts,
16. Protection of national monuments and objects and places of special artistic or historic importance, and
17. Promotion of international peace, security and solidarity, respect for national sovereignty and equality, non-interference in the internal affairs of other states, pacific settlement of international disputes, respect for international law and the Charter of the United Nations, strengthening fraternal relations among Muslim countries based on Islamic solidarity.

Quite admirable is the list of such fundamental principles of state policy which make Bangladesh a democratic and social welfare state. Part II of the Constitution having a long list of such high ideals may be lauded as the charter of social, economic and political democracy in this country. Full respect has been shown by the authors of the Constitution to the ideals of a liberal-democratic order. However, a critic may not appreciate clause (2) of Art. 25 that desires strengthening of relations with Muslim countries based on Islamic solidarity.

Fundamental Rights

Part III of the Constitution has a special significance of its own. It contains a long list of fundamental rights having a mandatory character. No law can prevail in this country that is inconsistent with the provisions of this Part. The Supreme Court is vested with the power of judicial review. Hence, any law of the state can be declared void by the High Court Division to the extent of being inconsistent with the fundamental rights. It has also been made clear in Art. 26 that it shall not apply to a law of constitutional amendment made under Art. 142 of the Constitution. The fundamental rights of the citizens may be enumerated as under:

1. All citizens are equal before law and are entitled to equal protection of law.

2. The state shall not discriminate against citizens on the grounds of religion, race, caste, sex, or place of birth in access to any place of public entertainment or resort, or admission to educational institutions. However, the state may make special provisions for the welfare and advancement of women, children and backward sections of the society.
3. Equality of opportunity has been guaranteed to all citizens in respect of recruitment to public services and no discrimination may be made on the gounds of religion, race, caste, sex, or place of birth. However, the state may make special provisions for the welfare and advancement of the backward sections of the citizens so as to give them adequate representation in the services of the republic, or for certain religious and denominational institutions. The state may also make discrimination on the basis of sex if it is warranted by nature.
4. No citizen, without the approval of the President, can accept any title, honour, award or decoration from any foreign state.
5. No action detrimental to the life, liberty, body, reputation, or property of any citizen or person shall be taken except in accordance with law.
6. No person can be arrested or detained without a cause. If he is arrested under a law in force as that time, he shall be informed of the cause and be produced before the nearest magistrate within twenty-four working hours. He shall have the right to defend himself through his lawyer. The state may make a law of preventive detention. If a person is arrested under this law, he may be put under detention for a period of six months, but the period may be extended on the recommendation of the Advisory Board consisting of three persons, two of them must be qualified to be appointed as the judge of the Supreme Court and one senior officer of the Government.
7. All forms of forced labour are prohibited. It shall not apply to the criminals in jail or in a situation required by law for a public purpose.
8. Personal liberty has been guaranteed. Hence, a person can be arrested under a law in force at the time of the commission of the offence; he cannot be punished for the same offence more than once; he cannot be forced to be a witness against himself; he cannot be subjected to cruel, inhuman or degrading punishment; and the case can be decided by an independent and competent court in an open and fair trial.

9. Every citizen has the freedom to reside, settle and move in the country and to leave or re-enter the country subject to any reasonable restrictions imposed by the state in the public interest.
10. Every citizen has the right to assemble and participate in public meetings and processions peacefully and without arms subject to any restriction imposed by law in the interests of public order and public health.
11. Every citizen has the freedom to form associations or unions subject to the restriction imposed by law in the interests or morality or public order.
12. Freedom of thought and conscience has been guaranteed. It also covers freedom of speech and expression and of the press. The state may impose reasonable restrictions in the name of national security, friendly relations with states, public order, decency, morality, contempt of court, defamation or incitement to an offence.
13. Every citizen has the freedom to do any trade, business, or occupation subject to the conditions laid down by the law of the state.
14. Subject to law, public order and morality, every citizen has the right to profess, practise and propagate a religion of his choice and to establish and maintain religious institutions. In educational institutions, no person can be forced to take part in instructions or ceremonies of a religion other than his own.
15. Every citizen has the freedom to keep, sell, transfer, or dispose of his property subject to any restriction imposed by the law of the state. Private property may be nationalised by the state in the public interest by the authority of law and on the payment of fair compensation.
16. Protection of home and correspondence and other means of communication is also guaranteed, but the state may impose restrictions in the interests of national security, public order, morality and public health.
17. For the protection of his fundamental rights, a citizen may move the High Court Division of the Supreme Court. The Parliament may make a law to authorise any other Court for this purpose without prejudice to the powers of the High Court Division.
18. The above provisions shall not apply to any provision of a disciplinary law relating to the members of a disciplined force for the purpose of ensuring proper discharge of their duties or the maintenance of discipline in that force.

19. The Parliament may make a law providing for indemnity in the case of a person in Government service, or any other person in respect of an act done by him in connection with the national liberation struggle, or the maintenance or restoration of the order in any part of the country, or validate any sentence passed, punishment inflicted, forfeiture ordered, or other act done in such area,
20. No law providing for any of the following matters shall be deemed to be void on the ground that it is inconsistent with, or takes away, or abridges any of the rights guaranteed by this Part of Constitution
    (*a*) compulsory acquisition, nationalisation, or requisition of any property, or the control or management thereof whether temporarily or permanently;
    (*b*) compulsory amalgamation of bodies carrying on commercial or other undertakings;
    (*c*) extinction, modification, restriction or regulation of the rights of directors, managers, agents or officers of such bodies, or of the voting rights of the persons owning shares or stocks (in whatever form) therein;
    (*d*) extinction, modification, restriction or regulation or rights of search for, or own minerals or mineral oil;
    (*e*) carrying on by the Government or by a corporation owned, controlled or managed by the government of any trade, business, industry or service to the exclusion of complete or partial or other persons, or
    (*f*) extinction, modification, restriction or regulation of any right to property, any right in respect of a profession, occupation, trade or business or the rights of employers or employees in any statutory public authority, or in any commercial or industrial undertaking.

Such a long list of fundamental rights guarantees and protects civil, political and economic freedoms of the citizens. The notable feature is that, despite being a theocratic state, the Constitution ensures freedom of conscience or faith and prohibits discrimination among the citizens on the grounds of religion, caste and race. In educational institutions nobody can be compelled to attend religious instructions or ceremonies of a different faith. Above all, right to constitutional remedies has been provided that places the judiciary in the capacity of the custodian of the fundamental law of the land.

51

STATE STRUCTURE

The political system of Bangladesh has all the trappings of a liberal-democratic order without deep and strong foundations. Banglabandhu Sheikh Mujib established a democratic system in 1972 and he subverted it three years after. In the general elections held in March, 1973, his Awami League secured 292 out of 300 seats in the Parliament. So he formed the government. Unfortunately, the conditions of civil war fomented by the Islamic fundamentalists and the Maoists forced him to declare 'emergency' in December, 1974. The fundamental rights of the citizens were suspended. In January, 1975 he replaced the parliamentary system by the presidential system and thereby he assumed the powers of the President. He banned all political parties and put the country under the iron hold of his own party renamed as Bangladesh Krishak Shramik Awami League (BAKSAL). After his assassination on 15 August, 1975, Ziaur Rahman established his fascists rule. He formed his Bangladesh Nationalist Party. He was assassinated on 31 May 1981 and his regime was forced out of power in March, 1982. Now Gen. Ershad established his fascist rule. He suspended the Constitution and put a ban on all political parties. Like his predecessors, he formed his Jatiyo Party in January, 1986. This military rule came to an end on 10 November, 1986. The suspended Constitution was revived. Once again, parliamentary system was restored. It shows that the political system of this country has witnessed frequent enactment of the drama of switching over from presidential system to parliamentary system and back resulting in the weakening of the democratic traditions under the rule of the leaders, both civilian and military, involved in the game of competitive authoritarianism.[1]

---

1. The term 'competitive authoritarianism' signifies a hybrid political regime displaying the trappings of democracy, especially elections, but not the substance. See Steven Levitsky and Lucan A. Way: "The Rise of Competitive Authoritarianism" in Mark Kesselman and Joel Krieger (eds.): *Readings in Comparative Politics* (Boston: Houghton Mifflin Company, 2006), p. 60.

President

Since Bangladesh has parliamentary form of government, the President is the ceremonial head of the Republic. He holds nominal authority as he is bound to act in accordance with the advice of his Ministers. He is elected by the members of Parliament in accordance with law. He must have three qualifications. First, he is a citizen of Bangladesh. Second, he has completed the age of 35 years. Third, he is qualified to be a member of the Parliament and that he has not been removed by the process of impeachment. He holds office for a term of five years from the date on which he enters upon his office. He shall continue to hold his office until his successor enters upon notwithstanding the expiration of his term. Moreover, like the United States, a person cannot have more than two terms. He may relinquish his office by tendering his resignation to the Speaker.

The President may be removed by the process of impeachment on the charge of violation of the Constitution or doing an act of grave misconduct. He may also be removed on the charge of physical or mental incapacity. In both the cases the procedure is a bit different. In case he is charged with violation of the Constitution or commission of an act of grave misconduct, the motion must be submitted to the Speaker having signatures of more than half of the total strength of Parliament. The motion shall be taken up for discussion at least 14 but not later than 30 days after the notice is so delivered. If the House is not in session, the Speaker may summon it. The Parliament may refer the matter for investigation to some Court or tribunal or any other body. The President shall have the right to defend his case either personally or through his representative. For the passage of such a motion, two-thirds majority of the whole House is required. If the office falls vacant on account of the passing of such a resolution, the Speaker shall act in the officiating capacity.

In the case of the charge of physical or mental incapacity, the motion must be signed by the absolute majority of the members of the House. If such a motion is presented to the Speaker, he shall forthwith summon the Parliament to discuss it. A resolution passed by the House shall empower the Speaker to set up a Medical Board and ask the President to appear before it within 10 days of the appointment of such a Board. The Board is required to submit its report within seven days. The President shall have the right to represent his case before this Board. After receiving the report of the Board, the Parliament may remove he President by passing a resolution by two-thirds majority of the whole House. If the office of the President falls vacant for any reason, the Speaker shall officiate until the new President enters upon his office.

Manifold are the functions and powers of the President. In the executive sphere, his functions and powers are:

1. He appoints the Prime Minister and other ministers on the recommendation of the Prime Minister. He appoints high functionaries of state like Chief Justice and other Judges of the Supreme Court, Chief Adviser and other Advisers of the Non-party Care-taker Government, Attorney-General, Chairman and other members of the Public Service Commission, Chairman and members of the Election Commission etc.
2. All administration is conducted in his name and he makes rules for the allocation and transaction of government business.
3. As head of the state, he maintains foreign relations. For this sake, he appoints his ambassadors to foreign countries and accepts the credentials of foreign envoys.
4. He is the Supreme Commander of the defence forces. As such, he appoints the chiefs of the armed forces.
5. By his prerogative of mercy, he may grant pardons, reprieves and respites and to remit, suspend or commute any sentence passed by any Court, tribunal or other authority.
6. If he is satisfied that a grave situation exists in which the security or economic life of the country or any part thereof is threatened by war or external aggression or internal disturbances, he may issue a proclamation of emergency.
7. He enjoys certain immunities. For instance, he shall not be answerable to any Court for anything done or omitted by him in the exercise of his functions. During his term of office, no criminal proceedings shall be instituted against him in any Court.

In the legislative sphere, his functions and powers may be enumerated as under:

1. He summons and prorogues the session of Parliament and may dissolve it at any time.
2. He may address the Parliament and may send messages to it. The first session of the Parliament after a general election and the first session of a new year begins with his inaugural address.

3. A bill passed by the Parliament requires his assent to it for having its place on the statute book. If a bill is submitted to him, he must take action on it within 15 days. In the case of a bill of constitutional amendment, he shall refer the matter to the verdict of people if it is related to the Preamble or Articles 8, 48, or 56 and then give his assent if it is approved in a referendum. He cannot exercise his veto power if it is a money bill. In the case of a non-money bill, he may assent to it, or may return it to the Parliament for reconsideration. If such a bill is passed by the Parliament by its absolute majority of the members, he must assent to it within seven days irrespective of the fact that his recommendations were honoured by the Parliament or not.
4. If the Parliament is not in session or it is dissolved and the situation so demands, he may promulgate an ordinance which shall have the force of law and shall remain in force upto 30 days beginning from the date of the session of Parliament.

The President has some financial powers. A money bill can be introduced in the Parliament with his recommendation. No demand for a grant shall be made except on the recommendation of the President.

The President has a number of other functions and powers which may be enumerated as under:

1. Until provision is made by the Parliament, the President may, after consultation with the Speaker, make rules regulating the recruitment and condition of service of persons appointed to the Secretariat of the Parliament which shall be regularised by a law of Parliament.
2. On receiving information from any person or source about the physical or mental incapacity of a judge of the Supreme Court or an act of gross misconduct done by him, the President may ask the Supreme Judicial Council to inquire into the matter and then take action on its report.
3. The President, in consultation with the Chief Justice, shall assign the area in relation to which each permanent bench of the High Court shall have its jurisdiction.
4. Subject to any law made by the Parliament, the Supreme Court may, with the approval of the President, make rules for regulating the practice and procedure of each Division of the Supreme Court and of any Court subordinate to it.

5. In case the office of the Auditor-General falls vacant for any reason, he may appoint some person qualified for the post to act in the officiating capacity.
6. The President may consult the Public Service Commission in matters relating to the appointments and promotions of public servants and their conditions of service.
7. Important functionaries of state like Comptroller and Auditor-General and Public Service Commission submit their annual report to the President and he causes them to be laid before the Parliament along with the statement of actions taken thereon.

The fact stands out that the President is the ceremonial head of the Republic and, as such, he is the 'dominant figure of the present Constitution and the keystone of the whole system of government.'[2]

Prime Minister and Cabinet

As pointed out above, Bangladesh has parliamentary form of government in which the President is the head of the State, the Prime Minister is the head of the Government. The President appoints the Prime Minister. He appoints other ministers on the advice of the Prime Minister. There is no ceiling on the size of the Cabinet. While all executive actions are taken in the name of the President, the real authority is vested in the Cabinet headed by the Prime Minister. It is given that not less than nine-tenths of the Ministers shall be appointed from among the members of Parliament and not more than one-tenth of them may be chosen from among persons qualified for election as members of Parliament. The President shall appoint a person as the Prime Minister who is a member of Parliament and who commands support of the majority of the members of Parliament. It is obvious that the President shall observe the tradition of inviting the leader of the majority party to form the government that has been converted into a written rule of the Constitution. The Cabinet is collectively responsible to the Parliament.

The Prime Minister may remain in office so long as he is a member of the Parliament and enjoys the support of the majority of the members of the House. He may submit his resignation to the President at any time. He

2. M. Nazrul Islam, *op. cit.*, p. 387.

shall continue to be in office until his successor enters upon. If the Prime Minister resigns and the President finds no chances of forming the alternative government, he may dissolve the Parliament. Formally, the ministers remain in office during the pleasure of the President. Actually, all ministers remain in office during the pleasure of the Prime Minister, for he may ask any minister to resign, and in case he does not oblige, he may advise the President to terminate his appointment.

The Constitution says nothing about the functions and powers of the Cabinet headed by the Prime Minister. However, a student of this subject may draw inferences from the text of various provisions as well and may elaborate them in the light of the traditions of other countries having parliamentary form of government. Hence, the functions and powers of the Cabinet may be enumerated as under:

1. It formulates national policy covering internal and external spheres and conducts administration accordingly.
2. The entire administration is conducted in the name of the President, but, in fact, it is done according to the decisions and advices of the Cabinet.
3. The Prime Minister advises the President to summon the session of the Parliament and read out the inaugural address prepared by the Cabinet.
4. The Cabinet moves a bill in the Parliament that is passed and becomes an act after receiving the assent of the President. The ministers know that the defeat of an official bill in the House amounts to the passing of a motion of no-confidence.
5. If very critical situation arises, the Cabinet may advise the President to make a proclamation of emergency. On the advice of the Cabinet, the President may revoke it as well.
6. All important appointments are made by the President on the advice of the Cabinet.
7. It is the duty of the Prime Minister to keep the President informed abort matters of domestic and foreign policy and submit for the consideration of the Cabinet any matter referred to him by the President.

It shows that the Prime Minister and his Cabinet constitute the real executive. As the head of this body, the Prime Minister holds the most important position so much so that he/she may become the working head of the State apart from being the head of the Government. However, it is possible if the Prime Minister enjoys the support of the majority in the House as well as of his or her party.

Non-Party Care-Taker Government

The provision of having a non-party care-taker government in really a distinctive feature of this Constitution. One may say that it is a novel arrangement. If the Parliament is dissolved by the President, or it stands dissolved by the expiration of its term, it shall be set up by the President within 15 days. It shall consist of a Chief Adviser and not more than 10 Advisers to be appointed by the President. The President shall appoint as Chief Adviser the person who among the retired Chief Justices of as Bangladesh retired last and, in case he declines the offer, or is not available for any reason, then the predecessor of the retired Chief Justice shall be picked up. It is obvious that this post shall be given to the retired Chief Justice of the Supreme Court or to a judge of the retired Appellate Division if no retired Chief Justice is available. In case no such person is available, then the President shall appoint any distinguished citizen qualified to be a judge of the Supreme Court after consultation with the leaders of major political parties. Finally, if no such person is available even after such a consultation with major political parties, the President himself shall hold the post of Chief Adviser.

The President shall appoint a number of Advisers from among the persons qualified to be the member of Parliament who are not the members of any political party or any organisation affiliated to any political party, and are not above 72 years of age. The Advisers shall be appointed on the advice of the Chief Adviser. They shall be collectively responsible to the President. Any Adviser may tender his resignation to the President. The Chief Adviser shall have the rank of the Prime Minister and other advisers shall have the rank of the ministers. This non-party care-taker government shall perform the functions of an interim government and shall stand dissolved when the new Prime Minister enters upon his office after the

Some Important Statements

Authoritarianism is a political system in which a small group of individuals exercises power over the state without being constitutionally responsible to the public. All decisions flow from the ruler, unfettered by political institutions of any sort.

—Patrick O'Neil

The position of the Parliament of Bangladesh is not comparable to the Parliament of Great Britain or the Congress of the United States of America. The supremacy of the legislature obviously testifies supremacy of the people. The sovereign will of the people can never be materialised in the absence of a powerful legislature.

—Prof. M. Nazrul Islam

Both Parliamentary and Presidential systems have advantages which deserve continuance, and each can be improved by taking advantage of the practices which have proved successful in the other. Recent tendencies are towards the adoption of the essential features of the Cabinet system; at the same time, a place is made for an executive with certain independent powers. *—Prof. R.G. Gettell*

election. Apart from performing routine functions of a provisional government, it shall render full assistance to the Election Commission for the holding of elections peacefully, fairly and impartially.

Parliament (House of the Nation)

The legislative powers of the Republic have been vested in the Parliament (Jatiyo Sangsad) which by its law may delegate its powers to any person or authority to issue orders or promulgate rules and regulations having the force of law. It shall consist of 300 members to be elected in accordance with law from single territorial constituencies by direct election. Then, 45 seats have been allotted to the women members who shall be elected by the members of Parliament on the basis of proportional representation with single transferable vote system. Women may have their place in the category of 300 members as well elected directly by the voters of the country.

A member of Parliament must be a citizen of Bangladesh and be above 25 years of age. A person shall be disqualified for election or for being a member of the Parliament if he is declared of unsound mind by a competent Court, or is an undischarged insolvent, or acquires the citizenship of a foreign state, or is convicted in a criminal case for at least two years unless a period of five years has elapsed since his release from the jail, or he holds an office of profit in the service of the Republic, or is disqualified under any law of Parliament. The offices of the President, the Prime Minister and Ministers have been exempted. In case the membership of a person is disputed with regard to his qualifications, the matter shall be decided by the Election Commission. A person may lose the membership of the House in case he does not take the oath within 90 days of the commencement of the session, or remains absent for 90 consecutive days without having the leave of the House, or tenders his resignation to the Speaker.

The Constitution has some important provisions to check the malady of political defections. A person shall forfeit the membership of Parliament in case he leaves the party on whose ticket he is elected, or he acts in the House against the directions of that party. An independent member may join any political party and then he shall be taken as elected on the ticket of that party. If, at any time, a question arises about the leadership of the Parliamentary party of a political party, the Speaker within seven days of being informed of it in writing by a person claiming leadership of the majority of the members of that party in Parliament, convene a meeting of all the MPs of that party according to Rules of Procedure and decide the matter by the division of votes. In case any member does not comply with the direction of the leadership so determined, he shall be taken as a defector and thereby lose his seat in the House.

A person can contest elections from not more than two constituencies. In case he is elected from both, he must abandon one seat and write a letter to this effect to the Chief Election Commissioner so that one of the two seats captured by him is declared vacant. In case he fails to deliver such information within 30 days of his election, his both seats shall be declared as vacant.

The President shall summon the session of the Parliament within 30 days after the declaration of results. A gap of not more than 60 days should occur between two sessions of Parliament. The normal term of the Parliament is of five years to be computed from the date of its first sitting. In case emergency is declared on account of the condition of war, the life of the House may be extended by a law of Parliament for one year at a time. But it cannot go beyond six months after the termination of emergency. An important point to be noted here is that the President may summon a special session of the dissolved Parliament in case a war breaks out and the emergency is declared. The first session of the House after a general election and the first session of a new year shall begin with the inaugural address of the President.

The House elects its Speaker and Deputy Speaker by absolute majority of the members and may remove them by the same majority. The procedure of Parliament shall be regulated by rules of procedure made by it. Presence of at least 60 members is required to hold the session. In the absence of quorum, the Speaker may adjourn the session. A Minister can speak in the House, but he cannot vote if he is not a member. The Speaker or Deputy Speaker can vote to break a tie. The Parliament acts with the help of many committees like Public Accounts Committee, Privileges Committee and a number of Standing Committees.

The functions and powers of the Parliament may be enumerated as under:

1. It makes laws and may amend or repeal any law in force. A bill must be passed by the House by absolute majority of the members. In case a bill is returned by the President for reconsideration, the House may pass it again by the same majority by honouring the recommendations of the President or not.
2. A non-money bill may be introduced by a Minister or by any member of the House, but a money bill can be introduced only by a Minister as it requires prior recommendation of the President.
3. The Parliament exercises its control over the Government. The Prime Minister with his Cabinet is collectively responsible to the House.
4. On the charge of wilful violation of the Constitution, or physical and mental incapacity, the Parliament may remove the President by following the process of impeachment. Such a motion must be supported by absolute majority of the House and after debate must be adopted by two-thirds majority of the whole House.
5. In case the President declares a state of emergency, its duration may be extended by the Parliament. In the event of war, the Parliament may extend its life by making a law to this effect for one year at a time.
6. The Parliament elects its Speaker and Deputy Speaker by absolute majority and may remove them also by passing a resolution by the same majority.
7. War can be declared and the Republic may participate in it with the assent of the Parliament.
8. Parliament may make a law to determine the boundaries of the republic, including the limits of territorial waters.

Composition of Parliament (2009)

Political Parties	*Seats*
1. Bangladesh Awami League	230
2. Bangladesh Nationalist Party (Jatiyobadi Dal)	29
3. Jatiyo Party	27
4. Jamaat-i-Islamic Bangladesh	2
5. Jatiyo Samajtantrik Dal	3
6. Workers Party of Bangladesh	2
7. Bangladesh Jatiyo Party	1
8. Liberal Democratic Party	1
9. Independents	4
10. Vacant	1
Total	300

Based on the results of general elections held in December, 2008. *Europa World Year-Book* (London: Routledge, 2010), Vol. I, p. 800

It may, however, be pointed out that the Parliament is not a powerful body in view of the fact that its authority is limited by the dominant role of the executive on the one side and by the system of judicial review on the other. In every country with a parliamentary system, the executive has unsurped the domain of the legislature. In a country with a powerful judiciary, that area has been further circumscribed by the role of active judiciary.

Judiciary

Chapter I of Part VI contains provisions relating to Judiciary with Supreme Court at the apex and subordinate Courts and administrative tribunals at the local level of government. The Supreme Court has Appellate Division and High Court Division. It shall have a Chief Justice and some Judges whose number shall be determined by an order of the President. The Chief Justice and the Judges appointed to the Appellate Division shall sit only in that Division, and the other Judges shall sit in the High Court Division. All the Judges, including the Chief Justice, shall be independent in the exercise of their judicial functions. The President shall appoint the Chief Justice and other Judges. A Judge must possess these qualifications: (i) He is a citizen of Bangladesh. (ii) He has been an advocate of at least 10 years standing in the Supreme Court, or he has held a judicial office in Bangladesh for at least 10 years, and that he possesses some other qualifications laid down in a law of Parliament.

The Judges retire on attaining the age of 67 years. A Judge may tender his resignation to the President at any time. He may be removed from office on some charge by an order of the President on the report of the Supreme Judicial Council consisting of the Chief Justice and two senior Judges of the Supreme Court. The functions of this body shall be to prescribe a code of conduct to be observed by the Judges, and to inquire into the capacity or conduct of a Judge or of any other officer having the status or rank of a Judge. The President shall ask this body to inquire if he receives a complaint or information from some source that a particular judge is physically or mentally unfit to do his job, or is involved in some act of gross misconduct.

In case the office of the Chief Justice is vacant for any reason, the President shall appoint the senior-most Judge of the Appellate Division to officiate. He may also appoint *ad hoo* Judges for a period of not more than two years. He may also authorise the Judges of the High Court Division to sit in the Appellate Division for a temporary period. A qualified person appointed as an *ad hoc* Judge may be appointed as a regular Judge by the President. The Chief Justice and a Judge of the Appellate Division cannot plead a case in any Court after retirement or removal from service. But a retired or removed Judge of the High Court Division may plead a case before the Appellate Division.

The seat of the Supreme Court shall be in the capital (Dhaka). The Judges of the High Court Division shall sit at the permanent seat of the Supreme Court and also at the seats of its permanent benches at Barisal, Chittagong, Comilla, Jessore, Rangpur and Sylhet. The Chief Justice may set up some other benches as well. The Chief Justice may determine the number of judges of each bench and may transfer a judge from one bench to another bench. The jurisdiction of each such bench shall be determined by the President in consultation with the Chief Justice.

The two Divisions of the Supreme Court have different jurisdictions. The High Court Division shall have such original, appellate and other jurisdictions as defined in the Constitution or in a law of Parliament. On the application of an aggrieved party, it may issue such orders or directions to any person or authority, including a functionary of the state, as may be appropriate for the enforcement of fundamental rights. It may issue prerogative writs in the nature of *habeas corpus, mandamus* and *prohibition* for giving relief to the aggrieved party. In case it is feared that the order of the Court may prejudice or interfere with the development programme or work of the State or in any way be harmful to the public interest, the Court shall give an opportunity to the Attorney-General to place his arguments before it takes any decision. The Appellate Division has the power to hear appeals in a matter decided by the High Court Division. It shall have the power to issue decrees, orders, directions or writs as may be necessary for doing complete justice. It may review its own judgments. This Division has also the power to give its advice to the President if it is sought by him on a question of law or a matter of public importance. The Supreme Court is also a Court of record. Its judgments are preserved and taken as precedents that must be followed by all other Courts of the country. Subject to the provisions of a law of Parliament, it has the power to make an order for the investigation of or punishment for any contempt of itself.

If studied from a critical viewpoint, it may be commented that the Supreme Court of Bangladesh is not a powerful body like its American and Indian counterparts despite the fact that the Constitution has ensured independence of judiciary. It has to exercise its powers in a way as provided in the Constitution as well as by a law of Parliament. The High Court Division may strike down a law if it is inconsistent with the provisions of Part III of the Constitution of course, but it cannot look into the competence of the Parliament in respect of making a law. The American Supreme Court may invoke the argument of 'due process of law' and the Indian Supreme Court may invoke the doctrine of 'competence'. But the case of the Supreme Court of Bangladesh is different. The Court cannot exercise its power of judicial review in relation to the enforcement of fundamental rights during times of 'emergency'. As Nazrul Islam observes: "Of course, the Supreme Court of Bangladesh is empowered to interpret the law and to enforce the basic rights under law, it has no jurisdiction to set limits to the legislative actions, or to prevent the executive from implementing the policies adopted by the Parliament of the Republic."[3]

3. Islam, *op. cit.*, p. 397.

52

POLITICAL PARTIES AND PRESSURE GROUPS

In every democratic state a number of political parties and numerous interest groups participate in the political process of the country. The nature and degree of such participation differentiates between democratic, semi-democratic and non-democratic systems. A look at the political pluralism of Bangladesh shows that here both the parties and the groups lack strong foundations and a well-institutionalised form. The rise and fall of the democratic system in this country may also be reckoned as an important factor in this regard. Rank opportunism and populism make the hallmarks of the whole scenario. It can be seen in the role of the leaders who usurp power, put a ban on political parties and then float a party of their own in the name of 'civilianising' their regime and thereby cheating the electorate. It applies to all parties that were in existence in East Pakistan and came into being after the liberation of the country in 1971.

Political Parties

Like other 'democratic' or 'semi-democratic' countries of the world, Bangladesh has its party system whose main characteristics may be enumerated as under:

1. Bangladesh is a multi-party state. The number of political parties, big and small, is very large, though a few of them have their place in the stasiological panorama of the country like Awami League, Bangladesh Nationalist Party and Jatiyo Party. Other parties like Workers Party of Bangladesh, Jamaat-i-Islami of Bangladesh, Jatiyo Party, Liberal Democratic Party and Communist Party have no significance at all.

2. All political parties are ridden with the evil of sharp factionalism. The groups of the defectors or break-away politicians play their part in creating conditions of political instability. It is a fact that the leaders in power attract such spineless politicians to join their political party. The result is that fragility haunts every political party that manages to be in power.
3. The element of ideology is altogether missing in the political parties in spite of the fact that Islam is the official religion. The fundamentalists try to push things in their own direction, the communists take to a different course. All professions of the leaders in the name of democracy and socialism look like a hoax. Secularism cannot have its place in the policies and programmes of any party and if the Awami League makes such a profession, it is just like its soft attitude towards theocracy.
4. As in India, so here political parties are known not by their principles but by the personality of their supreme leader. The names of Sheikh Mujibur Rahman and his daughter Sheikh Hasina are associated with the Awami League, Bangladesh Nationalist Party is the organisation of Ziaur Rahman and now his widowed wife Khalida Zia.
5. Happily, the Constitution has some provisions to check the evil of political defection. Art. 70 says that a member of Parliament cannot voluntarily leave the party on whose ticket he is elected and that he cannot ignore the directions of the leader of his party at the time of sitting in the Parliament.

Now we may have a brief look at the policies and programmes of some major political parties.

1. **Awami League:** Founded in 1949, it is the oldest party of Bangladesh. Its leader Sheikh Mujibur Rahman fought against the injustice done by the Punjabi-dominated government of West Pakistan. He raised the demand for 'autonomy' and led his colleagues to make the declaration of independence when President Yahya Khan frustrated his attempt to be the Prime Minister of Pakistan on the basis of the mandate of the people. However, after being the head of the state and government of Bangladesh, he took to the ways of authoritarianism by banning party system and putting the country under the iron hold of his Awami League, renamed as Bangladesh

Krishak Shramik Awami League. He established one-party state.[1] The situation was reversed after his assassination in 1975. Led by his daughter (Hasina) this party believes in four basic principles--Bengali nationalism, democracy, socialism and secularism. It perfers parliamentary form of government and aims at establishing a society free from exploitation. Thus, it desires improvement and modernisation of agriculture, equitable distribution of wealth and strengthening the foundations of a self-reliant economy.

2. **Bangladesh Nationalist Party:** Launched by President Ziaur Rahman in 1978, and now led by his widowed wife Begum Khaleda Zia, it prefers presidential system of government. It is an alliance of different shades of people ranging from the fundamentalists to the liberals. It rejects the case of Bengali nationalism and instead supports the case of Bangladeshi nationalism so as to accommodate the non-Bengali people in its ranks. It desires 'revolution' in the agricultural sphere and favours the system of mixed economy.

3. **Jatiyo Party:** Like Ziaur Rahman, President Gen. Ershad launched this party in 1982 for the purpose of 'civilianisation of military rule'. Thus, both the parties were accused of being 'sarkari dal'. It was also like a conglomerate alliance most of whom were the political defectors who sought to reap the benefits of political patronage. It sticks to five basic ideals—consensus on fundamental issues, protection of independence and sovereignty, Bangladeshi nationalism, establishment of Islamic ideals implying respect for the people of other faiths, and social progress along with economic emancipation.

---

1. One-party rule is of two types. One type may be found in communist and fascist countries where the ruling party becomes the state, the government, the society, the nation. Any opposition to its rule is mercilessly crushed. Its examples may be Italy under the Fascist party of Mussolini, Germany under the Nazi party of Hitler, Soviet Union under the Communist Party of Lenin, Stalin and their successors and China under Mao and his successors. The second type is one that is associated with colonial nationalism and state socialism in the developing countries. Here one powerful leader assumes all powers in his hands. He may ban party system and yet launch a party of his own and, after some time, may allow other parties to operate so as to alleviate their underground character. Its examples are Ghana under Nkrumah, Zaire under Mobuto, Tanzania under Nyrere and Bangladesh under Mujib, Zia and Ershad. Andrew Heywood: *Politics* (Houndmills, Basingstroke: Palgrave Foundations, 2005,) p. 260.

4. **Jamaat-i-Islami of Bangladesh:** Founded by Maulana Maudoodi in 1941, it is a body of religious fanatics that desires transformation of the society on Islamic principles. Thus, it desires rule of the Muslim theologians. It opposed the struggle of the Awami League for country's liberation. So it was banned by the Mujib government and then it became an under-ground organisation. Sometimes, it appears with the name of Islamic Democratic League. The fact is that it has hardly any place in the parliamentary democracy of the country,

5. **Communist Party:** It is a splintered body of the communists owing their allegiance to a foreign country once like the USSR and now China. Some of its members claim the origin of this party to the Communist Party of India founded by M.N. Roy at Tashkent in 1920. It believes in the establishment of socialism in the country in a scientific manner. It supports pro-people patriotic governments to lead the country towards a self-reliant economy and social progress. The fact is that, like the Jamaat-i-Islami, it has hardly any place in the parliamentary democracy of the country.

Party system has not been a successful affair in Bangladesh not for the reason of its unstable and fragile foundations as for the reason of the dominance of the institutions of civilian and military bureaucracy. The leaders of the political parties have miserably failed to keep the two sets of bureaucracy in check, or to maintain a balance between the politicians and the bureaucrats. Civilian bureaucracy thrives on the colonial foundations, while military bureaucracy has tasted the blood of power under Zia and Ershad. In developed political systems of the world, the hold of the bureaucracy is inevitable, not indomitable. Different is the case of a poor and backward state of the third world like Bangladesh where the civilian and the military bureaucrats form the 'partnership of conscience' and thereby create on 'over-developed state.'[2] As Islam says: "In fact, devising an effective way for the resolution of the conflict between political parties and dominant institutional groups as well as defining their respective roles has appeared to be the most formidable challenge to the politics of Bangladesh."[3]

---

2. Hamza Alavi: "The State in Post-Colonial Societies: Pakistan and Bangladesh" in Kathleen Gough and P. Sharma (eds.): *Imperialism and Revolution in South Asia* (New York: Monthly Review Press, 1973), pp. 145-47.
3. Nazrul Islam, *op. cit.*, p. 416.

Some Important Statements

One-party systems in Africa and Asia have usually been built around the dominant role of a charismatic leader and drawn whatever ideological identity they have possessed from the views of that leader. —***Andrew Heywood***

The colonial rulers had built up the bureaucracy as a separate class with special safeguards in their own interests. We do not want to keep this class—bureaucrats must change their mentality—they must realise that they are not rulers, they are servants. —***Prime Minister Sheikh Mujibur Rahman***

But after the emergence of Bangladesh, with the introduction of parliamentary government, when political elites became the supreme policy-makers and deliberately took various measures to curb the powers and privileges of the bureaucratic elites, it led to a conflict between the two sectors.

—***Prof. M. Nazrul Islam***

Pressure Groups

People have many interests and so many groups come into being for the sake of their protection and promotion. These interest groups are called pressure groups when they play a role to influence the actions of the government in their favour. They are known by various names as anonymous empire and unofficial government. The associations of the businessmen, traders, workers, peasants, medical professionals, teachers, students etc. become the subject of our study when their members fight for the sake of their interests. Their groups indulge in the act of 'lobbying' or influencing the legislators, administrators and other functionaries of the state so that decisions are taken as far as possible in their favour. It is possible that the decisions are reversed or modified or deferred in the face of the role of such groups which use constitutional, extra-constitutional as well as unconstitutional methods to achieve their aims.

If so, Bangladesh can be no exception. The Metropolitan Chamber of Commerce and Industry, the Bangladesh Medical Association, numerous registered and unregistered bodies of the workers, the peasants and other professionals have their place in this category. Some developed or well organised groups have their experts who give advice to the government and thereby manage to foster their aims and objects. Thus occurs the interlinking of the interest groups and the government.

However, the problem with this country is that even after 40 years of liberation, she is still beset with many uncertainties and controversies on fundamental issues. There exists a gross lack of consensus on important matters like official ideology, form of government, and economy of the country. Ceaseless debates and doubts over the role of the dominant institutional groups, intense factionalism in party politics and inadequate growth of institutions, exclusiveness of the ruling elites and the question of their legitimacy have perpetuated a state of serious political unrest and instability."[4]

4. *Ibid.*, p. 419.

Part-XV
Nigerian Constitution

The problem of Nigeria today is how to create a political system which is itself a present advance and containing the living possibility of further orderly advance.... The present system of government of Nigeria has many inconsistencies and by its nature is unsuited for experience in a Nigerian basin.

Arthur Richards

53

Constitution of Nigeria

There are some pertinent reasons behind the inclusion of the Nigerian Constitution in a work on major political systems of the world. It is a very big country of the African continent that remained under British colonial hold until the achievement of of independence on 1 October, 1960. Naturally, it received in legacy many features of the British Constitutional system as we may see in the cases of India and South Africa. It had a monarchical system that was replaced by the republican system on 1 October 1963. This big country has almost 250 tribal or racial communities. Hence, the federal system of the American model has been adopted. However, one striking point that differentiates it from other developing countries is that here the traditions of tribalism or racialism are very strong which act as an impediment in the establishment of a stable and progressive Nation-State. Military rule may be an exception in other countries, but here it is a routine affair. Like many other African countries, Nigeria is ill-known for national fragmentation, political instability, corruption and maladministration. A legend says, As Nigeria goes, so goes the rest of sub-Saharan Africa.

Constitution and Constitutionalism

Like other backward countries, Constitutionalism is a very serious problem here. The British rulers made many attempts to place this country under a Constitution. It is a fact that after establishing their colonial rule in the country, the British rulers put it under a Constitutional law in 1922. This system went on for about 24 years. It is, however, a different matter that during the inter-war period some important changes were made in the framework of the Constitutional rule. The Richards Constitution came into being in 1946 that was replaced by the Macpherson Constitution in 1951. This Constitution was amended in 1954 when a federal system with three provinces was established. It shows

Some Important Statements

Three reasons inspire us to study the Constitution of Nigeria. The first concerns Nigeria s size. With a population of about 90 million, Nigeria is by far the largest country in Africa and among the ten most populous countries in the world. The second reason to study Nigeria is that, unlike most other countries on the continent, Nigeria has a salutary combination of ***human and material resources*** to help it overcome the vicious cycle of poverty and autocracy that has become all prevalent in Africa. A third reason to study Nigeria is that it is a paradox.

R.A. Joseph, S.D. Taylor and Adigun Agbaje

The main characteristics of modern African politics.... would appear to have been fashioned by the colonial experience of the nineteenth and the twentieth countries. If there is any continuity in African political structure comparable to the continuity which de Tocqueville.... saw between the old regime and modern Europe it is not between pre-colonial and post-colonial Africa.

Peter Ekeh

Nigeria is not a nation. It is a mere geographical expression. There are no Nigerians in the same sense as there are English , Welsh or French . The word Nigeria is merely a distinctive appellation to distinguish those who live within the boundaries of Nigeria from those who do not.

Obafemi Awolowo

that long before federation was accepted in 1953, Nigeria seemed to have been moving progressively towards such a system of government.*f*[1] It was again amended in 1963 when monarchy was replaced by the republic. As a Nigerian writer observes: Republicanism in Nigeria has been regarded by some people as an act of rebirth or rediscovery, and so it was argued that there could be no complete rediscovery unless the country cast the name given to it by the British and adopted a new indigenous name that would reflect its pre-colonial history.*f*[2]

A new Constitution came into effect in 1979 that was a gift of the military rule. It reversed most of the democratic features of the existing Constitution so as to make it compatible with the requirements of a military rule. While realising the reality of the situation, a Nigerian writer commented. There is no gainsaying

1. O.I. Odumosu: *The Nigerian Constitution: History and Development* (London: Sweat and Maxwell, 1968), p. 227.
2. Turi Muhammadu: *The Nigerian Constitution of 1979: Framework for Democracy* (Enugu, Nigeria: Fourth Dimension Publishers, 1982), p. 90.

the fact that in a multi-national and multi-lingual society like ours with diverse cultures, creeds and religions, the task of producing a single document acceptable to all interest groups is not only arduous but also delicate.*f*[3]

The State of political instability continued which had its adverse impact on the progress of Constitutionalism. A new Constitution was framed in 1989 which could not be implemented. While keeping the recommendations of the Constitutional convention in 1994-95, the Government published the draft prepared by the National Constitution Committee on 7 December, 1998. Progress went on under the leadership of Obasanjo who was elected as the President on 27 February, 1999. After a lapse of about 16 years of military rule, this Constitution was inaugurated on 31 May, 1999. Now transition to civilian rule occured.[4] Then followed the elections in 2007 which showed the inauguration of civilian rule in this country.[5]

The alternation of the military and the civilian rules is the factor which may be described as a great impediment in the way of the establishment of a perfect Nation-State in this country. It has been well commented: Nigeria has changed its Constitution often in the search for perfection with constant Constitutional engineering and the inauguration of several Constitutions since colonial amalgamation in 1914. Although much attention has been focused on making Constitutions, there has been little effort made to ensure

3. *Ibid.*, p. 24. It is said that a British woman journalist Flora Shaw suggested the name Nigeria who had later married a renowned Governor-General Lord Lugard. Some leaders of this country suggested the name of Songhai for this country. However, many people did not appreciate it, because ancient Songhai Empire had included many non-Nigerian areas.
4. It is said that the Constitutions of 1964, 1979, 1989 and 1999 established in this country respectively the first, the second, the third and the fourth republics.
5. R.A. Joseph, S.D. Taylor and Adigun Agbaje: Nigeria*f* in Mark Kesselman, Joel Krieger and W.A. Joseph (eds.): *Comparative Politics at the Crossroads* (Lexington: D.C. Heath and Company, 1996), p.651.

Important Political Events

1. Nigeria achieved independence in October, 1960, adopted British Parliamentary system, Abubakar Tafawa Balewa became the Prime Minister.
2. Monarchy was replaced by a republic in October, 1963.
3. Gen. Aguiyi Ironsi captured power in January, 1966 and established military rule.
4. Gen. Yakubu Gowon wrested power in July, 1966.
5. Gen. Murtala Muhammed wrested power in February 1976; after some time he was assassinated and then Gen. Olusegun Obasanjo captured power.
6. In 1978 a Constitution of the American model was inaugurated. Alhaji Shehu Shagari became the President. It was a civilian rule.
7. Gen. Muhammed Buhari captured power in December, 1983.
8. Gen. Ibrahim Babangida captured power in August 1985. Now a new Constitution was framed that provided a two-party system. It could not come into effect.
9. Elections for the post of the President were held in March 1993. Bashir Tofa was defeated, Moshood Abiola won. But President Babangida cancelled the result of the election. Abiola was charged with treason and put under detention.
10. In August 1993 Babangida resigned. He appointed Gen. Sani Abacha as the Civilian President . A Constitutional Convention was set up. A new Constitution came into effect in May, 1999 that established civilian rule in the country.

that governments govern according to the Constitution and that the rule of law is enforced in place of capricious governance. In short, Nigeria has produced many Constitutions, but it has yet to entrench Constitutionalism.*f*[6]

Salient Features

The salient features of the Nigerian Constitution of 1999 may be enumerated as under:

1. **An Enacted, Written and Rigid Constitution:** It is a written document having 320 sections and sub-sections

6. V.A. Olorunsola: Questions on Constitutionalism and Democracy: Nigeria and Africa*f* in Dove Ronen (ed.); *Democracy and Pluralism in Africa* (Boulder: Lynne Rienner, 1986).

grouped into VIII chapters followed by six schedules. It is the creation of a Constitutional Convention. It is written in detail, for it has elaborate provisions relating to central, provincial and local governments and, in addition to that, relating to some Constitutional bodies and political parties. Like the American and Swiss Constitutions, its nature is rigid in view of the fact that a bill of Constitutional amendment must be passed in each house of Parliament by 2/3 majority and then it must be ratified by at least 2/3 of the State legislatures by the same majority. However, if such a bill is related to some important matter (as formation of a new State or of a local government, fundamental rights of the citizens, or process of amendment as given in Art. 9), then it must be passed by 4/5 majority of the whole house in each house of Parliament and then it must be ratified by 2/3 majority of the State legislatures. Such a bill must be passed in the legislature of a State by 2/3 majority of the members present and voting. It may be commented that this Constitution is more rigid than the Constitutions of America and Switzerland.

2. **Federal System:** Like the American and Swiss Constitutions, it has established federal system. The Constitution is the supreme law of the land. Powers have been distributed between the Centre and the States. The Centre can make a law on any item of the Exclusive Legislative List. The Centre and the States can make a law on any item of the Concurrent Legislative List, but the law of the Centre shall have over-riding effect in the situation of a conflict. The Supreme Court has been established to interpret the provisions of the Constitution from time to time and to settle Constitutional disputes between the Centre and the States. A notable point at this stage is that Federal Character Commission has been set up to maintain the federal system. As the tendencies of centralism have emerged in every federal system, same may be taken note of in the case of Nigerian system as well.

3. **Presidential Form of Government:** Like America, Nigeria has Presidential form of government. The President is the head of the State as well as of the government. He appoints

his ministers and distributes departments among them. Though there is no ceiling on the size of the council of ministers, it is required that there must be one minister from each State. All ministers work during the pleasure of the President. The President and his ministers cannot be the members of Parliament. If a member of the National Assembly is appointed as the President, he must leave the membership of the House of Parliament before taking the oath of office. The President is elected for a term of four years, but he may be removed on the charge of gross misconduct, or physical or mental incapacity.

4. **Checks and Balances:** As in America, so in Nigeria the system of checks and balances has been implemented. The legislative powers are vested in the National Assembly; executive powers are vested in the President; judicial powers are vested in the Courts. The Supreme Court is at the top. However, the powers of each have been checked by the powers of the other two organs of government. For eaxmple, all appointments made by the President must be confirmed by the Senate. If the President signs an international treaty, it cannot be put into effect unless it is ratified by the National Assembly. A bill passed by the National Assembly requires assent of the President. In case the President rejects a bill by the exercise of his veto power, it can be over-ridden if each House passes the same bill again by 2/3 majority. The Supreme Court has the power of judicial review. It can invalidate a law of the Parliament or an order of the President on the ground of unconstitutionality.

5. **Fundamental Objcetives and Directive Principles of State Policy:** In the Irish Constitution of 1937 some glorious principles were enshrined. Since then it has become a matter of deep appreciation. Hence, the Constitution-makers of many countries followed it whose instances may be seen in the Constitutions of India, China, Russian Federation and South Africa. These principles have been incorporated into Chapter II. It has been declared that the State shall be based on the ideals of Democracy and Social Justice. The motto of the State will be Unity, Faith, Peace and Progress. All corrupt practices

and the abuses of power shall be abolished. The natural resources of the country shall be used in the interest of all. The government shall frame a foreign policy that protects and promotes national interest and encourages international peace, security and cooperation. It also includes the duties of the citizens. For instance, they should abide by the Constitution of the State, should respect national flag and national anthem, and should make all efforts to protect the dignity of the motherland.

6. **Fundamental Rights:** Chapter IV of the Constitution has a long list of fundamental rights. Right to equality has been ensured to all citizens. Hence, there can be no discrimination on the grounds of religion, race, creed, place of birth, sex etc. The right to liberty has also been ensured. Hence, no citizen can be arrested without cause, nor can he be punished unless he is held guilty by a competent Court in a free and fair trial. Freedoms relating to thought, expression, faith, movement and residence or settlement in any part of the country have also been guaranteed. The aggrieved party may move the Federal High Court for the protection of his fundamental rights and the Court may issue necessary directives or instructions in this regard. However, such rights are not absolute. The State may impose reasonable restraints on their use or enjoyment in the public interest. The President may suspend the exercise of such rights during the period of emergency.

7. **Bicameralism:** Like other countries of the world, the Nigerian Constitution has adopted the model of bicameralism. The Senate and the House of Representatives are respectively the upper and the lower chambers of the National Assembly. The notable point is that both the houses have a term of four years and the Head of the State (President) cannot dissolve any house before the completion of its term. Three Senators are elected from each State and one Senator is elected from the Federal Capital Territory of Abuja. As there are 36 States, so the Senate has 109 members. The House of Representatives has 360 elected members. The members of both houses are elected directly. Like the national legislatures of America and Switzerland, this is not a

sovereign law-making body. It cannot make a law on a residuary subject and that its law may be struck down by the Supreme Court on the ground of unconstitutionality.

8. **Emergency Powers:** Section 305 of the Constitution has some provisions whereby the President may use his emergency powers. It may be done in some exceptional situations as war, breakdown of public order, natural disaster or calamity, or any event threatening the existence of the republic. Such a proclamation of the President must be approved by the Parliament within 10 days (within 2 days if the session is going on). The period of emergency may be extended and a resolution to this effect must be passed in each house of Parliament by special majority. The period may be extended for six months a time, but it may be done again and again. The emergency may be revoked at any time either by an order of the President or by a resolution of the Parliament. It is obvious that such an arrangement has been made to meet the national crisis. However, such provisions do not make the President an autocraft in view of the fact that the control of the Parliament is very much there on the exercise of such powers.

9. **Judicial Review:** Like the Supreme Court of the United States, the Supreme Court of Nigeria has been given the power to interpret the provisions of the Constitution from time to time as per necessity. It may review any law of the Parliament or an order of the President and declare it void on the ground of its being repugnant to the Constitution which is the supreme law of the land.

Salient Features of the Constitution

Features	Implications
1. An Enacted, Written and Rigid Constitution	This Constitution is the creation of a body; it has 320 sections and sub-sections grouped into VIII parts followed by six schedules; its process of amendment is very difficult.
2. Federal System	The Constitution is the supreme law of the land; it distributes powers between the Centre and the States; it establishes the Supreme Court to settle legal disputes between the Centre and the States.
3. Presidential Form of Government	The President is the head of the State as well as of the government; executive has been separated from the legislature.
4. Checks and Balances	An arrangement has been made whereby one organ has its checks on the other two organs of government so as to maintain the balance of power.
5. Fundamental Objectives and Directive Principles	The political system is based on some important ideals as Unity, Faith, Peace, Progress, Liberty, Equality and Justice.
6. Fundamental Rights	Rights relating to equality, liberty, non-exploitation, property etc. have been ensured to the citizens and their protection by the Courts has also been guaranteed.
7. Bi-cameralism	The Parliament or National Assembly has two chambers Senate as the upper or second chamber, the House of Representatives as the first or lower chamber. Both have a term of four years; no house can be dissolved prematurely.
8. Emorgency Powers	In the event of war, natural disaster or in some other grave situation, the President may defend the republic by declaring emergency covering whole country or some of its part.
9. Judicial Review	The Supreme Court can review the validity of any law of Parliament or an order of the President and may

	declare it void to the extent of being Unconstitutional.
10. Environmentalism	, The State shall improve environment and protect water, earth, air, forest and wild life.
11. Party System	, Each political party must be registered with the Independent National Electoral Commission. Only a member of any political party may take part in the elections.

10. **Environmentalism:** After the Stockholm Conference held in June 1972, the protection of environment became an important issue. Hence, the Constitutions framed after that have a distinct provision in this regard. The Constitutions of the Russian Federation and South Africa may be cited as its instances. This point was not included in the Indian Constitution framed in 1949, but it was adopted by the 42nd amendment of 1976. Chapter II of this Constitution has fundamental objectives and directive principles of State policy. It is given in section 20 that the State shall protect and improve environment and also protect water, air, earth, forest and wild life.

11. **Party System:** Party system is regarded as an extra-Constitutional development. The Constitution of a State has no provisions in this regard. However, the Constitution of Nigeria has set up a new precedent. Its Part III of Chapter VI has elaborate provisions about party system. It is necessary that political parties have their registration with the Independent National Electoral Commission and a person can take part in the elections if he is a member of any political party. The membership of a political party shall be open for all citizens, hence no discrimination can be done on any artificial ground. It is also required for each political party to submit its account of annual income and expenditure to the Independent National Electoral Commission. Some provisions have been made to prevent corruption or doing of any anti-national activity by the members of any political party.

Fundamental Objectives and Directive Principles of State Policy

Chapter II of the Constitution has a long list of such principles which have been designated as fundamental objectives of the State and directive principles of State policy. These may be numerated as under:

1. It shall be the duty and the obligation of all the organs of government and the persons exercising executive, legislative and judicial authority to respect these principles and act accordingly.
2. The federal republic of Nigeria is based on the ideals of democracy and social justice. Power resides in the people and the government derives power from them. The primary purpose of the government is the security and welfare of the people. People s participation in government has been ensured.
3. The Constitution has established federal system; its aim is national unity and security. Hence, primacy cannot be given to any racial or social group. Unity and diversity shall be maintained. So the motto of the federation shall be unity, faith, peace and progress.
4. For the sake of national integration, the State shall encourage the transit of people and goods throughout the country and also encourage inter-communal marriages; and develop private associations by eradicating racial, linguistic, religious and other class barriers.
5. The State shall abolish all corrupt methods and abuse of power; shall properly utilise natural resources and also encourage national prosperity and a self-reliant and dynamic economy. The material resources shall be used in the interest of all people.
6. The social system shall be based on the ideals of liberty, equality and justice. Equality of opportunity shall be ensured to all citizens. The State shall protect the dignity of the individual, save the people from exploitation, and eliminate discrimination among them on any artificial ground.
7. The State shall render social welfare services as to provide opportunities for employment and render assistance relating to medicine and health, and proper education of the people.
8. The State shall follow a foreign policy to protect and promote national interest, encourage African unity, improve international peace and security, respect international law,

discharge treaty obligations, and seek pacific settlement of disputes.

9. The State shall protect and improve environment and protect water, air, earth, forest and wild life.

10. The State shall strive to protect and promote national culture and encourage development of scientific and technical studies.

11. The national ethics shall be dicipline, integrity, dignity of labour, social justice, religious tolerance, self-reliance and patriotism.

12. It shall be the duty of each citizen to abide by the Constitution, to respect national flag, national anthem and its ideals and institutions, promote the feelings of common brotherhood, cooperate in maintaining peace and order, honestly declare his income to the concerned legal authorities, and sincerely pay his taxes.

Fundamental Rights

A long list of the fundamental rights of the citizens is contained in Chapter IV of the Constitution which may be enumerated as under:

1. Each citizen has the right to life. Nobody can be deprived of this right unless he has been held guilty of some criminal act by a competent Court. It is a different matter that he is killed in the suppression of some revolt, rebellion, mutiny or revolution, or somebody kills a person for the sake of self-defence or his opponent trying to snatch his property by means of violence, or some necessary step is taken to prevent the escape of a detained person. It simply means that no person can be deprived of this important right in an arbitrary manner.

2. Each citizen has the right to protect his dignity. Hence, he cannot be hurt or harmed in an inhuman manner. Nobody can be put in a State of slavery or servitude, nor can he be forced to do some work against his will. However, this provision shall not apply where such a step is taken at the instance of a Court, or it is in accord with the rules of civilian or military service, or it is made mandatory to deal with the

situation of emergency, or it is done to deal with a crisis that may harm the welfare of the community.

3. Personal liberty has been ensured. Hence, a person cannot be punished unless he is held guilty by a competent Court after following the procedure established by law. However, this provision shall not apply in some particular situations as the education and welfare of a person below the age of 18 years, or a person who is afflicted with a contagious disease, or is mentally disturbed, or is accustomed of using intoxicating goods, or is a foreign migrant trying to enter the country by illegal means, or some person is exiled or extradited from the country. If a person is detained in a legal manner, or his case has not been decided, then he cannot be detained for a period more than it is specified for committing such a crime.
4. The detained person shall have the right to take the help of a lawyer for his defence. Self-incrimination is prohibited. That is, a person cannot be forced to accept his crime or to be a witness against himself. If a person is arrested, he must be informed of the cause within 24 working hours and be shall be produced before a competent Court within reasonable time. Here the notable point is that in case a person is detained illegally, he may claim due compensation or public apology from that authority. However, this provision shall not apply in case the appropriate authority has detained him on the basis of a reasonable suspicion that he might have committed an act of murder.
5. If a person is arrested, the competent Court or tribunal shall hear the case within reasonable time. The person shall have the right to defend himself and all proceedings shall be conducted in an open manner.
6. A person may be arrested and prosecuted under a law that is in force at the time of commission of the crime. No person can be punished twice for the same crime. He can not be prosecuted in case he is pardoned by the President.
7. Privacy has been guaranteed to the citizens in matters relating to their personal life, their home, their correspondence, telephonic conversation and postal and telegraphic communications.

8. Freedoms of thought, expression, conscience or faith in any religion have been guaranteed to all citizens. Religious instructions may be imparted in any religious institution. The people may form their associations for protecting their interests, they may move or reside in any part of the country. But nobody can be a member of a secret organisation. Nobody can establish or operate radio, wireless or telephone for any purpose.
9. Each citizen has the right to keep or sell or transfer his movable and immovable property in the country. But the State may nationalise private property in the public interest by the authority of law and on the payment of due compensation. In the event of any injustice, the aggrieved party may protect his right by moving a competent Court.
10. Right to Constitutional remedies has also been guaranteed. If anybody s rights are offended, he may move the Federal High Court. Then, the Court may issue necessary directives, orders or writs for the protection of his fundamental rights. The National Assembly may make a law to extend the jurisdiction of the Federal High Court or to give financial help to the aggrieved party to meet the expenses.

No doubt, the Constitution has a comprehensive list of fundamental rights. However, some important points should also be noted. First, the law of the State must be such that may be proved reasonable in a democratic system. Second, if the President makes a declaration of emergency, then reasonable restrictions may be imposed on the exercise of these rights.

The notable point is that it is the first document which has ensured fundmental rights of the citizens and also made provisions for their protection by the Courts. Behind it may be seen the fact of public resentment that had become manifest in the referendum of 12 June , 1993. The people in general had raised their voice against racial, religious and regional divisions which had been coming since the days of the British colonial rule and the military rulers of the independent country had been following them. By their votes they took an important step to establish a democratic political system in their country in a true sense. This movement proved helful in the framing of the Constitution of 1999 in which is implicit the firm determination for creating a civil society by the guarantee of these fundamental rights.

Emergency Provisions

Section 305 of the Constitution is very important. It says that the President may declare emergency covering the country as a whole or any of its parts. Such a declaration may be made in certain exceptional situations as war in which Nigeria is involved, menace to the public order and security, natural calamity, or a threat to the existence of the republic. It is also possible that the President may declare emergency in a State on the recommendation of its Governor. The Governor may send his report to the President if the Legislative Assembly of that State passes a resolution to this effect by its 2/3 majority.

The Constitution has provisions which restrain the President from making misuse of his emergency powers. After the proclamation of emergency, its copy shall be sent to the presiding officers of the Senate and the House of Representatives. Both the houses shall meet immediately to consider the proclamation of the President. A resolution of approval must be passed in each house by 2/3 majority of all the members. This work must be done within 2 days if the Parliament is in session, otherwise within 10 days. The Parliament may extend the duration of emergency which cannot be of more than six months at a time. The President may revoke his order at any time, or the Parliament may do it if a resolution to this effect is passed in each house by the simple majority of votes.

After making a deep study of the provisions of the Constitution, it may be commented that the emergency is of two kinds covering country as a whole or any of its States. The country-wide emergency may be declared in many situations as physical involvement of the country in a war, or a serious menace to the existence of the republic, or some natural calamity, or the arising of some very serious situation that makes it indispensable for the President to take such a step. Such a declaration would cover the country as a whole or any of its parts. Declaration of emergency may be made in a State if there is breakdown of law and order, or there is some natural disaster or calamity, or there is imminent threat thereof. Such a declaration shall be made on the report of the Governor of that State. This is the same thing what is known as the President s rule in India.

In appearance, these provisions make the powers of the President not merely comprehensive but formidable. It is, however, not so in fact. The declaration of the President shall be presented in both houses of National Assembly immediately and it must be approved in each house by special majority. The duration of emergency may be extended for six months at a time. But the President may revoke it at any time, or the Parliament may do so in case a resolution to this effect is passed in each house by the simple majority of votes. It is true that such powers of the President do not make him an autocrat or a totalitarian, but it may also be added that such powers make the Centre highly powerful that may amount to the vitiation of the federal structure.

Federal System

Like the Constitutions of the United States of America and Switzerland, this Constitution has established a federal system in this country.[8]

In this regard, elaborate arrangements have been made which may be mentioned as under:

1. The Constitution is written and rigid. Its section 1 says that it is the supreme law of the land and its provisions are binding on all authorities and people in the country. Its process of amendment is very difficult. The bill of constitutional amendment must be passed in each house of Parliament by 2/3 majority of all the members and then it must be ratified by at least 2/3 majority of the States. Such a bill must be passed in the Legislative Assembly of each State by 2/3 majority of all members of the house. However, if it is related to some particular provisions of the Constitution (as formation

8. Section 318 of the Constitution has defined the federal character of Nigeria. It refers to the distinctive desire of the people of Nigeria to promote national unity, foster national loyalty and to give every citizen of Nigeria a sense of belonging to the nation.

of a new State or local government, fundamental rights of the citizens, or the process of amendment given in section 9), then it must be passed in each house of Parliament by 4/5 majority of all the members and then it must be ratified by at least 2/3 majority of the States. It is obvious that here effective participation of the States has been ensured in the process of amending the Constitution.

2. Distribution of powers is the key feature of a federal system. It is specified in Part I of the Second Schedule. The Exclusive Legislative List has 68 items on which the Centre can make a law. The main items of this List are: accounts of the government, arms and ammunition, banking, citizenship, creation of a State, currency and coinage, security of the country, foreign affairs, import and export, insurance, labour, post and telegraph, telephone and wireless, public revenue of the federation, railway, regulation of political parties, radio and television etc. The Concurrent Legislative List has 30 items as: collection of taxes, elections to the councils of the local governments, electricity and its generation, commercial and industrial development, institutions of scientific and technical research etc. on which both the Centre and the States can make laws. But in the event of conflict, the law of the Centre shall have over-riding authority. It may be inferred that, as in the United States, residuary subjects are with the States.
3. The Supreme Court has been established to interpret the provisions of the Constitution from time to time and to settle legal disputes between the Centre and the States. It has the power of judicial review whereby it may determine the constitutional validity of any impugned law made by the Parliament or an order issued by the executive. As such, it is the custodian of the Constitution.

A student of comparative politics may commont that the distribution of powers in Nigeria is such that it makes the position of the Centre very strong. All important items are contained in the Exclusive Legislative List which are with the Centre. Both the Centre and the States can make laws on the subjects of Concurrent Legislative List, but the law of the Centre shall have an over-riding authority in the event of a conflict. It has been made clear in section

68 of the

Some Important Statements

- Three principal themes have been apparent in the post- independence juncture. The first is the ever-present bane of Nigerian development: corruption and clientelism. The second theme is concerned with Nigeria s ethnic conflict and its embrace of a distinctive federalism, which has been proposed as a means of instigating and diffusing ethnic conflict. Finally, the pervasive role of highly politicised Nigerian military warrants attention. Each of these themes is closely inter-related and can be used to have played a significant role in the downfall of each successive post-independence regime.

R.A. Joseph, S.D. Taylor and Adigun Agbaje

- June 12 was a historical breakthrough, the day the ordinary people of Nigeria rose against the ethnic, religious, and regional prejudices and the divisive politics with which colonialism and political class had oppressed them for half-a-century. In doing this, they took a great step towards making Nigeria a truly viable and democratic polity.

Claude Ake

- Since 1914 the British government has been trying to make Nigeria into one country, but Nigerian people themselves are historically different in their backgrounds, in their religious beliefs and do not show themselves any sign of willingness to unite.......Nigerian unity is only a British creation for the country.

Abubakar Tafawa Balewa

Constitution that the Centre may make a law on any item that falls within the domain of any item of the Exclusive Legislative List either directly or indirectly.

Constant progress has been underway in the direction of federalism since 1954 as a result of which the number of the States has risen from 3 to 36 and the number of local governments has risen to 768 so as to strengthen the base of federalism.[9] According to authoritative sources, the motive is not to bring the government closer to the people, or to encourage development, or to make an adjustment in the demands of the racial minorities for autonomy. Instead, it has been a part of the strategy of the leaders that such small groups be kept apart and to make them dependent on the Centre by pampering them with financial doles. That is, the leaders have invariably adopted the strategies to keep them under their control instead of encouraging their participation in the administration of the country. It has displayed their peculiar attitude towards federalism.

The fact is that the federal system of this country is operated by the role of racial and religious communities. This fact also stands out that the African leaders are so much immersed in racial and religious bonds that they cannot think of any other mode of operation. Military rulers like Gowon, Obasanjo, Buhari, Babangida and Sani Abacha used power in their own ways and so they fiddled with the norms of a federal system.. The power of the Centre went on increasing which established the model of skewed federalism by transgressing into the autonomy of the States. So it is commented that this system is federal in disguise while being unitary. However, the role of racial diversity makes the establishment of a federal system indispensable. It is well commented;

Because federal system is also perceived as a tool of ethnic management, disputes about its application have tended to focus on ethnic representation rather than on representation of State interests.[10]

9. This figure is mentioned in section 1 (6) of the Constitution, but now the number has reached to 774. *Europa World Year Book* (2010), Vol. II, p. 3410.

10. Joseph, Taylor and Agbaje, *op. cit.*, p. 654.

54

State Structure

A liberal-democratic system has been established in Nigeria under the Constitution of 1999. Being a republic the President is the head of the State. He is also the head of the government as it has adopted Presidential form of government. The Parliament (National Assembly) is bi-cameral having Senate as its upper and House of Representatives as its lower chambers respectively. Executive and legislature have been separated. Powers have been distributed between the Centre and the States which make the system federal. Independent and impartial judiciary has also been provided. The Constitution has elaborate provisions relating to central, provincial and local governments. Constitutional status has been accorded to a number of other bodies like Independent National Electoral Commission, National Judicial Council, Federal Civil Service Commission etc. and political parties. After seeing such a comprehensive document, an impression may be formed that its makers have made serious efforts to establish a stable and strong liberal-democratic order in the country.

National Executive

Despite living under the British colonial rule, the makers of the Constitution replaced their Parliamentary system by the Presidental form of government of the American model. After the achievement of independence in 1960, Parliamentary system of the British model was established. Abubakar Tafawa Balewa was the Prime Minister. A military revolt occurred in January 1966 when Gen. Aguiyi Ironsi captured power. Such events occurred repeatedly as a result of which this country remained under the dictatorial rule of the military leaders who gave false assurances for the restoration of democratic system. As a matter of fact, it was not even the Presidential system of the American model, as it was the totalitarian rule of the military leaders who had converted the legislature into a non-entity and made judiciary an adjunct of the executive. On some occasions, elections were held which were like a farce. Though Abacha gave some big assurances, the general impression remained the same. The Constitution of 1999 embodies comprehensive provisions which restrain the powers of the President. The new system has been devised whereby one organ has its checks on the other two organs of government so that balance of power may be maintained that is regarded as the basis of a democratic system.[1]

President

Election, Term and Removal: Nigeria has Presidential form of government. So the President is the head of the State as well as of the government. He is elected by the voters directly for a term of four years. A person may hold this office once or twice either consecutively or with a break. He must possess these qualifications

1. He must be a natural born citizen of Nigeria.
2. He must be above 40 years of age.
3. He must be a member of some political party and that his name must have been sponsored by it.
4. He must be educated upto the School Certificate level or its equivalent.

The voters vote in favour of or against the candidates. It is required that the successful candidate must have at least 1/2 of the votes cast in at least 2/3 States and at least 1/4 of the votes cast in the Federal Capital Territory of Abuja. He must secure absolute majority of the total valid votes polled. It shall happen in case there is only one candidate in the field. If there are two or more candiates in the field, the successful candidate must secure largest number

1. Taking note of these events, some writers had commented in 1996: Nigeria's political history and recent experiences suggest that the country will again experience the unchallenged neo-patrimonial rule of the executive President and his handpicked cabinet, ineffectually checked by a weak legislature and judiciary, both vulnerable to executive and clientelist pressures.*f* R.A. Joseph, S.D. Taylor and Adigun Agbaje: Nigeria*f* in Mark Kesselman, W.A. Joseph and Joel Krieger (eds.): *Comparative Politics at the Crossroads* (Lexington: D.C. Heath and Company. 1996), p. 658.

Some Important Statements

- We, members of the armed forces, ...are committed to democracy, to the democratic process, and to our transition program. What we did was to annul the election, not the transition program. I have been mandated by the distinguished gathering .... to let you know that .... we shall install a democratically elected government on the 27th of August, 1993.

Gen. Ibrahim Babangida

- We, the people of the Federal Republic of Nigeria, having firmly and solemnly resolved, to live in unity and harmony as one indivisible and indissoluble sovereign nation under God, dedicated to the promotion of inter-African solidarity, world peace, international cooperation and understanding and to provide for a Constitution for the purpose of promoting the good government and welfare of all persons in our country, on the principles of freedom, equality and justice, and for the purpose of consolidating the unity of our people, do hereby make, enact and give to ourselves this Constitution.

Preamble to the Constitution of 1999

- In rejecting British Parliamentarism for America-style presidentialism, the framers of the 1979 Constitution of the second Republic argued that the new arrangement would lead to a more focused executive authority and facilitate the use of executive authority. According to them, the American model would also ensure (through the exercise of checks and balances and separation of powers), that no single arm of government would gain so much power as to put the liberties of citizens at risk. It was argued also that Presidentialism would promote political integration, since it authorised the head of the executive branch to appoint individuals from outside the legislature to the cabinet.

R.A. Joseph, S.D. Taylor and Adigun Agbaje

of votes in the polls and that he must secure at least 1/4 of the votes cast in 2/3 States and 1/4 of the votes cast in the Federal Capital Territory of Abuja. If it does not happen, then the Independent National Electoral Commission shall make arrangement for a new election within seven days after the declaration of the results of the cancelled election. Now only two candidates shall have the right to contest who had secured largest number of votes in the cancelled election. A candidate securing largest number of votes shall be declared elected.

After election, the President shall take the oaths of office and layalty in the presence of the Chief Justice of the Supreme Court and declare his assets and liabilities. His normal term is of four years. However, this term may be extended in case the country is physically involved in a war. A resolution to this effect must be passed in each house of Parliament by 2/3 majority. This duration may be extended again and again, but for not more than six months at a time. The President may resign whenever he so desires.

The President may be removed by the process of impeachment on two grounds gross misconduct and physical or mental incapacity[2]. Different are the procedures for both. If the President is charged with gross misconduct in the performance of his functions and powers, the petition must be signed by at least 1/3 members of Parliament. It shall be presented to the president of the Senate who will send its copy to the President and to all members of Parliament within 7 days. He shall also send the copies of the defence or explanation of the President to all members of Parliament. Then, within 14 days, all the members of the National Assembly shall decide whether the matter needs investigation. If such a resolution is passed, then the President of the Senate within next 7 days shall authorise the Chief Justice of the Supreme Court to set up an inquiry committee of 7 members. Such persons shall be included in this committee who are known for their impartiality and integrity of character, are not public servants, and are not the members of any legislative chamber or political party. This committee shall submit its report within 3 months. In case the President is held guilty, then within 14 days its report shall be discussed in both the houses of Parliament. The President shall be removed in case a resolution to this effect is passed in each house of Parliament by 2/3 majority of all the members.

If the President is charged with physical or mental incapacity, then the Executive Council (Cabinet) shall take the initiative. A resolution to this effect must be passed in its meeting by 2/3 majority of votes. Then the President of the Senate shall set up a committee of five doctors to examine him. If the report of the committee confirms the charge, then the Presidents of the Senate and the House of Representatives shall issue a communication to remove the President.

Functions and Powers: The President is the head of the executive. His powers are vast, which cover all areas of administration and may be enumerated as under

2. According to Section 143 (11), gross misconduct means a grave violation of this Constitution or a misconduct of such nature as amounts in the opinion of the National Assembly to gross misconduct.

1. He is the head of the State, hence all administration is carried in his name. He is the commander of all armed forces.
2. He determines the number of his ministers and appoints them. He must include at least one minister from each State. He administers to all ministers oaths of office and secrecy, distributes portfolios among them, and accepts their resignations. He may remove any minister.
3. He appoints the heads and members of many Constitutional bodies as Independent National Electoral Commission, National Population Commission, Federal Civil Service Commission, National Judicial Council etc. which are subject to Senatorial confirmation.[3]
4. In case the country is physically involved in a war, or there is some natural disaster or calamity, or there is any serious threat to the existence of the republic, he may declare a State of emergency.
5. He may pardon a person convicted by a Court at the top, or may commute his sentence. That is, he has the prerogative of mercy.
6. For maintaining foreign relations, he appoints his ambassadors and accepts the credential of foreign envoys. He represents his country in international conferences and makes treaties that must be passed by the Parliament.
7. He may deprive a person of his citizenship of Nigeria if he has been held guilty of a serious crime like treason.
8. He may entrust special responsibilities of the government to the Vice-President or to any minister by virtue of his discretionary powers. It is also required that he should hold regular meetings with his Vice-President and other ministers.

---

3. It is given in Section 154 (3) of the Constitution: In exercising his powers to appoint a person as Chairman or member of the Council of States, the National Defence Council, the Federal Judicial Service Commission and the National Security Council, the President shall not be required to obtain the confirmation of the Senate.*f*

9. By virtue of his discretionary powers, he may appoint additional members of the Civilian Security Council and Military Security Council.
10. If the office of the Vice-President falls vacant for any reason, then he shall nominate someone whose name must be approved by both the houses of Parliament.
11. He was veto power. When a bill is passed by the Parliament, it is referred to him for his assent. He may assent to it or not. In case he rejects a bill and the same bill is passed again by both the houses of Parliament by 2/3 majority of the members present and voting, then his assent is not required.
12. He may address any house of Parliament or both about affairs of administration and may send his message which shall be taken up for discussion at the earliest.
13. He shall remove a judge if the Senate passes the resolution of impeachment against him by its 2/3 majority of votes.
14. On the recommendation of the Finance Commission, he may present his proposals to the Parliament relating to the allocation of government revenues.
15. He causes to be laid before the Parliament annual account of the income and expeniture of the government.

It is clear that the President is the head of the State as well as of the government and has his counterpart in the President of the United States.

Vice-President

Section 141 of the Constitution says that there shall be a Vice-President. This office has been integrated with the office of the President. He must possess the same qualifications as are prescribed for the President. Both have a term of four years. The names of the team are sponsored by the political parties. Hence, election of both is held simultaneously. He takes the oath of office and loyalty in the presence of the President and declares his assets and liabilities. The process of removing him is also the same as has been prescribed for the removal of the President. It is given in Section 148 that the President shall regularly consult the Vice-

Disqualifications for President and Vice-President

1. declared as a lunatic or an undischarged insolvent by a competent Court,
2. convicted by any Court for dishonesty, fraud or murder,
3. being in the civil or military service of the Centre or of any State,
4. being a member of some secret organisation,
5. held guilty by some judicial inquiry commission or administrative tribunal for embezzlement or fraud.
6. submitting a forged certificate to Independent National Electoral Commission,
7. not being a citizen of Nigeria for any reason, or being loyal to some other country.

President and shall entrust to him responsibilities of administration. If the office of the President falls vacant for any reason (as death, resignation, permanent physical or mental incapacity, impeachment etc.), the Vice-President shall work in the officiating capacity for three months at the most. Fresh election for the post of the President must be held within this period. If the office of the Vice-President falls vacant for any reason, then the President shall nominate someone, but his name must be passed by both the houses of Parliament.

Executive Council

This is the cabinet of the President. It includes all the ministers appointed by the President. There must be one minister from each State who is domiciled there. All appointments are confirmed by the Senate. No minister can be a member of the National Assembly or of any other official body. All ministers work during the pleasure of the President. The President administers to them the oaths of office and secrecy and then they declare their assets and liabilities. If a minister is invited, he may address any house of the Parliament, but he cannot vote there. In this way, the executive and the legislature have been separated.

If studied critically, we may say that now the national executive is not as autocratic as it has been in the past under military rulers. Now the powers of the President have been effectively restrained. His appointments need Senatorial confirmation and foreign treaties signed by him require approval of both the houses of Parliament. In case he promulgates an arbitrary decree, it can be challenged in the Court. If he commits an act of gross misconduct , he may be removed by the process of impeachment. Thus, under the present Constitutional system, the Nigerian President resembles his American counterpart.

National Assembly

A totalitarian system finishes the legislalture. It is constituted just for the sake of display. The elections are postponed again and again on some pretext, or they are fully rigged. The leaders of the opposition and their parties and groups are ruthlessly suppressed. The military rulers adopt some other ways also. They set up some consultative or advisory bodies which are stuffed with their sycophants and are known by several names as Supreme Military Council, Ruling Council of the Armed Forces, Interim Ruling Council etc. Such bodies put the seal of legal validity on the undue actions of the military rulers. Under the Constitution of 1989, such a body of the civilian members (National Assembly) was set up in July 1992 which coud not do anything. It was a bicameral body. Its upper chamber (Senate) had 91 elected members, the lower chamber (House of Representatives) had 593 elected members. It was not proper to call them the members of Parliament, for they had not been given the power to deliberate or to move a proposal for legislation. However, under the present Constitution, the position of the National Assembly is virtually different. Though this Parliament is not as powerful as it should have been in a democratic set up, yet it cannot be described as a mere rubber stamp like its predecessor.[4]

---

4. Keeping in view the condition of that time, it was aptly observed: Not surprisingly, Nigeria s legislature has been a victim of country s political instability and its history of disorderly and unpredictable change. Legislative structures and processes have not operated free of abuse, neglect, or pre-emptory suspension by the executive arm for any appreciable length of time since independence. As such, the history of the legislature lacks any continuity, and thus has not been able to develop and function effectively as a vital component of a democratic system.*f* Joseph, Taylor and Agbaje, *op. cit.*, p. 665.

The Parliament of Nigeria, known by the name of National Assembly, is bicameral. Senate is its upper or second chamber, the House of Representatives is its lower or first chamber. Each State has three seats in the Senate and one seat has been given to the Federal Capital Territory of Abuja. There are 36 States. Hence, this chamber has 109 seats. The members are elected directly for a term of four years. To be a member of this chamber, it is required that he must be a citizen of Nigeria and be above 35 years of age. The chamber elects its President and Vice-president from among its members. The office of the presiding officer falls vacant on the dissolution of the chamber or on the loss of its incumbent s membership. The House of Representatives has 360 members who are directly elected for a term of four years. The country is divided into a number of constituencies keeping in view the proportion of the population as far as possible. It is required for a member of this house to be a citizen of Nigeria and be above 30 years of age. The house elects its Speaker and Deputy Speaker from among its members. The office falls vacant on its dissolution or on the loss of its incumbent s membership.

Following points are notable in this direction:

1. Both the chambers have a term of four years that begins with the first sitting of the house. This duration may be extended during emergency if a resolution to this effect is passed by both the houses. It may be extended for six months at a time.
2. All members are administered the oath of loyalty and each member makes a declaration of his assets and liabilities.
3. The proceedings of the house are conducted by the presiding officer or by his deputy during his absence. He can cast his vote to break a tie.
4. The presence of at least 1/3 members is necessary for conducting the business of the house. If there is a joint session, the same quorum is prescribed.
5. If there is a joint session, the President of the Senate shall preside, the Speaker of the House of Representative shall preside in his absence.
6. The proceedings of the house shall be conducted in the English language, but the members may make use of three languages

of the country-hausa, Ibu and Yoruba.

7. All bills (excluding one seeking amendment of the Constitution) are passed by the simple majority of the members present and voting. After a bill is passed by one house, it is referred to the other house where it must be passed within two months of the commencement of the financial year. If it does not happen, then the President of the Senate shall call a meeting of the joint committee of both the houses within 14 days. In case the matter remains unresolved, then the President of the Senate shall call a joint session of both the houses where it shall be discussed and passed by the simple majority of the members present and voting.
8. If a bill is passed by both the houses, it shall be referred to the President for his assent. The President must assent to it within 30 days. In case he uses his veto power, then the Parliament may over-ride it by passing the same bill again in its joint session by 2/3 majority of the members present and voting.
9. For the sake of maintaining peace and good governance in the country, the National Assembly may make a law on any item of the Exclusive Legislative List or the Concurrent Legislative List. The State Legislative Assemblies may also make a law on any item of the Concurrent Legislative List. If there is a conflict, the law of the Centre shall prevail, and the law of the State shall remain ineffective to the extent of being repugnant to the law of the Centre.
10. During times of war or emergency the National Assembly may make a law for maintaining peace and good governance in the country on any subject not mentioned in the Concurrent Legislative List as it may deem necessary for the sake of national security.
11. If emergency is declared in a State and the Legislative Assembly of that State is unable to make a law for any reason, then the National Assembly may make a law for that State on any item of the Concurrent Legislative List or on any residuary item. However, it cannot make a law to remove its Governor or Deputy Governor.

National Assembly (2007)

Palitical Parties	Seats Secured	
	Senate	House of Representatives
1. People s Democratice Party	78	258
2. All-Nigeria s Political Party	22	64
3. Action Congress	6	32
4. Progressive People s Alliance	1	3
5. Alliance for Democracy	1	1
6. Others	1	1
Total	109	359*

*one seat being vacant

Speaker of the House of Representatives David Mark

Some special provisions have been made for the composition and working of the National Assembly which may by enumerated as under:

1. Each house must meet at least for 180 days in a year.
2. It is also required that each member should be educated upto tenth standard and that he must be a member of any political party. That is, membership cannot be had by an illiterate or independent person.
3. In order to eliminate the evil of political defections, it has been laid down that an elected person cannot renounce the membership of his party by his choice or will. If he changes his party, he shall lose his membership. However, this provision shall not apply in case there is a split in the party as a result of which a new party is formed, or that party has its merger with some other party.
4. Here prevails the system of recall. In case more than half of the voters registered in an electoral constituency send their petition to the Independent National Electoral Commission and express want of confidence in that elected representative, then a referendum shall be held on it within 90 days and the decision shall be taken by the majority of votes in it.
5. After every ten years or whenever expedient, the Independent National Electoral Commission shall have the power to make alterations in the map of electoral constituencies, but its report must be approved by the National Assembly.

6. The National Assembly may make laws relating to elections and thereby outlaw some activities, make arrangement for suitable punishment to the guilty persons, and may enlarge the jurisdiction of the Independent National Electoral Commission.

If the functions and powers of the two houses of Parliament are compared, it appears that the Senate is more powerful for these reasons:

1. The appointments made by the President need Senatorial confirmation.
2. A money bill may be introduced in any house (that is, it may be introduced in the Senate) and that it must be passed by both the houses.
3. If there is a deadlock in the passing of a bill, then a joint seesion of a Parliment shall be held, which shall be presided by the President of the Senate. The Speaker shall do so in the event of his absence. It is a different matter that the House may have a stronger position in the joint session in view of its numerical strength, for the bill shall be passed by simple majority of the members present and voting.
4. If the President or the Vice-President is to be removed on the charge of gross misoconduct, then the resolution of impeachment shall be presented to the President of the Senate who will instruct the Chief Justice of the Supreme Court to set up an inquiry committee of eminent persons within 7 days. If the President or the Vice-President is to be removed on the ground of physical or mental incapacity, then it shall be initiated by the Executive Council (Cabinet). Then the President of the Senate shall set up a Committee of five medical experts and then take decision on the basis of its report.

However, the Nigerian Senate is not as powerful as the Senate of the United States, nor can it be for some pertinent reasons. It has a term of four years that is integrated with the term of the House of Representatives. Similarity may be noted in the point that its members are elected directly by the voters and that each State has its equal representation in the upper chamber. And yet its position is not that powerful in view of the fact that, leaving the case of confirmation of appointments made by the President, its each decision must be approved by the House of Representatives.

National Judiciary

In a totalitarian system the judiciary has the same truncated position that is assigned to the legislature. The military rulers prefer such persons as judges who interpret laws according to their wishes. It is possible that the provisions of the Constitution may allow judicial review, but a military ruler like Babangida or Abacha may make this power of the Courts ineffective by his decrees. President Babangida cancelled the results of the elections of 1993 and, while tilting to the side of the government, the Supreme Court ruled that such a matter did not fall within the domain of judicial review. The critics called it judicial terrorism . In June 1993, when Moshood Abiolo declared himself as the President, he was charged with treason and put behind the bars. When the Supreme Court granted him the relief of *habeas corpus*, the government of Abacha refused to honour it. A new order was issued specifying that a detained person could not move the Court for such a relief. Happily, the situation has now undergone a basic change.The Constitution of 1999 has incorporated such effective provisions which eliminate the possibilities of judicial terrorism or judicial imbecility.

By virtue of having a federal system, Nigeria has two-tiered judicial set up judiciary of the Centre and judiciary of the States. In the former, the Supreme Court stands at the top, followed by the Court of Appeal, Federal High Court, High Court of the Federal Capital Territory of Abuja, Sharia Court of the Federal Capital Territory of Abuja and the Customary Court of the Federal Capital Territory of Abuja. Eash State has a High Court, a Sharia Court and a Customary Court. Besides, both the Centre and the States have a number of their tribunals.

Supreme Court

In the domain of judiciary the Supreme Court is at the apex. It has a Chief Justice and 21 other judge whose number may be extended by a law of the Parliament. The President appoints them on the recommendation of the National Judicial Council which require Senatorial confirmation. Some special qualifications have been laid down for being a judge. He must be a citizen of Nigeria and must have been an advocate of at least 15 years standing.

In case the office of the Chief Justice falls vacant for any reason, the President may appoint the senor-most judge to officiate for a period of not more than three months, but his reappointment is prohibited. The presence of at least five judges is necessary to hear a case. The presence of at least nine judges is necessary if the Court has to interpret the provisions of the Constitution or to determine the validity of an impugned law or order of the State.

The original jurisdiction of the Supreme Court covers those cases which involve some law or fact relating to dispute between the Centre and the States. The National Assembly may enlarge its jurisdiction by its law. Its original jurisdiction does not cover criminal cases. The Court of Appeal is under it whose decision may be challenged in it. It has appellate jurisdiction in several matters as death sentence, dispute relating to the election of the President or Vice-President, vacancy of the post of the President or Vice-President, and protection of fundamental rights of the citizens. However, it is necessary to obtain leave of the Court of Appeal or of the Supreme Court before filing an appeal. In case the President has pardoned a person or commuted his sentence, it cannot be challenged in any Court. The Chief Justice makes rules of the proceedings of the Court and may amend them.

Court of Appeal

Below the Supreme Court is the Court of Appeal which has a Chief Justice and at least 49 judges. It must have at least three such judges who are well versed in Islamic law and three other Judges who are well versed in customary law. The National Assembly may change this system by its law. The President appoints the judges on the recommendation of the National Judicial Council which are subject to Senatorial confirmation. To be a judge it is required that he is a citizen of Nigeria and that he has a standing of at least 12 years as an advocate. If the post of the Chief Justice of this Court falls vacant for any reason, the President may appoint its senior-most judge to officiate on the recommendation of the National Judicial Council which may continue for three months. His reappointment is prohibited.

The presence of at least three judges is required to hear a case. Its original jurisdiction covers cases as irregularities in the election of the President or Vice-President or their office being vacant for any reason. There are several Courts under it as Federal High Court, High Court of the Federal Capital Territory of Abuja, Appellate Sharia Court of any State, Customary Court of Appeal, Military Court, or any tribunal set up according to a law of the Parliament whose decisions may be challenged in it. That is, this Court has appellate jurisdiction in civil and criminal cases. However, before filing an appeal, leave must be obtained either from the Lower Court or from this Court. The Chief Justice makes rules to conduct the proceedings of the Court and may amend them.

Federal High Court

It has a Chief Justice and some other judges whose number is determined by a law of the National Assembly. The President appoints them on the recommendation of the National Judicial Council which must be confirmed by the Senate. It is required that a judge is a citizen of Nigeria and that he has a standing of at least 10 years as an advocate. If the office of the Chief Justice falls vacant for any reason, the President shall apoint the senior-most judge on the recommendation of the National Judicial Council to officiate for a period of three months. His reappointment is prohibited.

The jurisdiction of this Court is limited to civil cases which are related to some matters as revenues of the government, taxation on commercial bodies, excise, import and export tax, banking and finacial institutions, patent, industrial disputes, navigation in Niger river, diplomatic representatives, citizenship and naturalisation, treason, extradition etc., The National Assembly may make a law to enlarge its jurisdiction. Its Chief Justice may make rules to regulate its proceedings and also amend them.

High Court for the Federal Capital Territory of Abuja

It has a Chief Justice and some judges whose number is determined by a law of the National Assembly. The President appoints them on the recommendation of the National Judicial Council which are subject to Senatorial confirmation. It is necessary that a judge is a citizen of Nigeria and that has a standing of at least 10 years as an advocate. In case the office of the Chief Justice falls vacant for any reason, the President, on the recommendation of the National Judicial Council, may appoint its senior-most judge to officiate. Such an appointment is made for three months at the most and reappointment is prohibited. The Chief Justice makes rules to conduct the proceedings of the Court and may amend them. Its jurisdiction covers hearing of the civil and criminal cases as assigned to it by the Federal High Court.

Sharia Court for the Federal Capital Territory of Abuja

It has a Chief Kazi and some other Kazis whose number is determined by a law of the National Assembly. The President appoints them on the recommendation of the National Judicial Council which must be confirmed by the Senate. To be a judge (Kazi) of the Court it is required that he is a citizen of Nigeria, has a standing of at least 10 years as an advocate, and has acquired special knowledge of Islamic law from an institution recognised by the National Judicial Council and has an experience of at least 12 years in practising such a law, or he is known for his ability in Islamic law. In case the office of the Chief Kazi falls vacant for any reason, the President shall appoint the senior-most kazi to officiate on the recommendation of the National Judicial Council for three months at the most. His reappointment is prohibited. Its jurisdiction is limited to the settlement of disputes relating to personal law of the Muslims as marriage, divorce, succession, protection of the non-adult, wakf, gift, will etc. The presence of at least three Kazis is required to hear a case.

Customary Court for the Federal Capital Territory of Abuja

It has a Chief Justice and some judges whose number is determined by a law of the National Assembly. The President appoints them on the recommendation of the National Judicial Council and are confirmed by the Senate. To be a judge, it is required that he is a citizen of Nigeria, has the standing of at least 10 years as an advocate, and has sufficient knowledge and experience of the laws and practices of the country. If the office of the Chief Justice falls vacant for any reason, the President, on the recommendation of the National Judicial Council, shall appoint the senior-most judge of the Court to officiate for three months at the most. His reappointment is prohibited. Its jurisdiction is limited to cases entrusted to it by the National Assembly or Federal Court. The presence of at least three judges is necessary to hear a case. The Chief Justice may make rules to regulate the proceedings of the Court and may amend them.

It is obvious that comprehensive arrangements have been made

Some Special Arrangements for Maintaining Independence and Impartiality of Judiciary

1. The President appoints judges of each federal Court on the recommendation of the National Judicial Council which require confirmation by the Senate.
2. A person cannot be appointed as a judge if he is a member of the National Judicial Council, Judicial Council of any State, or of the National Judicial Council of the Federal Capital Territory of Abuja. In case he has relinquished such an office, a cooling off period of at least three years must have elapsed.
3. The term of the judges is fixed and such persons may be appointed as judges who have special knowledge and experience in the field of law. They cannot hold any office of profit.
4. After appointment, a judge has to take the oath of loyalty and declare his assets and liabilities.
5. A judge may seek voluntary retirement after serving for 15 years or on completing the age of 65 years in the Supreme Court or of 60 years in some other Court. The retirement age of a judge is 70 years in the Supreme Court and 65 years in any other Court. He will be entitled to life long pension equal to his last salary and allowances and all other facilities as permissible under the law.
6. If a resolution is passed by the Senate by 2/3 majority of all the members against a judge charging him with a serious wrong, the President shall remove him forthwith.
7. After leaving the post of a judge, he cannot practise law in any Court.

by the provisions of the Constitution to maintain independence and impartiality of the judiciary. However, a critic may have an apprehension whether such measures may be translated into reality in a country badly ridden with corruption and favouritism.

Federal Executive Bodies

Each country has a number of executive bodies whose composition and working is governed by the laws made by the legislature or orders issued by the excutive departments. However, now a tradition is growing that some very important bodies should have their place in the provisions of the Constitution so that they have a special recognition and thereby act in a very effective manner. It is one the notable features of the Nigerian Constitution that it provides for a number of such bodies at the Centre and also in the States. A brief study of some of the important bodies deserves our attention.

Council of State: It is a very large body consisting of the President (who is its chairman), the Vice-President (who is its deputy chairman), all former Presidents, all former heads of the federal government, all former Chief Justices of the Supreme Court, President of the Senate, Speaker of the House of Representatives, all Governors of States and the Attorney General of Nigeria. The President takes its aid and advice before appointing the heads and the members of many important bodies as Independent National Electoral Commission, National Judicial Council, Federal Civil Services Commission and National Population Commission. He may also seek their advice from time to time as he deems necessary.

Independent National Electoral Commission: It has a head called Chief Electoral Commissioner and 12 members called Electoral Commissioners. They are appointed by the President subject to Senatorial confirmation. Such persons are appointed who are known for their impartiality and integrity of character. Its head must be of at least 50 years of age and other members of at least 40 years of age. The President also appoints local electoral commissioners for all the States and Federal Capital Territory of Abuja which must be confirmed by the Senate. Such persons shall be appointed who are known for their impartiality and integrity of character and be above 40 years of age. The function of this Commission is to conduct elections for the offices of the President, Vice-President, Senate, House of Representatives, Governors and Deputy Governors of the States. Hence, it superintends, directs and controls the elections, prepares electoral rolls and amends them, makes registration of the political parties and has its watch on their income and expenditure and ways of working. It makes rules relating to elections and performs all other functions assigned to it by a law of the Parliament.

National Judicial Council: It is a very large body consisting of the Chief Justice of the Supreme Court (who is its chairman), one senior-most judge of the Supreme Court (who is its Deputy Chairman), Chief Justice of the Court of Appeal, a retired judge (having been in the Supreme Court or in the Court of Appeal) selected by the Chief Justice of Nigeria, Chief Justice of the Federal High Court, five judges selected by the President from amongst the judges of the High Courts of the States and the Federal Capital Territory of Abuja (who will work for two years by rotation), a Chief

Political Parties and Interest Groups

A stable and well organised party system is very essential for operating a democratic system. However, in this country such a party system could not have its existence owing to sharp racial, religious and regional divisions or splits. It is a matter or surprise that the formation of many political parties and groups became faster due to the process of fragmentation and polarisation running together in this plural society. After achieving independence in 1960, the Northern People s Congress came to power, while the group of the people of the south (Yoruba Action Group) played the role of the opposition. After 1969 these organisations changed their names. Under the leadership of Shehu Shegari the Northern People s Congress became the National Party of Nigeria.

In 1989 the government of General Babangida issured a decree permitting only two party system. Thus emerged two parties National Republican Convention and Social Democratic Party. In a superficial sense, while the former represented the right, the latter represented the left on the political-ideological front. Section 220(1) of the Constitution of 1989 accorded legal recognition to these two parties only. Registration of the two parties with the Election Commission was also made mandatory. Still the cleavage between the north and the south continued. It is due to this that while Moshood a southerner, won the Presidential election in June 1993 and he declared himself as the President, he was thrown behind the bars. The Babangida regime annulled the results of the elections.

Thus in the third republic Nigeria remained like a two-party State having National Republican Convention of the northerners and Social Democratic Party of the southerners. Some splinter groups also emerged as People s Redemption Party, Great Nigerian People s Party, Nigerian Advance Party, Northern Elements Progressive Union. However, the two-party system of Nigeria could not be likened with the bi-party system of Britain or the United States for three reasons. First, the American and the British party system have extra-Constitutional growth, while the Nigerian system was imposed by the military regime. Second, while the British and the American systems operate in a democratic manner, the party system of Nigeria had to operate within a rigid framework set by the military administration. For instance, the registration of the two partes with the Election Commission and compliance with the rules framed by it was mandatory. Last, the British and the American party systems attach significance to certain principles of social and economic significance, the Nigerian party system banked upon the racial and communal competition between the northern and the southern parts of the country.

Notable changes have occured in this direction under the present Constitution. The bar to have only two political parties has been removed. However, in order to do away with the rampant evils of the party system,many effective provisions have been incorporated into the Constitution.[6] In the elections to the National Assembly held in 2007 many political parties took part as People s Democratic Party, All-Nigerian People s Party, Action Congress, Progressive People s Alliance and Alliance for Democracy. The present Constitution has made many effective and elaborate arrangements to regulate the organisation and working of the political parties which may be enumerated as under:

1. Now this country has a multi-party system. It is evident from the fact that many parties had taken part in the Parliamentary elections of 2007.
2. Now a person can take part in the elections of the President, Vice-President, Senate, House of Representatives, Governor, Deputy-Governor and local government councils at the base who is a member of any political party and whose name is sponsored by it. Not only this, all expenses of the candidate shall be borne by his party.
3. The names of the office bearers with their addresses must be registered with the Independent National Electoral Commission. The membership of a political party is open for all citizens of the country and in this regard there can be no

6. According to Section 229 of this Constitution, a political party covers any association whose activities include canvassing for votes in support of a candidate for election to the offices of the President, Vice-President, Governor, Deputy Governor, Senate, House of Representatives and State legislative bodies and local government councils.

discrimination on the grounds of race, religion, region etc. A copy of the Constitution of the party must be deposited in the office of the Independent National Electoral Commission. If any amendment is made in it, its information must be communicated to the Commission within 30 days.

4. No party can have a symbol that looks like the replica of any race or religion and a registered party cannot keep its activities confined to a particular region or part of the country. Its members should be the domicile of different parts of the country and its organisation must conform to the federal structure of the country.
5. The members of the managing committee must belong to different States of the Federation and they should represent at least 1/3 of the States.
6. Each party shall submit to the Independent National Electoral Commission its annual statement of income and expenditure, declare its assets and liabilities, cannot deposit its money in foreign banks and cannot accept foreign financial assistance. If any party receives foreign money, it shall remit it to the Independent National Electoral Commission within 21 days. The Commission may audit the income and expenditure of any party. In such a case, it shall send its report to the National Assembly.
7. The provisions of the Constitution of a party must conform to the fundamental objectives and directive principles of state policy mentioned in Part II of Chapter II of the Constitution.
8. No party can have its association with a secret organisation.[7]

---

7. According to Section 318 of the Constitution, secret society includes any person, association, group, or body of persons (whether registered or not) (*a*) that uses secret signs, oaths, rites, or symbols and which fosters the interest of its members and to aid one another under any circumstances without due regard to merit, fair play or justice to the detriment of the legitimate interests of those who are not members; (*b*) the membership of which is incompatible with the function or dignity of any public office under this Constitution and whose members are sworn to observe oaths of secrecy; or (*c*) the activities of which are not known to the public at large, the names of whose members are kept secret and whose meetings and other activities are held in secret.

9. No party can make use of physical force or methods of coercion. The National Assembly may make a law to ban such activities and the guilty person or persons may be awarded suitable punishment.
10. The National Assembly may by its law make the Independent National Electoral Commission effective, or may give necessary directions to it.

Taking note of these provisions, it may be commented that in this country praiseworthy attempts have been made to make the party system well organised and well regulated.

As there is a plural society in Nigeria, it is natural that there are many interest groups and organisations. It includes the unions of the formers, organisations of the traders and manufacturers and associations of many other professionals. For instance, the workers have their Nigerian Labour Congress which is a federation of many labour unions. There is a National Union of Petroleum Employees. When the military rulers took anti-labour measures, these unions resisted. They staged strikes and demonstration. The industrialists have their own organisations as Nigerian Associations of Chambers of Commerce, Industry, Mines and Agriculture. These organisations easily influence the government with their money power. This is the reason that corruption is rampant in every branch of administration and the attitude of the rulers has invariably been lenient towards them. Besides, there are many associations of the artists and the students. In 1987 was formed Civil Liberties Organisation.

As prevails in other democratic and semi-democratic countries, so is in this country. Some elite groups lead and operate such organisations. This tradition had its start in the pre-independence era and is still prevalent with some superficial distinctions. These chosen elements or elite groups foment racial, religious and regional differences and divisions in the country and create obstacles in the way of national integration. It is well commented: Political and economic elites act to create the perception that current social cleavages are fixed and immutable. By fostering divisions among the population, these elites deflect popular scrutiny of their own actions. Simply put, Nigerian elites maintain power by exploiting differences among ethnic groups, even as they promote cultural uniformity and homogeneity within their own specific groups. In many respects, therefore, governance in contemporary Nigeria is a throwback to the colonial era when, as indicated earlier, it was in the interest of the colonial authorities to emphasise inter-tribal disharmony while encouraging inter-tribal unity.f[8]

Problems of the Polity

Nigeria has not yet been able to establish its collective entity and a stable political system despite being a very big country of Africa and having been under the British colonial rule. Its reasons may be traced in deep racial, religious and cultural splits and in rampant corruption. A student may feel taken aback as to why this country is so poor and backward despite having abundant natural and mineral resources and large population and why the trends of national integration and political stabilisation have failed to strike their deep roots. For this, three reasons may be enumerated:

1. **Fragile Collective Identity and Rampant Corruption:** Without being a nation, Nigeria is a multi-national State. Here racial, religious and regional divisions have a formidable form as a result of which this country often remains ridden with conditions of civil war. The people in general are so callous that they cannot learn anything from the history of the disintegration of the multinational States like the Soviet Union and Yugoslavia. The leaders of this country are not merely racist or communalist, they are so corrupt that they have converted their polity into kleptocracy.[9] The leaders wrest power with the help of their supporters and then they give a long rope to their clients to mint money by both hands. Clientelism goes on that may be called patrimonialism or neo-

8. Joseph, Taylor and Agbaje, *op. cit.,* p. 657.

9. Kleptocracy means government by theft . For example, during military rule in Nigeria in the 1990s, officials stole more than one billion dollars from the State treasury. Patrick O Neil: *Essentials of Comparative Politics* (New York: W.W. Norton and Company, 2004), p. 262.

patrimonialism. It has the peculiar name of prebendalism in Nigeria.[10] It is rightly observed: Difficult crises threaten the progress of twenty-first century Nigeria. The adoption of a strict Islamic law code by several of Nigerian States has led to the fighting between Muslims and Christians that claimed more than 1600 lives between 2000 and 2002. The government also faces the daunting challenge of rebuilding its petroleum based economy which had been disrupted by corruption and mismanagement. In 2006 thirty one of thirty six governments were under federal investigation, mainly for corruption, and five had been impeached; according to one poll, only twenty-five per cent of Nigerians were satisfied with their new democracy.*f*[11]

2. **Low Political Culture:** The people of Nigeria lack the capacity to appreciate the significance of modern trends and to have faith in the values of a liberal democratic order and thereby strengthen their convictions or commitments in this regard. There has been a nasty alliance between bureaucracy and military since the times of British colonial rule that retards progress in the direction of democracy.

---

10. Prebendalism is a typical Nigerian word. It implies an extreme form of clientelism that refers to the practice of mobilising cultural and other sectional identities through corrupt inducements and behaviour by political aspirants and office holders. It is an institutionalised pattern of political behaviour that justifies the pursuit and the use of public office for the personal benefit of the officeholder and his clients; the official public purpose of the office is a secondary concern.*f* R.A. Joseph, S.D. Taylor and Adigun Agbaje, *op. cit.*, p. 648. So another writer comments: In attempting to fill the gaps, the patrons rely heavily on a system of relations linking rulers not with the public or even with ruled (at least, not directly) but with patrons, associates, clients, supporters and rivals who constitute the system.*f* J. Shola Omotola: Third World Politics and de-Institutionalisation of Power in Africa*f* in *African Review*, New Delhi, Vol. 3, No. 2 (July-December, 2011), p. 125.

11. Kwame Anthony Appiah and Henry Louis Gates, Jr. (eds.): *Encyclopaedia Africa* (Oxford: Oxford University Press, 2010), p. 243.

Some Important Statements

The power elites are men whose positions enable them to transcend the ordinary environment of ordinary men and women; they are in positions to make decisions having major consequences..... They run the machiney of the State and claim its prerogatives. The power elites are not solitary rulers. Advisers and consultants, spokesmen and opinion makers are often the captains of their thoughts and decisions.

C.W. Mills

The truth is that the big man has always been and remains a danger to society. This is really a dangerous undemocratic character whose track record shows nothing but corruption, waste, violence, human rights abuses, misplaced priorities, and a pathological commitment to the recycling of mediocrity.

J.O. Ihonvbere

The most dangerous dimension of the shadow of religion on Nigerian democracy has been the preservation of religious crises shrouded in ethnic garbs across the country.

J. Shola Omatola

3. **Structural Dualism:** Nigeria is a multi-ethnic, post-colonial State and one of the dominant feature of the post-coloniality in Africa and elsewhere is the structural coexistence and friction between the traditional and the modern in the cultural, social, economic, legal and political frameworks of society. In contemporary African social anthropology, this phenomenon is termed structural dualism . It implies, for instance, that the inherent colonial contradictions between communitarian and capitalist economies, traditional and modern political systems, as well as customary and common laws are far from settled in the present dispensation and that largely operated by indigeneous actor, the post-colonial States are starkly confronted with new dialectics in the context of both old (metropolitan forces) and new (post-colonial elites) interests. This feature both portrays the extremely unfinished nature of State-making and compounds the institutional and instrumental constraints of the central authorities in unifying the disparate ethnic nationalities into a modern nation-State.[12]

12. Kenneth Omeje: *High Stakes and Stake Holders; Oil Conflict and Security in Nigeria* (Burlington: Ashgate Publishers, 2006), p. 139.